Rape and the Legal Process

Second Edition

Jennifer Temkin

OXFORD
UNIVERSITY PRESS

OXFORD
UNIVERSITY PRESS

Great Clarendon Street, Oxford OX2 6DP

Oxford University Press is a department of the University of Oxford.
It furthers the University's objective of excellence in research, scholarship,
and education by publishing worldwide in

Oxford New York

Auckland Bangkok Buenos Aires Cape Town Chennai
Dar es Salaam Delhi Hong Kong Istanbul Karachi Kolkata
Kuala Lumpur Madrid Melbourne Mexico City Mumbai Nairobi
São Paulo Shanghai Taipei Tokyo Toronto

Oxford is a registered trade mark of Oxford University Press
in the UK and in certain other countries

Published in the United States
by Oxford University Press Inc., New York

Second edition first published 2002

First edition published by Sweet & Maxwell, London, 1987

British Library Cataloguing in Publication Data
Data available

Library of Congress Cataloging in Publication Data
Data available

ISBN 0–19–876354–9 (hbk.)
ISBN 0–19–876355–7 (pbk.)

1 3 5 7 9 10 8 6 4 2

Typeset by Hope Services (Abingdon) Ltd
Printed in Great Britain
on acid-free paper by
T. J. International Ltd., Padstow, Cornwall

RAPE AND THE LEGAL PROCESS

FOR ADAM AND FOR LARA

General Editor's Preface

It is a great pleasure to welcome to the Series a pathbreaking book in a new edition. Professor Temkin's writings on the response of the criminal justice system to rape have been widely acclaimed. The book deals both with the substantive ciminal law and with the whole range of legal processes, from investigative practices through the rules of evidence to sentencing and other measures. Jennifer Temkin brings to the work not only her knowledge of English law and comparative law, but also the understanding derived from her extensive empirical research and the experience of membership of the External Reference Group for the Sexual Offences Review. That review's report, *Setting the Boundaries* (2000), initiated a debate that will be re-kindled by proposals from the government for reform of the law of sexual offences. The timing of the book is therefore propitious, and its contents are likely to influence discussions of the subject for years to come.

Andrew Ashworth

Preface

This is not a book about why men rape women or other men. It does not seek to defend or attack the notion that rape is the product of a patriarchal society or that it is an extreme manifestation of what Professor Terence Morris has described as our society's predatory attitude towards women.[1] It will not talk of other societies such as that of the Minangkabau of Western Sumatra where rape, we are told, scarcely ever occurs.[2] Nor does it discuss the implications of rape as a crime in international law.[3] All this has been discussed cogently, and at times brilliantly, elsewhere. Indeed, it is discourse of this nature which has transformed our understanding of rape and ensured that those who experience and complain of it are no longer dismissed routinely as liars or fantasists, but are recognized increasingly as genuine victims.

Advances in thinking about rape have produced fundamental legal change in many countries. In England and Wales, however, law reform has proceeded at a measured pace. The purpose of this book is to examine some of the difficulties which rape presents for our criminal justice system and how these could and should be addressed. In Chapter 1, the plight of the rape victim and the response of the criminal justice system is discussed. Chapter 2 deals with the present law of rape in England and Wales and discusses law reform within the existing structure of sexual offences. Chapter 3 considers some of the more radical alternatives adopted in other common law jurisdictions. Chapter 4 examines aspects of the law of evidence as it applies to sexual offences. Finally, in Chapter 5, other methods of assisting rape victims are canvassed.

There are many people I should like to thank for the help they have given me in connection with this edition of the book. I am particularly indebted to Professor Andrew Ashworth who has been a source of great assistance and support. I am also very grateful to the following: Professors Barbara Krahe, Sally Lloyd-Bostock, Alan Saltzman, Annika Snare, Eva Smith and Graham Zellick, Mr Justice Robert Sharpe of the Ontario Court of Appeal, Judge Katarina Pahlsson, Dr Beth Grothe Nielsen, Janet Prescott, and the Danish

[1] See *The Times,* 20 Jan. 1982.

[2] See P. R. Sanday, 'Rape and the Silencing of the Feminine', in S. Tomaselli and R. Porter, eds., *Rape* (Oxford: Basil Blackwell, 1986) 84.

[3] On which see e.g. K. Askin, 'Sexual Violence in Decisions and Indictments of the Yugoslav and Rwandan Tribunals: Current Status' (1999) 93 AJIL 97; C. Chinkin, 'Rape and Sexual Abuse of Women in International Law' (1994) 5 EJIL 326.

Ministry of Justice. To this list should be added my children, Adam and Lara, to whom this book is dedicated.

Jennifer Temkin

University of Sussex
May 2002

Contents

Table of Cases

Table of Statutes

AUSTRALIA

GERMANY

ITALY

NEW ZEALAND

NORWAY

PAKISTAN

REPUBLIC OF IRELAND

SWEDEN

UNITED KINGDOM

Statutes

Statutory Instruments

UNITED STATES OF AMERICA

Table of Conventions and Agreements

Abbreviations

CJA 1991	Criminal Justice Act 1991
CJPOA 1994	Criminal Justice and Public Order Act 1994
CLRC	Criminal Law Revision Committee
ECHR	European Convention on Human Rights
OAPA 1861	Offences Against the Person Act 1861
SOA 1956	Sexual Offences Act 1956
SOA 1967	Sexual Offences Act 1967
SOA 1985	Sexual Offences Act 1985
SOAA 1976	Sexual Offences (Amendment) Act 1976
SOAA 1992	Sexual Offences (Amendment) Act 1992
SOAA 2000	Sexual Offences (Amendment) Act 2000
YJCEA 1999	Youth Justice and Criminal Evidence Act 1999

1

Rape, Rape Victims, and the Criminal Justice System

For over three decades in this country, public disquiet has been intermittently but vehemently expressed about rape[1] and the way it is handled by the criminal justice system. The principal areas of concern, which will be those considered in this chapter, are the experience of rape victims and their treatment by police and courts, the low reporting and conviction rates for rape, and the lenient treatment of rapists. It is felt that too many rapists are being permitted by the police and the courts to evade justice and that those who are convicted receive inadequate sentences. Rape does indeed pose a series of problems for the criminal justice system but the emphasis upon some of them is occasionally misplaced. The cry for harsher penalties, for example, can sometimes eclipse analysis and discussion of the very real plight of the victim.

The Victim's Experience

(a) The Experience of Rape

Individual accounts by victims of the physical and mental suffering which they have endured as a result of rape have formed a vital ingredient of the discourse on the subject.[2] Their reports are borne out by studies which confirm the existence of a rape trauma syndrome. According to Burgess and Holmstrom: 'This syndrome has two phases: the immediate or acute phase, in which the victim's lifestyle is completely disrupted by the rape crisis, and the long-term process, in which the victim must reorganise this disrupted

[1] In the footnotes to this book, titles which appear in the Select Bibliography are in Harvard style; others appear in full. On rape generally and why it is committed, see e.g. Brownmiller (1976); Clark and Lewis (1977); J. R. Schwendinger and H. Schwendinger, *Rape and Inequality* (Calif.: Sage, 1983); Russell (1984) Part II; Krahe (2001) ch. 8 and especially Smart (1989); N. Lacey, *Unspeakable Subjects* (Oxford: Hart, 1998).

[2] They are now too numerous to list but see e.g. 'Rape—Coping with the Memories', *Spare Rib*, No. 109, Aug. 1981, 20; *The Guardian*, 24 Oct. 1983; Toner (1982), ch. 10; J. Saward and W. Green, *Rape: My Story* (London: Bloomsbury, 1990); 'Looking Back, Looking Forward', *The Guardian*, 27 Nov. 1992; *The Guardian*, 5 Feb. 1992; Nancy Raine, *After Silence: Rape and My Journey Back* (London: Virago, 1999).

lifestyle'.[3] Whilst it is commonly supposed that in the immediate aftermath of the rape, the victim will be hysterical and tearful, Burgess and Holmstrom found that many victims have a controlled response in which they mask their feelings and appear calm and composed.[4] The acute phase, which may last for days or several weeks, is commonly characterized by sleep disturbance, decrease in appetite, and physical pain. Although many victims do not display signs of injury, they may none the less experience considerable bodily discomfort. Thus, one victim in the Burgess and Holmstrom study stated:

> I am so sore under my ribs. I can't sleep on my one side. The pain just stays there: it doesn't go away. I guess he really hurt me although the X-ray didn't show anything. . . . It hurts when I breathe and I can't wear any clothes that fasten. It hurts to swalow and bothers me to eat. I think he loosened my teeth because they hurt.[5]

The principal emotional reaction is commonly one of fear. Other feelings range from humiliation, degradation, guilt, shame, and embarrassment to self-blame, anger, and revenge.

Even after the first days or weeks in which the victim's reactions may be acute, in the succeeding months she may still experience physical and sexual problems, nightmares, intense nervousness, and fear. Many victims feel impelled to change their telephone numbers and their residence. Many are able to resume only a minimal level of functioning.[6] A New Zealand study concluded: 'Rape is an experience which shakes the foundations of the lives of the victims. For many its effect is a long-term one, impairing their capacity for personal relationships, altering their behaviour and values and generating fear.'[7]

In recent studies, some rape victims have been found to be suffering from post-traumatic stress disorder (PTSD).[8] A diagnosis of PTSD is applied to individuals who experience persistent psychological distress exclusively in response to a traumatic event which is outside the range of usual human experience and who manifest three distinct symptoms of at least a month's duration.[9] The first is the persistent and intrusive re-experiencing of the traumatic event. This may occur in recurrent, distressing dreams or recollections, or there may be sudden feelings that the event is re-occurring. The second is the persistent avoidance of stimuli associated with the trauma or the numbing of general responsiveness. This may be manifested by, for

[3] A. W. Burgess and L. L. Holmstrom, *Rape—Crisis and Recovery* (Bowie, Md., Prentice-Hall, Brady and London: 1979) 35.

[4] ibid. 36. [5] ibid. [6] ibid. 39–44.

[7] Young (1983), i, 34. See also Maguire and Corbett (1987), ch. 7.

[8] See e.g. W. O'Donohue and A. Elliott, 'The Current Status of Post-Traumatic Stress Disorder as a Diagnostic Category: Problems and Proposals' (1992) 5 Journal of Traumatic Stress 421; B. A. Clarke, 'Making the Woman's Experience Relevant to Rape: The Admissibility of Rape Trauma Syndrome in California' [1991] 39 UCLA LR 251 at 256–60.

[9] See American Psychiatric Association, *Diagnostic and Statistical Manual of Mental Disorders—Revised* (4th edn., Washington, 1994). This contains a widely recognized classification of mental disorders.

example, avoidance of activities, thoughts, or feelings arousing recollection of what happened, inability to remember an important aspect of the trauma, feelings of estrangement from others, and inability to have loving feelings. The third is persistent autonomic signs of anxiety, for example, insomnia, exaggerated startle response, and concentration difficulties. Thus, the range of symptoms covered by PTSD is narrower and more specific than those included in rape trauma syndrome. PTSD has been diagnosed in, for example, concentration camp victims, Vietnam war veterans, prisoners of war, victims of torture, disaster victims as well as in some victims of child sexual abuse.

Kilpatrick *et al.* found that victims of rape were considerably more likely than victims of other crimes to develop PTSD and that rape had a more negative impact than other crimes.[10] In a Northern Ireland study,[11] 70 per cent of the rape victims studied were found to be suffering from PTSD almost nine months later. The authors comment: 'Previous studies have shown that psychological symptoms present after this interval show little resolution with time. Thus the results would suggest that PTSD is likely to be a long term problem for a significant proportion of rape victims.'[12]

(b) The Experience of Reporting Rape

In addition to the trauma of the rape itself, victims have had to suffer further mistreatment at the hands of the legal system. Be it in England,[13] Scotland,[14] Australia,[15] Canada,[16] Scandinavia,[17] Russia,[18] or elsewhere,[19] the rough handling of complainants has been much the same. In 1982, English television viewers were shocked at the verbal brutality of Thames Valley police officers who were filmed interrogating a rape victim, but Rape

[10] D. G. Kilpatrick, B. E. Saunders, A. Amick-McMullan, C. L. Best, and L. J. Veronen, 'Victim and Crime Factors Associated with the Development of Crime Related Posttraumatic Stress Disorder' (1989) 20 *Behaviour Therapy* 199, 209–10.

[11] I. T. Bownes, E. C. O'Gorman, and A. Sayers, 'Assault Characteristics and Post Traumatic Stress Disorder in Rape Victims' (1991) 83 *Acta Psychiatrica Scandinavia* 27.

[12] At p. 29. Evidence of rape trauma syndrome or PTSD has so far not been admitted in this country to assist in establishing lack of consent, to explain delay in reporting, to respond to attacks on the credibility of the complainant by the defence, or to challenge rape myths. There are mixed views on the desirability of the use of such evidence although it is used in the United States for a variety of purposes: see e.g. Raitt and Zeedyk, (1997); F. Raitt and S. Zeedyk, *The Implicit Relation of Psychology and Law: Women and Syndrome Evidence* (London: Routledge, 2000), ch. 5; P. Rumney and M. Martin-Taylor, 'Male Rape Trauma Syndrome in the US Courts: *People v Yates*' (1997) 1 International Journal of Evidence and Proof 232.

[13] See generally on this, Heilbron Committee (1975); Toner (1982); London Rape Crisis Centre, Annual Reports, 1977 onwards; Adler (1987); Lees (1996, 1997).

[14] See e.g. Harper and McWhinnie (1983); Chambers and Millar (1983, 1986); Brown *et al.* (1992).

[15] See e.g. Scutt (1980); Wilson (1978); New South Wales Department for Women (1996); Easteal (1998).

[16] See e.g. Clark and Lewis (1977).

[17] See Snare (1983), 48.

[18] See *The Times*, 15 June 1994.

[19] See e.g. Young (1983) i.

Crisis Centre workers pointed out at the time that such interrogations were run-of-the-mill.[20] That the officers involved were well aware that the cameras were trained on them was itself of some interest, for some British policemen appeared to consider that harsh questioning, far from being undesirable, was precisely what was required. Thus, a complaint made by the father of one rape victim that his daughter had been questioned 'like a common criminal' was rejected by the Police Complaints Board which decided that the police had done their job correctly.[21] What was regarded as correct by some police officers may be gauged from the following advice extended by a detective sergeant to fellow officers in the pages of *Police Review*:

> It should be borne in mind that except in the case of a very young child the offence of rape is extremely unlikely to have been committed against a woman who does not immediately show signs of extreme violence. If a woman walks into a police station and complains of rape with no such signs of violence she must be closely interrogated. Allow her to make her statement to a policewoman and then drive a horse and cart through it. It is always advisable if there is any doubt of the truthfulness of her allegations to call her an outright liar . . . Watch out for the girl who is pregnant or late getting home one night; such persons are notorious for alleging rape or indecent assault. Do not give her sympathy. If she is not lying, after the interrogator has upset her by accusing her of it, then at least the truth is verified . . . The good interrogator is very rarely loved by his subject.[22]

In a study conducted by the Scottish Office Central Research Unit, 70 Scottish victims of sexual assault were interviewed. Forty were victims of rape, 28 of assault with intent to ravish. The views expressed by complainers on their interactions with CID officers and uniformed women police officers were mainly critical or negative. 'In the main the criticisms were concentrated . . . on the unsympathetic and tactless manner in which interviewing was often conducted.'[23] The researchers concluded that 'there is considerable scope for the development of police interviewing skills in relation to sexual assault complaints'.[24]

(i) False Allegations[25]

One important reason for the less than sympathetic behaviour of many police officers towards rape victims is the belief shared by many of them that complaints of rape are frequently false. In the Scottish study, of the critical comments received from complainers about the experience of reporting

[20] Film shown 18 Jan. 1982 on BBC Television in a series called *Police*.

[21] See *The Times*, 25 Mar. 1982.

[22] Firth (1975).

[23] Chambers and Millar (1983) 94.

[24] ibid 95. For further discussion of police treatment of rape victims, see Ch. 5.

[25] See also J. Jordan, 'True "Lies" and False "Truths": Women, Rape and the Police,' Ph.D. thesis, Victoria University of Wellington, New Zealand, discussed in Kelly (2002), 22; Ch. 2 under the heading 'Marital Rape: The Road to Reform in England and Wales'.

offences, 19 per cent related to the disbelief with which their allegations were received.[26] CID officers reportedly made comments such as 'Your statement is like a fairy tale', 'Don't talk rubbish', and 'You are making this up.'[27] Eighteen per cent of critical comments made by complainers concerned the number of times they were forced to repeat their story. It was explained to some that this was necessary because of the frequency of false complaints. It seems that lecture material distributed to the Scottish police gave repeated warnings about false complaining.[28] Many police officers interviewed in the survey expressed the view that false allegations were common.[29] However, the report notes: 'Despite a certain amount of rhetoric from police officers about the frequency of false complaining, individual officers were unable to document many individual cases which fitted into the category of false complaints'.[30]

Whilst it is clear that false allegations of rape are made to the police, there is no evidence that fabrication occurs more often in rape cases than in other crimes. Yet the myth persists. In a Howard League Working Party Report, for example, it is claimed that 'Some women and girls may well lay false charges out of malice, fear of pregnancy or to preserve their reputation in the face of a suspicious parent, husband or fiancé'.[31] However, little if any evidence in support of this proposition is provided. The report cites two very slight articles by police surgeons which purport to deal with the phenomenon of false complaining. Each is based on a tiny sample of cases. In the first,[32] the doctor concerned writes of 18 rape allegations made to the police, 14 of which he claims were false. Some of the cases were not in fact seen by him but by his senior surgeon. The conclusions arrived at were based on notes taken by each doctor. The article says little more than that in 14 cases intercourse with consent was eventually admitted. The only detail given is of one further case: 'One case was disproved on the grounds that it was totally impossible to have removed her extremely tight undergarments from her extremely large body against her will'.[33] Presumably the woman was able to remove the garments herself and might have done so if, for example, she was threatened. A third party would no doubt eventually have been able to do so too. This comment suggests that the writer's attitude towards rape allegations is a sceptical one. He states that the woman concerned subsequently admitted that the allegation was false. However, faced with a hostile or disbelieving authority figure, it seems not unlikely that some women, already traumatized, will wish to retract their statements in order to avoid further distress.

26 Chambers and Millar (1983) 78–9.
27 ibid. 79.
28 ibid. 84.
29 ibid. 85.
30 ibid. 86.
31 Howard League Working Party Report (1985) 68.
32 C. H. Stewart, 'A Retrospective Survey of Alleged Sexual Assault Cases' (1981) Police Surgeon 28.
33 ibid. 32.

The second article referred to in the Howard League Report as 'a more careful study'[34] was by N. Maclean,[35] a police surgeon working in Scotland. He claimed that out of 34 cases of alleged rape which he examined between 1969 and 1974, 10 were definitely and 6 probably fabricated, whilst the rest were definitely (15) or probably (3) genuine.[36] In each case, Maclean took a full history and medical examination as well as vaginal slides and swabs. He also interviewed the investigating officers and followed up each case. In the 10 cases classified as definitely fabricated, the complainant apparently admitted that her accusation was false. However, no information is given as to whether these confessions were made to Maclean himself or to the police or as to the type of interrogation which preceded them. It is most significant, however, that although it is stated that 'the most important evidence [to corroborate or disprove the woman's story] would be the finding of spermatozoa [and that] for this reason swabs and slides were taken in every case',[37] the police sent only 6 out of 31 slides and swabs to the laboratory. The author himself criticizes the police for this and states that this 'means the police are not obtaining what may be the only evidence that intercourse has occurred'. It seems clear that in the 10 cases classified as definitely fabricated, no laboratory tests were done. The police, it appears, were interested only in cases where the victim sustained injuries to her genitalia and it was only in these cases that samples were sent to the laboratory. None of the 'fabricated' cases involved such injury. The author states: 'If I found no such injuries I got the impression that the police no longer considered the case to be one of rape'.[38]

The writer's main interest seems to have been to develop a typology of the female fabricator. Thus, armed with the 10 cases which he classified as fabricated, he proceeded to consider those characteristics which they shared and those which distinguished them from the genuine cases. He found that, of the alleged fabricators, three were of low intelligence, two were under the care of the Social Work Department, two were prostitutes, one was very poor, and one belonged to a problem family.[39] 'Fabricators' reported later, most were not of dishevelled appearance, none seemed agitated or upset, few had injuries, and where they did, these were relatively insignificant.[40] It is of course precisely in cases of this type that complainers will be treated with most suspicion. Complaints involving prostitutes, women with little injury to show or who have delayed reporting, are likely to be considered bad cases to bring to court and are clear candidates for dismissal by the police. Moreover, women of low intelligence or who are severely socially disadvantaged are least likely to be able to withstand a forceful police interrogation. Burgess and Holmstrom's finding, that rape victims in the immediate aftermath of rape often show no emotion, has already been mentioned.[41] It

[34] n. 31 above. [35] Maclean (1979). [36] ibid. 30. [37] ibid. 38.
[38] ibid. 38. [39] ibid. 31. [40] ibid. 39. [41] See text at n. 4 above.

is by no means impossible, therefore, that upon further scrutiny some more cases in this modest sample might have been revealed to be genuine.

Women who are considered to have made false allegations of rape may be prosecuted for causing the wasteful employment of the police[42] or for attempting to pervert the course of justice.[43] Such prosecutions have serious consequences. They attract the attention of the press and there is no anonymity.[44] A conviction for attempting to pervert the course of justice will almost invariably result in a prison sentence.[45] Where a man is considered to have been wrongly imprisoned as a result of a false allegation, it has been made clear that severe punishment will be imposed.[46] Judicial comments when sentencing women on these occasions reveal that the old suspicions about rape complainants are alive and well. Thus in *Goodwin*, Lord Lane CJ commented: 'As everybody knows rape is an easy allegation to make and may be very difficult to refute'.[47] The difficulties of prosecuting and gaining convictions in rape cases are sufficiently well known today to make this obeisance to the seventeenth-century writings of Sir Matthew Hale hard to excuse.

Men who allege that they have been falsely accused of rape may also look to the civil courts for a remedy. Martin Garfoot successfully sued his accuser for defamation. She was ordered to pay damages of £400,000 and costs of £150,000. As well as financial ruin, she also faced the prospect of being struck off as a member of the Royal Pharmaceutical Society and thus prevented from practising her profession.[48] Extensive newspaper coverage of women labelled false accusers and their treatment by the legal system may intimidate and deter some victims from reporting rape, particularly where the rapist is not a stranger.

[42] Criminal Law Act 1967, s. 5(2).

[43] See e.g. *Gregson* (1993) 14 Cr App R (S) 85; *Goodwin* (1989) 11 Cr App R (S) 194; *Kyriakou* (1990) 12 Cr App R (S) 603. Judge David Bryant has suggested that there should be a special register of women who make false accusations of rape. This comment can only lend further credence to the myth that false allegations are a major problem in rape cases: see *The Times*, 5 Aug. 1999.

[44] There is considerable press interest in stories about false rape claims. See e.g. 'Rape Accusations Often False', *The Times*, 29 Apr. 1985; 'Woman Admits Kidnap and Sex Ordeal was a Fantasy', *The Times*, 26 Aug. 1983; 'Three Years' Custody for False Rape Claim' *The Independent*, 3 Dec. 1988; *The Times*, 8 Feb. 2000; *The Times*, 6 Apr. 2001.

[45] A woman who falsely accused a colleague of rape was put on probation for two years with a year of medical treatment because the judge had received a 'very moving' medical report on her. He commented that in the normal course of events she would have received a prison sentence of at least 18 months: see *The Times*, 24 Nov. 1993; see also *The Times*, 20 Jan. 1999.

[46] See *Kyriakou*, above, at 606.

[47] (1989) 11 Cr App R (S) 194, 196.

[48] See *The Times*, 8 Feb. 2001. For a slander action brought in similar circumstances, see the *Independent*, 11 May 1999. The former MP Neil Hamilton and his wife Christine have also threatened to bring a defamation action against a woman who accused them of being accessories to rape: see *The Times*, 29 Aug. 2001.

In the United States, police training programmes now place increasing emphasis on debunking the myth of widespread fabrication in rape cases.[49] Re-education about the plight of victims and the rape trauma syndrome has accompanied a transformation in police practice in some states. Thus Holmstrom and Burgess found that victim reactions to their encounters with the police were mainly favourable.[50] Similarly, Kelly in 1980 interviewed 100 adult female rape victims from four jurisdictions in the Washington metropolitan area. These women for the most part expressed satisfaction with their treatment by the police. Yet Kelly found that the same women also complained, often bitterly, about police behaviour. Her explanation of this paradox is 'that victims rated police and prosecutors highly because they expected to be treated so poorly'. Many had seen the film *Cry Rape* which had depicted rape victims being humiliated by the police. Thus, their satisfaction arose from receiving better treatment than they expected.[51]

In England, too, the police have altered their methods of handling rape cases but with mixed success.[52] These developments are discussed further in Chapter 5.

(c) The Victim in Court

If the police have behaved brutishly towards rape victims, it is the courts which may be said to have set the tone. Indeed, it is often claimed that in rape cases the complainant rather than the defendant is on trial.[53] Certainly, the focus of the court's attention is frequently upon her and rather less upon him. Yet the complainant generally has no legal assistance.[54] In England and Wales, counsel for the prosecution represent the State and will generally do no more than introduce themselves to complainants before the trial. Some prosecuting barristers are disinclined to do even that.[55]

[49] See e.g. O'Reilly (1984) 96. However lie detectors are still used in most states: see 'Fighting for Rape Victims' *The Chronicle of Higher Education*, 16 Apr. 1996.

[50] L. L. Holmstrom and A. W. Burgess, *The Victim of Rape: Institutional Reactions* (New York and Chichester: Wiley, 1978).

[51] Kelly (1982).

[52] See e.g. Blair (1985). Shapland *et al.* found that the sexual assault victims whose complaints had been accepted and recorded as crimes were more satisfied with their treatment by the police than the physical assault and robbery victims in their survey: see (1985: 87–8). Other studies are more critical: see Ch. 5.

[53] See e.g. Berger (1977). The Scottish study notes, 'The feeling of being "on trial" was common among complainers'. Out of 20 women interviewed whose cases went to court, about half thought that their experience at court had been even worse than expected: see Chambers and Millar (1986) 90–1. See also 'Raped Teenager's Court Ordeal Led to her Death', *The Times*, 19 July 2002.

[54] Discussed further in Ch. 5.

[55] Temkin (2000) 222–3. But see Report of the Royal Commission on Criminal Justice (1993), Cm. 2263, para. 52, 80 in which meetings between counsel and witnesses are encouraged. See also recommendation of HMCPSI Report (2002), para. 11.33. Barristers instructed by the CPS are now required to introduce themselves to victims at court: see K. Kneller, 152 NLJ, 26 Apr. 2002, 610. The CPS has published new guidance on the role of the prosecution

Much criticism of the treatment of rape victims in court has centred on the use of sexual history evidence to blacken their character. But other strategies commonly employed against them are equally oppressive and invidious. Newby identified three distinct tactics utilized by defence counsel in rape trials in Western Australia.[56] These are also in frequent use elsewhere.[57] The first tactic is continual questioning as to details of the rape. The woman is required 'to re-iterate again and again the details of the rape incident . . . The purpose is to test her story for inconsistencies and to attempt to twist her interpretation of events so as to make them consistent with an assumption of consent.'[58] The second strategy relates to cases where the victim and accused were known to each other. In such cases, questioning will be particularly detailed and the most intimate aspects of any pre-existing sexual relationship will commonly be rehearsed in court. Finally, the defence may seek to challenge the general character of the witness. This may include, but goes far beyond, references to her sexual past. The idea is to suggest to the court 'that this sort of woman, who behaves in this kind of way, in these circumstances is quite reasonably to be taken to be consenting'.[59] Thus, attention will be drawn to behaviour such as hitchhiking, excessive drinking or smoking, the wearing of 'seductive' clothing or the use of bad language.

The major concern here is the role of the judge during such cross-examinations. The law permits only relevant evidence to be adduced in criminal trials. What notion of relevance is it that permits prolonged questioning on matters of this kind? It is for judges to control the conduct of a trial. In rape cases, they appear all too often to give defence counsel free rein.[60]

But it is not only for their omissions to act that the judges must be castigated. Throughout the years in England, a steady stream of judicial

advocate: see www.cps.gov.uk. The Solicitor-General has announced a national network of specialist rape prosecutors in an attempt to increase the conviction rate: see 152 NLJ, 3 May 2002, 660.

[56] Newby (1980) 118–20.

[57] See e.g. Young (1983) i, ch. 7. Out of 64 trials examined in Young's study, complainants were cross-examined by more than one counsel in 25 per cent of cases because in each there were several defendants who were separately represented. The Scottish study also provides disturbing illustrations of defence tactics in rape trials: see Chambers and Millar (1986), 98–127. The authors state, 'In attempting to understand the complainer's experience at trial, defence tactics were of paramount importance. These included accusations of lying, insensitive and persistent questioning, harassment and intimidation . . . Defence questioning attempted . . . to discredit and demean the complainer's evidence and thereby influence the jury's perception of its veracity. Such questioning was commonplace in the trials studied and was largely unrestricted.' See, ibid. 126–7. For a recent Scottish illustration, see *The Times*, 19 July 2002, n. 53 above. See also S. Lees, 'Judicial Rape' (1993) 16 *Women's Studies International Forum* 11; Temkin (2000).

[58] Newby (1980) 119.

[59] ibid. 120.

[60] For discussion of the rules of evidence as they apply in rape cases, see Ch. 4. See also *CG v United Kingdom*, Application No. 43373/98, European Court of Human Rights, 19 Dec. 2001, [2002] Crim LR 313 which suggests that judges have considerable leeway to intervene.

utterances on rape has caused amazement and consternation. In 1982, Judge Wild in the Crown Court at Cambridge summed up to the jury thus:

Women who say no do not always mean no. It is not just a question of saying no, it is a question of how she says it, how she shows and makes it clear. If she doesn't want it, she only has to keep her legs shut and she would not get it without force and there would be marks of force being used.[61]

In the same vein, the late Sir Melford Stevenson remarked: 'It is the height of imprudence for any girl to hitch-hike at night. That is plain, it isn't really worth stating. She is in the true sense asking for it.'[62]

In 1988, Judge Sir Harold Cassell refused to jail a former policeman for the indecent assault of his 12-year-old stepdaughter. He said the man was driven to it because his wife's pregnancy had dimmed her sexual appetite causing 'considerable problems for a healthy young husband'.[63] Judge Raymond Dean told the jury in a case in 1990 that a verbal refusal of sexual intercourse might not be seriously intended: 'As the gentlemen on the jury will understand, when a woman says no she doesn't always mean it . . . Men can't turn their emotions on and off like a tap like some women can.'[64]

It is not surprising that victims have found rape trials a traumatic experience. Complainants interviewed in the New Zealand study found the experience of giving evidence in court 'negative and destructive'.[65] The report states: 'Three said that they considered the ordeal to be even worse than the rape itself, and one likened it to being crucified. Undoubtedly, the court proceedings added to and prolonged the psychological stress they had suffered as a result of the rape itself.'[66]

The conduct of rape trials is thus a second major problem confronting the criminal justice system. Undoubtedly, strict rules limiting the use of sexual history evidence can help to alleviate the victim's plight in court, but these alone are insufficient to protect her from needless distress and humiliation. Legal representation for complainants is one method of protecting their interests, and is currently provided as of right in Denmark, Norway, and Sweden.[67] But it would appear that a radical change in the attitude of coun-

[61] See Pattullo (1983), 20–1. [62] ibid. 21.

[63] See *The Times*, 15 June 1993.

[64] See *The Times*, 11 Apr. 1990. See further below under the heading 'Sentencing'. The utterances of some members of the Quebec judiciary are also noteworthy. In 1989, Judge Denys Dionne of the Quebec Court said: 'Rules are like women, made to be violated'. In 1993, Judge Raymonde Verreault of the same court sentenced a defendant to only 23 months' imprisonment for repeatedly sodomizing his 9-year-old stepdaughter on the ground that he had 'spared her virginity' and she had suffered no 'permanent scars'. In 1994, the Quebec Court of Appeal reduced to 90 days the sentence of a 44 year-old-man who had sexually assaulted his adolescent sister-in-law over a period of four years because the man was 'an asset to society': see *The Globe and Mail*, 15 Jan. 1994, 9 Dec. 1995.

[65] Young (1983), i, 124. One hundred and fifty victims were interviewed. [66] ibid.

[67] In Denmark, this provision was introduced by way of an amendment to the Civil and Criminal Code of Procedure in June 1980. In Norway, it was introduced by Act No. 66 of

sel and judges to sexual assault is also required. Continuing education programmes for judges should include re-education about sexual assault. Changes in the substantive law[68] might also be helpful in introducing new ways of thinking about this type of crime.

Reports, Prosecutions, and Convictions

(a) Rapes Recorded by the Police

In England and Wales, there has been a dramatic increase in the number of rape offences[69] recorded by the police in the years immediately following the Second World War until the present time. A comparison between the years 1947 and 1954 reveals a 22.5 per cent increase. The figures for 1976 and 1980 are, respectively, over four and five times that for 1947. There was an increase of 29 per cent in recorded rape offences in 1985 compared to 1984 and an increase of 24 per cent in 1986 compared to 1985. In 1987, there were 8 per cent more recorded rape offences than in 1986. The number of recorded rapes in 1991 was 19 per cent more than in 1990, 41 per cent more than in 1988, and more than double the number recorded in 1985. The 1993 figure was 11.8 per cent higher than the 1992 figure. By 2000/1, the number of recorded rape offences reached 8,593, a figure more than double that for 1992.

In the decade 1977–87, there was an average annual increase of 9.3 per cent in the figures of recorded rape.[70] With the exception of robbery, where the average annual increase was 9 per cent, there are no figures for other crimes which are comparable.[71] The average annual rise for all offences was 4 per cent. Between 1987 and 1997, the average annual increase in rape offences rose to 10.4 per cent. This was surpassed only by increases in drug offences but the average increase for all offences was only 1.7 per cent.[72] In the decade 1989/90 to 1999/2000, the number of recorded rapes rose by almost 150 per cent. The average annual increase for rape was 9.7 per cent, exceeded only by theft from a shop which averaged 10.3 per cent.[73] The average annual rise for all offences was 2.8 per cent.

12 June 1981, which amended the Criminal Procedure Act 1887. In Sweden, it was introduced in 1988 by the Legal Counsel for Injured Parties Act. The Danish scheme is discussed in detail in Ch. 5.

[68] See Chs. 2 and 3.

[69] The term rape in the criminal statistics includes rape, unlawful sexual intercourse with a defective (Sexual Offences Act 1956, s 7) or a mentally disordered patient (Mental Health Act 1959, s 128) as well as attempting, conspiring to commit, and aiding and abetting these crimes.

[70] *Criminal Statistics for England and Wales 1987*, Cm 498, Table 2.1, 28.

[71] The average annual increase for wounding or other act of violence against the person endangering life was 6.2 per cent.

[72] *Criminal Statistics for England and Wales 1997*, Cm 4162, table 2.1 33. However, for more serious offences of violence against the person it was 7.9 per cent.

[73] *Criminal Statistics for England and Wales 1999*, Cm 5001, table 2.1, 36.

Table 1.1. Rape offences recorded by the police, England and Wales

Year	Rape offences recorded by the police
1947[1]	240
1954[2]	294
1976	1,090
1980	1,225
1983[3]	1,334
1984	1,443
1985	1,842
1986	2,288
1987	2,471
1988	2,855
1989	3,305
1990	3,397
1991	4,046
1992[4]	4,142
1993	4,589
1997[5]	6,628
1999/2000	8,409
2000/2001[6]	8,593

Notes:

[1] See on this, Cambridge Dept. of Criminal Science Report (1957), 12 and app. 1.

[2] ibid.

[3] *Criminal Statistics for England and Wales 1983*, Cmnd 9349 (1984), 38 for figures between 1976 and 1983.

[4] See *Criminal Statistics for England and Wales 1992* (1993), Cm 2410, 48, which provides figures for recorded rapes from 1982 to 1992.

[5] The figures in Table 1.1 for 1997 onwards include male rape.

[6] See *Criminal Statistics for England and Wales 2000* (Cm 5312), Table 2.16, which provides figures for recorded rapes from 1993 to 2001. The figures for 1999/2000 and 2000/2001 cover the period April 1999 to March 2000 and April 2000 to March 2001. As from 1998, the statistics of recorded crime have been presented on a financial year basis.

The rise in recorded rape offences is probably mainly due to a change in attitudes which have become less tolerant of rape thus encouraging reporting, as well as leading to changes in the way police respond to and record rape allegations. However, it seems unlikely that the increases from 1946 onwards can be accounted for entirely in these terms.[74] As from 1995, the

[74] The rise in recorded rape offences over the past decade may be viewed in the context of the rise in recorded crimes of violence generally over this period: see R. Walmsley, *Personal Violence*, Home Office Research Study 89 (1986). However the rise in the reporting rate for rape substantially exceeds that for offences of violence against the person in all three decades mentioned above. Walmsley suggests that, since the conviction rate for rape has not kept pace with the rise in recorded offences, the rise in the incidence of rape is not as great as it seems: see ibid. 31 and 48. This fails to take account of the continuing difficulty in obtaining convictions in rape cases and the slow progress of reform in this area. The proposition that a rape takes place only in cases where a conviction results is manifestly unconvincing.

figures have been boosted by the inclusion of male rape. The figures for this have increased annually with 150 cases recorded in 1995 rising to 600 in 1999/2000, a rise of 19 per cent over the previous year and to 664 in 2000/2001, a further rise of 10.7 per cent.[75]

In other countries, too, increases in recorded rape have taken place.

Table 1.2. Offences of forcible rape recorded by the police in the United States

Year	Offences of forcible rape recorded by the police in the United States
1970	37,860
1982	77,763
1990	102,600
1991	106,593
1992	109,062
1999	89,110

In the United States between 1970 and 1982, reports of forcible rape more than doubled.[76] By 1990 the figure had increased by a further 32 per cent, rising in 1992 to a peak of 109,062.[77] Since then there has been an annual decrease.[78] In 1980, 71 out of every 100,000 females in the United States reported being victims of rape or attempted rape. This represented a 38 per cent increase over 1976.[79] By 1990, this figure had risen to 81 and by 1992 to 84 out of every 100,000 females.[80] By 1999, however, the figure had dropped to 64 out of every 100,000 females.[81] Several studies suggest that the level of reported rape in the United States is higher than in other Western nations and that this reflects the greater prevalence of rape in the United States.[82]

[75] Home Office, *Criminal Statistics* (2000), Table 2.1, 35; Home Office, *Criminal Statistics* (2001), Table 2.16. For further discussion of male rape, see Ch. 2 under the heading 'With a Woman or with a Man'.

[76] Federal Bureau of Investigation, *Uniform Crime Reports 1982* (Washington: United States Department of Justice, 1983). For the purpose of these statistics, forcible rape is defined as the carnal knowledge of a female forcibly and against her will. Assaults or attempts to commit rape by force or threat of force are also included.

[77] See *Uniform Crime Reports 1992* (Washington: United States Department of Justice, FBI, 1993), at 23 and annual volumes for previous years.

[78] Federal Bureau of Investigation, *Uniform Crime Reports 1999* (2000).

[79] Federal Bureau of Investigation, *Uniform Crime Reports 1980* (1981).

[80] See *Uniform Crime Reports 1992* (1993).

[81] *Uniform Crime Reports 1999* (2000).

[82] See e.g. Schiff, 'Rape in Other Countries' (1971) 11 Med Sci Law 3.

(b) Unreported Rape

It is universally recognized, however, that the number of offences recorded by the police is a small proportion of the number of rapes which actually take place. Victimization studies have been conducted to assess the true incidence of crime as against the number of crimes reported to the police.

(i) Unreported Rape in the United States

In the United States, a study published in 1967 and conducted by the National Opinion Research Centre involved 10,000 households and was aimed at discovering whether anyone in any of them had been a victim of any crime within the preceding 12 months.[83] This early study was not best calculated to unearth rapes whose victims had chosen not to report. Only one member of each household was interviewed and the interview was of 20 minutes duration. Yet this survey found that the estimated number of rapes per 100,000 population in 1965 was almost four times higher than the rate reported in the Uniform Crime Reports which are the official statistics of crime. Moreover, crimes revealed in the interviews were included in the figures only if seven rigorous criteria to establish their authenticity were fulfilled.[84] The United States National Crime Victimisation Survey (NCVS) of 1999 found 200,800 rapes and attempted rapes as compared with 89,110 recorded rapes. Only 37.5 per cent of forcible rapes were reported to the police.[85]

Other surveys suggest that the proportion of unreported rapes is much higher. Research conducted in 1978 by Diana Russell was, unlike the NCVS, geared specifically to ascertaining the incidence and prevalence of unreported rape and other forms of sexual assault in the San Francisco area.[86] Nine hundred and thirty randomly selected adult female residents living in San Francisco households were interviewed personally and privately by carefully trained female interviewers for, on average, 80 minutes. The study used the legal definition of rape in California and most other states at the time, namely, forced sexual intercourse or intercourse obtained by threat or force, or completed when the woman was drugged, unconscious, asleep, or otherwise totally helpless and hence unable to consent.[87] Of the 930 women, 44 per cent claimed at least one completed or attempted

[83] P. Ennis, *Criminal Victimization in the United States: A Report of a National Survey* (Washington: US Department of Justice, 1967).

[84] ibid. 4. See also Amir (1971); R. L. Dukes and C. L. Mattley, 'Predicting Rape Victim Reportage' (1977) 62 *Sociology and Social Research* 63.

[85] United States Department of Justice, Bureau of Justice Statistics, *Criminal Victimization in the United States, 1999*, Table 91 (Washington: United States Government Printing Office, 2000). The figures include male rape. The survey interviews about 80,000 people of 12 years old and upward, in 43,000 households, twice a year, about their experiences as victims of crime.

[86] Russell (1984), 34–48.

[87] ibid. 35.

rape, but out of 780 incidents of rape and attempted rape only 66 or 8 per cent were reported to the police. These figures include rape by husbands. If marital rape is excluded from the figures, 41 per cent of the women in the survey claimed rape or attempted rape. None of the marital rapes were reported to the police, so that out of the non-marital rapes 9.5 per cent, or approximately one in 10, were reported to the police.[88] The Russell survey also isolated the number of rapes and attempted rapes which interviewees had experienced in the 12 months prior to the interview (i.e. from mid-1977 to mid-1978). This number proved to be 13 times higher than the total incidence reported by the Uniform Crime Reports for females of all ages in San Francisco during 1978.[89] Russell estimated on the basis of her survey findings that there was at least a 46 per cent probability that a woman in San Francisco would be the victim of rape or attempted rape in the course of a lifetime.[90] Moreover, she suggested that 'there is no reason to believe that the percentage of raped women would be higher in San Francisco than in other cities [in the United States] of comparable size'.[91] She concluded that her survey bears out Johnson's assertion that 'sexual violence against women is part of the everyday fabric of American life'.[92]

In the United States, attempts have been made to improve the NCVS—a new questionnaire was introduced in 1992/3—in order to obtain a more accurate understanding of the level of unreported crime. In Canada[93] and Australia,[94] highly sophisticated methods have been developed to gauge the amount of unreported sexual crime. Canadian methodology, regarded as state of the art, has been replicated in Australia, Finland, and Iceland and is being developed for use in Sweden, Germany, and Ireland.[95] In Britain, however, our knowledge of the extent of sexual violence is far more limited.

[88] ibid. 35–6. Marital rape was excluded from the legal definition of rape in California at the time of the survey.

[89] ibid. 42–3. [90] ibid. 51. [91] ibid. 47.

[92] ibid. 71. For this assertion, see A. G. Johnson, 'On the Prevalence of Rape in the United States' (1980) 6 *Signs: Journal of Women in Culture and Society* 146. See also M. P. Koss, C. A. Gidycz, and N. Wisniewski, 'The Scope of Rape: Incidence and Prevalence of Sexual Aggression and Victimization in a National Sample of Higher Education Students' (1987) 55 *Journal of Consulting and Clinical Psychology* 162; M. P. Koss, W. J. Woodruff, and P. G. Koss, 'Criminal Victimization among Primary Care Medical Patients: Incidence, Prevalence and Physician Usage' (1991) 9 *Behavioural Sciences and the Law* 85; M. P. Koss, 'The Underdetection of Rape: Methodological Choices Influence Incidence Estimates' (1992) 48 *Journal of Social Issues* 61. For criticism of these studies, see N. Gilbert, 'The Phantom Epidemic of Sexual Assault' (1991) *Public Interest* 103. For a thorough review of the literature on prevalence rates for sexual aggression, see Krahe (2001), ch. 8.

[93] See Statistics Canada (1993); Johnson and Sacco (1995).

[94] Australian Bureau of Statistics, *Crime and Safety, Australia* (Canberra: Australian Bureau of Statistics, 1994).

[95] Walby and Myhill (2001), at 502.

(ii) Unreported Rape in Britain

Although there have been several useful small-scale studies which suggest a high level of unreported rape,[96] official or government-sponsored research has been noticeably lacking.[97] The British Crime Survey (BCS) has lagged behind in its methodology as far as sexual offences are concerned, although attempts are being made to improve it.[98] It has been suggested that, in any case, generic crime surveys like the BCS are not best placed to discover the true extent of crimes of violence against women and that, following the Canadian model, a survey dedicated specifically to such crime is required.[99]

In 1983, the BCS estimated that in England and Wales only 26 per cent of offences of rape and indecent assault were in fact recorded, although under-reporting was also found to be a feature of many offences.[100] The survey involved an interview in their homes with one person over 16 in each of about 11,000 households.[101] Only women were asked about their experience of sexual offences.[102] No rapes and only one attempted rape were revealed.[103] However, it was recognized that this was an inaccurate reflection of the amount of unreported rape which in fact occurs. The rape trauma syndrome involves feelings of extreme degradation, humiliation, and fear.[104] A rape victim is likely to feel inhibited about discussing the matter with an interviewer, particularly one who is male. A survey of this kind is better placed to reveal unreported crimes such as burglary and theft which do not carry the same emotional load. Moreover, sexual assault victims are frequently anxious not to reveal the incident to their families, members of which may well have been present or nearby during the interview. Although questions were asked in subsequent surveys about sexual assault, those conducting the BCS felt that its procedures produced unreliable estimates of the level of sexual victimization and therefore no estimates were

[96] See T. Jones, B. MacLean, and J. Young, *The Islington Crime Survey* (London: Gower, 1986); J. Hanmer and S. Saunders, *Well-Founded Fear: A Community Study of Violence against Women* (London: Hutchinson, 1984); Painter (1991). For discussion see Walby and Myhill (2001). See also Kelly (2002), 9–13; Hall (1985). For criticism of the methodology employed in the Hall study see B. Maclean (1985) 25 Brit J Criminol 390. In a small study of 22 men who had been raped, only two reported to the police: see Mezey and King (1992), 3–6.

[97] In a survey conducted by *Woman's Own* magazine, 25,000 women answered a questionnaire on rape. Of these, 12 per cent claimed to have been raped but out of these, 76 per cent did not report to the police: *Woman's Own*, 23 Aug. 1986.

[98] The 2001 BCS has evolved a new module on interpersonal violence including sexual violence: see Walby and Myhill (2001), 519 n. 1.

[99] Walby and Myhill (2001), at 507–8.

[100] *The British Crime Survey*, Home Office Research Study No. 76 (1983), 9. In 1984, it was found that 93 per cent of the sexual assaults uncovered in Scotland by the BCS were not reported to the police: *The British Crime Survey: Scotland*, Scottish Office Social Research Study (1984), 15.

[101] Home Office Research Study No. 76, 4.

[102] ibid. 54.

[103] ibid. 21. The number of sexual assaults revealed in the second British Crime Survey was also extremely low. See *Taking Account of Crime: Key Findings in the 1984 British Crime Survey*, Home Office Research Study 85 (1985).

[104] See above under the heading 'The Victim's Experience'.

published for over a decade.[105] But Percy and Mayhew of the Research and Statistics Directorate of the Home Office have now disclosed some of the unpublished findings.

It appears that, in 1993, for every 100 women there were 0.88 incidents of rape, attempted rape, and indecent assault. Aggregated for England and Wales, there were an estimated 190,000 such offences in 1993. This was over 15 times higher than the equivalent number of rapes and indecent assaults recorded by the police for that year, which numbered 12,000.[106] In the 1994 BCS, an attempt was made to try to improve measurement by using a Computer-Assisted Self Interview which allows respondents to answer a computer questionnaire. They thus avoid interaction with an interviewer and are able to complete the questions at their own pace.[107] A representative sample of 5,332 women aged 16–59 was used. As a result of this new methodology, it was estimated that 7.5 per cent of women in this age group in England and Wales had been sexually assaulted in 1993, a figure over ten times higher than the previous 1993 result.[108] An estimated 16.2 per cent of women in this age group had suffered unwanted sexual contact since the age of 16, with 6.3 per cent experiencing coerced sex[109] and 6.4 per cent attempted coerced sex.[110] Only 19 per cent of incidents classified by respondents as rape were reported to the police.[111] These disturbingly high figures are nevertheless acknowledged to be underestimates and are substantially lower than those in the 1992 Canadian survey in which the prevalence rate for unwanted sexual contact for women since the age of 16 was 25 per cent.[112]

(iii) Reasons for Non-reporting

There are many reasons why rape victims do not report. Out of 145 raped women in a study conducted by Women Against Rape (WAR), 55 per cent

[105] Estimates of rape and indecent assault were published in 1987: Percy and Mayhew (1997), 129. See now n. 109, below.

[106] ibid.

[107] ibid.

[108] Multiple victimization was found to be common: see ibid. 132. Widows were found to be at most risk of coerced sex although the figures were not high enough to arrive at a firm conclusion.

[109] i.e. forced into sex against their will. See now the 2000 British Crime Survey (Home Office, Research Study 237) which was conducted in the first half of 2000. Respondents were asked if they had experienced an incident of sexual victimization since age 16 and also in the last 12 months. The survey estimates that 61,000 women were the victims of rape in England and Wales during this 12-month period and that 754,000 women have been raped on at least one occasion since the age of 16. Women aged 16 to 24 were the most at risk.

[110] ibid. 133. Respondents were asked whether they regarded the incident as a crime deserving of punishment—a question not asked of other crime victims. This may be seen as an attempt to neutralize the impact of the survey's findings. However, most of those who described their experience as rape, attempted rape, or indecent assault answered this question affirmatively: see at 138–9.

[111] ibid. 140. In the 2000 survey, the police came to know about 20 per cent of the rapes, Home Office Rersearch Study 237, vii.

[112] Outside marriage or dating relationships only: see Percy and Mayhew (1997), Table 12, 144; Statistics Canada (1993); Johnson and Sacco (1995).

of those who did not report thought the police might be unsympathetic and 79 per cent thought that the police would be either unhelpful or unsympathetic. Thirty-one per cent felt too traumatized to face the prospect of police interrogation.[113] In two Australian studies, fear of the reaction of family members was also revealed as significant.[114] Snare suggests on the basis of Swedish research that rape by a stranger is far more likely to be reported than rape by someone well-known to the victim. Where there has been some initial voluntary contact, such as having a drink with the offender, she suggests that only one in ten cases is likely to be reported.[115] The WAR study provides some confirmation of this. Out of the same 145 victims, an estimated 60 were raped by a husband, boyfriend, family member, or man in authority. None of these cases was reported. A further 50 victims were estimated to have been raped by a friend, acquaintance, or workmate. Only 2 of these cases were reported. The remaining 10 reported cases all involved strangers.[116] Similarly, Russell found that 30 per cent of all rapes and attempted rapes by strangers which were revealed in her survey were reported to the police. This percentage was far higher than reports of rape to the police in respect of any other type of perpetrator, including acquaintances, family friends, personal friends, dates, boyfriends, and authority figures. Of all the rapes in her survey which were reported to the police, 55 per cent were by strangers. Yet stranger rapes represented only 17 per cent of the total number of rapes in the survey. Thus, stranger rape was disproportionately represented in the category of rapes reported to the police.[117] It may be that some victims believe that, unless the assault conforms to the stereotypical idea of rape, that is, by a stranger, their story is unlikely to be believed. Certainly 37 per cent of those who failed to report in the WAR study gave as a reason that 'they knew the man well or fairly well and did not think the police would take it seriously'.[118] Other reasons for non-reporting include 'feelings of shame, humiliation and self-blame; the desire to keep the rape secret . . . ; the wish to avoid . . . court appearances which are regarded as an ordeal; the wish to avoid trial by newspapers' publicity'.[119] Fear of retaliation is also an important factor.[120]

[113] Hall (1985), 108–13. In the *Woman's Own* survey, above n. 97, 25 per cent of victims did not report because they were afraid the police would not believe them, 17 per cent were afraid the police would be unsympathetic. For criticism of these findings, see G. Greer, 'Guess Who's Just Discovered Rape', *The Times*, 19 Aug. 1986.

[114] See Wilson (1978), Ch. 6; L. Henry, 'Hospital Care for Victims of Sexual Assault', in Scutt (1980), 170.

[115] Snare (1983), 66. See also L. Williams, 'The Classic Rape: When Do Victims Report' (1984) 31(4) *Social Problems* 459.

[116] Hall (1985), 127. In the *Woman's Own* survey above, p. 11, 11 per cent of those raped by a husband, 5 per cent of those raped by a boyfriend, and 43 per cent of those raped by a stranger went to the police.

[117] Russell (1984), 96–7.

[118] Hall (1985), 108.

[119] Smith (1989), 3. See also Kelly (2002), 9.

[120] See e.g. R. Bachman, 'Predicting the Reporting of Rape Victimizations' (1993) 20 Criminal Justice and Behaviour 254.

Of course, low reporting in itself is not necessarily a serious matter. Where victims fail to report crime because their experience of it was not particularly disturbing, it might be said to be pedantic to manifest disquiet. In the context of rape, however, non-reporting would appear to be quite unrelated to reactions of this sort. In Russell's survey, 85 per cent of those who described being extremely upset by the rape and 84 per cent of those who described having suffered considerable long-term effects failed to report the matter to the police.[121] If large numbers of victims, as the studies suggest, refrain from reporting out of fear that they will be treated without humanity or respect, this is indeed a grave indictment of the criminal justice system.

(c) 'No-Criming'

A second reason why the official statistics of recorded rape tell only part of the story is that women who do report rape do not necessarily have their complaints accepted by the police. Alternatively, complaints which are initially recorded as rape may subsequently be afforded a 'no crime' classification so that they do not enter the official statistics of recorded crime. Richard Wright, for example, found in his research into rapes and attempted rapes reported to the police between 1972 and 1976 in six English counties that, in about 24 per cent of the 384 cases made available to him, the police decided that no crime had taken place. Of these he writes: 'A number of them were clearly false. But it seemed equally clear to me that a significant proportion represented true rape offences.'[122] Similarly, in the Scottish Report, in 44 (22.4 per cent) out of a total of 196 cases of rape and assault with intent to ravish in the study sample, a no-crime classification was given to the crime report.[123] In 24 of the no-crime cases, the complaint was registered as withdrawn. However, the Report notes: 'It did not happen very often that complainers of their own accord and without encouragement withdrew their complaints'.[124] A study by Grace *et al.* of a sample of 335 rapes recorded by the police in England and Wales in 1985 found that 24 per cent of them were eventually no-crimed. The reasons given for no-criming were that the woman had withdrawn her allegation, had made a false allegation, was unwilling to testify or co-operate or was married to the suspect or that there was insufficient evidence.[125]

In America, the number of reported rapes which the police considered to be unfounded were, until 1976, specifically mentioned in the *Uniform Crime Reports*. Prior to 1975, the official 'unfounded rate' was about 18 per cent

[121] Russell (1984), 100.
[122] Wright (1980), 101.
[123] Chambers and Millar (1983), 38.
[124] ibid. 43.
[125] Grace *et al.* (1992), 6. The study considered only those cases which were initially recorded as rape by the police but were no-crimed after a month or more. It took no account of those which were no-crimed from the outset or within a month of recording. The true no-criming rate for this period would thus be greater. It was subsequently estimated to have been 45 per cent: see Harris and Grace (1999), Appendix B.

for most years.[126] Far more reported rapes than this, however, are thought to have fallen by the wayside. The *Uniform Crime Reports* returned to the theme in 1992 stating that the unfounded rate for rape that year was 8 per cent and that this was 6 per cent higher than for any other crime.[127] In their Canadian study, Clark and Lewis found that out of 116 cases of rape reported to the Toronto Police Department in 1970 involving complainants over 14 years old, 63.8 per cent were classified as unfounded.[128] However, the authors estimated that only 10.3 per cent of these were in fact unfounded.[129] In the majority of cases, the police used the 'unfounded' classification to cover cases which would be difficult to prosecute either because the rapist would be hard to trace or because there was insufficient corroborative evidence or because the victim was unlikely in their estimation to impress the jury favourably.[130]

In 1985 the Women's National Commission, an advisory group to the British government, issued a major report on rape in which some concern was expressed about the no-criming practices of the police.[131] This concern was taken up by the Home Office in a circular to all chief officers of police. It states: 'The only complaints which should be classified as "no crime" are those in which the complainant retracts completely and admits fabrication . . . There should be a clear distinction between unsubstantiated and false complaints. The former should remain recorded as crime whilst the latter should be recorded as "no crime".'[132] The Metropolitan Police had officially adopted a policy of this kind before the Circular was issued.[133] A study by Smith[134] of two London boroughs subsequently demonstrated that there had been a 50 per cent increase in criming between 1984 and 1986 and that the proportion of offences no-crimed dropped from 61 per cent in 1984 to 44 per cent in 1985 and to 38 per cent in 1986.[135] However, the study also revealed that no-criming continued to take place even where the allegation was not deemed to be false. Withdrawal of the complaint and insufficiency of evidence continued to be reasons given by the police for no-criming.[136] It concluded that it was difficult to fetter individual officers' discretion and that 'police officers are not complying with the advice which has been given'.[137]

A subsequent study by Gregory and Lees[138] looked at police recording practices in the London Borough of Islington from September 1988 to September 1990. It was found that out of 109 cases of rape and attempted rape reported during this period, 43 per cent were subsequently no-

126 Federal Bureau of Investigation, *Uniform Crime Reports* (1968–1974).
127 *Uniform Crime Reports 1992*, 24. 128 Clark and Lewis (1977), 34.
129 ibid. 38. 130 ibid. 58.
131 Women's National Commission (1985), para. 64.
132 Home Office Circular 69/1986: *Violence Against Women*, 11.
133 Home Office Statistical Bulletin, Issue 4/1986, 13 Mar. 1986. 134 Smith (1989).
135 ibid. 24. 136 ibid. 137 ibid. 25. 138 (1993).

crimed[139]—a higher rate than in any previous British study. Again, the reasons for no-criming were not confined to false allegations. Insufficiency of evidence, the victim's failure to substantiate the allegation (this included cases where she was unwilling to appear in court or to pursue the matter further or could not be contacted), a decision by the CPS to take no further action and the inability to identify the suspect, were all reasons given for no-criming.[140]

The most recent study to consider no-criming was conducted by Harris and Grace. This looked at nearly 500 incidents initially recorded as rape by the police in 1996. It was found that the no-criming rate had fallen to 25 per cent.[141] Although the most common reason for no-criming continued to be that the complaint was false or malicious (43 per cent), withdrawal of the complaint was the reason in 36 per cent of cases[142] and insufficiency of evidence in 15 per cent of cases. Thus, inappropriate use of the 'no crime' classification would appear to be a continuing problem. It was found that cases were least likely to be no-crimed where the complainant was under 13 or where violence had been used or where there was rape by an intimate.[143] Where violence was neither used nor threatened, cases were most likely to be no-crimed and the victim most likely to withdraw her complaint. It is not impossible that victims were encouraged to withdraw complaints in these circumstances. Victims were less likely to withdraw complaints where violence was used.

(d) Clear-Up Rates

The clear-up rate for rape in England and Wales has consistently been lower than that for other sexual offences with the exception of indecent assault on a female.[144] Since issues of consent as well as identity are particularly likely to arise with these offences, this is to be expected. The 1997 rate was the highest rate for 20 years, with other offences of violence enjoying a similarly high clear-up rate.[145] Since 1 April 1999, an offence cannot be classified as cleared up unless there is significant evidence to charge the suspect with a crime such that it would be likely to result in conviction.[146] This presumably explains, to some extent at least, the drop in the clear-up rate for all sexual offences in 1999.

139 ibid. 6.

140 ibid. 8.

141 However, this reduction was offset by the number of cases which had been classified as 'No further action'.

142 Home Office Circular 69/1986 specified that withdrawal of the complaint should only be classified as no-crime where it was accompanied by an admission that the complaint was false, see above.

143 However, rapes by intimates were likely to qualify for 'no further action'.

144 See Walmsley and White (1979), 54.

145 Home Office, *Criminal Statistics* (1998), 29.

146 Home Office, *Criminal Statistics* (2000), Appendix 2, para. 10.

Table 1.3. Clear-up rates, 1997, 1999

OFFENCE	Percentage cleared up in 1997[1]	Percentage cleared up in 1999[2]
Indecent assault on a female	71	55
Rape of a female	79	54
Rape of a male	80	60
USI[3] with a girl under 13	82	54
USI with a girl under 16	92	73
Incest	95	79
Buggery	94	78
Indecency between males	94	86

Notes:

[1] Home Office, *Criminal Statistics* (1998), Table 2.18, 47. For the purposes of the 1997 statistics as well as for previous years, an offence is said to be cleared up if a person is charged, summonsed, or cautioned for the offence, if the offence is admitted and taken into consideration by the court, or, in some cases if there is sufficient evidence to charge a person but the case is not proceeded with, for example because the offender is under the age of criminal responsibility or is already serving a long custodial sentence for another offence or because the victim is unable to give evidence. The clear-up rate is the ratio of offences cleared up in a year to offences recorded in the year: see Home Office, *Criminal Statistics* (1998), App. 2, para. 9.

[2] Home Office, *Criminal Statistics* (2000), Table 2.16.

[3] USI: unlawful sexual intercourse.

(e) Prosecution Rates

The prosecution rate for rape is low and has dropped dramatically over recent years. In the Scottish study, the Procurator Fiscal decided not to initiate proceedings in 30 per cent of cases sent to him by the police with a view to prosecution. This was a much higher no-proceedings rate than research revealed for other crimes of violence in Scotland.[147]

Table 1.4. Percentage of rapes recorded by the police in England and Wales resulting in court proceedings

Year	Rape of a woman (%)	Rape of a man (%)
1969–74	53	—
1980–82	55	—
1984–86	43	—
1987–89	43[1]	—
1990–92	42	—
1997	30	23
1999/2000	26	19

Notes:

[1] Similarly, in the Lees and Gregory study, of the 62 cases of rape and attempted rape reported at three London police stations between 1988 and 1990 only 27 (44 per cent) proceeded to court: Lees and Gregory (1993), 48.

[147] Chambers and Millar (1983), 10.

According to Smart, in England and Wales for the period 1969 to 1974, the percentage of rapes recorded by the police resulting in court proceedings was only 53 per cent.[148] This figure was obtained by taking the number of males proceeded against for rape as a percentage of the number of offences of rape recorded by the police.[149] As Table 1.4 indicates, applying this method to subsequent periods,[150] the percentage of males proceeded against for rape drops substantially so that in 1999/2000 it is under half of the 1969/74 figure. This closely resembles the finding, which can be deduced from the Harris and Grace study, in which only 27 per cent of the 362 cases of female rape recorded in 1996 and crimed by the police resulted in proceedings.[151]

The principal offence prosecution rate,[152] which showed signs of considerable improvement in the late 1970s and early 1980s, dropped from 65 per cent in 1977 to 49 per cent in 1999/2000 (Table 1.5, see page 24). The rate is based on the *Criminal Statistics* and is derived from the number of persons shown to have been proceeded against for rape as a percentage of the number of rapes cleared up[153] in the same year.

(f) Committals and Trials

The number of persons proceeded against in the magistrates' courts for rape offences[154] against women has mostly increased annually.[155] From 1979, the number of those committed for trial for rape offences each year was about 90 per cent of the number of persons proceeded against in the same

[148] C. Smart, *Women, Crime and Criminology* (London: Routledge and Kegan Paul, 1976), 118.

[149] The problem with this method is that the statistics of males proceeded against are compiled on an offender basis, whereas those of offences recorded by the police are offence based. However this method does enable comparisons to be made over a period of years.

[150] For the number of recorded offences of rape in each of the years mentioned see Home Office, *Criminal Statistics England and Wales*, vol. i (London: HMSO) and for the number of persons proceeded against, see *Criminal Statistics Supplementary Tables,* vol i. Recorded offences for 1999/2000 are compiled on a financial year basis but the supplementary tables continue to be compiled on a year to year basis. This means that the total figure for recorded rape offences used in this calculation includes offences recorded in the first three months of 2000.

[151] See Harris and Grace (1999), 12, 26.

[152] The *Criminal Statistics* do not record the total number of prosecutions for particular offences. Where proceedings involve more than one offence, it is only the principal offence which is recorded. For the meaning of principal offence, see Home Office, *Criminal Statistics 1997*, para. 31, 237. It is not possible to compare prosecution rates for different offences on the basis of the *Criminal Statistics*. This is because the recording of principal offences only does not have a uniform effect on all crimes. However, the principal offence prosecution rate is probably reliable for comparing the rates for a particular offence from year to year.

[153] For which see Table 1.3, n. 1, and n. 146 above.

[154] See above n. 69.

[155] See *Criminal Statistics Supplementary Tables*, Vol. 1, Table S1.1(A), 'Defendants Proceeded against at Magistrates' Courts by Offence, Sex and Result', annual volumes from 1979–2000.

Table 1.5. Rape. Principal Offence Prosecution Rate

Year	Per cent
1977	65
1978	69
1979	80
1980	78
1981	81
1982	75
1983	73
1984	67
1987	60
1989	57
1991	56
1992	53
1997	38
1999/2000	49

Table 1.6. Number of persons proceeded against for rape offences in magistrates courts; percentage of those proceeded against who are committed for trial; percentage proceeded against who are tried for rape

Year	No. proceeded against	Percentage committed	Percentage tried
1979	657	91	74
1987	1,048	82	61
1991	1,702	77	56
1992	1,648	72	56
1997	1,880	71	64
1999	2,054	67	67
2000	2,046	68	67

year. However, in 1987, the percentage dropped to 82 per cent and by 2000 it was 68 per cent[156] (Table 1.6). This is because of the dramatic increase in the number of cases in which proceedings are discontinued or the defendant is discharged on the ground of insufficient evidence. In 1985, there were two cases in which proceedings were discontinued and 69 defendants were discharged for lack of evidence. As Table 1.7 indicates, these figures have risen by leaps and bounds.[157]

[156] See ibid. for the number committed for trial each year.

[157] ibid. The number of persons who actually came up for trial at the Crown Court each year from 1979 to 1984 was on average 82 per cent of the number committed for trial each year but this percentage dropped to around 75 per cent from 1985 to 1987 and to 73 per cent in 1991 although it rose again to 79 per cent in 1992, to 90 per cent in 1997, and to over 100 per cent in 1999 and 2000. See *Criminal Statistics Supplementary Tables*, Vol. 2, Table S2.1(A), 'Defendants Tried and/or Sentenced at the Crown Court by Offence, Sex and Result', annual volumes from 1979–2000. (Those committed for trial do not necessarily come up for trial in the same year.)

Table 1.7. Rape cases discontinued or defendants discharged for lack of evidence

Year	Discontinued	Discharged for lack of evidence
1985	2	69
1991	180	189
1992	259	189
1997	317	201
1999	393	248
2000	387	229

Concern has been expressed that the CPS is generally too preoccupied with acquittal rates and too prone to discontinue cases where a conviction may be difficult to secure.[158] The recent joint report of the CPS and Constabulary Inspectorate into the prosecution of rape cases found some evidence of this.[159] Generally, it found that 'the prosecutor's approach too often tended to be one of only considering any weaknesses rather than also playing a more proactive role in seeking more information and trying to build or develop a case'.[160] This may help to explain why the number of defendants tried for rape in the Crown Court has not increased in line with the numbers proceeded against in the magistrates' courts. Indeed, in 1991 and 1992, the number tried was only 56 per cent of those proceeded against, rising to 67 per cent in 2000 (Table 1.6).[161]

(g) Conviction Rates

(i) Research Studies

In Wright's study, of the 255 rapes and attempted rapes carried out by solitary offenders in six counties of England between 1972 and 1976 which were investigated by the police as genuine ('no-crimed' cases were excluded from the sample), 240 men were involved and 204 men were actually arrested. Of these, 39 never appeared in court, either because charges were withdrawn by the complainant (8 cases) or because the prosecution decided not to proceed. Only 22 were found guilty of rape and 13 of attempted rape, a total of 17 per cent of those arrested. A further 65 were convicted of other offences in connection with the assault and 42 of a lesser offence such as indecent assault. Nine of these were not given a custodial penalty. Wright concluded:

[158] See e.g. *The Times*, 6 Dec. 1993.
[159] HMCPSI (2002), Executive Summary, para. 30.
[160] ibid., para. 31. See also Kelly (2002), 26–30.
[161] The number of those tried is not the same as the number coming up for trial. Not all defendants who come up for trial are tried.

Given the attrition of rape cases at every stage from the attack onwards, the rapist who receives a stiff fine must consider himself extremely unlucky. And the rapist who goes to gaol must believe that he was doubly unfortunate—the odds weigh heavily against that happening.[162]

In the Scottish study, a conviction was returned in only 25 per cent of a sample of 196 cases of rape and assault with intent to ravish recorded by the police in 1980 and 1981. Moreover, in over one-third of these, the conviction was for a lesser offence or for one which was not the subject of the original police report. The study sample included cases which were subsequently 'no-crimed'. If the 'no-crimed' cases are excluded, the conviction rate rises to 32 per cent, including convictions for lesser offences.[163] In the study by Grace *et al.*, out of a sample of 335 cases of rape or attempted rape recorded by the police in England and Wales in 1985 involving 327 suspects, only 27 per cent of cases resulted in a conviction for rape or attempted rape, although there were also convictions for other lesser offences. If the 'no-crimed' cases are excluded, the conviction rate rises to 35 per cent.[164] In the study by Lees and Gregory, an even lower conviction rate was found. Out of 109 cases of rape and attempted rape recorded by the police between 1988 and 1990, only 8 per cent resulted in convictions. If the 'no-crimed' cases are excluded, the conviction rate rises to 15 per cent.[165] However, in the most recent study by Harris and Grace, only 9 per cent of the sample of crimed rapes resulted in convictions for rape or attempted rape.[166]

A study by the Home Office found that of those committed for trial for substantive rape by the magistrates' courts in 1984 and 1985, only 48 per cent were convicted of rape, whilst a further 7 per cent were convicted of other sexual offences.[167]

Other studies suggest a high attrition rate in rape cases elsewhere. Thus, the New Zealand Report concluded: 'The chances that a rapist will actually be caught and convicted may be as low as 4 per cent, a figure which is probably much lower than that applying to most other serious offences'.[168] In Russell's study, of the 64 cases of rape and attempted rape reported to the police, six resulted in conviction. This represents 1 per cent of 670 rapes and attempted rapes revealed by the survey.[169]

(ii) Home Office Statistics

The official statistics show that in 1980 there were 416 convictions for rape offences in the Crown Court and in 1987 there were 423. In each year in-between apart from 1985, the number of convictions dropped below the

[162] Wright (1984), 400.
[163] Chambers and Millar (1983), 10.
[164] Grace *et al.* (1992), 5.
[165] Lees and Gregory (1993), 48.
[166] Harris and Grace (1999), 31.
[167] Home Office, *Statistical Bulletin,* Issue 4/89, (1989) Table 4. Substantive rape excludes attempted rape and other allied offences: see n. 69.
[168] Young (1983), 14.
[169] Russell (1984), 101.

Table 1.8. Convictions for rape offences against a female in the Crown Court

Year	No. of convictions
1980	416
1981	308
1983	308
1987	423
1988	504
1991	539
1992	492
1997	574
1999	598
2000	552

1980 figure. The first real increase came in 1988 when the figure rose to 504. It dropped back to 492 in 1992, rising again to 574 for rape of a female in 1997, 598 in 1999, but dropping back again in 2000 to 552.[170] Given that the number of recorded rapes doubled between 1980 and 1987 and the number of those proceeded against for rape in 1987 was 50 per cent more than the number proceeded against in 1980, it would seem to be remarkable that the number of convictions between 1980 and 1987 showed virtually no increase. It is similarly worthy of comment that the number of convictions in 1991 was 30 per cent more than the number in 1980, whereas the number of offences of rape reported to the police in 1991 was 230 per cent more than the 1980 figure and the number of persons proceeded against in 1991 was 145 per cent of the 1980 figure. There was an 11 per cent increase in the total number of convictions in 1999 as compared with 1991 but there was a 93 per cent increase in the number of offences recorded by the police and a 21 per cent increase in the number of persons proceeded against.

Table 1.9. Convictions for rape offences in the Crown Court as a percentage of reported cases in the same year

Year	Convictions as a percentage of reported cases
1979	32
1985	23
1989	18
1991	13
1992	12
1997	9
1999/2000	8

[170] See annual *Criminal Statistics Supplementary Tables*, Vol. 2, Table S2.1(A).

In 1979, the number of convictions for rape was 32 per cent of the number of reported cases in that year. This figure has dropped markedly over the years, falling to 8 per cent in 1999/2000 (Table 1.9).[171] Thus, to say that convictions have not kept pace with the number of recorded rapes or of those proceeded against would appear to be a massive understatement.

(h) Acquittal Rates

An acquittal rate for rape offences may be calculated in terms of the number of defendants acquitted of rape offences in the Crown Court each year as a percentage of the number of defendants tried for rape offences in the same year in the Crown Court.[172] On this basis, as Table 1.10 indicates, the acquittal rate for rape offences rose from 24 per cent in 1979 to 60 per cent in 1999.

Table 1.10. Acquittal rate for rape offences

Year	Acquittal rate
1979	24
1987	34
1991	43
1992	47
1997	51
1999	60
2000	57

Notes:
Figures for 1997 onwards include male rape.

That the conviction rate has dropped so markedly must be a matter of some concern. There is no easy explanation for this. A study by Lloyd and Walmsley comparing rape convictions in 1973 with those in 1985 found that there had been a marked increase in the proportion of rape convictions where the offender and victim were intimately known to each other as opposed to being acquaintances. Intimates were relatives, close friends, partners and ex-partners. The authors comment that it may be 'that the increases reflect a greater willingness . . . of the courts to convict' in such cases.[173] Grace *et al.* argue that such willingness does not appear to extend so readily to acquaintance rapes. Their study suggests that acquaintance rapes are

[171] The figures for 1997 and 1999/2000 include reports and convictions for male rape.

[172] The number of persons tried for rape is obtained by subtracting the total number of persons not tried for rape from the total for trial: see Annual Supplementary Tables, Vol. 2 Table S2.1(A).

[173] *Changes in Rape Offences and Sentencing*, Home Office Research Study No. 105 (1989), 11. But see Lees and Gregory (1993), p.45.

far more likely to result in acquittal than rape by strangers or intimates. Twenty-five per cent of the acquaintance rapes which came to court resulted in an acquittal as against 8 per cent of the stranger rapes and 11 per cent of the rapes by intimates.[174] It was found that if the complainant first met the defendant in a place such as a hotel, club, pub, or wine bar and the alleged attack took place indoors, the case was more likely not to result in a conviction.[175]

It might be tempting to conclude that one possible explanation for the drop in conviction rates is that more acquaintance rapes are being reported and are coming before the courts. However, the term acquaintance rape is almost devoid of meaning. It appears to be used to cover persons who could in no ordinary sense be described as acquaintances, for example, where the complainant had accepted a lift from the suspect, given him directions or where the suspect showed her round a house.[176] It is simply a ragbag category covering a multitude of different situations other than one involving a stranger whom the complainant had never seen before the attack, or a friend, lover, or member of the complainant's family. As such it can do little to explain the high acquittal rate in rape cases. Furthermore, in the subsequent study by Harris and Grace, it was found that out of those cases brought to trial, 25 per cent of the stranger rapes resulted in jury acquittals, as against 19 per cent of the acquaintance rapes and 14 per cent of rapes by intimates. If judge-ordered or directed acquittals are included, 25 per cent of stranger rapes resulted in acquittals as against 23 per cent of acquaintance rape and 23 per cent of rapes by intimates. Moreover, whereas 25 per cent of the stranger rapes resulted in a conviction for the full offence, this was true of 30 per cent of the acquaintance rapes and 23 per cent of the rapes by intimates.[177] Thus, not merely did stranger rapes have the highest acquittal rate but acquaintance rapes were more likely to result in a conviction for the full offence than either stranger rapes or rapes by intimates.

Rather more useful by way of explanation is the finding by Grace *et al.* that, in their sample, almost two-thirds of cases where the victim was injured resulted in a conviction of some kind whereas less than a third of cases where there was no evidence of physical injury resulted in conviction.[178] Yet Harris and Grace found that cases in which there was evidence of violence were often dropped. They concluded that there was a need for better evidence-gathering through photographs and medical reports.[179]

174 (1992), 17. The study looked at the cases which came to Crown Court from a sample of all offences initially recorded as rape in England and Wales during the second quarter of 1985: see at p. 2. See also Lees and Gregory (1993), 45.

175 (1992), p.26.

176 See Harris and Grace (1999), at 8.

177 At 31.There were 8 stranger rapes, 43 acquaintance rapes, and 44 rapes by intimates.

178 Grace *et al.* (1992), at 21.

179 Harris and Grace (1999), at 46. See also HMCPSI (2002), 4, para. 24.

The picture which thus emerges from the statistics is one in which the number of recorded offences of rape has radically increased, but the prosecution rate is dropping, as is the committal rate and the conviction rate. Thus, the attrition rate in rape cases after recording by the police is increasing.[180]

Appeals

A study of criminal appeals brought in 1996 revealed that there were more appeals in sexual offences than in any other offence category apart from offences of violence and that more convictions were quashed and more retrials ordered in sexual offence cases than in other offence categories apart from offences of violence.[181] The study does not provide information on specific sexual offences but clearly suggests that the attrition of rape offences may not end at Crown Court.

For those who subscribe to the ideal of the rule of law, the conviction rate for rape should be a cause for concern. The prosecuting authorities are unlikely to wish to expend undue time and energy prosecuting cases of this kind if convictions remain disproportionately hard to obtain. In suggesting the way forward to combat attrition, Harris and Grace recommend that further research be conducted into attrition rates in countries where better support for victims is provided.[182] Higher conviction rates may demand alterations in court procedures, in rules of evidence,[183] and in the substantive law.[184] They will certainly require changes in general attitudes and assumptions about sexual assault, which reforms within the criminal justice system may in themselves help to achieve.

Sentencing

The 1980s witnessed mounting concern about sentencing in rape cases. Various attempts to assuage public fears were made as a result but it was not until 1986 in *Billam*[185] that firm action was taken to try to deal with the relatively lenient approach to rape adopted by some judges.

[180] See also Kelly (2002), 13–17.

[181] J. Mattinson, *Criminal Appeals England and Wales, 1995 and 1996*, Home Office Statistical Bulletin, Issue 3/1998 (Research and Statistics Directorate, 1998), Tables 14 and 15.

[182] Harris and Grace (1999), at 49.The Scandinavian countries operate a system of legal representation for sexual assault victims which is considered in Ch. 5 of this book.

[183] Discussed in Ch. 4.

[184] Discussed in Chs. 2 and 3.

[185] [1986] 1 All ER 985.

(a) The Situation Prior To *Billam*[186]

(i) Sentencing in the Court of Appeal

In rape cases, the Court of Appeal generally took the view that sentences of imprisonment should be within a range of two to twelve years[187] with life imprisonment being a rarity. Those factors which the Court of Appeal considered to merit a sentence in the lowest bracket were clearly open to criticism. Rape of a girl of about the same age as the defendant who consented to some degree of familiarity, rape of a girl or woman who acted 'imprudently', or rape of a wife, would generally attract a light sentence of two to three years provided that not too much injury was caused.[188] Mitigating factors accepted by the Court of Appeal also sometimes appeared rather less than convincing.[189]

(ii) Sentencing in the Crown Court

Lenient sentences dispensed by trial judges were the source of much comment and public criticism in the 1980s. But it was as much the sentiments expressed by the judges and the attitudes they appeared to betoken as the sentences themselves which caused concern. In January 1982, for example, Judge Bertrand Richards declined to imprison a convicted rapist and imposed a £2,000 fine on him instead. The defendant was a businessman who had given a lift to a 17-year-old girl. The judge commented: 'I am not saying that a girl hitching home late at night should not be protected by the law, but she was guilty of a great deal of contributory negligence.'[190] In December 1982, sentencing in another rape case led to a public outcry and to a demand for change. Judge Stanley Price at Leeds Crown Court imposed a 12-month sentence with eight months of it suspended on a 26-year-old man who had raped and indecently assaulted a 6-year-old girl. The defendant spent 25 days in prison as a result. The judge, it seems, considered the case was essentially one of indecent assault. The fact remains, however, that penile penetration of the vagina, albeit slight, did take place and this in law is rape. This was apparently accompanied by several serious offences of

[186] For full discussion, see Temkin (1987), 16–19.

[187] Lower and higher sentences were occasionally seen. See further on this, Thomas (2nd edn., 1979), 112–17; Thomas *Current Sentencing Practice* (1979–), 2181–90/7. The tariff for the offence of wounding with intent to do grievous bodily harm under the OAPA 1861, s. 18 was similar.

[188] See Thomas (2nd edn. 1979), 113–14. Rape of a wife was then an offence only in certain limited circumstances, e.g. where a decree nisi of divorce had been granted or where the wife had obtained a non-molestation injunction against her husband: see pp. 80–1 below.

[189] See e.g. *Brimacombe* unreported, 20 Apr. 1971, CA (Cr Div) (Register No. 3783/B/70 cited in Thomas (2nd edn. (1979), 117 n. 1). For further examples, see Temkin (1987), 17.

[190] For report and comment on the case, see *The Times*, 6, 7, 8, 11, and 12 Jan. 1982.

indecency. The defendant's own solicitor expressed his complete surprise at the sentence and was reported to have said that his client 'would not have complained if he had been given at least a two-year immediate prison sentence'.[191] A year later, Judge Michael Argyle QC was criticized for imposing a suspended sentence in a serious case of attempted rape. His remarks to the defendant on the occasion were regarded as inappropriately indulgent. He is reported to have said:

> You have been all over the world and you are an experienced man. You have never seriously been across the law before . . . For goodness sake make this the last time. Once you put your hands around a woman's neck in drink anything can happen . . . You come from Derby which is my part of the world. Now off you go and don't come back to this court.[192]

(iii) Attempts to deal with the Criticism

In January 1982, a few weeks after the furore which greeted the decision of Judge Richards mentioned above, the Lord Chief Justice in *Roberts*[193] set out the general principles which should be applied in sentencing in rape cases. He emphasized that rape was an offence which should necessarily lead to a sentence of imprisonment save in exceptional circumstances.[194] He also indicated the situations in which higher sentences might be imposed.[195] However, nothing explicit was said about the level of sentencing in either normal or aggravated cases. The guidelines were thus too vague to be of much assistance.

In December 1982, in response to strong criticism in the press and by Members of Parliament following the sentence handed out by Judge Stanley Price, the Prime Minister announced that, as a general rule, for the future, only High Court judges or experienced circuit judges would try rape cases.[196] Whilst this announcement was sufficient to assuage public concern at the time, doubts were expressed as to whether senior judges would always be available and even if they were whether such a step would make any difference.[197]

Two years later, in November 1985, there was renewed criticism of lenient sentencing in rape cases. The immediate cause was the sentences imposed after the gang rape of two schoolgirls. Four of the youths concerned received seven years' youth custody, while two boys aged 14 and 15 were given three years' detention.[198] Mr David Mellor, a Home Office Minister,

[191] See *The Guardian*, 15 and 16 Dec. 1982; *The Times*, 16 Dec. 1982.
[192] See the *Daily Express*, 3 Dec. 1983; *The Guardian*, 6 Dec. 1983.
[193] [1982] 1 All ER 609.
[194] ibid. 610.
[195] e.g. gang rape, repeated rape, rape of very young or elderly.
[196] See *The Guardian* and *The Daily Telegraph*, 15 Dec. 1982; *The Times*, 16 Dec. 1982.
[197] See Z. Adler, 'Rape: Will Top Judges Pass Longer Sentences?' *The Times*, 7 Jan. 1983.
[198] See *The Daily Telegraph*, 19 Dec. 1985; *The Times*, 2 Feb. 1986; *The Guardian*, 22 Feb. 1986.

urged the Lord Chief Justice to issue new guidelines on sentencing in rape cases[199] and in February 1986, in *Billam,* these duly appeared.

(b) *Billam*

In *Billam,* Lord Lane CJ prefaced his remarks by noting that 'the nastiness of rape cases has certainly increased and what would 10 years ago have been considered incredible perversions have now become commonplace'.[200] He also expressed the view that sentences for rape had become too low.[201] His guidelines are far more specific than those suggested in *Roberts*, but similarly proceed on the basis that rape should entail a custodial sentence in all but the most exceptional circumstances. Exceptional circumstances were said to be illustrated by the case of *Taylor*,[202] in which a mentally retarded man raped a girl of 19 suffering from Down's Syndrome. The Court of Appeal reduced his sentence to probation on the grounds that the act was more in the nature of an indecent assault, the appellant had only a child-like understanding of the gravity of his actions, and the girl made very little protest.

(i) The Starting-Points

The guidelines stipulate five years as the starting-point for an adult pleading not guilty and with no mitigating circumstances.[203] This clearly represents an increase on past sentencing patterns.[204] The extent of this increase is indicated by Home Office figures for 1984 quoted in the judgment,[205] which show that only 18 per cent of those convicted for rape offences were imprisoned for over four and up to five years and only 8 per cent for more than five years. The guidelines further state that eight years should be the starting-point for two or more rapists acting together, for men who rape victims in the victim's own home, for those who abused positions of responsibility

199 See *The Times*, 20, 23 Feb. 1986.

200 [1986] 1 All ER at 986–7. Detective Chief Superintendent Thelma Wagstaff of the Metropolitan Police had earlier expressed a similar view when addressing a conference of the Howard League. She said that five years ago a victim would tell police that she had been raped, but 'Now the offender is also committing buggery, forcing the victim to have oral sex and urinating over her': see *The Guardian*, 21 Nov. 1985. See also p. 56 below. These assertions are supported by research findings: see C. Lloyd and R. Walmsley, *Changes in Rape Offences and Sentencing*, Home Office Research Study 105 (London: HMSO, 1989), 20–1.

201 [1986] 1 All ER at 987. See also *Darby* (1986) 8 Cr App R (S) 487. Shapland *et al.* found that the sexual assault victims in their study considered that the sentences meted out to their assailants were too low whereas this was not the view of the other victims in the survey: see Shapland *et al.* (1985), 72. In the Scottish study, 71 per cent of the sexual assault victims interviewed felt that the sentences given in their cases were too low: see Chambers and Millar (1986), 76–7, and 80.

202 (1983) 5 Cr App R (S) 241.

203 [1986] 1 All ER at 987.

204 See Temkin (1987), 20–2.

205 [1986] 1 All ER at 987.

over their victims, and for rape involving the abduction and holding captive of the victim.[206]

(ii) Aggravating Features

The guidelines state that the crime should be treated as aggravated if any one of the following eight factors is present: (1) violence is used over and above the force necessary to commit the rape; (2) a weapon is used to frighten or wound the victim; (3) the rape is repeated; (4) the rape has been carefully planned; (5) the defendant has previous convictions for rape or other serious offences of a violent or sexual kind; (6) the victim is subjected to further sexual indignities or perversions; (7) the victim is either very old or very young; (8) the effect on the victim, whether physical or mental, is of special seriousness. Where any one or more of these factors is present, a sentence substantially higher than the starting-point is to be given.[207] It is also stated that 15 years may be appropriate for those who conduct campaigns of rape and that in the case of perverted or psychopathic offenders, those with gross personality disorders and those who are likely to constitute a danger to women for an indefinite time, a sentence of life imprisonment is not unsuitable.[208]

(iii) Mitigating Features

Lord Lane mentioned two features which could mitigate the sentence. The first and most important is where the defendant pleads guilty. He suggested that a guilty plea should perhaps qualify the defendant for an even greater reduction in sentence than is usually the case because of the distress which a trial can cause to the victim. The extent of the reduction would depend upon the circumstances, including the likelihood of a finding of not guilty had the matter been contested.[209] There might also be some mitigation of sentence where the victim behaved in a manner calculated to lead the defendant to believe that she would consent to sexual intercourse.[210] But sexual familiarity falling short of so doing would not seem to qualify the defendant for a reduction.

(iv) Non-mitigating Features

Lord Lane went on to state that imprudence by the victim, such as accepting a lift from a stranger, and the victim's previous sexual experience should

[206] [1986] 1 All ER 985 at 987.

[207] [1986] 1 All ER 985 at 988.

[208] ibid 987–8.

[209] [1986] 1 All ER 988. See now Powers of Criminal Courts (Sentencing) Act 2000, s 152. Generally speaking, a plea of guilty may result in a reduction of between a quarter and a third of the sentence which would otherwise have been given: see Thomas (2nd edn., 1979), 52; Thomas (1979), 1061–4.

[210] [1986] 1 All ER 985 at 988.

not constitute grounds for moderating sentence, and the defendant's previous good character was similarly of only minor relevance.[211]

(v) Attempts

With respect to attempted rape, it was stated that the sentence should normally be less than for the completed offence, especially if the defendant desisted at a comparatively early stage. However, Lord Lane also indicated that attempted rape could be more serious than rape itself if aggravating features were present.[212]

(vi) Defendants under 21

Many rape defendants are under 21. Lord Lane favoured the imposition of custodial sentences on such offenders in most cases and considered that the sentence should be for the same length of time as an adult would spend in prison with some reduction to take account of the offender's age.[213]

Offenders who have reached the age of 18 but are under 21 may be sentenced to detention in a young offender institution.[214] Those who have reached 15 but are under 18 may be given a detention and training order, generally for a maximum of 24 months.[215] A similar sentence is available for those under 15 who are persistent offenders.[216] Where the boy is under 12, the court must additionally be of the opinion that only a custodial sentence would be adequate to prevent the offender from offending further before such a sentence can be imposed.[217] Alternatively, children under 18 may be sentenced to detention under the power originally conferred by the Children and Young Persons Act 1933, s 53(2)[218] for a period not exceeding that which could be imposed for an adult, so that lengthy sentences may be imposed. Detention will generally be in secure local authority accommodation, or in a young offender institution. The availability of the sentence under s 53(2) depends upon the case being tried on indictment. Lord Lane stressed that a magistrates' court dealing with a juvenile charged with rape should *never* accept jurisdiction to deal with the case but should invariably commit the case for trial to the Crown Court to ensure that this power could be used.[219]

(c) The Situation after *Billam*

In both *Roberts* in 1982 and *Billam* in 1986, Lord Lane made it clear that a custodial sentence should always be imposed for rape save in exceptional

211 ibid. 988. 212 ibid. 213 ibid.,

214 CJA 1982, s 1A as amended by CJA 1991. See now Powers of Criminal Courts (Sentencing) Act 2000, s 96.

215 Powers of Criminal Courts (Sentencing) Act 2000, s 100.

216 S 100(2)(a). 217 S 100(2)(b).

218 See now Powers of Criminal Courts (Sentencing) Act 2000, s 91. 219 At 988.

circumstances. But even before *Roberts,* in 1980 and 1981, 89 per cent of convicted rapists over 21 received custodial sentences. As Table 1.11 indicates, this percentage has risen steadily, reaching 99 per cent in 1997 and remaining more or less at that level.[220]

Table 1.11. Percentage of males over 21 convicted of rape who received custodial sentences

Year	Percentage custodial sentences
1980	89
1981	89
1984	91
1985	93
1987	94
1991	95
1997	99
1999	98
2000	98

In 1984, 31 per cent of all offenders who were sentenced to immediate custody for the full offence of rape[221] received sentences of five years or more (Table 1.12).[222] This figure rose to 79 per cent in 1987.[223] The number of offenders given more than 10 years or life increased from 25 in 1985 to 49 in 1987.[224] In 1987, sentences also increased for attempted rape with 40 per cent of convicted offenders receiving sentences of over five years as against 10 per cent in 1984.[225]

In 1984, of those sentenced to custody for rape offences[226] in the Crown Court, only 13 per cent were sentenced to five years or more. As Table 1.12 indicates, this percentage has risen dramatically over the years, reaching 74 per cent in 2000.[227] Thus, the *Billam* guidelines have made a clear impact on sentencing levels.

[220] *Criminal Statistics Supplementary Tables*, vol. ii. For the years 1980–97, table S2.1(E), for 1999, table S2.1(f), for 2000, table S2.1(g).

[221] i.e. rape itself and not attempted rape or offences connected with mentally defective patients which are generally included in the statistics.

[222] See Home Office, *Statistical Bulletin*, Issue 4/89, (1989) Table 7. This special issue provides information on rape between 1977 and 1987 which is not available for previous or succeeding years.

[223] ibid.

[224] ibid.

[225] ibid., para. 13. Figures for 1985 and 1986 unavailable.

[226] The *Criminal Statistics* produced annually by the Home Office provide statistics of rape offences. This category includes attempted rape and offences connected with mentally defective patients as well as rape. Figures are not provided for rape alone.

[227] *Criminal Statistics Supplementary Tables 1984–1999*, Vol. ii, Table S2.4. For 2000, Sentencing Advisory Panel (2001), 3.

Table 1.12. Percentage sentenced for five years or more for substantive and attempted rape and rape offences and number sentenced for over 10 years for substantive rape

Year	Percentage sentenced for five years or more for substantive rape	Number sentenced for over 10 years for substantive rape	Percentage sentenced for five years or morefor attempted rape	Percentage sentenced for five years or more for rape offences
1984	31	10	10	13
1985	42	25	–	25
1986	62	37	–	46
1987	79	49	40	61
1988	–	–	–	53
1989	–	–	–	53
1991	–	–	–	54
1992	–	–	–	59
1997	–	–	–	68
1999	–	–	–	75
2000	–	–	–	74

(i) Sentencing in the Court of Appeal

Any consideration of sentencing in the post-*Billam* era must take account of the power given to the Attorney General in 1988 to refer unduly lenient sentences to the Court of Appeal for review.[228] But a departure from the *Billam* guidelines will not in itself suffice to ensure that the sentence is raised. It is only where the sentence is unduly lenient that this will occur and this has been interpreted on more than one occasion to mean that there must have been some error of principle in the sentence so that public confidence would be damaged if it were not altered.[229] Even where this threshold requirement has been met, the Court of Appeal has adopted a 'double jeopardy' principle. It takes into account the fact that the defendant has been subjected to the sentencing process twice over and makes a reduction to compensate him for this. Thus, substituted sentences are frequently lower than the guidelines would indicate and since the extent of the reduction on this account is frequently not made clear, sentences altered through this mechanism are not always the best guide to interpreting the guidelines.

THE STARTING-POINTS

On the whole, the Court of Appeal is applying the five-year starting-point set out in *Billam*. The eight-year starting-points are also being observed with sentences frequently well above this level where aggravating features are present. Thus, rape with abduction or false imprisonment has attracted

[228] Criminal Justice Act 1988, ss 35–6. See *Attorney General's Reference No. 1 of 1989* (1989) 11 Cr App R (S) 409 for guidelines on sentencing in incest cases.

[229] See e.g. *Attorney General's Reference No. 5 of 1989* (1990) 90 Cr App R 358.

sentences of 10[230] and 13 years.[231] Where rape takes place in the victim's own home, sentences of 12 years are common[232] and 13[233] and 16-year[234] sentences have also been given.[235] The same is true of rape by men acting in concert, where sentences of 12 years and more have been dispensed.[236] Campaigns of rape have resulted in sentences of 15, 16, and 18 years.[237] Rape by a person in a position of authority or trust has tended to attract sentences at a lower level, with the Court of Appeal reducing sentences to eight years or less in several cases.[238] However, sentences of 12[239] and 15 years[240] have also been upheld in some cases of rape by a father.

AGGRAVATING FEATURES

In *Billam*, eight factors which would aggravate the offence were set out. It is noteworthy that of those cases which reach the Court of Appeal, there are relatively few in which aggravating features are not present. Some cases suggest a rule of thumb by which a year is added to the starting-point for each aggravation. In *Brown*,[241] for example, the defendant broke into the victim's home, threatened her with a knife, committed various sexual indecencies upon her, raped her twice and used violence above that which was necessary for the rape, causing her injury and pain. These four aggravating factors on top of the eight-year starting point for rape committed in the victim's home were said to warrant a sentence of 12 years which was reduced to nine on account of the defendant's guilty plea. But it is clear that more than this may be added, particularly where the starting-point is five years, extreme violence is used and the effect on the victim is grave. In *Rowe*,[242] for example, the defendant used serious violence against the victim as well as committing rape and buggery twice over and forcing her to perform oral

[230] *Malcolm* (1987) 9 Cr App R (S) 487.

[231] *Farmer* (1993) 14 Cr App R (S) 664; *Attorney General's Reference No. 10 of 1995* [1996] 2 Cr App R (S) 122.

[232] See *Gearing* (1987) 9 Cr App R (S) 465; *Hawkins* (1989) 11 Cr App R (S) 429; *Attorney General's Reference No. 1 of 1991* (1991) 13 Cr App R (S) 134.

[233] *Farag Mohammed Ali Guniem* (1994) 15 Cr App R (S) 91.

[234] *Williams* (1992) 13 Cr App R (S) 562; see also *Thomas* (1995) 16 Cr App R (S) 686—15 years upheld.

[235] For more lenient sentences, see *Attorney General's Reference No. 29 of 1996 (R v Fridye)* [1997] 1 Cr App R (S) 224; *Attorney General's Reference No. 44 of 1999 (R v Logan)* [2000] 1 Cr App R (S) 317.

[236] *Davids* (1991) 13 Cr App R (S) 468; *Jones* (1992) 13 Cr App R (S) 698.

[237] *Gibson* (1987) 9 Cr App R (S) 30 (15 years); *Paolucci* (1988) 10 Cr App R (S) 181 (16 years); *Henry* (1988) 10 Cr App R (S) 327 (18 years).

[238] *Lewis* [1990] Crim LR 11 (rape by father, seven years); *Baker* (1989) Cr App R (S) 513 (rape by stepfather, eight years); *H* (1993) 14 Cr App R (S) 414 (rape by father, six years); *Attorney General's Reference No 32 of 1992* [1993] Crim LR 716 (rape by uncle of 11-year-old niece, seven years). *Mason* (1995) 16 Cr App R (S) 860 (rape of 88-year-old dementia patient by nurse in nursing home, eight years).

[239] *Kirk* (1987) Cr App R (S) 261.

[240] *D* (1993) 14 Cr App R (S) 639. See also *R v M* [1996] 2 Cr App R (S) 286, 28 years reduced to 18 for rape of two stepdaughters on numerous occasions.

[241] (1992) 13 Cr App R (S) 382.

[242] (1989) 11 Cr App R (S) 342.

sex. The Court of Appeal noted her injuries and that it took her a month to recover from them. It added, 'How long it will take, if ever she does fully recover, to recover mentally from the ordeal, no-one can tell'. The sentence was reduced from 15 to 13 years. Thus, eight years was added to the starting-point of five for the four aggravating features—the extra violence, the repeated rape, the further sexual indignities, and the serious effect on the victim.

Similarly, in *Bojang*,[243] the defendant attacked a young woman who was walking home at night. He kicked her until she became unconscious, struck her on the head with a brick and broke her jaw. He then raped her and subjected her to further sexual indignities. He had previous convictions for indecent assault. The mental and physical effect on the victim was serious. Her jaw had to be fixed with wire and it remained wired for two months. The Court of Appeal reduced his sentence from 14 to 11 years on account of his guilty plea. Given that the starting-point for this offence was five years, the four aggravating features appear to have added six years to the sentence. The same is true of *Clarke*.[244] The defendant attacked a 53-year-old woman he had met at a club. He knocked her to the ground, punched her repeatedly about the face and mouth, breaking her dentures, gripped her throat, banged her head on the floor, and threatened to rip her tongue out. The Court had before it the report of the doctor who examined her when the police took her to hospital. It noted that the list of injuries covered more than a page and a half of the doctor's statement. It considered that the proper sentence without a guilty plea would have been 10 years. Since the starting-point here was again five years, this would have meant adding a further five years for grave violence and the effect on the victim. The guilty plea, however, reduced the sentence to eight years.

Previous convictions for rape have also added substantially to the sentence. In *Towler*,[245] the defendant raped a 15-year-old friend of his stepdaughter in her presence after he had taken them both for a ride in his car. He had one previous conviction for rape and one for attempted rape within 10 years of the existing offence. A sentence of 12 years was upheld. Assuming a starting-point of eight years given that the Court considered that there had been a breach of trust in this situation, and bearing in mind the guilty plea, at least six years appears to have been added on account of the previous convictions. In *Fenton*,[246] a sentence of life imprisonment was upheld on a defendant with a history of convictions for indecent assault who was considered to be very dangerous.

Now, under s 109[247] of the Powers of Criminal Courts (Sentencing) Act 2000, a person who is convicted of a serious offence who goes on to commit another serious offence when he is 18 or over, must receive a life

243 (1987) 9 Cr App R (S) 517.
244 (1990) 12 Cr App R (S) 10.
245 (1989) 11 Cr App R (S) 354.
246 (1992) 13 Cr App R (S) 85.
247 This provision was originally enacted as Crime (Sentences) Act 1997, s 2.

sentence on the second offence[248] unless there are exceptional circumstances relating to either of the offences or to the offender which justify its not doing so. The statute includes rape or attempted rape and unlawful sexual intercourse with a girl under 13 in the list of serious offences. Also on the list are other offences of violence including robbery, manslaughter, and attempted murder. It is not necessary for both the offences to be the same for this provision to apply.[249]

The list of aggravating features in *Billam* has not been treated as exhaustive. In *Hawkins*,[250] Lord Lane stated that the aggravating circumstances in the case included the tying up, blindfolding, and gagging of the victims. In *Cramer*,[251] Taylor LJ, as he then was, stated: 'It is not surprising perhaps that the learned Lord Chief Justice in dealing with the factors which should be treated as aggravating rape did not specifically anticipate and describe every wicked quirk or circumstance of conduct to which sadistic rapists might stoop. That does not mean that such circumstances as are not specifically mentioned in his list may not be extremely aggravating factors'.[252] In this case the fact that the three men involved in the rape of the victim laughed and treated the matter as a joke was considered to be 'an important aggravating feature'[253] since it added to the humiliation which the victim had experienced.

EFFECT ON THE VICTIM

The guidelines state that the offence is aggravated where its effect on the victim is of special seriousness. The effects of rape are almost invariably serious or very serious for its victims and it is not entirely clear what extra evidence is necessary for the effect to constitute an aggravating feature. Serious injury, whether physical or psychological, would seem to qualify as presumably would pregnancy or disease. In *Malcolm*,[254] it was suggested that if the victim had valid grounds for fearing that the defendant might have infected her with the HIV virus or if her blood actually contained it, a higher sentence might well be imposed. As the Common Serjeant of London noted at the trial: 'Any young woman following an attack on her must be anxious if not terrified, whether or not she has or might contract Aids which might be dormant in her body for years'. [255]

[248] See on this *Offen* [2001] 2 All ER 154 in which it was held that only if offenders constituted a significant risk to the public, could they be sentenced to life imprisonment under this section and this would not contravene Articles 3 and 5 of the ECHR. See also *Kelly No. 2* [2002] 1 Cr App R (S) 85; *Richards* [2002] 2 Cr App R (S) 91.

[249] Under ss 85 and 86 of the same Act the courts are empowered in the case of sexual or violent offences to extend periods of supervision after release and the length of time an offender can be required to serve if recalled after release. This is a further means of dealing with sex offenders who may constitute a continuing risk to the public.

[250] (1989) 11 Cr App R (S) 429.

[251] (1988) 10 Cr App R (S) 483.

[252] At 486.

[253] At 487.

[254] (1987) 9 Cr App R (S) 487.

[255] At 490.

Evidence of the effects of the rape should be brought to the attention of the sentencer by the prosecution[256] but it is not at all clear that this invariably occurs. There are cases in which it seems evident that the impact of the rape must have been severe but no specific evidence of this is brought forward. A Practice Direction issued by the Lord Chief Justice will now assist victims to provide their own statements about the effect the rape has had upon them.[257] The Direction states that victims will be told when they make their statements to the police that they have the chance, if they so wish, to make a victim personal statement. This can be made or updated at any stage prior to the disposal of the case.[258] The evidence of the effects of the offence on the victim must be served, prior to sentencing, on the defendant's solicitor in the proper form which is a witness statement or an expert's report.[259] The victim's personal statement, together with any supporting evidence, will be taken into account by the judge prior to sentencing. But the sentencer must not make assumptions unsupported by evidence about the effects of the offence unless these can be drawn from the nature or circumstances surrounding the offence. The opinions of the victim or her relatives as to what the sentence should be are irrelevant. Victims' personal statements place an added burden on the prosecution and the expense of obtaining an expert report may also act as a deterrent. None the less, it would seem highly desirable that a statement of the impact of the rape on the victim should be taken routinely from the complainant and served on the defence and that expert evidence should also be obtained wherever appropriate.

WIVES AND PARTNERS

There is nothing in the guidelines to suggest that there should be any reduction in sentence simply because the victim has or had a relationship with the accused. The guidelines do recognize that where the defendant is in a position of responsibility towards the victim, the starting-point for sentencing is eight years rather than five. Husbands and wives owe legal duties to one another and could be said to be in a position of responsibility towards each other but the guidelines have not been interpreted in this way.

[256] See e.g. *Attorney General's Reference No. 19 of 1992* [1993] Crim LR 83; *Williams* (1992) 13 Cr App R (S) 562; *Atkins* (1990) 12 Cr App R (S) 335; *Hobstaff* (1993) 14 Cr App R (S) 605.

[257] *Practice Direction* [2001] 4 All ER 640. This Practice Direction authorizes greater use of victim impact statements for all crimes. For further discussion, see e.g. E. Erez, 'Who's Afraid of the Big Bad Victim? Victim Impact Statements as Victim Empowerment and Enhancement of Justice' [1999] Crim LR 545; A. Sanders, C. Hoyle, R. Morgan, and E. Cape, 'Victim Impact Statements: Don't Work, Can't Work' [2001] Crim LR 447. In *Doe* (1995) 16 Cr App R (S) 718, 720, Sedley J upheld a sentence of six years and praised the use of a victim impact statement which 'served to illustrate the profound and enduring impact of this rape on the life and well-being of a young victim on the threshold of adult life'.

[258] It is generally improper for witness statements relating to the effects of both the rape and the trial on the victim to be obtained after the trial for presentation to the Court of Appeal: see *Ashmeil* (1988) 10 Cr App R (S) 126.

[259] Practice Direction [2001] 4 All ER 640. See also *Hobstaff* (1993) 14 Cr App R (S) 605.

In *Stockwell,* a pre-*Billam* case, the Court of Appeal reduced the defendant's sentence from three to two years. Farquarson J stated:

The principal contention, and the one indeed that affects us, was the fact that this was not rape of a strange woman or a woman hardly known, but the rape of a woman with whom the appellant had lived as man and wife—initially no doubt very happily—for upwards of 10 years. This does add a different dimension to the case and puts the sentence at the lowest end of the bracket.[260]

But, in *Thornton,*[261] a case involving the rape of a former partner, Lord Lane signalled a break with this approach. He stated that the pre-*Billam* cases gave very little assistance and raised the sentence from two to four-and-a-half years. 'The mere fact', he said, 'that the parties have . . . been living together and having regular sexual intercourse obviously does not licence the man, once that cohabitation or sexual intercourse has ceased, to have sexual intercourse with the girl willy-nilly. It is however a factor to which some weight can be given as was indicated in *Berry*'.[262] In *Berry* it was said that 'the violation of the person and defilement that are inevitable features where a stranger rapes a woman are not always present to the same degree when the offender and the victim had previously had a long-standing sexual relationship'.[263] Thus, more lenient sentences in marital rape cases were still held to be justified.

The approach in *Thornton* was followed in many subsequent cases.[264] However, *W,*[265] decided in 1993 after the marital rape exemption had been abolished,[266] marked a turning-point. Lord Taylor LCJ distinguished between marital rapes involving neither violence nor threats, where more lenient sentences could be given, and those where the conduct was gross and did involve threats or violence, where the *Billam* standard should apply. Whilst the drawing of any distinction between marital and non-marital rape may be criticized, the fact remains that marital rape cases which come before the courts *do* seem almost invariably to involve gross behaviour and/or, violence and threats,[267] and should therefore qualify for the *Billam* treatment. Indeed, some scholars might be surprised by the vignettes of married life that the case law affords.[268] Certainly, there has been a gradual trend towards tougher sentences in marital rape cases. In *WG,*[269] for example, a sentence of 10 years was upheld where H had continuously raped his wife over a period of several months and came perilously close to killing her by asphyx-

[260] (1984) 6 Cr App R (S) 84. See also *Larger* [1981] Crim LR 577.

[261] *Attorney General's Reference No. 7 of 1989* (1990) 12 Cr App R (S) 1.

[262] (1990) 12 Cr App R (S) 1, 6.

[263] (1988) 10 Cr App R (S) 13, 15.

[264] For discussion, see Rumney (1999).

[265] (1993)14 Cr App R (S)256.

[266] In *R v R* [1991] 4 All ER 481.

[267] If the sentencing reports are typical.

[268] See Ch. 2 under the heading 'The Phenomenon of Marital Rape' for the views of Professor Shorter on the state of marriage in the twentieth century.

[269] [2000] 1 Cr App R (S) 70.

iation.[270] The couple were cohabiting at the time[271] and he pleaded not guilty. In *H*,[272] a sentence of 10 years was reduced to seven. The couple were separated and H pleaded guilty. He had raped W anally, used violence, caused her physical injury and terrified her by brandishing a gun. He had also held her captive for four-and-a-half hours.[273]

But despite Lord Taylor's judgment, sentences continue almost invariably to fall short of the *Billam* standard. Indeed, even in *W* itself Lord Taylor does not appear to have applied it.[274] Thus, although sentencing has markedly increased in cases involving spouses and partners, they still benefit from a discount.[275] Both trial courts and the Court of Appeal continue to distinguish these cases from other rapes. Some decisions give cause for considerable concern. For example, in *Brown*,[276] in which the defendant raped his former partner, forced her to have oral sex, kicked her about the head and body causing her to bleed profusely and to require seven stitches in casualty, Lloyd LJ none the less stated: 'Having regard to the previous sexual relationship between these parties, the absence of any injury and the absence of any weapon, we regard the sentence of six years as too long'. It was therefore reduced to five years. Under *Billam,* the correct sentence would appear to have been at least seven years. In *Mahzer H.*,[277] a husband who pleaded not guilty was sentenced to five-and-a-half years' imprisonment for rape and false imprisonment of his wife. Under *Billam,* the starting-point in this case should have been eight years because of the false imprisonment. There were additionally at least four aggravating features which would have justified a sentence nearer to 12 years. First, the complainant had been kept a total prisoner in the home for about 10 weeks. Secondly, the false imprisonment was accompanied by conditions of extreme humiliation and deprivation. Thirdly, the rape had caused injuries to the anus. Finally, the sexual offences had lasted for a period of some hours. The Court of Appeal conceded that the sentence was lenient but took into account the experience of the judge who had heard all the evidence over the course of a three-week trial and the fact

[270] In *Dennis Mountaine* [1998] 2 Cr App R (S) 66, a sentence of 12 years for rape of a partner of 10 years was upheld in circumstances where there had been repeated rapes with violence.

[271] In most reported cases cohabitation has ceased at the time of the rape. Cases where the couple were cohabiting at the time of the rape tend generally to attract low sentences: see e.g. *T* [1993] Crim LR 983. In *M* [1995] Crim LR 344, the Court of Appeal was willing to depart considerably from the guidelines. It reduced the husband's sentence to 18 months on the ground that the parties were still cohabiting and sharing a bed and additional violence had not been used.

[272] [1999] 1 Cr App R (S) 470.

[273] See also *C* (1993) 14 Cr App R (S) 642 (six years upheld); *Hutchinson* [1993] Crim LR 718 (six years reduced to five); *K* (1990) 12 Cr App R (S) 451 (sentence of eight years upheld as 'entirely appropriate').

[274] See Rumney (1999), 250; K. Warner 'Sentencing in Cases of Marital Rape: Towards Changing the Male Imagination' (2000) 20 (4) LS 592.

[275] See e.g. the cases mentioned in n. 273 where some discount appears to have been given.

[276] (1993) 14 Cr App R (S) 434.

[277] *Attorney General's Reference No. 27 of 1998* [1999] 1 Cr App R (S) 259.

that H was a university graduate of good character. In *Toby F.*,[278] the trial judge entirely ignored the *Billam* guidelines and placed the husband on probation. He was depressed, had made an unsuccessful suicide bid and pleaded guilty. There were no fewer than six aggravating features in the case. Additional violence had been used. He had taped his wife's mouth so that she was unable to breathe and had become hysterical, tied her with rope to the bed and slapped her. He had used a Stanley knife to frighten her and rip off her clothes; the rape had been carefully planned; he had subjected her to other sexual indignities; the offence took a considerable period of time and the victim believed, with good cause, that she was going to be killed. The Court of Appeal raised the sentence to three-and-a-half years on the ground that the proper sentence was six years reduced to five for the depression and further reduced to take into account the double jeopardy element.

It is clear that judges need to reframe their understanding of marital rape. There is a lack of comprehension of the sheer terror which it may induce. A wife who has been raped in the home has no home. There is no safe place. Moreover, as Easteal argues, marital rape is a prime example of abuse of trust.[279] That element is usually missing from judicial evaluations of the damage caused. In *Billam* it was said that where the effect on the victim was of especial seriousness, higher sentences were justified, but the trauma of marital rape seems not to have been properly recognized or brought sufficiently to the attention of the courts.[280]

PROSTITUTES

The guidelines do not specify any reduction in sentencing where the victim is a prostitute, but it appears nevertheless that this will generally be regarded as a mitigating factor which will reduce sentence. In *Cole and Barik*,[281] two men threatened a prostitute with violence and raped her, one of them also forcing her to engage in oral sex. The Court of Appeal reduced their sentence of nine years to seven. The Court held that the law would uphold a prostitute's right to refuse sexual intercourse but 'a factor which the Court can take into account is that the prostitute is, in the nature of her trade, prepared to have intercourse with any man who pays for it and that the hurt that she may suffer as a result of the rape is to some extent different from that of another woman who would only be prepared to have sexual intercourse with a man whom she knows and respects'.[282] By way of exception, in *Masood* the Court upheld a sentence of nine years for rape of a 16-yearold prostitute and, declining to reduce the sentence on account of her prostitution, noted: 'it is only if courts are astute to

[278] *Attorney General's Reference No. 24 of 1999* [2000] 1 Cr App R (S) 275.

[279] Easteal (1998), 118.

[280] See further Rumney (1999).

[281] (1993) 14 Cr App R (S) 764.

[282] At 764. See also *Attorney General's Reference No. 28 of 1996 (R v Shaw)* (1987) 2 Cr App R (S) 206, in which a sentence of six years raised from four was given to a man who conducted a campaign against prostitutes—it was said in *Billam* that 15 years might be appropriate for campaigns of rape.

recognise the need for prostitutes to be protected that they can indeed get the protection which they require and only the courts can give'.[283]

Thus, although Lord Lane specifically stated that the victim's previous sexual experience was irrelevant, men who rape prostitutes, or present or former wives or partners, seem frequently to qualify for some reduction in sentence. To the extent that the justification for this is based on an express or implicit assumption that the trauma of the victim is less in these situations, it is of vital importance in individual cases that the true effect of the rape is brought to the attention of the court through statements from the witness and/or expert reports at the sentencing stage.

GUILTY PLEAS

It is plainly vital that full credit should be given to defendants who plead guilty, thereby ensuring that the complainant does not have to appear in court. Reductions have ranged generally from a quarter[284] to a third,[285] as is the case for other offences, but greater and smaller reductions[286] have also been given. For example, in *Attorney General's Reference No. 15 of 1992*,[287] a 55-year-old woman who was walking her dog in the woods was raped twice, threatened with a knife, indecently assaulted, and forced to engage in oral sex. Her attacker did not plead guilty until the DNA analysis was confirmed. A sentence of eight years, at the very least, was indicated under the guidelines, with some reduction to take account of the guilty plea, bearing in mind that the defendant had little chance of avoiding conviction. The defendant was of relatively low intelligence but was not mentally ill. His sentence of four years suggests a reduction for the guilty plea of more than a third. The Court of Appeal agreed that the sentence was lenient but concluded that it was not unduly so and refused to interfere with it. This decision seems hard to justify.

ATTEMPTS

Lord Lane did not indicate in the guidelines how much reduction should normally be made for an attempt but made it clear that in some circumstances no reduction was called for. This approach has been followed in several cases. A reduction of one year has been made in a number of cases[288] and, in a case involving the attempted rape of a 3-year-old, a sentence of eight years was reduced by Lord Lane to six.[289] *In Attorney General's Reference No. 15 of 1991*,[290] a man who broke into a woman's flat in the

[283] (1997) 2 Cr App R (S) 137 at 139.

[284] See e.g. *Brown* (1992) 13 Cr App R (S) 382; *North* (1989) 11 Cr App R (S) 437.

[285] See e.g. *McCue* (1989) 9 Cr App R (S) 17 (just over one-third).

[286] See *Clarke* (1990) 12 Cr App R (S) 10 for a smaller reduction.

[287] [1993] Crim LR 81.

[288] See *Williams* (1988) 9 Cr App R (S) 491; *Stone* (1989) 11 Cr App R (S) 537; *Burns* (1987) 9 Cr App R (S) 57.

[289] *McCarthey* (1988) 10 Cr App R (S) 443.

[290] (1992) 13 Cr App R (S) 622. See also *Attorney General's Reference No. 5 of 1996* (1996) 2 Cr App R (S) 434 in which a sentence of four-and-a-half years was given to a stepfather for attempted rape, indecent assault, and indecency with a child—the starting-point for positions of trust is eight years.

middle of the night and attempted to rape her was given a three-year sentence. Under the guidelines, eight years would have been appropriate for the full offence. The Court of Appeal concluded that although this was lenient, it was not unduly so and refused to interfere with it. Credit was given to the defendant for desisting when the woman told him to do so. However, this decision would appear to be out of line with others on attempted rape.

DEFENDANTS UNDER 21

In *Billam,* Lord Lane stated that juveniles should normally receive custodial sentences of the same length as adults with some reduction to take account of the age of the offender. Since then, appeals against custodial sentences imposed on juveniles have been uniformly unsuccessful and the sentences themselves have almost invariably been upheld. But the sentences imposed by trial judges have generally involved a very substantial reduction to take account of the age of the offender and might be criticized for their failure to take account of the age of the victims—they are almost invariably young or very young—and the serious effects of the rape. Thus, for example, in *Carlton and Staples*,[291] two juveniles with the help of a third held down and raped a 14-year-old girl and indecently assaulted another. Both girls were so traumatized that they took an overdose. The boys pleaded guilty and were sentenced to three years' detention. Adult offenders in the same circumstances would expect to receive sentences in the region of eight years. In *Connors*,[292] two boys of 14 and 15 raped a 14-year-old virgin. There was some evidence that the rape had been pre-planned. Again, sentences of three years' detention were imposed after guilty pleas. In *Reeve*,[293] a 14-year-old who raped his 4-year-old cousin on several occasions when acting as her babysitter was sentenced to two years' detention after a guilty plea, although he showed no remorse and appeared to blame the child. An adult in these circumstances would expect to receive at least three times this sentence. The imposition of a non-custodial sentence on a juvenile was challenged in *Attorney General's Reference No. 3 of 1993*,[294] in which a 15-year-old boy dragged a 15-year-old girl into the woods, raped her, and submitted her to forced oral sex. He did not plead guilty. The girl was a virgin and the psychiatric report before the court showed that she was experiencing PTSD as a result of the incident and would require treatment for some time into the future.[295] The Court of Appeal imposed a custodial sentence of two years. But even allowing for double jeopardy, the sentence an adult would expect to receive would have been in the region of three times longer for what was described as 'a serious case

[291] (1990) 12 Cr App R (S) 334.

[292] (1992) 13 Cr App R (S) 666.

[293] (1989) 11 Cr App R (S) 178.

[294] [1993] Crim LR 472.

[295] Judge John Prosser gave the boy a three-year supervision order on the ground that he came from a good family and a custodial sentence might result in his mixing with people who would teach him 'more bad habits'. He was also ordered to pay the victim £500 compensation. The judge stated 'It will give the girl the chance of a good holiday to help her get over the trauma': *The Times*, 8 Feb. 1993.

with aggravating factors'. It is not at all clear that Lord Lane contemplated reductions of this order.[296]

(ii) Sentencing in the Crown Court

It is of some significance that out of all cases referred by the Attorney General to the Court of Appeal on the grounds of undue leniency from the time when the power came into effect until the end of 1997, 17 per cent have involved sexual offences with 33 out of 66 being rape cases.[297] The References indicate that some judges are paying scant heed to the *Billam* guidelines and are imposing sentences which demonstrate a lack of appreciation of the gravity of the offence. The following are examples:

In *Attorney General's Reference No. 8 of 1991*,[298] a 13-year-old girl went to stay with her friend for the night. The friend's father raped her with force and ejaculated inside her. She was a virgin and the rape caused her great pain as well as trauma. The defendant pleaded guilty and showed some remorse. He was sentenced to 30 months' imprisonment. Under the *Billam* guidelines, the starting-point should arguably have been eight years as he was in a position of trust as far as the girl was concerned. Even if the starting-point was five years, the girl's age, evidence that the rape had been carefully planned, and the effect upon her were all aggravating factors. A sentence of between five and eight years bearing in mind the guilty plea would appear to have been indicated by the guidelines. A sentence of five years was substituted.

In *Attorney General's Reference No. 18 of 1991*,[299] the defendant entered the victim's flat during the night through an open window knowing that she was alone with her 9-month-old baby. He raped her while she was in bed with the baby and threatened to kill her. He was sentenced to three-and-a-half years' imprisonment. Under the guidelines, the starting-point should have been eight years for raping her in her own home. He did not plead guilty and, other than the fact that he eventually apologized to the victim, there were no mitigating features. A sentence of at least eight years should thus have been given. A sentence of six years was substituted.

In *Attorney General's Reference No. 33 of 1992*,[300] the defendant broke into a 61-year-old woman's house, wearing a mask and pretending to have another man with him. He raped her, tied her to the bed, gagged her, and threw a quilt over her head which interfered with her breathing. He also stole money from the house. When she managed to free herself to seek help, she was in an acutely distressed state. Twenty-six hours later, she suffered a severe stroke from which she died. The defendant pleaded guilty to rape but not guilty to manslaughter. The jury unanimously found him guilty of

[296] For sentences on older juveniles which are in line with sentences for adult offenders, see *Sisk* (1992) 13 Cr App R (S) 214; *Woods* (1987) 9 Cr App R (S) 256.

[297] Shute (1999), 608–23.

[298] (1992) 13 Cr App R (S) 360.

[299] 13 Cr App R (S) 624.

[300] (1993) 14 Cr App R (S) 712.

manslaughter. He was sentenced to seven years' imprisonment, made up of five years' imprisonment for the rape, three-and-a-half for the burglary and seven for the manslaughter to run concurrently. Since this was a rape in the victim's own home, the starting-point for the rape should have been eight years. Her age, his treatment of her after the rape, and its effect upon her were aggravating factors. His plea of guilty did nothing to save her any anguish since he had caused her death and therefore could justify little in the way of reduction of sentence. For the rape alone, therefore, a sentence of around double the one he received would have been called for under the guidelines. The sentence for rape was raised to nine years, with 11 for manslaughter to run concurrently.[301]

In *Attorney General's Reference No. 23 of 2000 (R v Bullock)*,[302] a woman was raped by a trusted friend in her own home whilst her children were in the next room. She was badly affected by the rape. The defendant, who was illiterate and of limited intelligence, pleaded guilty. He was put on probation for three years with a requirement that he attend a sex offender programme. This decision openly flouts the *Billam* guidelines. A custodial sentence for rape is mandatory save in exceptional circumstances of which there were none in the present case. The Court of Appeal substituted a sentence of two-and-a-half years' imprisonment.

Whilst a reference by the Attorney General can correct manifestly lenient sentences, the concern must be that only the very worst cases can be dealt with by this means. It is clear that in many other cases where no reference is brought, the guidelines have not been fully heeded.[303] This raises the question whether it is indeed only High Court judges or experienced circuit judges who are trying rape cases.[304] The rule is that if the offence is rape (in practice interpreted to include attempt, incitement, and conspiracy to commit rape) or a serious sexual offence against a child, the case must either be tried by a High Court judge or else a circuit judge who has the 'rape ticket', that is, has been approved to try such cases by the Senior Presiding Judge with the concurrence of the Lord Chief Justice.[305] Shute found that, of the 66 cases involving sexual offences referred for unduly lenient sentencing, seven were tried by High Court judges (who do not have to be ticketed) and almost all the rest by ticketed judges. Therefore, the rules were, for the most part, being observed.[306]

301 See also *Attorney General's Reference No. 3 of 1993*, above.

302 [2000] Crim LR 772.

303 In a study of sentencing for rape in 11 major Crown Courts in 1991 and 1992, Paul Robertshaw found that sentences of less than three years were dispensed in around 10 per cent of cases, and in two courts, sentences of this length were awarded in more than 15 per cent of cases. Given the five-year starting-point, this suggests that some courts are taking a broad view of mitigating circumstances or else that the guidelines are being insufficiently heeded. See 'Sentencing Rapists: First Tier Courts in 1991-92' [1994] Crim LR 343.

304 See above under the heading 'Attempts to Deal with the Criticism'.

305 *Practice Direction (Crown Court: Allocation of Business)* [1995] 1 WLR 1083

306 Shute (1999), at 623.

This system has, it seems, failed to put an end to overly lenient sentencing in rape cases. Furthermore, it has not put a stop to misguided and frequently foolish statements by some trial judges about rape and its victims.

In what has come to be known as the 'Vicarage Rape Case', the victim, a virgin, was subjected at knifepoint to rape, buggery, oral sex, and penetration with a knife-handle by two men who broke into her home. The men were sentenced to five and three years respectively for the rape and accompanying sexual assaults. In an appeal by a third defendant in the case, Lord Lane commented that sentences of ten and eight years would have been more appropriate.[307] But the trial judge, Judge Leonard, stated that he had been told that the trauma the victim suffered had not been so great.[308] The victim herself said subsequently that no one from court had asked her or anyone else how she felt.[309] In her own account of the case, she reveals that she had in fact experienced deep trauma and suicidal feelings as a result of the rape.[310]

In a subsequent case, the victim, who had formerly lived with the defendant, had obtained an injunction against him for his violent behaviour. He broke the injunction and raped her in the stairway leading to her flat. He pleaded guilty. Rougier J, in defiance of the guidelines, sentenced him to one year's imprisonment, saying, 'I am taking a gamble. I hope it is the right gamble'. He went on to state, 'I don't think it was such a shock to her as it might have been to many women' and described the victim as 'somewhat over-emotional'.[311] Alliot J, in another case, described a rape victim as 'a common prostitute and a whore'. Sentencing her rapist to three years' imprisonment despite the five-year starting-point, he commented: 'While every woman is entitled to complain about their body being violated, someone who for years has flaunted their body and sold it cannot complain as loudly as someone who has not behaved in this way'.[312] Another defendant who raped a teenage prostitute in a derelict garage was praised by Judge Arthur Myerson QC for complying with the wishes of the victim who, on realizing she was going to be raped, begged him to wear a condom. The judge stated that the defendant had shown 'concern and consideration by wearing a contraceptive' and commented that the victim had not suffered

[307] *R v Horsfield*, *The Times*, 9 June 1987. The defendants had also been sentenced to five years each for burglary to run consecutively so that their total sentences were ten and eight years. However, the low sentence for rape made them eligible for parole at an early stage. References to the Attorney General only became available in 1988.

[308] *The Times*, 5 Feb. 1987.

[309] *Observer*, 16 Sept. 1990.

[310] Saward and Green, *Rape—My Story*; see n. 2 above. For assumptions made by judges as to the amount of trauma suffered by the victim in cases where the victim has ostensibly forgiven the defendant, see *Hind* (1994) 15 Cr App R (S) 114 and *Hutchinson* (1994) 15 Cr App R (S) 134.

[311] *The Times*, 5 Aug. 1988; 138 NLJ, 12 Aug. 1988.

[312] *The Independent,* 1 Aug. 1991.

long-term effects.[313] The defendant was sentenced to three years' imprisonment.[314]

These cases all suggest that despite the fact that it is now only High Court judges or senior circuit judges who are trying rape cases, some of them have difficulty empathizing with the experience of the victim. It is also plainly unacceptable that victims should be the subject of derogatory judicial comment.[315] The need for re-education of the judges about sexual assault has already been emphasized. The Judicial Studies Board (JSB) is in charge of training for judges. Circuit judges with the 'rape ticket' are obliged to attend a two-day training session on serious sexual offences once every three years. There is no such obligation on High Court judges, although many choose to attend the course. The JSB provides training for judges by judges so that it is the judges themselves who set the agenda for the courses and are wholly responsible for their content. At the time of writing,[316] the course provides no specific input from victims' organizations and, whilst academic experts are brought in to cover a variety of matters, these do not include the impact of rape on victims, nor is it clear that gender awareness issues are sufficiently addressed.[317]

A further possibility which is worthy of consideration is to allow a prosecution appeal against sentence in all criminal cases as there is, for example, in Canada and several Australian states. Such a measure would be helpful in dealing with sentences which are manifestly too lenient. It might also lead to greater consistency in sentencing.[318]

(d) The Future of The Guidelines

In 2001,the Sentencing Advisory Panel issued a Consultation Paper expressing its decision to revisit the *Billam* guidelines. This was thought to be necessary for a number of reasons, including changes in the law, for example, the inclusion of male rape within the offence and also the increasing proportion of 'date rapes' coming before the courts.[319] The Panel invited

[313] *The Guardian*, 12 Apr. 1991. But in 1987, Judge Michael Coombe QC sentenced a company director to five life terms for the sadistic rape and torture of two prostitutes stating 'The fact that these two girls were prostitutes is neither here nor there.' *The Times*, 29 June 1987.

[314] See also n. 295 above and accompanying text.

[315] In a case in which a babysitter was found guilty of unlawful sexual intercourse with an 8-year-old, the latter was described by Judge Starforth QC as 'no angel': see *The Times,* 3 July 1993.

[316] August 2001.

[317] The content of the course changes every three years. Judges were formerly shown a video of a BBC documentary in the 'Everyman' series called 'No Great Trauma' in which the victim of the 'Vicarage Rape' case tells her story. The judges were then invited to discuss the video with Detective Inspector Carol Bristow who headed the enquiry in the case.

[318] See D. Thomas 'After the Rape Fine, the Case for Changing the System,' *The Times*, 1 Jan. 1982; 'Increasing Sentences on Appeal—A Re-examination' [1972] Crim LR 288. See also G. J. Zellick, 'The Role of Prosecuting Counsel in Sentencing' [1979] Crim LR 493.

[319] Sentencing Advisory Panel (2001), paras. 1, 2. The 2000 British Crime Survey found that women are most likely to be sexually attacked by partners or acquaintances. Current partners at the time of the attack were responsible for 45 per cent of rapes reported to the survey: see Home Office, Research Study 237 (2002).

responses and commissioned a study to be carried out by a market research organization to ascertain people's views on the relative seriousness of stranger rape, date rape, and relationship rape.[320] The latter was bound to be a complex exercise. Numerous studies show the widespread social acceptance of rape myths which are particularly related to non-stranger rape.[321] These include the myths that women who are raped have only themselves to blame or even that there is no such thing as rape. Indeed, the stranger-rape stereotype is deeply ingrained in our culture. As Barbara Krahe explains:

In everyday understanding, rape is commonly seen as an attack in the dark by a stranger on an unsuspecting victim who puts up physical resistance against her attacker. The more a specific incident differs from this prototypical representation of the 'real rape' the smaller the number of people prepared to consider it as rape. This reduction of the 'real rape' stereotype to stranger assaults affects the way in which people evaluate and respond to the fate of rape victims. Victims whose experiences deviate from the real rape stereotype . . . are more likely to be blamed for the assault and less likely to receive sympathetic treatment from others. Moreover the real rape stereotype affects women's self-identification as victims of rape.[322]

However, despite common perceptions, numerous studies point clearly both to the serious nature and to the devastating impact of non-stranger rape on victims. Koss *et al.* have summed up existing research findings on acquaintance rape as follows:

The acquaintance rapist is more likely to kiss the victim, verbally abuse her throughout the assault, commit rape repeatedly, and demand secrecy after the attack (Bownes, O'Gorman, & Sayers, 1991). Furthermore, contrary to stereotypes that date rape is 'rapette', women raped by acquaintances are at least as affected as those raped by strangers (Katz, 1991). There has been a uniform failure to find differences in psychometrically assessed symptom severity between the two classes of victims (Atkeson et al., 1982; Frank, Turner & Stewart, 1980; Girelli, Resick, Marhoefer-Dvorak & Hutter, 1986; Katz, 1991; Koss, Dinero, Seibel & Cox, 1988). Some

[320] This is in line with Home Office policy which is to consult the public on sentencing reforms: see Home Office, www.fairer-sentencing.co.uk.

[321] See e.g. P. Easteal, 'The Cultural Context of Rape and Reform', in Easteal (1998), ch. 1; P. Easteal, 'Beliefs about Rape: A National Survey', in Easteal, ed., *Without Consent: Confronting Adult Sexual Violence* (Canberra: Australian Institute of Criminology, 1993), 21–34; R. Barber, 'Judge and Jury Attitudes to Rape' (1974) 7 Australian and New Zealand Journal of Criminology 157; N. Barnett and H. Field, 'Sex Differences in University Students' Attitudes towards Rape' (1977) 2 *Journal of College Student Personnel* 93; M. R. Burt, 'Cultural Myths and Supports for Rape' (1980) 38 *Journal of Personality and Social Psychology* 217; N. Malamuth *et al.*, 'Testing Hypotheses Regarding Rape: Exposure to Sexual Violence, Sex Differences and the Normality of Rape' (1980) 14 *Journal of Research in Personality* 121; D. Carmody, 'Rape Myth Acceptance among College Women: The Impact of Race and Prior Victimisation' (2001) 16 *Journal of Interpersonal Violence* 424; G. Muir *et al.* 'Rape Myth Acceptance among Scottish and American Students'(1996) 136 *Journal of Social Psychology* 261; C. Ward, *Attitudes Towards Rape* (London: Sage, 1995); Toner (1982), ch. 2; Blair (1985), 23–8.

[322] Krahe (2001), 186.

reports have noted increased distress among acquaintance rape victims compared with stranger victims (Ellis, Atkeson & Calhoun, 1981; Stewart, 1982). Some evidence suggests that acquaintance rape is associated with different cognitive impacts than stranger rape. For example, acquaintance rape victims, whose trust was most violated by their rape, experienced more self-blame and negative changes in self-concept than those women assaulted by strangers (Katz & Burt, 1988).[323]

The results of the study commissioned by the Panel[324] show that respondents did indeed reflect cultural stereotypes in their comments and responses.[325] However, in group discussion as well as in individual interviews they proved able to move beyond these stereotypes and 'in general, the relationship between the offender and victim was not seen as relevant to the sentence that should be passed.'[326] Furthermore, the majority of respondents were of the opinion that the sentence for *any* rape should be high, at least five years and not reduced below that level in any circumstances.[327] The study findings have been taken on board by the Panel in formulating its proposals for a revision of the guidelines.[328]

The Sentencing Advisory Panel's Proposals

After reflection on current sentencing practice, the results of its study, and the responses to its Consultation Paper, the Panel now proposes a reformulation of the guidelines along the following lines:

1. The same guidelines should apply in principle to male and female rape.[329]
2. There should be no inherent distinction between anal and vaginal rape.[330]

[323] M. P. Koss, L. A. Goodman, A. Browne, L. F. Fitzgerald, and N. F. Russo, (1994). The research mentioned in the text is as follows: B. Atkeson, K. S. Calhoun, P. A. Resick, and E. M. Ellis, 'Victims of Rape: Repeated Assessment of Depressive Symptoms' (1982) 50 *Journal of Consulting and Clinical Psychology* 96–102; I. T. Bownes, E. C. O'Gorman, and A. Sayers, 'Rape—A Comparison of Stranger and Acquaintance Assaults' (1991) 31 Medicine Science and Law 102–7; E. M. Ellis, B. H. Atkeson, and K. S. Calhoun, 'An Assessment of Long-Term Reactions to Rape' (1981) 90 *Journal of Abnormal Psychology* 263–6; E. Frank *et al.*, 'Initial Response to Rape: The Impact of Factors within the Rape Situation' (1980) 2 *Journal of Behavioral Assessment* 39–53; S. A. Girelli *et al*, 'Subjective Distress and Violence during Rape: Their Effects on Long-Term Fear' (1986) 1 Violence and Victims 35–45; B. L Katz, 'The Psychological Impact of Stranger versus Non Stranger Rape on Victims' Recovery' in A. Parrot and L. Bechhofer, eds., *Acquaintance Rape: The Hidden Crime* (New York: Wiley, 1991), 251–69; B. L. Katz and M. R. Burt, 'Self-Blame in Recovery from Rape', in A. W. Burgess, ed., *Rape and Sexual Assault*, ii (New York: Garland, 1988), 151–8; M. P. Koss, T. P. Dinero, C. A. Seibel and S. L. Cox 'Stranger and Acquaintance Rape. Are there Differences in the Victim's Experience?' (1988) 12 *Psychology of Women Quarterly* 1; A. Stewart, 'The Course of Individual Adaptation to Life Changes' (1982) 42 *Journal of Personality and Social Psychology* 1100–13. See also Russell (1982), 191–2, 204.

[324] Sentencing Advisory Panel, Research Report No. 2, *Attitudes to Date Rape and Relationship Rape: A Qualitative Study* (May 2002).

[325] ibid., para. 5.8. [326] ibid. [327] ibid.

[328] Sentencing Advisory Panel, Advice to the Court of Appeal on the Sentencing of Rape, (May 2002, internet, Sentencing Advisory Panel).

[329] ibid. para. 12. [330] para. 15.

3. Relationship rape, acquaintance rape, and stranger rape should be treated as being of equal seriousness.[331]
4. The starting-point of a five-year custodial sentence should be considered appropriate only for a single offence of rape of an adult victim by a single offender.[332]
5. A starting-point of eight years should apply where the rape is committed by two or more offenders; the offender is in a position of responsibility towards the victim; the offender abducts the victim; rape of a child or especially vulnerable victim; racially aggravated rape; repeated rape in the course of one attack; and rape by a man who is knowingly suffering from a life-threatening disease whether it is communicated or not.[333]
6. The following aggravating factors should increase the sentence beyond the starting point:
   (i) use of violence over and above force necessary to commit the rape;
   (ii) use of a weapon to frighten or injure;
   (iii) an especially serious physical or mental effect on victim;
   (iv) further degradation of the victim;
   (v) offender has broken into victim's place of residence;
   (vi) presence of children during the rape;
   (vii) covert use of drugs to overcome victim's resistance;
   (viii) a history of sexual assaults or violence against the victim.[334]
7. Guilty pleas should not qualify for maximum credit, that is, a discount of about one third, where the plea is entered at a late stage and the victim suffers additional distress as a result. Only timely pleas should qualify for the maximum credit.[335]

The overall impact of this revised approach to sentencing in rape cases will be to reflect current concerns about the offence and above all its grave consequences for victims irrespective of their relationship with the offender. As such the proposals are truly welcome.

[331] para. 26. [332] para. 32. [333] para. 34. [334] para. 32. [335] para. 42.

2

Defining and Redefining Rape

In Chapter 1, the difficulties associated with processing rape were described. But the law itself constitutes a further problem for the criminal justice system. This chapter will focus on the law of rape in England and Wales, its relationship with other sexual offences,[1] and the options for reform within the present framework of the law.

Before 1994, the definition of rape contained five constituent elements.[2] There had to be (1) sexual intercourse (2) with a woman which was (3) unlawful and which took place (4) without consent, (5) knowingly or recklessly. Under present law,[3] there has to be (1) sexual intercourse (2) with a person (3) without consent (4) knowingly or recklessly. The elements of the law as it was and as it is will now be discussed in turn.

Sexual Intercourse

(a) The Legal Definition of Sexual Intercourse

Until 1994, vaginal penetration by the penis alone constituted sexual intercourse which is required to be proved for the crime of rape.[4] Concern about the phenomenon of male rape, which the law characterized as buggery, led

[1] Rape is the most serious of a diverse collection of offences in English criminal law which involve sexual conduct. The two principal offences designed to cover sexual aggression are rape and indecent assault but there are also other offences which deal with sexual coercion. For example, it is an offence under SOA 1956, s 2 to procure sexual intercourse by threat which need not be a threat of violence and under s 3 it is an offence to procure sexual intercourse by fraud. Certain consensual sexual acts between adults remain criminal. Anal intercourse between two adult males is an offence if the act is not regarded as taking place in private (see SOA 1956, s 12(1)). An act of gross indecency between males amounts to an offence in similar circumstances. The term 'gross indecency' is not defined by statute nor has it been judicially defined. It seems that such an act may take any form but usually consists of mutual masturbation or some form of intercrural or oral-genital contact which falls short of the offence of buggery or attempted buggery. See further on this, the Wolfenden Committee Report, Cmnd 247 (1957), 248; Cambridge Dept. of Criminal Science (1957), 349. There are several offences which deal with sexual activity involving minors. For example, it is an offence to have sexual intercourse with a girl under 16, and to touch her indecently amounts to the crime of indecent assault whether or not she consents. Homosexual acts with boys under 16 are also prohibited regardless of consent. A man or woman who has sexual intercourse with an animal commits the crime of buggery. See further Smith and Hogan (1999), ch. 14. For criticism of the present law, see Home Office *Setting the Boundaries* (2000).

[2] SOAA 1976, s 1(1).

[3] See SOA 1956, s 1(1) as amended by CJPOA 1994, s 142.

[4] See *Gaston* (1981) 73 Cr App R 164; [1981] Crim LR 406. See also SOA 1956, s 44.

in that year to an expansion of the definition to include penile penetration of the anus of a male or a female.[5] Forced acts of oral sex and penetration by objects or other parts of the body remain collectively subsumed under the heading of indecent assault, a crime which covers a multitude of activities, some of which are less than grave.[6] The maximum penalty for indecent assault when perpetrated against a woman was formerly two years' imprisonment,[7] rising to five where she was under 13.[8] In 1985, it was raised to 10 years' imprisonment regardless of the victim's age.[9] The penalty remains substantially lower than for rape which is regarded with extreme gravity and carries a maximum penalty of life imprisonment.[10]

In their study of 115 rape victims, Holmstrom and Burgess found that vaginal penetration by the penis had been accompanied by forced fellatio in 22 per cent of cases, cunnilingus in 5 per cent, anal intercourse in 5 per cent, urination on the victim or her clothes in 4 per cent, and insertion into the vagina of an object in 1 per cent of cases respectively.[11] Wright and West, in a study of all incidents recorded by the police as genuine rapes or attempted rapes in six English counties over a five-year period from 1972 to 1976, found that of a total of 297 cases, fellatio took place in 30 incidents, cunnilingus in 13, buggery in 12 and other sexual acts usually involving masturbation in 38.[12] Forced fellatio was particularly common where the assailant had been drinking and was unable to sustain an erection or reach orgasm.[13] Holmstrom and Burgess found that forced fellatio was twice as common in multiple assailant rape whereas cunnilingus only featured in single-assailant rape,[14] but these differences do not appear in Wright and West's larger sample. A later study by Smith of all cases of rape or attempted rape reported to the police during the three year period 1984 to 1986 in two London boroughs, found that 12 per cent of a total of 450 cases involved a combination of sexual acts including anal intercourse, oral sex, digital penetration, or penetration by objects, a smaller proportion of cases than in the Wright and West sample.[15]

An incident of sexual assault thus frequently involves a number of different sexual acts. English law continues to differentiate sharply between them. The narrow definition of rape and its failure until 1994 to encompass any

[5] CJPOA 1994, s 142. Discussed below under the heading 'With a Woman or with a Man'.

[6] Broadly speaking, any sexual touching of a person without consent will amount to an indecent assault. See further Smith and Hogan (1999), 471–7.

[7] SOA 1956, s 14.

[8] Indecency with Children Act 1960.

[9] SOA 1985, s 3(3). The CLRC proposed this increase in penalty: see CLRC (1984), para. 4.8.

[10] See SOA 1956, sched. 2.

[11] Holmstrom and Burgess (1980), 431.

[12] Wright and West (1981), 29.

[13] Wright, *New Society*, 1980, 124.

[14] Holmstrom and Burgess (1980), 431.

[15] Smith (1989), 13. See, however, the remarks of Lord Lane in *Billam* noted in Ch. 1, p. 33, at n. 200. Victims are not always willing to disclose other sexual assaults such as anal intercourse: see below under the heading 'With a Woman or with a Man'.

form of sexual assault other than vaginal penetration may be attributed to the early origins of the offence. Historically, the law of rape was concerned particularly with theft of virginity, abduction, and forced marriage.[16] In the twelfth century, the author of Glanvill, describing the manner in which a complaint of rape was to be made, had the rape of virgins in mind when he wrote: 'A woman who suffers in this way must go, soon after the deed is done, to the nearest vill and there show to trustworthy men the injury done to her, and any effusion of blood there may be . . . '.[17] Later, in the thirteenth century, Bracton described the special appeal which could be brought where a virgin was raped and the severe penalty which would ensue upon conviction:

Among other appeals there is an appeal called the rape of virgins. The rape of virgins is a crime imputed by a woman to the man by whom she says she has been forcibly ravished against the king's peace. If he is convicted of this crime [this] punishment follows: the loss of members, that there be member for member for when a virgin is defiled she loses her member and therefore let her defiler be punished in the parts in which he offended. Let him thus lose his eyes which gave him sight of the maiden's beauty for which he coveted her. And let him lose as well the testicles which excited his hot lust. *Punishment of this kind does not follow in the case of every woman*, though she is forcibly ravished, but some other severe punishment does follow . . . In times past, the defilers of virginity and chastity [suffered capital punishment] as did their abettors since such men were not free of the crime of killing especially since virginity and chastity cannot be restored.[18]

Although Bracton alleged that the rape of non-virgins was also punishable, this does not appear to have been the practice of the courts. Indeed in 1244, Thurkleby J disallowed a widow's appeal of rape 'because a woman can only appeal concerning rape of her virginity'.[19] Eventually in 1275 the first Statute of Westminster appears to have provided that the ravishment of any woman was an offence punishable with a penalty of two years' imprisonment and ransom and in 1285 the second Statute of Westminster turned this into a capital offence. However, it is noteworthy that even as late as the nineteenth century, the courts were still discussing whether, in the case of a young girl, there was penetration sufficient to constitute rape where the

[16] See particularly J. B. Post, 'Sir Thomas West and the Statute of Rapes, 1382' (1980) 53 *Bulletin of the Institute of Historical Research* 24. For further discussion, see Brownmiller (1976), 23–30; Toner (1982), ch. 5. It is noteworthy that under the Treason Act 1351, still in force, it is treason to violate the King's eldest daughter [yet] unmarried. On Muslim law, see F. Mernissi, 'Virginity and Patriarchy' (1982) 5 *Women's Studies International Forum* 183 at 187.

[17] R. de Glanville, *Treatise on the Laws and Customs of the Realm of England commonly called Glanvill,* Book XIV, 6 (ed. G. D. G. Hall, London: Nelson, 1965), 175. This sentence is repeated by Bracton, n. 18 below.

[18] ed. S. E. Thorne, (Cambridge, Mass.: Belknap Press of Harvard University Press, 1968), vol. ii, 414 (emphasis added).

[19] PRO Just 1/175, m44d. See Post (1978), 150 and 153.

hymen remained intact.[20] Sexual offences introduced into the law at a much later stage continued to reflect this preoccupation with penile penetration of the vagina. In a series of crimes, the words 'sexual intercourse' are used exclusively in this sense. Thus, it is an offence to procure a woman to have sexual intercourse by threats[21] or false pretences[22] in any part of the world. These offences were apparently introduced to combat the white slave traffic.[23] It is equally an offence to administer drugs to a woman for a similar purpose[24] or to procure a girl under 21[25] or a defective[26] to have sexual intercourse with a third party in any part of the world. Equivalent statutory offences to deal with men who procure women by threat to perform any other sexual acts or who administer drugs or procure for third parties for such purposes do not exist. Similarly, it is an offence for a man who is a member of staff or a manager of a hospital to have sexual intercourse with a mentally disordered female patient.[27] It is no offence for him to engage in other sexual acts with her, unless these are otherwise unlawful, although it is an offence for him to commit an act of buggery or gross indecency with a male patient who is mentally disordered.[28] Since a variety of conduct is included within the term gross indecency,[29] the protection afforded to male patients from sexual exploitation is greater than it is for female patients. The crimes of detaining a woman against her will with the intention that she shall marry or have unlawful sexual intercourse,[30] and taking an unmarried girl under the age of 18 out of the possession of her parent or guardian with the intent that she shall have sexual intercourse,[31] are restricted in the same fashion. It seems likely that the two latter offences were conceived to protect the interests of wealthy fathers by seeking to ensure that their daughters did not contract unsuitable marriages or forfeit their virginity and become less eligible. Today, the main justification for retaining the offences described in this paragraph must be the protection of women and men from sexual exploitation. If this is the case, the argument for so narrow a definition of sexual intercourse would seem hard to sustain.

The crime of incest is a further case in point. It may be committed where sexual intercourse takes place between a man and his daughter, sister, or half-sister, mother or granddaughter irrespective of whether the relationship is traced through 'lawful wedlock', and irrespective of whether consent is present.[32] It therefore covers conduct which is already penalized by the crimes of rape and unlawful sexual intercourse with a girl under 16.[33]

[20] See *Hughes* (1841) 9 C & P 752; *Russen* (1777) 1 East PC 438.
[21] SOA 1956, s 2(1). [22] SOA 1956, s 3(1).
[23] See Williams (1983), 558 and 562. [24] SOA 1956, s 4(1).
[25] SOA 1956, s 23(1). [26] SOA 1956, s 9(1).
[27] Mental Health Act 1959, s 128(1)(a). Wives are excluded. [28] SOA 1967, s 1(4).
[29] See n. 1 above. [30] SOA 1956, s 17. [31] SOA 1956, s 19(1). See also ss 25–7.
[32] ibid. s 10. [33] ibid. ss 5 and 6.

However, since it applies whatever the age of the woman, it also extends to behaviour which is not otherwise dealt with by the criminal law. But the offence is confined to sexual intercourse. Thus, a man may have sexual relations other than vaginal intercourse with his mother, daughter, granddaughter, or sister provided that she is over 16[34] and provided she gives her consent in the legal sense of the term.[35]

Eugenic considerations may be regarded as a justification for confining incest to sexual intercourse. Certainly there appears to be a high risk that the child of an incestuous union between father and daughter or brother and sister will have serious congenital defects. The risk remains, although it decreases where the relationship is further removed.[36] However, 'eugenic considerations were by no means crucial to the passage of the Incest Act' in 1908[37] and the protection of children from sexual exploitation by parents was regarded as far more significant.[38] But the sexual exploitation of a child does not only take the form of vaginal penetration by the penis. Other sexual acts may well be involved. Sometimes indecent assault of a small child is a preliminary to sexual intercourse when the child reaches puberty. Thus, Sandra Butler writes:

> In many situations in which the father is the aggressor, the eldest daughter is the first to be victimised, and the earliest sexual contact can begin when the child is as young as 5 or 6, with genital fondling, mutual masturbation and oral-genital contact . . . Explicit genital intercourse frequently does not begin until the girl reaches puberty . . . When sexual activity continues for years, the child feels a deepening responsibility to keep the relationship hidden from everyone, and her father is free to escalate the level of sexuality between them.[39]

The responsibility which parents have to ensure that sexual acts do not take place between themselves and their children is surely not confined to sexual intercourse. The breach of the special trust that exists between a child and a parent is no less violated where sexual acts other than vaginal penetration are induced or performed. The view of most experts is that 'whatever form the assault takes, the scarring of the child can be deep and lasting'.[40] Once it is conceded that there are grounds other than eugenic ones for a separate

[34] The Sexual Offences (Amendment) Act 2000 lowered the age of consent to acts of buggery to 16 for both boys and girls.

[35] See below under the heading 'Without Consent'.

[36] This was the conclusion arrived at, on modern evidence, by the CLRC and by the Policy Advisory Committee (PAC) which was set up in 1975 to assist in the CLRC's deliberations on sexual offences: see CLRC (1984), para. 8.9. See also CLRC (1980), paras. 113–15. For a bibliography of the extensive nineteenth-century literature on the subject, see Wolfram (1983).

[37] See Wolfram (1983).

[38] V. Bailey and S. Blackburn, 'The Punishment of Incest Act 1908: A Case Study in Law Creation' [1979] Crim LR 708.

[39] Butler (1978), 31–2. See also S. Forward and C Buck, *Betrayal of Innocence—Incest and its Devastation* (Middlesex, England: Penguin Books, 1981), 130.

[40] Butler (1978), 5.

offence of incest, then the question which inevitably arises is why the crime should be confined to sexual intercourse.

(b) Reform

(i) Rape, Indecent Assault, Buggery

The CLRC was unanimously of the view that the definition of sexual intercourse for the purposes of the law of rape should continue to be penile penetration of the vagina.[41] It was opposed to any form of integration between the three offences of rape, indecent assault, and buggery. Now that the CJPOA 1994 has rejected this approach and the law has moved on from its early origins, the question arises whether rape should be confined in its scope to penile penetration of the vagina and anus or should include other acts of penetration, as is the case elsewhere.[42]

THE SEX OFFENCES REVIEW

Submissions received by the Sex Offences Review (SOR) from organizations and members of the public highlighted concerns about the scope of the offence of indecent assault and, in particular, that serious penetrative assaults which did not come within the umbrella of rape could be prosecuted only as indecent assault.[43] It might be thought that, whilst forced insertion of the penis into the mouth may be less intrusive and distressing than anal and vaginal penetration, the difference is not so great as to justify its inclusion in a lesser offence category. Penetration by objects and parts of the body other than the penis are also grave assaults which might, with justification, be covered by the law of rape.[44] If they were, this would seem to require that rape become a gender-neutral offence.[45] Certainly, it would be hard to justify confining the offence to male perpetrators. To do so, unless penalty structures were altered, would mean that such assaults, when performed by a woman, would amount to an indecent assault punishable with a maximum of 10 years' imprisonment but, when perpetrated by a male, would amount to rape, punishable with a maximum of life imprisonment. It is possible that this could be challenged under Articles 8 and 14 of the ECHR.[46]

41 CLRC (1984), paras. 2.45–2.47.

42 All the Australian states have moved away from the traditional approach favoured by the CLRC: see M. Heath, 'Disputed Truths—Australian Reform of the Sexual Conduct Elements of Common Law Rape', in Easteal (1998), ch. 2, 19–21.

43 Home Office, *Setting the Boundaries*, (2000), vol. i, para. 2.3.1. The SOR was set up by the Home Office in 1999 to review the law on sexual offences.

44 The definition of sexual intercourse for the purposes of the Swedish law of rape is about to be widened to include other sexual acts including penetration by parts of the body other than the penis: Swedish Government Factsheet, 'Violence against Women', 21 Apr. 1999.

45 See e.g. Crimes Act 1958 (Victoria), s 35.

46 Article 8 protects the right to private life which includes sexual activities. Article 14 prohibits discrimination. It could be argued that the law would be discriminating in the way that it dealt with identical sexual assaults depending on whether they were perpetrated by a male or female so that there would be discrimination in the way that private life was protected.

Some members of the Review favoured expanding the offence of rape to become a gender-neutral offence covering a wide range of penetrative acts. Such an approach has been widely adopted in Australia. In Victoria, for example, sexual penetration for the purposes of rape means 'the introduction (to any extent) by a person of his penis into the vagina, anus or mouth of another person or the introduction (to any extent) by a person of an object or a part of his or her body (other than the penis) into the vagina or anus of another person'.[47] The majority, however, was opposed to this and the Review's final recommendation was that rape should continue to be confined to acts of penile penetration.[48] As sexual abuse is mainly perpetrated by men, there is an argument that an offence of rape should reflect this and that rape should continue to be an offence that can in law be perpetrated only by a male, albeit that women can be liable as accessories.[49] The Report, however, expresses the matter differently. It states:

> We felt rape was clearly understood by the public as an offence that was committed by men on women and men. We felt that the offence of penile penetration was of a particularly personal kind, it carried risks of pregnancy and disease transmission and should properly be treated separately from other penetrative assaults.[50]

Emphasis on the public understanding of rape and the particular risk of pregnancy, echoes the reasoning of the CLRC[51] and is not entirely convincing. The argument appears to be that if the public thinks that a particular law covers certain activities and in fact it does cover these activities, then it should for that reason continue to cover only these activities. Quite apart from the limitations on law reform in general which such an argument would appear to justify, neither the CLRC nor the SOR took steps to discover how the public perceives the ambit of the law of rape. Nor would there have been any point in doing so, for, if the views of the public are of any significance at all in this context, then it must be its view of what the law ought to be rather than what it is. As to the risk of pregnancy,[52] the fact that pre-pubertal, menopausal, sterilized, and infertile women as well as those who practise contraception are all covered by the law of rape suggests that this distinction is not of overriding significance. Moreover, historically, since the issue was virginity, the possibility of pregnancy does not emerge as a central consideration in the offence of rape. Hale declared that proof of the

[47] Crimes Act 1958 (Victoria), s 35.

[48] Home Office, *Settting the Boundaries*, (2000), vol. i, para. 2.8.5.

[49] See J. Temkin, 'Literature Review of Research into Rape and Sexual Assault' in Home Office, *Setting the Boundaries*, vol. 2, (2000), 83.

[50] Home Office, *Setting the Boundaries*, (2000), vol. i, para. 2.8.4.

[51] See CLRC (1980), para. 45. The CLRC did not mention the risk of disease. The Review favours a broader definition of sexual intercourse for rape than that which was proposed by the CLRC.

[52] The CLRC stated 'The risk of pregnancy is a further and important distinguishing characteristic of rape'.

emission of seed was unnecessary[53] and, in the nineteenth century, although there was some doubt about this, East expressed himself to be firmly against such a requirement. He stated that upon penetration, 'The quick sense of honour, the pride of virtue which nature hath implanted in the female heart . . . is already violated past redemption and the injurious consequences to society are in every respect complete'.[54] Today, section 44 of the SOA 1956 makes it clear that sexual intercourse is established upon proof of penetration alone.[55] On the other hand, pregnancy or the fear of it will undoubtedly serve substantially to exacerbate the trauma of some women. The same is true of disease transmission which could ultimately be life-threatening.[56] The risk of disease transmission otherwise than through penile penetration is negligible.

As well as covering oral penetration by the penis, the Review proposes that penile penetration of the genitalia should also be included in rape[57] as it is in Victoria and New South Wales.[58] This would preclude argument which sometimes occurs, particularly where children are concerned, as to whether the penis actually entered the vagina or not. Thus the concept of penetration would extend to the external as well as the internal organs. The rigid demarcation between the two which currently exists and is explicable in terms of the history of the offence is not necessarily justifiable. Such assaults are highly intimate invasions of private areas of the body. In terms of the rationale put forward in the Report, they may also carry with them the risk of pregnancy and disease.

The Review further recommends that the crime of indecent assault should be sub-divided and renamed. It assumes that penetration of the body, by whatever means, is generally more traumatic than other forms of sexual contact. It proposes that there should be a gender-neutral offence of sexual assault by penetration carrying a maximum penalty of life imprisonment, whilst other non-penetrative assaults should be charged as sexual assaults with a maximum of 10 years as at present.[59] Nomenclature was carefully considered.[60] 'Sexual assault' was preferred to 'indecent assault' which was thought to be inappropriate and trivializing. 'Aggravated sexual assault' to

[53] IPC 628. Hale states: 'But the least penetration maketh it rape or buggery, yea altho there be not emissio seminis . . . And therefore I suppose the case in my Lord Coke's 12 Rep. 36.5 Jac. that faith, there must be both, *viz.* penetratio and emissio seminis to make a rape or buggery is mistaken and contradicts what he saith in his Pleas of the Crown.'

[54] 1 East PC 437.

[55] The same applies for other offences involving sexual intercourse. See also *Marsden* [1981] 2 QB 149.

[56] For the most recent review of sexual assault and sexually transmitted infections, see H. Lamba and S. M. Murphy, 'Sexual Assault and Sexually Transmitted Infections: An Updated Review' (2000) 11(8) Int J STD AIDS 487–91.

[57] Home Office, *Setting the Boundaries*, (2000), vol. i, para. 2.8.5

[58] Crimes Act 1958, s 35; New South Wales Crimes Act 1900, s 61H(1)(a).

[59] Home Office, *Setting the Boundaries*, (2000), vol. i, paras. 2.9.2 and 2.14.4.

[60] See paras. 2.14.2 and 2.14.4.

cover penetrative assaults was also rejected in case it be thought that assaults falling outwith this category were less than serious.[61]

The scope of the new offence of sexual assault by penetration would be broad, covering penetration of the vagina, anus, or external genitalia by objects or parts of the body other than the penis. As the Report notes:

> Penetration comes in many forms. Men put their penis into the vagina, anus and mouth. Other parts of the body (notably fingers and tongues) are inserted into the genitalia and the anus. Objects are inserted into the vagina and anus of victims. Both men and women may perform such penetration. These are all extremely serious violations of victims which can leave them physically and psychologically damaged for many years.[62]

In cases where the complainant is unsure as to the means of penetration—a child is often uncertain whether it was an object, a penis, or some other part of the body—it is proposed that sexual assault by penetration should be charged.[63] The offence of sexual assault would thus be severely limited in its scope and confined mainly to sexual touching.[64]

A two-tier offence might encourage plea-bargaining. However, since the maximum penalty for sexual assault would remain high, this need not result in unacceptably low sentences. Taken as a whole, the Review's proposals would effect a substantial upgrading of non-consensual sexual activity to reflect the seriousness with which such behaviour is now regarded.

TRANSSEXUALS

A further issue is whether the penetration of an artificially constructed vagina should also amount to rape. Such an act would, at the very least, amount to an indecent assault under present law since, whatever view is taken of the effect of a sex change operation, the new organ must surely be recognized as a sexual one. Given that the risk of pregnancy is not of overriding significance in the law of rape,[65] and that the offence is now concerned purely with sexual violation with the penis, the authenticity of the vagina does not appear to be a critical matter. Recognition that the law of rape covers penetration of an artificial vagina would not conflict with case law in other areas which has resolutely refused to recognize that a male to female transsexual ceases to be male after a sex change operation.[66] A man

[61] Unpublished minutes of Sex Offences Review. The CLRC rejected the idea of dividing the offence in terms of penetrative and non-penetrative acts on the ground that the latter would become trivialized: see CLRC (1984), para. 4.19. The SOR's proposal avoids this by retaining the maximum 10-year penalty for such acts and by its choice of nomenclature.

[62] Home Office, *Setting the Boundaries*, (2000), vol. i, para. 2.8.2.

[63] para. 2.9.

[64] The demarcation between the two offences could give rise to questions whether the defendant simply touched the outside of the genitals or penetrated within.

[65] See above, under the heading, 'The Sex Offences Review'. See also CLRC (1980), para. 45.

[66] See *Corbett v Corbett* [1970] 2 All ER 33; *R v Tan* [1983] 2 All ER 12. But see now *Goodwin v The United Kingdom*, Application No. 28957/95, ECtHR, 11 July 2002.

commits rape if he has sexual intercourse with a *person* whether vaginal or anal.[67] Thus whether or not a male to female transsexual is a woman or a man is of no consequence. All that is required is that a vagina is penetrated. The only issue therefore is whether or not the word vagina should be taken to include one that is artificially constructed. In rare cases, women with congenital abnormalities may also require the surgical construction of a vagina.

During the parliamentary debate on the CJPOA 1994 which changed the definition of rape, there was no discussion of this issue nor has it yet been considered by the Court of Appeal.[68] One problem is that the artefact created by the surgeon in a sex change operation, described in *Tan*[69] as 'an artificial vaginal pocket', is not anatomically a vagina at all. The question is whether this matters. An artificial pocket may be penetrated. On the other hand, not all acts of penile penetration are currently covered by the crime of rape. However, if rape expands to cover all forms of penile penetration as the SOR recommends, the stronger the argument becomes for including penile penetration of an artificial vagina within rape if the law is not to be seen as discriminatory. In Victoria the legislation specifically states that vagina includes a surgically constructed vagina for the purposes of the law of rape.[70]

In the case of a female to male sex change operation, the legal issue becomes more complex. Since rape can only be perpetrated by a male, the person concerned would have to be recognized by the criminal law as a male before this could be classified as rape. To do so would run counter to present law.[71] The Sex Offences Review has brushed such difficulties aside and has recommended that rape should include penile penetration by and of, surgically reconstructed male or female genitalia and that this should be made clear in legislation.[72] It states: 'If modern surgical techniques could provide sexual organs, the law should be clear enough to show that penetration of or by such organs would be contained within the scope of the offence. The law must give protection from all sexual violence.'[73]

Similarly, for the purposes of the proposed offence of sexual assault by penetration, it proposes that legislation should make clear that references to genitalia include surgically reconstructed genitalia.[74]

[67] SOA 1956, s 1(2).

[68] It was the opinion of Hooper J in the unreported case of *Matthews*, tried at Reading Crown Court in October 1996, that an artificially constructed vagina was included within s 142. See M. Hicks and G. Branston, 'Transsexual Rape—A Loophole Closed?' [1997] Crime LR 565 at 565.

[69] ibid. at 19.

[70] Crimes (Sexual Offences) Act 1991, s 3 amending s 39 of the Crimes Act 1958. See also New South Wales Crimes Act 1900, s 61H(1)(a).

[71] See n. 66.

[72] Home Office, *Setting the Boundaries*,(2000), vol. i, paras. 2.8.5.

[73] At para. 2.8.4.

[74] para 2.9.2.

(ii) Incest

The CLRC shared the view of the Policy Advisory Committee that 'the primary aim of the law against incest is the protection of the young and vulnerable against sexual exploitation within the family'[75] and rejected the idea that eugenics was the law's principal justification.[76] It commented further:

> It is not merely a question of unlawful sexual intercourse with a person who may not be in a position to give true consent. There is also a special dimension, the violation of the role of the family, which adds to the harmful consequences of incest. A child who suffers abuse at the hand of a stranger can expect comfort and protection from his or her family; incest victims often have no-one to whom to turn—those who should support have been the cause of the suffering.[77]

These considerations clearly apply with equal force to other acts of sexual exploitation within the family such as buggery and oral sex. Indeed, the CLRC consistently treated buggery as a particularly grave form of abuse. Moreover, the Policy Advisory Committee expressed the view that 'some indecent acts other than sexual intercourse, especially if repeated over any length of time, can perhaps be as harmful as sexual intercourse, and . . . they represent just as much an abuse of the familial relationship as acts of sexual intercourse'.[78] Despite all this, however, both committees took the view that incest should be confined to vaginal penetration by the penis on the ground that the case for extending the offence had not been made out.[79]

Under present law, a father who commits buggery on his 16-year-old daughter or has oral sex with her can be criminally liable only for the offence of rape or indecent assault, for which lack of consent must be proved. It is not at all clear that the type of threat which might be used in this kind of situation would be considered sufficient to vitiate consent. The father might, for example, threaten that he will inform the girl's mother of previous sexual activity between them if she does not comply.[80] The offence of procuring sexual intercourse by threat does not, of course, apply here although the CLRC proposed that acts of gross indecency procured by threat should become an offence.[81] However, threats may not always be easy to establish. Prosecutions are seldom brought for procuring sexual intercourse by threat. A father's position of power and influence in the home may render any form of direct threat unnecessary, particularly where the girl is of low intelligence, immature, or dependent. In such cases, she would clearly be left, under the CLRC's proposals, without any protection from the criminal law at all.

75 CLRC (1984), para. 8.11. 76 ibid., para. 8.10. 77 ibid., para. 8.11.
78 ibid., para. 8.38. 79 ibid.
80 See discussion below under the heading 'Without Consent'.
81 CLRC (1984), para. 4.29.

It is further the case that a father who persuades his 14-year-old daughter to perform an act of fellatio on him or to masturbate him is not criminally liable. This is because the crime of indecent assault requires the defendant to do something to the victim. There is no indecent assault if the defendant, without force or threats or indecent touching, induces the victim to do something to him. Where the girl is under 14, this gap in the law is filled by the Indecency with Children Act 1960. The CLRC recommended that the age be raised to 16 under this legislation.[82] However, in the family situation, girls above 16 may well be in need of the law's protection.

Under the CLRC's proposals, therefore, fathers who have sexual intercourse with their daughters of 16 years old or more would commit the serious offence of incest whatever the circumstances. Fathers who choose instead to commit acts of oral sex or buggery on them would commit no offence save where the girl's consent was lacking in the narrow legal sense[83] or where it was obtained by threat, which might be difficult to prove. The Committee's position is hard to defend. Far preferable is the approach taken by the SOR which closely reflects the law in Victoria, Australia.[84] The SOR proposes that a new offence of familial sexual abuse should replace incest[85] and this would cover all acts involving penetration of the mouth, vagina, genitalia, or anus by any part of the body or by an object.[86] Fathers who induce their daughters under the age of 16 to fellate or masturbate them would be liable for a new offence to be called adult sexual abuse of a child.[87]

(iii) Other Offences

In its Working Paper, the CLRC discussed several offences apart from rape which require proof of sexual intercourse. It concluded that vaginal penetration by the penis should remain the focus of sexual offences legislation.[88] In its final report, however, the CLRC reconsidered that approach. It proposed that the offence of taking an unmarried girl out of the possession of her parents with intent to have sexual intercourse should include both boys and girls provided that they were under 16. It should also encompass an intent to have anal intercourse or to commit an act of gross indecency since such conduct 'would be regarded by many as more serious than abduction for the purposes of sexual intercourse'.[89]It further recommended that the crime of administering a drug to enable a man to have sexual intercourse

[82] CLRC (1984), para. 7.13. As did the SOR, see Home Office, *Setting the Boundaries*, (2000), vol. i, 145.

[83] The CLRC considered that consent should be regarded as vitiated only in a very narrow set of circumstances: see below under the heading 'Without Consent'.

[84] Crimes Act 1958, s 44.

[85] This would cover blood and adoptive relationships, stepparents and foster parents and other persons living in the household and in a position of trust or authority over a child: see Home Office, *Setting the Boundaries*, (2000), vol. i, para. 5.6.13.

[86] ibid., para. 5.5.9.

[87] For which see text at n. 625 below.

[88] For a more detailed discussion of the Working Paper, see Temkin (1987), 34.

[89] CLRC (1984), para. 13.8.

with a woman should be extended to protect males and to cover acts of gross indecency.[90] A new offence was also proposed to penalize the procuring of acts of gross indecency by threats or intimidation.[91]

The SOR, however, has taken a very different approach. Rather than focusing on vaginal penetration by the penis, it would extend the ambit of certain offences so that they cover all acts involving penetration of the mouth, vagina, genitalia, or anus by any part of the body or by an object. This would include the existing offences of administering drugs to stupefy a woman,[92] procuring by threat or fraud, and a new offence of assault to commit rape or sexual assault by penetration.[93] However it also proposes several new offences which would cover an even broader range of conduct. Thus, by way of substitute for the offence of burglary with intent to rape, there would be a new offence of trespass with intent to commit a serious sex offence which would be defined to include the intent to commit rape, sexual assault by penetration, sexual assault or adult sexual abuse of a child.[94] Similarly, a new offence of abduction with intent to commit a serious sex offence is proposed with a similar definition of serious sexual offence.[95] Thus, under the new scheme of auxiliary offences recommended by the SOR, none would be confined to vaginal penetration, some would cover a wide range of penetrative acts, whilst others would cover non-penetrative sexual assaults as well. The reason for the distinction is not always clear. It might be thought, for example, that the offence of procuring by threat or fraud should cover sexual touching.

With a Woman or with a Man

Until 1994, rape was the most gender specific of all crimes: only a man could be the actual perpetrator,[96] only a woman the victim. In common parlance, however, the word rape has always been used to describe the sexual assault of men as well as women. Increasing concern about the phenomenon of male rape began to be voiced in this country in the early 1990s.[97] Once thought to happen almost exclusively in the prison context—although its occurrence in British penal institutions was generally denied—it came to be recognized that male rape was yet another instance of largely hidden sexual crime. Prior to 1994, it was legally classified as buggery, a category which also included intercourse with animals, consensual and non-consensual anal intercourse

[90] ibid., para. 2.113. [91] para. 4.31.

[92] Home Office, *Setting the Boundaries*, (2000), vol. i, para. 2.19.3.

[93] para. 2.15.3. [94] para. 2.16.3. [95] para. 2.17.

[96] Until the law was changed by the Sexual Offences Act 1993, there was a presumption in England and Wales, although not in Scotland, that a boy under 14 was incapable of sexual intercourse and could not therefore be guilty of rape: see *Groombridge* (1836) 7 C & P 582. Women may be liable as accomplices to rape.

[97] See e.g. G. C. Mezey and M. B. King (1992), 'Speaking out on the Last Taboo', *The Times*, 6 Sept. 1992.

with a female, and consensual anal intercourse with a male. Moreover, although buggery of a male without consent was regarded as a separate statutory offence,[98] the annual criminal statistics did not record the number of such offences reported each year. Male rape was thus effectively concealed from view.

Unpublished figures obtained from the Home Office[99] reveal that in 1973 there were only 5 prosecutions for non-consensual buggery of a male over 16 rising to 24 in 1989, 25 in 1990, 31 in 1991, and 38 in 1992. The number of convictions was 15 in 1989, 13 in 1990, 14 in 1991, and 15 in 1992. There are several explanations for these low figures.

Research has revealed that rape is a highly traumatic experience for male victims. A particular feature of the trauma for some is the challenge to sexual identity and masculinity.[100] There is a reluctance to report the matter, in part because of the shame involved, but also because 'any claim that he consented projects on to him a homosexual identity. Where the victim is homosexual, this can lead to considerable feelings of guilt, which tend to act as a deterrent to reporting. Where the victim is heterosexual, the very fear of being thought a homosexual may well stop him from reporting'.[101] A further critical factor was that male victims were denied anonymity.[102]

In 1986, Survivors, now a registered charity, was set up in London to provide a helpline and counselling service for male victims of sexual abuse. In 1992, the Metropolitan Police set up the first pilot project in the country in which 26 officers were trained to deal with male victims and rape suites were made available for them.[103] The growing recognition that sexual assault was a problem for men as well as for women led to increasing demands for a change in the law.[104] It was pointed out that the maximum penalty of 10 years' imprisonment for buggery of a male over 16 without consent was too low and could not be justified given that the maximum for rape or buggery of a woman without consent was life imprisonment.[105] The simplest expedient would have been to follow the CLRC's proposal and raise the penalty for non-consensual buggery of a male to life imprisonment[106] which was what it had been prior to 1967. The CLRC also recommended that non-consensual buggery of a male or a female should become

[98] See *Courtie* [1984] AC 463.

[99] The author is grateful to the Home Office Statistical Division for these figures.

[100] See S. Turner, 'Surviving Sexual Assault and Sexual Torture', in Mezey and King (1992), 75–87.

[101] Z. Adler, 'Male Victims of Sexual Assault—Legal Issues', in Mezey and King (1992), 128.

[102] Anonymity for victims of buggery was introduced in the Sexual Offences (Amendment) Act 1992 but it was subject to certain limitations: see s 4. As a result of CJPOA 1994, s 142, male rape victims acquired the same right to anonymity as female rape victims.

[103] See Morgan-Taylor and Rumney (1994), at 1493.

[104] e.g. *The Times* spoke out strongly for legal change: see 'Indecent Anomaly', *The Times*, 29 Oct. 1992.

[105] Morgan-Taylor and Rumney (1994), at 1490.

[106] CLRC (1984), para. 3.7.

a separate offence.[107] However, given that the term buggery is also associated with consensual acts, and would have remained in use in that sense under the CLRC's proposals,[108] this solution would have continued to disguise the true nature of the conduct involved.

It was proposed instead that male rape should be taken out of the category of buggery and placed in the category of rape. This would bring the offence into the open and ensure that it was treated with appropriate seriousness. There was also an argument that such a step would benefit female victims as well. By bringing men within the scope of the offence, some improvement might result in the way that victims were treated by the criminal justice system. However, the disadvantage of this approach was that rape would then cease to 'emphasise the reality that sexual violence is predominantly committed by men against women'. Rape would no longer 'underline the protection of the sexual autonomy of women'.[109]

In 1991, Harry Cohen MP unsuccessfully introduced a Sexual Offences (Amendment) Bill into Parliament which was designed *inter alia* to alter the definition of rape to include anal rape of a male or a female.[110] The Criminal Justice and Public Order Act 1994 finally succeeded in changing the law.[111]

Since then the number of offences of male rape recorded by the police has increased exponentially. In 1995, 150 offences were recorded. This rose to 231 in 1996, 347 in 1997, 504 in 1998/9, 600 in1999/2000, and 664 in 2000/1.[112] Early research into the treatment of male rape victims by the criminal justice system since the Act came into effect suggests that male victims are suffering the same shoddy treatment in court as has always been meted out to female victims.[113]

If male rape has come out of the closet, it is not clear that the same can be said of anal rape of a woman which was also subsumed into the law of rape by the CJPOA 1994.[114] It is clear that this is a particularly traumatic experience for women. Jill Saward, the victim of the Ealing Vicarage rape case, commented eight years after her ordeal: 'For me that (i.e. anal rape) was the hardest thing to come to terms with. I still have physical problems bleeding.'[115] She also described her meeting with another rape victim: 'There was one woman who had been seeing a counsellor for two years and asked to

[107] para. 3.8. [108] para. 6.20.

[109] R. Leng, 'The Fifteenth Report of the Criminal Law Revision Committee: Sexual Offences—The Scope of Rape' [1985] Crim LR 416 at 417. See further Young (1983), i, 113–16.

[110] The Bill would also have brought forced fellatio and marital rape within the scope of the offence.

[111] s 142.

[112] Home Office (1998), 47; Home Office Statistical Bulletin (July 2001), *Recorded Crime*, 28. From 1998 figures are on a financial year basis, from April to March of the following year.

[113] See P. Rumney, 'Male Rape in the Courtroom: Issues and Concerns' [2001] Crim LR 205.

[114] s142. [115] 'Why I Must Never Forget', *The Times*, 28 Feb. 1994.

meet me. One of the first things I asked was whether buggery had occurred . . . This woman said that nobody had ever asked her that and she was ashamed to mention it. You do feel ashamed.'[116]

Rape statistics do not record the number of offences of anal rape perpetrated against women. Such research evidence as there is indicates that anal rape is unlikely to be perpetrated on its own but rather in combination with other sexual assaults.[117] It is important that women should feel able to mention this experience when reporting rape so that due account can be taken of it medically and psychologically as well as in sentencing. It is at least worth considering whether separate recording of offences of anal rape against women would be helpful and might assist in bringing this offence into the open.

OTHER OFFENCES

Many sexual offences are gender specific as to victims. There are separate offences for acts perpetrated by males against females, by males against other males, by males against female children, and by males against male children. Often these offences carry different penalties for what is essentially similar behaviour. Thus there are separate offences of indecent assault of a woman[118] and indecent assault of a man.[119] Until 1985, the penalty for the former was a maximum of two years' imprisonment whilst it was 10 years for the latter. It is now 10 for both.[120] It is a separate offence for a man to have sexual intercourse with an under-age girl, the maximum penalty for which is only two years where she is over 13, life where she is under 13.[121] A man who commits an act of gross indecency with a boy under 16 commits the offence of indecency between men for which the maximum penalty is five years where the perpetrator is over 21.[122] A maximum penalty of life imprisonment applies in these circumstances where the offence is buggery.[123]

Many offences only extend protection to women. Thus, for example, it is not an offence to procure a man by threats or false pretences for sexual purposes or to administer drugs to a male for such purposes, or to abduct a male or to procure a male under 21 for sexual purposes nor can a male be the victim of incest. It is not an offence for a woman to induce or permit a boy under 16 to have sexual intercourse with her.

Much of the explanation for these inconsistencies and differences lies in the piecemeal fashion in which the law has evolved. It should be a matter for

[116] ibid. In Philip Roth's novel, *The Human Stain* (London, Jonathan Cape, 2000), it is suggested ironically that Monica Lewinsky would not have spoken to others of her affair with President Clinton had he subjected her to anal intercourse: see ch 3.

[117] See Smith (1989), 13.

[118] SOA 1956, s14.

[119] SOA 1956, s15.

[120] SOA 1985, s3(3).

[121] SOA 1956, second schedule.

[122] ibid. as amended by CJPOA 1994 s144(3)(a) and by SOAA 2000, s1(1)(b).

[123] SOA 1956 s37(3) and Sched. 2, para. 3(a) as amended by CJPOA 1994 s144(2)(a).

concern that the law provides so little protection for female children between the ages of 13 and 16 and fails sufficiently to recognize that males can also be the victims of sexual coercion.

The CLRC's conviction that both rape and incest should be confined to vaginal penetration by the penis,[124] precluded any discussion in its Report of gender neutrality in either context. Yet the case for expanding incest, at least, to include male as well as female victims is strong.[125] The abuse of power, the breach of the special trust between parent and child which are the hallmarks of incest, are clearly as significant where the victim is a boy. The law may in this instance have a role to play in drawing the attention of society in general and professionals in particular to the fact that boys, too, may be the objects of sexual exploitation within the family. The CLRC did, however, recommend that certain other crimes[126] become gender neutral and extend to other sexual acts.

The Sex Offences Review, with an eye to the ECHR, and the likelihood of challenge to existing law, has embraced the concept of gender neutrality, adopting it as a governing principle, so that all sex offences would become neutral as to victims and all but rape and possibly indecent exposure become neutral as to perpetrators. It proposes the abolition of the crimes of buggery, gross indecency, and unlawful sexual intercourse.[127] Instead, in addition to the offences of sexual assault and sexual assault by penetration,[128] there would be new offences of adult sexual abuse of a child to protect children from sexual interference by adults of 18 or over[129] and a crime of familial sexual abuse to replace incest.[130] All would be gender neutral.

Some will no doubt argue that the SOR should have pursued its gender-neutrality policy exhaustively to include all sexual offences. In the case of rape, it has chosen instead to highlight the reality of male sexual violence by confining the offence to penile penetration.[131] Similarly, research suggests that indecent exposure, as a species of sexual assault in public, is very much a male phenomenon. Gender neutrality in this context would suggest a problem that does not exist.[132]

[124] See discussion above at 60, 65.

[125] There is clear evidence that boys can be victims of sexual abuse within the family: see e.g. A. W. Burgess, ed., *Child Pornography and Sex Rings* (Lexington, Mass.: Lexington Books, 1984).

[126] i.e. administering a drug to a woman for the purpose of obtaining sexual intercourse, the abduction offences, and the offence of procuring sexual intercourse by threat: see CLRC (1984), paras. 2.113(3), 13.14, 4.29.

[127] Home Office, *Setting the Boundaries*, (2000), vol. i, 144, 145.

[128] paras. 2.19 and 2.14.

[129] For which the penalty would be a maximum of 10 years' imprisonment where the child was between 13 and 16 years old, life where the child was under 13.

[130] Home Office, *Setting the Boundaries*, (2000), vol. i, 146.

[131] See ibid., para. 2.8.4.

[132] See ibid., para. 8.2.8.The Report specifically invites views on this matter.

Unlawful Sexual Intercourse

The SOAA 1976 reflected the common law in defining rape as unlawful sexual intercourse without consent. Unlawful here meant outside marriage.[133] Hence rape within marriage was not generally an offence.[134] The marital rape exemption has now been abolished in England and Wales[135] and rape is defined simply as sexual intercourse without consent.[136]

(a) The Phenomenon of Marital Rape

It is said that, for women, home is often the most dangerous place to be. In India, dowry deaths—the murder of a wife for a disappointing dowry—are not uncommon and almost invariably connived at by the legal system.[137] Much the same was true of wife battering in Britain until Erin Pizzey and others exposed the phenomenon in the 1970s[138] and legislation was introduced to combat it.[139] If this has not been entirely successful,[140] recognition of the problem has at least been achieved. By a strange process of intellectual compartmentalization, however, other forms of violence within the family may be ignored, or at least not recognized for what they are. It is often pointed out that the statistics of murder include many domestic killings, the implication being that the figures are not therefore quite as grave as they seem.[141] Rape was formerly the least acknowledged form of violence within the home. The Policy Advisory Committee 'did not see marital rape as a serious social problem'.[142] Sir Melford Stevenson described it as 'the

[133] cf. *Chapman* [1959] 1 QB 100; *Jones* [1973] Crim LR 710.

[134] Unsuccessful attempts to make it an offence were made during the passage of the Act through Parliament.

[135] See *R v R* [1991] 4 All ER 481; CJPOA 1994, s142.

[136] SOA 1956, s1(2).

[137] India announced that in 1983, 258 women were burned to death in New Delhi alone in dowry-related crimes (a reduction on the 1982 figure). Prosecutions and convictions for these offences are extremely rare. See M. Mukhopadhyay, *Silver Shackles: Women and Development in India* (Oxford: Oxfam, 1984); G. Mukherjee, *Dowry Death in India* (Delhi: South Asia Books, 1999); P. Mishra, *Women in South Asia: Dowry Death and Human Rights Violations* (Delhi: Authorspress, 2000).

[138] See Pizzey (1974).

[139] e.g. Domestic Violence and Matrimonial Proceedings Act 1976, Domestic Proceedings (Magistrates' Courts) Act 1978.

[140] See e.g. Women's National Commission (1985), ch. IV; A. Cretney and G. Davis, 'Prosecuting Domestic Assault' [1996] Crim LR 162; L. Kelly *Domestic Violence Matters: An Evaluation of a Development Project*, Home Office Research Study 91 (1999); C. Mirrlees-Black and C. Byron *Domestic Violence: Findings from the BCS Self-Completion Questionnaire*, Home Office Research Study 86 (1999).

[141] See e.g. T. Morris and L. Blom-Cooper, *Murder in England and Wales since 1957* (London: *The Observer*, 1979), 8, in which the authors contrast killings committed in the course of other crimes such as robbery with domestic killings and refer to the former as 'more serious killings'.

[142] CLRC (1980), para. 32.

rarest possible offence'.[143] Professor Shorter implicitly denied that the problem existed for twentieth-century women. Writing of two centuries ago, he stated:

We may thus think of the subordination of women as the result of three different kinds of victimisation. 1. Women were victimised by men, in the form of limitless sexual access. Men's conjugal rights exposed women to an endless series of unwanted and unplanned pregnancies.[144]

He contrasted the position of modern women:

Then between 1900 and 1930 these various sources of victimisation came to an end. Women gained access to relatively safe abortion, and thus gained control over their own fertility. Men themselves acquired a more responsive attitude to women. In short, a physical basis for equality between the sexes was established. The men were now remoulded by the modern family into affectionate husbands, and quite unlike the earlier contemptuous brutal males.[145]

He added: 'In our own time, a married woman who dislikes her husband's advances can leave the marriage'.[146] However, in England and Wales women in general did not acquire access to relatively safe abortions until 1967 and then only on a limited basis.[147] Whilst they were less oppressed by childbearing than they had been previously, there was no basis for assuming that this had led to equality within the sexual sphere of marriage or that it was a simple matter to leave the marriage. Before the 1970s, one reason why wife battering was not perceived as a social problem was because it was argued that those suffering it could leave and those who stayed could not be suffering. It was left to Erin Pizzey to reveal that many, if not most, physically abused women had nowhere else to go.[148]

That rape in marriage happens and not infrequently is now firmly established. One of the most thorough and systematic studies to reveal this was conducted by Russell in San Francisco in 1978.[149] Of a random sample of 644 female householders who were or had been married, 87 or 14 per cent had been the victims of rape or attempted rape by their husbands or ex-husbands.[150] Since some women would no doubt have been unwilling to disclose experiences of marital rape (a few openly refused to do so), the 14 per cent figure is, if anything, a conservative one. Of particular interest

[143] *The Times*, 7 Nov. 1980.

[144] E. Shorter, *A History of Women's Bodies* (Middlesex, England: Penguin, 1984), p. xii.

[145] ibid. 296.

[146] *The Guardian*, 23 Feb. 1983.

[147] The Abortion Act 1967 permits abortions only where in the view of two doctors certain conditions are fulfilled. It does not give women control over their own fertility.

[148] See Pizzey (1974).

[149] See Russell (1982; 2nd edn., 1990).

[150] Russell (1982), 57. Of the 87 cases, 74 were rapes and nine attempted rapes. The remaining four involved acts of forced oral, anal, or digital sex or attempts to commit such acts. Women were only asked about rape in the sense of vaginal penetration by the penis. The four women who had been otherwise assaulted volunteered this information and it was decided to include it in the final figure.

in the light of Professor Shorter's remarks, is the finding that many women in the survey who were not raped did not consider that they had the right to refuse sex with their husbands. They submitted 'even when they had no desire for sex or were repulsed by the idea'.[151] Russell also found that economic factors were highly significant in determining whether a sexually abused wife remained with her husband. She states: 'Our quantitative analysis has shown that wives who were primary bread-winners at the time their husbands first raped them were more likely to take effective action'.[152] In their study of 60 battered women, Hilberman and Munson found that 'sexual assaults were common, women describing being beaten and raped in front of the children'.[153] But Russell found that although battered wives were frequently raped as well, rape in marriage was by no means confined to women who were the recipients of other forms of domestic violence.[154]

By contrast with the United States, there was formerly little information on the extent of marital rape in the UK although a number of reported criminal cases revealed instances of marital rape[155] and women's organizations had long been aware of the problem.[156] But Kate Painter's thorough and comprehensive quantitative study of marital rape in Britain, conducted in 1989, may now be said to provide the final answer to those who have argued that marital rape is a rare event in this country.[157]Out of a representative sample of 1,007 married women, it was found that 14 per cent or one in seven had been raped by their husbands.[158] Painter points out that 'if this finding is generalised to all married women aged between 18 and 54, it means that over one and a quarter million (1,370,000) women who are or have been married have been raped by their husbands'.[159] In almost half of the rapes violence was threatened or used.[160] One in five women were pregnant at the time. Half of the wives raped with violence had been raped six times or more.[161] The study echoes previous findings in revealing that marital rape was the commonest form of rape.[162] In the survey it was seven

[151] Russell (1982), 58. [152] ibid. 329.

[153] E. Hilberman and M. Munson, 'Sixty Battered Women' (1977–8) 2 *Victimology* 462. According to a spokeswoman for Scottish Women's Aid, 10 per cent of battered women who sought assistance from their Falkirk and Grangemouth refuge had also been forced to have sex or to perform degrading sexual acts. *The Times*, 24 Dec. 1984.

[154] Russell (1982), 90–1.

[155] e.g. *Morgan* [1976] AC 182; *Cogan and Leak* [1976] QB 217; *Larger* [1981] Crim LR 577; *Clarke* [1949] 2 All ER 448; *Miller* [1954] 2 QB 282; *O'Brien* [1974] 3 All ER 663; *Steele* [1977] 65 Cr App Rep 22; *Caswell* [1984] Crim LR 111; *Thain* (1983) 147 JP 477.

[156] See e.g. R.Hall, S. James, and J. Kertesz, *The Rapist Who Pays the Rent* (Bristol: Falling Wall Press, 1981). This describes a study conducted by Women Against Rape which revealed that 60 out of 1,236 women who responded to a questionnaire on women's safety had been raped by their husbands.

[157] Painter (1991).The survey itself was conducted by Ark Market Research Company. See now Home Office, Research Study 237 (2002) p. vii, in which it was found that 45 per cent of rapes reported to the survey were perpetrated by current partners at the time of the attack.

[158] Painter (1991), 1. [159] ibid. [160] ibid. [161] ibid.

[162] See e.g. Resnick *et al.* (1991), 329–30.

times more common than rape by a stranger and twice as common as rape by acquaintances or boyfriends.[163] Social class and geography were found to be significant. Wife rape was higher among women lower down the social scale, with women in social class DE twice as likely to be raped and three times more likely to be raped with violence than women in social class AB.[164] Wives who were economically independent were found to be no less vulnerable to rape.[165] The highest reported incidence of marital rape occurred amongst those who were separated or divorced at the time of the survey. Fifty-nine per cent of all those in the survey who had been threatened and raped and 51 per cent of those who had been hit and raped during their marriage were divorced or separated.[166]

(b) The Law

(i) The Origins of the Marital Rape Exemption[167]

With certain limited exceptions, married men in England and Wales were exempt from liability for rape of their wives until 1991,[168] although they could be prosecuted for any accompanying assault or violence.[169] The exemption has generally been attributed to the seventeenth-century writings of Sir Matthew Hale,[170] and whilst this is in some measure correct, it is best understood in the context of the evolution of the law of rape as a whole.

It has been pointed out above that historically the law of rape was exclusively concerned with the protection of virginity.[171] In medieval times, the normal presumption of the courts was that any history or implication of consent on the part of the woman was a valid defence to an appeal of rape. The thirteenth-century eyre records testify vividly to the fact that at that time previous or subsequent sexual intercourse with the same man was fatal to such an appeal. Thus, in 1202 at the Lincolnshire Assize, the defendant was acquitted of rape, having successfully argued in his defence that '*tunc et prius et post fuit succuba eius*'[172]—she had lain with him both before and afterwards. Similarly, at the eyre at York in 1218–19, one Aldusa de Eton brought an appeal of rape against Simon son of Alan. He was acquitted on the ground that 'he had her for almost a year with her goodwill'.[173] At the Warwickshire Eyre of 1221, one Reginald was found not guilty of the rape

163 Painter (1991), 1. 164 ibid. 2. 165 ibid. 26. 166 ibid. 25.

167 I am indebted for his assistance on this matter to Dr J B Post.

168 *R v R* [1991] 4 All ER 481.

169 *Miller* [1954] 2 QB 282. For the view that the exemption might also have applied to certain acts which would otherwise have constituted indecent assault, see *Caswell* [1984] Crim LR 111.

170 1 PC 629. 171 See p. 57 above.

172 D. M. P. Stenton, *The Earliest Lincolnshire Assize Rolls. A. D. 1202–1209* (Lincoln: Lincoln Record Society, 1926), No. 909.

173 D. M. P. Stenton, *Rolls of the Justices in Eyre Being the Rolls of Pleas and Assizes for Yorkshire, in 3 Henry III 1218–1219* (Seldon Soc. 56, 1937), No. 669.

of Margery daughter of Aelfric 'because a long time before this he had her of her own free will, and again two years afterwards in the house of her father, and they say no cry was raised'.[174] It was decided that whilst Reginald should go free, it was Margery who should be placed in custody for her false appeal. In 1240 a rape defendant was acquitted on the ground that 'before and since, he has lain with her [the complainant] often and not by force'.[175] In 1249, an appeal of rape failed '*quid fuit precognita*'—because the defendant had known the complainant before.[176] The Statutes of Westminster apparently extended the law of rape to cover all women, not merely virgins,[177] but there is nothing in them to suggest that a man could be liable for rape of a woman with whom he had previously had consensual sexual intercourse. Moreover, it is of interest that in 1279 a defendant was acquitted of rape because 'he was betrothed to J [the complainant] before he lay with her'.[178] Betrothal appears to have carried with it a presumption of consent.

In the thirteenth-century context, liability for marital rape would clearly have been quite inconceivable. From the later Middle Ages onwards, there is very little in the way of pleas, verdicts, and judgments on rape.[179] The seventeenth century, however, saw the notorious trial of Lord Castlehaven[180] as well as the pronouncements on rape of Sir Matthew Hale. It has been suggested that Lord Castlehaven's case is authority for the proposition that a man can be liable for rape of his wife.[181] But Castlehaven was indicted as *praesens, auxilians and confortans* for holding his wife down to facilitate her rape by 'one of his minions'.[182] His liability was thus as a principal in the second degree. The case could, however, have paved the way for such a development in the law. It is significant that the court held that 'in a criminal case of this nature, where the wife is the party grieved and on whom the

[174] F. W. Maitland, *Select Pleas of the Crown 1200–1225* (Seldon Soc. 1, 1887), No. 166.

[175] C. E. H. Chadwyck Healey, *Somersetshire Pleas* (Somerset Record Society, vol. II, 1897), No. 1120.

[176] C. A. F. Meekings, *Crown Pleas of the Wiltshire Eyre, 1249* (Wiltshire Archaeological Society Records Branch, vol. XVI, 1960), Nos. 310–11.

[177] See Post (1978), 150 and 153.

[178] PRO Just 1/876, m. 50.

[179] Hanawalt looked at 15,952 indictments from eight widely scattered counties over the years 1300–48. Rape accounted for about 0.5 per cent of them. See B. A. Hanawalt, *Crime and Conflict in English Communities, 1300–1348* (Cambridge, Mass.: Harvard University Press, 1979), Table 3, p. 66. For a similar picture, see B. H. Putnam, ed., *Proceedings before Justices of the Peace in the Fourteenth and Fifteenth Centuries: Edward III to Richard III* (London: Spottiswoode, Ballantyne, 1938). From the late sixteenth century, rape was tried at the assizes. In his investigation of indictments at the assizes in Elizabethan Essex, J. A. Sharpe found that from 1559 to 1603, there were only 28 cases of rape. He suggests that this indicates that rape was brought to trial with 'surprising infrequency': see *Crime in Early Modern England* (London: Longman, 1984), 49. Moreover the assize records of Elizabeth I and James I reveal nothing about the law of rape itself. For the records themselves, see J. S. Cockburn, ed., *Calendar of Assize Records* (London: HMSO, 1975).

[180] 3 St Tr 401 (1631).

[181] Freeman (1981), 10.

[182] 3 St Tr 401 (1631), 402.

crime is committed, she is to be admitted a witness against her husband'[183] and there is no specific mention of a marital rape exemption by any party at any stage of the proceedings. Sir Matthew Hale was to ensure, however, that the law did not proceed in this direction.

When Hale came to survey the law of rape in the seventeenth century, he was confronted by centuries in which very little had been said about the matter.[184] He would have been able to look at Bracton and the medieval law as well as at Lord Castlehaven's case. Faced with such a dearth of modern authority, Hale had plenty of scope to steer the law in a different direction and this, to some extent, he did. Thus, he pronounced against the rule that a man could not be liable for the rape of his concubine, stating that concubinage was evidence of consent, but no more than this since the woman could withdraw from cohabitation and thus withdraw her consent.[185] It follows from this that any woman who had previously had consensual sexual relations with a man would similarly be protected if on a subsequent occasion she refused consent and he raped her. The question therefore arose as to whether a wife should be treated any differently in this respect. It was Hale's opinion that she should be. He took the view that her consent alone could not be retracted since it was given for all time as part of the contract of marriage.[186] Hale's choice to retain the medieval approach to consent in the case of married women only was to shape the course of the law up to the last decade of the twentieth century.

(ii) Hale's Rationale for the Marital Rape Exemption

Hale justified the marital rape exemption in the following terms: 'The husband cannot be guilty of rape committed by himself upon his lawful wife, for by their mutual matrimonial consent and contract the wife has given up herself in this kind unto her husband, which she cannot retract'.[187] This explanation may have convinced Hale but was plainly based on a fiction which became over the centuries increasingly hard to justify. The contractual analysis did not bear scrutiny. In the words of Appleton CJ '. . . the rights, duties and obligations of [marriage] rest, not upon . . . agreement, but upon the general law of the State . . . They are of law, not of contract.'[188] Even if a wife had expressly agreed to sexual intercourse on demand, such a promise would not in English law have been contractually binding upon her. Under matrimonial law, moreover, by consenting to marriage, a wife did not impliedly consent to have sexual intercourse with her husband as and when

[183] ibid. 414. [184] See n. 179 above.

[185] 1 PC 628–9. He also refused to accept the medieval view that subsequent pregnancy was a manifestation of consent.

[186] 1 PC 629. [187] 1 PC 629.

[188] *Adams v Palmer* (1863) 51 Maine 480 at 483.

he pleased.[189] If he considered that she was refusing intercourse unreasonably, his remedy was a matrimonial one.[190] He could not take the law into his own hands.[191]

Yet despite the dubious basis for the exemption, in England and Wales it remained largely unchallenged. Legal history appears to record a silence on the matter until the nineteenth century.

(iii) Nineteenth-Century Developments

In 1885, Parliament passed the Criminal Law Amendment Act. This created several offences designed to protect women from sexual exploitation. Under sections 3(1) and (2), it became a crime to procure women by threat[192] or by false pretences[193] to have sexual intercourse in any part of the world. But wives, alongside common prostitutes and women of known immoral character, were excluded from the protection of section 3(2). Husbands were equally exempt from liability under section 3(1) as well as for the offence under section 3(3) of administering drugs to a woman with intent to stupefy her and enable a man to have sexual intercourse with her.[194] Parliament was thus taking the marital exemption into realms uncontemplated even by Hale, who believed that it was one thing for a man to have sexual intercourse with his wife without her consent, quite another for him to force her into sexual intercourse with others. Commenting on *Lord Castlehaven's* case, he stated: 'Tho in marriage she hath given up her body to her husband, she is not to be by him prostituted to another'.[195] In 1951, prostitutes and immoral women were brought fully within the scope of the legislation,[196] but wives remained unprotected.

Hale is unlikely to have approved of a further development which took place in connection with this legislation. The three offences mentioned above were originally introduced to deal with men who procured women for the benefit of third parties. It came to be accepted, however, that a defendant who procured a woman by the means proscribed in order to have sexual intercourse with her himself was equally within their scope.[197] As a result, a husband who, for example, drugged his wife in order to have

[189] Excessive sexual demands could on the contrary be sufficient to establish grounds for divorce, cf. *Holborn v Holborn* [1947] 1 All ER 32.

[190] Namely, divorce or separation. A decree for restitution of conjugal rights (now abolished) was not available in these circumstances: see *Forster v Forster* (1970) 1 Hag Con 144; *Orme v Orme* (1824) 2 Add 382.

[191] cf. *Jackson* [1891] 1 QB 671. Under the Matrimonial Causes Act 1965, s 1(1)(*b*), rape by the husband was a ground for divorce.

[192] Now replaced by the SOA 1956, s 2(1).

[193] Now replaced by the SOA 1956, s 3(1).

[194] See now SOA 1956, s 4(1). The 1885 statute used the phrase 'unlawful carnal connection' for each offence. This has always been interpreted to exclude intercourse within marriage. See e.g. Hawkins, PC i, ch. 41, s1. See also *Chapman* [1959] 1 QB 100.

[195] 1 PC 629.

[196] By the Criminal Law Amendment Act 1951.

[197] See *Williams* (1898) 62 JP 310.

sexual intercourse with her was exempt from liability under section 3(3), even though a wife's implied consent and contract could hardly be said to extend to being overpowered and stupefied by drugs for the purpose of intercourse. Curiously, husbands are still exempt today from liability for this offence[198] even though they may now be liable for procuring by threat or false pretences.[199]

As for the marital rape exemption itself, there was little in the way of judicial comment on the matter until *Clarence* in 1888.[200] Clarence had sexual intercourse with his wife knowing that he was suffering from venereal disease and without disclosing this fact to her. He was charged with unlawfully and maliciously inflicting grievous bodily harm and with assault occasioning actual bodily harm. Rape was not charged but there are *dicta* on the subject from six of the 13 judges who sat in the case.

Two centuries after Hale's pronouncement, Pollock B unequivocally expressed his support for the marital rape exemption in similar terms. He stated: 'The husband's connection with his wife . . . is done in pursuance of the marital contract and of the status which was created by marriage and the wife . . . has no right or power to refuse her consent'.[201] The other judges were less enthusiastic. Indeed, Wills J appeared to query the very existence of a marital rape exemption. He commented:

> If intercourse under the circumstances now in question constitute an assault on the part of the man, it must constitute rape, unless indeed, as between married persons rape is impossible, a proposition to which I certainly am not prepared to assent, and for which there seems to me to be no sufficient authority . . . I cannot understand why, as a general rule, if intercourse be an assault, it should not be rape.[202]

The second and less sweeping challenge to Hale came from Smith J who, whilst accepting the contract and consent analysis, suggested that the consent could in certain circumstances be revoked by the wife. Thus, he stated:

> Until the consent given at marriage be revoked, how can it be said that the husband in exercising his marital right has assaulted his wife? The utmost the Crown can say is that the wife would have withdrawn her consent if she had known what her husband knew . . . In my judgement, in this case, the consent given at marriage still existing and unrevoked, the prisoner has not assaulted his wife.[203]

Two judges took the view that whilst the matrimonial consent could not be revoked by the wife, this consent had a restricted ambit. It did not apply to sexual intercourse under certain circumstances, as where the husband's

[198] However, it is possible that H could be held liable under the OAPA 1861, s 24. Similarly, a husband who procured intercourse with his wife by threatening, e.g. to kill her, could not formerly be liable under the SOA 1956, s 2(1) but could still, presumably, have been held liable for assault.

[199] CJPOA 1994, s 142.

[200] (1888) 22 QBD 23. For further discussion of this case, see Scutt (1977).

[201] (1888) 22 QBD 23 at 63–4. [202] ibid. 33. [203] ibid. 37.

conduct was of a particularly outrageous nature. Thus, Field J postulated the case of a wife in poor health who refused intercourse and who was forced to comply by her husband who enlisted the aid of a third party to subdue her. He asks: 'Would anyone say that the matrimonial consent would render this no crime?'[204] Similarly, Hawkins J stated:

By the marriage contract a wife no doubt confers upon her husband an irrevocable privilege to have sexual intercourse . . . But this marital privilege does not justify a husband in endangering his wife's health and causing her grievous bodily harm . . .[205] I can readily imagine a state of circumstances under which a husband might deservedly be punished with the penalty attached to rape.[206]

The fifth judge, Stephen J, appears to have considered that the wife's consent to sexual intercourse would in certain circumstances be vitiated. He stated: 'If we apply [the fraud vitiates consent] idea to the present case, it is difficult to say that the prisoner was not guilty of rape, for the definition of rape is having connection with a woman without her consent'.[207]

Thus, towards the end of the nineteenth century, five judges were prepared to voice their reservations about the marital rape exemption. Nothing bolder was to emerge from the English judiciary until over a century later. Rather, until then, the exemption was consistently upheld and Hale's rationale cited, often without criticism. There was scarcely any reiteration of the suggestion made in *Clarence*, that either a wife could unilaterally in certain circumstances withdraw her consent, or else that the ambit of consent was restricted so that a wife was not deemed to consent to her husband where his conduct was egregious.[208] The judges were willing to concede little more than that separation agreements, divorce, and certain other matrimonial orders which were not available in Hale's time, must have some effect upon the exemption.

(iv) Twentieth-Century Developments

The first case to raise the issue of marital rape after *Clarence* was *Clarke* in 1949.[209] The wife had obtained a separation order containing a non-cohabitation clause from the magistrates' court. In these circumstances, it was held that the husband could be liable for rape. The exemption itself was upheld and the Hale rationale invoked. There was no suggestion that consent could be revoked otherwise than by a court order. Thus, Byrne J stated:

The position, therefore, was that the wife, by process of law, namely marriage, had given consent to the husband to exercise the marital right during such a time as the

204 (1888) 22 QBD 23 at 57–8. 205 ibid. 33. 206 ibid. 177.
207 ibid. 43.
208 In *Miller* [1954] 2 QB 282 at 288, Lynskey J, having examined *Clarence*, stated '. . . there may be circumstances in which a woman would be entitled to refuse that which is dangerous to her health'.
209 [1949] 2 All ER 448.

ordinary relations created by the marriage contract subsisted between them, but by a further process of law, namely, the justices' order, her consent to marital intercourse was revoked. Thus, in my opinion, the husband was not entitled to have intercourse with her without her consent.[210]

In *Miller*, in 1954,[211] the wife had petitioned for divorce, after which her husband attacked and raped her, causing her actual bodily harm. The court refused to accept that by petitioning for divorce she had revoked her consent. It was held that 'an act of the parties or . . . an act of the courts' was necessary to revoke consent,[212] and it was suggested that an agreement to separate, particularly if it included a non-molestation clause, would suffice. Similarly in *O'Brien* in 1974, it was the pronouncement by the court of a decree nisi of divorce which was held to revoke 'a wife's implied consent to marital intercourse'.[213] Even as late as 1977, Lane LJ in *Steele*[214] cited Hale's rationale and upheld the marital exemption without query or question. In this case, the husband had raped his wife following an undertaking to the court not to molest her. It was because this undertaking was the equivalent of a court order and was fully enforceable by the court that he was convicted of the offence. However, it was also stated that the exemption would be displaced if the parties by 'an agreement between themselves [have] made it clear . . . that the wife's consent to sexual intercourse with her husband . . . no longer exists'.[215] An agreement to separate containing a non-cohabitation clause was suggested as an example of this. This statement paved the way for and was indeed reiterated in *Roberts*[216] in which the Court of Appeal held that consent had, on the facts, been terminated where there was a formal deed of separation, even though this lacked both a non-cohabitation and a non-molestation clause. But the Court did not appear to regard a formal agreement as essential which suggested that the exemption no longer applied to couples living apart by mutual consent.

THE HUSBAND AS ACCESSORY

Hale's statement that a wife is not to be by her husband prostituted to another[217] also influenced judicial thinking in the twentieth century. In *Cogan and Leak*,[218] it was held that a husband could be liable for rape if he forced his wife to have sexual intercourse with a third party who was unaware of her lack of consent. The novelty of the decision lay in the characterization of the husband as principal in the first degree acting through the innocent agency of the third party. The reasoning on this point, however,

[210] ibid. 448–9.
[211] 2 QB 282.
[212] ibid. 290. See also n. 208 above, for a further situation in which it was suggested that consent might be revoked.
[213] [1974] 3 All ER 663, 664.
[214] (1977) 65 Cr App Rep 22.
[215] ibid. 25.
[216] [1986] Crim LR 188.
[217] 1 PC 629.
[218] [1976] QB 217.

attracted much criticism and it was proposed that the husband should, in future, be held liable as an accessory in these circumstances.[219]

ABOLITION OF THE EXEMPTION IN ENGLAND AND WALES

Academic writers, with a striking degree of unanimity, argued the case for the abolition of the marital rape exemption.[220] They drew attention to the injustice of exempting husbands but not cohabitees. They explained that the exemption might have seemed appropriate in Hale's time but was incompatible with the status of married women in the twentieth century. They pointed out that the existence of other remedies for wives in this situation was no reason for disentitling a wife to the protection of the criminal law and that the possibility of bringing charges for assault or wounding was an inadequate substitute for a rape prosecution which focuses upon the denial of another's sexual autonomy and integrity. 'The exemption', it was said, 'has nothing to support it'.[221] In the words of Professor Glanville Williams, it was 'no more than an authentic example of male chauvinism'.[222]

It was also demonstrated to those who doubted it[223] that marital rape can be highly traumatic for victims. Russell concluded from her survey that 'just over one third of the marriages in which wife rape occurred (34%) involved extreme trauma (two victims attempted suicide), 30% involved considerable trauma, 19% involved some trauma, 1% involved none, and in 9% the degree of trauma was not ascertainable.'[224] Similarly, Painter found that almost half of all wives who had been raped sought medical attention, one in four for physical injuries and one in three for psychological problems.[225]

Russell also sought to compare the impact of wife rape with the impact of rape by strangers and others, and found that 65 per cent of women raped by a relative who was not a husband and 61 per cent of women raped by a stranger reported being extremely upset, as against 59 per cent of women raped by a husband and 33 per cent raped by a friend, date, or lover. Fifty-two per cent of women raped by a husband and 52 per cent of women raped by a relative (not a husband) reported that the rape had a great effect on their lives, whereas the same effect was reported by only 39 per cent of those raped by a stranger and 22 per cent by a friend, date, or lover. She concluded that wife rape was one of the more upsetting kinds of rape.[226]

219 See the Law Commission, *Criminal Law: Codification of the Criminal Law—A Report to the Law Commission* (Law Com No. 143, 1985) HC 270, cl. 30, 187.

220 See e.g. Freeman (1981); Mitra (1979); Scutt, 'Consent in Rape' (1977);) Temkin (1982).

221 Freeman (1981), 28.

222 Williams (1983), 237.

223 See e.g. N. Morris and A. L. Turner, 'Two Problems in the Law of Rape' (1952–5) 2 Qld LJ 256.

224 Russell (1982), 204.

225 Painter (1991), para. 4.8.1.

226 Russell (1982), 191–2.

But there were also powerful voices against abolition.[227] The CLRC could not make up its mind about the matter. Its vacillations are implicated in the legislative failure to take timely action. In its Working Paper in 1980 it supported, by a majority, abolition of the exemption, subject to a requirement that the DPP's consent be required before prosecutions were brought.[228] But in its Report in 1984, it abandoned this position. The Committee were divided and could agree only that the husband's immunity should be lifted where the couple were living apart. It was the first to acknowledge that this proposal was unsatisfactory given the legal difficulties which were bound to ensue in determining the circumstances in which it could be said that cohabitation had ceased.[229]

The Law Commission took over the matter and produced a Working Paper in 1990.[230] It provisionally concluded that the immunity should be abolished entirely and invited public comment.[231] There was overwhelming support for this proposal amongst a broad spectrum of the community. The Council of Circuit Judges, however, favoured retention of the exemption when the spouses were cohabiting. Its main concern was with false allegations and the 'spite and malice' of wives. [232] It stated: '. . . having regard to the number of acquittals in rape trials, many allegations of rape are or may be both untruthful and persisted in with considerable determination . . . This is the position in non-matrimonial cases. Our experience suggests that anger and bitterness are no less prevalent inside the matrimonial relationship.'[233]

Similarly, the Criminal Bar Association, the Family Law Bar Association, the General Council of the Bar and the majority of the London Criminal Courts' Solicitors' Association considered that the consent of the DPP should be required before a prosecution for marital rape was brought, to counter the danger of false allegations.[234]

If it is worrying that circuit judges and some other lawyers' organizations still harbour ideas of this kind, it is of even greater concern that the Law Commission failed directly to confront the mythology surrounding false allegations. Indeed, the Commission itself referred on several occasions to false allegations in rape cases, thus lending credence to the idea, so far totally unproven, that this is a particular danger where rape is concerned.[235]

R v R.[236] In Scotland in 1989, the High Court of Justiciary in *Stallard v HM Advocate*[237] held that the fiction of implied consent by a wife to intercourse

[227] Notably and surprisingly Professor Glanville Williams: see e.g. 'The Problem of Domestic Rape' 141 NLJ, 15 Feb. 1991, 205; 'Rape is Rape' 142 NLJ, 10 Jan. 1992, 11.

[228] CLRC (1980), paras. 37, 42.

[229] CLRC (1984), paras. 2.55–2.85.

[230] Law Commission (1990).

[231] See on this J. Temkin, 'Law Commission Report: Rape within Marriage' (1993) 2 International Review of Victimology 345.

[232] Law Commission (1992), para. 3.41.

[233] ibid., para. 346.

[234] paras. 4.2 and 4.3.

[235] See paras. 4.28, 4.32, 4.39, 4.40.

[236] [1991] 4 All ER 481.

[237] 1989 SCCR 248.

with her husband as a normal incident of marriage had 'no useful purpose to serve today in the law of rape in Scotland'. In repudiating the law as it was set out by Baron Hume[238] on the ground that the status of women had changed, Lord Justice-General Emslie undoubtedly emboldened the English judiciary and set the stage for Lord Lane's final renunciation of Hale's doctrine.

In *R*, the defendant was held guilty at his trial of attempted rape of his wife. Owen J ruled that withdrawal of either party from cohabitation, accompanied by a clear indication that consent to sexual intercourse had been terminated, would exclude immunity irrespective of whether there was any agreement on these matters.[239] This decision seemed to conflict both with *Roberts* and with *Steele*. It was followed by that of Simon Brown J who, in 1990, in *C*[240] at the Crown Court in Sheffield, held that there was no marital rape exemption in English law. However, subsequently, in *J*,[241] again in the Crown Court, Rougier J held the reverse, declaring that the position was made quite clear in the SOAA 1976 which used the word 'unlawful' advisedly to mean outside marriage. Since Parliament had spoken on the matter, there was nothing more that the courts could do.

Before the Law Commission had time to publish a final report, *R* went up to the Court of Appeal. After surveying the authorities, Lord Lane LCJ announced that the 'husband's immunity as expounded by Hale CJ no longer exists'.[242] He declared: 'This is not the creation of a new offence, it is the removal of a common law fiction which has become anachronistic and offensive and we consider that it is our duty having reached that conclusion to act upon it'.[243]

The House of Lords upheld the decision to public acclaim.[244] However, there was criticism in academic quarters from those who considered that Rougier J's position on the matter was the correct one. It was not for judges to create new offences. This was a fundamental breach of the rule *nulla poena sine lege*. In usurping Parliament's supreme role in the law-making process, the decision was said to have 'serious constitutional implications'.[245] It was also pointed out that, simply to sweep away the old law on the ground that it was anachronistic and morally repugnant was not the common law way. There were other routes to achieving the same result which would have been consistent with the principles of statutory interpretation and preserved the delicate balance between judicial and legislative roles.[246] Rather than pretending, as the House of Lords did, that the word

[238] *Commentaries on the Law of Scotland respecting Crimes*, vol. (i) (4th edn., Edinburgh: Bell and Bradfute, 1844), 306 ed. B. R. Bell.

[239] [1991] 1 All ER 747.

[240] [1991] 1 All ER 755.

[241] [1991] 1 All ER 759.

[242] [1991] 2 All ER 257,265.

[243] At p. 266.

[244] See e.g. Editorial, *The Independent*, 24 Oct. 1991.

[245] See A. T. H. Smith, *Letter, The Times,* 26 Oct. 1991.

[246] See Giles (1992).

'unlawful' in the statute was simply superfluous and without meaning,[247] it could have been interpreted more broadly, building on the previous case law.[248] In other words, it was less the decision itself that was perceived as the problem, more the House of Lords' blatant assumption of law-making powers.

The European Court of Human Rights to which the husband in *R* finally appealed entirely rejected this type of criticism.[249] The Court unanimously held that there was no breach of Article 7 of the European Convention. It recognized and accepted the need for judicial interpretation and clarification of doubtful points of law and the progressive development of the criminal law through judicial law-making. It held that, provided that the resultant development is consistent with the essence of the offence and could reasonably be foreseen, there would be no breach of Article 7.[250] In this instance it noted that there had been an evolution consistent with the essence of the offence. This evolution had reached a stage where judicial recognition of the absence of immunity had become a reasonably foreseeable development of the law.[251] Moreover, the abandonment of the immunity was in conformity with the fundamental objectives of the Convention, the essence of which is respect for human dignity and freedom.[252]

Had Parliament acted more expeditiously, this saga could have been avoided. It was clear that the problem of sexual violence within marriage could no longer be ignored. The CPS, with highly commendable persistence, was bringing case after case of marital rape before the courts. Trial judges were coming to different decisions. It was necessary to put an end to the uncertainty and there was no indication of any parliamentary intervention on the horizon. The Court of Appeal and the House of Lords did what had to be done. If the methodology was faulty, the result was not.

Despite the reservations of some parts of the legal community, the decision in *R* was finally ratified by the legislature in 1994. It may be that had the ECHR been incorporated into the law of England and Wales at an earlier stage, the battle to secure a basic human right for married women might have been far less arduous and protracted.[253]

[247] See [1991] 4 All ER 488–9.

[248] Giles (1992), 411–12.

[249] *CR v The United Kingdom* (1996) 21 EHRR 363.

[250] para. 34

[251] para. 41.

[252] para. 42.

[253] The decision in *X and Y v The Netherlands* 8 EHRR 235 (26 Mar. 1985) confirmed that there was a positive obligation upon a state under Article 8 to protect the private life of individuals, private life in this instance being interpreted to include freedom from sexual abuse. The denial of such protection to married women alone would arguably have been in breach of Articles 8 and 14.

THE LAW ELSEWHERE

Other jurisdictions with the common law legacy were less tardy in abolishing the exemption.[254] In 1980, the Israeli Supreme Court held that a Jewish husband resident in Israel could be convicted of raping his wife and that the English common law rule should no longer apply. Bechor J who gave the judgment of the court stated: 'English common law holds that a woman must submit herself totally to her husband. This is an outrage to human conscience and reason in an enlightened country in our time.'[255]

In Australia in 1976, judicial scepticism about Hale's doctrine was expressed in *Caldwell v R*.[256] In 1980, the influential 'Australian Women's Weekly' published a questionnaire about sexual abuse to which 30,000 women responded.[257] Thirteen per cent of them revealed that they had been the victims of marital rape.[258] The Government of New South Wales apparently took this finding into consideration in deciding to abolish the immunity.[259] In the 1980s, most Australian states followed suit[260] as did Canada[261] and New Zealand.[262] In the Republic of Ireland, the exemption was abolished by the Irish Parliament in 1990,[263] several months before the decision of the House of Lords in *R*.

In the United States, the position is far less satisfactory. Seventeen states together with the District of Columbia have now abolished the exemption in its entirety. However, the remaining thirty-three states still exempt husbands for rape in certain circumstances, for example, where the husband has not used force because the wife was either temporarily or permanently mentally or physically impaired. Furthermore in Connecticut, Iowa, Minnesota, and West Virginia, cohabitants enjoy immunity in the same circumstances as husbands. In Delaware, even dating partners enjoy immunity in certain

[254] It is also the case that in Denmark, Sweden, and Norway, no exemption exists: see Freeman (1981), 26–7; G. Geis, 'Rape in Marriage' (1978) 6 Adelaide LR 284. In Germany, marital rape became a crime in 1996 but punishable only with a maximum of five years' imprisonment.

[255] *Jerusalem Post*, international edn., 28 Sept.–4 Oct. 1980. See also, 'A Wife's Right to Say No' (1981) 55 ALJ 59.

[256] [1976] WAR 204.

[257] 13 Feb. 1980.

[258] *Australian Women's Weekly*, 23 July 1980, 30.

[259] Crimes (Sexual Assault) Amendment Act 1981, sched. 1, para. 4. See also Russell (1982), 72.

[260] See Victoria Crimes (Amendment) Act 1985, s 10 amending the Crimes Act 1958, s 62(2); Western Australia Acts Amendment (Sexual Assaults) Act 1985, s 10; Tasmania Criminal Code Amendment Act 1987 (Sexual Offences) Act 1987, s 18; Queensland Criminal Code, Evidence Act and Other Acts Amendment Act 1989, s 31; South Australia Criminal Law Consolidation Act 1935, 1992 (SA), s 73(3).

[261] Criminal Law Amendment Act, SC 1980–81–82, c. 125, s 6. The present law is contained in the Canadian Criminal Code, s 246.8. See also Law Reform Commission of Canada, Report No. 10, *Sexual Offences* (1978), 16.

[262] Crimes Amendment Act (No. 3) 1985, s 2.

[263] Criminal Law Rape Amendment Act 1990, s 5.

circumstances.[264] Legislation of this type is regressive even by the standards of seventeenth-century England. Although there was clear authority at that time for the proposition that a man could not be guilty of the rape of a woman who lived with him outside marriage, Hale himself curtailed it by stating that cohabitation was not a defence but merely some evidence of consent.[265] By the standards of some United States legislators, therefore, Hale was a doughty defender of women's rights.

(c) Processing Marital Rape Cases

It was anticipated by some that abolition of the marital rape exemption, though an important symbolic reform, would be unlikely to give rise to many prosecutions. Whilst no statistics are published as to the number of marital rapes prosecuted annually, sentencing[266] and press reports reveal a stream of cases which have come before the courts since *R* was decided.

(i) Compellability

Where a prosecution is brought for marital rape, a wife may decide, whether out of fear of further violence or for some other reason, that she does not wish to testify against her husband. The question arises whether she should be a compellable witness. A divorcee or a cohabitant is compellable in the same way as any other witness. The Law Commission was surprised to find that compellability was controversial and was vehemently opposed by some women's organizations. In its Working Paper, it had expressed itself in favour of it and this view was shared by the majority of respondents who commented individually.[267] The Report points out that the CPS is used to taking into account the wishes of victims who do not wish to pursue a prosecution and that very often no prosecution takes place in these circumstances.[268] It is of interest that the Council of Her Majesty's Circuit Judges thought that the great majority of judges would be unwilling to commit a wife for contempt if she refused to testify.[269] The Law Commission also noted that the defence of duress is available to a wife in these circumstances.[270] If a wife who refuses to testify is unlikely to suffer a penalty,[271] it might be thought that the case for compellability is, if anything, stronger. It will encourage the faint-hearted, reluctant, or capricious witness to steel

[264] This was the situation in 1998: see P. Mahoney and L. M. Williams, 'Sexual Assault in Marriage', in J. Jasinski and L. Williams, eds., *Partner Violence: A Comprehensive Review of 20 Years of Research* (Calif.: Sage, 1998); National Clearinghouse on Marital and Date Rape (1998) (www.vaw.umn.edu).

[265] 1 PC 628.

[266] Sentencing in marital rape cases is dealt with in Ch. 1 under the heading 'Sentencing'.

[267] Law Commission (1992) para. 4.12. [268] para. 4.25. [269] para. 4.27.

[270] ibid.

[271] Fines have occasionally been imposed in domestic violence cases: see para. 4.26, n. 28.

herself, but for those who, having weighed up the risks, genuinely conclude that their interests will not be served by testifying in court, no penalty is likely to ensue.

The Commission proposed that it should be made clear in legislation that wives in rape cases are compellable witnesses. This would clarify and be consistent with section 80 of the Police and Criminal Evidence Act 1984 which makes them compellable in cases of domestic violence.[272] However, it is unclear whether any further legislation on this matter is necessary. Professor Dennis states that the Law Commission's concern on this point is misplaced since the 1984 Act clearly covers the case already.[273] Certainly, section 80(3) specifies that where the offence charged involves an assault on the wife she is compellable. Since assault is assumed to cover battery, every rape will involve a battery and therefore rape should be covered. When Parliament passed the legislation in 1984, buggery of a wife was an offence even if rape was not. The legislature must have intended that assault covered buggery since otherwise there would be compellability for the minor offence of assault but not for the major offence of buggery. If buggery was included, then rape must be covered as well.[274]

(ii) Anonymity

Unlike complainants in rape cases, defendants do not enjoy the benefit of anonymity. Section 4(b) of the SOAA 1976 provides that after a person is accused of a rape offence 'no matter likely to lead members of the public to identify a woman as the complainant shall be published in writing or broadcast'. Since to reveal the name of a husband rapist may well result in the identification of the complainant herself, newspapers are left with the choice of either not mentioning the name of the husband or else disguising the fact that the situation is one of marital rape. The problem is that if different newspapers choose each alternative, then readers who see several newspapers may be able to identify the complainant. This issue of 'jigsaw' identification was considered by the Law Commission which proposed that, in order fully to protect the wife from unwanted publicity, anonymity should extend to husbands charged with rape so that they would benefit from anonymity to the same extent as their wives.[275] This reflects the views of those responding to the Working Paper. It was further recommended that anonymity should also extend to husbands charged with attempted rape, burglary with intent to rape, and assault with intent to rape but not to those charged with incitement, conspiracy, or being an accomplice to rape of a wife even though anonymity is given to wives in these cases.[276] Whilst there might have been some justifiable reluctance to extend anonymity too widely

[272] para. 4.13. [273] Dennis (1999), 418. [274] See ibid.
[275] Law Commission (1992), para. 4.42.
[276] See SOAA 1976, s7(2) as amended by Criminal Justice Act 1988, s158(6).

as far as defendants are concerned, there is clearly a risk that the wife might be identified in these cases as well if the husband was not given anonymity.

The Commission recognized that in cases where cohabitants were involved, the same considerations might sometimes apply as in marital rape cases. But it considered that its brief was confined to marital rape alone and that, besides, in relation to anonymity, the position of cohabitants was not altogether similar to that of married couples.[277] Thus it was argued that cohabitants do not necessarily share the same surname. But what if they do? It was further argued that

> cases of marital rape will be likely to involve, or to cause apprehension of, the revelation of intimate details of the marital relationship during the course of the proceedings. The latter publicity, if it identifies those involved by name, can be particularly distressing for all family members and, in general terms, seems likely to be more damaging to a husband and to his relationship with other members of the family than it would be to a cohabitant.[278]

This is puzzling. It hardly needs stating that, whilst cohabitation may be a temporary situation, very often it is not and the couple, who may well have children, are in every respect, including relationships with other family members, like a married couple. It is not at all obvious why in these circumstances the failure to enter into the formalities of marriage would reduce distress to family members. As to whether publicity would be more or less damaging to a husband than to a male cohabitant, it is again unclear why marriage should make any difference here, but, more significantly, the Law Commission based its proposals principally on protection of the wife not on damage to the husband. The fact is that a woman who is a cohabitant rather than a wife, especially if she shares a common surname with her partner, may well be identified if his name is revealed and for this reason requires further protection. It should be perfectly possible to limit this protection to cohabiting couples who do share the same surname—in these cases the relationship is also likely to be more established—but it is not clear that such a limitation would be justified.

The Law Commission's proposals on anonymity in marital rape cases have not been implemented so that the possibility of jigsaw identification remains a problem today. Whatever the issues regarding cohabitants, the Commission was surely right to conclude that this was no reason for withholding the remedy in marital rape cases.

[277] Law Commission (1992), para. 4.42.   [278] ibid.

Without Consent

(a) Background to the Present Law

According to the present legal definition, rape is sexual intercourse which takes place without consent.[279] But originally the law of rape required that sexual intercourse occur against the victim's will. This necessitated the use or threat of force or violence by the defendant and resistance by the victim. Once rape ceased to be a capital offence, however, the judges became willing to broaden its scope.[280] It was in *Camplin*[281] that it was first established that rape could take place even though there was no force threatened or used, provided that the victim did not consent to intercourse. It thus became rape to have intercourse with a woman who was insensible through drink. In 1872, it was held that it was similarly rape to have intercourse with a sleeping woman.[282] These decisions paved the way for *Flattery*[283] and *Williams*[284] in which rape was held to have been committed where the defendant, using neither force nor the threat of it, obtained the victim's consent to intercourse by fraud as to the nature of the act. Similarly, in 1885, a man became liable for rape if he impersonated a woman's husband to have sexual intercourse with her.[285]

Some judges in England and Wales appear, however, to have been unaware of the shift in emphasis which had taken place in the law. Thus, in 1911, in *Dimes*,[286] the jury was directed that the prosecution had to establish that the defendant had acted violently and against the will of the prosecutrix. The trial judge emphasized that the facts failed to disclose any bruising of the victim's thighs or any other sign of struggle. In *Harling*[287] in 1938, Hilbery J expressed the view that 'a charge of rape requires to be sustained by evidence which satisfies the jury first of all that there was carnal knowledge, secondly that it was by force, and thirdly that it was without consent'. In the course of his summing up to the jury, he stated:

> In order to constitute the offence of rape . . . the prosecution must satisfy you that he effected his purpose by overcoming such resistance as the girl offered, you being satisfied that she was offering resistance and that he was overcoming it. Did he convince you that no force was used to effect this purpose? If he did, then he is not guilty of rape, and you must acquit him . . .[288]

[279] SOA 1956, s 1(1).

[280] Rape ceased to be a capital offence in 1841. For discussion of this development, see K. L. Koh, 'Consent in Sexual Offences' [1968] Crim LR 81.

[281] (1845) 1 Cox CC 220.

[282] *Mayers* (1872) 12 Cox CC 311.

[283] (1877) 2 QBD 410.

[284] [1923] 1 KB 340.

[285] Criminal Law Amendment Act, s 4, re-enacted as SOA 1956, s 2 and then as CJPOA 1994, s 142(3).

[286] 7 Cr App R 43.

[287] [1938] 1 All ER 307.

[288] ibid.

On appeal, not merely was no criticism levelled at this direction, but Humphreys J himself stated that 'where . . . the charge is one of rape it is necessary that the prosecution should prove that the girl or woman did not consent and that the crime was committed against her will'.[289] As late as 1965, in *Howard*,[290] Lord Parker LCJ appeared to consider that in cases of rape other than where a child was involved, it was up to the prosecution to prove that the woman had physically resisted. A decade later, in *DPP v Morgan*, the trial judge stated:

> The crime of rape consists in having unlawful sexual intercourse with a woman without her consent and by force. 'By force'. Those words mean exactly what they say. It does not mean there has to be a fight or blows have to be inflicted. It means that there has to be some violence used against the woman to overbear her will or that there has to be a threat of violence as a result of which her will is overborne.[291]

The Heilbron Report expressed the following criticism of this type of approach:

> It is wrong to assume that the woman must show signs of injury or that she must always physically resist before there can be a conviction for rape. We have found this erroneous assumption held by some and therefore hope that our recommendations will go some way to dispel it.[292]

It recommended that 'as rape is a crime which is still without statutory definition, the lack of which has caused certain difficulties, we think that this legislation should contain a comprehensive definition of the offence which would emphasise that lack of consent (and not violence) is the crux of the matter'.[293] In response to the proposals of the Heilbron Committee, the SOAA 1976 was passed. This expressly defined rape as sexual intercourse with a woman without her consent.[294]

(b) Problems with the Present Law

The 1976 Act made no attempt to set out what was meant by the phrase 'without her consent'. This absence of definition of the key element of the offence has meant its parameters are unclear, nor can any assistance be sought from other sexual offences in which consent is the key element since nowhere is the phrase defined by statute and the courts have also fought shy of providing a definition.

However, before 1976, as mentioned above, it was well established that in the following situations consent would be regarded as absent:

1. where the defendant has used force to procure intercourse;
2. where the defendant has threatened the victim with force to procure intercourse;

[289] ibid. 308. [290] [1965] 3 All ER 684. [291] [1976] AC 182, 186–7.
[292] Heilbron Committee (1975), para. 21. [293] ibid., para. 84. [294] s 1(1).

3. where the victim fears force;
4. where the defendant has perpetrated a fraud on the victim as to the nature of the act he is intending to carry out, for example, the victim is deceived into believing that she is to undergo an operation;[295]
5. where the defendant impersonates the victim's husband;[296]
6. where the defendant has sexual intercourse with the victim who is asleep;[297]
7. where the defendant has sexual intercourse with the victim who is so overcome with drink that she is insensible.[298]

But even in these situations there was and is a lack of clarity as to the precise scope of the law. For example, it is not clear to what extent threats of force to third parties will vitiate consent.

The *Concise Oxford Dictionary* gives 'voluntary agreement' as its first meaning of consent. There are many situations other than those set out above in which it might be thought that consent is absent. Sexual intercourse may, for example, have been secured by kidnapping or false imprisonment which did not involve force, or by trickery of various kinds. The victim might have been subjected to threats of eviction or of dismissal from a job. Similarly, compliance may be secured by fears other than of force. It is not clear whether in any of these situations the victim's consent will be regarded as absent.

The only response which the law has offered in recent years to deal with the issue of consent is the decision in *Olugboja*[299] in which it was held that it was up to the jury to decide in each individual case whether or not the victim had consented to sexual intercourse. Consent was a question of the victim's state of mind at the time. The judge would need to instruct the jury that there is a difference between consent and submission. A person who submitted to sexual intercourse may or may not have consented to it. It was up to the jury to decide whether, if the victim submitted, that submission should be regarded as consent. The jury would decide this 'applying their combined good sense, experience and knowledge of human nature and modern behaviour to all the relevant facts of the case'.[300]

The decision in *Olugboja* is radical in that it appears to seek to overturn the old approach of the common law altogether. It appears to suggest that in every case of rape, consent will be an issue for the jury to decide on the facts. Fixed categories of cases in which the law recognizes that consent is absent should no longer apply. Thus, even where force is used or threatened, the issue of consent would remain one for the jury to decide.

[295] *Flattery*, above.

[296] This has recently been expanded to cover the impersonation of any other person so that the victim believes that she is having sexual intercourse with somebody other than the defendant himself: *Elbekkay* [1995] Crim LR 163.

[297] *Mayers*, above. [298] *Camplin*, above. [299] [1981] 3 All ER 1382.

[300] At 449.

Academic commentators have responded in different ways to this decision. Smith and Hogan have stated that the distinction between consent and submission is 'so vague that both judges and juries may have quite different ideas as to its application'.[301] Certainly, in *McAllister*,[302] the jury demonstrated its confusion over the matter by specifically requesting the judge to clarify the distinction between consent and submission. Simon Gardiner,[303] on the other hand, has hailed the decision as a considerable breakthrough in advancing the legal protection of sexual autonomy. In depicting consent as the state of mind of the individual complainant, he argues, it permits the jury to decide in each case whether consent was present. 'Solicitude for the individual'[304] is thus the hallmark of the decision. In his view, after *Olugboja* there are no longer any certainties or fixed standards. Sexual autonomy 'can only be about individual choice'.[305]

It is hard to agree with this point of view. Rather it seems that *Olugboja* does little to increase the protection of sexual autonomy. The decision, in transforming issues of law into issues of fact for the jury, makes for uncertainty. There is no reason to welcome this. There is no way of telling in advance of a court hearing whether in law consent is present or not. In this way the law fails to meet a minimum requirement of clarity, certainty, and comprehensibility. Moreover, by failing to spell out or provide any criteria by which lack of consent can be judged, much oppressive behaviour is likely to go unpunished. Neither prosecutors nor juries can be expected to wander far from common understandings of rape as forcible violation.

The decision in *Olugboja* has been ratified by further decisions of the Court of Appeal.[306] In *Larter and Castleton*,[307] a 14-year-old girl was raped whilst she was asleep. If the old common law had been applied she would as a matter of law have been held not to have consented if the jury was satisfied that she was asleep at the time. The Court of Appeal, however, upheld *Olugboja* and stated that consent was an issue for the jury. This suggests that the law is indeed shifting away from a 'categories' approach. On the other hand, in *Linekar*,[308] a case involving sexual intercourse by fraud, the Court of Appeal effectively held that the law recognized only two types of fraud which would negative consent and that the categories of rape by fraud were closed.

Thus the law at present on the issue of consent in rape is afflicted by a threefold uncertainty. First, there is the uncertainty generated by the absence of any statutory provision defining consent. Secondly, there is the decision in *Olugboja* itself that seeks to abandon a legal standard of non-consent in favour of jury decisions on individual cases. Finally, there is the uncertainty as to the extent to which *Olugboja* has indeed displaced the old common law.

301 Smith and Hogan (1999), 459.
302 [1997] Crim LR 233.
303 Gardiner (1996). See also Scutt (1977).
304 Gardiner (1996), 287.
305 ibid. 292.
306 See e.g. *Malone* [1998] Crim LR 834.
307 [1995] Crim LR 75
308 [1995] 3 All ER 69.

(c) Consent and Police Attitudes

The absence of a clear definition of consent has left the police with some leeway to interpret the law for themselves. In so doing, they would appear to be influenced by what they consider will be necessary to prove the matter in court as well as by their own, sometimes unenlightened, opinion of what 'true' rape really is.

A report by the Central Research Unit of the Scottish Office described the approach of Scottish policemen to rape cases. Scottish law developed slightly differently from English law requiring that sexual intercourse take place against the victim's will, which, in general, meant that some force or the threat of it was necessary.[309] The report, however, suggested that 'There were grounds for thinking that in some cases detective officers were interpreting the law in a stricter fashion than might be required by a court of law'.[310]

The report suggests that the police regard true rape as occurring where one or preferably two of the following criteria are met: (1) the complainer is attacked in her own home by intruder(s); (2) a 'respectable' complainer is attacked by strangers; (3) the complainer is severely beaten up; (4) the complainer is attacked by assailants wanted by or known to the police for crimes of violence (especially against women); (5) the assailant uses a weapon; (6) the assailant is apprehended at the scene of crime.[311] This suggests that the police are most likely to interpret an event as rape where it shares some of the characteristics of familiar and conspicuously criminal activity.

But it is not only in Scotland that police appear to over-emphasize violence in connection with rape. Wright[312] looked at 255 rapes or attempted rapes investigated by the police as 'genuine' offences in six English police areas. Some form of physical violence was directed against the victim in about 80 per cent of cases. Usually this was limited to 'rough treatment' (defined as pushing, slapping, or roughly handling the victim but not punching or kicking her), but in 13.6 per cent of cases the violence was extreme. Victims who suffered physical violence were also threatened in 43.4 per cent of cases. In 6.6 per cent of cases, the victim was subject to intimidation only. Thus, a total of 86.8 per cent of victims whose cases were regarded as genuine were subjected to violence or intimidation and half of these were subjected to both.[313] More recent research found that women in London and Sussex who reported rape to the police and were positive about the way they had been treated, were more likely to have reported immediately and to have been violently raped by a stranger than those who were negative about their

[309] See e.g. *Chas. Sweenie* (1858) 3 Irv 109. But see now *Lord Advocate's Reference No. 1 of 2001* SLT, 26 Apr. 2002, 266–490.

[310] Chambers and Millar (1983), 91.

[311] ibid. 87.

[312] Wright (Cropwood, 1980).

[313] ibid. 106. Calculations derived from Wright's figures.

treatment by the police.[314] The use of violence, it seems, is the extra factor which, for many police officers, turns non-consensual sex into rape. There is a clear case for setting out in legislation other circumstances in which consent may be regarded as vitiated so that police officers as well as prosecutors may be encouraged towards a broader interpretation of the meaning of rape.

(d) Consent and Normal Heterosexual Relations

There is a view, which was favoured, for example, by the CLRC[315] and Professor Glanville Williams,[316] that where a woman has sexual intercourse with a man, she should be regarded in law as having consented to it save in exceptional circumstances, as where violence or the threat of it is used. One reason for this may be a desire to protect from criminal liability men whose conduct is not universally regarded as criminal. Certainly, the use of some coercion in sexual relationships has not always traditionally been frowned upon. Thus, Rousseau wrote:

> To win this silent consent is to make use of all the violence permitted in love. To read it in the eyes, to see it in the ways in spite of the mouth's denial . . . if he then contemplates his happiness, he is not brutal, he is decent. He does not insult chasteness; he respects it; he serves it. He leaves it the honour of still defending what it would have perhaps abandoned.[317]

Interviews conducted by Toner several centuries later suggest that attitudes have not altogether changed. She noted:

> A senior police officer and a police surgeon, both very pleasant and helpful, admitted that in their courting days they had indeed persevered and had sexual intercourse despite protests from the women they were with; an actor asked in fascination how it could possibly be called rape if a woman had gone so far before protesting; a dentist [stated] 'I have had it with dozens of women against their will. I am normal, so that sort of rape must be normal.'[318]

Sometimes the reluctance to label coercive behaviour as criminal takes extreme forms. In a case involving a brutal sexual assault by a guardsman, Slynn J, stated: 'It does not seem to me that the appellant is a criminal in the sense in which that word is used frequently in these courts. Clearly he is a man who, on the night in question, allowed his enthusiasm for sex to overcome his normal behaviour'.[319] Thus, for some, it seems, there is a continuum of

[314] Temkin (1997), 521; Temkin (1999), 33.

[315] CLRC (1984), para. 2.29 discussed by Temkin (1987), 66–7.

[316] See Williams (1983), 552–8.

[317] J. J. Rousseau, *Politics and the Arts* (trans. Bloom, Glencoe, Ill.: Free Press, 1960).

[318] Toner (1982), 107.

[319] See Pattullo (1983), 19–20. The case provides an example of a mere assertion by the defendant being treated as exculpatory. The defendant's normal behaviour cannot have been known to the judge.

non-consent, and rape is a point far along it. The question is whether, as MacKinnon suggests,[320] that point is further on from that at which people feel violated.

It is no coincidence that Rousseau also believed that women were incapable of the development and education required for citizenship and 'must be trained to bear the yoke from the first . . . and to submit themselves to the will of others'.[321] A law which fails to protect a woman's right to refuse sexual intercourse, fails to uphold her human right to bodily integrity, as well as her right to full and equal citizenship. John Stuart Mill recognized this when, speaking of wives, he wrote:

> Far from pretending that wives are in general no better treated than slaves . . . no slave is a slave to the same lengths and in so full a sense of the word as a wife is [for her husband] can claim from her and enforce the lowest degradation of a human being, that of being made the instrument of an animal function contrary to her inclinations.[322]

In the new millennium, the criminal process still fails to protect sexual autonomy. Amongst those who influence the development of the law, it is still far from accepted that the overriding objective of the law of rape and allied offences should be the protection of sexual choice, that is to say, the protection of the right to choose, whether, when, and with whom to have sexual intercourse so long as that choice does not impinge on the same right of others.

(e) Reforming the Law on Consent[323]

(i) The Options

On the assumption that the current basic structure of the crime of rape is retained, there are at least four options for tackling the problem of consent:

OPTION 1: *OLUGBOJA*

The decision in *Olugboja* raises a fundamental question which is whether the issue of consent should be left as a matter for the jury to decide in each case on an individual basis, or whether the law should attempt to set out the circumstances in which consent will be deemed to be present or absent. If the *Olugboja* approach were preferred, there would need, at least, to be clarification as to whether the old common law categories still apply. The CLRC, however, was critical of the decision, stating 'It is in our opinion inherently

[320] C. MacKinnon, 'Feminism, Marxism, Method, and the State: Towards Feminist Jurisprudence' (1983) 8 *Signs: Journal of Women in Culture and Society* 649.

[321] J. J. Rousseau, *Emile* (trans. B. Foxley, London: Dent, 1911). See further C. Pateman, 'Women and Consent', paper presented to the Annual Meeting of the Conference for Political Thought, New College, Oxford, 4–6 Jan. 1979.

[322] *The Subjection of Women* (London: Longmans, 1869).

[323] See also Ch. 3, 166–77.

unsatisfactory to leave what constitutes an offence to be determined on the facts of each case'.[324] Similarly the SOR has rejected it,[325] as has the Law Commission.[326]

OPTION 2: A STATUTORY DEFINITION OF CONSENT

This involves creating a statutory provision which incorporates a definition of consent into the law. For example, Canadian law provides: 'Consent means the voluntary agreement of the complainant to engage in the sexual activity in question'.[327] In Australia, the laws of the Northern Territory and Victoria each provide that consent is 'free agreement'[328] and in Tasmania, consent means 'consent which is freely given by a rational and sober person so situated as to be able to form a rational opinion upon the matter to which the consent is given'.[329] But these definitions beg the question of when an agreement to have sexual intercourse is to be regarded as voluntary or free. To answer this question, the legislation in each place sets out a list of circumstances in which consent will be deemed to be absent.[330]

The circumstances in which the law should deem consent to be absent are a matter of policy and the balancing of a series of different considerations. A modern law of rape should seek to protect sexual autonomy and sexual choice but it cannot seek to curb all incursions into autonomy. Some may be left to lesser offences, some to be dealt with by the civil law or by regulatory bodies, and some must be left for the individual to deal with as part of the business of living in the world. Also material to the scope of consent is the issue of punishment. In most jurisdictions, rape and other sexual assaults carry heavy penalties.

Whilst the list of situations in which consent will be deemed to be absent varies in different jurisdictions and some are more comprehensive than others, since all are non-exhaustive, the question of what constitutes a free agreement still, to a lesser or greater extent, remains.

OPTION 3: A COMPREHENSIVE LIST OF SITUATIONS WHERE CONSENT WILL BE DEEMED TO BE ABSENT

This option would involve the creation of a statutory provision that sets out all the circumstances in which consent will be deemed to be absent. Whilst this might promote certainty, it would deprive the law of flexibility.

324 CLRC (1984), para. 2.25.

325 Home Office, *Setting the Boundaries*, (2000), vol. i, para. 2.10.

326 Law Commission (2000), paras. 2.5–2.12.

327 Canadian Criminal Code, s153(2). For further discussion of the Canadian law, see Ch. 3, 173.

328 Northern Territory of Australia, Criminal Code, s 192; Victoria, The Crimes (Rape) Act 1991, s 36.

329 Tasmania, Criminal Code 1924, schedule 1, ch. 1, s 2A.

330 The Australian Capital Territory has legislation that contains a lengthy non-exhaustive list of situations where consent will be regarded as absent but there is no accompanying definition of consent: Crimes Act 1900, s 92P.

OPTION 4: THE APPROACH OF THE CRIMINAL LAW REVISION COMMITTEE AND THE LAW COMMISSION

The CLRC did not consider adopting a definition of consent and was unanimously in agreement that 'it would be impracticable to define what is meant by absence of consent'.[331] Instead, it proposed that statute should simply set out which threats[332] and which types of fraud[333] should negative consent but should otherwise remain silent on the matter. Uncertainty as to the full scope of the offence of rape would thus remain. In its Consultation Paper, the Law Commission mainly sought to follow this approach[334] which has been adopted, broadly speaking, in New South Wales.[335] However, in its Policy Paper its position on the matter has shifted. It has concluded that there should be a statutory definition of consent. Consent should be defined as 'subsisting, free and genuine agreement'.[336] 'Free' would signify that it was not obtained by duress and 'genuine' that it was not obtained by deception or as a result of a mistake.[337] The threats and deceptions which would vitiate free, genuine agreement would be set out in statute. However, where there were no threats or deceptions, statute would give no indication as to when consent would be absent. It is not clear to what extent the old common law categories would continue to apply.

The Law Commission's proposed definition of consent is unusual compared with that of other jurisdictions in requiring that the consent be subsisting. Such a requirement arose from the Commission's original consideration of consent in the context of offences against the person.[338] It would appear that in the absence of any threat or deception, the burden of proof would be upon the prosecution to prove that there was no subsisting agreement.[339] This will be a simple matter where the parties are strangers but where there is or has been a sexual relationship between them, this requirement would be an open invitation to the defence to argue that the complainant had, say, consented to anal sex in the past and there was a tacit agreement that this was now an established part of their sexual life together. The defence could even argue, quite simply, that in the context of their relationship, sex took place without expressions of consent and consent was always assumed. The Commission proposes that the agreement could be implied and non-verbal.[340] Where such an assertion is made by the defence, the prosecution would have to prove either that there was no such agreement or else that the agreement had been withdrawn.[341] But, even if it did so, the defendant would be able to argue that he honestly believed that there

331 CLRC (1984), para. 2.18.
332 ibid., para. 2.29.
333 ibid., para. 2.25.
334 Law Commission (1995), 202 and 205.
335 New South Wales Crimes Act 1900, s 61R(2).
336 Law Commission (2000), para. 2.12.
337 ibid., para. 2.10.
338 See Law Commission (1995), 199.
339 Law Commission (2000), para. 2.13–2.17.
340 ibid., para. 2.11.
341 See ibid., para. 2.11.

was a subsisting agreement and would thus, under the Commission's proposals, be exonerated if the jury accepted this contention.[342] The law has long recognized that consent must be to the particular act of intercourse at the very moment it takes place. This is the essence of sexual autonomy. To suggest otherwise, would risk taking us back to that early stage of the law when consent on one occasion was consent for all time.[343] Any difficulties which the criminal justice system has at present with prosecuting cases of rape by non-strangers would be substantially and unjustifiably increased by this proposal.

(ii) The SOR's Proposals

The SOR has chosen Option 2, proposing that consent should be defined in law as 'free agreement'.[344] It also recommends that legislation should include a list of circumstances, such as the following, in which free agreement would be deemed to be absent:[345]

1. Where a person submits or is unable to resist because of force or fear of force;
2. submits because of threats or fear of serious harm or serious detriment of any type to themselves or another person;
3. was asleep, unconscious, or too affected by alcohol or drugs to give free agreement;
4. did not understand the purpose of the act, whether because they lacked the capacity to understand, or were deceived as to the purpose of the act;
5. was mistaken or deceived as to the identity of the person or the nature of the act;
6. submits or is unable to resist because they are abducted or unlawfully detained;
7. has agreement given for them by a third party.[346]

The prosecution would need to prove the existence of one of these circumstances beyond reasonable doubt. The list is not intended to be exhaustive and 'free agreement' would remain open to judicial interpretation where different circumstances arose.[347] There is no suggestion that in non-listed situations it should be left to the jury to decide the issue. The *Olugboja* approach has thus been decisively rejected.

Consent obtained by force or fear of force. The SOR proposes that free agreement should be regarded as absent 'where a person submits or is unable to resist because of force or fear of force'.[348] It explains that this would include 'force to a person, their child etc.'.[349] It is clear that it intends that

342 See ibid., para. 7.34.
343 See above 'The Origins of the Marital Rape Exemption'.
344 Home Office, *Setting the Boundaries*, (2000), vol. i, para. 2.10.5.
345 ibid., para. 2.10.6.
346 para. 2.10.9. 347 para. 2.10.7. 348 para. 2.10.9. 349 ibid.

force or fear of force to any third party should vitiate consent.[350] Clearly, where violence is used against third parties to secure consent, there can scarcely be said to be free agreement. It does not propose that such fear should be based on reasonable grounds. Again, a complainant who fears violence to herself or another, albeit that her fear was unreasonable, has not freely agreed. The words chosen by the SOR were not intended for drafting purposes and are best avoided in legislation. 'Submit' is ambiguous and 'unable to resist' raises the question of whether she could have resisted, a throwback to the common law before the developments of the nineteenth century.[351] It would also be unfortunate if the prosecution were forced on each occasion to prove a causal connection between violence or fear of violence and the agreement to have intercourse. It would be preferable for legislation simply to specify that force or the honestly held fear of force against herself or any third party will vitiate free agreement.

Consent obtained by threat. The SOR proposes that free agreement should be regarded as absent where 'a person submits or is unable to resist because of threats or fear of serious harm or serious detriment of any type to themselves or another person'.[352] This proposal is substantially different from that of the CLRC and of the Law Commission in its Consultation Paper.

The CLRC proposed that only express or implied threats of immediate force against the victim or another person should suffice for rape. Threats which, on a reasonable view, could not be carried out immediately would not qualify, even if the victim thought that they could be carried out immediately. It recommended that all other threats should be dealt with under section 2 of the SOA 1956 which makes it an offence to procure a woman to have sexual intercourse by threats or intimidation. It proposed that the penalty under this section should be raised from two to five years' imprisonment.[353]

The CLRC's proposal has little to commend it. The requirement that the threat must *on a reasonable view* be capable of being carried out immediately ignores the reactions of the victim herself and her state of fear and knowledge at the time. People who are afraid may not be capable of taking a reasonable view. Moreover, a requirement that the threat be one of *immediate* force would discount the legitimate fear of the complainant that she would be subjected to serious violence in the future. The common law did not necessarily require the threat of force to be immediate and it would seem strange for the modern law to be more restrictive in this respect. Is a young woman who is threatened that she will be gang-raped the following week or month or at some point in the future if she does not submit, to be held to have consented when she fears that this is likely to happen? Where a person commits a crime under duress, the immediacy requirement has been held in

[350] See Home Office, *Setting the Boundaries*, (2000), vol. i, para. 2.10.9.
[351] See above under the heading '(a) Background to the Present Law'.
[352] Home Office, *Setting the Boundaries*, (2000), vol. i, para. 2.10.9.
[353] CLRC (1984), para. 2.29.

several cases not to prevail.[354] It would be remarkable indeed if a victim was to be denied the protection of the law on the ground that the threat was not an immediate one. Moreover, an immediacy requirement would lead inevitably to lengthy cross-examination and argument over whether or not the threat was immediate, believed to be immediate, or could have been resisted or avoided so that it was not immediate. This would be a retrograde step. A law which fails to protect against all threats of violence cannot lay claim to the protection of autonomy.

In its Consultation Paper, the Law Commission proposed that the test should depend on the victim's own belief as to the immediacy of the threat and whether the victim believed the threat would be carried out before she could free herself from it.[355] Whilst this was clearly an improvement on the CLRC recommendation, it is unrealistic to expect victims, in a moment of fear, to address their minds to such calculations. In many other jurisdictions no such requirements have been thought to be necessary.[356] The Law Commission has now shifted its position and has abandoned any immediacy requirement from its proposal.[357]

The CLRC's proposal also confined threats to those of violence. The Law Commission, in its Consultation Paper, went slightly beyond this, recommending that a threat of force should be taken to include a threat of detention or abduction.[358] But what of threats to commit another criminal offence against the victim, threats to accuse anyone of a criminal offence or to expose a secret which would be highly damaging to the victim's interests. The Australian Capital Territory includes a threat publicly to humiliate or disgrace, to use extortion against or to harass physically or mentally.[359] Tasmania includes 'threats of any type'[360] and the Northern Territory and Victoria similarly include fear of harm of any type.[361] The Californian Penal Code includes threats to use the authority of a public official to incarcerate, arrest, or deport the victim or another where the victim has a reasonable belief that the perpetrator is a public official.[362] The present penalty for rape might be thought to argue for confining its scope to the most serious threats and assigning lesser threats to section 2 with an amended penalty. However, the virtual desuetude of section 2 must raise concerns as to whether threats consigned to it would ever be pursued within the criminal justice system.[363]

354 See e.g. *Hudson* [1971] 2 All ER 244.

355 Law Commission (1995), para. 27, 205.

356 In New Zealand, the Australian Northern Territory, Tasmania, Victoria, Australian Capital Territory and Queensland there is no such restriction.

357 Law Commission (2000), para. 6.25.

358 Law Commission (1995), para. 6.34.

359 Crimes Act 1900, s 92P.

360 Criminal Code Act 1924, schedule 1, part 1, ch. 1, s 2A(2).

361 Criminal Code, s 92; Crimes (Rape) Act 1991, s 36.

362 s 261.

363 For a rare instance of a prosecution under section 2 of the SOA 1956, see *R v Harold* (1984) 6 Cr App R (S) 30 in which an attempt to procure sexual intercourse by a threat to tell the complainant's employer that she had been a prostitute led to a sentence of 12 months' imprisonment with 8 months suspended.

Both the SOR and the Law Commission have now proposed that consent be vitiated where any serious harm has been threatened.[364] Seriousness would be determined subjectively.[365] Hence a threat to a child or a learning disabled person that the witches will take her away if she does not agree to sexual intercourse would suffice if this was experienced by the victim herself as serious. Given the general reluctance to report rape even of the most serious type, it can safely be predicted that threats which appear trivial will seldom be reported.

If threats of serious harm will vitiate consent, this proposal seems to leave little scope for a section 2 offence. If a threat was serious to the victim and she agreed to intercourse because of it, rape or sexual assault will be committed. If she did not regard the threat as serious, it can scarcely be argued that any criminal liability should arise even for an offence with a lower penalty. Recognizing this, the Law Commission proposes that section 2 should be repealed.[366] The SOR, however, considers that section 2 should remain but suitably redrafted so that it becomes gender neutral and applies to all acts of sexual penetration.[367]

There is an argument for retaining section 2. Juries may not be willing to convict of rape men who obtain agreement to sex by the use of trivial threats, even though these threats were serious to the complainant. Where the threats are objectively trivial, a lesser offence might seem to a jury to be more appropriate. Section 2 could be retained to give the prosecutor choices, whilst recognizing that this would involve a continuing overlap between section 2 and the offences of rape and sexual assault. The alternative is to confine the threats capable of vitiating free agreement to a specified list as in other jurisdictions. This would involve difficult and arbitrary choices as to which threats should be included and excluded.

The Law Commission proposes that *implied* threats of serious harm should also vitiate free agreement[368] whilst the SOR proposes that *fear* of serious harm or serious detriment of any type, even in the absence of a threat or implied threat, should have the same effect.[369] In Victoria and the Northern Territory fear of harm of any type will vitiate consent.[370] However, the Australian Model Criminal Code Officers Committee took a different view. It was not convinced that fear of, say, substantial economic harm or job loss should be dealt with by the criminal law at all.[371] Certainly, it seems legiti-

[364] Home Office, *Setting the Boundaries*, (2000), vol. i, para. 2.10.9; Law Com (2000), para. 6.25.

[365] Home Office, *Setting the Boundaries*, (2000), vol. i, para. 2.10.9; Law Com (2000), para. 6.21.

[366] Law Commission (2000), para.6.29.

[367] Home Office, *Setting the Boundaries*, (2000), vol. i, para. 2.18.7.

[368] Law Commission (2000), para. 6.25.

[369] Home Office, *Setting the Boundaries*, (2000), vol. i, para. 2.10.9.

[370] Victoria Crimes (Rape) Act 1991, s 36; Northern Territories Criminal Code, s 192.

[371] Model Criminal Code Officers Committee (1996), 57.

mate for the law to distinguish between situations where specific threats are uttered or implied by conduct and those where there are no such threats but the victim fears serious harm will befall her if she does not comply. For example, she may fear that if she does not agree to sex with her boss, she will lose her job. In the absence of any express or implied threats to that effect, her fears may be quite irrational. Whilst it is unlikely that cases of this sort would come to court, in the absence of threats express or implied, her fears should at least be required to be based on reasonable grounds.

Where a person is asleep, unconscious, or too affected by alcohol or drugs to give free agreement.[372] The SOR seeks to reflect the common law by proposing that consent should be vitiated where the victim is asleep or unconscious. Where the victim was drunk, consent issues are particularly likely to arise. She may have drunk so much that she loses her inhibitions and becomes more willing than she might otherwise have been to have sexual intercourse. She consents at the time although she may afterwards regret it. In a rape trial, the defence will always seek to argue that this was the case since such a state of affairs is not rape. Alternatively, she may have become so drunk that she becomes insensible. At common law it is rape for a man to have sexual intercourse with a woman who is insensible through drink.[373] The SOR's proposal would cover this situation. However, there is likely to be a point before this when the victim cannot be said to have consented. This was recognized in *Malone*[374] where a 16-year-old girl was too drunk to walk and had to be carried home. She was too drunk to resist Malone or effectively to communicate her unwillingness to have intercourse with him, even though she was aware of what he was doing. The SOR's formula would be apt to cover this situation as well since the girl was too affected by alcohol to be able to give free agreement.

In *Malone* it was also noted: 'It is not the law that the prosecution, in order to obtain a conviction for rape, have to show that the victim was either incapable of saying no or putting up some physical resistance or did say no or put up some physical resistance'.[375] Under the SOR's proposals, consent will automatically be vitiated whenever the victim is proved to have been insensible or so drunk that she lacked the capacity to consent. However, the issue in each case must be whether the victim freely agreed or whether, as a result of her intoxication, she did not freely agree. It must be open to the prosecution to demonstrate that, although not necessarily incapable, she did not freely agree to sexual intercourse on the occasion in question.

Drug-assisted rape. A further provision may be necessary to deal with drug-assisted rape which is now officially recognized as a problem in the United Kingdom.[376] Such offences are frequently pre-planned and may involve

[372] Home Office, *Setting the Boundaries*, (2000), vol. i, para. 2.10.9.
[373] *Camplin* (1845) 1 Cox CC 220.
[374] [1998] Crim LR 834.
[375] [1998] Crim LR 834, 835.
[376] See Sturman (2000).

more than one offender.[377] Whilst Rohypnol is the drug best known in this context, other drugs such as GHB (Gamma Hydroxy Butyrate), Zopiclone, Dixtromethorpine, Prometazine, and Midazolam or alternatively alcohol have been found in drug-rape samples.[378] The drugs are placed in any kind of drink, without the victim's knowledge and with the purpose of raping her. The combination of drink and drugs will have a very powerful effect. Alcohol, cocaine, or ecstasy may then be administered to disguise the drug in order to avoid detection.[379]

The SOR's formula will catch drug-assisted assault where victims are rendered unconscious or mentally or physically incapacitated. However, in some cases, complainants 'consent' to acts which they normally consider abhorrent.[380] The drugs may arouse them sexually (for example, GHB is a sexual stimulant), and they may feel that they are enjoying what is happening. The law needs to be clear that consent which is induced by drugs which have been administered without the victim's knowledge or consent[381] does not constitute free agreement.[382]

Consent obtained by fraud or mistake. In the Australian Capital Territory,[383] a fraudulent representation of any fact made by the defendant or by a third party to the defendant's knowledge will vitiate consent. The CLRC took a very different approach, recommending that the only frauds which should be sufficient to negative consent for the purpose of the law of rape should be those recognized by the common law as having this effect, namely, frauds as to the nature of the act and frauds as to identity. It proposed that there should be a statutory provision to this effect.[384] Arguably, there is a sound reason for drawing the line at this point.[385] In such cases there is no agreement to intercourse with the defendant—the victim, through his deception, either does not realize that it is a sexual act that he has in mind or else does not realize who he is. Thus the fraud goes to the very root of the transaction. The victim has been deprived of the choice of whether or with whom to have sexual intercourse. The same cannot be said of other frauds. For example, where the defendant promises to marry the victim if she has intercourse with him when he has no intention of doing so, she is at least agreeing to sexual relations and with him albeit that she has been deceived.

377 See Sturman (2000), 20, 23.

378 At 89–90; see also 'Operation Leopold' Police Review, 22 Sept. 2000.

379 Sturman (2000), 24. Photographs or videos may be taken of the rape for pornographic purposes: see pp. 21 and 24*d*. There are now internet sites which encourage drug-assisted rape: see p. 98.

380 Sturman (2000), 14.

381 This would include awareness of the properties of the drug.

382 Under present law, SOA 1956, s 4 may be charged. This is the offence of administering drugs to obtain or facilitate intercourse which carries a maximum penalty of two years' imprisonment.

383 Crimes Act 1900, s 92P.

384 CLRC (1984), para. 2.25.

385 See Temkin (1982), 401–6. See also Model Criminal Code Officers Committee (1996), 57.

Such frauds should, in the CLRC's view, be dealt with under section 3 of the SOA 1956, which makes it an offence to procure sexual intercourse by false pretences.[386] The Court of Appeal in *Linekar*[387]accepted this approach.

The SOR proposes that free agreement should be absent where a person is deceived as to the identity of the person, the nature of the act, or the *purpose* of the act.[388] It has thus accepted the CLRC's approach but has included a further, related situation. For example, the defendant may deceive the victim into thinking that a vaginal examination is required for medical reasons when this is not the case at all. A woman who consents to a vaginal examination in these circumstances cannot be said to have freely agreed to the defendant touching her for sexual purposes. By including deception as to the purpose of the act, the SOR's proposal would ensure that there is no unnecessary debate as to whether the victim was mistaken as to the nature of the act in such circumstances.

In *Tabassum,*[389] the defendant deceived women as to his qualifications by making out that he was a breast cancer specialist. The women permitted him to examine their breasts but all testified that, had they known that he had no relevant qualifications, they would never have done so. The jury found him guilty of indecent assault. Sir John Smith is critical of the decision on the ground that it goes beyond the common law in that there was no deception as to the *nature* of the act and because, in his view, it was not clear that the defendant had a sexual purpose.[390] The Law Commission has proposed that deception as to identity should include deception as to the possession of a professional qualification or other authority to do the act.[391] This would deal precisely with the *Tabassum* situation and would be a useful addition to the SOR's proposals in cases where the defendant's purpose is unclear.

In proposing that frauds as to identity should vitiate consent, the SOR seeks to do no more than follow the law as set out in *Elbekkay*.[392] It explains 'The victim may think, for example, that it is her husband or partner who has slipped into bed with her; she would consent to sex with him but not with the defendant—who took advantage of her mistake. The free agreement was to have sex with one particular person, not the one who was present and impersonating another.'[393] Hence, where the defendant deceives the victim into believing that he is David Beckham and she has sexual intercourse with him on that basis, this would not vitiate consent. She has willingly had sexual intercourse with the person whom she sees present before her even though she has been tricked as to his real identity.

386 CLRC (1984), para. 2.25. 387 [1995] 3 All ER 70.
388 Home Office, *Setting the Boundaries*, (2000), vol. i, para. 2.10.9.
389 [2000] Crim LR 686. 390 ibid. 687–9.
391 Law Commission (2000), para. 5.25. This would involve reversing the decision in *Richardson* [1998] 2 Cr App R 200 which would be a welcome result.
392 See [1995] Crim LR 163.
393 Home Office, *Setting the Boundaries*, (2000), vol. i, para. 2.10.9.

A further issue is whether, in the absence of fraud, a *mistake* by the victim as to the nature of the act or as to identity should be regarded as vitiating consent. It would be hard to argue that consent is present in this situation since her state of mind is the same whether a fraud is perpetrated or not. The defendant's liability would depend on whether he deliberately took advantage of what he knew to be her mistake or alternatively decided not to disabuse her where he realized she might be mistaken. In New Zealand, the Northern Territory, Victoria, and New South Wales consent is regarded as vitiated in these circumstances.[394] The SOR has similarly included mistakes as to identity or the nature of the act in its list of situations in which consent will be vitiated.[395]

In its Consultation Paper, the Law Commission was prepared to consider whether other serious frauds should be regarded as capable of vitiating consent. It invited consideration of a specific proposal that the existing categories of fraudulent rape be expanded to cover fraud as to HIV status and that a comparable offence be created to cover females who perpetrate a similar fraud.[396] This proposal might be thought to have certain attractions. A person who expressly lies about HIV status deliberately places the life of the deceived party at risk. Neither fraud by impersonation nor fraud as to the nature or purpose of the act can compare in terms of the potential seriousness of the outcome. On the other hand, a deception as to HIV status is very different from those frauds. The victim of a fraud as to HIV status, in common with the victim of a fraud as to marital intentions, would have been content to have had sexual intercourse with the defendant were it not for a particular circumstance. Both the SOR and the Law Commission favour the retention of the existing offence of procuring a woman by false pretences, suitably altered to make the offence gender neutral and applicable to all acts of penetration. The offence would thus become obtaining sexual penetration by deception.[397]Arguably, frauds as to HIV status should be dealt with, if at all,[398] with this offence. The Law Commission has now declined to make any proposal on the matter.[399]

394 Crimes Act 1961, s 128A; Criminal Code, s192; Crimes (Rape) Act 1991, s 36; New South Wales Crimes Act 1900, s 61D(3).

395 Home Office, *Setting the Boundaries*, (2000), vol. i, para. 2.10.9. The Law Commission does not make a specific proposal relating to mistakes save where these are induced by deception and it may be concluded that it did not consider that consent should be vitiated by mistakes alone: see Law Com (2000), paras. 5.10–5.35. Mistakes as to the purpose of the act are not included in the SOR's proposals. In the absence of a deception, this could cast the law's net too wide.

396 Law Commission (1995), paras. 6.19 and 6.80.

397 Law Commission (2000), para. 5.45; Home Office, *Setting the Boundaries*, (2000), vol. i, para. 2.18.7.

398 Organizations such as the Terrence Higgins Trust do not consider that use of the criminal law is helpful in these circumstances. It is thought that this would run counter to the idea that individuals should take responsibility for their own sexual health and could act as a deterrent to regular testing.

399 Law Commission (2000), para. 5.27.

Where the person submits or is unable to resist because they are abducted or unlawfully detained. Rape has traditionally been understood in terms of the use of force. In its Consultation Paper, the Law Commission provisionally proposed that force should include detention or abduction.[400] In Victoria,[401] the Northern Territory,[402] and the Australian Capital Territory[403] statute specifically states that consent is vitiated where the person submits because she or he is unlawfully detained. The SOR proposes a similar provision.[404] This would apply whether or not force is used.

Where agreement is expressed by a third party not the victim. Under the SOR's proposals,[405] free agreement must be expressed by the complainant herself and not by a third party. Thus consent will be vitiated where it is expressed by a third party alone. This would seem to be a minimum requirement if autonomy is to be protected.

It may be concluded that the list of situations in which free agreement would be vitiated under the SOR's proposals would bring the law to a place beyond but not far from where the common law can reach at the moment. However, the list is capable of introducing greater clarity and certainty as well as spelling out basic principles of autonomy in this area.[406] One situation which has not been separately included is where agreement is obtained by an abuse of authority. The difficult issues which arise in this type of case will now be considered.

(f) Abuse of Power, Authority, or Position of Trust

A person may exploit a position of power in order to have sexual relations with another. The question is whether, in the case of adults, the criminal law has a role to play in these situations—it scarcely intervenes at present.[407] If so, the matter to be resolved is whether consent should be regarded as vitiated in such circumstances so that there is liability for rape or sexual assault or whether it is desirable to create new and lesser offences specifically geared to this type of conduct.

The circumstances in which an abuse of power may occur vary considerably and may be thought to require different solutions.

Where there is no practical means of escape. The victim may submit to sexual intercourse in the absence of threats or fear of violence where the defendant is in a position of power or authority and there is no practical means of escape. Men and women compelled to live in institutional settings from which they are

[400] Law Commission (1995), para. 6.36.
[401] The Crimes (Rape) Act 1991, s36.
[402] Criminal Code Act, s192.
[403] Crimes Act 1900, s 92P.
[404] Home Office, *Setting the Boundaries*, (2000), vol. i, para. 2.10.9.
[405] ibid.
[406] It is unlikely that the list approach to the consent problem can achieve much more than this: for discussion of the impact of the Canadian provision, see Ch. 3, 175–6.
[407] For a rare instance, see e.g. Mental Health Act 1959, s128.

unable to discharge themselves, such as prisons, and elderly people in residential care might find themselves in this situation. Prison officers and residential care workers are in a position of power that may border on the absolute. In this situation, where the victim is utterly unwilling to have intercourse and submits purely out of fear of the possible consequences of refusal, consent may be said to be absent. There is no free agreement to sexual intercourse.

Where the victim still has choices. An employer, without using threats, may abuse his position of power to have sexual intercourse with an employee. She again is entirely unwilling but submits out of fear that she might lose her job or be treated otherwise unfavourably. It is less obvious that consent ought to be regarded as absent here since the employee has alternative courses of action available to her.

Abuse of a professional relationship. One instance of this is where doctors, psychiatrists, therapists, and counsellors take advantage of those who have come to them for help at a time when they are emotionally or mentally vulnerable. Whilst most cases of this sort will not come to light, POPAN reports that this is a growing problem.[408] Schulhofer explains that a patient in therapy 'must learn to lower her psychological defences, to discuss her innermost thoughts and fears and to place an extraordinary degree of trust in her therapist. The psychological dynamics of therapy are powerful . . . When doctor-patient relationships evolve from the professional to the sexual, serious harm to the patient usually results.'[409]

A patient may not wish to have sexual relations with her therapist but may fear that he will otherwise terminate the therapy, a result which she is too dependent or emotionally disturbed to contemplate. Alternatively, she may welcome the therapist's advances or be too confused to resist them. Therapy 'distorts the patient's awareness of the dangers of a sexual encounter'.[410] Breaches of trust of this nature can have tragic consequences including patient suicide.[411] Schulhofer argues that patients cannot make an adequately informed decision and are best treated as incapable of giving a valid consent.[412]

It might be thought that situations of this kind are best dealt with through the disciplinary codes of the professional bodies concerned. However, many of those who describe themselves as therapists do not belong to a professional body. Further regulation is one response but it is not clear that even those who do belong to a professional body can be sanctioned sufficiently.[413] An alternative approach is the use of civil actions but the law of

[408] POPAN (Prevention of Professional Abuse Network) Annual Report 1998–9 reports about 130 enquiries that year relating to sexual abuse; see further Home Office, *Setting the Boundaries*, (2000), vol. i, paras. 4.8.8–4.8.15.

[409] Schulhofer (1998), 210–11.

[410] ibid. 220.

[411] See ibid. 217.

[412] ibid. 226.

[413] See e.g. 'Woman Seeks Action against Psychologist', *The Guardian*, 4 June 1999.

tort has not been especially responsive where the damage is emotional. The question is whether it is appropriate for the criminal law to intervene in this situation. Given the harm caused by sexual exploitation of this type and the consequent need to protect vulnerable members of the community, there is plainly an argument that it should do so.

Alternative Solutions

There are different ways of approaching the problem of abuse of authority. The Canadian law states that, for the purposes of the crime of sexual assault, consent is vitiated 'where the defendant induces the victim to engage in the activity by abusing a position of trust, power or authority'.[414] The Australian Capital Territory has a similar provision[415] and Tasmania provides that consent is not freely given where it is procured by reason of the person being overborne by the nature or position of another person.[416] The breadth of these provisions is likely to lead to difficulties of interpretation but they would potentially cover all three situations discussed above. The SOR's proposal that consent should be regarded as absent where the victim submits because of fear of serious detriment of any type would also potentially cover at least some of the circumstances mentioned, although a prosecution for rape inevitably imposes a heavy burden on the prosecution.

By contrast, the SOAA 2000, section 3 creates a separate offence based on abuse of trust which is highly specific in its coverage.[417] It criminalizes an abuse of trust in certain designated situations involving victims under the age of 18 without reference to and irrespective of consent. It would be possible for this type of provision to be introduced for adults. That there should be criminal liability in certain designated situations involving the abuse of trust of vulnerable adults has been recognized in American law. For example, in the District of Columbia sexual abuse of a patient or client is an offence punishable by a maximum of 10 years' imprisonment. The defendant is liable if he

> purports to provide in any manner, professional services of a medical, therapeutic or counselling nature and engages in a sexual act with another person who is a patient or client where the nature of the treatment or service provided and the mental, emotional or physical condition of the patient or client are such that the defendant knows or has reason to know that the patient or client is impaired from declining participation in the sexual act.[418]

In Colorado, the crime of sexual assault in the third degree is committed where the victim is 'in custody of law or detained in a hospital or other institution and the defendant has supervisory or disciplinary authority over the

[414] Canadian Criminal Code, s 153.1(3)(c). [415] Act 1900, s 92P.

[416] Criminal Code Act 1924, schedule 1, part 1, ch. 1, s 2A(2)(b).

[417] It was introduced as a palliative for those opposed to the main purpose of the Act which was to reduce the age of consent to homosexual acts from 18 to 16.

[418] Criminal Code of the District of Columbia, Articles 22–4115 and 4116.

victim and uses this position of authority, unless incident to a lawful search, to coerce the victim to submit'.[419] Schulhofer argues vigorously for the need for an abuse of trust provision to cover adults on probation or parole or detained in a hospital, prison, or other custodial institution where the defendant has supervisory or disciplinary authority over such persons or is engaged in providing professional treatment, assessment, or counselling of a mental or emotional illness.[420] Both the Netherlands and Germany have specific provisions in their penal codes dealing *inter alia* with sexual exploitation by therapists.[421]

The SOR has recommended that

> there should be offences of a breach of a relationship of care to prohibit: sexual relationships between a patient with a mental disorder, whether inpatient or outpatient and any member of staff, whether paid or unpaid; sexual relationships between a person in residential care and a member of staff, whether paid or unpaid; sexual relationships between a person receiving certain care services in the community and designated care providers whether paid or unpaid and sexual relationships between doctors and their patients and therapists and clients.[422]

The introduction of specific offences to deal with specific abuse of trust situations would seem to be a useful alternative to treating these offences as rape or sexual assault where consent is the issue. They would require careful drafting to secure the degree of definitional certainty which is necessary for a criminal offence and would inevitably entail far lower penalties than those for rape or sexual assault.

(g) The Consent of Children

Where rape is alleged against a child of any age, it is still necessary to prove beyond reasonable doubt that the child did not consent. There is no automatic assumption that a child cannot consent to sexual intercourse. In the case of *Howard*,[423] which involved a 6-year-old girl, Lord Parker CJ held that consent was to be assessed differently in the case of girls under 16. The prosecution would need to show that the victim's understanding or knowledge was such that she was not in a position to decide. He held that 'it would be idle for anyone to suggest that a girl of that age (i.e. 6) had sufficient understanding and knowledge to decide whether to consent or resist'.[424] However, he commented: 'There are many girls under 16 who know full well what is happening and can properly consent'.[425]

419 Criminal Code, ch. 171, 18–3–404.

420 Schulhofer (1998), 283–4.

421 See Home Office, *Setting the Boundaries*, (2000), vol. i, 69.

422 Home Office (2000), vol. i, para. 4.8.15. This proposal does not appear to include sexual relationships with prisoners and those in authority over them—an unjustifiable exclusion.

423 [1965] 3 All ER 684.

424 At 685.

425 ibid.

It is not clear from this decision what it is that a child must fail to understand or know. Must she lack knowledge of the facts of life or an understanding of the significance of sexual relations before consent will be deemed to be absent? Today, even fairly young children may know the facts of life, but an understanding of the broader issues associated with sexual relations will be absent.

It is clear that no fixed standard by which consent can be judged has been set in the case of children under 16. Under present law, children under 10 years old cannot be liable for criminal offences but they can be held to have consented to sexual intercourse. It may be argued that pre-pubertal children are incapable of giving meaningful consent to sexual intercourse. In its Consultation Paper, the Law Commission approached the issue somewhat differently. It provisionally recommended that the victim should be regarded as lacking the capacity to consent if 'she is unable by reason of age or immaturity to make a decision for herself on the matter in question'.[426] It recommended that the victim 'should be regarded as unable to make a decision by reason of age or immaturity if at the time the decision needs to be made he or she does not have sufficient understanding and intelligence to understand the information relevant to the decision including information about the reasonably foreseeable consequences of deciding one way or another'. In determining whether the victim has sufficient understanding and intelligence 'a court should take into account his or her age and maturity as well as the seriousness and implications of the matter to which the decision relates'.[427]

There is circularity about this recommendation. A person will be deemed to lack capacity to provide a valid consent if, by reason of age or immaturity, she is unable to make a decision. Immaturity is gauged by lack of understanding and intelligence. Understanding and intelligence are gauged by age and maturity as well as by the seriousness of the matter itself. The extent to which emotional as well as cognitive factors are to be taken into account in assessments of maturity is also not entirely clear. Thus a very bright 11-year-old might understand the implications of sexual intercourse but entirely lack the emotional maturity to make such a decision.

The disadvantage of the Law Commission's approach is that it would require an investigation into capacity in every case even those involving young children. Arguably in such cases an investigation is unnecessary and oppressive. One solution might be for an age to be set below which capacity to consent would be deemed to be absent in sexual matters. Above that age and below the age of 16 an amended version of the Law Commission's capacity test could apply. A man having intercourse with a child below the given age would thus be guilty of rape provided that he had the necessary *mens rea*.

[426] Law Commission (1995), 57. [427] ibid.

The Law Commission has come round to this view. It has proposed that there should be an age below which consent should be deemed to be absent.[428] It does not specify what that age should be but suggests that 13, the age originally contemplated by the SOR,[429] may be too high. The Commission is surely right to conclude that, for the purposes of rape and sexual assault, the age should be set fairly low. Children of 12 will attend senior school and may well have entered into puberty. Whilst it is clear that many such children are pressured into sexual relations[430] and may lack maturity and judgement, they may nevertheless have some understanding of the implications of a sexual relationship. It is suggested that the age should be set at 10, the age of criminal responsibility, so that children below that age should be regarded as incapable of giving consent. Such children will almost invariably be pre-pubertal and will lack the maturity and knowledge to make decisions on sexual matters.[431] As for children above the chosen age, the Law Commission has now proposed an amended test which it claims to be simpler. It proposes that a person under the age of 16 should be regarded as having the capacity to consent to an act only if he or she is capable of understanding (1) the nature and reasonably foreseeable consequences of the act and (2) the implications of the act and of its reasonably foreseeable consequences.[432] Whilst it may be an improvement to formulate the test in positive rather than negative terms, the second limb of the test is opaque and seems to require further adjustment. If it is proposed that this formula be used for legislation, the difference between implications and reasonably foreseeable consequences would need further clarification.

(h) The Consent of the Mentally Impaired

It is presumed in law that people who are mentally impaired consent to sexual intercourse unless it can be proved beyond reasonable doubt to the contrary. Any notion of consent must comprehend some degree of knowledge and understanding on the part of the victim as to the type of act that the defendant is contemplating. But how much knowledge and understanding is required? The law gives no firm answer. In *Fletcher*,[433] a nineteenth-century case involving a mentally impaired 13-year-old girl, the view was expressed that the girl consented even if she merely acted out of 'animal instinct'.

[428] Law Commission (2000), para. 3.18.

[429] The final draft of the SOR report does not contain a proposal for an age below which consent should be deemed to be absent where rape or sexual assault is charged: see Home Office, *Setting the Boundaries*, (2000), vol. i, para. 3.5.11. Earlier drafts did include such a proposal.

[430] See Report of the Social Exclusion Unit, *Teenage Pregnancy* Cm 4342 (London: The Stationery Office, 1999); A. Mullins and J. McCluskey, *Teenage Mothers Speak for Themselves* (London: National Children's Home, 1999).

[431] For the *mens rea* requirement where such children are concerned, see below under the heading 'The *mens rea* of rape: young and mentally disabled victims'.

[432] Law Commission (2000), para. 3.16.

[433] (1859) Bell CC 63.

Presumably this meant that no knowledge or understanding of the meaning or implications of sexual relations was necessary provided that she appreciated that the defendant intended to insert his penis in her vagina. Palles CB, in the later case of *Dee*,[434] deplored this view. He held that, 'Consent is the act of man, in his character of a rational and intelligent being, not in that of an animal. It must proceed . . . from the will sufficiently enlightened by the intellect to make such consent the act of a reasoning being'.[435]

Given Article 8 of the ECHR which protects the right to private life, the question is whether the standard suggested by Palles CB is too high and would interfere with the right of the mentally impaired to engage in sexual relations. The European Court of Human Rights has frequently held that sexual activity is an aspect of private life covered by Article 8. 'Particularly serious reasons'[436] are therefore required to justify a criminal prosecution relating to consensual sexual activity in private. However, in this instance, the issue is when sexual activity entered into by those with mental disabilities can be said to be consensual.[437] Moreover, the Strasbourg Court has recognized the importance of ensuring that the rights of vulnerable people not to be subjected to sexual abuse should be upheld. This was recognized in *X and Y v The Netherlands*[438] which establishes that states must in principle provide protection from sexual molestation in such cases.

The Supreme Court of Victoria in *Morgan* approved a less demanding test than that which was advocated by Palles CB.[439] It was held that a woman must be regarded as having the capacity to consent to intercourse unless it is proved that she lacked the knowledge or understanding to comprehend either (*a*) that the man intended to insert his penis into her vagina or, if that were not proved, that (*b*) what was proposed was an act of sexual connection as distinct from an act of a totally different character. Thus, under (*b*) if the defendant has deceived the victim by telling her, for example, that what he intends to do is to perform an operation on her, consent will not be regarded as present. But she would not be required to understand, for example, that this was an act which could result in pregnancy or disease. The *Morgan* test was preferred by Professor Glanville Williams on the ground that 'a low requirement of understanding is necessary to prevent men who have intercourse with willing but sexually innocent girls from being convicted of rape'.[440] He also considered

[434] (1884) 15 Cox CC 579. [435] ibid. 593.

[436] *Dudgeon v UK* (1982) 4 EHRR 149, para. 36.

[437] Even where the activity is clearly consensual, attempts to regulate it may not fall foul of Article 8: see *Laskey and others v UK* (1997) 24 EHRR 39.

[438] (1986) 8 EHRR 235; see also *Dudgeon*, above. Article 14 prohibits unequal treatment between persons in a relevantly similar position (see *National and Provincial Building Society v UK* (1998) 25 EHRR 12, para. 88). However, the mentally impaired are not in a similar position to those without mental impairment. For further discussion, see B. Emmerson and A. Ashworth, *Human Rights and Criminal Justice* (London: Sweet and Maxwell, 2001), chs. 8 and 18.

[439] [1970] VR 337. [440] Williams (1983), 571.

that such a low standard was necessary in 'order not to forbid sexual expression to women of subnormal intelligence'.[441] He pointed out that there are statutory provisions which limit sexual relations with those whose intelligence and social functioning are 'severely impaired'. What, however, of those women who do not meet the strict statutory criteria? In the light of the pronouncements of the European Court of Human Rights,[442] it is not clear that this low test would or should pass muster.

The problem at present is that the law does not appear to have set any clear standard for consent in the case of the mentally impaired. In its Consultation Paper, the Law Commission addressed this issue by provisionally proposing that a person should be regarded as lacking capacity to consent if he is unable by reason of mental disability to make a decision for himself on the matter in question.[443] Mental disability is defined as a disability or disorder of the mind or brain, whether permanent or temporary, which results in an impairment or disturbance of mental functioning. A person would be deemed to be unable to make a decision for himself on the matter in question if he is unable at the time to understand or retain the information relevant to the decision including information about the reasonably foreseeable consequences of deciding one way or another or he is unable to make a decision based on that information.[444]

This formula was designed to be used in relation to sexual offences and offences against the person. It is not entirely clear what information would be thought to be relevant to a decision to have sexual intercourse and whether the understanding and retaining of *information* is necessarily the issue in sexual offences. On the other hand, understanding reasonably foreseeable consequences would clearly be relevant. These might be thought to include the risk of pregnancy and disease. The Law Commission formula in practical terms would appear to add to the *Morgan*[445] formula (which it is assumed it would wish to incorporate) a requirement that the person concerned should understand the possible consequences of the decision. This does not set a particularly high standard—it is less demanding than the standard it proposes for children[446]—but the Commission was concerned to respect the choices made by the mentally disabled. It rejected the approach taken in Ireland where section 54 of the Criminal Law (Sexual Offences) Act 1993 contains an unqualified prohibition against sexual intercourse with a person who is mentally impaired.

The Law Commission has now amended its proposed test, removing the emphasis on the ability to understand and retain information and bringing the test closer to that which it recommends for capacity in children.[447] It is

[441] Williams (1983), 571.
[442] See *X and Y v The Netherlands*, above.
[443] Law Commission (1995), 56.
[444] ibid. at 57.
[445] (1970) VR 337.
[446] See above under the heading 'Consent of Children'.
[447] Law Commission (2000), paras. 4.44 and 4.84.

thus open to similar criticism. Under the new test, which has the support of the SOR,[448] a person would be regarded as lacking capacity if at the material time:

(*a*) he or she is by reason of mental disability unable to make a decision for himself or herself on whether to consent to the act: or

(*b*) he or she is unable to communicate his or her decision on that matter because he or she is unconscious or for any other reason.

(1) A person should be regarded as being unable to make a decision on whether to consent to an act if:

(*a*) he or she is unable to understand

(i) the nature and reasonably foreseeable consequences of the act; and

(ii) the implications of the act and its reasonably foreseeable consequences; or

(*b*) being able so to understand, he or she is none the less unable to make a decision; and

(2) mental disability should mean a disability or disorder of the mind or brain, whether permanent or temporary, which results in an impairment or disturbance of mental functioning.

Whilst the Law Commission and the SOR are agreed as to a definition of capacity, there is some disagreement as to the application of the test. The Law Commission is mindful of the need to secure freedom of sexual expression for those with learning disabilities, even those who are so disabled that they do not even understand that sexual intercourse can result in pregnancy. It proposes that even where there is a lack of capacity to consent and *mens rea* is present, the law should none the less state that in certain circumstances there should be no liability for rape or sexual assault.[449] The type of circumstances which the Commission has in mind are where both parties have learning disabilities and lack capacity under the proposed test and where there is no obvious exploitation involved.[450] It proposes that in the chosen circumstances there should be an evidential burden on the defence to show that the sexual intercourse was consensual and that both parties lacked capacity. The prosecution would then have the burden of proving that exploitation was involved which it could do by showing that, for example, threats, deception, or force were used.[451] The Commission also contemplates a further exemption where the defendant does have capacity but where the circumstances were non-exploitative. In such cases, the burden of proof would lie on the defence to establish the non-exploitative circumstances in which the sexual act took place. The justification claimed for shifting the burden of proof is that otherwise an abusers' charter would be created.[452] The SOR rejects this approach, considering that there should be

[448] Home Office, *Setting the Boundaries*, (2000), vol. i, para. 4.5.13.
[449] Law Commission (2000), para. 4.72.
[450] para. 4.74. [451] paras. 4.75–4.76. [452] para. 4.77.

no legally enshrined exemptions from liability and recognizing the potential of learning disabled persons themselves to be abusers. It states 'It seems wrong for the criminal law to withdraw completely from this area. If an abuser is capable of telling right from wrong and has the capacity to know about sex and understand broadly its consequences, he or she should not be immune from prosecution, nor should such behaviour be condoned by carers.'[453] It proposes that in addition to rape and sexual assault, offences dealing specifically with those who have sexual relations with the learning disabled should be retained and revised. This would give prosecutors the option of offences carrying lower penalties. It should be left to prosecutors whether to prosecute and if so for which offences.[454] It is suggested that this approach is to be preferred. It provides greater protection for the learning disabled and avoids a legal structure which is highly complex. There is every reason to think that the exempting provisions proposed by the Law Commission in cases where both parties lack capacity would indeed lead to an abusers' charter, since the burden of proof on the prosecution would be such as to deter prosecutions from being brought. Ultimately, it has to be recognized that there is 'a considerable diversity of people with mental impairment in terms of extent of impairment, living circumstances and sexual interest and knowledge'.[455] Providing that the test of capacity is not too high, prosecutors are best left to determine when legal action is or is not appropriate.

The *Mens Rea* of Rape

(a) Background

(i) DPP v Morgan[456] *and its Implications*

The mental element of rape was considered by the House of Lords in *DPP v Morgan*. In this case, Morgan invited three strangers to have sexual intercourse with his wife. He told them, so they alleged, that she was 'kinky' and was likely to struggle to get 'turned on'. Morgan denied having said this. All four had sexual intercourse with her, using violence to overcome her resistance. The three strangers claimed, *inter alia*, that they believed Mrs Morgan was consenting. The trial judge directed the jury that, unless their belief was based on reasonable grounds, it could not constitute a defence to rape. They were convicted of rape, whilst Morgan was convicted of aiding and abetting. They all appealed against conviction to the Court of Appeal and finally to

[453] Home Office, *Setting the Boundaries*, (2000), vol. i, para. 4.72.

[454] ibid. vol. i, paras. 4.6.3, 4.7.2

[455] Law Reform Commission of Victoria Report No.15, *Sexual Offences Against People with Impaired Mental Functioning* (1988).

[456] [1976] AC 182.

the House of Lords. It was held by Lords Hailsham, Cross, and Fraser, with Lords Simon and Edmund-Davies dissenting, that there could be no conviction of rape where a man honestly believed that a woman consented to sexual intercourse and that his belief did not have to be reasonable. However, the proviso was applied and the convictions upheld. The speeches of Lords Cross, Hailsham, and Simon in the case are all of some interest and merit further scrutiny.

LORD CROSS

Lord Cross paid some attention to matters of policy raised by the case. He stated:

> To have intercourse with a woman who is not your wife is, even today, not generally considered to be a course of conduct which the law ought positively to encourage and it can be argued with force that it is only fair to the woman and not in the least unfair to the man that he should be under a duty to take reasonable care to ascertain that she is consenting to the intercourse and be at the risk of a prosecution if he fails to take such care.[457]

He was, however, dissuaded from holding that a man's belief in consent must be reasonable because of the wording of section 1 of the SOA 1956, which provides that it is an offence for a man to *rape* a woman. He considered the ordinary meaning of the word rape and concluded that in ordinary parlance rape does not connote sexual intercourse with a woman in the belief that she consents. If the argument for imposing a requirement of reasonableness is a forceful one as Lord Cross suggests, then it is curious that he should consider that the ordinary use of the term rape is a good enough reason for forgoing such a requirement. Moreover, Lord Cross's appeal to the meaning of the word rape in common usage and the ordinary man's understanding of rape is no more than a pretext for introducing his own view of what rape means. Thus, he states:

> Rape, to my mind, imports at least indifference as to the woman's consent . . . To the question whether a man, who has intercourse with a woman believing that she is consenting to it, though she is not, commits rape, I think that he [the ordinary man] would reply, 'No. If he was grossly careless then he may deserve to be punished but not for rape.'[458]

However, perhaps the most surprising aspect of Lord Cross's speech is the apparent complacency with which he viewed the implications of his decision. For he considered that had the defendants been subtler in the presentation of their defence, they might have been acquitted.[459] Had they conceded the truth of Mrs Morgan's amply corroborated testimony instead of challenging it and simply argued belief in consent, on the basis of her husband's assertions as to her sexual proclivities, they might have been believed.

[457] p. 203. [458] p. 203. [459] p. 204.

Mrs Morgan testified that her husband had dragged her from the bedroom which she shared with her small son. She had yelled to her children to fetch the police. Her assailants had covered her face and pinched her nose so that she could not breathe. They had grasped her by the wrists and feet and dragged her to the neighbouring room. She was held down on the bed whilst a variety of sexual acts were performed on her. It is curious that Lord Cross could entertain with equanimity the prospect of an acquittal in circumstances such as these.

LORD HAILSHAM

Lord Hailsham held that the mental element required for rape was intent and that there was ample authority in support of this proposition. He cited Archbold's assertion that 'rape consists in having unlawful sexual intercourse with a woman without her consent by force, fear or fraud',[460] claiming that the *mens rea* of rape was indicated by the words 'force, fear or fraud'.[461] These words, however, as counsel for the respondent correctly pointed out,[462] do no more than indicate the circumstances in which consent may be negatived. They do not apply to the *mens rea* of the offence and can certainly shed no light upon whether or not belief in consent must be reasonable.

Lord Hailsham further cited four nineteenth-century cases. One of these, *Tolson*,[463] was a case on bigamy. In the remaining three, which did involve rape or assault with intent to commit rape, the jury was directed that 'Both the charges require an intent . . . to commit the act by force against her [the victim's] will'.[464] None of these cases, however, involved the issue raised by *Morgan*, namely, whether a mistaken belief in consent can negative liability for rape even where the mistake is unreasonable. Indeed, there was no known English authority on this question. *Morgan* appears to have been the first case in which the issue was raised in this country. The likelihood is, that had the matter come before the courts in the nineteenth century, they would have held, at most,[465] that mistake was a defence which would excuse a defendant from liability only where it was based on reasonable grounds.[466] Indeed, in *Tolson* this was expressed to be the case even where the crime was held to be one requiring proof of a mental element.[467]

460 *Pleading, Evidence and Practice in Criminal Cases* (38th edn., London: Sweet & Maxwell, 1973), para. 2871. Archbold cites East and Hale as authority for this proposition but neither writer used this formula. Indeed, rape by fraud was not accepted until much later on.

461 [1976] AC 182, 211. 462 p. 198. 463 (1889) 23 QBD 168.

464 This was the direction in *Wright* (1864) 4 F & F 967, 968. Similar directions were given in *Stanton* (1844) 1 Car & K 415 and *Lloyd* (1836) 7 C & P 318.

465 They are likely to have held that there was strict liability in relation to the 'against her will' element of the offence given that rape required force, fear, or fraud. This is the case today in many American states: see Cavallaro (1996).

466 cf. *Tolson*, above. 467 See ibid. 187.

Lord Hailsham accepted the contention of modern academic writers that mistake is not a defence but is rather a matter of *mens rea*. If the *mens rea* of a crime is intention, then the defendant who makes an honest mistake has no *mens rea* and is therefore not guilty. If, on the other hand, the crime is one of negligence, the defendant may be acquitted only if his belief is reasonable. The acceptance of such reasoning required Lord Hailsham to address anew the question of the mental element required for lack of consent in rape, since the nineteenth-century judges upon whom he relied had never had the matter presented to them in these terms. Lord Hailsham, however, used twentieth-century reasoning and applied it to nineteenth-century cases. From the latter, he chose to derive the proposition that intent is the *mens rea* for all elements of the offence of rape[468] and to this he added recklessness. Having done so, he concluded, as a matter of 'inexorable logic',[469] that a mistaken belief in consent meant that the defendant lacked *mens rea*. The implications of this approach were not discussed; social policy considerations were, for the most part, neatly by-passed. The inexorable logic was in fact sleight of hand.

LORD SIMON OF GLAISDALE

Of the five law lords who delivered speeches in *Morgan*, it was only Lord Simon whose decision was at all influenced by social policy considerations. Speaking of the requirement that a mistake be reasonable in many areas of criminal law and applying this to rape, he stated:

> The policy of the law in this regard could well derive from its concern to hold a fair balance between victim and accused . . . A respectable woman who has been ravished would hardly feel that she was vindicated by being told that her assailant must go unpunished because he believed, quite unreasonably, that she was consenting to sexual intercourse with him.[470]

It will be argued here that the protection of all women, not merely those who might be classified as 'respectable', is undermined by the approach of the majority in *Morgan*.

(ii) The Aftermath of Morgan

The decision of the House of Lords in *Morgan* met with widespread public disapproval. It was hailed as the 'rapists' charter'. In the Commons, Mr Jack Ashley MP was given leave by an overwhelming majority of the House of Commons (228 votes to 17) to introduce a Bill which would have imposed a requirement of reasonableness where a mistaken belief in consent was alleged.[471] The Government's response was to set up a committee chaired by a judge (Mrs Justice Heilbron) to look into the matter. The Heilbron

[468] See n. 464 above. [469] [1976] AC 182 at 214. [470] At 221.
[471] HC Deb., vol. 892, cols. 1412–16 (21 May 1975).

Committee took the view that the majority decision of the House of Lords was correct in principle, that it would neither cloud the real issues in rape trials nor encourage juries to accept bogus defences. It concluded, echoing the sentiments of Professor John Smith, that the appropriate *mens rea* for rape was intention and recklessness and to go further 'would be to extend the definition of a grave crime to include conduct which, however deplorable, does not in justice or in common sense justify branding the accused as a guilty man'.[472]

The Sexual Offences (Amendment) Bill introduced in 1976 was designed to implement the Heilbron Committee's proposals. Clause 1 reproduced the decision in *Morgan* and confirmed that the *mens rea* of rape was intention and recklessness. The Heilbron Committee's endorsement of the decision, together with that of the National Council for Civil Liberties and the Criminal Bar Association, had succeeded in removing most of the opposition to it. There was little debate on the clause but what little there was displayed a lack of understanding both about the legal significance of *Morgan* and its implications for women. Thus, for example, the Minister of State at the Home Office, in defence of the decision, asserted:

> A crime must be deliberate or reckless intent to do something that society brands as criminal. Only that justifies punishment. In civil legislation, there is clearly room for fault to be penalised if it is merely a mistake. We do that in relation to negligence generally in the civil courts, but not in the criminal courts.[473]

Of course, the criminal law does and always has penalized mistakes.[474] Any suggestion that the civil law alone deals with mistaken conduct is clearly erroneous. The Minister went on to concur with Peter Bottomley MP that the outcry which followed *Morgan* was not because the House of Lords had changed the law but because the public mistakenly thought it had done so.[475] It has already been pointed out that there was no authority on the precise issued raised by *Morgan*, so that in that sense the House of Lords could not be said to have *changed* the law. On the other hand, the law relating to mistake was uncertain before *Morgan*. The case was a departure from much pre-existing authority to the effect that a mistake to excuse must be reasonable. In that sense *Morgan* had authorized a clear change of direction in the law.

There were further misconceptions about the effect of the inclusion of recklessness in the *mens rea* of rape. Thus, Robin Corbett MP, who introduced the Bill, asserted:

472 Heilbron Committee (1975), para. 76.

473 HC Deb., vol. 905, col. 830, (13 Feb. 1976).

474 See e.g. *Tolson* (1889) 23 QBD 168; *Rose* (1884) 15 Cox CC 540; *Chisam* (1963) 47 Cr App R 130.

475 HC Deb., vol. 905, col. 833.

> We must tread carefully, because my postbag suggests that allegations of rape can arise from previously non-sexual relationships, where the man goes too far and persuades himself in the passion of the moment that 'No' means 'Yes'. However, we now have a chance to remove the fear from the minds of women that for too long the attitude to rape has been based on the unspoken belief that, in the end, no woman will refuse the sexual advances of a dominant man and that 'No', whatever the circumstances in which it is said, is simply a 'tease' and that women never mean it. However, perhaps put more simply, one benefit of the Bill will be to increase the respect for women and for their right—because that is what it is—to say 'No' and to be understood to mean 'No'.[476]

But a man who persuades himself 'in the passion of the moment' that No means Yes, or who believes that women who say 'No' never mean it is not reckless and would escape liability.[477] The Bill did nothing to affect this situation and did not therefore uphold a woman's right to say 'No'. Jack Ashley's Bill would have come far closer to doing so by requiring that belief in consent must be reasonable.

Several MPs argued that men were in need of protection in certain sexual situations and that *Morgan* and clause 1 were necessary in order to provide it. The Minister of State asserted:

> There may be a point at which the woman has not resisted physically, at which the man has applied no physical violence or physical pressure, and yet the woman is not consenting. It may be difficult in certain circumstances for the man to understand that she is not consenting.[478]

John Lee MP, made a similar point: 'This is, above all, an intimate field of emotional human relationships where rationality is not always to be expected of human beings. I use the phrase "She did not say 'Yes', she did not say 'No'" and that represents a hazardous situation.'[479]

In seduction situations of this kind, where a woman fails to register lack of consent and no violence is used or threatened, the decision in *Morgan* is largely irrelevant, since the prosecution will generally be quite unable to establish beyond reasonable doubt that the woman's consent was lacking.[480] The case for the prosecution is lost regardless of the issue of *mens rea*. Indeed, it is unlikely that a prosecution in these circumstances would be launched. However, even if the defendant were prosecuted and conceded

[476] ibid., col. 833.

[477] The term reckless has now been extended to cover the person who could not care less (see below under the heading 'Recklessness'), but where the defendant believes in consent he will not be liable: for the situation where the defendant believes in consent but at the same time could not care less whether the victim is consenting or not: see Shute (1996), at 686–7.

[478] HC Deb., vol. 905, col. 831 (13 Feb. 1976).

[479] HC Deb., vol. 892, cols. 1415–16.

[480] John Lee was not describing a situation where the victim was insensible through drink, asleep, or too mentally disabled to be capable of giving consent where the prosecution would be able to establish lack of consent.

lack of consent, he would certainly be acquitted in these circumstances even if the law required his belief in consent to be both honest and reasonable.

There are situations in which the defendant's case could rest on an application of the decision in *Morgan*, because his belief in consent was possibly honest, though certainly unreasonable. One is where the circumstances resemble those which arose in *Morgan* itself.[481] A has sexual intercourse with a woman at the invitation of B. The woman struggles and protests but B explains that this is mere play-acting. A believes him. A second situation is where the woman explicitly states that she does not consent and attempts to resist. The defendant, because of his superior strength, is able without much force to overcome her. He, believing that women always behave in this way, interprets her 'no' as 'yes', her resistance as token resistance. Alternatively, the defendant may, by his conduct, have so terrified the victim, that she does not dare register her non-consent. He may, for example, have broken into her home or have violently assaulted her before attempting to have sexual intercourse. He interprets her lack of protest as consent.[482] Finally, honest but unreasonable mistakes could arise in situations involving children or the mentally disabled. The matter which ought to have been debated in Parliament is whether a man should have the law's protection in circumstances such as these. Talk of the ambiguities which may arise in sexual situations is largely irrelevant in a discussion of the rights and wrongs of *Morgan*.

(b) A Woman's Right to Say 'No'

The unequal status which women still possess in society results in a situation in which what they have to say is for many purposes discounted or reinterpreted for them. So it is in the context of sex. Women who expressly state that they do not consent to intercourse may nevertheless be considered to consent to it. Resistance may be dismissed as token. To justify a treatment of women which denies their autonomy, resort has been had to a ragbag of ideas about female and male sexuality, varying from the bogus to the irrelevant and culled formerly from medicine and latterly from psychoanalysis. Thus, for centuries it used to

[481] A similar situation arose in *Cogan and Leak* [1976] QB 217.

[482] See Toner (1982), ch. 1, in which the unreported case of *Stapleton* (Old Bailey, 26 Sept. 1975) is described. Stapleton broke into the victim's flat and had sexual intercourse with her without her consent. He alleged that he believed she was consenting because (through fear) she hardly protested. He was acquitted of rape. See also *Sansregret* [1984] 1 WWR 720 in which the defendant, the complainant's former lover, broke into her home, threatened to kill her, punched her in the face, made her strip, tied her hands, and indulged in other terrifying behaviour. In order to stay alive, the complainant tried to calm him and did not desist when he had sexual intercourse with her. At his trial, he alleged honest belief in consent and was acquitted. The judge stated: 'He saw what he wanted to see, heard what he wanted to hear, believed what he wanted to believe'. An appeal by the Crown was allowed and a verdict of guilty substituted: for discussion of the Canadian law see below under the heading 'The SOR's proposal'.

be thought that even if a woman expressed her lack of consent in every way within her power, if she conceived as a result of the intercourse, she must in fact have consented.[483] As late as 1812, Dr Samuel Farr, whose book *Elements of Medical Jurisprudence* was published for the benefit of coroners and courts of law, articulated this view. He wrote:

> With respect to the next question, whether a woman, upon whom a rape hath been committed can become pregnant? It may be necessary to enquire how far her lust was excited, or if she experienced any enjoyment. For without an excitation of lust, or the enjoyment of pleasure in the venereal act, no conception can probably take place. So that if an absolute rape were to be perpetrated, it is not likely she would become pregnant.[484]

Today, a man who argues an honest but unreasonable belief in consent is often appealing, whether directly or indirectly, to one or more of the following ideas about female and male sexuality.

(i) *Woman as Masochist/Rape Fantasist*

There is a view that women are by nature masochistic[485] and derive pleasure from pain in sexual encounters. It is also thought that some women enjoy fantasies of rape.[486] Some psychoanalytic writing appears to lend support to these assumptions.[487] However, generalizations about the sexuality of women are of no more relevance in a criminal trial than generalizations about sadistic tendencies or pornographic fantasies in men. At issue in a rape case is whether this particular woman at this particular time consented to this particular act of sexual intercourse. If it were assumed, however, that a particular complainant did have an unconscious desire to be raped, could this be relevant to the defendant's liability? John Forrester argues[488] that Freud himself would have answered this question in the negative since he clearly considered that a subject's unconscious desires should play no role whatsoever in evaluating whether or not there was a conscious wish for an event to take place. To be mindful of unconscious motivations in such an evaluation would, in Freud's view, have led to injustice. Similarly, Glanville

483 Britton expressed this view at the end of the thirteenth century: see F. M. Nichols, ed., *Britton: An English Translation and Notes* (Washington DC: J. Byrne & Co., 1901), bk. I, ch. 24, para. 7, p. 95.

484 At 42–3. Hale, it seems, had more sense and rejected this view: 1 PC 445.

485 For a different view, see P. J. Caplan, *The Myth of Women's Masochism* (London: Methuen, 1986).

486 The *Sun* newspaper was criticized by the Press Council for being 'grossly insensitive' in printing the results of its 'great 1986 sex survey' in an edition which also contained a front-page photograph of a rape victim. *The Sun* claimed that its survey revealed that rape was a favourite female fantasy. See *The Guardian,* 11 Aug. 1986.

487 See e.g. H. Deutsch, *The Psychology of Women* (New York: Grune and Stratton, 1945). For criticism of Deutsch, see Brownmiller (1976), 319–22.

488 Forrester (1986), 57 and 61–3. Forrester also points out that Freud himself had little if anything to say on the subject of rape. See ibid. 58.

Williams appears to have discounted the relevance of unconscious motivation in the assessment of a defendant's *mens rea*.[489] It would seem to follow that unconscious motivation should be regarded as similarly irrelevant where the complainant's wishes are concerned. In practice, of course, it would be extremely hard to establish any such unconscious desires in the complainant. But what of the complainant who consciously fantasizes about rape? Should her fantasy be regarded as relevant to her claim of non-consent? Of course, both men and women harbour sexual fantasies which they would be horrified to see realized. However, Professor Williams considered that the possible existence of such fantasies, whether conscious or unconscious, should in certain circumstances be investigated in rape cases. He observed:

> That some women enjoy fantasies of being raped is well authenticated, and they may, to some extent, welcome a masterful advance while putting up a token resistance.
>
> A little still she strove and much repented
> And whispering 'I will ne'er consent' consented.
>
> This possibility needs consideration where the man was well known to the woman and where it is clear that she was not intimidated.[490]

This passage has been criticized by Forrester, who writes:

> It slides from recognising the existence of rape *fantasies* to inferring from their existence a woman's conscious consent. It is beside the point whether a woman enjoyed the masterly advance or not; what is at issue is whether she consented. . . . If the seduction misfires, if the woman does not consent, then there is no reason for attenuating the degree of her non-consent . . . a seduction that ends in rape is still rape.[491]

It seems strange, moreover, that Professor Williams failed to mention male rape fantasies or to suggest that these might be considered in assessing whether the defendant was prepared to override the victim's wishes.

Where the defendant, in the face of evidence that a woman demonstrated lack of consent, alleges belief in consent on the basis of information given him by a third party, he may well, whether expressly or impliedly, be appealing to the idea of female masochism. In *Morgan*, the defendants specifically alleged that they had been told that Mrs Morgan could be 'turned on'[492] only by struggle and resistance. A man may be willing to believe another who claims that a particular woman has a liking for sado-masochism or has other sexual preferences. If the law grants him a defence in these circumstances, then he may have sexual intercourse with her and use violence upon her with impunity. Neither the law of rape nor assault can touch him. Such

[489] *Criminal Law: The General Part* (2nd edn., London: Stevens, 1961), ch. 2, 36.

[490] G. Williams, *Textbook of Criminal Law* (1st edn., London: Stevens, 1978), 197. A similar passage appears in the 2nd edn.: see Williams (1983), 238.

[491] Forrester (1986), 65.

[492] [1976] AC 182, 206.

a state of affairs is hard to justify. Whatever one man tells another about a woman's sexual inclinations and whether or not she demonstrates her unwillingness,[493] it is hard to see why a man should be able to rely for consent on the word of another man or why there should be no obligation upon him to consult her himself.

(ii) Woman as Whore

It is believed by some that women who say no to sexual intercourse are merely playing sexual games and their 'no' means 'yes'. Alternatively, particular women may be viewed in this light. A man may believe that a woman who has consented to him before or consented frequently to others will consent again and that her 'no' is equally a sham. Once again the question arises whether a man who persists in believing that a woman consents, despite an active demonstration by her that such consent is denied, should have a defence to rape. It may be argued that some men, in the heat of the moment, may genuinely be mistaken. In the words of Michael Alison, MP:

> We are talking about the disposition of the mind in the passion of sexual intercourse . . . The mind is profoundly volatile. There is a sense of all rational control or deliberation seeping away or being under much less deliberative control. It is almost inherent in the nature of the passions and the acts we are concerned with that feeling overcomes or ceases directly to control and regulate action. It is part of the natural spontaneity of the action, and it is bound to be like this.[494]

This depiction of male sexuality might be regarded as convenient and self-serving rather than accurate. It is suggested that where a woman registers unwillingness, a man does have the capacity and should be required to ascertain whether or not her consent is present.

The ultimate question which arises in this area of law is whether a commitment to subjectivism should override all other considerations regardless of circumstances or social cost. As Toni Pickard has saliently pointed out, it is possible for a man to ascertain whether a woman is consenting or not with minimal effort. She is there next to him. He has only to ask. Since to have sexual intercourse without her consent is to do her great harm, it is not unjust for the law to require that he inquire carefully into consent[495] and, it may be added, process that information carefully as well. An unreasonable mistake in this context might be described in Pickard's words as 'an easily avoided and self-serving mistake produced by the actor's indifference to the separate existence of another'.[496] Moreover, where a woman dares not register her non-consent because of a man's violent or frightening behaviour,

[493] See *Cogan and Leak* [1976] QB 217.

[494] In the debate on the Sexual Offences (Amendment) Bill: see HC Deb., vol. 905, col. 826 (13 Feb. 1976).

[495] 'Culpable Mistakes and Rape: Relating *Mens Rea* to the Crime' (1980) 30 U Tor LJ 75, 83.

[496] ibid.

the law is permitting him to benefit from his own wrong if it grants him a defence on the basis of an honest but unreasonable belief in consent.

(c) Reckless Rape

As a result of *Morgan* and the SOAA 1976, recklessness became an established part of the *mens rea* of rape. Section 1(1) of the SOA 1956 now makes it clear that the defendant can be guilty of rape only if he knew that the other person was not consenting to sexual intercourse with him or else he was reckless as to whether that person was consenting or not. The term 'reckless' clearly covers the situation in which the defendant realizes that there is a risk that the victim may not be consenting but deliberately presses on regardless. It has also been interpreted in cases such as *Satnam and Kewal*[497] to mean that he could not care less whether the victim was consenting or not. This formulation seems highly appropriate. Arguably, it is precisely such an attitude of mind which the law should seek to punish and the language is robust enough for any jury to understand.[498]

The Law Commission in its Draft Code adopted the recommendation of the CLRC that a man should be liable for rape where he is aware that the victim may not be consenting or does not believe that she is consenting.[499] Such a formulation would seem to cover, if less vividly, more or less the same ground as 'could not care less'. A person who could not care less may not have given any thought to whether or not the other was consenting precisely because he could not care less. A person who does not believe the other is consenting may similarly have given no thought to the matter. Neither formulation is strictly in accordance with mainstream orthodoxy about the appropriate reach of the criminal law. This demands that those who have failed to think should not ordinarily be criminally liable. There will be few cases, however, of defendants who fail to think about whether the other person is consenting or not. This situation is perhaps most likely to occur where there has been some consumption of alcohol or drugs.

In an apparent rejection of mainstream orthodoxy, the Law Commission in its Consultation Paper on Consent stated that a failure to address one's mind to the issue of whether a woman is consenting or not is 'a violation of her rights, in that it fails to give proper value to her existence as a human being and thereby to accord her full human status'.[500] Both the Law

[497] (1984) 78 Cr App R 149.

[498] It is of interest that judges and practitioners attending the Legal Practitioners' Conference held in 1999 by the Home Office in connection with the SOR expressed strong support for this formula on the ground that it was simple for juries to understand.

[499] CLRC (1984), paras. 2.38–9, see Temkin (1987), 88–9; Law Commission, *A Criminal Code for England and Wales* (1989), Law Com No. 177, clause 89, p. 76.

[500] Consultation Paper No. 139, 95.

Commission[501] and the SOR[502] have now confirmed their support for the 'could not care less' formulation, and consider that it does and should cover situations where the defendant, because he couldn't care less, has failed to give any thought to whether the victim is consenting or not.[503]

(d) Mistaken Belief in Consent: *Morgan* reassessed

Although the decision in *DPP v Morgan* still applies in England and Wales,[504] it now holds only limited sway in the rest of the common law world. Whilst it has been followed in four states of Australia, namely, Australian Capital Territory, New South Wales, South Australia, and Victoria,[505] it has been rejected in New Zealand which requires that belief in consent be reasonable and this is also the position in the Code jurisdictions of Australia, namely, Queensland, Western Australia, the Northern Territories, and Tasmania.[506] Canadian law has placed firm restrictions on its use.[507] American law has no truck with it at all. In most American states, a mistaken belief in consent is no defence but, in those states where it is a defence, the mistake invariably has to be both honest and reasonable.[508]

(i) The Law Commission's Consultation Paper

In its Consultation Paper, the Law Commission demonstrated commendable awareness of the broader issues of sexual autonomy surrounding the *Morgan* decision. It was prepared to reach beyond conventional legal wisdom and invited views on a proposal that the law should be changed so that the defendant would be held liable for rape if he has sexual intercourse with a victim who does not consent, where he does not realize that the victim does not consent but that fact should be obvious to him and he was capable of appreciating that fact.[509] With its simplicity, this formula clearly has much to commend it. However, it falls short of specifically requiring any effort on the defendant's part to ascertain consent even in situations where there can be no excuse for failing to do so. A man who has sexual intercourse with a non-protesting

501 Law Commission (2000), paras. 7.9 and 7.35.

502 Home Office, *Setting the Boundaries*, (2000), vol. i, para. 2.12.6.

503 For a similar approach taken in the New South Wales Court of Appeal, see *Kitchener* (1993) 29 NSWLR 696; *Tolmie* (1995) 37 NSWLR 660.

504 It is not entirely clear whether it has been affected by the decision in *Satnam and Kewal* (n. 497 above) in the rare situation in which the defendant simultaneously believes in consent but could not care less whether the victim is consenting or not: see Shute (1996), 687.

505 See *Halsbury's Laws of Australia* (Sydney: Butterworths, 1991–), para. 130–2025.

506 New Zealand Crimes Amendment Act (No. 3) 1985 amending s 128 of the Crimes Act 1961; QLD Criminal Code, s 24; WA Criminal Code, s 24; Tasmania Criminal Code, s 14; Northern Territory Criminal Code, s 32.

507 See below under the heading 'The SOR's Proposal'.

508 See Cavallaro (1996); Dana Berliner, 'Rethinking the Reasonable Belief Defence to Rape' (1991) 100 Yale Law Journal 2686.

509 Law Commission (1995), para. 7.24.

woman, having been assured of her consent by a third party, should be obliged to ascertain this for himself. His liability should not depend on whether or not she was able in the circumstances to demonstrate her lack of consent.

(ii) The Law Commission's Policy Paper

By contrast with its reflective Consultation Paper, the Law Commission's Policy Paper simply avoids the issues. It declares that it cannot take a view on the question of principle raised by *Morgan* since this is 'a highly contentious area of social relations'.[510] Furthermore, it cannot seek to depart from *Morgan* in the absence of evidence that it is not working and is failing to deliver convictions of those who ought to be convicted.[511] This position is both extraordinary and unacceptable. It was not the position taken in the Consultation Paper. Certainly, if a law reform body feels that it cannot address socio-legal issues involving matters of principle, it would seem to be arguing for its own demise. By opting for the status quo, it does, of course, express a view on the matter.[512] As far as a requirement of evidence is concerned, the Commission's position is disingenuous. There are plenty of issues of which it could be said that decision-making would be enhanced if empirical evidence were available, but the Commission does not generally feel constrained by its absence. Besides, empirical evidence would, in this instance, be almost impossible to obtain. In rape trials the issue of belief in consent will almost never arise on its own. A direction on consent as well as belief in consent will be given. The jury does not provide reasons for its decisions nor is research into these reasons permitted so that the impact of *Morgan* on the jury's decision will generally be unascertainable.

The Commission further rejects the idea of introducing a requirement of reasonableness on the ground that it is not clear whose reasonableness would be applied.[513] It mentions the problems caused by this concept in the context of the provocation defence. The two situations are, however, quite different. It is certainly doubtful whether the law on provocation has been cast appropriately. The defence requires the reaction of the defendant in killing another human being to be that of a reasonable man.[514] Since killing is not generally regarded as the province of reasonable men, this requirement is indeed curious and has been reshaped by the judges so that the reasonable man is now tempered with some of the accused's characteristics.[515] However, in rape cases, the problem, if there is one, can relate only to differences in sexual attitudes. Not all men, it is true, would concede that all women should have autonomy over their own bodies and lives or that their 'no' should be taken to mean 'no'. But such a view is one which society must

[510] Law Commission (2000), para. 7.29.
[511] para. 7.31.
[512] para. 7.34.
[513] para. 7.21.
[514] Homicide Act 1957, s 3.
[515] See now *R v Smith* [2000] 4 All ER 289.

reject as unreasonable since to do otherwise is to countenance a denial of women's basic human rights.

The Law Commission goes on to discuss the issues raised by the YJCEA 1999 which permits evidence of the victim's sexual history to be admitted where the defendant asserts belief in consent.[516] This creates a considerable loophole in the protection which the new law affords to complainants and has been heavily criticized.[517] However, arguably, so long as the law permits belief in consent as a defence, it is hard to justify excluding evidence which might support it. In debate on the Youth Justice and Criminal Evidence Bill, the government held out the hope that the law as set out in *Morgan* would be amended and the loophole closed.[518] The Law Commission has, however, refused to be drawn into this exercise. It takes the view that *if* there are problems with the sexual history provisions, then it is these which must be reformulated. [519] It refuses, in any case, to accept the need to consider *Morgan* in the light of the sexual history provisions because it appears to believe that sexual history evidence is only rarely used in rape trials. It mentions the views expressed by a number of judges at a number of seminars[520] and concludes: 'The experience of the bench . . . is that these days no competent defence counsel would dream of alienating the jury by seeking to ask offensive and intrusive questions about the complainant's previous sexual history'.[521]

This flies in the face of the research evidence[522] and the considered view taken in *Speaking up for Justice*.[523] Given the Commission's demand that there be evidence before it will contemplate a change in the law on *Morgan*, it is strange, to say the least, that anecdote should be preferred to the research evidence which is available on the use of sexual history evidence. The Law Commission's remarks indicate that it is out of sympathy with the aims of the new legislation on sexual history evidence and is not prepared to assist in facilitating them. If the Commission had, as a matter of principle, concluded that *Morgan* should be retained, it could not be blamed if it refused to abandon that principle in order to let the government off the hook on sexual history evidence. However, since the Commission does not appear

516 Law Commission (2000), paras. 7.20 and 7.24.

517 See Ch. 4 under the heading 'Belief in Consent'.

518 See statement of Minister of State at the Home Office, Paul Boateng, YJCE Bill, Standing Committee E, 24 June 1999, col. 207.

519 Law Com (2000), para. 7.24.Certainly, it is noteworthy that in New South Wales which has adopted the *Morgan* decision, if the defendant pleads belief in consent based on the victim's past sexual conduct, evidence of this is permitted only in limited circumstances: see discussion in Ch. 3 under the heading 'Belief in Consent'. However, in drawing up the provisions of the YJCEA there has been a need for caution given Article 6 of the ECHR.

520 This echoes the approach of the CLRC to sexual history evidence, see CLRC (1984), paras. 2.86–2.90.

521 Law Commission (2000), para. 7.24.

522 See Ch. 4 under the heading 'The Operation of Section 2'.

523 See Ch. 4 under the heading 'The YJCEA 1999'.

to wish to engage with matters of principle,[524] its position on this issue seems weak.

Despite its disclaimers, the Law Commission does go on to propose some slight attenuation of the *Morgan* position. Under present law, where belief in consent is at issue, the judge must instruct the jury that the reasonableness of the defendant's belief may be taken into account in assessing its honesty.[525] The Commission recommends some additional jury directions. The jury should be told to have regard to whether the defendant availed himself of any opportunity to ascertain whether the victim consented.[526] This is simply intended as a pointer to the jury. It would still be able to acquit him despite his failure to do so. On the other hand, the Law Commission recommends that the jury be told that where the belief in consent arose solely out of the defendant's voluntary intoxication through drink or drugs, he has no defence.[527] This represents the law at present as stated in *Woods*[528] but it is clearly useful for the jury to have it spelt out in this way. The only objection to the formula proposed is use of the word 'solely' which does not appear in *Woods* and is capable of distracting the jury. A jury is best instructed that where belief in consent arose out of voluntary intoxication, the defendant has no defence.

(iii) The SOR'S Proposal

The SOR has also balked at full-scale rejection of *Morgan* although many of its members were in favour of such a step.[529] It leaned instead towards the solution adopted in the Canadian Criminal Code which provides that where belief in consent is alleged:

> It is not a defence . . . where
> a) the defendant's belief arose from his
> (i) self-induced intoxication
> (ii) recklessness or wilful blindness: or
> (b) the defendant did not take reasonable steps in the circumstances known to him at the time to ascertain that the victim was consenting.[530]

The SOR proposes that a defence of honest belief in free agreement should not be available where there was self-induced intoxication, recklessness as to consent, or if the defendant did not take all reasonable steps in the circumstances to ascertain free agreement at the time.[531]

Whilst the SOR's recommendation falls short of dispatching *Morgan*, it is to be preferred to the Law Commission's latest proposal. It will preclude the *Morgan* defence not merely where the defendant was drunk as in the

[524] para. 7.29.

[525] SOAA 1976, s 1(2).

[526] Law Commission (2000), para. 7.44.

[527] ibid.

[528] (1982) 74 Cr App R 312.

[529] Home Office, *Setting the Boundaries*, (2000), para. 2.13.8. The External Reference Group was unanimously opposed to *Morgan* and in favour of an objective approach.

[530] Canadian Criminal Code, s 273.2.

[531] Home Office, *Setting the Boundaries*, (2000), para. 2.13.14.

Commission's proposal, but also where he failed to take reasonable steps to ascertain consent and where he was reckless. In the latter case, where he has a belief in consent but at the same time he could not care less, he will be liable.[532] Finally, the SOR's reframing of the defence as belief in free agreement, is an improvement on the Law Commission's proposal which is still expressed in terms of belief in consent. In raising the defence, the defendant will have to give evidence that he believed that the victim freely agreed to what occurred. The burden will then be upon the prosecution to prove that he had no belief in free agreement. This may be easier to discharge in some situations than having to prove an absence of belief in *consent*. For example, where the defendant breaks into the victim's home and she is too terrified to register her non-consent, it may be easier for the prosecution to prove that there was no belief that she freely agreed to sexual relations with him than to prove an absence of belief in consent.

(iv) Canadian Jurisprudence

HONEST BELIEF AND THE HUMAN RIGHTS OF VICTIMS

The Canadian provision, on which the SOR's proposal is modelled, should be considered in the context of its own jurisprudence. The Supreme Court of Canada has examined the issue of mistaken belief in consent in great depth and on several occasions.[533] In *Park* the court recognized, as the Law Commission did in its Consultation Paper,[534] that the mistaken belief in defence issue raises fundamental questions about human rights. As L'Heureux-Dubé J expressed it:

> The current common law approach to the *mens rea* of sexual assault may perpetuate social stereotypes that have historically victimised women and undermined their equal right to bodily integrity and human dignity[535] . . . This court must strive to ensure that the criminal law is responsive to women's realities rather than a vehicle for the perpetuation of historic repression and disadvantage.[536]

In the earlier case of *Dagenais v Canadian Broadcasting Corp.*,[537] the Supreme Court held that the common law must develop in a way that is consistent with the values of the Canadian Charter of Rights and Freedoms. Accordingly, L'Heureux-Dubé concluded that the *mens rea* of sexual assault had to be approached having regard to section 15 of the Charter which provides that 'every individual is equal before and under the law and has the right to equal protection and equal benefit of the law without discrimination'.[538]

[532] See above n. 477.

[533] See *Pappajohn v The Queen* [1980] 2 SCR 120; *Sansregret v The Queen* [1985] 1 SCR 570; *R v Osolin* [1993] 4 SCR 595; *R v Park* [1995] 2 SCR 836; *R v Ewanchuk* [1999] 1 SCR 330; *R v Davis* (1999) 29 CR (5th) 1 (SCC).

[534] See above under the heading 'The Law Commission Consultation Paper'.

[535] [1995] 2 SCR 836, para. 38.

[536] para. 51.

[537] [1994] 3 SCR 835.

[538] [1995] 2 SCR 836, para. 51.

Similarly, in *Ewanchuk*,[539] L'Heureux-Dubé adverted to the Convention on the Elimination of All Forms of Discrimination against Women, pointing out that discrimination includes gender-based violence and that parties to the Convention were supposed to ensure that rape laws afforded adequate protection to women.[540]

THE 'AIR OF REALITY' TEST

In *Pappajohn* and later in *Osolin* and *Park*, the Supreme Court of Canada confirmed that it is not sufficient for the defendant simply to assert a belief in consent. He is obliged in satisfying the evidential burden to set the defence on its feet by giving it 'an air of reality', in other words by providing some supporting evidence for the belief. The 'air of reality' test has to some extent been codified in section 265(4) of the Canadian Criminal Code which provides:

> Where the defendant alleges that he believed that the victim consented to the conduct that is the subject matter of the charge, a judge, *if satisfied that there is sufficient evidence and that, if believed by the jury, the evidence would constitute a defence* shall instruct the jury when reviewing all the evidence relating to the determination of the honesty of the accused's belief, to consider the presence or absence of reasonable grounds for that belief. (emphasis added)

In *Park* the Supreme Court emphasized that the mistaken belief defence should never be put to the jury unless there is a proper basis for it in the evidence. There must be a 'real factual basis' for the defence.[541] Courts must 'filter out irrelevant or specious defences' which may confuse the finder of fact.[542] A mere assertion of belief will not do. The totality of the evidence for the defendant 'must be reasonably and realistically capable of supporting that defence'.[543] Ideally there should be 'independent' evidence corroborating his testimony.[544] The accused should be able to point to evidence tending to show that the victim communicated consent to him on the actual occasion in question or else risk a finding by the jury that he was reckless or wilfully blind to the victim's absence of consent.[545] In *Osolin* McLachlin J explained the matter as follows:

> The defendant's mere assertion of his belief is not evidence of its honesty. The requirement that the belief be honestly held is not equivalent to an objective test of what the reasonable person would have believed. But nevertheless it does require some support arising from the circumstances. A belief which is totally unsupported is not an honestly held belief. A person who honestly believes something is a person who has looked at the circumstances and has drawn an honest inference from them. Therefore, for a belief to be honest there must be some support for it in the circumstances. A person who commits a sexual assault without some support in the cir-

[539] [1999] 1 SCR 330. [540] At paras. 68–75.
[541] *Per* L'Heureux-Dubé J [1995] 2 SCR 836 at para.11. [542] ibid.
[543] para. 20. [544] para. 18. [545] At para. 45.

cumstances for inferring the consent of the complainant has, at very least, been wilfully blind as to consent.[546]

The Supreme Court made a useful distinction between situations where the defendant believed that the victim *would* consent and those where he believed she *did* consent. The 'air of reality' test would not be satisfied where the defendant believed that the victim *would* consent where he is aware or wilfully blind or reckless as to lack of consent at the actual time of the sexual activity.[547]

In England and Wales, the courts have not adopted 'the air of reality test' but they have sought to ensure that the Morgan defence does not needlessly distract juries.

In *Taylor,*[548] Lord Lane LCJ made it clear that there is no general requirement that a *Morgan* direction be given in all rape cases. In a judgment which anticipates some of the Canadian jurisprudence he stated: 'The nature of the evidence and of course particularly the evidence given by the complainant and the defendant will determine whether or not such a direction is advisable . . . There must be room for mistake in the case before such a direction is required'.[549]

Thus Lord Lane was emphasizing that to justify a direction on mistaken belief, the facts of the case and, in particular, the evidence of the two parties must suggest that there was the possibility that a mistake could have arisen. Failing this, there is simply no room for a belief in consent defence.[550] The facts of *Adkins*[551] provide an illustration. In that case, the victim testified that A barged into her flat, pushed her into the bedroom, ignored her protests, and raped her. Afterwards he had warned her about going to the police. His story was that not merely had she consented but she had participated enthusiastically. He never alleged belief in consent. If the jury believed her story there was no room for a belief in consent defence, nor was there if it believed his story. In *Adkins* the Court of Appeal rejected the contention that the trial judge should have directed the jury on belief in consent. Roch LJ held that 'Such a direction need only be given when the evidence in the case is such that there is room for the possibility of a genuine mistaken belief that the victim was consenting. In our view this accords with the basic principle that the jury should not be subjected to unnecessary and irrelevant directions.'[552]

CIRCUMSTANCES IN WHICH MISTAKEN BELIEF IN CONSENT WILL BE NO DEFENCE

In *Ewanchuk,* the Supreme Court of Canada held that where the defendant claims belief in consent, the trial judge must first determine whether there is

546 [1993] 4 SCR 595 at 649–50.

547 *Park per* L'Heureux-Dubé J at para. 24. For a less robust version of the 'air of reality' test, see *Davis* above.

548 (1985) 80 Cr App R 327.

549 At 330.

550 See also *Haughian v Pearson* (1985) 80 Cr App R 327.

551 [2000] 2 All ER 185.

552 At 191.

evidence which lends an air of reality to the assertion. If so, then the question is whether he honestly believed that the victim had communicated consent by her own words or her actions. If there is no such belief the defence cannot succeed. Neither can it succeed if the belief is reckless or results from wilful blindness.[553] Moreover, the defence will also fail if the defendant is aware of one of the factors which negatives consent under section 273.2 of the Code.[554] In these circumstances, his belief is in something which is not regarded as consent in law and his mistake of law is no defence.[555] Section 273.2 states that consent is vitiated where:

(*a*) the agreement is expressed by the words or conduct of a person other than the complainant,
(*b*) where the complainant is incapable of consenting to the activity,
(*c*) where the defendant induces the complainant to engage in the activity by abusing a position of trust, power, or authority,
(*d*) the complainant expresses, by words or conduct, a lack of agreement to engage in the activity,
(*e*) the complainant, having consented to engage in sexual activity, expresses by words or conduct a lack of agreement to continue to engage in the activity.

Thus the Canadian law goes a long way towards importing a requirement of reasonableness into the law without formally doing so. Indeed, by ruling out the defence in certain circumstances, it might be thought to be preferable to the New Zealand approach which leaves the jury to determine whether the mistake was reasonable or not.

APPLYING CANADIAN JURISPRUDENCE TO HONEST BELIEF IN CONSENT SITUATIONS

It has already been noted that the decision in *Morgan* could result in the defendant's acquittal in a number of situations including the following:[556]

(1) the defendant has sexual intercourse with the victim at the invitation of another man, X. She struggles and protests but X explains that this is mere play-acting and the defendant believes him;
(2) the victim explicitly states that she does not consent and attempts to resist. The defendant, because of his superior strength, is able without

[553] The concept of wilful blindness was utilized in this context in *Sansregret v the Queen* [1985] 1 SCR 570. As defined by Professor Glanville Williams *Criminal Law: The General Part* (London: Stevens & Sons, 1961) para. 57), it is a species of recklessness but in this more recent articulation it may cover gross negligence.

[554] [1999] 1 SCR 330 at paras. 64 and 65.

[555] For further discussion of the mistake of law approach to the honest belief defence, see Ch. 3 under the heading 'Consent', subsection (c) Canada, especially nn. 118 and 119 and accompanying text.

[556] See above under the heading '(b) The Aftermath of *Morgan*'.

much force to overcome her. He, believing that women always behave in this way, interprets her 'no' as 'yes' and her resistance as token;[557]

(3) the defendant has so terrified the victim by his conduct that she dare not register her non-consent. He may, for example, have broken into her home or violently assaulted her before attempting to have sexual intercourse. He interprets her lack of protest as consent.

An application of the Canadian jurisprudence to these three situations would suggest that in none of them would the defence succeed. Indeed, it is unlikely that this defence would be put to the jury. In all three cases, there has been no communication of consent by the victim herself at the time of the event in question to warrant any belief in consent by the defendant. The same would apply if the defendant believes that the victim consents because of what he has heard about her sexual behaviour from other men. This is evidence of his belief that she *would* consent, not evidence of belief that she *did* consent. Moreover, in the first two situations the defendant has made a mistake of law which, according to *Ewanchuk*, would be no defence.

However, it is not clear that under the SOR's proposals, the honest belief in consent defence would similarly fail in all three situations. Much would depend on whether the jury decides that the defendant was reckless. It would need to be made much clearer in the jurisprudence that the defendant is reckless as to consent where there has been no communication of consent by the victim herself at the time in question. The same would apply where the defendant's belief in consent was based on his knowledge of her sexual history. It would be necessary for the judges to make it clear that a belief that she *would* consent is not evidence of belief that she *did* consent. Given that a claim of honest belief in consent is now a gateway to the admission of sexual history evidence, this would be particularly significant.[558]

In the first situation, the defendant's belief in consent would also be based on a mistake of law since the SOR has proposed that consent would not exist where it is expressed by a third party. It should therefore be no defence.[559] But this highlights the fact that the list of circumstances in which consent would be vitiated under the SOR's proposals is narrower than in the Canadian provision. It seems reasonable that consent should be regarded as absent where the victim specifically communicates that she is not consenting. If this were added to the SOR's list of non-consent situations, a belief in

[557] Of this example, the Law Commission comments: 'He is relying on an attitude towards other people which is no longer acceptable. The question is whether society should state clearly that a man who ignores a woman's express refusal will not be permitted to claim that he did not think she meant it.' Law Commission Consultation (1995), para. 7.19.

[558] YJCEA 1999, s 41: see above under the heading 'The Law Commission's Policy Paper'.

[559] It has been pointed out that 'few distinctions have given more difficulty than that between mistake of fact and mistake of law', Smith and Hogan (1999), 80. However, since in this situation 'the defendant intends the occurrence of that event which the law forbids' his mistake should arguably be no defence: see ibid.

consent where the defendant was aware that the victim had communicated her lack of consent would be based on a mistake of law and should therefore be regarded as no defence.

(v) Young and Mentally Disabled Victims

Special consideration needs to be given to the situation where the victim is a child or young person or is mentally disabled. If the victim fails to make any demonstration of lack of consent because she does not appreciate the nature of the act or lacks the capacity to understand its significance a number of different possibilities need to be explored. First, the defendant might argue that he believed in the victim's consent since she permitted penetration. If he knew full well that she had no understanding of the act then he clearly has no defence. If consent does not exist where a woman lacks understanding of the nature of the act and the defendant knows of her lack of understanding or was aware that she might not understand, then he must have the requisite *mens rea* for the offence. Alternatively, the defendant may have considered the possibility that the victim did not understand the nature of the act but have dismissed it from his mind, although the risk was, given his own capacities, an obvious one. Here the defendant is likely to be judged reckless since it appears that he could not care less. A further situation might arise in which the defendant alleges belief in consent on the basis of the victim's consent to penetration but where it did not occur to him that she might not understand the nature of the act, although the risk of this was obvious. Again, he will be liable if his failure to consider that she might not appreciate the nature of the act was due to his own recklessness. Under the SOR's proposals unless the defendant took all reasonable steps in the circumstances known to him at the time to ascertain consent, the defence would not apply.

Under the Law Commission's proposal,[560] it will be assumed that consent is absent where the child is under a certain age. It would follow that if a defendant knew she was under that age or was reckless as to this matter, he would not be able to plead belief in consent.

Sexual Assaults against Children

(a) **Background to the Present Law**

Historically, the crimes of rape and carnal knowledge, that is, sexual intercourse with a girl under the age of consent, were not clearly differentiated and there was disagreement amongst commentators as to whether the former included the latter. Certainly, the first Statute of Westminster in 1275

[560] See above under the heading 'The Consent of Children'.

did not distinguish between the two and made it a single criminal offence, punishable with a maximum penalty of two years' imprisonment, either to ravish a woman against her will or to have sexual intercourse with a girl who was under age. Coke and Hale assumed that the relevant age, which the Statute did not specify, was 12 since that was the age of marital capacity.[561] The second Statute of Westminster in 1285 made rape a capital offence but did not mention carnal knowledge. However, under legislation passed in the reign of Elizabeth I, it was specifically stated to be a felony to have carnal knowledge of a girl under 10.[562] That felony was again assumed to be rape by Hale.[563] Whilst Hale considered that carnal knowledge of a girl under 12 was rape, Blackstone and East concluded that once the girl was over 10 but under 12, the offence was still governed by the first Statute of Westminster but was not rape, merely a misdemeanour.[564] Indeed, East expressed the view that carnal knowledge of a girl under 10 was not 'properly speaking a rape' although he implies that it was generally considered to be so.[565]

By the nineteenth century, however, the two offences had clearly become quite separate. Legislation passed in 1828 made it a specific felony, punishable with death, to have carnal knowledge of a girl under 10.[566] Where she was over 10 and under 12 it was a misdemeanour punishable with imprisonment with or without hard labour for such term as the court should decide.[567] That the age of consent should remain at 12 seems to have been taken for granted by the Commissioners on Criminal Law.[568] In this they may have been influenced by the fact that this was still the age of marital capacity.[569] Their only concern was that the law was too harsh. They were understandably opposed to the death penalty but also proposed in 1843[570] that where the child had reached 10 years of age, the maximum penalty should be three years' imprisonment, a clear indication that they did not view the offence as particularly grave. The penalties were reduced first in 1841[571] and again in 1861.[572]

The absence of provision in the criminal law throughout the centuries to protect young girls against sexual exploitation was compounded by the

[561] See Coke PC ch. 11, Hale 1 PC 631. [562] 18 Eliz I c 7, s 4. [563] 1 PC 630.

[564] E. H. East, *A Treatise of the Pleas of the Crown* (London, 1803), ch. 10, s 2. W. Blackstone, *Commentaries* (Oxford: Clarendon Press, 1769), vol. iv, 212.

[565] East, above. [566] 9 Geo IV c 31, s XV11. [567] ibid.

[568] See Fourth Report of Her Majesty's Commissioners for Revising and Consolidating the Criminal Law, article 88 (First Commission, 1839).

[569] And remained so until the Age of Marriage Act 1929.

[570] Seventh Report of her Majesty's Commissioners for Revising and Consolidating the Criminal Law, article 27.4 (First Commission, 1843).

[571] The penalty for carnal knowledge of a girl under 10 was reduced in 1841 from death to transportation for life: 4 and 5 Vic c 56.

[572] For carnal knowledge of girls under 10 the penalty was reduced to penal servitude for a maximum of life and minimum of three years or to imprisonment for no more than two years with or without hard labour. For girls above 10 the penalty became three years' penal servitude or imprisonment for no more than two years with or without hard labour: 24 and 25 Vic c 100.

activities of the ecclesiastical courts. The ecclesiastical offence of fornication was used to punish not merely their seducers but, more often, the girls themselves, particularly if pregnancy resulted.[573] Moreover, lower temporal courts were also prone to punish fornicators with carting, stocking, whipping, or imprisonment in the house of correction.[574] But, by the eighteenth century, it was mainly girls of the rural lower class who were the recipients of punishment since young men and upper-class girls seemed to be able to avoid the jurisdiction of the courts.[575] Not merely were young upper-class girls less likely to be charged with fornication but they were indirectly protected by the offences created to safeguard the property interests of their fathers. Indeed, the age of consent where a woman of property was involved was in many respects effectively 16. Statutory offences reflective of pre-existing common law,[576] were introduced in 1557[577] with the express aim of ensuring against the abduction and defloration of young heiresses by worthless suitors. It was made an offence punishable with two years' imprisonment to take an unmarried girl under 16 out of the possession of her parents *against their will* with the penalty rising to five years if defloration or marriage accompanied the abduction. Moreover, her property would throughout her lifetime be held and enjoyed by her next of kin and on her death her husband would be excluded from inheriting. Over the centuries these offences were interpreted strictly in order to ensure paternal interests.[578]

By the latter half of the nineteenth century it remained the case that a girl who had reached her twelfth birthday was left utterly unprotected from coercive sexual behaviour. The only available offence was rape, which was hard to establish, and rarely prosecuted. Wealthy girls had the protection of the abduction offences, but in Victorian times they were in any case far less vulnerable to sexual exploitation than their working-class counterparts. The preservation of Victorian values was contingent upon the sexual exploitation of working-class women and children who provided the vast prostitute

[573] See R. Houlbrooke, *Church Courts and the People during the English Reformation 1520–1570* (Oxford: Oxford University Press, 1979).

[574] See K.Thomas, 'The Puritans and Adultery: The Act of 1650 Reconsidered' in D. Pennington and K. Thomas, eds., *Puritans & Revolutionaries: Essays in Seventeenth Century History Presented to Christopher Hill* (Oxford: Clarendon Press, 1978) 257–82 in which examples of such interventions are given in the fifteenth, sixteenth, and seventeenth centuries.

[575] See S. Staves, 'British Seduced Maidens', in *Eighteenth Century Studies*, vol. xiv (1981), 109, at 123.

[576] See *R v Twistleton and others* 2 Keb 432, Mich T, 20 Car 11, in which it was stated to be a common law offence to abduct a girl under 16 from her father's custody and that the statute of 1557 (n. 577, below) did no more than increase the penalty for this conduct.

[577] Ph and M c 8.

[578] See *R v Mankletow* (1853) Dears CC 159; *R v Robins* (1844) 1 Car and K 456, in which it was held that the girl's consent was no defence and *R v Timmins* (1860) Bell, CC 276 in which it was held that even a temporary appropriation of the girl would suffice. Tortious remedies were also available to fathers in these circumstances.

population of the cities.[579] It was the plight of the children and young girls which moved reformers like Josephine Butler.[580] But her campaign to raise the age of consent met with bitter and determined opposition. A turning-point was reached when a Royal Commission, set up to look into the operation of the Contagious Diseases Acts,[581] proposed that the age of consent be raised to 14.[582] Yet every legislative attempt to do so[583] was thwarted until 1875 when, for the first time, it became a misdemeanour to have sexual relations with a girl between the ages of 12 and 13.[584] In the face of the obvious inadequacy of this legislation, Josephine Butler continued her work with the result that a House of Lords Select Committee was set up to look into child abduction and prostitution. In its Report of 1882 it recommended raising the age of consent to 16.[585] The government finally agreed to promote the Criminal Law Amendment Bill but this encountered fierce opposition in Parliament. That middle- and upper-class men should be brought within the criminal law for consorting with under-age working-class prostitutes was clearly anathema to many who spoke in the debates.[586] The conflict between the reformers[587] and what came to be referred to as the 'vice lobby' is written on the face of the 1885 statute which eventually came into law. On the one hand, the Act was expressed to be for 'the protection of women and girls' and a panoply of offences introduced. On the other hand, these were hedged about with corroboration requirements, exemptions where the woman was a 'common prostitute', and, in the case of the new offence of carnal knowledge of a girl of 13 and under 16, a three-month time limit. A

[579] The youth of prostitutes is alluded to in the papers of the Select Committee on the State of the Police of the Metropolis: see e.g. Parliamentary Papers 1817, vol. vii, 54. Prostitutes imprisoned in Bridewell prison were noted by the committee to include girls of 14: see PP 1818, vol. viii, 30. The Committee was keen to investigate the existence of brothels devoted to children alone: see PP 1816, vol. v, 127, 147.

[580] *Personal Reminiscences of a Great Crusade* (2nd edn., London: Horace Marshall, 1898), 224.

[581] Report of the Royal Commission upon the Administration and Operation of the Contagious Diseases Act, PP 1871, vol. xix. The Commission received evidence that girls as young as 12 were being hospitalized for contagious diseases: see 'Analysis of Evidence', 23.

[582] It commented 'We think a child of 12 years can hardly be deemed capable of giving consent and should not have the power of yielding up her person': see ibid., para. 59.

[583] Private Members Bills were introduced in 1872, 1873, and 1874.

[584] Offences against the Person Act, s 4. The maximum penalty was two years' imprisonment with or without hard labour.

[585] See *Report from the Select Committee of the House of Lords on the Law Relating to the Protection of Young Girls,* Parliamentary Papers 1882 Cmnd 344. For the campaign led by the Booths, the Salvation Army, and William Stead, the editor of the *Pall Mall Gazette* in support of this proposal, see M. Pearson, *The Age of Consent: Victorian Prostitution and its Enemies* (Newton Abbott: David and Charles, 1972).

[586] See e.g. Captain Price, HC Deb., vol. ccc, cols. 777–8 Hansard, ser. 3 (31 July 1885); the Earl of Milltown, HL Deb., vol. ccxcvi, col. 1441, Hansard, ser. 3 (13 Apr. 1885).

[587] See Sir Baldwin Leighton who declared: 'The working classes . . . would deeply feel and deeply resent any trifling with . . . this Bill [and] were getting exceedingly impatient at the manner in which all these social questions, greatly affecting their interest, were put on one side'. HC Deb., vol. ccxcviii, cols. 1181–2, Hansard, ser. 3 (22 May 1885).

defence where the defendant made a reasonable mistake that the girl was above 16 was also included.[588] Moreover, the offence was made a misdemeanour only and punishable with a maximum of two years' imprisonment.[589] Thus whilst the symbolic gains were substantial, the practical effect of the new legislation was strictly limited.

The legacy of the bitter conflict over the 1885 legislation continues to this day. The limitations imposed on prosecutions in order to placate the 'vice lobby' continue to affect the efficacy of the offence of unlawful sexual intercourse (USI) with a girl over 13 and under 16.[590] The low penalty remains the same, there is still a time limit on prosecutions although this was gradually extended to a year,[591] and, most significantly, there is still a mistake of age defence which now exists in the more limited form of the 'young man's defence'.[592] This applies where the defendant is under 24, has not been charged with this offence before, and has an honest belief on reasonable grounds that the girl was above 16. The burden of proof in establishing the defence is upon him on the balance of probabilities.

The Impact of the 'Young Man's Defence'

In a major study of sexual offences conducted by the Cambridge Institute of Criminology between 1950 and 1954, 3,000 cases involving sexual offences were investigated. It was found that the proportion of offenders recorded by the police as having committed carnal knowledge of girls aged 13 to 16 who were not brought before the courts was much higher (46%) than for men charged with other heterosexual offences (12%). One of the principal reasons for this was considered to be the existence of the 'young man's defence'.[593] Today, there is a reluctance to prosecute young men who are not much older than the girl herself. Older men are more likely to be prosecuted. Often the dividing line between rape and USI is hard to discern. The prosecution rate for unlawful sexual intercourse with a girl over 13 but under 16 remains very low as compared with other heterosexual offences. The Home Office Research Unit found that in 1973 it was 25 per cent as compared with 81 per cent for rape, 83.5 per cent for incest, 63 per cent for buggery, and 66 per cent for unlawful sexual intercourse with a girl under 13.[594] In 1987, there were 2,699 offences recorded under section 6. This figure has dropped steadily over the decade and fell to 1,112 in 1997[595] with

[588] See Criminal Law Amendment Act 1885, ss 2, 3, and 5. [589] s 5.

[590] Now contained in SOA 1956, s 6.

[591] See Prevention of Cruelty Act 1904 (six months); Criminal Law Amendment Act 1922 (nine months); Criminal Law Amendment Act 1928 (12 months).

[592] The Criminal Law Amendment Act 1922 which effected this change was itself replaced by the Sexual Offences Act 1956, s 6(3). In *Kirk* (*The Times*, 26 June 2002), it was held that the defence was not incompatible with Articles 6 and 14 of the ECHR.

[593] Cambridge Dept. of Criminal Science (1957), 48.

[594] Walmsley and White (1979), 42. [595] *Criminal Statistics 1997*, table 2.15.

1,237 in 2000.[596] The number of prosecutions for the offence has similarly dropped over the decade. In 1987, there were 360, 13 per cent of the number of recorded offences in that year[597] as against 153 in 1997, 14 per cent of recorded offences, and 169 in 1999,13 per cent of recorded offences.[598] The report by the Social Exclusion Unit on Teenage Pregnancy[599] notes the effect of the young man's defence on prosecution policy. It also refers to the concern, expressed by organizations such as Barnardo's, that men who target and abuse children may exploit the defence and it may lead to cases not being investigated.[600] Certainly, the attraction for punters of under-age prostitutes has not abated.[601]

(b) The CLRC's Proposals

The age of consent was considered by the Policy Advisory Committee (PAC) which recommended that it should remain at 16.[602] It took the view that 'there has been no significant increase in recent times in the level of psychological maturity of girls under 16 and that [these girls] face greater problems today than their mothers did at their age'.[603] This recommendation was supported by the CLRC, which noted that the policy behind the law was the protection of young girls.[604] Both committees further considered whether sexual intercourse with a girl under 13 should continue to be punishable with life imprisonment or whether the age limit for this offence should be reduced to 12. The PAC strongly advised that 13 should remain the age limit. It argued that girls of 12 are at a vulnerable stage of their lives, in particular because they are usually in their first year at a senior school and there is a risk that they will imitate behaviour, including the sexual ways, of older girls.[605] The CLRC again accepted this recommendation.[606]

But the CLRC also recommended that there should be a full-scale extension of the young man's defence to cover men of all ages. It proposed that, whether the girl was under 13 or under 16, a man who believed that she was over 16 should not be guilty of any crime even though his belief was entirely unreasonable. Moreover, the burden of proof should be upon the prosecution and not on the defence as at present.[607] If implemented, this proposal

596 Home Office Statistical Bulletin, *Recorded Crime England and Wales* (2001), 12/01, 28.

597 *Criminal Statistics Supplementary Tables*, vol. 1 (1987), table S1.1(A).

598 *Criminal Statistics Supplementary Tables 1997, 1999*, vol. 1, table S1.1(A).

599 Cm 4342 (London: The Stationery Office, 1999).

600 At 47–8.

601 See J. Ennew, *The Sexual Exploitation of Children* (Cambridge: Polity Press, 1986), at 82.

602 *Report on the Age of Consent in Relation to Sexual Offences* (1981), Cmnd 8216. The PAC was set up to advise the CLRC on issues relating to sexual offences.

603 Working Paper on the Age of Consent in Relation to Sexual Offences (1979), para. 23.

604 CLRC (1984), para. 5.4.

605 ibid., para. 5.5.

606 ibid., para. 5.6. The PAC recommended that the age of consent to male homosexual acts should be reduced from 21 to 18.

607 CLRC (1984), para. 5.26.

would afford men charged with USI even greater protection from prosecution and conviction than they enjoyed under the 1885 Act. It could serve only to undermine the purpose of an age of consent which the CLRC purported to support. But the CLRC considered that the law should be brought into line with the law of rape[608] even though the practical implications of an honest belief defence in the two situations are quite different. A defence of honest belief that a girl is over 16 would have a far greater impact than the defence of honest belief in consent in the context of rape. On a charge of unlawful sexual intercourse, if sexual intercourse has taken place, mistake of age would be the only defence available so most men would plead it. The defendant might state that he honestly thought at the time that the girl was above 16 and that he never thought to enquire, or that the girl was dressed up and wearing make-up. Mistakes about age are, after all, easy to make, particularly if no questions need be asked. In many cases, it would be very hard for the prosecution to prove beyond reasonable doubt that he was lying. In a rape case, by contrast, men generally plead consent. A defendant who says he believed in consent when the girl had demonstrated her lack of it may very well not be believed. A plea of honest belief that a girl is above 16 would thus be far more likely to be pleaded and with far greater success than a plea of honest belief in consent on a rape charge. The CLRC proposal would ensure that it became far harder to acquire convictions in section 6 cases than it is at the moment. The number of not guilty pleas would certainly increase which would mean that more young girls would have to be subjected to the trauma of giving testimony in court. This in turn would discourage prosecutions. The CLRC proposed that the defence should also become available to all age-related sexual offences so that an honest belief that a person was above the age of consent irrespective of its reasonableness could always be a defence.[609]

If implemented, the CLRC's proposals would critically undermine the protection which the law gives to under-age girls and boys. As Lord Simon recognized in *Morgan*, it is the role which the criminal law has in protecting girls under 16 from sexual exploitation and abuse which justifies the present law.[610] This role, which applies equally for boys and girls, cannot effectively be pursued if strict *mens rea* principles are applied, however appropriate these may be to other areas of the criminal law.

(c) Recent Developments

Whilst Parliament has, wisely, ignored the CLRC's proposals, the House of Lords now seems determined to implement them itself. In *B v DPP*,[611] the defendant was charged under section 1(1) of the Indecency with Children

[608] CLRC (1984), para. 5.14.
[609] See CLRC (1984), paras. 6.10, 6.14, 7.28.
[610] [1976] AC 182 at 221.
[611] [2000] 1 All ER 833.

Act 1960 which makes it an offence, punishable with a maximum of two years' imprisonment, to commit an act of gross indecency with or towards a child under the age of 14. The House of Lords was asked to decide whether the section imported a requirement of *mens rea* on the question of age or whether it should be read as imposing strict liability. Heavy reliance was placed on the decision in *Sweet v Parsley*,[612] in which it was held that whenever a section is silent as to *mens rea* there is a presumption that *mens rea* should be read into it. On that basis, it was held that, since there was nothing in the statute itself which displaced that presumption, the section should be interpreted as requiring *mens rea.* Moreover, the burden of proof should be on the prosecution to prove that the defendant lacked an honest belief that the victim was 14 years or over. The House of Lords considered that it was up to Parliament to indicate either expressly or by necessary implication that liability was strict otherwise a requirement of *mens rea* would be imported. That this decision renders the section very hard to enforce was not their Lordships' concern. The CLRC's proposals discussed above were mentioned with approval. Neither Lord Nichols nor the rest of their Lordships were prepared to 'attach much weight to a fear that it may be difficult sometimes for the prosecution to prove that the defendant knew the child was under 14 or was recklessly indifferent about the child's age'.[613] However, the House of Lords did make the important concession that the defendant should be guilty where his belief in consent was coupled with recklessness in the sense that he was indifferent to the matter.[614]

Sir John Smith has hailed this decision[615] even though he concedes that if a Minister had been asked during debate in Parliament, he or she would probably have stated that liability under the section was strict. He urges the courts to go further and dismantle strict liability elsewhere, even under section 5 which seeks to protect children under 13.[616] Spurred on, perhaps, by such distinguished enthusiasm, the House of Lords in *K*[617] has declared that *mens rea* must also be imported into section 14 of the SOA 1956 so that the prosecution will have to prove that a man charged with the indecent assault of a girl under 16 had no honest belief that she was 16. Lord Millett who concurred with the rest of their Lordships was at least prepared to acknowledge that this was certainly not Parliament's intention when the offence was introduced and that its aim was to protect young girls. The *mens rea* requirement as formulated in *K* would again appear to impose liability on reckless

612 [1969] 1 All ER 347.

613 [2000] 1 All ER 833 at 839.

614 See also Lord Steyn and Brook LJ in the court below: ibid. at 851. This suggests recklessness as interpreted in *Satnam and Kewal.* For further discussion of the relationship between honest belief and recklessness, see above nn. 477 and 532 and accompanying text.

615 [2000] Crim LR 404–9. But for criticism of it, see J. Horder, 'How Culpability Can and Cannot be Denied in Under-Age Sex Crimes' [2001] Crim LR 15.

616 [2000] Crim LR at 407–9.

617 [2001] UKHL 41; [2001] 3 All ER 897. See now *Fernandez* (*The Times*, 26 June 2002), which applies the same principle to s 15 (indecent assault of a boy under 16).

defendants as well as on those who have actual knowledge that the girl was over 16. A man who fails to think about the girl's age where the risk that she is under 16 is obvious is reckless in the *Caldwell* sense of the term and should be liable since he has no honest belief in consent.

There have been other decisions on age-related offences which have been decided differently. In *Land*[618] the defendant was charged under section 1(1)(c) of the Protection of Children Act 1978. This makes it an offence to take or permit to be taken any indecent photograph of a child or to have possession of such indecent photographs with a view to their being distributed. Again, the statute does not specify any requirement of *mens rea*. The court noted that it did provide certain specific defences to a charge under the section. It held that liability must be strict for, had Parliament wished to extend the defences open to a defendant, it would have done so. It took into account the policy of the statute and its purpose which is 'to protect children from exploitation and degradation'.[619] In *London Borough of Harrow v Shah and Shah*[620] charges were brought under section 13 of the National Lottery Act 1993, s 13(1)(c) and the National Lottery Regulations 1994, regulation 3 after an employee of the defendants had sold lottery tickets to a boy under 16. The question once again was whether strict liability applied to the age requirement. The Divisional Court held that it did on the ground that the offence was not truly criminal in character so that the need to import *mens rea* as set out in *Sweet v Parsley* did not apply and the offence dealt with an issue of social concern. Strict liability would encourage greater vigilance.

An absurdly inconsistent position now obtains with regard to age-related requirements in sexual and allied offences. The need for parliamentary intervention is clearly urgent. Indeed, given the chaotic state of the law relating to the protection of children of both sexes from sexual exploitation, a radical overhaul of this whole area is long overdue.

(d) The Proposals of the Sex Offences Review

Under present law there are a variety of sexual offences relating to children which do not form a logical and coherent whole. There is a range of inconsistent penalties, defences, and age thresholds. Under sections 5 and 6 of the Sexual Offences Act 1956, it is an offence, punishable with a maximum of life imprisonment, for a man to have sexual intercourse with a girl under 13 and an offence punishable with a maximum of two years' imprisonment if the girl is over 13 and under 16. It is not an offence for a woman to have sexual intercourse with a boy under 16. But any sexual touching of a girl or boy under 16 falling short of rape or buggery is covered by the crime of indecent assault under sections 14 and 15 and carries a maximum penalty of

[618] [1998] 1 All ER 403. [619] At 407. [620] [2000] Crim LR 692.

10 years' imprisonment. Under section 12, it is an offence of buggery carrying a maximum penalty of life imprisonment to have anal intercourse with a boy or girl under 16. Other homosexual acts with a boy under 16 are punishable with five years' maximum under the section 13 offence of indecency between men. Under the Indecency with Children Act 1960, it is also illegal to commit an act of gross indecency with or towards a child under 14 and this offence carries a maximum penalty of 10 years. A person over 18 who engages in sexual activity with a person under that age and in so doing abuses a position of trust commits an offence under section 3 of the SOAA 2000 for which the maximum penalty is 5 years' imprisonment. As to the age requirement, some offences involve strict liability, others now require *mens rea*, the young man's defence applies only to section 6, and, in the case of the abuse of trust offence, there is a defence if the defendant 'did not know and could not reasonably have been expected to know' that the victim was under 18.[621]

The SOR has proposed a total dismantling of the present structure of sexual offences dealing with children and its replacement with a set of new offences in order to provide far greater protection for children against sexual exploitation.[622] It favours preservation of the age of consent[623] and abolition on time limits for prosecutions. It recommends the repeal of sections 5 and 6 together with sections 12 to 15 of the Sexual Offences Act 1956 and the Indecency with Children Act 1960.[624] Instead, a new gender-neutral offence of adult sexual abuse of a child would be introduced covering all sexual acts involving adults of 18 or over and children of under 16.[625] Where a person under 18 is the perpetrator, an offence of sexual activity between minors would apply.[626]

Careful consideration was given to the mental element of the new offences. The report is adamant that, as is the position under section 5, there should be no defence where the child is under 13.[627] As far as children over 13 and under 16 were concerned, the Report noted that it is all too easy to claim an honest mistake and hard to disprove it. Moreover, some men specialized in targeting young girls.[628] On the other hand, it accepted the need to be just to truly innocent defendants.[629] The compromise proposed is that mistake of age should provide a defence where the victim is 13 or over, where it is based on reasonable grounds, and where the defendant has taken all reasonable

[621] SOAA 2000, s 3(2)(a). A man who was acquitted under SOAA 1956, s 6 as a result of the young man's defence could, prior to *K*, nevertheless be convicted on a second count for an indecent assault under s 14.

[622] Home Office, *Setting the Boundaries*, (2000), vol. i, ch. 3.

[623] A recent study found that one in five girls aged 13 to 15 would like to see the age of consent raised to 18: see *The Times*, 8 Sept. 2000. It confirmed the findings of The Social Exclusion Unit's Report that girls are frequently pressured into early sexual activity: see n. 599 above, at 42–3.

[624] Home Office, *Setting the Boundaries*, (2000), vol. i, 143–5.

[625] para. 3.6.5.

[626] para. 3.9.13.

[627] para. 3.5.10.

[628] para. 3.6.12.

[629] ibid.

steps to ascertain age. It should be available on one occasion only and should, like the young man's defence, be limited by the age of the defendant.[630] What that age should be was a matter on which views were invited but the Report notes the suggestion by Barnardo's that no defence should be available where there was a five-year differential between victim and perpetrator.[631] In decisively rejecting the CLRC's approach, the SOR has moved once again in the direction of the law in Canada and Australia. In Canada, a mistake of age defence can be used only where the defendant took all reasonable steps to ascertain age[632] and, in Australia, it is recommended in the Model Criminal Code that there be a reasonable belief requirement.[633] On the other hand, the far stricter approach taken in most American states which makes under-age sex a strict liability offence, or even statutory rape, has been rejected[634] although there is no reason to think that it would have been outlawed by the ECHR.[635] The SOR's solution seems to offer a fair compromise between different sides of the debate. If legislation is to provide proper protection for children, the precise nature of the *mens rea* and defences for the new offences will need to be spelt out clearly in statute.

The SOR did not consider that its proposals for the new offences of adult sexual abuse of a child and sexual activity between minors removed the need for a separate offence of incest in relation to children. On the contrary, it concluded that the law should make special provision for sexual abuse within the family in order to increase protection and provide appropriate remedies. It has accordingly proposed the recasting of the offence to include a far wider range of relationships which reflect modern configurations of family life.[636] Moreover, as previously noted,[637] unlike under present law, the range of prohibited sexual activity covered by the new offence would include far more than vaginal penetration by the penis.

Conclusion

From its earliest origins, rape was a narrowly defined offence. In the last decade, steps have been taken to broaden its scope: the marital rape exemption has been abolished and liability for rape has been extended to cover sex-

[630] paras. 3.6.13, 3.6.14, 3.6.16. [631] para. 3.6.16.

[632] Canadian Criminal Code, s 150.1(4)

[633] Home Office, *Setting the Boundaries*, (2000), vol. i, para. 3.6.8

[634] ibid. [635] See *Salabiaku v France* (1988) 13 EHRR 379.

[636] The new offence would be called familial sexual abuse. To the list of relations included in the existing offence of incest would be added uncle and aunts related by blood. Adoptive parents would be treated as natural parents; sexual relations between adoptive siblings would be prohibited until 18. Stepparents and foster parents would also be included in the list. Sexual penetration between adult close family members would be an offence irrespective of the age of the parties. The position as far as stepparents and adult stepchildren was left open: see Home Office, *Setting the Boundaries*, (2000), vol. i, ch. 5.

[637] See text at n. 86 above.

ual acts apart from vaginal penetration by the penis. If the proposals of the SOR are implemented, the scope of the offence will become broader still. The same will be true of other allied offences, such as incest and obtaining sexual intercourse by threat, which will include within their scope acts apart from sexual intercourse whether performed against males or females. But whilst the review has proposed a major overhaul of offences against children, the basic structure of non-consensual sexual offences against adults will remain the same. In Chapter 3 more fundamental alternatives will be considered.

3

Alternative Approaches

In its Report on Sexual Offences in 1984,[1] the Criminal Law Revision Committee concluded that, whilst certain adjustments to it might be desirable, the law of rape was basically sound. The Committee did not, however, consider the crime in context. It did not look at rape as a social problem nor did it have regard to the difficulties which rape poses for the criminal justice system. Its approach to the reform of sexual offences was legalistic in the sense that it was mostly concerned with the law itself, its consistency and logicality, its relationship to other laws of a similar kind and to the criminal law as a whole.

By contrast with this approach to reform, radical reform of rape laws was introduced elsewhere in the 1970s and 1980s. This was far more closely associated with the feminist movement. In some places, women were directly responsible for its introduction, whilst in others feminist ideas clearly influenced the lawmakers.[2]

The hallmark of radical reform was a rejection of the existing legal framework in favour of the introduction of new offences with a different emphasis. Rape tended to be presented as a crime of violence with sexual overtones rather than as simply a sexual offence. Distinctions resting on the mode of penetration were abandoned. But the aim of radical reform was not merely to change the law's approach so that it became more in tune with perceptions of sexual assault which were current at the time, but to address directly the problem of processing rape. Thus, radical reform restructured rape offences in ways that it was hoped would facilitate the prosecution process without jeopardizing the interests of the accused. Furthermore, it was perceived to have an educative and symbolic function as well as a practical one.

Examples of radical reform, proposals for it, and attempts to obtain it may be drawn from all parts of the globe. In Italy in 1979, an ad hoc committee of women drafted a Rape Bill and proceeded to launch a 'signature campaign' to gather support for it. The Bill would have altered the definition of rape, which at the time was classified in the Italian Penal code as a 'crime against morals and custom', so that it became a crime of violence against the person. It would have abolished distinctions between vaginal intercourse and other sexual acts and prohibited cross-examination of the victim about her personal and sexual life. Interviews conducted by Tamar Pitch with

[1] CLRC (1984). [2] See further Temkin (1986), 16, 26–36, and 40.

members of the committee revealed that the campaign's objectives included increasing public awareness of the issue of sexual assault and gaining recognition for the principle that violence against women was a serious offence.[3] The Italian campaign was to come to naught,[4] but in a number of English-speaking jurisdictions, reform proposals along very similar lines were implemented before and after it.

In Michigan, the Women's Task Force on Rape was set up in 1973. It was responsible for drafting a Bill and a campaign which resulted in the introduction of radical and influential legislation in 1974.[5] In 1972, two years before it was enacted, 90 people in Michigan were convicted of unlawful carnal knowledge, as the offence of rape was termed under the statute then in force. However, in the same year in Detroit alone, at least 3,370 alleged victims of rape were treated in hospitals and 900 rapes were reported to the police. The aims of the legislation and the expectations of those responsible for it were summarized thus:

> From the earliest articulation of the problem [of rape] it was argued that antiquated statutes provide little protection for the victim and hinder effective prosecution. Michigan's Criminal Sexual Conduct statute held the promise of change that would be both instrumental and symbolic in impact: properly implemented it could bring about improvements in the criminal justice system, the conviction rate and the treatment of victims.[6]

In 1981, radical reform was also introduced in New South Wales, Australia, with similarly broad aims in view. The Premier of New South Wales described the new legislation as follows:

> This is an historic measure and one of the most important reforms this Government has ever presented to Parliament. . . .These reforms are designed to protect the victims of rape from further victimisation under the legal process; to encourage rape victims to report offences to the authorities; to facilitate the administration of justice and the conviction of guilty offenders.[7]

In both Michigan and New South Wales, it was also intended that the legislation should play an educative and symbolic role. Thus, the New South Wales statute was designed to 'serve an educative function in further changing community attitudes to sexual assault'.[8] It was hoped that the Michigan

[3] T. Pitch, 'Critical Criminology, the Construction of Social Problems, and the Question of Rape' (1985) 13 International Journal of the Sociology of Law 35.

[4] For the reform which was eventually enacted in Italy in 1996, see Note by A. J. Everhart, 'Predicting the Effect of Italy's Long Awaited Rape Law Reform on "the Land of Machismo"', (1998) 31 Vanderbilt Journal of Transnational Law 671.

[5] See Marsh *et al.* (1982), ch. 2.

[6] J. C. Marsh, N. Caplan, A. Geist, G. Gregg, J. Harrington, and D. Sharphorn, 'Criminal Sexual Conduct in Michigan: The Law Reform Solution' Research Paper prepared for the National Center for the Prevention and Control of Rape, National Institute of Mental Health (1981).

[7] NSW *Hansard*, Legislative Assembly, 18 Mar. 1981.

[8] ibid.

reform would 'confront and change cultural norms'.[9] In Canada, the aims of the women's pressure groups which played a major role in bringing about reforming legislation were described as follows:

Their original intentions were to lessen the humiliation experienced by the victim in a rape trial and to send a symbolic liberating and educational message to the rest of society, advising all that it was no longer acceptable to assault sexually (or batter, or ultimately to subjugate) women.[10]

Those advocating reform along broadly similar lines also stressed the importance of this educational function:

Irrespective of its ability either to discourage certain forms of behaviour, or to bring offenders to justice, the law should delineate and prohibit behaviour which is socially abhorrent. And more than this, the law should adopt the role of community educator. It should condemn behaviour which is exploitative, violent, and/or involves the violation of one person's liberty by another.[11]

This chapter examines the legislation passed in Michigan,[12] New South Wales,[13] and Canada,[14] and considers whether it fulfilled the expectations of radical reform.

The Shape of Radical Reform

The legislation in Michigan, New South Wales, and Canada has five central features in common. First, it involves a gradation scheme. Secondly, it makes some attempt to deal with the problem of consent. Thirdly, it does not use the term rape. Fourthly, it removes the exemption from liability of certain males. Finally, it substantially alters the rules of evidence in sexual assault cases. The first four of these features will now be considered whilst the fifth is discussed in Chapter 4.

[9] Marsh *et al.* (1982), 4.

[10] L. Snider, 'Legal Reform and Social Control: The Dangers of Abolishing Rape' (1985) 13 International Journal of the Sociology of Law 337, 352.

[11] N. Naffin, *An Inquiry into the Substantive Law of Rape,* Women's Adviser's Office, Dept. of the Premier and Cabinet, South Australia (1984), 11.

[12] Criminal Sexual Conduct Act 1974, No. 226 Mich Public Acts [1974], 77th Sess (effective 1 Apr. 1975), amending No. 328 Mich Public Acts [1931], Mich Comp Laws 750.1.568 (1970).

[13] Crimes (Sexual Assault) Amendment Act, 1981, amending the Crimes Act 1900. The law came into effect 14 July 1981.

[14] Criminal Law Amendment Act SC 1980–81–82, c. 125. The Act amending the Canadian Criminal Code was passed in 1982 and came into force 4 Jan. 1983.

Gradation

(a) Advantages and Disadvantages

In each of the jurisdictions under consideration, the crime of rape ('unlawful carnal knowledge' in Michigan) was abolished and the conduct which it covered redistributed between several new offence categories to form an integrated ladder of offences with a graduated penalty scheme.

One attraction of gradation is that it arranges sexual offences thematically and offers a coherent, organized framework which appears to fit within a modern code of criminal law rather better than old-style sexual offences which are, by contrast, somewhat disparate in form. For example, in Canada, the offences of rape, attempted rape, sexual intercourse with the feeble-minded, and indecent assault on a male and a female were abolished. A new, three-rung ladder of sexual assault offences, namely, sexual assault (maximum penalty 10 years), sexual assault with a weapon (maximum penalty 14 years), and aggravated sexual assault (maximum penalty life), replaced them.

Gradation schemes have a number of objectives.[15] One of these is to improve reporting, prosecution, and conviction rates. It was believed that gradation would encourage more women to report to the police since there were lower maximum penalties for some types of rape. It was felt that high penalties deterred some women who were reluctant to see a man imprisoned for life.[16] By reclassifying the conduct involved in such a way as to distinguish the grave from the less grave, it was also hoped to discourage unwarranted pleas of not guilty and to overcome both the reluctance of prosecutors to bring charges and of courts to convict. For, as Kalven and Zeisal noted, often when juries acquit of rape, their 'stance is not so much that involuntary intercourse under these circumstances is no crime at all, but rather does not have the gravity of rape'.[17]

If a gradation system has an effect of this kind, it might seem to have much to commend it. But it might be thought that there are dangers and disadvantages in such schemes. There is first the problem of plea-bargaining. It could be argued that defendants who might otherwise have been acquitted could be persuaded to plead guilty to lesser offences. Alternatively, defendants might be able to strike favourable bargains and get off more lightly than they deserve. It has to be recognised, however, that plea-bargaining is a clear feature of the system's operation under traditional rape laws. Indeed, because of the difficulty of securing convictions for rape, there is a clear incentive for the prosecution to accept pleas to lesser offences.[18]

[15] For further discussion, see Young (1983), vol. i, 104–12.

[16] ibid. 108.

[17] Kalven and Zeisel (1966), 250.

[18] See e.g. Chappell's study of plea-bargaining in Seattle, Washington before reform was introduced: Chappell (1977), 305.

In Michigan prior to the reforms, the conviction rate for rape was extremely low. Between 1972 and 1974, for example, no more than eight convictions per month were recorded.[19] Defendants would, however, plead guilty to lesser offences such as assault, assault and battery, and assault with intent to commit rape, which carry low penalties. Richard Wright reported surprisingly similar findings in England.[20] More recently, Harris and Grace traced the progress of rapes recorded in 1996 in England and found that plea-bargaining remained a pronounced feature of the system.[21]

Traditional rape laws, therefore, also involve some sort of gradation and may well encourage plea-bargaining. English law, for example, provides an offence of rape and attempted rape on the one hand, with maximum penalties of life imprisonment, and indecent assault on the other, with a maximum penalty of 10 years' imprisonment.[22] There is nothing in between. Indecent assault is not designed to cover situations where the penis has entered the vagina, although it appears to be used even where this has occurred. The alternative for prosecutors is to accept a plea to a non-sexual offence such as assault occasioning actual bodily harm or unlawful wounding which carry maximum penalties of five years' imprisonment. The object of radical legislation was to introduce a more refined and coherent form of gradation which would ensure, *inter alia*, that guilty defendants were not able to bargain their way into sentences which were far lighter than they deserved. Legislation in the jurisdictions under consideration inserts extra tiers into the structure of sexual offences and introduces a more graduated scheme of penalties. This was intended to enable prosecutors to strike bargains at an appropriate penalty level. It was also designed to ensure that defendants were convicted of offences which reflected the fact that the crime committed was one of *sexual* violence.

A further advantage of gradation was thought to be that it would give judges far more guidance in sentencing than under existing laws which were regarded as affording far too much discretion to the judiciary. It does, however, limit the sentencing powers of the judge. Under the present English law of rape, a judge has complete discretion as to sentencing and may take into account a variety of factors. But it is worth reiterating that traditional rape laws frequently give rise to light sentences for lesser offences.

Quite apart from their implications for sentencing, other objections may be raised to gradation schemes. Gradation clearly rests on the premise that rape encompasses a range of behaviour which is not of uniform gravity. As one advocate of gradation argued: 'Rape can range from a non-consensual

[19] Marsh *et al.* (1982), 29.

[20] Wright (1984), 399. For similar findings in Scotland, see Chambers and Millar (1986), 57–9 and 79.

[21] Harris and Grace (1999), 32.

[22] SOA 1985, s 3(3) raised penalty from two years.

act accompanied by violence and physical injury to the victim, pack rape, rape of a tiny child right through to "date rape" or so-called petty rape'.[23]

But the assumption that rapes differ as to seriousness begs the question: which rapes are more serious than others? As the CLRC discovered when it attempted to provide a two-tier system of indecent assaults, it was not at all clear which conduct ought to be consigned to the more and which to the less serious category.[24] Certainly, the view that there is such a thing as 'petty rape' and that date rape is somehow less serious than certain other forms of rape would today be regarded by many as anathema. In England and Wales, the SOR decisively rejected the idea that there were categories of rape which could be described as lesser forms of the offence.[25]

The emphasis in the Canadian gradation schemes is on violence, so that, broadly speaking, the more it is used or threatened, the more serious the offence becomes. It might be argued that this approach downgrades sexual intercourse without consent where little violence or none at all is used. A contrary view is that there is more potential for the recognition of the gravity of non-violent assaults within a gradation scheme than there is where a unitary offence of rape is retained. For where rapes are not differentiated, it tends to be assumed by police and prosecutors that true rape is rape with clear indications of violence. By specifically designating non-consensual sexual intercourse as a distinct offence and non-consensual sexual intercourse accompanied by degrees of violence as separate offences, the criminality of the former is emphasized.

But many feminist commentators[26] now regret what they regard as the desexualization of rape and believe that legislation which has sought to achieve this has been an unfortunate mistake.[27] Certainly, to focus on violence is to miss the point that sexual coercion takes many forms, only some of which involve any violence at all. Arguably, gradation schemes shift what is a sentencing matter to centre stage. Centre stage should be the sexual violation. The use of violence is a factor to be regarded along with others by the judge when sentencing. If the purpose of the law on sexual offences is the protection of sexual autonomy, then the law needs to make that statement clearly. By focusing on the violence of the conduct, the law simply reiterates the message which is already conveyed by offences against the person, namely, that violence is wrong. Young's New Zealand study, which involved interviews with victims, demonstrated that the New South Wales

[23] H. Coonan, 'Rape Law Reform—Proposals for Reforming the Substantive Law', in Scutt (1980), 40.

[24] CLRC (1984), 38–42.

[25] Home Office, *Setting the Boundaries*, (2000) vol. i, paras. 2.8.7–2.8.8.

[26] See e.g. C. McKinnon, *Feminism Unmodified: Discourses on Life and Law* (Cambridge, Mass.: Harvard University Press, 1987), 86.

[27] See V. Bell, 'Beyond the "Thorny Question": Feminism, Foucault and the Desexualisation of Rape' (1991) 19 International Journal of the Sociology of Law 83; C. Mackinnon, *Towards a Feminist Theory of the State* (Cambridge, Mass.: Harvard University Press, 1989), ch. 9.

and Canadian models were not in keeping with the way in which most victims described their experience of rape. He states:

> Victims who had been beaten felt that the act of sexual intercourse rather than the assault was the primary injury. . . . Any legislation highlighting the violent component of the offence at the expense of the sexual violation involved would therefore seem to be at odds with the perception of many victims.[28]

Moreover, as Professor Carol Smart wisely observes, it was naïve to think that the transposition of rape into a crime of violence would necessarily work as a strategy for facilitating the successful prosecution of rape in the courts. Violence in a sexual context may be presented as ambiguous, if not pleasurable.[29]

Not all gradation schemes desexualize rape or focus exclusively on violence. But if violence is abandoned as an organizing theme, it becomes far more difficult to construct a ladder of offences. Legislation passed in Victoria in 1980 illustrates the difficulty.[30] It created a two-rung ladder of offences of rape. The sexual dimension was retained. The offence with the higher penalty was committed where there were aggravating circumstances. These included the use of serious violence, the carrying of an offensive weapon or explosive, the performance of an act which was likely seriously and substantially to degrade or humiliate the victim, and where the perpetrator was aided or abetted by another person who was present at the time. But the selection of aggravating circumstances was open to the objection that it was random and arbitrary. That rape is in itself degrading and humiliating seems to have been denied. It could equally well be argued that aggravating factors should focus upon the impact that the rape has had upon the victim—whether she has been seriously mentally traumatized, lost her reproductive capacity, become pregnant or HIV positive. To elevate any circumstances above others will always be hard to justify and will detract fundamentally from the issue of autonomy which should be central. The offence of aggravated rape was finally abolished in Victoria in 1991.[31]

Thus, gradation may satisfy the instinct for neatness but it is not clear that gradation schemes which focus on levels of violence can be justified theoretically or ideologically. On the other hand, the more sophisticated Michigan scheme which does not seek to deny the sexual element of sexual abuse and, whilst emphasizing violence, does not exclude certain other forms of coercion, is cumbrous and complex. Gradation, if it is to be successful, requires a simple structure of offences. Without a coherent organizing theme, such simplicity cannot be achieved. Arguably there is no such theme.

[28] Young (1983), 109. [29] Smart (1989), 46.
[30] The Crimes (Sexual Offences) Act 1980, No. 9509/1980.
[31] Crimes (Rape) Act 1991, No. 81/1991.

(b) Gradation in New South Wales, Canada and Michigan

(i) New South Wales

In New South Wales, as a result of legislation passed in 1981, the Crimes Act 1900 provided as follows:

SEXUAL ASSAULT CATEGORY 1—INFLICTING GRIEVOUS BODILY HARM WITH INTENT TO HAVE SEXUAL INTERCOURSE

s 61B (1) Any person who maliciously inflicts grievous bodily harm upon another person with intent to have sexual intercourse with the other person shall be liable to penal servitude for 20 years.

(2) Any person who maliciously inflicts grievous bodily harm upon another person with intent to have sexual intercourse with a third person who is present or nearby shall be liable to penal servitude for 20 years.

SEXUAL ASSAULT CATEGORY 2—INFLICTING ACTUAL BODILY HARM, ETC., WITH INTENT TO HAVE SEXUAL INTERCOURSE

s 61C (1) Any person who—

(a) maliciously inflicts actual bodily harm upon another person; or
(b) threatens to inflict actual bodily harm upon another person by means of an offensive weapon or instrument, with intent to have sexual intercourse with the other person shall be liable to penal servitude for 12 years.

(2) Any person who—

(a) maliciously inflicts actual bodily harm upon another person; or
(b) threatens to inflict actual bodily harm upon another person, with intent to have sexual intercourse with a third person who is present or nearby shall be liable to penal servitude for 12 years.

SEXUAL ASSAULT CATEGORY 3—SEXUAL INTERCOURSE WITHOUT CONSENT

s 61D (1) Any person who has sexual intercourse with another person without the consent of the other person and who knows that the other person does not consent to the sexual intercourse shall be liable to penal servitude for 7 years or, if the other person is under the age of 16 years, to penal servitude for 10 years.

(2) For the purposes of subsection (1), a person who has sexual intercourse with another person without the consent of the other person and who is reckless as to whether the other person consents to the sexual intercourse shall be deemed to know that the other person does not consent to the sexual intercourse.

SEXUAL ASSAULT CATEGORY 4—INDECENT ASSAULT AND ACT OF INDECENCY

s 61E (1) Any person who assaults another person and, at the time of, or immediately before or after, the assault, commits an act of indecency upon or in the presence of the other person, shall be liable to imprisonment for 4 years or, if the other person is under the age of 16 years, to penal servitude for 6 years.

The aim of this gradation scheme was to 'place primary emphasis upon the violence factor in sexual assault rather than upon the element of sexual contact'.[32] It will be seen that Category 1, which carried a maximum penalty of 20 years, was confined to the malicious infliction of grievous bodily harm with intent to have sexual intercourse either with the victim or with a third party who was present or nearby. Category 2, with its maximum penalty of 12 years, covered the infliction of actual bodily harm with intent to have sexual intercourse with the victim or a third party who was present or nearby. It also covered a threat to inflict such harm upon a person with intent to have sexual intercourse with that person provided that the threat was made with an offensive weapon or instrument. Where, however, the defendant threatened one person with actual bodily harm with intent to have sexual intercourse with another, no offensive weapon or instrument was necessary.[33] All other forms of non-consensual penetration fell within Category 3, which carried a maximum of seven years. Category 4 consisted of indecent assaults falling short of penetration where the maximum was four years if the victim was over 16 and six years if the victim was under 16.

Penetration of the body by whatever means is generally more traumatic than other forms of sexual contact and there is a clear case for distinguishing sexual assaults according to whether or not penetration is effected. This distinction was maintained in the New South Wales scheme. Thus, for the purposes of the first three categories, sexual intercourse was defined gender neutrally to include penetration of the vagina or anus by any part of the body or by an object; introduction of the penis into the mouth and cunnilingus; as well as the continuation of any such intercourse.[34] Where the defendant had no intention to commit any of these acts, the sexual assault fell into Category 4, which was also gender neutral. It is noteworthy, however, that Categories 1 and 2 did not require actual penetration to take place. Where the victim was subjected to serious violence, an intention to have sexual intercourse was all that was required. However, in many cases, that intention would be established by evidence that sexual intercourse in fact took place.

A major problem with the New South Wales scheme was that Categories 1 and 2 were too narrowly defined. Sexual intercourse which was obtained by a threat to strangle the victim or to beat her senseless ranked only as a Category 3 offence if no weapon was used. The same applied to gang rape, rape of the particularly old or young, and rape accompanied by a non-injurious assault calculated to degrade the victim—such as urination or defecation upon her. It seems strange that rapes such as these carried a lower

[32] Woods (1981), 7, 12.

[33] This was designed to cover cases in which a man threatens to injure or have sexual intercourse with a child if its mother refuses sexual intercourse. See Woods (1981), 15.

[34] Crimes Act 1900, s 61A(1). Penetration of the external parts of the female genitalia was added to the list in 1992.

penalty than a Category 2 case in which the defendant threatened violence against one party with the aim of securing intercourse with another, but where no violence was perpetrated and sexual intercourse did not in fact take place. In England and Wales, the *Billam* guidelines set out a starting-point of eight years' imprisonment for two or more rapists acting together, for men who rape victims in the victim's own home, for those who abuse positions of responsibility over their victims, and for rape involving abduction.[35] Yet all of these could have amounted merely to Category 3 offences in New South Wales with a maximum penalty of seven years.

Judges in New South Wales were highly critical of the 1981 legislation for placing 'an unwarranted emphasis on the means used to obtain intercourse while paying too little attention to the act of intercourse itself'.[36] By relegating sexual intercourse without consent to a third category offence, the legislation effected in the words of Hunt J 'an unwarranted down-grading of the humiliation and the degrading aspects of sexual assault'.[37]

A gradation system which fails to afford adequate recognition to the horror which the community may feel about certain forms of rape lays itself open to attempts at circumvention. These may undermine the objectives of gradation. In New South Wales, this is precisely what occurred. It seems that in order to increase the penalty in certain cases, prosecutors combined Category 3 charges with charges for other offences such as burglary. Moreover, in *Smith*,[38] it was held that the legislation did not in fact create a ladder of alternative offences. Rather, each of the offences had to be charged where the facts warranted it. For example, where there was sexual intercourse without consent preceded by the infliction of actual bodily harm on the victim, charges would need to be brought under both Categories 2 and 3. It has been commented that this development 'demonstrates the uncertainty and ambiguity inherent in the New South Wales approach'.[39]

The gradation scheme just described was abandoned after eight years. However, the reconfiguration of offences which took place in 1989[40] does not appear to be a vast improvement.

Sexual assault, formerly the Category 3 offence with a seven-year maximum penalty, has now become the basic offence with a maximum penalty of 14 years' imprisonment.[41] In addition, an offence of aggravated sexual assault has been introduced, carrying a maximum penalty of 20 years' imprisonment.[42] This comes into play where any one of the following aggravating factors exists:

(1) at the time of, or immediately before or after, the commission of the offence, the alleged offender maliciously inflicts actual bodily harm on the alleged victim or any other person who is present or nearby; or

[35] See Ch. 1 under the heading 'Sentencing'.
[36] Young (1983), 109.
[37] *R v Smith* [1982] 2 NSWLR 569, Supreme Court of New South Wales.
[38] ibid.
[39] Young (1983), 111.
[40] Crimes (Amendment) Act 1989, No. 198.
[41] Crimes Act 1900, s 61I.
[42] Crimes Act 1900, s 61J(1).

(2) at the time of, or immediately before or after the commission of the offence, the alleged offender threatens to inflict actual bodily harm on the alleged victim or any other person who is present or nearby by means of an offensive weapon or instrument; or
(3) the alleged offender is in the company of another person or persons; or
(4) the alleged victim is under 16 years; or
(5) the alleged victim is (whether generally or at the time of the commission of the offence) under the authority of the alleged offender; or
(6) the alleged victim has a serious physical disability; or
(7) the alleged victim has a serious intellectual disability.[43]

The offence of aggravated sexual assault has all the disadvantages of the offence abolished in the state of Victoria in 1991.[44] The selection of aggravating factors seems entirely random and serves only to curtail higher sentences in other cases. The experiences of victims who do not come within the aggravated offence are necessarily downgraded.

The new scheme preserves the old Category 2 offence, referred to now as assault with intent to have sexual intercourse. The penalty for this offence has been raised to a maximum of 20 years.[45]

The Category 4 offence of indecent assault has been split into indecent assault,[46] with a raised maximum penalty of five years, and aggravated indecent assault,[47] with a maximum penalty of seven years' imprisonment, rising to 10, if a child under 10 is involved. The circumstances of aggravation partially resemble those for aggravated sexual assault.[48]

Thus, this new configuration of offences deals with some of the objections to the old gradation scheme by raising penalties across the board. It is now less obviously a ladder of offences. There is a basic offence, an aggravated form of the offence, and what appears to be a separate offence of assault with intent to have intercourse. The offence of indecent assault is now also split into two. The theme of violence remains but it has been attenuated by the inclusion of certain other factors mainly relating to the characteristics of the victim.

(ii) Canada

The Canadian Criminal Code provides as follows:

SEXUAL ASSAULTS

Sexual Assault (Level 1)

s 271 (1) Every one who commits a sexual assault is guilty of

(a) an indictable offence and is liable to imprisonment for 10 years (maximum); or
(b) an offence punishable on summary conviction and liable to imprisonment for a term not exceeding 18 months (maximum).

[43] s 61J(2). [44] See text at nn. 30–1 above. [45] s 61K.
[46] s 61L. [47] s 61M. [48] See s 61J(2)(c)–(g).

Sexual Assaults Involving Bodily Harm, Weapons, or Third Parties (Level 2)
s 272 Every one who, in committing a sexual assault,

(a) carries, uses, or threatens to use a weapon or an imitation thereof,
(b) threatens to cause bodily harm to a person other than the complainant,
(c) causes bodily harm to the complainant, or
(d) is a party to the offence with any other person,

is guilty of an indictable offence and is liable to imprisonment for 14 years (maximum). (Minimum four years if firearm is used.)

Aggravated Sexual Assault (Level 3)
s 273 (1) Everyone commits an aggravated sexual assault who, in committing a sexual assault, wounds, maims, disfigures, or endangers the life of the complainant

(2) Every person who commits an aggravated sexual assault is guilty of an indictable offence and liable to . . . imprisonment for life (maximum). (Minimum four years if firearm is used.)

Of the three gradation schemes under discussion, the Canadian is the simplest in so far as it creates only three degrees of offence. These three new offences replace the old crimes of rape, attempted rape, sexual intercourse with the feeble-minded, and indecent assault on a male or a female. Anal intercourse remains a separate offence punishable with a maximum of 10 years' imprisonment.[49] The three offences are gender neutral so that both homosexual and heterosexual conduct is covered and males and females can be both victims and perpetrators.

The ladder of sexual offences closely resembles the ladder of assault offences but has considerably higher maximum penalties. Thus, the offence of assault carries a five-year maximum penalty as against 10 for sexual assault. Assault with a weapon carries a maximum of 10 years as against 14 for sexual assault with a weapon. Aggravated assault carries a maximum of 14 years as against life for aggravated sexual assault.

By contrast with New South Wales, the Canadian legislation draws no distinction between penetration and other sexual acts. This is because in Canada the view that rape is less a crime of sex and more a crime of violence has been pursued with particular fervour. In its Working Paper No. 22, the Canadian Law Reform Commission stated that one of its objectives was to 'direct attention away from rape as a sexual offence and towards the right of every person to be free from physical assault'.[50] It was considered that to focus on penetration would be to continue to emphasize the sexual as against the violent aspects of the offence. It seems also to have been hoped that detailed and embarrassing cross-examination of the complainant as to whether penetration had actually taken place would cease to be necessary with a reform of this kind.[51] But if rape is indeed about violence and not

[49] Unless the parties consent and are married or over 18: Canadian Criminal Code, s 159.
[50] *Sexual Offences* (Ottawa: Law Reform Commission of Canada, 1978), 21.
[51] See Boyle (1984), 46.

about sex, then it is not entirely clear why it should be distinguished from other offences of violence and why it should not be subsumed within the law relating to offences against the person. The Canadian law might be said to suffer from an inherent contradiction. It attempts to represent rape and allied offences as crimes of violence and yet imposes penalties that far exceed those for violent crimes.

Several objections may be raised to the Canadian scheme. First, the legislation nowhere defines what is meant by a sexual assault. The meaning of the term is obviously crucial, particularly since there is a substantial difference in penalty between assault and sexual assault. The predictable result of this has been a plethora of cases in which the courts have been called upon to rule in what circumstances an assault may be described as sexual. This situation was not merely anticipated but welcomed in certain quarters. Thus, in its submission to the Standing Committee on Justice and Legal Affairs about the proposed new law, the National Action Committee on the Status of Women commented:

> We agree with the decision not to define sexual assault specifically. This will allow judges to interpret the offence as they best determine. And as the number of women appointed to the judiciary increases, we feel certain that the definition developed will be in the best interests of the victim.[52]

This assertion of confidence in the judiciary may, with hindsight, be thought to have been misplaced. In *Chase*, for example, it was held that breasts were not included within the meaning of the term sexual, which covered only the primary sex organs. Breasts, it was said, were no more sexual than men's beards, and erogenous zones were not necessarily sexual, for otherwise 'a person [could] be liable to conviction for stealing a good-night kiss'.[53] This decision was followed by a succession of cases in which the issue was simply whether assaults involving the breast were necessarily sexual.[54] The decision in *Chase* eventually reached the Supreme Court of Canada. It held that a sexual assault was perpetrated if, from the point of view of a reasonable person, it was committed in circumstances of a sexual nature such that the sexual integrity of the victim was violated. The test does not turn on the part of the body touched. In this instance the grabbing of the victim's breasts was a sexual assault.[55]

The bewildering lack of certainty and clarity which has resulted from the new law is clearly undesirable for victims and may deter some from pursuing a complaint. It may also have a negative effect on prosecutors who may be inclined to settle for a plea of guilty to assault instead.

52 'Sexual Offences: Crimes of Aggression—A Brief in Response to Bill C–53' (1982).

53 (1984) 40 CR (2d) 282; 55 NBR (2d) 97 at 102.

54 See *Gardynik* (1984) 42 CR (3d) 362: *Ramos* (1984) 42 CR (3d) 370; *Dare* BC Co Ct, 24 May 1984 (unreported); *Cook* (1985) 46 CR (3d) 129. For discussion of these cases, see Temkin (1987), 103.

55 (1987) 37 CCC (3d) 97 (SCC).

Objection may also be taken to the new offences on the ground that rape has been substantially downgraded as a crime where the specified aggravating factors do not exist. Rape and a pinch on the bottom may now occupy the same offence category and both may be dealt with in summary proceedings and punished with a maximum of 18 months' imprisonment.[56] The same is true of the rape and sexual assault of children. Authority figures, who are generally responsible for it, do not need to use the violence required to raise the offence to a higher category.

A further possible drawback to the Canadian scheme is the structure of the intermediate offence carrying the 14-year penalty. In common with Category 2 of the 1981 New South Wales legislation, it has been said that this offence is 'more significant for what it fails to include [than] for what it does include'.[57] Thus, threats to cause bodily harm to the complainant other than those involving a weapon[58] are not included, although such threats will suffice if they are aimed at a third party. On the other hand, actual injury to a third party will not suffice, although injury to the complainant will. Unlike in Michigan, injury has not specifically been defined to include psychological injury.[59]

The distinction between the intermediate and the aggravated offence has also given rise to adverse comment. One writer, for example, states:

> An offender armed with a knife is in the same 14 year category as one armed with a blunt instrument. Both use their weapons; the knife inflicts a minor cut in a non-dangerous area. The knife carrier is now vulnerable to aggravated sexual assault charges. The club-carrier strikes a blow to the victim's head, causing brain damage; there is, however, no external manifestation and no danger to the life of the complainant. This second hypothetical offender remains in the 14 year bracket.[60]

There are therefore clear disadvantages associated with the Canadian scheme. Moreover, unlike that of New South Wales, its penalty structure remains substantially[61] unamended.

(iii) Michigan

As a result of the Criminal Sexual Conduct Act 1974, Michigan law now provides as follows:

[56] Raised from six months.

[57] Watt (1984), 107.

[58] Weapon is given a wide definition under the Canadian Criminal Code and includes 'anything that is designed to be used as a weapon or anything that a person uses or intends to use as a weapon, whether or not it is designed to be used as a weapon'.

[59] See Los (1994) at 33–4. However, under section 245 of the Code, bodily harm includes any hurt or injury that interferes with the health or comfort of the complainant and that is more than merely transient or trifling in nature. In the English case of *Ireland* it was held also to include psychiatric injury: [1997] 4 All ER 225.

[60] P. Nadin-Davis, 'Making a Silk Purse?—Sentencing: The "New" Sexual Offences' (1982) 32 CR (3d) 28 at 39.

[61] See n. 56 and accompanying text.

MCL 750.520*b* (1) A person is guilty of criminal sexual conduct in the first degree if he or she engages in sexual penetration with another person and if any of the following circumstances exists:

(a) That other person is under 13 years of age.

(b) That other person is at least 13 but less than 16 years of age and the actor is a member of the same household as the victim, the actor is related to the victim by blood or affinity to the fourth degree to the victim, or the actor is in a position of authority over the victim and used this authority to coerce the victim to submit.

(c) Sexual penetration occurs under circumstances involving the commission of any other felony.

(d) The actor is aided or abetted by one or more other persons and either of the following circumstances exists:

(i) The actor knows or has reason to know that the victim is mentally defective, mentally incapacitated or physically helpless.

(ii) The actor uses force or coercion to accomplish the sexual penetration. Force or coercion includes but is not limited to any of the circumstances listed in subdivision (*f*)(i) to (v).

(e) The actor is armed with a weapon or any article used or fashioned in a manner to lead the victim to reasonably believe it to be a weapon.

(f) The actor causes personal injury to the victim and force or coercion is used to accomplish sexual penetration. Force or coercion includes but is not limited to any of the following circumstances:

(i) When the actor overcomes the victim through the actual application of physical force or physical violence.

(ii) When the actor coerces the victim to submit by threatening to use force or violence on the victim, and the victim believes that the actor has the present ability to execute these threats.

(iii) When the actor coerces the victim to submit by threatening to retaliate in the future against the victim, or any other person, and the victim believes that the actor has the ability to execute this threat. As used in this subdivision, 'to retaliate' includes threats of physical punishment, kidnapping, or extortion.

(iv) When the actor engages in the medical treatment or examination of the victim in a manner or for purposes which are medically recognised as unethical or unacceptable.

(v) When the actor, through concealment or by the element of surprise, is able to overcome the victim.

(g) The actor causes personal injury to the victim, and the actor knows or has reason to know that the victim is mentally defective, mentally incapacitated, or physically helpless.

(2) Criminal sexual conduct in the first degree is a felony punishable by imprisonment in the state prison for life or for any term of years.

750.520*c* (1) A person is guilty of criminal sexual conduct in the second degree if the person engages in sexual contact with another person and if any of the following circumstances exists:

(a) That other person is under 13 years of age.

(b) That other person is at least 13 but less than 16 years of age and the actor is a member of the same household as the victim, or is related by blood or affinity to the fourth degree to the victim, or is in a position of authority over the victim and the actor used this authority to coerce the victim to submit.

(c) Sexual contact occurs under circumstances involving the commission of any other felony.

(d) The actor is aided or abetted by one or more other persons and either of the following circumstances exists:

(i) The actor knows or has reason to know that the victim is mentally defective, mentally incapacitated or physically helpless.

(ii) The actor uses force or coercion to accomplish the sexual contact. Force or coercion includes but is not limited to any of the circumstances listed in sections 520*b*(1)(*f*)(i) to (v).

(e) The actor is armed with a weapon, or any article used or fashioned in a manner to lead a person to reasonably believe it to be a weapon.

(f) The actor causes personal injury to the victim and force or coercion is used to accomplish the sexual contact. Force or coercion includes but is not limited to any of the circumstances listed in section 520*b*(1)(*f*)(i) to (v).

(g) The actor causes personal injury to the victim and the actor knows or has reason to know that the victim is mentally defective, mentally incapacitated or physically helpless.

(2) Criminal sexual conduct in the second degree is a felony punishable by imprisonment for not more than 15 years.

750.520*d* (1) A person is guilty of criminal sexual conduct in the third degree if the person engages in sexual penetration with another person and if any of the following circumstances exists:

(a) That other person is at least 13 years of age and under 16 years of age.

(b) Force or coercion is used to accomplish the sexual penetration. Force or coercion includes but is not limited to any of the circumstances listed in section 520*b*(1)(*f*)(i) to (v).

(c) The actor knows or has reason to know that the victim is mentally defective, mentally incapacitated, or physically helpless.

(2) Criminal sexual conduct in the third degree is a felony punishable by imprisonment for not more than 15 years.

750.520*e* (1) A person is guilty of criminal sexual conduct in the fourth degree if he or she engages in sexual contact with another person and if either of the following circumstances exists:

(a) Force or coercion is used to accomplish the sexual contact. Force or coercion includes but is not limited to any of the circumstances listed in section 520*b*(1)(*f*)(i) to (iv).

(b) The actor knows or has reason to know that the victim is mentally defective, mentally incapacitated, or physically helpless.

(2) Criminal sexual conduct in the fourth degree is a misdemeanour punishable by imprisonment for not more than two years, or by a fine of not more than $500.00, or both.

The Michigan gradation scheme is by far the most comprehensive of the three under discussion. Unlike the Canadian scheme, it distinguishes heavily between penetration and other forms of sexual assault. Sexual penetration is defined by the statute as 'sexual intercourse, cunnilingus, fellatio, anal intercourse or any other intrusion, however slight, of any part of a person's body or of any object into the genital or anal openings of another person's body'.[62] Where sexual penetration is present together with a full range of aggravating factors, criminal sexual conduct in the first degree is committed. Aggravating factors include, for example, where the defendant is armed with a weapon or where he causes injury to the victim and threatens her with future physical punishment, extortion, or kidnapping. Where sexual penetration takes place without the specified aggravating factors but in circumstances which include, *inter alia*, the use of force or coercion, criminal sexual conduct in the third degree is committed. Thus, where sexual penetration takes place, there are two degrees of offence as against three in both Canada and New South Wales.

Where there is no sexual penetration but some other form of sexual conduct, there is a similar two-tier structure of offences. Sexual contact 'includes the intentional touching of the victim's or actor's intimate parts or the intentional touching of the clothing covering the immediate area of the victim's or actor's intimate parts, if that intentional touching can reasonably by construed as being for the purpose of sexual arousal or gratification'.[63] Similarly, 'intimate parts' is defined to include the primary genital area, groin, inner thighs, buttock or breasts of a human being'.[64] Where sexual contact takes place in aggravating circumstances (which are the same as for a first-degree offence), criminal sexual conduct in the second degree is committed. In the absence of these factors, but where, *inter alia*, force or coercion is used, the crime concerned is criminal sexual conduct in the fourth degree. It will be noted that where there is no penetration but aggravating circumstances exist, the maximum penalty which can be imposed is heavier than in cases where there is sexual penetration but aggravating circumstances are absent.

The Michigan scheme has avoided some of the pitfalls into which the New South Wales and Canadian models appear to have fallen. It cannot be criticized for trivializing certain forms of rape by setting maximum penalties which are too low. The dividing line between the categories would seem to be less arbitrary and illogical. Moreover, the sexual aspect of the offence cannot be said to have been in any sense downgraded.[65] A further advantage is that it spells out precisely and in detail exactly what forms of conduct are

[62] 750.520*a*. [63] 750.520*a*(k). [64] 750.520*a*.

[65] The traumatic effect of sexual assault is recognized in the definition of personal injury which includes mental anguish: see 750.520*a*(*j*).

included within each degree of offence. It thus considerably reduces the discretion of police officers, prosecutors, and judges so that charges may be brought and maintained at the correct level. These positive aspects of the Michigan law have, however, been achieved at the expense of simplicity. If the scheme is comprehensive, it may also be said to be open to the criticism that it is an unwieldy instrument for judges and juries to use. Indeed, it has been described as a 'law professor's dream', and far too complicated for easy day-to-day use.[66] But research suggests that criminal justice personnel, including the judiciary, have, after training, learned to live with the legislation. Spohn and Horney noted that 'judges, prosecutors and defence attorneys whom we interviewed in Detroit spoke approvingly of the clarity and precision of the new statute'. They did, however, feel that it could be confusing for juries.[67]

Consent

Defendants who plead not guilty to rape generally do so on the ground that the victim consented. In the New Zealand study, for example, out of the 79 defended cases examined, consent was the principal defence in 49 cases and a subsidiary defence in a further nine. It thus featured as an issue in 73 per cent of cases.[68] In a more recent English study, it was found that consent was relied upon in 62 per cent of cases involving acquaintances and half of those involving intimates. Where stranger rapists were involved, the defendant was more likely to deny the offence altogether.[69]

The non-consent requirement undoubtedly gives rise to a host of problems. It ensures that the complainant rather than the defendant is the object of attention at the trial. The prosecution must prove beyond all reasonable doubt that there was no consent and the defence will be irresistibly tempted to raise that doubt by suggesting that the complainant is the type of person who might well have consented. The South Australian Report noted:

> Lack of consent of the victim, as one of the key external elements of rape, is clearly a problem. It creates difficulties for the jury (in interpreting its meaning), for the victim (in focusing the trial on her behaviour) and for the Crown (in endeavouring to overcome the stereotyped notions of consenting sexual relations from which the jury is likely to derive its interpretation of consent).[70]

The Tasmanian Law Reform Commission expressed the matter even more forcefully: 'The present focus on consent virtually demands that a defence counsel who is doing his job properly must challenge the sexual conduct and

[66] Chappell (1977), 303.
[67] Spohn and Horney (1992), 103.
[68] Young (1983), 73.
[69] Harris and Grace (1999), 20.
[70] Criminal Law and Penal Methods Reform Committee of South Australia, Special Report: *Rape and Other Sexual Offences* (1976), 24.

personal integrity of the complainant and attempt to present her in the most unfavourable light'.[71]

One way of approaching the problem of consent through law reform is to change the rules of evidence relating to corroboration and sexual history. In Canada, New South Wales, and Michigan, attempts were also made to tackle the non-consent requirement itself.

(a) New South Wales

In Categories 1 and 2 of the 1981 New South Wales scheme,[72] the word consent was not mentioned. In both instances, the focus of attention was placed entirely upon the actions of the defendant. Symbolically, an arrangement of this type may have much to commend it, but in practical terms its impact ought not to be over-estimated.

SEXUAL ASSAULT CATEGORY 1: INFLICTING GRIEVOUS BODILY HARM WITH INTENT TO HAVE SEXUAL INTERCOURSE

Category 1 made it an offence maliciously to inflict grievous bodily harm upon another person with intent to have sexual intercourse. However, it is precisely where the infliction of grievous bodily harm has taken place that rape is most easily established under a traditional rape law, so that the absence of a non-consent requirement in these circumstances is not particularly significant. Grace *et al.* found that 'the correlation between injury and outcome was highly significant', with almost two-thirds of those cases where the victim was injured resulting in conviction.[73] Moreover, there is abundant evidence to suggest that whilst a significant minority of victims suffer serious physical injury, most victims who report rape do not. Although 20.4 per cent of the victims studied by Amir in Philadelphia had been brutally beaten before, during, or after the rape,[74] other studies suggest a fairly low percentage of serious injury. Certainly, in the New Zealand study, it was found that of the 83 cases looked at, 41 per cent of complainants had no injuries at all, 42.2 per cent had only minor injuries, and only 15.6 per cent required medical treatment or hospitalization.[75] Similarly, Wright found that most of the victims in his sample had received no injuries. Serious injury occurred in fewer than 6 per cent of attacks.[76] Again, out of 196 victims in the Scottish sample, only 5.6 per cent were seriously injured.[77] More recently, Grace *et al.* found that whilst 79 per cent of victims in their study suffered 'some type of physical violence over and above the alleged rape, the least serious type of manual violence was the most common, with 56 per

[71] Tasmanian Law Reform Commission (1982), para. 44.
[72] Categories 1 and 2 are set out under the heading 'Gradation' above.
[73] (1992), 21. [74] Amir (1971), 155. [75] Young (1983), 87.
[76] Wright (1980), Cropwood Conference Series 111.
[77] Chambers and Millar (1983), 20.

cent of alleged victims suffering rough treatment or physical restraint'.[78] Thus, an offence of the Category 1 type is only ever likely to cater for a small minority of reported cases.[79] Category 1 was abolished in 1989.[80]

SEXUAL ASSAULT CATEGORY 2: INFLICTING ACTUAL BODILY HARM WITH INTENT TO HAVE SEXUAL INTERCOURSE

The Category 2 offence, formerly contained in section 61C, was retained in 1989 as section 61K. It covers situations where the defendant, with intent to have sexual intercourse, inflicts actual bodily harm or threatens to inflict such harm with a weapon. Again, there is no explicit requirement of lack of consent. Actual bodily harm need not be serious harm and it has been held in English law to include psychiatric injury.[81] Since victims will commonly sustain actual bodily harm, many rapes potentially come within this category.

But is an offence of inflicting actual bodily harm with intent to have sexual intercourse capable of excluding issues of consent entirely from the court's consideration? The answer to this question is clearly no. Consent will remain an important issue. It is likely to form the basis for an assertion that the injury was not inflicted with the requisite intent. For example, the defendant might argue that the injury was not inflicted with intent to have intercourse but occurred *after* consensual intercourse or was inflicted during a quarrel, after which there was reconciliation and consensual sexual intercourse took place. Similarly, where the defendant is charged with threatening the complainant with an offensive weapon or instrument with intent to have sexual intercourse, he may state that he brandished a knife to persuade the victim to hand over money, or for some other purpose unconnected with sexual intercourse and that sexual intercourse in fact took place with consent.

On the other hand, there may be a number of situations in which the victim's consent to sexual intercourse would be excluded from consideration. For example, the defendant would presumably not be able to say that he injured the complainant intending to have sexual intercourse with her but she then consented. But what if he asserts that the victim is a masochist who consented to the injury and subsequently to the intercourse? Two distinct issues are raised here. The first is the extent to which consent to injury can be a defence in circumstances such as these. In the English case of *Brown*,[82] it was held that consent was not a defence where assault occasioning actual bodily harm was charged. Therefore, the prosecution would not, in English

[78] (1992), 21.

[79] Swedish research suggests that stranger rapes which are those most likely to be reported involve less violence than rape by a person previously sexually involved with the woman where graver injury is more likely. See Snare (1983), 61.

[80] Crimes (Amendment) Act 1989.

[81] *Ireland* [1997] 4 All ER 225.

[82] [1993] 2 ALL ER 75.

law, be prevented from establishing actual bodily harm on the ground that the victim consented to it.

The second issue is whether, if the victim is a masochist or if the defendant and the victim were involved in sado-masochism, the prosecution will be able to establish that the assault was committed *with the intention* of having sexual intercourse, assuming that the requisite intent is construed as 'purposive and not foresightful' as Dr Woods suggests.[83] Take the case of the masochist whose partner inflicts harm upon her because it is only in these circumstances that she will have sexual intercourse. Here the defendant has clearly occasioned actual bodily harm with the purpose and intent of having sexual intercourse. In the case of sado-masochism, the couple may derive sexual pleasure and stimulation from inflicting and receiving injury. In so far as sexual stimulation is often geared towards sexual intercourse, the purpose of their violent activity may well be regarded as sexual intercourse where there is evidence that this subsequently took place. The requirement of intent will thus, once again, be fulfilled. On the other hand, the defendant should not be liable where he inflicts actual bodily harm before or during intercourse but without aiming thereby to have or continue having sexual intercourse.[84]

Where a couple are involved in sado-masochism, they are unlikely to report the matter to the police. In the unlikely event that a prosecution was brought in these circumstances, and it was clear that a sado-masochistic pact existed between the parties, the judge could take this into account in sentencing. However, it may be thought that where sado-masochism takes place between adult consenting parties and the injury sustained is not serious, the law should not intervene at all.

Cunliffe suggests that a mere bruise or a love bite would also bring a defendant within the offence.[85] It is of course possible that where either is inflicted as part of the preliminaries to intercourse, a defendant could be brought within such an offence even where the recipient fully consented to such acts. Although the chances of a complaint's being made or a prosecution's being brought in these circumstances seem remote, it is conceivable that a prosecutor with censorious views could make use of the legislation for purposes for which it was not intended. Homosexual couples might be a possible target.[86]

Cunliffe also objects to the offence on the ground that a man could be liable where he engaged in consensual sexual intercourse if this resulted in either the rupture of a woman's hymen, the transmission of a sexual disease, or her

[83] Woods (1981), 13.

[84] See further K. Warner, 'The Mental Element and Consent under the New "Rape" Laws' (1983) 7 Crim LJ 245.

[85] Cunliffe (1984), 281.

[86] The legislation is gender neutral so that homosexual activity may be covered.

pregnancy.[87] Rupture of the hymen could theoretically amount to the offence where D deliberately set out to do so in the belief that he would thereby be able to have sexual intercourse with the woman. However, he should be able to argue that the hymen was ruptured during and as a consequence of intercourse and that it was not deliberately ruptured with the aim of having sexual intercourse.[88] Precisely the same is true where a venereal disease is communicated or pregnancy ensues. Even if it is assumed that actual bodily harm has been inflicted in these circumstances,[89] D has inflicted it *during* intercourse but has not inflicted it *in order to have* or continue having sexual intercourse.

It is clear that the issue of consent is not effaced from this offence. If this is the case, what advantage, if any, does it have over a traditional rape provision? One advantage is that it relieves the prosecution of the burden of proving sexual intercourse, which is helpful where precise forensic evidence is lacking. It is certainly true, moreover, that, at any rate in the first instance, there is no need for the prosecution to provide evidence of anything more than the actual bodily harm or threat of it and the necessary intention. However, a traditional rape offence such as the English offence of rape should not require much more than this in equivalent situations. As Professor Glanville Williams pointed out: 'If the prosecution gives evidence that violence was used, this should be enough to discharge the evidential burden on the issue of consent and take the case to the jury. . . . The defence will then be under the practical necessity of giving evidence to establish consent.'[90] The same would apply to a threat of violence. It is clear, furthermore, that a defendant charged with inflicting actual bodily harm with intent to have sexual intercourse, who seeks to do no more than deny the prosecution's assertion that injury was inflicted with intent to have sexual intercourse, is entitled to have his claim placed before the jury.[91] There would be no evidential burden on him in these circumstances. It may be concluded, therefore, that the advantages which this offence can afford to the prosecution are by no means as great as they might at first sight appear to be.

A study conducted by the New South Wales Department for Women looked at 150 hearings which took place over a one-year period between 1994 and 1995 in the NSW District Court.[92] It found that in practice this offence was hardly used. In only eight hearings in the study (5%), was this offence the principal charge and only 16 charges out of 310 were brought for this offence.[93] The study concludes: 'It seems that the intended purpose of this section was not being realised'.[94]

[87] Cunliffe (1984), 278 at 281.

[88] It is only rarely that the hymen completely covers the vaginal opening so that rupture is necessary in order to effect intercourse.

[89] According to Woods, 'inflicts' means 'causes' in this context. See Woods (1981), 14. See also *Burstow* [1997] 4 All ER 225. For further discussion, see Smith and Hogan (1999), 428–9.

[90] Williams (1977), at 158. The advantage of the New South Wales provision is that it clarifies this position.

[91] See Williams (1977). [92] Report (1996), 1. [93] ibid. 76. [94] ibid.

SEXUAL ASSAULT: SEXUAL INTERCOURSE WITHOUT CONSENT[95]

Under the 1981 scheme, sexual assault was the Category 3 offence. Unlike Categories 1 and 2, it required proof of non-consent. Under the new 1989 regime, sexual assault becomes the basic offence. Liability both for sexual assault and aggravated sexual assault arises where sexual intercourse takes place without consent. Consent has thus been restored to centre stage.

The legislation makes some attempt to list circumstances in which consent will not be regarded as present, but the list is short and is not intended to be comprehensive. Section 61R provides as follows:

> For the purposes of subsection 61I and 61J and without limiting the grounds upon which it may be established that consent to sexual intercourse is vitiated—
> *(a)* a person who consents to sexual intercourse with another person—
> (i) under a mistaken belief as to the identity of the other person; or
> (ii) under a mistaken belief that the other person is married to the person,
> is to be taken not to consent to the sexual intercourse; and
> (*a*1) a person who consents to sexual intercourse with another person under a mistaken belief that the sexual intercourse is for medical or hygienic purposes is taken not to consent to the sexual intercourse;[96] and
> *(b)* a person who knows that another person consents to sexual intercourse under a mistaken belief referred to in paragraph *(a)* or (*a*1) is to be taken to know that the other person does not consent to the sexual intercourse; and
> *(c)* a person who submits to sexual intercourse with another person as a result of threats or terror, whether the threats are against, or the terror is instilled in, the person who submits to the sexual intercourse or any other person, is to be regarded as not consenting to the sexual intercourse; and
> *(d)* a person who does not offer actual physical resistance to sexual intercourse is not, by reason only of that fact, to be regarded as consenting to the sexual intercourse.

It will be noted that the section overrules the decision in *Papadimitropolous*,[97] in which it was held that a victim who mistakenly believed that she was married to the defendant at the time of sexual intercourse none the less consented to it. Moreover, husband impersonation, which constituted rape at common law, has been extended so that any mistake as to the other person's identity is deemed to negative consent.

(b) Michigan

The old Michigan law which preceded the 1974 reform placed an extremely heavy burden of proof upon the prosecution which had to prove beyond reasonable doubt both that force had been used by the defendant and that the victim was unwilling. This meant that, once the prosecution had established

[95] This offence (Category 3) is set out under the heading 'Gradation', above.
[96] This provision was not included in the original 1981 legislation.
[97] (1958) 98 CLR 249.

the use of force, it had to go on to prove that the victim had 'resisted to the utmost from the inception to the close of the attack'.[98] It was only in the more enlightened judgments that it was held that resistance was unnecessary where the complainant was overcome by fear.[99]

One of the main aims of the Michigan legislation was to lighten the prosecution's burden. It was felt that once evidence of force had been adduced, it should not be necessary for the prosecution to show in its evidence in chief that the victim had not consented. The 1974 legislation would appear to have accomplished this objective. It is made plain in the statute that the prosecution no longer has to establish that the complainant resisted.[100] Indeed, the word consent does not appear in the legislation at all. In its evidence in chief, the prosecution need do no more than adduce evidence of one of the circumstances required by the offence of criminal sexual conduct.[101] However, it is now well established that the defence will frequently be able to raise the issue of consent.[102] For example, the Act makes it an offence to engage in sexual contact or penetration in circumstances in which the actor causes personal injury to the victim and force or coercion is used to accomplish the contact or penetration. The statute provides a non-exhaustive list of the situations in which force or coercion will be deemed to have been used. The prosecution will discharge its evidential burden in a case such as this by adducing evidence of contact or penetration accompanied by personal injury and the use of force. The defence will then be able to argue that the complainant consented to sexual intercourse and that force was not used in order to accomplish the contact or penetration. Arguably, the defence has no evidential burden to discharge in this situation,[103] for, since the defence is seeking to do no more than deny the basic elements of the prosecution's case, any assertion of consent by the defence should be placed before the jury. This view has not, however, been taken by the courts, which have generally insisted upon some evidence of consent before a jury direction on consent is required.[104]

With respect to certain other forms of criminal sexual conduct, however, the legislation has, on the face of it, succeeded in ruling out consideration of consent altogether. Thus, for example, criminal sexual conduct in the first degree is established where the defendant engages in sexual penetration with

[98] *People v Geddes,* 301 Mich 258 at 261, 3 NW 2d 266 at 267 (1942).

[99] e.g. in cases of gang rape at gunpoint. See e.g. *People v Jackson* 42 Mich App 468 (1972).

[100] See MCL 750.520(i) which provides 'A victim need not resist the actor'.

[101] See e.g. *People v Stull* 338 NW 2d 403 (Mich App 1983). The offence is set out in full under the heading 'Gradation', above.

[102] The significance of consent was played down in *People v Nelson* 261 NW 2d 299 (1978). However, in subsequent decisions it has been recognized that consent remains a defence. See e.g. *People v Hearn* Mich App 300 NW 2d 396 (1981).

[103] For a contrary view, see e.g. Dor, 'Justice after Rape: Legal Reform in Michigan', in M. J. Walker and S. L. Brodsky eds., *Sexual Assault: The Victim and the Rapist* (Lexington, Mass. and London: D. C. Heath, 1976), 149, 154.

[104] See e.g. *People v Paquette* Mich App 319 NW 2d 390 (1982).

another and the actor is armed with a weapon or any article used or fashioned in a manner to lead the victim reasonably to believe it to be a weapon.[105] It is similarly established where the defendant engages in sexual penetration with another and this occurs 'under circumstances involving the commission of any other felony'.[106] The victim's consent would seem to be immaterial in both instances. It has been held, however, that consent is still a defence in these circumstances.[107] If this is the case, then it should be up to defending counsel to set it on its feet and persuade the judge to place the matter before the jury. Where sexual intercourse takes place before the barrel of a gun, it seems quite appropriate that it should be up to the defence to discharge an evidential burden with respect to consent. It is similarly arguable that it should be up to the defence to provide a proper foundation of evidence for an assertion that a woman who has been robbed by a man none the less subsequently consented to sexual intercourse with him. There is judicial support for this view.[108]

Under the Michigan regime, the only circumstances in which consent is now entirely excluded from consideration are precisely those where consent is not an issue under English law, namely, where children or the mentally disabled are concerned. Research into the operation of the Michigan law suggests that so far as judges, prosecutors, and defence counsel are concerned, consent remains an important issue. But it was also found that the significance of consent had decreased as a result of the legislation, as had the importance of resistance by the complainant.[109]

(c) Canada

The Canadian legislation of 1982 did very little to tackle the issue of consent. Section 265(1)*(a)* of the Canadian Criminal Code provides: 'A person commits an assault when, *without the consent of another person*, he applies force intentionally to that other person' (emphasis added). Lack of consent remains, therefore, an integral part of the crime of sexual assault at all three levels. The legislation originally did no more than provide a short list of situations in which consent would not be deemed to exist for the purpose both of assault and sexual assault offences:

For the purposes of this section, no consent is obtained where the complainant submits or does not resist by reason of

[105] In *People v Davis* 300 NW 2d 497 (1980), the defendant was held to be armed with a weapon when his rifle was lying six feet away.

[106] Criminal Sexual Conduct Act, 1974, s520*b*.

[107] See *People v Hearn* above; *People v Thompson* 117 Mich App 324 NW 2d 22 (1980).

[108] See *People v Hearn* 115 above; *People v Thompson* Mich App, above.

[109] Marsh *et al.* (1982), 51–2. However, prosecutors interviewed by Spohn and Horney considered that the law did not go far enough since it was left up to the judge whether to give an explicit jury direction that resistance was not required: see (1992), at 163.

(a) the application of force to the complainant or to a person other than the complainant;
(b) threats or fear of the application of force to the complainant or to a person other than the complainant;
(c) fraud;
(d) the exercise of authority.[110]

By including fraud without confining it to fraud as to the nature of the act or husband impersonation and also including the exercise of authority, the list went considerably beyond the categories of non-consent at common law.[111] However, the provision had certain drawbacks. First, it was not made clear whether or not the list was intended to be exhaustive. Secondly, it did not include mistakes other than those occasioned by fraud. Thirdly, criteria such as 'fraud' or 'exercise of authority' are exceedingly vague and arguably provide too much scope for judicial interpretation. Finally, the wording of the subsection seemed to invite the defence to argue that the complainant's submission did not occur *by reason of* the factors mentioned.

The decision of the Supreme Court of Canada in *Seaboyer*[112] to strike down the sexual history provisions contained in the Canadian Criminal Code produced a second phase in the history of sexual offences law reform in Canada. In 1992, the Canadian government, working with a coalition of women's groups, responded to the outcry which greeted the decision by delivering a new reform package containing three key elements. In addition to new sexual history provisions, a determined attempt was made to tackle both the issue of consent as well as the plea of honest belief in consent.[113] It is of interest that, as far as consent was concerned, the chosen method was not to redefine sexual offences so as to exclude consent altogether from the definition as had been tried in Michigan and New South Wales. It was decided instead to build on the existing Canadian legislation, first by defining consent and then by expanding the list of situations in which consent was to be regarded as absent. This approach is very much in line with 'second wave' legislation passed in Australia.[114] The new provision, which does not displace but adds to the old one, also establishes that the statutory list of non-consent situations is non-exhaustive.[115] Section 273.1 now provides:

[110] Canadian Criminal Code, s 265(3).

[111] See, however, *Petrozzi* (1987) 35 CCC 3d 528 (BCCA) where it was held that the broad fraud provision in fact went no further than the common law, covering only frauds as to identity and the nature of the act. However, in *Cuerrier* [1998] 2 SCR 371 a much broader approach was taken and it was held that fraud as to HIV status would vitiate consent. The majority held that there were no limitations or qualifications on the term 'fraud'.

[112] [1991] 2 SCR 577.

[113] For further discussion of the plea of honest belief in Canadian law, see Ch. 2 under the heading 'The *Mens Rea* of Rape'.

[114] See in particular The Crimes (Rape) Act 1991, Victoria. See also Ch. 2, 'Reforming the Law On Consent', pp. 96–116 for the proposals of the SOR.

[115] s 273(3).

(1) . . . 'consent' means, for the purposes of sections 271, 272, and 273, the voluntary agreement of the complainant to engage in the sexual activity in question.
(2) No consent is obtained . . . where
(*a*) the agreement is expressed by the words or conduct of a person other than the complainant;
(*b*) the complainant is incapable of consenting to the activity;
(*c*) the accused induces the complainant to engage in the activity by abusing a position of trust, power, or authority;
(*d*) the complainant expresses, by words or conduct, a lack of agreement to engage in the activity;[116] or
(*e*) the complainant, having consented to engage in sexual activity, expresses, by words or conduct, a lack of agreement to continue to engage in the activity.

Taken in combination, the two lists appear to provide a wide range of situations where consent will be regarded as absent. The new law includes abuse of a position of trust or power. This was in response to growing concern about sexual exploitation by, for example, doctors and priests.[117] The new consent provision was also intended, by means of an ingenious strategy, to limit unmeritorious claims of belief in consent.[118] For example, by stating that there is no consent where agreement is expressed by a third party, the defendant would not be able successfully to plead mistaken belief in consent in those circumstances since his mistake would constitute a mistake of the criminal law which in law is no defence. Similarly, where the victim expressly declines to have sexual intercourse with the defendant, his belief that she was nevertheless consenting would constitute a mistake as to the criminal law since under the statute consent does not exist in those circumstances. Again, therefore, he would have no defence.[119]

The high hopes which the women's lobby vested in the new law may, once again, have been misplaced. It was thought that, by defining consent to mean voluntary agreement, this would underline that 'consent requires active, hence verifiable (not projected) conduct freely chosen (not coerced or presumed)' and that it would focus law enforcement 'on the specific sexual interaction in dispute, not on past history or self serving myths'.[120] Given

[116] In *M (ML)* (1994) 3 CR 4th 153 (SCC) it was held that silence does not signify consent and that there was no need for the complainant to express her lack of consent. In *Ewanchuk* (1999) 22 CR (5th) 1 (SCC) 330,the Supreme Court held that there was no such thing as implied consent from conduct. Consent was subjective to the complainant.

[117] See Boyle (1994), 147 and discussion in Ch. 2 under the heading 'Abuse of Power, Authority, or Position of Trust', pp. 107–10.

[118] See McIntyre (1994), 297.

[119] This approach was specifically endorsed by the Supreme Court of Canada in *Ewanchuk* [1999] 1 SCR 330 but is criticized by D. Stuart: see *Canadian Criminal Law: A Treatise* (4th edn., Ontario: Carswell, 2001), 302. For exposition of the concept of mistake of law, see Smith and Hogan (1999), 82–4. See also Ch. 2, text at nn. 554, 555.

[120] See McIntyre (1994), 306. However, it has been suggested that the list of non-consent situations does no more than reflect male expectations and interests and that a list of the coercive pressures that operate on women in the real world would look very different: see

the chequered history of sexual assault law reform in Canada, the women's lobby ought perhaps to have taken a leaf out of the Michigan reformers' book by seeking to ensure detail and specificity in the law. The new provisions continue in some respects to be vague and offer a sitting target for judges who are out of sympathy with them.[121] Research conducted into the effect of the 1992 reforms after the first three years of their operation was unable to find any evidence that the definition of consent had had any impact at all on the practice of the courts.[122] It remains to be seen whether the subsequent decision of the Supreme Court of Canada in *Ewanchuk*,[123] which strongly supported the new provisions, will eventually influence the way they are treated in practice.

(d) Solving the Problem of Consent[124]

It may be concluded that the problem of consent is unlikely to vanish whatever means are adopted to deal with it. Realistically, it is likely to remain an issue in the majority of sexual assault cases. There are, however, three strategies which might be worth considering. First, there may be a case for shifting the evidential burden of establishing consent onto the shoulders of the defence in certain cases, such as where there is evidence of serious injury inflicted by the defendant, where weapons are used,[125] or where sexual intercourse takes place in the context of the commission of another grave offence.[126] Generally speaking, as a matter of practical necessity, the defence will have to produce evidence of consent in these circumstances. But there could be a formal requirement that the defence 'lend an air of reality' to its plea by providing a 'real factual basis' for it rather than making a mere assertion of consent.[127] A failure to produce such evidence would then ensure that the issue of consent was not left to the jury. Secondly, legislation could

T. B. Dawson, 'Legal Structures: A Feminist Critique of Sexual Assault Law Reform' (1985) 14 *Resources for Feminist Research* 40; Boyle (1994), 141.

121 See e.g. *Petrozzi* (1987) 35 CCC (3d) 528 (BCCA) discussed above.

122 C. Meredith, R. Mohr, and R. Cairns Way, *Implementation Review of Bill C–49* (Ottawa: Dept. of Justice, 1997), 42.

123 [1999] 1 SCR 330.

124 See also discussion in Ch. 2, 96–116.

125 Wright (*New Society* 1980), 124 found that in 20 per cent of the cases in his survey, the victim was threatened with a weapon. A similarly high proportion of cases (19%) in which weapons were carried by defendants was found in the Scottish survey: Chambers and Millar (1983), 19. In Amir's study, weapons were used in 21 per cent of cases (1971), 153; in Clark and Lewis's Canadian study the figure was 13 per cent (1977), 67; Young's New Zealand study also recorded that in 20 per cent of cases submission was obtained by the threat or use of a weapon (1983), 36. On the other hand, Grace *et al.* found that weapons were rarely used (1992), 21.

126 In Wright's study, in one out of ten cases, rape took place in the context of a non-sexual rime such as burglary or robbery: Wright, *New Society* (1980), 124.

127 See discussion of Canadian cases of *Pappajohn, Osolin,* and *Park* in Ch. 2 under the heading 'The SOR's proposal'.

codify existing law[128] by providing that the prosecution need not adduce evidence of resistance or words or conduct indicating absence of consent in order to establish lack of consent. Moreover, in those cases where the evidential burden of establishing consent is on the defence, evidence of lack of resistance or absence of such words or conduct should not suffice. Finally, there is something to be said for a statutory definition of consent coupled with a well-defined, non-exhaustive list of situations in which consent will be negatived.[129]

Abolition of the Word 'Rape'

In the 1970s and 1980s where radical reform was introduced, there was a clear preference for use of the term 'sexual assault' rather than rape. In Michigan, Canada, and New South Wales the word rape is not used in the legislation. The Michigan statute creates a crime of criminal sexual conduct to replace the old offence of carnal knowledge. In Canada and New South Wales, rape has been abolished in favour of new offences of sexual assault.

There are, certainly, arguments in favour of such a change in terminology. In its Report on Sexual Offences, the Canadian Law Reform Commission stated: 'The Commission has come to the conclusion that the very use of the word "rape" attaches a profound moral stigma to the victims and expresses an essentially irrational folklore about them'.[130] Similarly, explaining the use of the term sexual assault in the New South Wales legislation, Woods stated: 'It was widely believed that the term "rape" involved an unacceptable stigma for victims'.[131] This is not to say that sexual assault carries no stigma, but the term is vaguer and the stigma arguably less. The word rape also conjures up certain stereotypical images: it is too often associated with psychopaths, strangers, and violence. Juries may therefore be reluctant to impose the stigma of it on an offender save in the most extreme cases. They may consider that many forms of non-consensual sexual intercourse are not so grave as to be labelled rape. It has already been suggested that this is the reaction of many policemen. Thus, in order to distance the law from preconceived cultural notions about rape, rapists, and rape victims, a new terminology may be thought to be desirable. Moreover, where there has

[128] See *Malone* [1998] 2 Cr App R 454.

[129] For the proposals of the SOR to this effect, see Ch. 2 under the heading 'Without Consent'. In the United States a further strategy is being explored. Courts have been persuaded to admit evidence that the complainant was suffering from rape trauma syndrome in order to rebut the defence of consent. See e.g. *State v Marks,* 231 Kan 645, 647 2d 1292 (1982), *State v Liddell,* 685 P 2d 918 (Mont 1984), and *State v Huey* 145 Ariz 59, 699 2d 1290 (1985). See also, Comment, 'Expert Testimony on Rape Trauma Syndrome: Admissibility and Effective Use in Criminal Rape Prosecution' (1984) 33 Am UL Rev 417; J. Rowland, *Rape: The Ultimate Violation* (London and Sydney: Pluto Press, 1986); P. A. Frazier and E. Borgida, 'Rape Trauma Syndrome—A Review of Case Law and Psychological Research' (1992) 16 Law and Human Behaviour' 293.

[130] Report No. 10 (1978), 12.

[131] Woods (1981), 7.

been a radical restructuring of sexual offences, use of the term rape to cover conduct which bears little resemblance to the offence as it is generally understood might also deter juries from convicting.

More recently, some jurisdictions have shied away from the term sexual assault. In Western Australia, the offence is now referred to as 'sexual penetration without consent' and in the Northern Territory as 'sexual intercourse without consent'. The Australian Model Criminal Code Officers Committee preferred this approach and has proposed that the offence be called 'unlawful sexual penetration'.[132] Whilst this type of nomenclature might be thought to be preferable to sexual assault in that it steers away from a conceptualization which focuses upon violence, the terminology might be criticized as too neutral and bland given the nature of the conduct involved.

There is now a growing preference among feminist thinkers for a return to the term 'rape' where penetrative offences are concerned.[133] This is the term used in Victoria, Tasmania, Queensland, and South Australia. It has the decided advantage of conveying the full horror of the event. It stigmatizes the conduct which is important if the public is to view it with an appropriate degree of revulsion. By contrast, where rape is disguised as sexual assault, the conduct involved is downgraded or in the words of a Texan judge 'sugarcoated'.[134] Abandonment of the term rape may well have serious repercussions for the way in which the offence is processed and dealt with by the criminal justice system. Spohn and Horney quote a prosecutor in Chicago who felt that the new terminology served only to confuse jurors 'who often wondered why we didn't just charge the guy with rape'.[135] As the Law Reform Commission of Victoria put it: 'The main argument for retention regardless of the form and substance of the law is that the term rape is synonymous with a particularly heinous form of behaviour'.[136]

Evidence

The radical reform packages introduced in Michigan, Canada, and New South Wales all contained changes to the law of evidence as it applied in sexual cases. In all three jurisdictions, greater restrictions were placed on the use of sexual history evidence. In Canada and New South Wales, corroboration requirements were substantially modified—there were no such requirements in Michigan—and changes were introduced to the rules surrounding evidence of recent complaint. These changes are considered in Chapter 4.

[132] Discussion Paper (1996), 29.

[133] See e.g. J. Bargen and E. Fishwick, *Sexual Assault Law Reform: A National Perspective* (Canberra: Office of the Status of Women, 1995), 60.

[134] Spohn and Horney (1992), 161.

[135] ibid.

[136] Discussion Paper No. 2, *Rape and Allied Offences: Substantive Aspects* (1986), 51, n. 9.

Abolition of the Exemptions for Certain Males

In Canada[137] and New South Wales,[138] abolition of the marital rape exemption was an essential part of the reform package. In Michigan, it proved to be politically impossible in 1974 to change the law in this way[139] and abolition was not achieved until 1988.[140] In Canada[141] and New South Wales,[142] the exemption from rape and attempted rape which boys under 14 had formerly enjoyed at common law was also abolished.

Monitoring Radical Reform

(a) Michigan

In Michigan, efforts have been made to monitor the effects of radical law reform.[143] An early study conducted by Marsh *et al.* found that the Criminal Sexual Conduct statute had radically affected conviction rates and also affected arrest rates. Thus, whereas in the period 1972 to 1974, eight forcible rape convictions were achieved per month, after the legislation, between 1976 and 1978, there were 21 convictions per month.[144] Between 1975 and 1978, a conviction was obtained in 70 per cent of cases in which a warrant of arrest was issued by the Detroit Police Department for a criminal sexual conduct offence.[145] This they described as an 'astonishingly high rate' in US terms.[146] A study of arrests made by this department between January 1975 and May 1979 revealed that twice as many warrants were issued for first-degree offences as for the other three offences put together. Thus, crimes which conformed to the traditional image of rape were more likely to be pursued. It was also found that they were more likely to result in convictions for the original charge than the other three degrees in which plea-bargaining was more common.[147]

Interviews were conducted with criminal justice officials to assess their views of the changes which the new legislation had effected. Out of 157 people taken from a cross-section of officials and crisis centre staff, 44.1 per cent attributed the improved chances which a prosecutor had of winning a

[137] Canadian Criminal Code, s 278. The complainant spouse is also a competent and compellable prosecution witness: Canada Evidence Act, s 4(2).

[138] Crimes Act 1900, s 61T.

[139] See Marsh *et al.* (1982), 15.

[140] PA 1988, No. 138: effective 6 June 1988. See now MCL 750.520.

[141] s 147 of the Canadian Criminal Code was amended so as to exclude the sexual assault provisions from the exemption.

[142] See now Crimes Act 1900, s 61S.

[143] For a study of the reforming legislation in Washington, see W. Loh, 'The Impact of Common Law Rape Reform Statutes on Prosecution, An Empirical Study' (1980) 55 Washington LR 543.

[144] Marsh *et al.* (1982), 29.

[145] ibid. 32.

[146] ibid. 36.

[147] ibid. 33–7.

case to the sexual history restrictions and 25.8 per cent attributed it to the degree structure.[148] However, despite the concrete achievements of the legislation, the study revealed that much that was hoped for from it had not been achieved. Thus, for example, although sexual history evidence had become less significant, it was still sometimes admitted improperly or introduced through innuendo.[149] The legislation did not appear to have affected reporting rates or the attitudes of many officials towards sexual assault. A slight majority of defending counsel interviewed claimed that they had not altered their way of handling rape cases as a result of the legislation.[150] Moreover, a series of interviews conducted by the Battelle Law and Justice Centre with prosecutors in the Wayne County District Attorney's Office also indicated a 'business as usual' attitude despite the presence of the new law. Duncan Chappell observed:

> In Wayne County, the filing prosecutors wielded . . . power in a conservative fashion with respect to criminal sexual conduct cases, removing from the system what they termed 'bad rapes' and keeping 'good rapes'. One prosecutor described a 'good rape' as 'one where a nurse is coming home from work to her husband and family. She is dragged off the street and into an alley where her clothes are torn and she is sexually assaulted'. The same prosecutor described a 'bad or bullshit, Mickey Mouse rape' as 'one where some broad living on welfare and screwing the government and living with some guy goes out all night and then says she was raped.' Clearly the prosecutors' personal attitudes loomed large in the decision making, the legal definition of criminal sexual conduct in one of its degrees playing a minor role in determining which cases got filed.[151]

Later research by Spohn and Horney covers a longer period up to 1984 and evaluates the impact of the legislation in Detroit rather than the whole of Michigan. They found that there had been a significant increase in reporting in Detroit from the time of the implementation of the new law. This was not matched by increases in the reporting of other violent crimes such as robbery and assault.[152] The authors suggest that the increase is likely to have occurred as a result of publicity surrounding the new law.[153]

Spohn and Horney also found that the indictment rate, that is, the number of cases prosecuted as a percentage of reports, 'increased by 18 percentage points following reform of the rape laws. Thus not only were there more indictments simply because of an increase in the number of cases reported but prosecution of these cases was more likely following the legislative changes'.[154] However, the research found that this increase in the prosecution rate was not matched by the likelihood of conviction, which did not change. More convictions were being obtained as a result of an increase in

[148] Marsh *et al.* (1982), 45. [149] ibid. 60–1. [150] ibid. 52.

[151] Chappell (1977), 304. [152] (1992), 87.

[153] (1992), 102. Contrast the finding of Marsh *et al.* that there had been no increase in reporting in Michigan as a whole: see discussion above.

[154] (1992), 90.

cases coming through the system, but there was no change in the percentage of charges resulting in conviction.[155] It had been expected that the new law would encourage juries to convict on lesser charges. However, it was found that prosecutors declined to ask judges to instruct juries that they could convict on lesser charges for fear that juries would become too confused by the sheer complexity of the degree structure.[156] Thus, by contrast with the findings of Marsh *et al.,* the authors found no increase in the conviction rate in Detroit and no significant increase in the percentage of convictions on the original charge. This finding, the authors concede, 'represents a failure of reformers' expectations'.[157] However, they also note quite fairly that the fact that the conviction rate has remained constant is itself an achievement: 'If the increase in indictments represented more borderline cases entering the system, a decline in convictions might have followed. In fact the overall number of convictions increased suggesting that defendants in these borderline cases *are* being convicted.'[158] Contrary to expectation, it was found that there was no obvious increase in plea-bargaining.[159] This may have been due to the strict regulation of this by the prosecutor's office and its insistence that complainants be consulted first.[160]

Spohn and Horney found strong support for the reforms among criminal justice officials in Detroit.[161] A programme of seminars and training sessions had been introduced which may have assisted in this. However, in common with Marsh *et al.,* they also found that the reforms had little impact on the way criminal justice officials assessed the strength or weakness of particular types of reported rape cases.[162] They suggest that officials' judgements of likelihood of conviction may accurately reflect their observations of jury behaviour in Detroit.[163] In Michigan, as is often the case in the United States, a defendant may waive his right to jury trial with the consent of the prosecutor and the approval of the court. He will then have a bench trial, which is trial by judge alone.[164] It was found that bench conviction rates were 64 per cent whereas jury conviction rates were only 52.9 per cent.[165] Unlike criminal justice officials, juries do not receive training. Such success as there has been in Michigan as far as conviction rates are concerned would have been considerably reduced if the only mode of trial were jury trial.

The authors also conclude that any success achieved in Michigan as far as reporting and prosecution rates are concerned is associated with the limited discretion which the law affords to criminal justice officials.[166] Other factors, such as the location of the Rape Counselling Centre in Detroit within the Detroit Police Department, were also regarded as significant.[167]

155 ibid. 156 ibid. 161. 157 ibid. 104. 158 ibid.
159 ibid. 91. 160 ibid. 64. 161 ibid. 172. 162 ibid. 115–16.
163 ibid. 129.
164 Defendants may prefer a bench trial where the facts of the case are particularly unpleasant or it is likely that previous misconduct will be revealed in court.
165 Spohn and Horney (1992), 72. 166 See ibid. 172–3. 167 ibid.

(b) New South Wales

As was the case in Michigan, in New South Wales, monitoring of the 1981 legislation also took place shortly after it came into effect. The Bureau of Crime Statistics and Research concluded that its findings[168] provided grounds for 'cautious optimism' about the effects of the new legislation on the processing of sexual assault cases.[169]

However, more recent research suggests that there was every reason to remain cautious.

A study conducted by the New South Wales Department for Women looked at all 150 sound-recorded sexual assault hearings in the NSW District Court over a one-year period between May 1994 and April 1995.[170] By this time, as noted above, there had been some alteration to the gradation system in New South Wales.[171]

It was found that out of 111 trials in which D pleaded not guilty mainly to principal charges of sexual assault, aggravated sexual assault, and assault with intent to have sexual intercourse,[172] only 34 out of 111 cases resulted in conviction.[173] Thus there was an acquittal rate of 69 per cent. Given that one of the purposes of a gradation scheme is to facilitate convictions, such a rate is surprisingly high and no advertisement for the sexual assault scheme. Moreover, the majority of the offences charged (59%) were at the lowest level, that is, sexual assault, with only 19 per cent charged with aggravated sexual assault[174] and only 5 per cent with assault with intent to have sexual intercourse.[175] It might have been anticipated that by bringing charges at the lowest level, convictions would be easier to obtain. Of the 150 hearings, 39, that is, 26 per cent, resulted in a guilty plea.[176] Since a gradation scheme is intended to encourage guilty pleas, this result seems equally disappointing. Thus, 73 out of 150 hearings resulted in a conviction, an overall conviction rate of 49 per cent.

The vast majority (76%) of those convicted of sexual assault (maximum penalty 14 years) in the NSW study received sentences of imprisonment of 30 months or less.[177] Sixty-five per cent of those convicted of aggravated sexual assault (maximum penalty 20 years) received sentences of between three and four years.[178] Seventy-seven per cent of those charged with assault with intent to have sexual intercourse (maximum penalty 20 years) also received sentences of four years or less.[179] It is true that in New South Wales

[168] For a detailed analysis of these findings, see Temkin (1987), 151–3.

[169] New South Wales Bureau of Crime Statistics and Research, *Interim Report 2—Sexual Assault—Court Outcome, Acquittals, Convictions and Sentence* (1985), 68.

[170] New South Wales Dept. for Women (1996), 1.

[171] See above under the heading 'Gradation'.

[172] For the full list of offences, see NSW Department for Women (1996), table 2, 79.

[173] New South Wales Dept. for Women (1996), 3.

[174] ibid. [175] ibid. 76. [176] ibid. 3. [177] ibid. 301, fig. 4.

[178] ibid. 303, fig. 7. [179] ibid. 304, fig. 9.

remissions are not available for prisoners so that these sentences represent the period actually served in prison. Nevertheless, there must be some concern that the ladder of offences has resulted in a low level of sentencing particularly where, as is most often the case, the basic sexual assault offence is charged.

The NSW research further found that, despite the fact that the law had made them optional, corroboration warnings were given in all but 14 cases.[180] Moreover, sexual experience material was raised in 95 instances in the 111 trials studied and admitted into evidence in 84 per cent of the instances in which it was raised.[181]

These findings do not give cause for optimism.

(c) Canada

In Canada, the Federal Department of Justice conducted a wide-ranging evaluation of the sexual assault law reforms which it published in 1990.[182] This evaluation, together with subsequent research, provides an illuminating picture of sexual assault and criminal justice in the aftermath of the 1983 reforms.

Reporting rates appear to have increased exponentially. Roberts found that the number of complaints of sexual assault remained relatively stable in the six years prior to the implementation of the reforms but that it increased by 127 per cent in the six years succeeding it.[183] There was also a rise in the reporting of non-sexual crimes of violence, but this does not compare to the rise in reports of sexual assaults.[184] One of the goals of the reforms had been to increase reporting rates and it has been claimed that the reform has been successful, directly or indirectly, in this respect.[185] However, it is unlikely to have been the *content* of the reform package that was responsible for this, but rather the change in public attitudes towards sexual assault and child sexual abuse and publicity for these reforms which might have prompted victims to come forward. It is also worth noting that after 1983 a number of important changes took place in the treatment of sexual assault victims which may well have encouraged reporting. These included the emergence of sexual assault centres, police-based victim/witness assistance programmes, and hospital forensic units. Moreover, reporting rates vary considerably in different parts of Canada. In Quebec they remain low,[186] suggesting that attitudes to reporting have not changed uniformly throughout Canada. Experimental research conducted by the Centre of Criminology at the University of Toronto into whether the change of nomenclature from rape to sexual assault was likely to influence reporting behaviour produced

[180] ibid. 8. [181] ibid. 10. [182] Canadian Department of Justice (1990).
[183] Roberts (1990). [184] Roberts and Grossman (1994), 73. [185] ibid.
[186] ibid. 68

a negative result. Subjects who participated were no more likely to report the crime where it was labelled sexual assault rather than rape. The results indicated that the label had few significant effects upon subjects' reactions.[187]

An examination of police handling of this vast increase in reports of rape reveals that offences are overwhelmingly classified at the lowest level (Level 1) save where stranger rape is concerned. Indeed, in 1989, 96 per cent of reports of rape were classified as Level 1.[188] Moreover, the proportion of cases classified at the two higher levels decreased each year from 1983 to 1990 so that by 1990, 436 cases were classified at Level 3 (1%) as against 685 in 1983 (5%). In 1990, 31,401 cases were classified at Level 1 (96%) as against 12,241 in 1983 (88%).[189]

Roberts found that the percentage of reports treated by the police as unfounded was not affected by the legislation and remained constant at 15 per cent as against 7 per cent for other crimes against the person.[190] Moreover, the increase in reporting rates has not translated itself into comparable increases in charging rates. Indeed, although the figures for the arrest and charging of sexual assault cases did change dramatically after 1982, research into the period between 1982 and 1991 demonstrates that the detection and charging of non-sexual crimes of violence also rose considerably. Moreover, the proportion of sexual assaults charged was smaller than for non-sexual crimes of violence.[191] After the first flush of enthusiasm following the enactment of the legislation, there was an increasing discrepancy between arrest and charge rates for sexual assault.[192]

Classification of offences at the lowest level was found to be manifest at every level in the system. Mohr found that convictions for the Level 1 (lowest-level) offence frequently involved defendants who had used weapons or had caused bodily harm to the complainant of a serious nature and were thus classifiable as Level 2 or Level 3 offences. Many of these cases did not involve plea-bargaining.[193] Indeed, plea-bargaining does not appear to have increased markedly as a result of the new legislation,[194] presumably because the police are classifying cases at the lowest level in any case. It was also found that, because of the structure of the gradation scheme, some extremely grave assaults on children only managed to be squeezed into the Level 2 category because of factors which were almost incidental to the true horror of the assault which had occurred.[195] In *Jondreau*,[196] a stranger rapist subjected a 7-year old girl to anal

[187] M. G. Grossman, *Canadian Legislative Changes in the Area of Sexual Aggression: An Experimental Survey (1990)*, (Toronto: Centre of Criminology, University of Toronto, 1990).

[188] Mohr (1994), 164 and 180. [189] ibid. 67. [190] Roberts (1990), 33.

[191] B. Schissel, 'Law Reform and Social Change: A Time-Series Analysis of Sexual Assault in Canada' (1996) 24 Journal of Criminal Justice 123.

[192] ibid. 127.

[193] Mohr (1994), 165. For the different levels of the sexual assault offence, see above pp. 159–60.

[194] Clark and Hepworth (1994), at 128. [195] Mohr (1994), 165–6.

[196] (1986) Carswell Ont 1037, 18 OAC 120.

intercourse and attempted vaginal intercourse, defecated on her, and ordered her to swallow faeces. It was possible to charge him at Level 2 only because he had also threatened to kill the child's mother.

Conviction rates have been unaffected by the reforms. The overall number of convictions has risen but the proportion of cases resulting in conviction has remained constant.[197] Nuttall found that defendants charged with sexual assault were frequently convicted of non-sexual crimes.[198]

Mohr found that sentencing at Level 1 ranged from a suspended sentence and probation to imprisonment, although, where serious violence was involved, prison sentences were generally given and were clearly higher than other Level 1 cases.[199] Some judges adopted a three-year starting-point[200] but there was no firm guideline judgment equivalent to *Billam* in England and Wales and sentencing was very much a matter of discretion. The exercise of this discretion not infrequently gave rise to sentences which were unjustifiably low. In particular, a gradation scheme which so clearly singles out violence as the dominating theme has led to low sentences where judges feel that violence was lacking. For example, in *Desbiens*,[201] D locked a 16-year-old in the house where she was babysitting, threatened her with a knife, raped her, made her perform fellatio, and told her that she would be killed if she reported what had happened. He was charged at Level 2. The judge commented:

> Leaving your victim in a sexual assault case unharmed apart from the assault is something that deserves more than a little attention. . . . The weapon represented a threat, but it was not used, and as much as I can do so, I want to give an accused full marks for that.

D was sentenced to two years' imprisonment, raised to four on appeal. It is likely that under the *Billam* regime he would have been sentenced to at least eight years.

It was expected that the emphasis on violence rather than sex in the Canadian scheme would result in far less detailed and, for the complainant, unnerving questioning about the sexual aspects of the offence. However, even this possible advantage has not materialized. It has been noted that 'the specific nature of sexual acts remains extremely important in the practice of the courts and the complainant has to answer questions focused directly on those aspects. The presence or absence of penetration remains an extremely important consideration in sentencing'.[202]

197 Canadian Department of Justice (1990).

198 S. Nuttall, *Toronto Sexual Assault Research Study (*Ministry of the Solicitor General, 1989).

199 Mohr (1994), 165, 167.

200 ibid. 169.

201 1985 Carswell Sask 379, 43 Sask R 169 (Saskatchewan Court of Appeal).

202 Los (1994), 37.

Conclusion

Radical reform of the type discussed in this chapter may be evaluated in terms of the statistics of reports, prosecutions, and convictions. If rape reports appear to have increased substantially, so have they elsewhere, with England and Wales affording a prime example.[203] It is difficult to pinpoint precisely the factors responsible for an increase in the reporting of rape offences. It may be that *any* changes which are perceived by victims to indicate that the criminal justice system has forsworn its hostility towards them may encourage reporting and that the exact nature of the reform package is immaterial.

The impact of the reforms on prosecution and conviction rates has been manifestly disappointing. Radical reformers did not sufficiently reckon with the attitudes and practices of those who administer the law, from police officers to jurors. The low level of sentencing, for which gradation is in no small measure responsible, should also give cause for concern. Moreover, radical legislation was also intended to make a break with past history and the unfortunate saga of mistreatment of rape victims by the criminal justice system. It was hoped to make a new beginning, free of some of the old associations. But even on this level, its results are disappointing as the continued use of sexual history evidence and corroboration warnings in New South Wales illustrates. Legal change of this kind was supposed to have had symbolic and political importance for women as well as for society as a whole. But, arguably, in New South Wales and Canada, rape has been downgraded with no obvious practical benefit to compensate.

[203] See Ch. 1 under the heading 'Reports, Prosecutions, and Convictions'.

4

Evidence

The evidential rules as they apply in sexual assault cases have been and remain a cause for some concern. They are implicated in the low conviction rate for rape. In England and Wales, as elsewhere in the common law world, steps have been taken to remove some of their worst excesses, but it is not clear that change has gone far enough. This chapter will focus on the evidential law relating to recent complaint, sexual history, collateral finality, the previous misconduct of the accused, and corroboration.[1]

Recent Complaint

In a criminal trial, there is a general rule that the statements of a testifying witness, previously made out of court, are inadmissible as evidence of the facts stated. This prohibition emanates from the rule concerning hearsay evidence in the criminal trial.[2] It is equally the case that a statement made by a witness on a previous occasion which supports his testimony at the trial itself cannot be used as evidence of his consistency.[3] Such testimony is considered on the one hand to be self-serving and on the other hand to be superfluous and time-wasting, since the assertions of a witness at trial are in general assumed to be true.[4] The latter assumption does not, however, appear to apply in the case of rape victims whose testimony at trial has, on the contrary, always been treated with the greatest suspicion. For this reason, an exception to the rule prohibiting evidence of previous consistent statements was made in her case. She is permitted to give evidence that she complained of the rape to a third party in order to combat the assumption that might otherwise be made that her testimony is false. The origins of this exception would appear to go back to the Middle Ages when it was essential for a victim of rape to raise the hue and cry if an appeal of rape were to succeed.[5] Attitudes had changed but little by the eighteenth century when Hawkins referred to the strong presumption against the complainant in a case of rape if she made no complaint within a reasonable time of the alleged outrage.[6]

[1] For further discussion of aspects of the law of evidence in sexual cases, see Childs and Ellison (2000); Temkin 'Rape and Criminal Justice at the Millennium' (2000); Temkin (2002).

[2] See Tapper (1999), 271.

[3] ibid.

[4] See Tapper (1999), 272.

[5] ibid. 273.

[6] 1 PC ch. 41, s 9.

The recent complaint exception permits the complainant to give evidence that at the earliest reasonable opportunity she voluntarily and without prompting reported the rape to a third party.[7] This evidence is regarded as relevant to her credibility, since it indicates a consistency between her conduct and her statement at the trial.[8] Moreover, where consent is in issue, it may be used to show that her conduct was inconsistent with her consent.[9] However, the jury must be directed that it is not evidence that the events in question actually occurred or that the complainant's allegations are true—a distinction which may understandably elude many juries.[10]

The trend in twentieth-century cases has been towards an expansion of the recent complaint exception to cover sexual offences in general and to permit some latitude in the construction of promptness. In *Valentine*,[11] the Court of Appeal demonstrated how far some judicial attitudes have progressed as far as sexual victimization is concerned. Roch LJ stated:

> We now have greater understanding that those who are the victims of sexual offences, be they male or female, often need time before they can bring themselves to tell what has been done to them; that some victims will find it impossible to complain to anyone other than a parent or member of their family whereas others may feel it quite impossible to tell their parents or members of their family.[12]

The Court confirmed that evidence of recent complaint would be admissible if the complaint were made at the first reasonable opportunity and within a reasonable time of the alleged offence. What was reasonable would depend upon the character of the individual complainant and the circumstances of the case. Approving the approach taken in *Cummings*,[13] the Court of Appeal held that it would be reluctant to interfere with the decision of the trial judge who admitted such evidence where the right principles had been applied and the judge had directed himself to the question of whether the complaint was made as early as was reasonable in the circumstances. In *Valentine* itself, the complainant was permitted to give evidence of a complaint made in the region of 20 hours after the rape and the decision confirms that complaints made considerably later than this may, in the right circumstances, also qualify.[14] However, developments in this area have not all been positive. In *White*,[15] the Privy Council, in an appeal from the Court of Appeal in Jamaica, held that unless another witness testified to the complaint, no evid-

[7] *Osborne* [1905] 1 KB 551.

[8] *Sparks* [1964] AC 964.

[9] It follows that, in the case of a child, where consent is not at issue and the child does not give evidence either in person or by means of a video-recording, no evidence of recent complaint may be adduced.

[10] See CLRC (1972), para. 232.

[11] [1996] 2 Cr App R 213.

[12] At 224.

[13] [1948] 1 All ER 551.

[14] See e.g. *R v Peter M* (Court of Appeal, Criminal Division No. 1999/7320/Z2, 2000 WL 1213017), in which a complaint in the form of a letter written in 1988 following abuse occurring between 1983 and 1987 was admitted.

[15] *White v Regina* [1999] 1 Cr App R 153.

ential significance could be attached to it and the jury should be warned against doing so. This requirement is novel and no English authorities were cited by Lord Hoffmann in support of it.[16] If adopted, it will severely undermine the recent complaint exception in a variety of situations, as where the recipient of a complaint cannot be called as a witness[17] or where, as in *Kincaid,*[18] the witness is confused as to the exact time of the complaint. The Privy Council stressed that, although it was not forbidden for the complainant, in the course of giving her evidence, merely to mention that she spoke to someone after the incident, care must be taken not to give the impression that this in any way supported her credibility. It also held that the complainant ought not to have been permitted to say that she had told five people 'what had happened' since this was an evasion of the hearsay rule.[19]

This attack on the recent complaint exception demonstrates some lack of understanding of its rationale and confirms that suspicious attitudes about the veracity of complainants remain as entrenched as ever. For, in essence, the import of the decision is that the word of the complainant that she made a complaint is not to be trusted unless it is corroborated by nothing less than the evidence of the recipient or a third party who heard the complaint. In the absence of such evidence, where the complaint is mentioned, the jury must be warned against setting any store by it as far as her credibility is concerned. The negative impact of such a warning on the jury, however it is couched, is not to be under-estimated. It is to be hoped that the decision will not be followed in this jurisdiction.[20] Certainly, this was not the approach of the Law Commission which considered that 'where the witness is available to be asked about the circumstances in which the earlier statement was allegedly made, the risk of manufacture should go to weight, not admissibility'.[21]

(a) Late Complaints

The other side of the coin as far as the recent complaint rule is concerned is that rape victims who do not complain promptly to a third party can expect to be cross-examined about this by the defence, and the judge too may comment adversely on the matter in his summing-up to the jury. Indeed, Australian and Canadian decisions in the 1970s emphasized the importance of the judge's doing so on the ground that 'the failure to complain at the first

[16] He cited *Kincaid* [1991] 2 NZLR 1 and *Fletcher* (1996), an unreported Jamaican case.

[17] The recipient may, for his own reasons, deny receiving the complaint or be unknown or untraceable.

[18] Above.

[19] [1999] 1 Cr App R at 159–60.

[20] The circumstances in which the appeal arose in *White* were unusual and readily distinguishable. The complainant had allegedly made complaints to five individuals but none was called as witness. In the course of a defective summing up, the trial judge commented that it was the police rather than the complainant who should be blamed for this failure.

[21] Law Commission (1997), para. 10.15.

reasonable opportunity is a circumstance which tells against the truthfulness of the complainant's evidence'.[22] These cases revealed a total lack of understanding about rape victims and of knowledge about the rape trauma syndrome, for many perfectly genuine rape victims fail to report rape to a third party, either immediately or at all. In his study of 70 rape victims who did not report to the police, Paul Wilson found that about 50 per cent never told anyone until they were interviewed for the study or had told someone weeks or months later in conjunction with a discussion on other matters.[23] Similarly, one-third of the women in the Women Against Rape study who claimed to have been raped or sexually assaulted as adults had suffered one such attack without telling anyone about it.[24] In a survey published by the Australian Bureau of Statistics, it was found that the majority of women victims did not report rape and those who did very often delayed before telling anyone at all.[25] Victims decline to complain of rape for a variety of reasons. They may be too traumatized, too embarrassed, too scared of encountering a judgemental attitude, or too full of quite unjustified guilt feelings about what has occurred.[26] The emphasis on the importance of recent complaint is therefore quite unjustifiable and it also presents yet another barrier to prosecution and conviction in rape cases. In England, Adler's Old Bailey study confirmed that defending counsel could be relied upon to point out forcefully to the jury any delay in reporting. A significantly lower conviction rate was revealed in such cases.[27] It has now been held in *Greenwood*[28] that the Crown is entitled to adduce evidence to explain absence of complaint provided that it is admissible and not hearsay evidence.

(b) Alternative Approaches

(i) Abolition

There has been some criticism of the recent complaint doctrine as an exception to the rule against previous consistent statements. In particular, it has been suggested (somewhat remarkably in view of the reasons for it) that it gives an advantage to the complainant which is not enjoyed by the defendant in a rape trial.[29] Professor Tapper, who favours its abolition, suggests that the way forward is 'to reform what is still shown to be wrong in the law of procedure as it applies to sexual offences directly, rather than seek to

22 *Boyce* (1975) 23 CCC (2d) 16 at 33–4. See also *Kilby v The Queen* (1973) 129 CLR 460 at 465; *Kistendey* (1976) 29 CCC (2d) 383.

23 Wilson (1978), 62–3.

24 Hall (1985), 142. In the year preceding the 2000 BCS, the BCS estimated that 61,000 women were the victims of a rape in England and Wales: see Home Office Research Study 237, p. vi. But in 1999/2000, only 8,409 offences of rape against females and males were recorded by the police: see p. 12, 16–17 above.

25 Crime and Safety Survey, NSW, Cat. No. 4509.1, Apr. 1994.

26 See Wilson (1978), 58–65.

27 See Adler (1987), 119.

28 [1993] Crim LR 770.

29 See Cross and Tapper (1985), 263.

counterbalance one injustice by a different anomaly'.[30] It is not at all clear what procedural reforms are envisaged. But whatever they are, this does not address the basic issue. Procedural reforms will not create an assumption that a woman who says she has been raped is telling the truth in the face of an abundance of prejudicial myths concerning women who allege rape,[31] the inevitable paucity of evidence to support her claim, and the mostly unbridled efforts of defence counsel to discredit her. She will continue to be in a different position from most other witnesses. Professor Tapper suggests that evidence of recent complaint should be permitted only if it falls within a further exception to the prior consistent statement rule, namely, to rebut an allegation of recent fabrication.[32] But this exception has been narrowly construed and in *Oyesiku*[33] the Court of Appeal warned that great care was called for in applying it. Evidence of recent complaint would rarely become admissible under this head. If a timely complaint made by the alleged victim could not be mentioned, many of those serving on juries would wonder why, if she were telling the truth, she did not report the rape to someone right away. This would be a further nail in her coffin. The abolition of the exception would serve only to place a further impediment in the way of prosecutions in rape cases.

The negative consequences of abolition have been amply illustrated by the Canadian and South Australian experience.Section 275[34] of the Canadian Criminal Code provides: 'The rules relating to evidence of recent complaint in sexual assault cases are hereby abrogated'. This provision would appear to have the effect of disallowing the prosecution from adducing evidence of recent complaint as well as disallowing the judge from directing the jury as to any adverse inference to be drawn from a failure to produce such evidence.[35] This might be described as throwing the baby out with the bath water. Those who argued for such a provision appear to have done so on the ground that the recent complaint exception stems from a prejudiced attitude towards the testimony of complainants in sexual assault cases. Whilst this is certainly true, abolition of the exception does not do away with the prejudice. Instead, it deprives the complainant of the opportunity to adduce evidence which might tend to support her credibility in a situation in which she continues to be viewed with disbelief and suspicion.

[30] Tapper (1999), 279.

[31] e.g. that women frequently fabricate rape allegations; that rape is consensual sex which the woman afterwards regrets; that rape allegations are easy to make and hard to disprove; that genuine rape victims report to the police immediately. On rape myths, see also Ch. 1, under the heading 'The Future of the Guidelines'.

[32] Tapper (1999), 279. This exception applies only where 'the credit of the witness is impugned . . . on the ground that his account is a late invention or has been lately devised or reconstructed': see *Oyesiku* (1971) 56 Cr App R 240, 245. See also *Tyndale* [1999] Crim LR 320.

[33] Above.

[34] Formerly s 246.5.

[35] For further discussion of the effects of s 275, see Paciocco and Stuesser (1999), 307–8.

It is no surprise that numerous attempts have been made to circumvent section 275 by seeking to introduce recent complaint evidence through other avenues permitted by the law of evidence.[36] There has been a certain judicial willingness to accommodate these attempts but often this has involved distorting other evidential rules. For example, in *Page*,[37] the complainant reported sexual assault to the police immediately after the event. Counsel for the prosecution sought to have evidence of her complaint adduced in court by way of the *res gestae* doctrine. Statements made during the *res gestae*, that is, while the actual events themselves were occurring, are admissible by way of further exception to the rule against previous consistent statements.

It was argued somewhat optimistically in *Page* that any complaint made at the first reasonable opportunity should be regarded as part of the *res gestae* and hence admissible. Whilst the court rejected this contention, it was prepared to concede that a complaint which amounted to a spontaneous exclamation in response to the events in question could be regarded as part of the *res gestae*. Although it considered that the *res gestae* principle could not be invoked on the facts in question, it was prepared nevertheless to allow the Crown to adduce evidence that a complaint was made to the police shortly after the event and also to permit other witnesses to describe the complainant's emotional condition and state of dress. The court justified this on the ground that evidence of the fact of a complaint by the victim of any crime is always admissible on the issue of the victim's credibility as a witness. But Schiff has noted that 'both the premise and the conclusion of the argument are wrong'.[38] The court did not permit details of the complaint,[39] thus reverting to Canadian law as it was in the nineteenth century when evidence of recent complaint but not details thereof was admitted as evidence.

Where no complaint has been made, section 275 prevents the judge from directing the jury to draw adverse inferences. However, it does not prevent defence counsel from cross-examining the complainant as to a failure to make an immediate complaint and from drawing this failure to the attention of the jury. Although Crown counsel will be able to respond in these circumstances by adducing evidence of complaint, recent or otherwise, the complainant may very well not have complained to anyone except eventually to the police. Expert evidence to counter the myth that genuine complainants always report rape at the first opportunity and to explain why most do not is not generally admitted.[40] The Supreme Court of Canada has now held that a trial judge should instruct a jury that there is no inviolable rule on how people who are the victims of trauma like a sexual assault will behave, that in assessing the credibility of a complainant, the timing of the

[36] See Schiff (1993), 890 n. 28.

[37] (1984) 40 CR (3d) 85.

[38] Schiff (1993), 890 n. 28.

[39] For support for this approach, see Watt (1984), 185–6.

[40] See *R v DD (*2000) 2 SCR 275.

complaint is simply one circumstance to consider in the factual mosaic of a particular case, and that a delay in disclosure, standing alone, will never give rise to an adverse inference against the credibility of the complainant.[41] Whilst such a direction, if given, would certainly be helpful, it does not sufficiently challenge common prejudiced assumptions.

Empirical research has revealed that only the defence has benefited from the Canadian 'reform'. Whilst it has not hindered the defence from raising the issue of delayed reporting in cross-examination, the prosecution has found it harder to support the complainant's credibility.[42] That the legislature has acted mistakenly emerges ever more clearly. This became obvious too in South Australia where the recent complaint exception was abolished in 1976. It was restored in 1984 after it was recognized that abolition had created a series of problems, including depriving the complainant of an opportunity to adduce evidence in support of her credibility, substantially disadvantaging the prosecution and seriously prejudicing the complainant's credibility in the eyes of the jury.[43] In the Australian Capital Territory, however, evidence of recent complaint by the victim and the terms of such complaint may no longer be admitted in sexual assault proceedings.[44]

(ii) Model Directions

In New South Wales (NSW), the issue of recent complaint has been approached quite differently. Prosecuting counsel may adduce evidence of recent complaint and this will be regarded as evidence of the complainant's consistency. As a result of the Crimes (Sexual Assault) Amendment Act 1981,[45] where the victim did not complain immediately, and evidence is given or a question asked about the matter, it is now obligatory for the judge, under section 405B of the Crimes Act 1900, to warn the jury that this does not necessarily betoken falsehood on the part of the complainant and that there may be good reasons why a victim of sexual assault may hesitate or refrain from complaining about the assault.[46] This will not prevent the judge from stating, in any particular case, that the facts are indicative of fabrication. Other Australian states have similar provisions.[47] The Victorian legislation provides additionally that 'A judge must not warn or suggest in any way to the jury that the law regards complainants in sexual cases as an unreliable class of witness'.[48]

[41] ibid.

[42] See Clark (1993), 1–2, 31–40.

[43] See Model Criminal Code Officers Committee (1996), 187.

[44] Evidence (Amendment) Ordinance (No. 2) 1985 (ACT) inserting s 76c(1) Evidence Act 1971. However a special warning must be given to the jury in the case of late complaint: see below under the heading 'Model Directions'.

[45] Schedule 1(14).

[46] Crimes Act 1900, s 405B.

[47] See ACT Evidence Act, s76C; Tasmanian Criminal Code, s 371A: Western Australia Evidence Act, s36BD; Northern Territory Sexual Offences (Evidence and Procedure) Act, s 4.

[48] Crimes Act 1958, s 61(1).

Dr Woods explained the reasons behind the NSW provision as follows:

> The reasons for late complaint or the absence of recent complaint may be subtle and difficult to understand or express. Section 405B is designed as a compulsory warning to the jury (as well as to the judge and counsel) that even though a rape victim may have difficulty in articulating in the witness box the painful self-reflections he or she felt after the offence occurred, such difficulty should not be necessarily taken as indication of fabrication. . . . The section thus serves to alert the court to a point of considerable importance. The pressure to dismiss rape allegations where the 'hue and cry' has not been immediately raised has certainly been a factor in deterring legitimate reports and prosecutions of sexual assault. The section will be 'a signpost', it is hoped, not only for courts but also for investigating police and prosecutors.[49]

This approach may seem to have much to commend it. It appears to represent a positive and imaginative step in the direction of dismantling the stereotype of the genuine rape victim. However, the unfortunate history of the operation of these provisions is not encouraging. In *Davies*,[50] the New South Wales Court of Criminal Appeal chose severely to undermine the effect of the new provisions. It held that, in addition to giving the directions required by section 405B, the trial judge should generally continue to direct the jury in accordance with the decision taken by the High Court of Australia in 1973 in *Kilby v The Queen*[51] that the absence of a complaint or the delay in making one can be taken into account in evaluating the evidence of the complainant and in determining whether to believe her. The result of *Davies* is that in some cases the jury will receive a section 405B warning coupled with an old-style *Kilby* direction, an absurd situation that can only result in total confusion. In *Crofts*,[52] the High Court of Australia dealt with an appeal concerning the Victorian mandatory directions. It echoed the decision in *Davies* and held that they too did not prevent a judge from offering a *Kilby* direction, commenting that the section did not 'convert complainants in sexual misconduct cases into an especially trustworthy class of witness'.[53]

A recent Australian study has demonstrated that judges in New South Wales frequently fail to give the section 405B warning and give the *Kilby* direction instead.[54] A separate study found that in Victoria, although statutory warnings were given more often, many judges had a negative attitude towards them and in some cases made comments which undermined their force.[55] The lesson seems to be that old attitudes die hard and that innovation which is not supported by judicial education is bound to falter.

[49] Woods (1981), 26. In New Zealand, a far less satisfactory provision has been enacted. It is up to the judge whether he explains to the jury that there may be good reasons for failure to complain: see Evidence Amendment Act (No. 2) 1985, s 3.

[50] (1985) 3 NSWLR 276.

[51] (1973) 129 CLR 460.

[52] (1996) 88 Crim R 232.

[53] At 250.

[54] New South Wales Dept. for Women (1996), 211.

[55] See Attorney General's Legislation and Policy Branch (Victoria), Report 2 (1997), 70–1.

(iii) Expert Evidence

Simon Bronitt has suggested a different approach. He argues that the best way of assisting and educating both the jury and the trial judge about the characteristic reactions of victims to traumatic events is through expert evidence of Rape Trauma Syndrome (RTS). In this way the myths and misconceptions surrounding delayed complaints would be effectively challenged.[56] Alternatively, he suggests that the many victimization studies which illustrate why victims are reluctant to report sexual abuse could be brought to the attention of the court through expert evidence.[57] This is easier said than done. There has been a marked reluctance to allow experts to give psychological or psychiatric evidence. As Lawton LJ stated in *Turner:* 'Jurors do not need psychiatrists to tell them how ordinary folk who are not suffering from any mental illness are likely to react to the stresses and strains of life'.[58] Although the *Turner* principle is now applied a little more flexibly, the basic approach to expert evidence is that it is permitted only where it is deemed to be strictly necessary: 'An expert's opinion is admissible to furnish the court with scientific information which is likely to be outside the experience and knowledge of a judge and jury'.[59] It may be argued that judges and jurors are not generally familiar with scientific findings about reactions to trauma, which are very often counter-intuitive. But scholars too have voiced misgivings about any attempt to admit RTS evidence to support the complainant's credibility in rape cases.[60] There is the fear, *inter alia,* that those who do not suffer the symptoms of RTS will be disbelieved. But this argument seems less compelling where RTS evidence is used only to demonstrate that victims are frequently too traumatized to report immediately. There is something to be said for prosecutors attempting to introduce such evidence for this limited purpose. The judicial response might be, however, that such evidence carries with it the danger that juries might, by the application of erroneous logic, conclude that if rape victims commonly fail to report rape immediately, then this complainant who failed to report immediately must be a rape victim. Since the judge would need to point this out, and it would be hard to control how this was done, it might be thought that the whole exercise was counterproductive.

[56] S. Bronitt 'The Rules of Recent Complaint', in Easteal (1998), 50–3. [57] ibid.

[58] [1975] QB 834, 841. A sentiment recently repeated in *Gilfoyle* [2001] 2 Cr App R 57. See now *R v DD (*2000) 2 SCR 275 (Canada).

[59] *Turner* [1975] QB 834, 841.

[60] The many concerns about the admission of RTS evidence include the fear that rape victims will be pressured to respond appropriately; that by medicalizing the impact of rape on victims, they may come to be regarded as sick or dysfunctional, see Raitt and Zeedyk (1997), 558–61; and that RTS 'simply empowers the "psy" professions to speak for women', see Smart (1989), 47.

(iv) Expansion of the Recent Complaint Exception

An entirely different approach to the recent complaint exception is to permit its use more freely. There is growing support for the view that the rule against prior consistent statements is in any case too broad. Very often such statements are an important part of the story and have much to say about the alleged victim's experience. The Law Commission has wisely proposed that evidence of prompt complaint should be admissible in a broad range of offences whenever 'the witness claims to be a person against whom an offence to which the proceedings relate has been committed' and subject to certain conditions, including that the complaint was made 'as soon as could reasonably be expected after the alleged conduct'. Furthermore, it proposes that such statements should be admissible not merely to support the victim's credibility, as is the case at present, but as evidence of the truth of the assertions which they contain.[61] This proposal is warmly to be welcomed. It is hard for juries or anyone to make the distinction between the two and yet the failure of a judge to direct the jury as to this distinction may, at present, lead to a successful appeal.[62]

The Law Commission's proposals may be less radical than law enacted in New South Wales. Under section 66 of the New South Wales Evidence Act 1995, first-hand hearsay may be admitted in criminal trials where the maker of the representation is available to testify, provided that 'when the representation was made, the occurrence of the asserted fact was fresh in the memory of the person who made the representation'. It follows that a report of a sexual assault made by a victim while it was fresh in her memory may be admissible as evidence of the facts stated, subject to the discretion of the judge. The 'fresh in her memory' test is apt to cover complaints made some time after the event itself, even years afterwards, whereas the Law Commission formula would apply only to those complaints that were made 'as soon as could be reasonably expected after the alleged conduct'. Under both formulae, where the temporal line is drawn will depend heavily upon the judge in each case.

Sexual History Evidence

It is well known that one of the most distasteful features of rape trials is the tactics employed by defence counsel to discredit the complainant. This has often taken the form of dredging up her past sexual history by cross-examining her about previous sexual relationships or suggesting that she has a 'bad reputation for chastity'.[63]

[61] Law Commission (1997), 154–8.

[62] See *Islam* [1998] Crim LR 575. However, in *McNeill* 162 JP 416, Apr. 1998, the conviction was upheld.

[63] See e.g. *Tissington* (1843) 1 Cox CC 48 and *Greatbanks* [1959] Crim LR 450.

In the nineteenth century, certain rules became established in England so far as such evidence was concerned.[64] Evidence that the complainant had had sexual intercourse with other men in the past was considered to be relevant to her credibility, that is, it tended to show that she was not a trustworthy witness.[65] Evidence that she was a prostitute or had a bad sexual reputation in the community[66] or had had previous sexual intercourse with the defendant himself[67] was considered to be relevant both to her credibility and to the issue of consent. In the twentieth century, these rules were still being applied and the judges had done little if anything to moderate them or to regulate the use of such evidence.

In 1975, the Heilbron Report noted that sexual history evidence was largely irrelevant and that its admission was not merely traumatic and humiliating for the victim but was also 'inimical to the fair trial of the essential issues'.[68] Certainly jury prejudice against the complainant appears to have been one of the consequences of its use. In the United States, Kalven and Zeisel found that rape ranked extremely low in percentage of waivers of jury trial and low in guilty pleas. This may partly be explained in terms of their further finding that in rape cases the jury 'often harshly scrutinises the female complainant particularly, it would seem, where she has a sexual history'.[69] They instanced one brutal case in which three men kidnapped a girl from the street at 1.30 p.m., took her to an apartment, and raped her. It transpired that the young unmarried girl had two illegitimate children. The judge described the jury's acquittal of the defendants in this case as a 'travesty of justice'.[70]

A further consequence of the use of sexual history evidence is that it deters victims from reporting the offence. It was also suggested in a recent Home Office Report that one reason why women who do report rape to the police subsequently withdraw their complaints is because they are 'deterred by the prospect of cross-examination in public on their previous sexual history'.[71]

The Heilbron Committee proposed that the use of sexual history evidence should be firmly regulated. It recommended the introduction of a statutory provision which would exclude evidence of the complainant's past sexual history with men other than the defendant. The judge would have discretion to admit such evidence in two situations only. First, if it concerned previous incidents of a strikingly similar nature to the incident in question and it would be unfair because of its relevance to exclude it. Secondly, if the

64 For a full discussion of these rules, see Temkin (1984).

65 See *Cockcroft* (1870) 11 Cox CC 410; *Holmes* (1871) LR 1 CCR 334 and *Riley* (1887) 18 QBD 481.

66 See *Tissington* and *Greatbanks*, above, and also *Barker* (1829) 3 C & P 589 and *Clarke* (1817) 2 Stark 241.

67 *Riley* (1887) 18 QBD 481; *Cockcroft* (1870) 11 Cox CC 410.

68 Heilbron Committee (1975), para. 89.

69 Kalven and Zeisel (1966), 249.

70 ibid. 251.

71 Home Office, *Report of the Interdepartmental Working Group* (1998), 68.

defence sought to adduce it in order to counter evidence by the prosecution as to the complainant's sexual history, for example, that she had been a virgin.[72] This proposal, however, was never implemented and section 2 of the Sexual Offences (Amendment) Act 1976, was passed instead.[73]

(a) The Operation of Section 2

Section 2 placed a general embargo on the use of sexual history evidence, but permitted the defence to apply, in the absence of the jury, for leave to include it. The judge was left to decide whether it would be unfair to the defendant to exclude such evidence and, if it was thought to be unfair, to accede to the defence's request.[74] On the face of it, this solution would appear to have been less than satisfactory. It was after all the judges who had failed to control the use of sexual history evidence and were thus largely responsible for the problem in the first place. The Heilbron Committee's proposal would have given the judges far less scope to decide when such evidence should be admitted. In Scotland, a not dissimilar scheme to section 2 was introduced by section 36 of the Law Reform (Miscellaneous Provisions) (Scotland) Act 1985. This legislation, whilst it excludes evidence of previous sexual behaviour, provides certain exceptions, including one which permits the judge to include such evidence where it would be 'in the interests of justice to do so'. The judges are thus effectively given *carte blanche*.[75]

Section 2 was soon given a broad interpretation. In the leading case of *Viola*, the Court of Appeal held that 'if the questions are relevant to an issue in the trial in the light of the way the case is being run, for instance relevant to the issue of consent as opposed merely to credit, they are likely to be admitted'.[76] Thus, all was left to depend on what view the trial judge took

[72] Heilbron Committee (1975), paras. 134–8.

[73] Section 2 provided as follows: '(1) If at a trial any person is for the time being charged with a rape offence to which he pleads not guilty, then, except with the leave of the judge, no evidence and no question in cross-examination shall be adduced or asked at the trial, by or on behalf of any defendant at the trial, about any sexual experience of a complainant with the person other than that defendant. (2) The judge shall not give leave in pursuance of the preceding subsection for any evidence or question except on an application made to him in the absence of the jury by or on behalf of a defendant; and on such an application the judge shall give leave if and only if he is satisfied that it would be unfair to that defendant to refuse to allow the evidence to be adduced or the question to be asked. (3) In subsection (1) of this section "complainant" means a woman upon whom, in a charge for a rape offence to which the trial in question relates, it is alleged that rape was committed, attempted or proposed. (4) Nothing in this section authorises evidence to be adduced or a question to be asked which cannot be adduced or asked apart from this section.' For a detailed analysis of the legislative history of s 2, see Temkin (1984).

[74] *Viola* [1982] 1 WLR 1138 at 1142. See also *Lawrence* [1977] Crim LR 492; *Mills* (1978) Cr App R 327. For a discussion of judicial interpretation of s 2, see Temkin (1984, 1993).

[75] The Scottish law was regarded as unsatisfactory: see Scottish Executive Justice Department, *Redressing the Balance: Cross-examination in Rape and Sexual Offence Trials* (2000). It has now been replaced by the Sexual Offences (Procedure and Evidence) (Scotland) Act 2002.

[76] (1982) 75 Cr App R125 at 130.

as to the relevance of the sexual history to an issue in the trial. But in a series of cases, the Court of Appeal also made it clear that it was prepared to oversee such decisions and to impose its own broad view of relevance.[77] Lord Bingham LCJ expressed his own attitude to this question in debate in the House of Lords: 'The simple truth is that on an issue of whether a complainant consented to sexual relations with the defendant, the fact that the complainant has behaved promiscuously on other occasions. . . . may well—I emphasise "may well"—be relevant'.[78] He also gave the hypothetical example of a woman who had sexual relations with four different men on four separate occasions the week before an alleged rape. If counsel wishes to question her about these incidents, he said, 'no rational person would think that those questions were irrelevant'.[79] But he offered no explanation as to why such evidence was relevant. That a woman has had consensual sexual relations with some or many men in the near or distant past is a reflection of current sexual mores[80] and can shed no light on whether she consented to this particular defendant on the occasion in question. Relevance is in the mind of the beholder and all too often it can be swayed by stereotypical assumptions, myth, and prejudice. As L'Heureux-Dubé J explained in the Supreme Court of Canada's decision in *Seaboyer*:

> Regardless of the definition used, the content of any relevancy decision will be filled by the particular judge's experience, common sense and/or logic . . . There are certain areas of enquiry where experience, common sense and logic are informed by stereotype and myth . . . This area of the law has been particularly prone to the utilisation of stereotype in the determination of relevance.[81]

Her words are amply illustrated by research into the operation of section 2. Adler studied rape trials at the Old Bailey in 1978–9.[82] Of the 85 per cent monitored, there were 50 cases, involving 80 defendants, where a not guilty plea was entered. Applications under section 2 were made on behalf of 32 (40%) of these defendants. Over 75 per cent of them were successful. In most cases, defence counsel argued that the sexual history evidence in question was relevant to the issue of consent. However, what they and the judges considered to be relevant to consent in some cases gives cause for concern. For example, evidence that a complainant under 17-years-old was not

[77] See Temkin (1993).

[78] Hansard vol. 595 No. 13, 15 Dec. 1998, col. 1236.

[79] Hansard vol. 597 No. 32, 8 Feb. 1999, col. 55. This contention was firmly rejected by the Minister of State at the Home Office: see Hansard, Standing Committee E, 24 June 1999, col. 211.

[80] The 1994 survey on sexual behaviour in Britain demonstrates that sexual relations before marriage are almost universally approved: A. M. Johnson *et al.*, *Sexual Attitudes and Lifestyles* (Oxford: Blackwell, 1994), 236. Latest figures show a rise since the 1994 survey in the number of sexual partners women have in a lifetime: see *The Times*, 31 Nov. 2001.

[81] *R v Seaboyer, Gayme* (1991) 83 DLR (4th) 193, 228.

[82] Adler (1982, 1987). See also Temkin (1984) for discussion of this research.

a virgin was admitted on this ground.[83] The judge stated that it was necessary to admit such evidence in case the jury thought that she was one.[84] Since young people of both sexes have commonly had sexual intercourse before the age of 17,[85] it was unnecessary and prejudicial to have permitted this fact to be specifically mentioned to the jury. Evidence that the complainant had previously had sexual intercourse with black men was admitted where the defendant was black and evidence of a sexual relationship with an older man was admitted where the defendants were older than the complainant.[86] In the former case, the judge explained his decision to allow the application as follows: 'I allowed the cross-examination not in order to show that she was promiscuous or a woman of loose or low morals . . . but it was simply to show, in fairness to these defendants, that it is manifest that [the complainant] was not averse to having sexual relations with coloured men.'[87]

It would seem to follow from this reasoning, with its undertone of prejudice, that evidence of past sexual relations with disabled men could be admitted where the defendant was disabled, with non-Caucasians where the defendant was non-Caucasian, and with men from any minority, ethnic or religious group if the defendant belonged to such a group, provided that in each case the complainant did not share this particular characteristic. Such understandings of relevance argue the case for tighter legislation.

Adler also found that defence counsel in many cases simply by-passed section 2 altogether and made reference to the complainant's sexual history without troubling to apply for leave of the court.[88] Research has revealed a similar practice in Scotland.[89]

Adler's findings were echoed in later studies. In her analysis of 31 rape trials which took place in 1993, Lees found that irrelevant questions about sexual history were frequently asked in cross-examination.[90] For example, one complainant was asked whether she was a single mother, another who was allegedly raped by a West Indian was asked: 'Do you often sleep with ethnics?' In a third case, the white complainant was questioned about the colour of the father of her baby and whether he was a Rastafarian.[91]

Interviews with a number of defence counsel in the Scottish study revealed that 'they would do what they could to suggest that a woman was of "easy virtue" precisely because they believed that juries were swayed by it'.[92] In a

83 See Adler (1987), 78 and 84.

84 See Temkin (1984), 974.

85 In a recent survey, 66 per cent of women between the ages of 16 and 19 considered that sex before marriage was not wrong at all: see L. Jarvis, K. Hinds, C. Bryson, and A. Park, *Women's Social Attitudes: 1983–1998* (London: The Women's Unit, Cabinet Office, 2000), 212.

86 Adler (1987) 79; Temkin (1984), 974–5.

87 Temkin (1984), 975. See further Z. Adler, 'The Relevance of Sexual History Evidence in Rape: Problems of Subjective Interpretation' [1985] Crim LR 769. For a different view, see D. Elliot, 'Rape Complainants' Sexual Experience with Third Parties' [1984] Crim LR 4.

88 Adler (1982), 673; (1987), 86–7.

89 Brown *et al.* (1992), 17.

90 Lees (1996), 134.

91 ibid. 134–7.

92 Brown *et al.* (1992), 73.

study which included interviews with ten highly experienced barristers who between them had prosecuted and defended in hundreds of rape trials, it was found that most of them would frequently apply to the judge to have sexual history admitted under section 2.[93] A leading QC invariably did so because, as he put it, 'if the complainant could be portrayed as a "slut" this was highly likely to secure an acquittal'.[94] Barristers were often put under pressure by the defendant himself to bring out the woman's past sexual history in court. As one barrister explained: 'Defendants often want you to dig up every piece of smut there is about the complainant'.[95] The barristers were all agreed that trial judges carefully scrutinized applications under section 2 but none seemed to have encountered too much difficulty in persuading the judge to admit the evidence. The QC, who was himself licensed to try rape cases, explained: 'A judge has to be indulgent if the defence can set up half a good reason why they need to go into the sexual history'.[96]

In other jurisdictions, legislation similar to section 2, in that it gives full scope to the judge to determine when sexual history evidence should be admitted, has also been passed without much success. This is true of Australia, where in all states, save New South Wales, legislation is of this kind. Henning and Bronitt have pointed out that 'the principal structural flaw of these legislative schemes is their failure to define the key concepts for determining admissibility' leaving the judges free rein to apply their 'common sense assumptions'.[97] In Victoria, a study by the Rape Law Reform Evaluation Project showed that sexual experience evidence is still admitted in a significant number of committal and trial proceedings.[98] Similarly, the South Australian legislation was considered by many to have failed.[99] In Canada, such legislation, passed in 1975 and deemed to be ineffective, was repealed in favour of a much stricter statutory regime, but there has been a reversion to a scheme which allows the judge to determine the relevance of the evidence in each case, taking into account a series of factors in arriving at a decision.[100]

(b) The Youth Justice and Criminal Evidence Act 1999

Despite growing concerns about the doubtful efficacy of section 2, the CLRC in 1984 expressed its satisfaction with the existing law[101] on the basis

[93] Temkin (Journal of Law and Society, 2000) 234. [94] ibid. [95] ibid.

[96] ibid. 235. [97] In Easteal (1998), 85.

[98] See Attorney General's Legislation and Policy Branch (1997), 127.

[99] See e.g. Woods (1981), 31.

[100] Criminal Law Amendment Act, SC 1975 c C–93 revised s 142 of the Canadian Criminal Code. s 142 in its revised form forbade the use of sexual history evidence save where the judge was satisfied that 'to exclude it would prevent the making of a just determination of an issue of fact . . . including the credibility of the complainant'. The 1975 provision was replaced in 1982 by s 276 of the Canadian Criminal Code. In 1992 a new s 276 was substituted for the old one. On the limited efficacy of the 1992 provisions, see Meredith *et al* (1997).

[101] CLRC (1984), paras. 2.86–2.90.

of advice it had received from some Old Bailey judges. However, this did not put a stop to the debate or to growing dissatisfaction with the section 2 regime.[102] The turning-point came in 1998 with the publication of *Speaking Up for Justice,* the Report of a Working Group set up by the Home Office.[103] This Report concluded that there was 'overwhelming evidence that the present practice in the courts is unsatisfactory and that the existing law is not achieving its purpose'.[104] It proposed that the law be changed.[105] By the end of the same year, the Labour Government responded by introducing the Youth Justice and Criminal Evidence Bill which contained a new scheme to control sexual history evidence far more rigorously. The proposed scheme was slightly modified to take into account amendments introduced in the House of Lords. Sections 41 to 43 of the Youth Justice and Criminal Evidence Act (YJCEA) 1999 now provide as follows:

41 Restriction on evidence or questions about complainant's sexual history

(1) If at a trial a person is charged with a sexual offence, then, except with the leave of the court—

(a) no evidence may be adduced, and
(b) no question may be asked in cross-examination, by or on behalf of any accused at the trial, about any sexual behaviour of the complainant.

(2) The court may give leave in relation to any evidence or question only on an application made by or on behalf of an accused, and may not give such leave unless it is satisfied—

(a) that subsections (3) or (5) applies, and
(b) that a refusal of leave might have the result of rendering unsafe a conclusion of the jury or (as the case may be) the court on any relevant issue in the case.

(3) This subsection applies if the evidence or question relates to a relevant issue in the case and either—

(a) that the issue is not an issue of consent; or
(b) it is an issue of consent and the sexual behaviour of the complainant to which the evidence or question relates is alleged to have taken place at or about the same time as the event which is the subject matter of the charge against the accused; or
(c) it is an issue of consent and the sexual behaviour of the complainant to which the evidence or question relates is alleged to have been, in any respect, so similar—
    (i) to any sexual behaviour of the complainant which (according to evidence adduced or to be adduced by or on behalf of the accused) took place as part of the event which is the subject matter of the charge against the accused, or

[102] See e.g. Lees (1996), 251; A. McColgan, 'Common Law and the Relevance of Sexual History Evidence' (1996) 16 Oxford Journal of Legal Studies 275.

[103] Home Office, *Report of the Interdepartmental Working Group* (1998).

[104] ibid., para. 9.64.

[105] ibid., para. 9.70.

(ii) to any other sexual behaviour of the complainant which (according to such evidence) took place at or about the same time as that event, that the similarity cannot reasonably be explained as a coincidence.

(4) For the purposes of subsection (3) no evidence or question shall be regarded as relating to a relevant issue in the case if it appears to the court to be reasonable to assume that the purpose (or main purpose) for which it would be adduced or asked is to establish or elicit material for impugning the credibility of the complainant as a witness.

(5) This subsection applies if the evidence or question—

(a) relates to any evidence adduced by the prosecution about any sexual behaviour of the complainant; and

(b) in the opinion of the court, would go no further than is necessary to enable the evidence adduced by the prosecution to be rebutted or explained by or on behalf of the accused.

(6) For the purposes of subsections (3) and (5) the evidence or question must relate to a specific instance (or specific instances) of alleged sexual behaviour on the part of the complainant (and accordingly nothing in those subsections is capable of applying in relation to the evidence or question to the extent that it does not so relate).

(7) Where this section applies in relation to a trial by virtue of the fact that one or more of a number of persons charged in the proceedings is or are charged with a sexual offence—

(a) it shall cease to apply in relation to the trial if the prosecutor decides not to proceed with the case against that person or those persons in respect of that charge; but

(b) it shall not cease to do so in the event of that person or those persons pleading guilty to, or being convicted of, that charge.

(8) Nothing in this section authorises any evidence to be adduced or any question to be asked which cannot be adduced or asked apart from this section.

42 Interpretation and application of section 41

(1) In section 41—

(a) 'relevant issue in the case' means any issue falling to be proved by the prosecution or defence in the trial of the accused;

(b) 'issue of consent' means any issue whether the complainant in fact consented to the conduct constituting the offence with which the accused is charged (and accordingly does not include any issue as to the belief of the accused that the complainant so consented);

(c) 'sexual behaviour' means any sexual behaviour or other sexual experience, whether or not involving any accused or other person, but excluding (except in section 41(3)(c)(i) and (5)(a) anything alleged to have taken place as part of the event which is the subject matter of the charge against the accused; and

(d) subject to any order made under subsection (2), 'sexual offence' shall be construed in accordance with section 62.

43 Procedure on applications under section 41

(1) An application for leave shall be heard in private and in the absence of the complainant.

In this section 'leave' means leave under section 41.

(2) Where such an application has been determined, the court must state in open court (but in the absence of the jury, if there is one)—

(a) its reasons for giving, or refusing, leave, and

(b) if it gives leave, the extent to which evidence may be adduced or questions asked in pursuance of the leave,

and, if it is a magistrates' court, must cause those matters to be entered in the register of its proceedings.

(3) Rules of court may make provision—

(a) requiring applications for leave to specify, in relation to each item of evidence or question to which they relate, particulars of the grounds on which it is asserted that leave should be given by virtue of subsections (3) or (5) of section 41;

(b) enabling the court to request a party to the proceedings to provide the court with information which it considers would assist it in determining an application for leave;

(c) for the manner in which confidential or sensitive information is to be treated in connection with such an application, and in particular as to its being disclosed to, or withheld from, parties to the proceedings.

The above provisions offer the advantage of a more structured approach to decision-making.[106] But they have been criticized by women's groups[107] and the question remains whether they have been drawn too widely to make a significant difference to the operation of the law in this area. There must also be some concern that zealous defence counsel will succeed in undermining the legislation by frequent challenges under Article 6 of the ECHR which provides the right to a fair trial and specifically under Article 6(3)(d) which provides a right to examine or have examined witnesses.[108] In seeking to determine whether the provisions favour defendants too generously or, to the contrary, are so restrictive that they prevent the court from hearing relevant evidence,[109] it is instructive to compare them with similar legislation introduced elsewhere, including the former Canadian legislation which has now been repealed on constitutional grounds.

[106] See Home Office, *Report of the Interdepartmental Working Group* (1998).

[107] See e.g. R. Hall and L. Longstaff, 'Sexism Still Part of New Rape Law', *The Times,* 13 July 1999.

[108] See discussion below under the heading 'Sexual History Evidence and Human Rights'.

[109] For this view, see Birch (2000), 249. See also D. Birch, 'Rethinking Sexual History Evidence: Proposals for Fairer Trials' [2002] Crim LR 531.

(c) Sexual History Evidence in Michigan, New South Wales, and Canada

Many American statutes set out a general rule excluding sexual history evidence and designate several specific and circumscribed exceptions to it.[110] The Michigan Criminal Sexual Conduct Act is a radical example of this type of legislation in that it includes only two narrowly drawn exceptions to the rule of exclusion. Section 520j provides as follows:

(1) Evidence of specific instances of the victim's sexual conduct, opinion evidence of the victim's sexual conduct, and reputation evidence of the victim's sexual conduct shall not be admitted under sections 520b to 520g unless and only to the extent that the judge finds that the following proposed evidence is material to a fact at issue in the case and that its inflammatory or prejudicial nature does not outweigh its probative value:
(*a*) Evidence of the victim's past sexual conduct with the actor.
(*b*) Evidence of specific instances of sexual activity showing the source or origin of semen, pregnancy, or disease.

The Michigan approach is the one most favoured in the United States. Twenty-five states have adopted it, in the sense that they set out a rule of exclusion with narrow exceptions to it so that judicial discretion is excluded. However, US rape-shield laws need to be interpreted against the backdrop of the US Constitution and, in particular, the Sixth Amendment, which guarantees the right to confront and cross-examine witnesses. It has been interpreted to permit evidence in certain limited situations which are not included in the rape-shield legislation itself.[111]

In New South Wales, section 409B(3) of the Crimes Act 1900, takes a similar approach to the Michigan legislation but with the provision of more exceptions to the exclusionary rule. It reads:

In prescribed sexual offence proceedings, evidence which discloses or implies that the complainant has or may have had sexual experience or a lack of sexual experience or has or may have taken part or not taken part in any sexual activity is inadmissible except—
(*a*) where it is evidence—
  (i) of sexual experience or a lack of sexual experience of, or sexual activity or a lack of sexual activity taken part in by, the complainant at or about the time of the commission of the alleged prescribed sexual offence; and
  (ii) of events which are alleged to form part of a connected set of circumstances in which the alleged prescribed sexual offence was committed;
(*b*) Where it is evidence relating to a relationship which was existing or recent at the time of the commission of the alleged prescribed sexual offence, being a relationship between the accused person and the complainant;

[110] See Berger (1977).

[111] See e.g. *People v Wilhelm* (1991) 190 Mich App 574.

(*c*) where
(i) the accused person is alleged to have had sexual intercourse, as defined in section 61A(1), with the complainant and the accused person does not concede the sexual intercourse so alleged; and
(ii) it is evidence relevant to whether the presence of semen, pregnancy, disease or injury is attributable to the sexual intercourse alleged to have been had by the accused person;
(*d*) where it is evidence relevant to whether—
(i) at the time of the commission of the alleged prescribed sexual offence, there was present in the complainant a disease which, at any relevant time, was absent in the accused person; or
(ii) at any relevant time, there was absent in the complainant a disease which, at the time of the commission of the alleged prescribed sexual offence, was present in the accused person;
(*e*) where it is evidence relevant to whether the allegation that the prescribed sexual offence was committed by the accused person was first made following a realisation or discovery of the presence of pregnancy or disease in the complainant (being a realisation or discovery which took place after the commission of the alleged prescribed sexual offence); or
(*f*) where it is evidence given by the complainant in cross-examination by or on behalf of the accused person, being evidence given in answer to a question which may, pursuant to subsection (5), be asked, and its probative value outweighs any distress, humiliation or embarrassment which the complainant might suffer as a result of its admission.

Section 246.6 of the Canadian Criminal Code as enacted in 1982 and repealed in 1992 stated:

(1) In proceedings in respect of an offence under section 246.1, 246.2 or 246.3, no evidence shall be adduced by or on behalf of the accused concerning the sexual activity of the complainant with any person other than the accused unless
(*a*) it is evidence that rebuts evidence of the complainant's sexual activity or absence thereof that was previously adduced by the prosecution;
(*b*) it is evidence of specific instances of the complainant's sexual activity tending to establish the identity of the person who had sexual contact with the complainant on the occasion set out in the charge; or
(*c*) it is evidence of sexual activity that took place on the same occasion as the sexual activity that forms the subject matter of the charge, where that evidence relates to the consent that the accused alleges he believed was given by the complainant.

The main features of the above regimes will now be examined and compared with the YJCEA. It will be seen that, while the four provisions have aspects in common, they are also different in ways that merit attention.

(i) The Rule of Exclusion

Under each of the four regimes, there is a rule forbidding the use of sexual history evidence. Each allows certain exceptions to this rule. There are some critical differences between the rule of exclusion in each place.

APPLICATION TO PROSECUTION AS WELL AS TO DEFENCE

The exclusionary rule in section 41(1) of the YJCEA expressly applies only to defence evidence. The same was true of the Canadian rule. Thus, the prosecution is free to adduce sexual history evidence as it pleases if it considers it expedient to do so. The Michigan legislation has been interpreted in this way as well so that there is nothing to prevent the complainant from testifying to lack of previous sexual experience.[112] By contrast, the rule of exclusion in New South Wales applies equally to the prosecution. The argument in favour of such a course is that prosecuting as well as defending counsel may seek to introduce such evidence where it is not strictly necessary and where it might be damaging to the complainant to do so. Indeed, Scottish research has demonstrated that the prosecution not infrequently adduces sexual history evidence.[113]

PREVIOUS SEXUAL BEHAVIOUR WITH THE DEFENDANT

Under the YJCEA, evidence of previous sexual relations with the accused is as much excluded as evidence relating to sexual relations with a third party. The same is true in Michigan and New South Wales. In all three cases, however, as will appear below, defending counsel may apply for leave to introduce such evidence, which may be permitted in certain circumstances. The Canadian rule, however, did not apply to evidence concerning previous or subsequent sexual relations with the defendant. This meant that such evidence might be adduced freely by the defence without seeking the leave of the court. It cannot be assumed, however, that sexual history evidence of this kind will necessarily be relevant. The evidence may, for example, relate to a single incident which took place many years prior to the event in question. It seems preferable to apply the embargo to the accused as well.

EVIDENCE OF SEXUAL REPUTATION

This is evidence of the general sexual reputation of the complainant rather than of sexual conduct with particular individuals. Under section 41(1)(b) of the YJCEA, the rule of exclusion applies only to sexual behaviour. There is no express reference to evidence relating to sexual reputation nor is there any suggestion in the *Explanatory Notes*[114] that sexual behaviour encompasses sexual reputation. There is, however, a clear indication that it was intended to exclude it. Under section 41(6), reputation evidence would not appear to be admissible under the exceptions to the rule of exclusion since it is expressly provided that the evidence of sexual behaviour must relate to specific instances of conduct. If it is not admissible under the exceptions to the rule of exclusion, it must *a fortiori* follow that it is not admissible where

[112] *People v Mooney* 216 Mich App 367 (1996).

[113] Chambers and Millar (1986), 138–9.

[114] *Explanatory Notes*, YJCEA 1999.

those exceptions do not apply. However, it would have been preferable for this to be spelt out clearly in section 41(1)(b).

In Michigan, by contrast, evidence of sexual reputation is expressly subject to the general rule of exclusion but according to the statute, may be admitted if it comes within the two exceptions to the rule. In New South Wales, under section 409B(2), such evidence is expressly banned in all circumstances.

The Canadian provisions appear once again to have been weaker than those of the other three jurisdictions. In Canada, such evidence did not seem to be subject to the general rule of exclusion, but was dealt with separately under section 246.7, which merely provided that evidence of sexual reputation could never be adduced 'for the purpose of challenging or supporting the credibility of the complainant'. This suggested that evidence of sexual reputation was freely admissible where it was relevant to an issue in the case. Since what is relevant to the issue of consent may be broadly interpreted by some judges and defence counsel, this section left a large loophole in the law.

EVIDENCE OF SEXUAL BEHAVIOUR AND EXPERIENCE

In New South Wales, the rule of exclusion applies to sexual experience and the lack of it and to sexual activity and the lack of it. The purpose of specifically excluding evidence of sexual experience was to 'cover the suggestion that the complainant was promiscuous'.[115] Under the YJCEA, the rule of exclusion is limited to sexual behaviour. The *Explanatory Notes* assume that sexual behaviour includes sexual experience and also includes what it describes as 'secondary evidence of sexual behaviour such as abortions'.[116] It should in that case also exclude questions concerning the colour of the complainant's baby, whether she has children by different men, or is a single parent.

(a) Previous 'false' complaints. The view expressed in the Explanatory Notes to the YJCEA is 'that evidence that does no more than show that the complainant has a history of making unproved complaints of sexual offences' would not be treated as evidence of sexual behaviour and would not therefore be excluded.[117] As Lord Williams of Mostyn, Minister of State at the Home Office, explained: 'A history of false complaints or false complaints about sexual behaviour is admissible because it goes to credibility. But it is not evidence about sexual behaviour: it is about untruthful conduct on prior occasions. There is a very clear difference.'[118] This view has now been adopted by the Court of Appeal in *R v T*.[119] Yet such evidence might very well imply that the complainant has had consensual sexual intercourse and then falsely claimed that it was rape. As such this would appear to be

[115] Woods (1981), 34.
[116] *Explanatory Notes*, para. 145.
[117] ibid., para. 150.
[118] Hansard vol. 598, 8 Mar. 1999, col. 34.
[119] [2002] 1 All ER 683.

an example of 'secondary evidence' and hence subject to the rule of exclusion.[120]

It is very easy to allege that the complainant is a liar who has made false complaints of rape in the past. Indeed, this practice is not at all unknown amongst rape defendants. Women who have been raped and otherwise sexually abused may very well have had this experience more than once. Women frequently withdraw complaints of rape and rape prosecutions frequently fail. Neither outcome means that the allegations were false. In Michigan, it has been held that a defendant may cross-examine the complainant regarding prior false accusations of a similar nature because the basis for doing so is not that she was unchaste but that she lied about similar charges in the past.[121] However, the Michigan courts have made it clear that before the admission of such evidence will even be considered, they require concrete evidence that any prior accusation was indeed false and the relevance of the evidence will need to be demonstrated.[122] This approach clearly has much to commend it. It is to be preferred to that of the Court of Appeal in *R v T* which, whilst requiring that the defence should have a proper evidential basis for asserting that false allegations had been made in the past, seemed content that the judge should simply seek assurances from the defence that this was the case. There would appear to be no obligation on the judge to investigate further. The Court merely commented that it would be professionally improper for those representing the defendant to seek to elicit evidence about the complainant's past sexual behaviour under the guise of previous false complaints. This leaves open the question of what would suffice to satisfy the evidential burden and how far counsel should go in making enquiries into this matter. Would firm assurances by the accused that the complainant has lied in the past suffice? If not, what further evidence is required?

(b) Previous sexual abuse. In New South Wales, one contentious issue has been whether or not the rule of exclusion operates to exclude evidence of previous sexual abuse of a child. It was suggested in *R v PJE*[123] that it excluded only evidence of consensual sexual experience. But there is nothing in the statute to suggest that the words 'sexual experience' should be interpreted in this way. The YJCEA uses the term 'sexual behaviour' rather

120 In NSW, in a series of cases, it has been held that the rule of exclusion would exclude evidence of previous false complaints: see e.g. *R v M* (1993) 67 A Crim R 549. However, these cases have all arisen where the defendant has alleged that no sexual relations took place with the complainant. Under the YJCEA such evidence would be admissible in these circumstances under s 41(3)(a).

121 *People v Mikula* (1978) 84 Mich App 108.

122 *People v Williams* (1991) 191 Mich App 269; *People v Garvi* (1986) 148 Mich App 565. For a similar approach by the Pennsylvania Superior Court see *Commonwealth v Boyles* 595 A 2d 1180 (1991).

123 Unreported, CCA NSW, 9 Oct. 1995.

than sexual experience. It is not clear whether this term would cover an incident in which a child has been the passive object of abuse. Where a child has been forced to perform an active role, then questions or evidence about this would seem clearly to be prohibited. A sensible reading of the section would cover both situations and the *Explanatory Notes*, as mentioned above, clearly envisage that behaviour includes experience.[124] This would not, of course, preclude such evidence being adduced under one of the exceptions to the rule.[125]

(ii) Exceptions to the Rule of Exclusion

There are four express exceptions to the rule of exclusion under the YJCEA. These are wide enough to encompass a range of behaviour and are broader than the range of exceptions in the other three jurisdictions.

EVIDENCE RELATING TO A RELEVANT ISSUE IN THE CASE WHICH IS NOT AN ISSUE OF CONSENT

The first exception to the rule of exclusion contained in section 41(3)(a) of the YJCEA will permit evidence of sexual behaviour where it relates to an issue which is not an issue of consent. This will permit sexual history evidence in a number of different situations.

(a) Belief in consent. Section 42(1)(b) expressly provides that belief in consent is not 'an issue of consent'. This means that subject to section 41(4) and (6), the defence is free to adduce any evidence of past sexual behaviour irrespective of the time or circumstances in which it took place if it has a bearing on his honest belief in consent. The other three jurisdictions do not have an exception of this breadth. In New South Wales, evidence to support belief in consent is permitted only where it is based on conduct that took place at or about the same time as the conduct which is the subject-matter of the charge. The Canadian provision was similar. The Michigan exceptions do not permit evidence on this ground at all.

Strong objection to this exception has been taken by women's groups who have contended that it will create a substantial loophole in the law.[126] The scope of this exception would be reduced if the substantive law were changed so that a defendant who claimed belief in consent could be acquitted only in certain limited circumstances[127] or if his belief in consent had to be reasonable as well as honest.

Unlike the Canadian and NSW legislation, the YJCEA does not contain an express exception which permits evidence of past sexual conduct with the accused himself. However, he will be able to argue that such evidence is

124 See *Explanatory Notes*, para. 145.
125 See below under the heading 'Sexual Offences Where Consent is not the Issue'.
126 R. Hall and L. Longstaff, 'Sexism Still Part of New Rape Law', *The Times*, 13 July 1999.
127 See Ch. 2 under the heading 'The SOR's Proposals', pp. 130–1.

admissible to show honest belief in consent. He should be able successfully to put forward this argument even if a requirement of reasonableness were imported into the law, unless, for example, the relationship was casual and far back in time.[128]

(*b*) *Evidence relating to identity.* Where the accused alleges that he did not have sexual intercourse with the complainant at all, section 41(3)(a) of the YJCEA will permit him to adduce any evidence to support this contention since this is evidence which does not relate to the issue of consent. The Canadian provision was similar. Both are wider than equivalent provisions in NSW and Michigan in so far as they permit any such evidence. The Michigan provision permits only evidence of specific instances of sexual activity showing the source or origin of semen, pregnancy, or disease whilst the New South Wales provision additionally permits evidence of injury.

Thus, under all four schemes, the defence will be able to argue, for example, that the semen found on the complainant's body, her pregnancy, or the disease she has contracted are attributable to someone else. It is clearly fair that he should be able to adduce such evidence to dissociate himself from the event in question. Exceptions of this kind do not entitle the accused to 'probe generally into the sexual behaviour of the complainant'.[129] As Berger has commented: 'In contrast to the use of these facts [i.e. pregnancy, sexual disease etc.] to evince consent or lack of veracity, here the evidence . . . does not exploit sexist stereotypes of women and accordingly is less innately offensive'.[130]

Section 41(3)(a) would apply even where there is no evidence of semen, injury, pregnancy, or disease, provided that the evidence tends to establish the identity of the person who did have sexual contact with the complainant on the occasion in question. It seems fair that in such circumstances the defendant should nevertheless be able to provide evidence of specific instances of sexual activity in order to show that someone else and not he was the man responsible.

(*c*) *Motive to lie.* Under section 41(3)(a), the court may give leave to admit evidence of sexual behaviour where it 'relates to a relevant issue in the case which is not an issue of consent'. Under section 42(1)(a), '"relevant issue in the case" means any issue *falling to be proved* by the prosecution or defence in the trial of the accused' (emphasis added). This formula seems to reflect that which was used in *Viola* in which it was said that evidence of sexual history could be admitted if it was 'relevant to an issue in the trial *in the light of the way the case is being run*'.[131] It is potentially capable of a broad

[128] But under the SOR's proposals he would not be able to do so if, for example, he was reckless as to consent or drunk since in those circumstances the honest belief defence would not apply: see Ch. 2 under the heading 'The SOR's Proposals'.

[129] Woods (1981), 37.

[130] Berger (1977), 58.

[131] (1982) Cr App R 125 at 130; emphasis added.

construction. Thus, if the complainant's motivation became an issue in the case, it would, arguably, be possible to question her about previous sexual behaviour if this were relevant to it. It remains to be seen whether the courts will accept such an argument. Neither the Canadian nor the Michigan exceptions would permit such evidence, although it is permitted in limited circumstances in New South Wales.[132] In the United States, it has been held in numerous cases that such evidence is admissible under the Sixth Amendment.[133]

(d) Sexual offences where consent is not the issue. Unlike section 2 of the SOAA 1976, which applied only to rape, the sexual history provisions of the YJCEA extend to a range of sexual offences, including those against children below the age of consent. However, the new legislation appears to give with one hand and take away with the other. Evidence of sexual behaviour which is not relevant to the issue of consent will be admissible. This means that, in prosecutions for unlawful sexual intercourse, previous sexual behaviour evidence, including evidence of previous sexual abuse, is prima-facie admissible and may be used to undermine the complainant's case. The accused might argue, for example, that he did not have sexual intercourse with the girl and that her evidence and sexual knowledge were based on certain specific relationships she had had with other men. Great care is clearly required before such evidence is admitted. In Michigan, in *People v Morse*,[134] the defendant sought to prove that the victims had been sexually abused in the past by their mother's partner who had pleaded guilty to charges brought against him. The Court of Appeals held that under the Sixth Amendment such evidence would not be precluded if it were to show that the victim's inappropriate sexual knowledge had not been learnt from him and that they had a motive to lie. But such evidence could be admitted only where an in camera hearing determined that there had been a conviction of criminal sexual conduct involving the children and that the facts were sufficiently similar to be relevant.[135]

EVIDENCE OF SEXUAL BEHAVIOUR AT OR ABOUT THE SAME TIME AS THE SEXUAL ACTIVITY IN QUESTION

Under section 41(3)(b) of the YJCEA, where the issue is consent, evidence of sexual behaviour may be admitted if it occurred at or about the same time

[132] Under s 409B(3)(e) but this exception does not appear to be much used. Lord Hope in *R v A* [2001] 3 All ER 1, 27 considered that s 41(3)(a) was a gateway to admitting such evidence. See also *R v T* above. But see *R v Mokrecovas* [2002] 1 Cr App R 226.

[133] See e.g. *Daniels v State* 767 P 2d 1163 (Alaska CA 1989). *Castro v State* 591 So 2d 1076 (Florida DCA 1991).

[134] (1998) 231 Mich App 424.

[135] See also the decision of the Pennsylvania Superior Court in *Commonwealth v Wall* 606 A 2d 449 in which evidence of previous sexual abuse of the complainant was admitted under the Sixth Amendment despite Pennsylvania's rape-shield law, where there was a conviction of a third party for this abuse and the evidence was more probative than prejudicial.

as the sexual activity which is the subject-matter of the charge. There are several criticisms that might be made of this exception.

First, there may be some difficulty in distinguishing between sexual behaviour which took place *at the same time* as the event which is the subject-matter of the charge and sexual behaviour which is *part of the event* which is the subject-matter of the charge. Under section 42(1)(c), if the behaviour is part of the event, then it may be freely mentioned and is not subject to any restriction. If, on the other hand, it took place at the same time as the event, it is banned unless it is permitted under section 41(3)(b).

Secondly, the exception is arguably too broad. The Canadian law contained a similar but much narrower provision. It applied only where the defendant alleged *belief* in consent on the basis of the sexual conduct of the complainant on the same occasion. No such restriction applies under the YJCEA.

The New South Wales legislation also provides a similar but narrower exception. It permits evidence of contemporaneous sexual behaviour only where it forms part of a set of circumstances *connected* to the sexual behaviour which is the subject-matter of the charge. By contrast, under the YJCEA, it will be possible for evidence of sexual acts which are entirely unconnected to the alleged rape to be admitted in court provided that they occurred at or about the same time. According to the *Explanatory Notes*, the phrase 'at or about the same time' is not expected to be interpreted to mean more than 24 hours before or after the alleged rape.[136] Thus, if the complainant had sexual intercourse with her partner within 24 hours of the rape, this evidence could be admitted. The reason for doing so would be based on a mythical assumption that if a woman has genuinely been raped she would not act in this way.[137] Indeed, in the NSW case of *Morgan*,[138] it was stated that such behaviour would be 'contrary to human experience'. There is, however, no substance to this myth. There are many different reactions to trauma. The complainant may be seeking in this way to extinguish the rape experience. Moreover, one consequence of rape is that a woman's partner may react with anger and jealousy[139] and sexual intercourse may take place at his insistence or to provide reassurance to both parties of the continuing strength of their relationship. Such evidence is irrelevant to the issue of consent and, because of the myth, highly damaging to the complainant.

Thirdly, there is a clear danger that 'at or about the same time' could be interpreted more widely than 24 hours before or after the alleged rape. Certainly, this has been the experience in New South Wales where sexual

[136] *Explanatory Notes* (1999), 25. Evidence of sexual conduct admitted in *Viola* [1982] WLR 1138 would thus have been able to be admitted under this exception.

[137] This myth seems to have had some influence in *Viola*.

[138] (1993) 30 NSWLR 543 at 550.

[139] See e.g. D. Orr, 'The Real Meaning of Rape', *The Independent*, 19 May 1999.

intercourse between the complainant and the defendant two weeks before the alleged incident was admitted under the equivalent exception.[140] However, in *R v A*,[141] the House of Lords declined to give the phrase a broad interpretation. Indeed, Lord Steyn stated that it could not be interpreted to extend the temporal restriction to days, weeks, or months.

It is noteworthy that in Michigan, where there is no exception of this kind, it was held that the refusal to permit evidence of sexual behaviour close in time to the alleged events did not violate the defendant's right to confrontation.[142]

SIMILAR BEHAVIOUR

The YJCEA contains a third exception to the rule of exclusion which the other three legislative schemes eschewed. It was not part of the original Bill but was added in response to criticism in the House of Lords by Baroness Mallalieu. She provided the example of a woman with a Romeo and Juliet fantasy who is in the habit of inviting men to re-enact the balcony scene by climbing into her bedroom from the balcony. If, after such an episode, she alleges rape, the defence should, it was argued, be able to adduce evidence of all the other similar occasions when her consent was freely given.[143] This less than telling scenario, which was described by Lord Lester as 'extreme, hypothetical and curious',[144] nevertheless persuaded the government to introduce a further exception to accommodate it.

In order for previous sexual behaviour to be admitted under section 41(3)(c), the previous behaviour of the complainant must be 'so similar . . . that the similarity cannot reasonably be explained as a coincidence'. This wording seems to owe its inspiration to *DPP v Boardman*,[145] which dealt with the circumstances in which the previous misconduct of the defendant could be admitted in a criminal trial under the similar fact doctrine. It was held that the test was whether there was such a striking similarity between the accused's alleged conduct and his previous conduct that it would be an affront to common sense to assert that the similarity was explicable on the basis of coincidence. Translated into the context of sexual history evidence, this approach appears to require that the evidence of past sexual acts which took place with the complainant's consent, are so similar to her behaviour during the event in question, that her behaviour cannot reasonably be explained otherwise than that she consented on this occasion as well.

[140] *McGarvey* (1987) 10 NSWLR 632. [141] [2001] 1 All ER 1 at 15.

[142] In *People v Wilhelm* (1991) 476 NW 2d 753, the defendant sought unsuccessfully to have evidence admitted that, earlier on in the same evening as the alleged rape, he had seen the complainant in a bar displaying her breasts and allowing others to touch them.

[143] Hansard vol. 597 (2) Feb. 1999, col. 45. [144] ibid., col. 47.

[145] [1974] 3 All ER 887.

The Government intended that this should be a narrow exception.[146] Indeed, it is hard to conceive of any cases that will fall within it. The Romeo and Juliet case makes the point. It cannot be argued that, just because the complainant consented to men in the past who came to her via the balcony, there is no reasonable explanation other than that she consented to the accused on the occasion in question when he arrived by the same route. The issue is one of consent, which must be given on each occasion to each man. The complainant may like to indulge her Romeo and Juliet fantasy, but, equally, she may change her mind if, on further perusal, the accused looked more like fat old Friar Laurence than Romeo. This formula which might fit well where previous misconduct of the accused is concerned—four previous brides of the accused found dead in the bath do suggest that the presence of a fifth dead bride in his bath is scarcely likely to be a coincidence—can rarely, if ever, be applicable in the context of consent. Consent is to a person not to a circumstance. Had the exception simply insisted upon a striking similarity between the complainant's conduct on previous occasions and her conduct on the occasion in question, as Heilbron recommended, it would have opened the door more readily to the admission of past sexual history.

But the narrowness of the exception under section 41(3)(c) is to be applauded since it is hard to justify an exception based on similarity. The idea was rejected in New South Wales where it was pointed out that there would be difficulties in determining when a similarity was sufficiently striking:

> Just what elements would make one act of sexual intercourse strikingly similar to another? The essential act does, after all, have a fairly simple and readily identifiable characteristic—how much further would the strikingly have to go? Would the pick up point have to be a wine bar or would a coffee shop be sufficiently similar? Would a mini-skirt/wine bar/missionary position combination be sufficiently strikingly similar to a pair of jeans/coffee shop/unorthodox position combination? What about the afternoon episode on the one hand with the cocktail hour or after theatre episode on the other? The possible variables are clearly so countless as to require no further elaboration of this point.[147]

But even if such an exception were drawn very narrowly so as to require a *modus operandi* which was quite unique, other objections to it might be raised. Arguably, it draws unjustifiable and irrational distinctions between some complainants and defendants and others. Or as Roger Court trenchantly put it:

> Why should the female who confines her sexual activities to, say, 7.45 on Thursday nights in thongs, be at a greater risk in this connection than one who goes at it

[146] Hansard, Standing Committee E, 24 June 1999, col. 224. But see discussion of *R v A* below, under the heading 'Sexual History Evidence and Human Rights'.

[147] New South Wales Dept. of Attorney General, *Report on Rape and Various Other Sexual Offences* (1977), 29.

24 hours a day in all sorts of places and in all sorts of attire? Or, vice versa, why should the male who succumbs to the seduction of the Thursday night 7.45 in thongs be at an advantage to the victim of the 24 hours a day seductress?[148]

That an exception based on past similar conduct has not been adopted more widely is of little surprise. Its basis is questionable and it provides an open invitation to an interpretation which could fundamentally undermine the very purpose of this type of legislation.

EVIDENCE TO REBUT PROSECUTION EVIDENCE

It has been noted above that the YJCEA does not prevent the prosecution from adducing sexual history evidence. Section 41(5) also contains an exception to the rule of exclusion which permits the defence to challenge any such prosecution evidence. This approach was also taken under the Canadian provisions. The New South Wales provisions contain a similar exception, so that evidence of sexual history or its absence which the prosecution has disclosed or implied may be questioned.[149] The Michigan provisions do not contain an exception of this kind.

Whether or not it is fair to permit the defence to counter the assertions of the prosecution about sexual history, there is no justification for permitting this exception to open the floodgates by enabling the defence broadly to cross-examine the complainant about her sexual past. Accordingly, under section 41(5) and (6) of the YJCEA, questioning by the defence must 'go no further than is necessary to enable the evidence adduced by the prosecution to be rebutted or explained'. It must also 'relate to a specific instance or instances of alleged sexual behaviour on the part of the complainant'. The Canadian legislation similarly provided that evidence might be admitted by the defence if it was 'evidence that rebuts evidence of the complainant's sexual activity or absence thereof that was previously adduced by the prosecution'. In other words, the section did not permit the complainant to be subjected to cross-examination unless the defence were in possession of evidence which rebutted the prosecution's claim.

The New South Wales provision is far less satisfactory. It does not require any firm evidence from the defence but will allow it freely to cross-examine

[148] New South Wales Dept. of Attorney General (1977), 29.

[149] s 409B(5) provides as follows: 'In prescribed sexual offence proceedings, where the Court or Justice is satisfied that—*(a)* it has been disclosed or implied in the case for the prosecution against the accused person that the complainant has or may have, during a specified period or without reference to any period—(i) had sexual experience, or a lack of sexual experience, of a general or specified nature; or (ii) taken part or not taken part in sexual activity of a general or specified nature; and *(b)* the accused person might be unfairly prejudiced if the complainant could not be cross-examined by or on behalf of the accused person in relation to the disclosure or implication, the complainant may be so cross-examined but only in relation to the experience or activity of the nature (if any) so specified during the period (if any) so specified.'

The existence of this exception is curious given that the prosecution is barred from adducing sexual history evidence in the same way as the defence.

the complainant provided that the questions are confined to the matters raised by the prosecution and provided that the defendant would be 'unfairly prejudiced'[150] if such cross-examination were not permitted. This latter phrase gives *carte blanche* to the judges to permit such cross-examination whenever they wish to do so. It is not surprising therefore that this exception has proved to be a ready vehicle for the inclusion of sexual history evidence.[151] Prosecution evidence can easily be construed by willing judges to imply the complainant's sexual experience or the lack of it. Moreover, research shows that where the prosecution has not explained the precise purpose for which the evidence is being adduced, it is difficult to confine or control defence cross-examination on these matters.[152] There is clearly a danger that the section 41(5) exception may also prove to be a trap, particularly for inexperienced prosecuting counsel and especially since the YJCEA places no restriction on the use of sexual history evidence by the prosecution.

It is noteworthy that in Michigan it was held in *People v Mooney*[153] that where the victim had given testimony about her lack of sexual experience, the defence was not permitted to cross-examine her on this matter and that this did not violate his confrontation right.

(iii) Exceptions Omitted from the YJCEA

EVIDENCE OF SEXUAL RELATIONS WITH THE DEFENDANT

It has been noted above that such evidence is subject to the rule of exclusion under the YJCEA as well as in New South Wales and Michigan. But whereas in New South Wales and Michigan, a specific exception exists to the rule of exclusion so that defending counsel may apply for such evidence to be included, there is no such exception under the YJCEA. There is, however, ample scope to adduce such evidence under the four exceptions which are set out under the Act. Thus, as mentioned previously, under section 41(3)(a), if the defence argues belief in consent on the basis of a prior relationship, then the evidence would certainly be admissible. Where the complainant had sexual contact with the accused 'at or about the same time' as the alleged rape, this will be admissible under section 41(3)(b). In the unlikely event that she has had sexual relations with him before in circumstances that were so similar to the event in issue that the similarity cannot reasonably be explained as a coincidence, this evidence will be admissible under section 41(3)(c).[154] Finally, where the prosecution adduces evidence about her sexual behaviour, the defence will be able to adduce evidence to rebut or explain it under section 41(5). Thus, if she states in examination-in-chief that she has never had a sexual relationship with the accused, the defence would be able to rebut this.

[150] See n. 149. [151] Henning and Bronitt (1998), 88. [152] ibid. at 91.
[153] 216 Mich App 367.
[154] See now *R v A* [2001] UKHL 25, 3 All ER 1, discussed below at p. 224.

The approach which the Michigan and New South Wales legislation takes to evidence of a previous sexual relationship with the accused is open to criticism. The Michigan exception applies irrespective of the circumstances in which sexual conduct between defendant and complainant took place. However, such evidence is by no means always permitted and may be excluded on the ground that it is more prejudicial than probative.[155] On the other hand, the New South Wales exception specifically recognizes that evidence of sexual conduct with the defendant is by no means necessarily relevant. It provides that such evidence may be admitted 'Where it is evidence relating to a relationship which was existing or recent at the time of the commission of the alleged prescribed sexual offence'. However, Dr Woods states that the relationship which is existing or recent could be merely 'a nodding acquaintance'.[156] If this is so, the exception is arguably too broad since it would permit any evidence of sexual history with the defendant however far back in time provided that a non-sexual relationship, however vestigial, existed at the time of the rape. By contrast, rape-shield legislation enacted in Missouri renders admissible 'evidence of the sexual conduct of the complaining witness with the defendant where *this* is reasonably contemporaneous with the date of the alleged crime'.[157] Had an exception along broadly similar lines been included in the YJCEA, it would not have undermined the purpose of the legislation and would have prevented the possibly damaging intervention by the House of Lords in *R v A*.[158]

EVIDENCE OF DISEASE

The New South Wales legislation provides a further exception which does not appear in the YJCEA or in the Canadian or Michigan provisions. Under section 409B(3)(d), evidence may be admitted

> where it is relevant to whether—
> (i) at the time of the commission of the alleged prescribed sexual offence, there was present in the complainant a disease which, at any relevant time, was absent in the accused person; or
> (ii) at any relevant time, there was absent in the complainant a disease which, at the time of the commission of the alleged prescribed sexual offence, was present in the accused person . . .

There is a case for permitting a defendant to adduce evidence of the presence or absence of a sexual disease in himself or the complainant if this tends to confirm that he did not have sexual intercourse with the complainant on the occasion in question. Section 409B(3)(d), however, does not confine the use of such evidence to cases where the defendant denies having intercourse with the victim. Yet it is hard to envisage any circumstances in which it would genuinely be necessary to adduce such evidence where the plea is consent. A

[155] See e.g. *People v Adair* (1996) 550 NW 2d 505.
[156] Woods (1981), 36.
[157] Mo Rev Stat, s 491.015.
[158] [2001] UKHL 25, 3 All ER 1: see below p. 224.

defendant seeking to discredit the complainant in the eyes of the jury could hardly do better than to adduce evidence that he contracted venereal disease as a result of having intercourse with her. This exception would appear to permit him to do so regardless of the relevance of such evidence to any issue in the case. A study conducted by the NSW Department for Women of 70 trials in which sexual experience material had been admitted did not record a single instance in which application was made under this exception and there is no case law on the matter.[159]

(iv) Excluding Evidence which falls within the Exceptional Categories.

Under the YJCEA, admission of evidence falling within one of the four exceptions is by no means automatic. Under section 41(4), evidence will not be regarded as relating to a relevant issue in the case and coming within the exceptions contained in section 41(3) if it appears to the court to be reasonable to assume that its main purpose is to impugn the credibility of the complainant. Moreover, under section 41(6), for the purposes of all four exceptions, the evidence must relate to specific instances of sexual behaviour. Finally, before admitting evidence which technically falls within one of the exceptional categories, the judge must, under section 41(2), be satisfied that a 'refusal of leave might have the result of rendering unsafe a conclusion of the jury or the court on any relevant issue in the case'.

The New South Wales and Michigan legislation similarly vest in the judge a discretion to *exclude* evidence even where it does fall within one of the exceptions. In New South Wales, the judge may exclude evidence where its probative value does not 'outweigh any distress, humiliation or embarrassment which the complainant might suffer as a result of its admission'. But the purpose of 'rape-shield' legislation such as this is equally to limit the inclusion of evidence which impedes the course of justice by distracting jurors and unfairly prejudicing them against the victim. The Michigan formula seeks to reflect this. A Michigan judge may admit evidence in the exceptional categories only where it is 'material to a fact at issue in the case and its inflammatory or prejudicial nature does not outweigh its probative value'. The failure of the Canadian legislation to include any discretion to exclude was a further weakness in its provisions.

Use has been made of the discretion in Michigan to exclude, for example, evidence of previous sexual relations with the defendant.[160] However, the experience in New South Wales has been that evidence which falls within one of the exceptional categories is almost always admitted even where it is of minimal relevance to the issues in the case.[161] There is clearly a danger that the same approach could be adopted here.

159 (1996), 232. 160 See e.g. *People v Adair* (1996) 550 NW 2d 505.

161 M. Kumar and E. Magner, 'Good Reasons for Gagging the Accused' 2 (1997) UNSW Law Journal 311 at 327.

(v) Procedure

Strong procedural provisions are an important accompaniment to laws which seek to control sexual history evidence. But these differ markedly in each of the four jurisdictions.

NOTICE

In Michigan,[162] a defendant wishing to adduce sexual history evidence has to give notice of his intention to do so. Notice provisions seek to ensure that only genuine and considered applications are made to introduce sexual history evidence. They also serve to give the prosecution some warning of what is in store. In Michigan, the requirements are stringent and non-compliance may lead to an exclusion of evidence which would otherwise be admissible.[163] The defence must, within 10 days after the arraignment on the information, file a written motion and offer of proof. Failing this, it is only where new information is discovered during the course of the trial that the judge may consider its admissibility.[164] In Canada, a notice requirement applied only where the defence sought to produce evidence under exception *(c)* of section 246.6(1), namely, evidence of sexual activity on the same occasion as the alleged assault. A failure to comply would result in automatic exclusion of the evidence. There are no notice provisions under either the YJCEA or the NSW legislation, which may be regarded as a weakness in both.

HEARING THE APPLICATION

Under the YJCEA, applications to the court for permission to introduce sexual history evidence must be made in the absence of the public, the press, the jury, and all witnesses apart from the accused.[165] In Canada, the jury and members of the public were excluded from the hearing.[166] In Michigan, an in camera hearing may be ordered[167] and in New South Wales only the jury is automatically excluded.[168] There is clearly a strong case for excluding the public as well as the jury. One English judge put the matter thus:

> . . . sometimes in cases the members of the jury have relatives or friends who come to court with them, for perfectly proper reasons, natural interest in what is going on, and they sit in the public gallery. If they heard what went on in the absence of the jury, they might hear something which the judge has decided the jury should not be told. There is another reason as well, quite apart from that reason. If the judge

[162] Criminal Sexual Conduct Act, s 520J(2).

[163] See *People v Powell* (1993) 201 Mich App 516.

[164] For the argument that these notice provisions are unconstitutional see *People v Williams* Mich App 289 NW 2d 863 (1980). However, the US Supreme Court has ruled that they are not in themselves unconstitutional: see *Michigan v Lucas* 111 (1991) S Ct 1743.

[165] YJCEA, s 43 and see *Explanatory Notes*, para. 152.

[166] s 246.6(3). They remain so under the present law. See Canadian Criminal Code, s 276.2(1).

[167] Criminal Sexual Conduct Act 1974, s 520J(2).

[168] Crimes Act 1900, s 409B(6).

decides that the complainant should not be asked about her previous sexual experience but it comes out during the hearing in the jury's absence, then it is a little unfair, do you not think, that members of the public who might know this complainant—a neighbour, maybe, who knows about the case and has come along to hear it—should hear all about that complainant's past if it has been private up until that moment.[169]

Under the YJCEA, the complainant is also excluded from the application.[170] In NSW and Michigan, the complainant is not excluded, nor was she under the Canadian provisions. It is not entirely clear why a complainant who wishes to hear the allegations made against her in such an application should not be able to attend. The Canadian provision ensured that she did not have to give evidence at such a hearing if she did not wish to do so.[171]

No precise indication is given in any of the four statutes as to what form the hearing should take. However, Dr Woods envisaged that in New South Wales a trial within a trial should take place[172] and it was suggested that the same would apply in Canada.[173]

Under section 43(2) of the YJCEA, the court must state in open court, but in the absence of the jury, its reasons for giving or refusing leave and the extent to which evidence may be adduced or questions asked in pursuance of the leave. The New South Wales legislation contains a similar provision which requires that after the hearing the court or justice 'shall, before the evidence is given, record or cause to be recorded in writing the nature and scope of the evidence that is so admissible and the reasons for that decision'.[174] This requirement will both ensure that the judge considers the application with all due deliberation and also that defence counsel knows the limits of the questions which may be asked and the evidence which may be adduced.

A New South Wales study of 111 trials found that in 70 of them (63%) sexual experience evidence was admitted on a total of 79 occasions. It was found that, in 35 per cent of these, no application was made but the evidence was simply admitted with the connivance of the court and lack of protest from prosecuting counsel. Similarly, evidence of sexual reputation was admitted in 13 trials but in nine of these, no application was made and no objection was raised by counsel or judge.[175]

[169] See J. Temkin, 'Evidence in Sexual Assault Cases: The Scottish Proposal and Alternatives' (1984) 47 MLR 625, 646 n. 36.

[170] This was also the case under the Law Reform (Miscellaneous Provisions) (Scotland) Act 1985, s 36(2). See also, Scottish Law Commission, *Evidence: Report on Evidence in Cases of Rape and Other Sexual Offences,* No. 78 (HC 28, 1983), para. 5.22.

[171] s 246.6(3) specifically provided that the complainant was not a compellable witness at such a hearing. This remains the case; see Canadian Criminal Code, s 276.2(2).

[172] Woods (1981), 40. [173] Watt (1984), 196. [174] s 409B(7).

[175] New South Wales Dept. for Women (1996), 228, 230, 232. See also Adler (1987), 85–7.

(vi) Sexual History Evidence and Human Rights

It may be concluded on the basis of the above analysis of the four regimes that, taken as a whole, it is the YJCEA which is the most protective of the accused and therefore the weakest, with the exceptions it provides to the rule of exclusion affording the best opportunities to the defence to override the rule of exclusion. The absence of notice provisions is also a procedural weakness. It is only where there is an allegation of a previous sexual relationship between the parties that the YJCEA is more protective of the complainant. This situation, as explained below, has now been changed.

The Canadian sexual history provisions discussed above were challenged on the ground that they infringed the Canadian Charter of Rights and Freedoms. In *Oquataq*,[176] it was said that their purpose was to protect the complainant from humiliation and to encourage victims to report the offence but that they operated unfairly against the accused. They were challenged principally on the basis that they violated sections 7 and 11(d) of the Charter which provide as follows:

7. Everyone has the right to life, liberty and security of the person and the right not to be deprived thereof except in accordance with the principles of fundamental justice.

11. Any person charged with an offence has the right . . . to be presumed innocent until proven guilty according to law in a fair and public hearing by an independent and impartial tribunal.

In 1991 the Supreme Court of Canada in *Seaboyer*[177] ruled by a majority that section 276 was unconstitutional, expressing a preference for a discretionary provision. The principal objection was that the exceptions to the rule of exclusion were drawn too narrowly and prevented relevant evidence being adduced. There was particular concern that the exceptions to the rule of exclusion did not permit evidence that supported a mistaken belief in consent, similar fact evidence and evidence that went to bias or to motive to fabricate. As previously discussed, the equivalent provisions under the YJCEA do, expressly, permit such evidence in the first two situations and also appear to do so in the third.

The NSW provisions have also faced heavy criticism from some quarters of the judiciary and have been challenged by defence counsel by invoking the common law right to a fair trial.[178] This strategy has resulted in the courts ordering a stay of proceedings in several cases. Intervention by the Court of Criminal Appeal has been required to put a stop to this practice.[179] Despite the fact that the exceptions to the rule of exclusion have, at the insistence of

176 (1985) 18 CCC (3d) 440.

177 [1991] 2 SCR 577.

178 See e.g. *Dietrich* (1992) 177 CLR 292.

179 *PJE* (unreported NSW CCA Oct. 1995) referred to by Henning and Bronitt (1998), 92.

the Court of Appeal, been very generously interpreted,[180] there remains heavy pressure to repeal the provisions and substitute an anodyne discretionary alternative.[181] The cases in which the provisions have been challenged and a stay ordered have involved allegations of child sexual abuse, where consent is not the issue, but in which the defence has sought to introduce evidence of previous sexual abuse of the child, or evidence of allegedly false allegations of sexual assault previously made by the child.[182] Again, the YJCEA would permit such evidence in such circumstances.[183]

The NSW experience is particularly instructive. Two empirical studies, one conducted by the NSW Bureau of Crime Statistics and Research, the other by the Department for Women, both indicate that the legislation has made some progress in excluding unnecessary and irrelevant evidence.[184] The NSW Law Reform Commission similarly concluded that the legislation appeared to be achieving its goals.[185] On the other hand, a concerted attempt has been made by some members of the legal profession and judiciary to undermine it. This illustrates the cardinal importance of judicial training in relation to the new law, for, without some awareness of all the issues involved, the provisions under the YJCEA could meet a similar fate. In Michigan, it seems, such awareness does exist. The courts appear to have had no difficulty grasping both the reasons for the legislation and its significance. As a result, constitutional challenge has had only limited success and the rape-shield law is fully operative and intact.

The rape-shield provisions under the YJCEA were bound to provoke controversy,[186] even though it is clear that every effort was made to secure a fair balance between the interests of the accused and those of the complainant. The Heilbron Committee considered that the main reason for excluding sexual history evidence was because it was generally of singular irrelevance to the issues in a rape case.[187] To exclude irrelevant evidence is not an injustice to the accused. Of course, occasions may arise where sexual history evidence

[180] See *R v McGarvey* [1987] 10 NSWLR 632; *Dimian* (1995) 83 A Crim R 358; *R v M* (1993) 67 A Crim R 549.

[181] See e.g. comments in *R v Morgan* (1993) 30 NSWLR 543. The Australian Model Criminal Code Officers Committee has recommended tentatively that the Model Criminal Code adopt a discretionary approach: see Model Criminal Code Officers Committee (1996), 175.

[182] See e.g. *Morris* unreported (Court of Criminal Appeal NSW Oct. 1990) discussed by NSW Law Reform Commission (1997), 2.

[183] See above under the heading 'Sexual offences where consent is not the issue'.

[184] See Bonney (1987) and NSW Dept. for Women (1996), 248–53.

[185] (1997) at 24.

[186] See N. Kibble, 'The Sexual History Provisions: Charting a Course between Inflexible Legislative Rules and Wholly Untrammelled Judicial Discretion' [2000] Crim LR 274.

[187] Heilbron Committee (1975), para. 92. See also *Oyston v UK*, Application No. 42011/98, ECtHR, 22 Jan. 2002 (admissibility decision) in which the ECtHR approved restrictions on the right to cross-examine witnesses about sexual history evidence in order to safeguard the interests of victims, provided that the defence was not precluded from asking the complainant about matters central to his defence.

ought to be included. Experience has shown that decisions on such matters cannot be left at large for the judges to determine. The YJCEA, in seeking to impose a structured approach to decision-making in this area, has included a generous range of exceptions to the rule of exclusion. Taken as a whole, it permits sexual history evidence in a wider range of circumstances than those permitted by the three alternative schemes discussed here. Indeed, there is some concern that the range of circumstances is too broad.

The one area in which the new provisions were particularly vulnerable to challenge was in relation to evidence of sexual relations with the defendant.[188] In *R v A*,[189] the defence sought to have admitted evidence of a previous sexual relationship which he alleged he had had with the complainant, as evidence bearing on the issue of consent. It was contended that there was no obvious way of bringing such evidence within any of the four exceptions to the rule of exclusion. The House of Lords considered that this was a likely flaw in the provisions but was not prepared to hold that they were, as a whole, incompatible with the ECHR. It decided instead to exercise its interpretative duty under section 3 of the Human Rights Act 1998 with a view to achieving compatibility with Article 6. It therefore read into section 41(3)(c) (the similarity exception) an interpretation that evidence could be admitted where it was 'so relevant to the issue of consent that to exclude it would endanger the fairness of the trial under Article 6'.[190] Lord Steyn, who gave the leading opinion, entered the caveat that due regard should always be paid to the importance of seeking to protect the complainant from indignity and humiliating questions,[191] and made clear that a prior relationship with the accused would not always be relevant. However, since no clarification was offered as to when it would be irrelevant, it seems likely that such evidence will generally be admitted in the future for fear of a successful appeal. It must be hoped that the House of Lords has not now opened the door to a wide interpretation of the provisions even in cases which do not involve previous sexual relations with the accused. Certainly, Lord Hope for one was against the addition of a broad overall discretion,[192] but this may be precisely what has been achieved. However, in the subsequent case of *R v Mokrecovas*,[193] the Court of Appeal dismissed an appeal against the trial judge's ruling that evidence of alleged sexual behaviour with a third party, the defendant's brother, could not be admitted since it did not fall within any one of the exceptions. The Court declared that admitting such evidence would invade her privacy, subject her to humiliating accusations, and drive a coach and horses through section 41. It may be that the general tenor of the opinions in *A* which were broadly supportive of the new law, will ensure

[188] See discussion above p. 217. See also N. Kibble, 'The Relevance and Admissibility of Prior Sexual History with the Defendant in Sexual Offence Cases' [2001] Cambrian Law Review 27; Birch (2000), 249.

[189] [2001] UKHL 25, 3 All ER 1.

[190] At 18.

[191] ibid

[192] At p. 35, para. 109.

[193] [2002] 1 Cr App R 226.

that trial judges interpret it in accordance with legislative intent. Without research into the operation of the new law, it will be hard to tell.

The Collateral Finality Rule

This rule is intended to ensure that where a witness is cross-examined and the cross-examination relates to credibility rather than to an issue in the case itself, then the witness's answers to questions are final and no evidence may be called to rebut them. This is in the interests of finality since otherwise evidence could be called endlessly to challenge the credibility of the witness. This doctrine has, however, been under attack, particularly in sexual cases,[194] where it has been suggested that the rule should not apply and that evidence in rebuttal should be able to be called. Thus, in *Nagrecha,*[195] the defence alleged that the complainant had made false allegations of sexual assault against other men in the past. In cross-examination, she denied having made any allegations of a sexual nature. The judge refused to allow the defence to call evidence to rebut this assertion. The Court of Appeal considered that such evidence should have been allowed. It appeared to accept Professor Tapper's argument that the line between relevance to credibility and relevance to the issue in sexual cases was often too fine to be drawn[196] and concluded that the evidence was material to her credibility and to the issue in the case. The appeal was allowed on that basis. But, as the trial judge so rightly pointed out, even if allegations had been made by her in the past and even if they were untrue, this was not to say that the present allegation was false and to explore them would have been to wander considerably off-track. In *Neale,*[197] perhaps in response to the incisive criticism of *Nagrecha* by Professor Birch,[198] the Court of Appeal dismissed another attempt to circumvent the collateral finality rule in a case involving the indecent assault and rape of a child. However, the rule was again bypassed in the later case of *David.*[199] It would be singularly unfortunate if sexual assault cases were to be treated as an exception to the collateral finality rule so as to permit further oppressive treatment of complainants.

The Previous Misconduct of the Accused

The general rule in criminal cases is that the accused's previous misconduct or convictions cannot be revealed during the trial.[200] The accepted explanation for this is the prejudice which might result where the jury has

194 See e.g. *Funderburk* [1990] 1 WLR 587.
195 [1997] 2 Cr App R 401.
196 Tapper (1999), 313.
197 [1998] Crim LR 737.
198 [1998] Crim LR 65–7.
199 [1999] Crim LR 909.
200 See Tapper (1999), chs. 8 and 9.

this information. Too much weight might be attached to previous convictions and guilt too readily assumed. Alternatively, where previous misconduct has not resulted in a conviction, the jury might think that he was deserving of punishment in any case, whether or not he had committed the crime alleged.[201] It is thus only in exceptional circumstances that evidence of previous misconduct or convictions may be admitted.

(a) Use of Previous Misconduct Evidence by the Prosecution in Examination-in-Chief

A man charged with rape might have committed sexual assaults on previous occasions whether or not they have resulted in convictions. The general rule, known misleadingly as the similar fact rule,[202] is that evidence of the accused's previous convictions and past misconduct cannot be led as evidence by the prosecution. The principal exception was previously set out in *Boardman*,[203] in which it was held that such evidence could be adduced only where there was a striking similarity between it and the conduct alleged by the prosecution in the present case. 'The similarity would have to be so unique or striking that common sense makes it inexplicable on the basis of coincidence.'[204] The *Boardman* test was interpreted rigidly in some cases. In *Brooks*,[205] for example, in which the accused was charged with incest with his three daughters, it was held that the similarities had to be both useful[206] and truly striking before previous misconduct evidence could be admitted. Similarities which were no more than 'the common coin of evidence in cases of father/daughter incest' would not suffice.[207]

The complainant in a sexual assault trial is in a different position from most other witnesses in that it is not necessarily assumed initially that what she is saying is true. On the contrary, the prosecution faces a supremely hard task in pushing aside the haze of suspicion which surrounds her, fending off the routine onslaughts against her character, and proving the case beyond reasonable doubt. Clearly, evidence that the accused has sexually assaulted other members of the same family is highly probative and of the utmost importance in supporting her claim. That it is fair and appropriate for the prosecution to be able to adduce such evidence was finally recognized by the House of Lords in *P*,[208] a radical decision which has finally cast aside the strait-jacket imposed by *Boardman*. It was decided in *P*, which again involved sexual abuse by a father, that the test of admissibility should be the probative force of the evidence and whether this was sufficiently great to make it just to admit it, notwithstanding its prejudicial effect. Striking sim-

201 For further discussion, see Law Commission (1996), 124–6.
202 See Tapper (1999), 333.
203 [1974] 3 All ER 887.
204 ibid. *per* Lord Salmon at 913.
205 (1991) 92 Cr App R 36.
206 At 42.
207 At 43.
208 [1991] 3 All ER 337.

ilarity was held to be but an instance of this. By overruling cases such as *Brooks*, the door has been opened more widely to permitting evidence of the accused's previous sexual misconduct, particularly in cases where sexual abuse by a parent or stepparent is concerned. The decision in *P* has been bolstered by *Z*,[209] in which it was held that where the accused has been charged with an offence and acquitted, this does not preclude the conduct concerned from being adduced in evidence at a later trial where another offence is charged. The House of Lords considered that there was no infringement of the double jeopardy rule in these circumstances since the evidence was led in order to prove that he was guilty of a *subsequent* offence.

Whilst the decision in *P* is a welcome step forward, there are difficulties associated with it.[210] These include the interpretation of probative value and the assessment of when evidence is more probative than prejudicial. This will be a matter for the judge to decide in each case and it will be hard to predict that decision in advance. However, it seems clear that the decision in *P* is unlikely to prove to be an easy avenue for the inclusion of evidence of the defendant's past misconduct. In their Crown Court study, Zander and Henderson found that it was used extremely rarely.[211] McEwan has also noted that prosecutors' experience is that courts tend to exclude such evidence for fear of an appeal.[212]

(i) The Law Commission's Provisional Proposals[213]

Having considered various options, the Law Commission provisionally proposed that the decision in *P* should be placed on a statutory footing. The statute would specify that evidence of the accused's previous misconduct would be admissible in examination-in-chief if it was relevant to a fact in issue and its probative value outweighed the risk that if admitted it might result in prejudice. If it did so, the evidence might none the less be excluded if it might mislead, confuse, or distract the fact-finders or cause undue waste of time.[214]

The Commission also provisionally proposed that, in order to assist in the assessment of what is probative and prejudicial, the legislation should expressly set out the factors which the court should take into account.[215] On the probative value side would be included:

1. the extent to which the evidence suggests that the defendant has a propensity to act in the manner alleged;
2. any similarities between the facts revealed by the evidence[216] and those now alleged;

209 [2000] 3 All ER 385.

210 See on this Dennis (1999), 592–4.

211 According to defence barristers who responded to their survey, out of 66 cases where the jury learnt of previous convictions, it was used in only two cases: see Zander and Henderson (1993), paras. 4.6.1, 4.6.6, and 4.6.7

212 McEwan (1997), 95.

213 Law Commission (1996).

214 Law Commission (1996), 262.

215 Law Commission (1996), at 262–3.

216 i.e. the facts pertaining to the previous misconduct.

3. the extent to which such similarities may reasonably be attributed to coincidence;
4. any dissimilarities between the facts revealed by the evidence and those now alleged.

On the prejudice side, the factors would be:

1. the risk of the fact-finders attaching undue significance to the evidence in question in determining whether the defendant is guilty as charged; and
2. the risk of their convicting the defendant on the basis of his or her conduct on some other occasion or occasions, rather than because they are satisfied that he or she is guilty as charged.

It is not clear that this statutory scheme would be much of an improvement as far as sexual offences are concerned. First, it would not be productive of any more certainty or predictability. The weight to be attached to any one of the factors mentioned would remain a matter for the judge, as would the final overall weighing of the evidence on both sides. This uncertainty is likely to discourage complainants. Secondly, there is a distinct possibility that, in sexual cases, the statutory formula, by specifically spelling out the factors on the prejudice side, would be likely to ensure that evidence of previous sexual misconduct is admitted even more rarely than it is at present. Where the accused has committed sexual offences in the past, the judge might think that the jury might attach too much weight to this, or, alternatively, convict on the basis that he was deserving of punishment in any case. Certainly, the probative value of the evidence would have to be very high indeed to tip the balance in favour of admitting it. The Commission specifically rejected the option of admitting prejudicial evidence if it has significant probative value,[217] insisting that the probative value should outweigh the risk of prejudice. Moreover, the court would be able to exclude evidence even if its probative value did outweigh the risk of prejudice, if it was likely to mislead, confuse, or distract the fact-finders or cause undue waste of time.[218] No such limitation was specified in *P*. The Commission suggests that undue waste of time could result where the accused disputes the previous misconduct evidence.[219] In sexual cases, where the alleged previous misconduct has not resulted in prosecution or conviction, as would frequently be the case, he would almost inevitably dispute it.

Thus, under these proposals, past misconduct evidence would, if anything, be admitted in even fewer sexual cases than at present. A subsequent comment which the Commission makes in relation to the Oxford study[220] is revealing in this context: 'The Oxford Report shows that if jurors are aware of a defendant's previous conviction for a sexual offence they are likely to find it exceptionally easy to convict that defendant of another sex

[217] Law Commission (1996), paras. 10.67–10.68. [218] ibid., para. 10.82, 183.
[219] ibid. [220] See below under the heading 'The Oxford Study'.

offence'.[221] This suggests that the Commission considered that in most cases the prejudice to the accused would be too overwhelming to admit such evidence. The conclusions which the Commission has drawn from the Oxford study are queried below.[222]

(ii) *The Law Commission's Final Report*[223]

In its final Report, the Law Commission has essentially opted for the same approach. It proposes that leave may be given to adduce evidence of the accused's bad character on two conditions.[224] First, the evidence has substantial probative value in relation to a matter in issue which is itself of substantial importance in the context of the case as a whole. Secondly, in all the circumstances, the evidence carries no risk of prejudice to the defendant or, taking account of the risk of prejudice, the interests of justice nevertheless require the evidence to be admissible in view of its probative value, the availability or lack of availability of other evidence on the matter and the importance of the matter in the context of the case as a whole.[225] In deciding upon these two conditions, the court must have regard to certain specified factors and to any others it considers relevant. These factors are the nature and number of the events or other things to which the evidence relates, their timing, and, where it is suggested that their probative value rests on similarity, the nature and extent of the similarities and dissimilarities or, where identity is the issue, the extent to which the evidence tends to show that the same person was responsible.[226] By contrast with the provisional proposal, the judge is not required to consider similarities and dissimilarities where these are not relied upon by the prosecution.

(iii) *Background Evidence*[227]

Under the present law, the similar fact rule does not apply to evidence which forms either part of the background to the offence charged or is part of the *res gestae*, that is, part of the story itself. Hence, evidence of the previous bad conduct of the accused can be more or less freely admitted in these circumstances, regardless of whether they meet the criteria set out in *P*. This type of background evidence can be immensely important in sexual cases. In *Rearden*,[228] for example, R was charged with the rape of a 10-year-old girl. The court allowed the jury to hear from the complainant that he had raped

[221] Law Commission (1996), para. 9.37.

[222] See below under the heading 'The Oxford Study'.

[223] Law Commission (2001). See also the Government's White Paper *Justice for All*, Home Office (2002), paras. 4.54–4.59, which suggest that the Government intends to follow the Law Commission's recommendations.

[224] No leave would be required where the evidence has to do with the central facts of the case: see Law Commission (2001), 204, para. 3.

[225] Law Commission (2001), Draft Bill, 214.

[226] ibid. 212.

[227] See Law Commission (2001), paras. 10.1–10.7.

[228] (1864) 4 F and F 76.

her on several occasions before she told her mother, on the basis that this was virtually all part of the same offence. The Law Commission is now proposing that background evidence should be brought within a tight framework of control so that it would only be possible to admit it if three conditions were met.[229] These are that the court would find it difficult or impossible to understand other evidence in the court without it, that the value of the evidence for understanding the case as a whole is substantial, and that either it carries no risk of prejudice or its value for understanding the case as a whole is such that, taking account of the risk of prejudice, the interests of justice require it to be admissible. This should ensure that courts hear rather less background evidence than they do at the moment.

(iv) Alternative Solutions

In the United States, the Federal Rules of Evidence which apply in the Federal courts and have influenced the codes of many US states have, since 1994, included special provisions for sexual cases.[230] These are in marked contrast to the approach taken by the Law Commission. Rule 413 provides that where the defendant is accused of an offence of sexual assault, evidence of his commission of another offence or offences of sexual assault is admissible and may be considered for its bearing on any matter to which it is relevant. Under Rule 414, where the defendant is charged with child molestation, evidence of another offence or offences of child molestation is admissible and may be considered for its bearing on any matter to which it is relevant. Rule 415 applies the same approach to civil cases involving sexual assault and child molestation. Under all three rules, notice must be served on the defence of the intention to offer evidence of the relevant past misconduct and there must be disclosure of this evidence, including the statements of witnesses, no longer than 15 days before trial.[231] It has now been confirmed in numerous cases[232] that a judge would still be able to exclude such evidence under Rule 403 which gives the court a discretion to exclude relevant evidence 'if its probative value is substantially outweighed by the danger of unfair prejudice, confusion of the issues, or misleading the jury, or by considerations of undue delay, waste of time or needless presentation of cumulative evidence'.

The advantage of this new regime from the prosecutor's point of view is that evidence of sexual assaults committed by the accused in the past is, if relevant, prima-facie admissible rather than the reverse. The Law

[229] Law Commission (2001) 214, cl 7.

[230] Rules 413–15 were introduced in the Violent Crime Control and Law Enforcement Act 1994, Pub L No. 103–322, s 320935(a), 108 Stat 1796, 2135–7.

[231] Rule 413(b), rule 414(b), rule 415(b).

[232] See e.g. *United States v Enjady* 134 F 3d 1427, 1431–3 (10th Cir. 1998); *United States v Guardia* 135 F 3d 1326 (10th Cir. 1998); *United States v Larson* 112 F 3d 600 (2d Cir. 1997); *United States v Le Compte* 131 F 3d 767 (8th Cir. 1997).

Commission rejects this approach.[233] Its reasons for doing so are unconvincing and appear to have been either shaped or confirmed by a study which it commissioned and which was carried out at the Oxford Centre for Socio-Legal Studies.

THE OXFORD STUDY[234]

The Oxford study looked into the effect on mock juries of knowing that the accused has a previous conviction. It focused, in particular, on the effects of the similarity or otherwise of a previous conviction to the offence currently charged and whether it made a difference that the previous conviction was recent or old.[235] The Commission was particularly keen to discover the effect on a jury of knowledge that the accused had a previous conviction for indecent assault of a child (IAC) in the light of calls that such convictions should be made known in child sexual abuse trials.[236] The research was therefore also specifically concerned with the impact on juries of knowledge of a previous conviction of IAC.[237]

Each mock jury was shown one video of one trial. There were 24 different videos: eight involved a trial for handling stolen goods (HSG), eight involved a trial for indecent assault on a woman (IAW), and eight involved a trial for causing grievous bodily harm with intent, contrary to section 18 of the OAPA 1861.[238] None of the videos involved trials for indecent assault on a child. Each of the eight videos in the three groups differed according to the information given about the accused's previous conduct. The different information given was as follows:[239]

(1) D had a previous similar recent conviction;
(2) D had a previous similar old conviction;
(3) D had a previous dissimilar recent conviction;
(4) D had a previous dissimilar old conviction;
(5) D had no previous convictions, that is, D was of good character;
(6) No mention was made of either good character or previous convictions;
(7) D had a previous recent conviction for indecent assault on a child;
(8) D had a previous old conviction for indecent assault on a child.

The main research findings were as follows:

1. Participants who were told of a *recent similar* conviction rated the defendant as significantly more likely to have committed the crime with

[233] Law Commission (1996), para. 9.38; Law Commission (2001), para. 6.57. For support for the Law Commission's approach, see M. Childs, 'The Character of the Accused' in Childs and Ellison (2000).

[234] Described in appendix D of Law Commission (1996). See also Lloyd-Bostock (2000).

[235] Law Commission (1996), appendix D, para. D.2.

[236] See Lloyd-Bostock (2000), 736.

[237] Law Commission (1996), appendix D, para. D.2.

[238] ibid., para. D.6.

[239] ibid., para. D.7

which he was charged than when they were told he had a dissimilar conviction or no convictions.[240]

2. Where participants were told of an *old* conviction, their rating of the likelihood of the defendant's having committed the offence for which he was charged did not differ significantly from that of those participants to whom no mention was made of previous convictions or of good character.[241]
3. A *dissimilar* previous conviction reduced the likelihood of a guilty verdict.[242] Indeed, a dissimilar previous conviction was associated with a lower perceived probability that the accused committed the offence than where no information about previous convictions was given and even where he was of good character.
4. A previous conviction for IAC produced the highest rate of guilty verdicts. Where the accused had a previous conviction for IAC, this produced 'a consistent and for some offences significant increase in ratings of likelihood that he would commit *dissimilar* offences'.[243]

The study was set up to look at the impact on the perceived likelihood that the accused committed the offence in question of previous convictions which were recent, old, similar, and dissimilar and a previous conviction for IAC. *It does not purport to provide information about the impact of any other specific offences, including any other sexual offences*. But it did also consider the participants' impressions of the defendant, depending on whether he had previous convictions for IAC, IAW, section 18, HSG, or where they were told that he was of good character or where nothing was said about his character. Some interesting differences emerged between assessments of the accused where he had a previous conviction for IAC and where he had a previous conviction for IAW:

1. Where participants were asked how likely it was that the accused had committed criminal offences in the past which he got away with, they considered that this was most likely where he had a previous conviction for IAC but, in the case of IAW, this was considered to be less likely than for any other category save where he was of good character.[244]
2. When participants were asked if they would let the accused take a job where he would look after money and other valuables, they were markedly more willing to do so in the case of a person with a previous conviction for IAW than for any other category, whereas in the case of IAC they were more unlikely to do so than in any other category apart from HSG.[245]
3. When participants were asked whether the accused deserved punishment, he was most likely to be considered to deserve it where he had a

[240] Law Commission (1996), appendix D, para. D.21, 329.
[241] ibid., para. D23, 329.
[242] Lloyd-Bostock (2000), at 746.
[243] ibid. 749.
[244] ibid. 751.
[245] ibid.

previous conviction for IAC but less likely to deserve it where he had a previous conviction for IAW than in any other category save HSG.[246]

These results may have been influenced by the fact that no details were provided of any of the previous convictions, and participants may have assumed that the previous conviction for IAW involved a relatively minor sexual assault such as that in the trial video.[247] It is only in assessments of credibility and trustworthiness that defendants with previous convictions for IAW came close to defendants with previous convictions for IAC. Ratings of likelihood that the accused would lie on oath were lower for IAW than for IAC but not substantially so,[248] assessments of his truthfulness when giving evidence were higher for IAW than for IAC but not substantially so,[249] and assessments of trustworthiness, though certainly higher for IAW than for IAC, were lower than assessments in the other categories.[250]

Professor Lloyd-Bostock, who carried out the study, concluded that

> when participants were told that D had a previous conviction for IAC, his testimony was least believed and he was perceived as most likely to commit the kind of crime he was on trial for (which in no case was indecent assault on a child), least trustworthy, most deserving of punishment, most likely to have committed crimes he has got away with and most definitely not given a job where he would look after children as well as most likely to tell lies in court.[251]

But, given the structure of the study, the findings as far as previous convictions for IAW are concerned are strictly limited. The study was not designed to provide information about the impact of such convictions. Other sexual assaults against adults were not considered at all. However, in its discussion, the Law Commission persistently fails to acknowledge this. Thus, discussing the prejudicial effect of the defendant's criminal history, it states:

> The Oxford Report clearly suggests that a previous conviction for a sexual offence and in particular for an indecent assault on a child is highly prejudicial. Mock jurors told that D had such a previous conviction were not only more likely to believe that D had committed the offence charged but were also less likely to believe his evidence: Appendix D, paras. D.36–D41.[252]

Whilst it was found that a previous conviction for IAC was prejudicial, the study does not permit the drawing of such conclusions as far as other sexual offences are concerned. Indeed, as has been demonstrated, in some respects jurors were far more positive towards defendants with previous convictions for IAW than for IAC. Although jurors were more likely to believe that the accused committed the offence charged if previously convicted of IAC, no such conclusion can be drawn from the study concerning a previous conviction for

[246] ibid. 750. [247] i.e. touching the complainant's breast without her consent.
[248] ibid. 749. [249] ibid. [250] ibid. 750. [251] ibid. 748.
[252] Law Commission (1996) appendix D, 147 n. 45.

IAW. Moreover, whilst credibility ratings for IAC and IAW were closer than for other categories, there were differences between them.

Again, on the theme of the prejudicial impact of sexual assault convictions, the Law Commission states:

> The Oxford Report clearly suggests that in a sexual offence case, where the jury are told that the defendant has a similar previous conviction, they are much more likely to convict. Both the similarity of the previous conviction to the current charge and the abhorrent nature of the previous conviction increase the likelihood of conviction. See Appendix D, para. D.28.[253]

Paragraph D.28, however, is concerned exclusively with the impact of a conviction for IAC. No reference is made to the impact of convictions for any other offences, including sexual ones. This is because the study was not designed to shed light on the impact upon convictions of any previous convictions other than for IAC.[254]

The Law Commission goes on to state: 'It must be remembered that the Oxford Report shows that if jurors are aware of a defendant's previous conviction for a sexual offence, they are likely to find it exceptionally easy to convict that defendant of another sex offence'.[255] Again, it cites in support of this statement paragraph D.28 of appendix D which, as mentioned above, says nothing of the kind but deals exclusively with the impact of a conviction of IAC. In fact, the report shows that participants told of *any recent similar offence* rated the defendant as significantly more likely to have committed the crime with which he was charged than when they were told he had a dissimilar conviction or no convictions. The effect did not hold where the similar conviction was old.[256] Moreover, as McEwan points out, only 32 per cent of the sample in fact voted guilty even where the conviction was both recent and similar. She comments: 'The fact that conviction rates were low in any case suggests that there is no reason to think that defendants with criminal records are automatically condemned'.[257] Whilst the evidence against the accused in the mock trials, excluding previous convictions, was not particularly strong,[258] the comment is none the less a valid one.

The heavy reliance on the Oxford study is further illustrated by the comments of the Law Commissioner responsible for the Consultation Paper.[259]

253 Law Commission (1996) appendix D, 146 n. 41.

254 Indeed, whilst it was found that a previous conviction for IAC produced the highest rate of guilty verdicts in the study, a previous conviction for IAW produced the lowest: see ibid. 334, fig. 3. However, the numbers involved as far as IAW were concerned were so small that conclusions cannot be drawn from this.

255 ibid. 148, para. 9.37.

256 ibid., para. D.24, 329.

257 McEwan (1997), 100.

258 See Lloyd-Bostock (2000), 740.

259 Silber (1997), 125–33. See also Law Commission (2001), 88–9.The findings of the Oxford Study are also misrepresented in the Auld Report: see Auld (2001), para. 119, in which he states 'The Oxford study indicated that a jury would be more likely to convict if they know that D either had a conviction for a similar offence or for indecent assault irrespective of the offence charged'.

Conceding the 'substantial probative value' of previous misconduct evidence in cases of sexual assault, he stated:

> It is precisely in those cases that the risk of prejudice is at its highest according to the Oxford study . . . It will be remembered that the Oxford study shows that if jurors are aware of a defendant's previous convictions for sexual offences, they are likely to find it exceptionally easy to convict him of another sex offence.[260]

Indeed, so perturbed was he with the implications of this 'finding' for sexual cases where previous misconduct evidence was admitted that he declared: 'I have in mind an even more stringent warning than that which is normally given'.[261]

Quite apart from the fact that the Oxford study does not purport to shed light on the impact on juries of convictions for sexual offences other than IAC, it clearly has severe limitations as far as its implications for law reform are concerned. Each jury sat through a 30-minute video containing only 'the controversial and central prosecution and defence evidence'.[262] Two witnesses were called for the prosecution, only the defendant for the defence.[263] When the defendant was called to the witness box, attention was focused on his previous conviction by mentioning it in a voice-over.[264] The judge also referred to it in his summing up afterwards and then gave the Judicial Studies Board specimen direction which was current at the time.[265] Crucially, the judge did not sum up the evidence in the case.[266] After the video, participants were asked to fill in a questionnaire and participate in a 30-minute discussion following which a second questionnaire was administered. This second questionnaire included questions, focusing again on the defendant and designed to elicit impressions of him.[267] It is not clear that a study of this kind can shed light on how real jurors would react when they are called upon to assess liability after a trial which may well last several days, when a variety of witnesses are called for both sides, including expert witnesses. In real trials, there is far more scope for impressions of the defendant to be diffused with a multitude of other impressions. Real jurors have the benefit of weighing all the evidence after direction by the judge.

OTHER ARGUMENTS FOR AND AGAINST THE FEDERAL RULES

In addition to invoking the Oxford study, the Law Commission sets up various weak arguments in favour of the Federal Rules and treating sexual offences differently which it then proceeds happily to demolish:

'Sexual offences should be treated differently because of the particular psychology of the perpetrators'.[268] This argument is patently weak and the

[260] Silber (1997) 130–1. [261] ibid. 130. [262] ibid., para. D.9.
[263] ibid. [264] ibid., para. D.11. [265] ibid., para. D.11, 326.
[266] Lloyd-Bostock (2000), 741.
[267] Law Commission (1996), appendix D, para. D.16.
[268] Law Commission (1996), para. 9.24.

Commission has no trouble dispatching it. Sexual offenders are not necessarily psychologically abnormal. It cannot therefore be assumed that, if the accused has a conviction for a sexual offence, he is psychologically different from the rest of the population and hence more likely to have committed the offence alleged.

On the other hand, it is plain that some sexual offenders *are* psychologically abnormal. McEwan argues that, given that some sexual offending is pathological, notably serial or sadistic offending, there is a case for an exceptional rule in such cases.[269] The problem here is distinguishing which sexual offenders fall into this particular category. The identification of serial offenders is fraught with difficulty. The number of sexual offences committed by any given defendant is not generally known.[270] As sexual offences are infrequently reported and hard to prosecute successfully, serial offenders do not commonly leave a trail of previous convictions for sexual offences. Classification of offending as sadistic is also problematic.[271] In psychological terms, sadism needs to be seen in terms of the motivation and inner world of the offender as well as his behaviour. Thus, it might be hard and somewhat arbitrary to distinguish between sexual offenders on the basis which McEwan suggests.

'Sexual offenders should be treated differently because of the particular danger they pose to society'.[272] A second argument dismissed by the Commission for treating sexual offences differently is that they are 'abhorrent and increasingly prevalent'.[273] Clearly, their increased prevalence is debatable and other offences are equally abhorrent.

The Commission suggests that, since sexual offenders suffer more opprobrium than other offenders, this could support an argument that they require more rather than less protection from wrongful conviction.[274] To increase the hurdles and decrease the chances of conviction for sexual offences because of the stigma they attract would be hard to justify, given the seriousness of these offences. Besides, this seems to ignore the stigma attracted by a range of non-sexual offences. Moreover, stigma does not necessarily attach to all types of sexual offending.[275]

The Commission further suggests that, since large numbers of sexual assaults do not result in charges let alone convictions, it is not clear that a

[269] [1997] Crim LR 96

[270] For example, a sample of 37 rapists attending a sex offender treatment programme who were asked how many rapes they had committed, reported committing 433 rapes previously but had been charged with 66 offences: Weinrott and Saylor (1991), at 291.

[271] See e.g. R. A. Prentky and R. A. Knight, 'Identifying Critical Dimensions for Discriminating Among Rapists'(1991) 59 *Journal of Consulting and Clinical Psychology* 643, 652.

[272] Law Commission (1996), para. 9.27.

[273] ibid., para. 9.28, 145.

[274] ibid., para. 9.30, 146.

[275] e.g. sexual assaults involving touching an adult woman.

change in the law of evidence would discourage potential attackers.[276] However, it is likely that the present rules of evidence are part of the problem as far as poor conviction rates are concerned. The Commission concludes from the Oxford study that previous misconduct evidence, if admitted, *would* affect conviction rates in sexual cases.[277] If so, this might encourage more victims to report, more prosecutions to be brought, and might deter more potential offenders. Since the Commission appears to doubt that all those who commit sexual offences are psychologically abnormal,[278] at least some should be capable of responding rationally to real threats of imprisonment.

'Sexual offences should be treated differently because of the particular problems they pose in gathering evidence'.[279] The Commission rejects this argument on three different grounds. First, it points out that, where the rape is a stranger rape, the police may 'round up the usual suspects' who will be previous sexual offenders. There would be a risk that the defendant would be convicted on the basis of his previous convictions.[280] This may be an argument for excluding stranger rape cases from special rules for sexual offences, but it is not an argument for rejecting such rules in the majority of cases which are not stranger rape cases.

But the Commission goes on to argue that, even where the accused is known to the complainant, if she or others know that he has a record, she may be more likely to accuse him and the police may be more likely to charge him.[281] This is less than convincing. If he has indeed raped her, the fact that she is encouraged to report by the knowledge that he has raped others is entirely irrelevant. The problem, if there is one, can only possibly arise where she is lying. There is no evidence at all to suggest that fabrication is a particular problem in rape cases. The chances that a complainant will deliberately make a false allegation of rape against a man in the knowledge that he has convictions for previous similar offences seem, at best, remote. Within an adversarial system, there are many safeguards to protect the accused from wrongful conviction in these circumstances.

The Law Commission goes on to argue that probative value is not everything. The prejudicial effect must also be taken into account and the new Federal Rules do not make it clear whether they are subject to Rule 403.[282] Again, this is not an argument for rejecting this option. It is an argument for making it clear whether or not prejudicial effect should be built into the equation. That Rule 403 does apply has now been confirmed in numerous cases.[283]

276 Law Commission (1996), para. 9.29, 146.
277 See discussion above under the heading 'The Oxford Study'.
278 See Law Commission (1996), paras. 9.26–9.27.
279 ibid., para. 9.30.
280 ibid., para. 9.32, 146.
281 ibid., para. 9.33, 147.
282 ibid., para. 9.34.
283 See above under the heading 'Alternative Solutions'.

The Commission mentions a further argument, which is that the rules of evidence should be neutral, consistent, and uniform and that exceptions should not be made.[284] But exceptions are made at present. In England and Wales, previous convictions for handling may be adduced by the prosecution in handling cases[285] and, evidence of the accused's 'known character', which would include any convictions, may be adduced in prosecutions under section 1(2) of the Official Secrets Act 1911. It is also the case that, in the magistrates' jurisdiction, the trier of fact is frequently aware of the accused's past record.[286] In New Zealand, there is a similar provision for handling cases[287] and previous convictions for poisoning may be adduced in poisoning cases as well.[288] The Law Commission favours abolishing the special handling rules[289] and bringing the official secrets exception within the framework which it recommends for all offences.[290] However, even if the evidential rules were rendered uniform in all respects, it would be a mistake to suppose that consistency is to be equated with neutrality. The treatment of all offences in a uniform manner may not necessarily secure fairness. The law of evidence should not exist as a construct set apart from the context in which it operates. Sexual offences may require special measures if victims are to be treated no less favourably than victims of other offences.

THE CASE FOR THE NEW FEDERAL RULES

There is a case, which has not been put by the Commission, for treating sexual offences differently and for the type of approach taken in the Federal Rules. It may be summarized as follows:

(a) Sexual offences are particularly difficult to prosecute. Sexual offences are, for many different reasons, particularly difficult to prosecute. Generally, there is an absence of neutral witnesses and the medical evidence is likely to be equivocal. Often, sexual abuse is accompanied by threats not to reveal what has occurred. In this way it remains secret and vital evidence may be lost.

(b) The importance of credibility in sexual assault cases. In sexual assault cases, issues of credibility are uppermost precisely because of the lack of evidence. Most rape cases turn on the issue of consent. By his plea of not guilty, the accused is asserting that the complainant is lying and has fabricated a rape charge against him. A barrage of myths surround women who report rape, the most potent of which is that women commonly make false accusations for a variety of reasons and that a substantial proportion of the

[284] Law Commission (1996), para. 9.35.
[285] Theft Act 1968, s 27(3).
[286] See Darbyshire (1997), 106–7.
[287] Crimes Act 1961, s 258.
[288] Evidence Act 1908, s 23.
[289] Law Commission (1996), para. 14.13; Law Commission (2001), para. 11.55.
[290] Law Commission (2001), para. 11.61.

rapes reported to the police are false.[291] Thus, the complainant in a rape trial is at a disadvantage from the outset. No comparable myths surround other crime victims. In the case of children, further myths abound. Children are considered commonly to be natural liars and there is a reluctance to believe the word of a small child against that of an adult. Men who rape may be otherwise respectable citizens—doctors, businessmen, police officers, men with wives and families. Knowledge that the accused has committed rape on other occasions is a vital factor in assessing the plausibility of conflicting claims. It is evidence which will 'illumine the credibility of the charge'.[292] Where vital information about him is concealed, the chances of an accurate verdict are highly unlikely.

It is also the case that in rape trials the jury is likely to be invited to consider the complainant's mode of dress and her behaviour immediately before and during the incident to suggest that, at the very least, she brought what happened upon herself and that the accused is consequently undeserving of punishment.[293] A jury might see these claims in a different light if his record as a sexual predator were revealed.

(c) Evidence of previous sexual offending is highly probative. Evidence of past sexual offending may very well be not merely relevant but highly probative. It demonstrates that the accused has on one or more occasions crossed the Rubicon between fantasy and reality. He has lacked the boundaries in his sexual behaviour and effective inhibitions against acting on his sexual impulses that society expects. This is particularly the case where offences against children are concerned. 'A defendant's history of child molestation provides evidence that children are within his zone of sexual interest.'[294] He is more likely therefore to have committed the offence. Mathematical probability is also a consideration. In cases where multiple victims come forward quite independently with similar stories, it is highly improbable that they are all fabricated.[295]

(d) Misleading juries. The past sexual misconduct of the accused may well be a vital piece in the jigsaw. By depriving the jury of this information, it is being misled and its decision-making proceeds on an improper basis. The argument for withholding information demonstrates a fundamental lack of trust in the institution of the jury. If juries cannot be trusted with information about the accused's past misconduct, particularly with a suitable direction from the judge, this casts substantial doubt on their capacity to try criminal cases. There is serious hypocrisy at work here. If juries are integral to our system and a bastion of freedom, as the rhetoric so often proclaims, then they must be trusted and treated in an adult fashion. We do this in relation to many types of evidence which are considered to be potentially

[291] See e.g. Torrey (1991); Williams and Holmes (1981); Karp (1994), 21. [292] ibid.
[293] See Temkin (2000), 231–4. [294] Karp (1994), 53. [295] See ibid.

dangerous, such as eyewitness evidence. There is no suggestion that such evidence should be banned, even though in this case it has certainly led on occasions to wrongful convictions.[296] It frequently happens that juries convict a defendant on some charges and acquit him on others, indicating that they are quite capable of acting on judicial directions, sifting evidence and discerning when the burden of proof has or has not been satisfied.[297]

(e) The problem of serial rape. Studies indicate that many men who commit sexual offences are repeat offenders. Some have committed dozens, others hundreds of sexual offences. But they are seldom prosecuted or convicted for most of this sexual offending.[298] This happens, partly at least, because of an unwillingness to adjust outdated laws, which in turn discourages victims from reporting. An acknowledgement of the distinctive character of sexual offences and the way they are dealt with in court demands solutions which may not be necessary in dealing with other offences. Where the state refuses to place boundaries on offending behaviour, such behaviour is encouraged. In the case of adolescent sexual offenders in particular, sexual violence may become a habit unless society imposes sanctions.[299] Unchecked, sexual offending may become more violent and can sometimes escalate into murder.[300] It is the duty of the state to protect its citizens and laws which prevent this need to be amended.

(f) Other systems. The rule preventing the fact-finder from hearing about the accused's previous convictions seems to be unique to the English-speaking world. No such rule exists in Continental jurisdictions.[301]Article 6 of the ECHR has not been interpreted as forbidding reliance on previous convictions of the accused.[302] Moreover, even in English-speaking jurisdictions, the rule is far less rigidly adhered to in America, Canada, and New Zealand than it is in England and Wales. In America, long before the new Federal Rules were introduced, states commonly made exceptions in sexual cases so that evidence of previous sexual offending was admitted to show 'lustful disposition'.[303] Alternatively, pursuant to the decision in *People v Molineux*,[304] it was admissible to provide evidence of motive, plan, intent, or identity, provided the evidence was more probative than prejudicial.

[296] See Danna (1996), 308.

[297] See e.g. *Blackstock* (1979) 70 Cr App R 34; *Christou* [1996] 2 All ER 927.

[298] See e.g. Weinrott and Saylor (1991); G. G. Abel *et al.*, 'Self-Reported Sex Crimes of Nonincarcerated Paraphiliacs' (1987) 2 Journal of Interpersonal Violence 3.

[299] See e.g. National Children's Home (1992), para. 3.20.

[300] Spencer mentions the case of Colin James Evans a compulsive child molester who provided child-minding services. When charged with assault, his previous convictions were withheld from the jury. After his acquittal he murdered one of his victims: J. R. Spencer, *The Times*, 13 Aug. 1992.

[301] See Damaska (1994); Law Commission (1996), appendix B paras. B104–119.

[302] See Law Commission (1996), Appendix B, para. B104.

[303] See Danna (1996), 283.

[304] 61 NE 286 (NY 1901) for further discussion see Danna (1996), 281–4.

These exceptions continue to be applied. Thus, the new Federal rules essentially reflect the common law practice of many state courts and have withstood constitutional challenge. Several states have now adapted and incorporated them.[305] Neither New Zealand nor Canada adopted the strict regime which applies in England and Wales to restrict cross-examination of a defendant about his previous convictions.[306]

A PROPOSAL FOR REFORM

Now that it has been established that Rule 403 applies to Rules 413 to 415, their impact is likely to be far less than their critics feared. There can be no doubt that it is right that Rule 403 should apply.[307] Evidence of previous sexual offending, though relevant, may be less than highly probative because, for example, of lapse of time and dissimilarity with the alleged offence. The main difference between the new rules and English law is the starting-point. In English law, the similar fact rule dictates that there is a presumption of inadmissibility which can be displaced where the conditions set out in *P* apply. Under Rules 413 to 415, there is a presumption in favour of admissibility which can be displaced upon application of Rule 403. Thus, whilst the starting-points are different, the finishing points may be less so. The result is likely to be that more evidence will be admitted under the Rules than under *P*, but this will depend on judicial attitudes. It is suggested that where the defendant is charged with a crime of sexual assault, including sex with a person under the age of consent, evidence of previous sexual assaults, including sexual activity with minors, should be admissible as evidence. There should be discretion to exclude such evidence where its probative force is not sufficiently great to outweigh its prejudicial effect. Where the evidence is admitted, the judge should administer an appropriate warning to the jury to the effect that it must not be assumed that the defendant committed the crime alleged merely because of his past misconduct.[308]

305 Namely, Arizona, California, and Indiana: see Arizona Rule of Evidence 404(c); California Evidence Code, Rule 1108; Ind Code Ann, s 35–37–4–15(a) (Michie, 1998).

306 See discussion below under the heading 'Cross-examination of the Accused'.

307 As indeed was envisaged by those who were responsible for the introduction of the new rules: see Karp (1994), at 19.

308 This proposal is unlikely to result in the admission of previous convictions in many cases. For example, in 1985, only 18 per cent of those convicted of rape or attempted rape had previous convictions for sexual offences and only 3 per cent had previous convictions for rape: see Home Office *Statistical Bulletin* Issue 4/89 (1989), table 10. For the more far-reaching proposal put forward by Professor Spencer for all criminal cases, see Auld (2001), para. 118, 565–6. This proposal finds some favour in the Report: see ibid. para. 120. See also *Criminal Justice: The Way Ahead* (Cm 5074, HMSO, 2001), para. 3.51 in which the government mentions the possibility of admitting previous convictions in all cases 'where relevant providing the prejudicial effect does not outweigh the probative value'. The Labour Party manifesto also stated that there is 'a strong case for a new presumption' to that effect: see Auld (2001), para. 113, 564. See also n. 223 above.

(v) Contamination and Collusion

The relaxation of the similar fact regime brought about by *P* prompted familiar fears of false allegations. Where several complainants are involved, there is concern that they may have colluded to concoct a story, or else that, in discussing the matter between themselves, each one's account of what happened may have been contaminated.[309] In *H*,[310] the House of Lords dealt robustly and, it is submitted, appropriately with such fears. It was held that the issue of contamination was generally one for the jury to determine. Save in exceptional cases, it was not for the judge to enquire into contamination and collusion in a *voir dire* so that, if either were established, evidence could be withheld from the jury. It was for the jury to evaluate the complainant's evidence, if necessary with a suitable direction from the judge on the issue of collusion, where this question was raised. Lord Griffiths recognized that the defence was likely to allege contamination in cases where alleged victims were known to each other. He considered that allegations of contamination should not stand in the way of the jury's hearing all the evidence and making its own decision on the weight which should be attached to it.[311]

The decision in *H* again illustrates the growing sensitivity of the judiciary to the problem of sexual abuse and its recognition of the artificial barriers which evidential laws have placed in the way of the successful prosecution of these cases. But it has been heavily criticized. Professor Tapper considers that the issue of contamination is relevant to admissibility and that it should be decided before the jury hears the evidence.[312] He favours the decision of the High Court of Australia in *Hoch v R*,[313] which, if adopted here, would effectively ensure that where parties who know each other are the alleged victims of abuse, evidence which satisfies the test in *P* would nevertheless be excluded. In this way the decision in *P* would be as good as nullified in such cases to the considerable detriment of victims of sexual abuse. The Law Commission, although initially inclined towards Professor Tapper's view,[314] has now endorsed the approach recommended in *H*.[315]

But the Commission was concerned about a situation in which evidence of previous misconduct by the accused was admitted in accordance with *P* 'but it later transpires that the evidence has been seriously affected by contamination or collusion'.[316] In *H*, the House of Lords concluded that where it became clear, after the admission of previous misconduct evidence, that 'no reasonable jury could accept the evidence as free from collusion', then the judge should direct the jury that the evidence could no longer be relied

[309] See discussion by Tapper (1999), 361–4.
[310] [1995] 2 All ER 865.
[311] At 878.
[312] Tapper (1999), 362–4.
[313] (1988) 165 CLR 292.
[314] Law Commission (1996), paras. 10.99–10.105.
[315] Law Commission (2001), para. 15.23.
[316] Para. 10.100.

on for any purpose adverse to the defence.[317] The Commission, however, did not consider that juries could be trusted in this way. Citing the Oxford study once again, it concluded that the prejudicial impact of previous misconduct evidence was too great to take the risk.[318] In its Consultation Paper, it provisionally recommended instead that

> where a judge is satisfied, after hearing all the evidence, that a conviction would be unsafe because, *in the light of the risk of contamination or collusion*, the probative value of any evidence admitted is outweighed by its likely prejudicial effect and the risk that the jury may be misled, confused or distracted, the judge should discharge the jury and consider whether to order a retrial or to enter a verdict of not guilty.[319]

Thus, whereas the House of Lords proposed that only in cases where there was clear evidence of collusion should a jury be directed not to rely on the evidence for purposes adverse to the defence, the Commission's proposal related to cases where there was a risk of either collusion or contamination. It is likely that children who are related or have lived in the same household as the accused would discuss the matter if a prosecution were brought. The defence would inevitably allege contamination and a risk of collusion in every case of this kind.

In its final report, the Commission has stood by its provisional proposal but the recommendation is now that the jury should be discharged or an acquittal directed where the judge is satisfied that the evidence is contaminated and that a conviction would be unsafe.[320] The language of risk appears to have been abandoned. None the less, under this proposal, given the breadth of the concept of contamination, if the prosecution applied to take the route mapped out by *P*, it would frequently run the risk that the trial would be aborted in mid-stream. It might well prefer to avoid such a risk so that the jury would be deprived of hearing evidence that would substantially support the complainant's evidence, particularly in child sexual abuse cases. If implemented, this proposal would be likely to erode much of the progress which has been made in this area.

(vi) Joinder and Severance

Where the accused is charged with several separate offences, the question arises whether these should all be dealt with at a single trial or whether the judge should sever the indictment and order separate trials. Where, applying *P*, the evidence of one offence could be used as evidence in support of the commission of another offence, there is clearly no objection to trying both offences together. It is where this is not the case that the question of separate trials arises.

Rule 9 of the Indictment Rules 1971 allows joinder of different counts in the same indictment if the counts are 'founded on the same facts or form or

[317] [1995] 2 All ER at 877. [318] See Law Commission (1996), paras. 10.100–10.101.
[319] ibid., para. 10.05; emphasis added. [320] Law Commission (2001), para. 15.37.

are part of a series of offences of the same or similar character'. Thus there is no requirement under Rule 9 that the different counts conform to the strict standard demanded by *P*. However, section 5(3) of the Indictments Act 1915 states that where the judge considers 'that a person accused may be prejudiced or embarrassed in his defence by reason of being charged with more than one offence in the same indictment', the judge may order separate trials.

Criticism about severance of counts and the ordering of separate trials in sexual offence cases has increasingly been voiced. There is legitimate concern that serial rapists are avoiding justice altogether where judges exercise their discretion to order separate trials, insisting that the evidence on each count be admissible on the other counts if they are to be heard together.[321] In sexual cases, where issues of credibility are uppermost, it is important that the single trial option is chosen. The complainant's account of a sexual assault perpetrated against her is less likely to be dismissed by the jury, after the usual efforts to undermine her credibility by the defence, where there is other evidence against the accused. However, in 1996, a proposed amendment to the Criminal Procedure and Investigations Bill, which would have made it more difficult for judges to order separate trials for sexual offences, was defeated. In the debate, it was noted by Tessa Jowell MP that 'trial judges' readiness to hear cases separately denies juries crucial information about the extent of the allegations made against some serial rapists'.[322]

JUDICIAL INTERPRETATION OF RULE 9

In *Ludlow v MPC*,[323] it was held that, where the counts are for offences of a similar character, they should normally be tried together since this was 'the manifest intention of the Act' subject to the discretion under section 5(3).[324] The judge should not exercise this discretion unless there existed 'some special feature' which would cause embarrassment or prejudice and severance would be 'in the interests of justice.'[325]

The Court of Appeal has been reluctant to interfere with a trial judge's decision on these matters. However, in *Brooks*,[326] decided before *P*, it was held that separate trials should have been ordered where the evidence on each count of incest was not strikingly similar and was thus inadmissible as evidence on the other counts. In *Cannan*,[327] it was suggested that 'it may well be that often the judge in sexual cases will order severance'.

In *Christou*,[328] by contrast, the House of Lords, in another case involving sexual abuse of children, refused to quash the conviction where the trial judge had not exercised the discretion to sever. It confirmed that this was a matter for the judge, who was not obliged to sever where the evidence on

321 See *The Times*, 2 Feb. 1994; Lees (1996), 191–209.
322 Hansard, 12 June 1996, col. 357.
323 [1971] AC 29.
324 At 41.
325 ibid. *per* Lord Pearson.
326 (1991) 92 Cr App R 36.
327 (1991) 92 Cr App R 16.
328 [1996] 2 WLR 620.

each count did not meet the standard set down by *P* for admissibility on the other counts, despite a decision to the contrary in *P* itself.[329]

The decision in *Christou* is warmly to be welcomed. The Lord Chief Justice made it clear that, in considering whether to sever, the court must consider not merely fairness to the accused but fairness to the prosecution and those involved in it.[330] He was confident that, where juries were instructed that evidence on one count could not be used on another count, they were capable of putting that into effect. Cases in which juries convicted on some counts and acquitted on others demonstrated their ability to do so.

Christou should offer encouragement to judges to resist routine severance in sexual cases. It is disappointing that in its Consultation Paper the Law Commission sought to query this approach. It criticized the present position as illogical and asked for views as to 'whether the courts should sever charges where prejudicial evidence is not interadmissible between different charges, *especially in sex cases*'.[331] Such an approach would involve turning back the clock to place yet another obstacle in the way of convictions of rapists. If there is a problem, it lies in the rigidity of the approach to admissibility, and it is this, not cases like *Christou,* which are ripe for reform. The Law Commission's final proposal would create a presumption in favour of severance where the defence requests it and bad character evidence is admissible on one count but inadmissible on another count. The court would be able to resist this only where it was satisfied that the accused could receive a fair trial without severance.[332] This regrettable approach would be likely to ensure a trend in the direction of severance.

(b) Cross-Examination of the Accused

Section 1 of the Criminal Evidence Act 1898 provides the accused with a shield so that he cannot generally be cross-examined about his previous offences and bad character. Section 1(f)(ii), however, deprives him of his shield where 'the nature or conduct of the defence is such as to involve imputations on the character of the prosecutor'. Barristers defending in rape trials where consent is the issue will routinely employ strategies which involve casting imputations on the character of the complainant. Research involving in-depth interviews with 10 barristers who were highly experienced in prosecuting and defending in rape trials revealed that the discrediting of the complainant was the central defence strategy in rape cases.[333] The main aim was to undermine the victim in the eyes of the jury. As one barrister explained: 'You'll put your chap's facts and obviously controvert her facts. They're less important than undermining her personality. It sounds sinister but that's

[329] [1991] 3 All ER at 348.
[330] [1996] 2 All ER at 937.
[331] Law Commission (1996), 263; emphasis added.
[332] Law Commission (2001), para. 16.21.
[333] Temkin (2000), 231.

what you're trying to do, make her sound and appear less credible.'[334] The strategy of discrediting the complainant was found to involve several different tactics. These included maligning the victim's behaviour at the time of the incident, maligning her clothes and maligning her sexual character. Applications would regularly be made to admit sexual history evidence.[335]

Apart from section 41 of the YJCEA 1999, present law does little to restrain defence strategy. The decision in *Turner*[336] ensured that, despite section 1(f)(ii), the accused would not forfeit his shield in a rape case where he alleged consent. This decision has been broadly interpreted so that, in practice, the defence in a rape trial may cast imputations on the behaviour and character of the complainant with relative impunity provided that this is directed at establishing consent. As the Heilbron Committee commented:

> We have received evidence which suggests that in practice the rule in *Turner's* case has come to be very widely interpreted in favour of the accused, so that where the defence is consent, the cross-examination can go to considerable lengths with no risk of letting in the accused's record, if there is one.[337]

Rape is thus treated differently from all other offences. It is *sui generis*.[338] In no other situation can an accused expect to sling mud without receiving some back. Not only will a mere allegation of consent result in no loss of the shield, but neither, very often, will evidence adduced to support this defence irrespective of whether it discredits the complainant. In every other case, the casting of imputations, even where necessary to enable the accused to establish his defence, will result in the loss of the shield unless judicial discretion is exercised to disallow such evidence. This blatant discrimination in favour of the accused in rape cases cannot be justified. It is bound to be a factor in the persistent difficulty in obtaining convictions in rape cases. Where defects in the character or behaviour of the complainant are revealed but those of the defendant are concealed, the jury is bound to be misled.[339] There is much

[334] Temkin (2000), 231.

[335] ibid. 231–5. Defence practice in the United States is similar. For example, in the trial of William Kennedy Smith in Florida, the complainant's medical records were revealed in order to argue that she had a long-standing psychological disorder which, defence counsel argued, might explain why she had falsely accused Smith of raping her. It was claimed that she was suffering the emotional impact of at least two abortions and one miscarriage and that she was a man-hater. The defence also devoted much attention to the allegedly seductive quality of her underwear, even though it was not alleged that Smith had seen it before the rape occurred. However, the jury was not told that three women had come forward with very similar allegations against Smith. Each, entirely independently, told a similar tale of rape. This evidence was ruled inadmissible. Smith was acquitted.

[336] [1944] 1 All ER 599.

[337] Heilbron Committee (1975), para. 127. A similar situation would appear to prevail in Scotland. See Brown *et al.* (1992) 73. But see now the Sexual Offences (Procedure and Evidence) (Scotland) Act 2002, s 10.

[338] Or so it was suggested by Devlin J in *R v Cook* [1959] 2QB 340, 347.

[339] For an excellent analysis, see S. Seabrook, 'Closing the Credibility Gap: A New Approach to s 1(f)(ii) of the Criminal Evidence Act 1898' [1987] Crim LR 231.

to be said for overruling the decision in *Turner* and subsequent cases which confirmed it[340] so that, at the very least, rape is treated on a par with all other offences.

The rigid regime imposed by the Criminal Evidence Act 1898 has not been followed in Canada or New Zealand. In Canada, the accused may be cross-examined about his previous convictions in exactly the same way as any other witness, although details of the offences may not be mentioned and there is a discretion to limit this type of cross-examination.[341] In New Zealand, the position is similar. Defendants are in the same position as far as cross-examination as other witnesses, subject to the court's discretion to limit cross-examination on previous convictions. Where the convictions relate to an issue in the trial, they are more likely to be admitted than where they are relevant to credibility.[342]

(i) The Law Commission's Provisional Proposals

LOSING THE SHIELD

In its Consultation Paper, the Law Commission provisionally recommended the approach taken by the Australian Commonwealth Evidence Act 1995. In all criminal cases, an accused would forfeit his shield only if the imputations cast 'do not relate to the witness's conduct in the incident or investigation in question'.[343] This formula has clear advantages in certain situations as, for example, where the accused wishes to assert that there was improper police behaviour during the investigation. At present, defendants with criminal records are constrained from doing so for fear of losing their shield. However, as far as rape trials are concerned, it is not at all clear that this formula would achieve justice.

(a) Imputations about the complainant's behaviour on the occasion in question. Under the Law Commission's provisional proposal, imputations about the complainant's behaviour in the incident in question would not result in the defendant's losing his shield. It has been noted above[344] that maligning the complainant's behaviour at the time of the rape is part of the defence strategy of discrediting her. In sexual assault cases where everything hinges on credibility, there can be no justification for permitting one side to undermine the credibility of the other without redress. The point is illustrated by the facts of *Turner* itself. The complainant alleged that, while on her way to visiting her mother, she encountered some soldiers and that one of them, Turner, raped her. He alleged that having just met her, she volunteered to perform an act of gross indecency on him and that she then consented to sexual intercourse. This was clearly an imputation on her character

[340] See *Selvey v DPP* [1970] AC 304. [341] Paciocco and Stuesser (1999), 272.
[342] Law Commission (1996), appendix B, paras. B.69–B.71.
[343] Law Commission (1996), para. 12.70. [344] Text at n. 334 above.

and the trial judge permitted evidence to be adduced that Turner had a previous conviction for assault with intent to ravish. The Court of Appeal considered that this evidence should not have been admitted. Under the Law Commission's provisional proposals, which echo the Court of Appeal's decision in this respect, the accused would not lose his shield in these circumstances. Indeed, no matter how damaging the allegations made about the complainant's conduct during the incident, he would not lose his shield. A further problem with this proposal is that it would raise questions as to the boundaries of the incident and when precisely it began and ended. If it is alleged that the complainant offered to perform oral sex on the accused having just met him, would this be regarded as part of the incident if the offer were made 24, 36, or 48 hours before he allegedly raped her?

(b) Where the defence is permitted to adduce sexual history evidence. Section 41 of the YJCEA 1999 permits the admission of sexual history evidence in certain prescribed circumstances. This evidence is likely to be highly damaging to the prosecution. For example, the accused may allege that he believed that the complainant was consenting because he knew of previous incidents in which she had had sexual intercourse with his friends and could see no reason why she would not also consent to him.[345] Alternatively, he may allege that, on the night in question, she had had sexual intercourse with his friends.[346] But, in order to be admitted, the evidence has to pass the gateway set by section 41(4). It may be adduced only if the judge considers that it is related to a relevant issue in the case. If the main purpose of it is to impugn her credibility, it will not be regarded as relating to a relevant issue in the case. Evidence which passes the hurdle set by section 41(4) would not result in the accused's losing his shield under the Australian law which the Law Commission proposed to follow. This is because under section 104(4)(b) of the Commonwealth Evidence Act 1995, leave may not be granted to the prosecution to cross-examine the accused about his previous misconduct unless the defence 'has been permitted to adduce evidence which tends to prove that a witness called by the prosecution has a tendency to be untruthful and which is relevant mainly or solely to that witness's credibility'. Thus under section 41(4) sexual history evidence may not be admitted where its purpose is to impugn the complainant's credibility. Under section 104(4)(b), unless its main purpose is to impugn her credibility, the accused will not lose his shield. Hence, under the Law Commission's provisional proposal, where the court permitted the use of sexual history evidence, the accused would never lose his shield.[347]

345 Such evidence is potentially admissible as a result of s 41(3)(a).

346 Such evidence is potentially admissible under s 41(3)(b).

347 Law Commission (1996), para. 12.71. Contrast Sexual Offences (Procedure and Evidence (Scotland) Act 2002, s 10.

WHERE THE ACCUSED HAS NO CRIMINAL RECORD AND THERE IS NO KNOWN PREVIOUS MISCONDUCT

Any scheme under which the accused forfeits his shield if imputations are cast on prosecution witnesses clearly applies only where he *has* previous convictions or evidence of his previous misconduct is available. Whilst the majority of defendants who come before the courts have criminal convictions, this is not always the case. In such circumstances, or where previous misconduct is unknown, defendants are free under present law to attack the character of prosecution witnesses with impunity, the only restrictions being those which are imposed by the YJCEA 1999 in sexual cases. But the scope of the 1999 Act is limited. Although section 41 is designed to include an embargo on secondary evidence of sexual behaviour, such as abortions,[348] it is most unlikely that it would be construed to apply to other humiliating and frequently irrelevant evidence relating to clothing, underwear, and make-up even though such evidence has clear sexual connotations. Some American 'rape-shield' legislation, by contrast, goes beyond barring sexual history evidence and extends specifically to other evidence commonly used in sexual offence trials. Thus, three states have widened the embargo on sexual history evidence so that it applies to the complainant's mode of dress as well.[349] The Utah Rules of Evidence place a ban on evidence which may have sexual connotations, such as evidence about the victim's dress, speech, or lifestyle.[350] The Scottish Law Commission also originally proposed that evidence tending to show that the alleged victim in sexual cases was not of good character should be excluded, as well as evidence of sexual behaviour.[351] This was in recognition of the difficulty of distinguishing sexual character from general character.[352] However, this approach was not adopted in the legislation which followed.

The Law Commission discusses the possibility of a further option, referred to as Option D, which would apply in all criminal cases and set limits to the extent to which bad character evidence of witnesses other than the accused might be adduced in the first place. It suggests that 'it would be possible to adopt a rule that bad character evidence must be of more than trivial weight or of significant or substantial weight before it can be admitted'.[353] This is the position under the Australian Commonwealth Evidence Act 1995.[354] Alternatively, it suggests that the formula used under the now

[348] *Explanatory Notes*, para. 145.

[349] Namely, Georgia, Florida, and Alabama. For an interesting discussion of this legislation, see A. Sterling, 'Undressing the Victim: The Intersection of Evidentiary and Semiotic Meanings of Women's Clothing in Rape Trials' [1995] 7:87 Yale Journal of Law and Feminism 87.

[350] Rule 412: see Advisory Committee Note http://courtlink.utcourts.gov/rules/ure/0412.htm.

[351] Scottish Law Commission, *Evidence: Report on Evidence in Cases of Rape and other Sexual Offences*, No. 78 (HC 28, 1983), app. A, 30.

[352] See Brown *et al.* (1992), 73.

[353] Law Commission (1996), para. 12.91.

[354] s 103.

defunct Sexual Offences (Amendment) Act 1976 could be disinterred and made to apply in all cases. Thus, bad character evidence would be admissible only where the judge considered that it would be unfair to the defendant to exclude it, since it might reasonably lead the fact-finder to take a different view of the evidence. Either approach would leave it in the hands of the judges to determine when bad character evidence should be admitted. It seems unlikely that such approaches would exclude much of the evidence which defence barristers commonly see fit to adduce in sexual cases, as previous experience of the Sexual Offences (Amendment) Act indicates.

WHERE THE ACCUSED CLAIMS THAT HE IS OF GOOD CHARACTER

Under present law, where the accused gives evidence of his own good character or asks questions of prosecution witnesses with a view to establishing his own good character, he may also lose his shield.[355] Moreover, character is deemed to be indivisible so that where he states or implies that he is of good character, say, in financial matters, evidence may be adduced that he has previous convictions for sexual offences.[356] The Law Commission was provisionally in favour of changing this rule.[357] It considered that 'there is no necessary connection between different character traits'[358] and that psychological studies demonstrate that it is hard to predict future behaviour from the existence of any particular character trait. It cites approvingly the words of the Australian Law Reform Commission on this matter: 'A person's character is not so highly integrated as to motivate trans-situational consistency of behaviour. Rather valid predictions about human behaviour are unlikely unless an individual is placed in similar situations.'[359] It fails to note, however, that such theories are constantly changing and that the fortunes of 'trait theory' have ebbed and flowed over the past few decades.[360] The Commission also relies upon theories concerning 'the halo effect' which concern perceptions of character. It states: 'There is a tendency for people to form a complete, integrated impression of another person's personality even where only limited information about that person is available to them'.[361]

In response to these two separate bodies of theory, neither of which is effectively scrutinized by the Commission, it recommends that character should no longer be treated as indivisible. The accused should be open to cross-examination only on that part of his or her character or truthfulness about which an assertion of good character has been made.[362] But this proposal is puzzling given the Commission's own analysis. If it is the case that

355 Criminal Evidence Act 1898, s 1(f)(ii).

356 See e.g. *Winfield* (1939) 27 Cr App R 139.

357 Law Commission (1996), para. 11.42.

358 ibid., para. 11.6.

359 para. 6.13.

360 See Danna (1996), at 286–7; S. M. Davies, 'Evidence of Character to Prove Conduct: A Reassessment of Relevancy' 27 Crim L Bull 504.

361 Law Commission (1996), para. 6.19.

362 At para. 11.42.

'valid predictions about human behaviour are unlikely unless an individual is placed in similar situations', then there can be no reason to permit cross-examination about character unless the situation is a similar one. As far as the 'halo effect' is concerned, the Commission concedes that the Oxford study suggests quite the reverse, namely, that juries frequently resist the halo effect.[363]

The Law Commission's proposal would have unsatisfactory consequences as far as sexual offences are concerned. Many of those who are charged with a sex offence do not have previous convictions for sexual offences. This is because of low reporting and conviction rates. They are, however, highly likely to have convictions for other offences.[364] There are connections between sexual offences and other types of offending. Sibling incest offenders are often thieves; bigamists may well have previous convictions for deception offences; and rapists are frequently violent men committing a disproportionate number of other kinds of violent offences.[365] As Soothill and Francis have noted: '. . . many sexual offenders come from the general pool of offenders and perhaps we separate off sexual offenders at our peril'.[366] Under the Law Commission's proposal, those charged with sex offences are likely to be advantaged over other defendants. Indeed, a reverse halo effect is likely to be created. A man charged with rape would be able to point to the fact that he had never been convicted or charged with a sexual offence before, confident that his previous convictions for other offences would not be disclosed. He would emerge as a far more wholesome character than in fact he is. The present law deters him from creating a false impression of his character in this way.

In a case where the convictions are 'spent, minor or wholly irrelevant', the Commission recommends that the jury should be told that the accused has 'no relevant convictions'.[367] Again, this begs the question of what is irrelevant, whether spent convictions for sexual offences are irrelevant, and whether judges will necessarily be aware of the unusual connections which exist between sexual and other offences. Similarly, it recommends that, where the evidence adduced to rebut the assertion of good character is 'directly relevant' to the accused's propensities, the fact-finder should not be directed to treat the evidence as bearing solely on his credibility.[368] But

[363] Law Commission (1996), para. 6.29.

[364] For example, a study of 142 imprisoned rapists found that 86 per cent had a previous criminal record. The vast majority (72%) had convictions for theft and 47 per cent for minor assault (D. Grubin and J. Gunn, *The Imprisoned Rapist and Rape* (London: Institute of Psychiatry, 1990), 18–20). In a study of 210 cases of men arrested for serious sexual assault, most of whom were subsequently convicted, 84 per cent had criminal records with 73 per cent having at least one conviction for theft, 56 per cent for burglary, 50 per cent for violence and 32 per cent for a sexual offence: Davies *et al.* (1997), 164.

[365] K. Soothill and B. Francis, 'Sexual Reconvictions and the Sex Offenders Act 1997' 147 NLJ 5 Sept. 1997 1285–6.

[366] ibid. 1285.

[367] Law Commission (1996), 205, n. 52.

[368] Law Commission (1996), para. 11.45.

again, this begs the question of when evidence of previous convictions is directly relevant. Certainly, without further training about sexual offences, judges are likely to miss possible linkages. Moreover, under the Commission's proposal, the judge would also have discretion not to deprive the accused of his shield even if he does make an assertion of good character.[369] Thus, even if the accused asserts his good character in the sexual sphere, the judge would not be bound to permit the prosecution to adduce evidence of his past sexual misconduct.

THE DEFENDANT WHO DOES NOT GIVE EVIDENCE

Under present law, as a result of the decision in *Butterwasser*,[370] if the accused chooses not to give evidence, he is free to sling as much mud as he likes at the complainant and other prosecution witnesses without fear of redress. Whilst it is true that defendants who decline to testify now run the risk[371] that the judge will invite the jury to draw adverse inferences from this, a judge will not inevitably give such a direction.[372] Moreover, it is a risk which might well be worth taking. The impact of a sustained attack on the complainant's character is likely so to affect the jury that any such adverse inferences will be of little consequence. The Royal Commission on Criminal Justice rightly condemned this state of affairs and recommended that the accused should lose his shield in these circumstances.[373] In its final report, the Law Commission has also rejected the *Butterwasser* approach.[374]

(ii) The Law Commission's Final Report[375]

The Law Commission has now decided to jettison the 1898 Act altogether and with it the so-called 'tit-for-tat' principle. It has also rejected the notion of indivisibility of character. In cases where the accused suggests that another person has a propensity to be untruthful, the prosecution would be able to adduce evidence of the accused's bad character but only in so far as it indicates his propensity to be untruthful and only where a series of further conditions are fulfilled.[376] Likewise, it is proposed that leave might be given to adduce evidence of the accused's bad character where he is responsible for an assertion which creates a false or misleading impression about himself, provided again that certain conditions are fulfilled.[377] Only those aspects of his bad character which are considered to be of substantial relevance in refuting the specific assertion made would be admissible.[378] The objections to this approach have already been canvassed.[379]

[369] At para. 11.43.

[370] [1948] 1 KB 4.

[371] CJPOA 1994, s35.

[372] *Cowan* [1995] 3 WLR 818; see also *Murray v UK* (1996) 22 EHRR 29.

[373] Report of the Royal Commission on Criminal Justice (Cm 2263, London, 1993), ch. 8, para. 34.

[374] See (2001), para. 4.65 and clause 10(5), 218.

[375] Law Commission (2001).

[376] See p. 205 at para. 9.

[377] At 206.

[378] See para. 13.28.

[379] See above under the heading 'Where the Accused Claims That He Is Of Good Character'.

In the case of other witnesses, the Commission has pursued and developed Option D.[380] Evidence of the bad character of witnesses would be admissible where this has to do with the offence charged. No sanction would be attached to the admission of such evidence.[381] Attention has been drawn to the disadvantages of this scheme as far as complainants in sexual cases are concerned.[382] Where the evidence of bad character falls outside this envelope, leave would need to be sought and would be given only if it passed a test of substantial probative value.[383] Bad character would be defined as evidence that a person has committed an offence or has behaved or is disposed to behave in a way that in the opinion of the court might be viewed with disapproval by a reasonable person.[384] It is not clear that this definition, with its emphasis on bad behaviour, would cover much of the evidence that is commonly used to undermine the credibility of complainants. Thus, for example, evidence that the complainant suffers from depression or anxiety, evidence concerning her clothing or that she lives in a squat seem unlikely to count as evidence of bad character and thus would not be subject to any control. Where evidence does amount to evidence of bad character and leave is given, there would be no question of the accused's losing his shield. In the case of sexual history evidence, if this amounted to evidence of bad character, this would theoretically have to pass both the barriers erected in section 41 and the substantial probative value test, but the Report notes that the latter test would almost certainly be satisfied in every case.[385] Again, the admission of sexual history evidence would never lead to the accused's losing his shield.

Since the new controls on bad character evidence would be unlikely to add a great deal to section 41, this regime would have a limited effect on the status quo in sexual offences, and the defence would continue to enjoy considerable freedom to undermine the complainant's credibility. Moreover, with the abolition of the 'tit for tat' principle, complainants would be worse off than at present, since occasionally defendants in rape trials do lose their shield under the existing law.

(iii) A Proposal for Reform

The Law Commission has considered a number of options to deal with the problems raised by the defence's casting imputations on prosecution witnesses or alternatively seeking to show the accused's good character. None of these options would be likely to operate in a satisfactory or fair way in sexual cases. By adopting the Australian model discussed in the

[380] See p. 249.

[381] Law Commission (2001) 204, para. 3.

[382] See above under the heading 'Imputations about the complainant's behaviour on the occasion in question'.

[383] See Law Commission (2001) 205, para. 6, i.e. 'substantial probative value in relation to a matter in issue in the proceedings, which is of substantial importance in the context of the case as a whole'.

[384] 204, para. 2.

[385] para. 9.45.

Consultation Paper, the accused would forfeit his shield only where imputations did not relate to the witness's conduct in the incident or investigation in question. He would thus be free to cast aspersions on the complainant's conduct during the incident without fear of redress. The use of sexual history evidence by the defence under the exceptions set out in section 41 of the YJCEA would fail to trigger any loss of the shield. It is also not at all clear that the type of routine undermining of the complainant's character indulged in by defence counsel would generally lead to the defendant's losing his shield. Now, in its final Report, the Law Commission proposes the repeal of the 1898 Act and its substitution by a provision which would seek to do no more than place limits on the extent to which the credibility of prosecution witnesses could be attacked. In practice, this would leave complainants in sexual cases with not much more than section 41 and with even less protection than at present. Furthermore, the proposal that the accused's character should no longer be regarded as indivisible is likely to shift the balance further in favour of the accused in sexual offence trials.

The issue is essentially one of fairness. Sauce for the goose must be sauce for the gander. Sir John Smith expressed it thus: 'The problem for the jury, in the end, is to decide whether they are satisfied beyond reasonable doubt that the woman rather than the man is speaking the truth; and if the characters of both are bad, it looks a bit one-sided if they know of hers but not of his'.[386] So long as this is the case and the complainant is exposed whilst the accused's character remains uncovered, this can only deter victims from pursuing prosecutions, given the exceptional importance of credibility in sexual cases. The starting-point must be that any undermining of the complainant's character must be met by similar treatment of the accused. But it is not sufficient to express this in terms of a general formula. There should be a statutory provision to the effect that, where evidence is adduced for the defence with the purpose of undermining the complainant's character, including evidence about her way of life, previous convictions, clothing other than on the occasion in question where belief in consent is alleged, or sexual or medical history, including a history of previous sexual abuse, then evidence of the accused's previous convictions and past misconduct should be admitted.[387] Where the accused asserts his own good character, the indivisibility of character rule should continue to apply in sexual cases. Section 41 of the YJCEA 1999 should be extended expressly to cover evidence concerning clothing and make-up. There would thus be an embargo on such evidence save in those exceptional circumstances which it specifies.[388]

[386] J. C. Smith [1976] Crim LR 97 at 105.

[387] If the previous convictions were for sexual assault, these could have been admitted already under the proposal put forward above: see under the heading 'A Proposal for Reform', at 241. See also Sexual Offences (Procedure and Evidence) (Scotland) Act 2002, s 10.

[388] See above under the heading 'The Youth Justice and Criminal Evidence Act 1999', at p. 201.

Corroboration

In Pakistan, as part of the Government's Islamization programme introduced in 1977, it has become an imprisonable offence known as *zina* for a man and woman to have sexual intercourse outside marriage.[389] The *Zina* Ordinance which created this offence also created the offence of *zina-bil-jabr,* which is rape. It provides that, for the offence of rape to be established, the accused must either confess, or at least four Muslim adult male witnesses must give eyewitness evidence of the act of penetration. The evidence of these witnesses is acceptable only if the court is satisfied that they are truthful people who abstain from major sins. In the event that no such evidence is available, the court may conclude that intercourse was consensual and that the crime of *zina* has therefore been committed. In *Mina v State,*[390] Jehan Mina, a 15-year-old, became pregnant as a result of an alleged rape. In the absence of the requisite witnesses, she was convicted of *zina* on the basis of her illegitimate pregnancy and sent to prison where the child was born. In *Bibi v State,*[391] Safia Bibi, a 16-year-old, half-blind domestic servant met the same fate, having alleged that she was pregnant after repeated rape by her employer and his son. Since corroboration of the sort required is inevitably lacking, women who allege rape in Pakistan are liable to be held in prison for extended periods on charges of *zina* where they run a distinct risk of rape by the police.[392]

No such blatantly discriminatory provisions exist in the English law of evidence; however, the common law rules relating to corroboration were less than satisfactory as far as their implications for women were concerned.

(a) The Old Common Law Rules

Generally, in England and Wales, the evidence of a single witness, if believed, is sufficient to prove the case against the accused.[393] There are, however, some exceptions to this rule. With certain sexual offences which involved procuring a woman for the purposes of prostitution,[394] the victim's evidence alone was incapable of securing a conviction. There had to be some additional confirmatory evidence which implicated the accused person and tended to confirm his guilt. This is known as a corroboration requirement. It was abolished in the case of these offences in 1994.[395] For the remaining

[389] The Offence of *Zina* (Enforcement of Hudood) Ordinance VII of 1979. See Quraishi (1999).

[390] 1983 P.L.D. Fed. Shariat Ct. 183. [391] 1985 P.L.D. Fed. Shariat Ct.120.

[392] See Quraishi (1999), 3–4. Amnesty International, *Pakistan: Torture, Deaths in Custody and Extrajudicial Executions* (London: Amnesty International, 1993), 11–12.

[393] This is not the case in Scotland where conviction on the uncorroborated evidence of a single witness is not allowed.

[394] See SOA 1956, ss 2–4, 22, and 23. [395] CJPOA 1994, s 33.

sexual offences, whether or not consent was an ingredient of the offence, corroboration was not actually required, but the judge was obliged to warn the jury of the danger of convicting solely on the basis of the evidence of the complainant. The judge was, however, also entitled to state that the jury might choose to convict even in the absence of corroborating evidence if the defendant's guilt was clear beyond reasonable doubt. Provided that the warning was administered, a conviction could not be quashed on appeal merely because of the absence of corroboration. But where the warning was not given, the conviction would be quashed by the Court of Appeal, even though there was abundant corroborative evidence, unless it decided that the case merited application of the proviso to section 2(1) of the Criminal Appeal Act 1968, in which case the conviction would stand because 'no miscarriage of justice had actually occurred'.[396]

Corroboration requirements and warnings in sexual cases were, until recently, well established throughout the common law world. Their rationale rested on the alleged proclivities and weaknesses of women. Women, it was said, might fabricate sexual assault out of jealousy, spite, revenge, or because of a tendency to tell lies and fantasize. The beginning of wisdom in this context was the well-worn statement by Sir Matthew Hale: 'It must be remembered that it [rape] is an accusation easily to be made and hard to be proved, and harder to be defended by the party accused, tho never so innocent'.[397] Of course, rape is one of the hardest charges to bring, which is why most women never report it. Warren Young noted: 'The empirical evidence in our study tends to demonstrate . . . that rape is *not* a charge easily to be made and that a complaint to the police is usually made at considerable personal cost to the complainant . . .'.[398]

Those who argued in favour of the corroboration warning stressed that it was not merely that many women who alleged rape were liars but that they might be extremely adept at concealing the fact. Professor Glanville Williams urged that juries were particularly likely to be deceived by 'girl[s] of tender years whose appearance makes a strong appeal to the[ir] sympathy and protective feelings'.[399] Wigmore in similar vein wrote:

> The unchaste (let us call it) mentality finds incidental but direct expression in the narration of imaginary sex incidents of which the narrator is the heroine or the victim. On the surface the narration is straightforward and convincing. The real victim, however, too often in such cases is the innocent man; for the respect and sympathy naturally felt by any tribunal for a wronged female helps to give easy credit to such a plausible tale.[400]

[396] See CLRC (1972), para. 176. See further Cross and Tapper (1985), 222–3. On the issue of the corroboration warning where accomplices to rape were concerned, see *Olaleye* [1986] Crim LR 458.

[397] 1 PC 634.

[398] Young (1983), 140.

[399] 'Corroboration—Sexual Cases' [1962] Crim LR 662, 663. See also CLRC (1972), para. 186.

[400] J. H. Wigmore, *A Treatise on the Anglo-American System of Evidence in Trials at Common Law* (3rd edn., Boston: Little, Brown, 1940), para. 924A.

Indeed, Wigmore considered that, because the danger of fabrication was so overwhelming, female complainants, particularly young ones, should be subjected to medical or psychiatric examination to assess their credibility.[401] Moreover, it has been suggested that he was not above doctoring his sources to prove the point. Having scrutinized the authorities upon which Wigmore relied for his assertions about the mendacity of young girls, Bienen concluded: 'Wigmore writes as a man convinced, apparently so convinced that he actually suppressed factual evidence contradicting his assertions'.[402]

The explanation for the corroboration warning did not remain concealed from the public gaze in the writings of learned scholars. On the contrary, every sexual assault victim who had the temerity to permit a prosecution to be brought was required to be publicly humiliated by the judge's recitation of the reasons for the warning. In some cases, the judges went to town. Thus, Sutcliffe J at the Old Bailey in April 1976 told the jury: 'It is well known that women in particular and small boys are liable to be untruthful and invent stories'.[403] Barbara Toner quotes the following judicial explanations for the warning given in three different cases:

1. JUDGE: Whatever the advocates of Women's Lib say, the experience of the courts has been that charges of sexual attacks are so easily made, but so difficult to refute. For example, doctors don't examine without someone being present. It is so difficult to refute because it appears in private. There may be reasons why women make such unjust allegations: fantasies, for example, or spite. I won't enumerate the causes. Let me speculate that the defendant was the boyfriend of the complainant's sister some years ago. This hasn't been investigated and probably isn't true. But if the complainant thought that the defendant let her sister down, that would be a possible cause. You couldn't suppose that this is a reason because no such evidence was given, but it's an illustration of what I'm saying. False accusations have been made and are desperately difficult to disprove.
2. JUDGE: This is a sex case. Experience has shown that women can and do tell lies for some reason, sometimes for no reason at all.
3. JUDGE: It is well known that in sex cases women sometimes imagine things which various ingredients in their make up tend to make them imagine.[404]

In every one of the warnings which has been quoted here, it was made clear that the reason for giving it was not because complainants in sexual cases, be they male or female, were prone to lie, but specifically because women were prone to lie about sexual matters. It was thus to protect men from the alleged fabrication of women that the corroboration warning owed its

[401] This suggestion appeared for the first time in the 1934 supplement to the 1920 edition of Wigmore's treatise. For further discussion, see Bienen (1983), at 239. In Germany complainants in rape cases are frequently subjected to psychological testing to provide an assessment of their credibility: see J. Hunter and K. Cronin, *Evidence, Advocacy and Ethical Practice: A Criminal Trial Commentary* (Sydney: Butterworths, 1995), 363–4.

[402] Bienen (1983), 241.

[403] See Pattullo (1983), 18.

[404] Toner (1982), 218. See also *Taylor* (1985) 80 Cr App R 327 at 332; Adler (1987), 162.

justification. Indeed, in Canada prior to the 1982 reform, the warning was required only for sexual offences involving female victims.[405] In England, although the warning had to be administered regardless of whether the object of the offence was male or female, the need for corroboration still tended to be seen in terms of female complainants. In *Gammon*, for example, the trial judge in directing the jury on corroboration stated: 'We who have had long experience of these cases know that the evidence of a girl giving evidence of indecency by a man is notoriously unreliable, and you look in those cases for some other evidence making it likely that her story is true. It does not apply nearly as much in the case of boys.'[406] But there is no evidence which indicates that women or girls are prone to make false allegations of rape. These directions were based purely on supposition and myth. Moreover, far from its being difficult to shake an allegation of rape, the problem lies in securing a conviction for it.

In England and Wales, the corroboration warning did not merely have to be administered in sexual assault cases. The evidence of accomplices and the sworn evidence of children would also be the occasion for such a warning. Indeed, in *DPP v Kilbourne*, Lord Hailsham went so far as to state that the categories of those for whom a warning was required were not closed. He included within it persons of 'admittedly bad character'.[407] In *Bagshaw*,[408] the warning was held to have been required in the case of three male patients at Rampton Hospital who alleged maltreatment by some of the nurses there. The patients concerned were criminals convicted of serious offences. One was a violent schizophrenic who suffered from paranoia and hallucinations. The other two were extremely violent epileptics. One suffered from hallucinations and the other was described as paranoid. The court did not consider that those sent to hospital under the Mental Health Act constituted a class of persons in respect of whom a warning had always to be given, but took the view that, in some cases involving patients detained in special hospitals, a warning would be necessary. Thus, sexual assault victims kept company with children, accomplices to crime, severely disordered criminals prone to delusion and paranoia, and 'persons of admittedly bad character'. What, it may be asked, did they all have in common? The answer which the law gave was that they all had a propensity to tell lies. Women were thought to lie because they were women; children because they too were not considered to understand the difference between fantasy and reality, truth and fiction; and accomplices because it was in their interest to incriminate the principal defendant and exculpate themselves. Many scholars pointed to the preposterousness of the reasoning behind the corroboration warning in the case of sexual assault victims. Professor Dennis wrote:

[405] See Boyle (1984), 155–7.
[406] (1959) 43 Cr App Rep 155, 159.
[407] [1973] AC 729, 740.
[408] [1984] 1 All ER 971.

It is truly extraordinary to say that all female victims of sex crimes are presumed to be perjurers or fantasists unless the jury is convinced otherwise . . . As a result of [*Bagshaw*] women victims are treated less favourably by the law of evidence than mental patients to whom a general corroboration requirement does not apply.[409]

In the subsequent case of *Spencer*,[410] which also concerned allegations by patients against nurses at Rampton, it was held that in cases which were analogous to those in which a corroboration warning was required owing to the potential unreliability of a witness, it was simply necessary for the judge to make plain the difficulties and dangers of convicting on the basis of that witness's evidence alone. There was no need for the words 'danger' or 'dangerous' to be used, as had been wrongly held in *Bagshaw*. Furthermore, the same was true even in the three types of case in which a warning was always required.[411] It was up to the judge how it should be phrased. In *Spencer*, the male complainants were described as men of bad character who 'were mentally unbalanced . . . anti-authoritarian, prone to lie or exaggerate and [who] could well have old scores which they were seeking to pay off'.[412] The case confirmed that the evidence of witnesses of this variety was to be treated as on a par with that of sexual assault victims.

(b) Problems Associated with the Corroboration Warning

(i) Forensic Evidence

Quite apart from its dubious rationale, corroboration in sexual assault cases gave rise to a host of difficulties. First, it is not all evidence which is capable of amounting to corroboration and corroborative evidence is not always available. One reason for the latter problem is undoubtedly deficiencies in the police collection of forensic evidence. This was the subject of unfavourable comment by, amongst others, the London[413] and Edinburgh Rape Crisis Centres[414] and, more recently, in the Home Office study by Harris and Grace.[415] The Scottish Report also remarked that, although medical examination of the complainant should take place without delay in order to avoid the deterioration of forensic evidence, in some cases in the sample there were considerable delays before a medical examination took place.[416]

409 'Corroboration Requirements Reconsidered' [1984] Crim LR 316, 326.

410 [1986] 2 All ER 928.

411 i.e. cases involving a sexual offence, the evidence of an accomplice or the sworn evidence of a child.

412 [1986] 2 All ER 928, 937.

413 See *Rape: Police and Forensic Practice—Submission by the Rape Counselling and Research Project to the Royal Commission on Criminal Procedure* (London: Only Women Press, 1981), 9–14.

414 *First Report* (Edinburgh: Edinburgh Rape Crisis Collective, 1981), 13.

415 Harris and Grace (1999), p. xiv, para. 5.

416 Chambers and Millar (1983), 97–8.

The Report also noted: 'In analysing case records and in discussion with police surgeons the researchers were struck by the number of references to what seemed to be inadequacies and inconsistencies in the procedures and practices surrounding the medical examination and collection of forensic evidence'.[417] If the collection of forensic evidence by the police was erratic and unsatisfactory, this was, of course, an argument for improving police procedures. It is of interest, however, that the existence of a corroboration warning did not have the effect of ensuring efficiency in this respect. Of course, the absence of corroborating evidence was likely to influence the decision to prosecute.

(ii) Judges and Juries

Judges were free to express the corroboration warning in their own terms, but whatever phrases they selected, there was an inherent complexity in the warning which could not be circumvented. A large majority of judges in the New Zealand study claimed that the warning often confused the jury, for, as Warren Young pointed out: '. . . the form of the warning—to the effect that it is dangerous for the jury to convict on the complainant's uncorroborated evidence, but that they may do so if they are satisfied beyond reasonable doubt of the defendant's guilt—is almost a contradiction in terms'.[418]

If the warning did indeed confuse the jury, what effect did this confusion have? It would seem likely, particularly in view of the very low conviction rate for rape, that juries were persuaded to acquit as a result of it. Where corroborating evidence was lacking, even if the case against the defendant was strong, the chances of an acquittal must have been high. One crown prosecutor in New Zealand explained how this could happen:

> One can have a case where the complainant has been an impressive witness whose evidence has been given fully and fairly; she may have been proved to have made a complaint to her mother or friend immediately after her return home in a shocked or tearful state; the accused may have made statements to the police which it can be shown are untrue; there may be medical and scientific evidence consistent with force being used on the complainant. None of this, however, would amount to corroboration and the jury retires to consider its verdict with the solemn warning about the dangers of convicting ringing in its ears. The qualification that they may convict if they think fit notwithstanding the warning, tends to become lost in the mass of words which are required to give effect to the warning itself.[419]

Even where there was corroborating evidence, the judge had nevertheless to administer the warning. By suggesting to the jury that complainants in rape cases sometimes lie, this might well have sown the seeds of doubt in its collective mind, even though the required evidence was there in abundance.

[417] Chambers and Millar (1983), 106. [418] Young (1983), 141. [419] ibid. 140.

Empirical research on a limited basis attempted to shed some light on the precise effects of the corroboration warning. In the LSE jury project,[420] people were recruited to act as jurors in experiments conducted under laboratory conditions so that they could be observed and their deliberations recorded and analysed. The 'jurors' were asked to listen to a tape-recording re-enacted from the transcript of a real trial and then to reach a verdict upon what they had heard. An attempt was made to assess the effect of the corroboration warning by giving the same rape case to several juries but administering the corroboration warning to only half of them. It was anticipated that convictions would be fewer where the warning was administered, but this was not what was found. Evidence capable of amounting to corroboration was available against one of the defendants and it emerged that the willingness of jurors to convict him was markedly greater when the corroboration warning *had* been given.

The researchers commented:

A possible explanation lies in the fact that the judge, after giving the warning, must then state whether particular pieces of evidence may amount to corroboration, and in so doing causes the jurors to favour convicting. Alternatively it may lie in the form of the corroboration warning generally in use at present, which obliges the judge, after telling the jury of the danger of convicting on uncorroborated evidence, then to state that they may nevertheless convict. The suggestion of our figures is that, at any rate in its present form, the corroboration warning may be positively detrimental to the accused. Those who place some faith in the value of a corroboration warning should perhaps pause to consider their position.[421]

Whilst these findings are of some interest, they must, as the researchers themselves conceded, be treated with some reserve. The experiment was conducted on an extremely small scale with only four juries. It took place in laboratory conditions, requiring each 'juror' to return his individual verdict. No communal decision was taken. Since no one formula was required to express the warning, the language which the judges used was all-important. Clearly, some judges expressed the warning more vividly than others. It is not clear what language was used in the experiment. Moreover, although it was found that the jury's willingness to convict was markedly greater where the warning had been given, this related to a situation in which there was evidence capable of amounting to corroboration.[422] This finding was not duplicated where no such evidence existed.

If juries were mystified by the corroboration warning, judges too had their problems with it. The judge was required to warn the jury of the danger of

[420] See 'Juries and the Rules of Evidence' [1973] Crim LR 208. See also V. Hans and N. Brooks, 'Effects of Corroboration Instructions in a Rape Case on Experimental Juries' (1977) 15 OHLJ 701.

[421] [1973] Crim LR at 220.

[422] Where the judge states that certain evidence is capable of amounting to corroboration, this is, after all, a positive comment about the evidence against the accused.

relying on uncorroborated evidence, instruct it to look for corroborating evidence, explain the technical, legal meaning of corroboration, and state which specific items of evidence in the case were and which were not capable of amounting to corroboration.[423] In New Zealand, Young noted that errors in judges' summings-up on corroboration resulted in a disturbing number of mistrials in rape cases.[424] In England, too, there were frequent cases in which there was ample corroborating evidence but, because the judge failed to administer the warning, the conviction had to be quashed.[425] Similarly, it was noted that 'such technical questions as "what is corroboration?" and "was the jury warned in the right terms?" were a fertile source of appeals'.[426] One of the difficulties was that it was not entirely clear what evidence would suffice for corroboration. For some time, for example, it was not resolved whether or not lies told by the defendant could be corroborative. It was finally held in *Lucas*[427] that they could be, provided that no fewer than four criteria were fulfilled. The judge's task in directing the jury in such cases was thus a formidable one.[428] In *Reeves*,[429] the Court quashed a conviction after the trial judge had given the corroboration warning but had failed to identify to the jury the evidence capable of amounting to corroboration. The Court of Appeal held that it was precisely because it was so difficult to identify corroborative evidence that this task was an important feature of the summing-up.

(c) Reform in England and Wales

The requirement of a corroboration warning in sexual cases owed its existence to misogynistic fantasy. The reasons for it had no basis in proven fact. On this ground alone, and quite apart from the many difficulties to which its application gave rise, there was a strong case for its abolition. The defendant, like all other defendants is, after all, protected by the requirement that his guilt must be established beyond reasonable doubt. His counsel has every opportunity to point out any weakness in the prosecution case and the judge will do the same.

This was not the view of the Criminal Law Revision Committee, however, which in 1972 declared its acceptance of the traditional rationale for the corroboration warning and proposed no more than a cosmetic change in its form.[430] Eight years later, in its *Working Paper on Sexual Offences*, the Committee did no more than reiterate its earlier view.[431] In its Final Report

[423] See P. Mirfield, 'Corroboration after the 1994 Act' [1995] Crim LR 448 at n. 2.

[424] Young (1983), 141.

[425] See Cross and Tapper (1985), 222.

[426] ibid. 237.

[427] [1981] 2 All ER 1008.

[428] See e.g. *R. v R.* [1985] Crim LR 736, in which the conviction was quashed because of the judge's direction on corroboration where lies told by the defendant were involved.

[429] (1978) 68 Cr App R 331.

[430] CLRC (1972), para. 186.

[431] (1980), para. 49. For criticism of the Working Paper, see Temkin (1982), 418.

on Sexual Offences published in 1984, the Committee simply failed to discuss the corroboration issue at all.

It was not until seven years later that the Law Commission recommended that the law on corroboration be changed.[432] Section 32(1)(b) of the Criminal Justice and Public Order Act 1994 accordingly abolished the requirement that the judge must warn the jury about the dangers of convicting on the uncorroborated evidence of the complainant.[433] However, judges remain free to give a warning if appropriate on the facts. In *Makanjuola*,[434] the Court of Appeal demonstrated its unequivocal support for the policy and purpose of the legislation. Lord Taylor LCJ stated that there would need to be an evidential basis for suggesting that the evidence of the witness might be unreliable which went beyond a mere suggestion by defence counsel. He held that it was a matter of discretion for the judge as to whether or not a warning should be given and in what terms. The Court would not interfere with the exercise of this discretion save where it was '*Wednesbury* unreasonable'.[435] The Court emphasized that the 'florid regime of the old corroboration rules' was not required in those cases where a warning was considered necessary and that 'attempts to re-impose the straitjacket of the old corroboration rules are strongly to be deprecated'.[436] In *R*,[437] the succeeding Lord Chief Justice demonstrated his strong support for his predecessor's approach and held that, even where the events in question had taken place many years before the trial, this did not necessarily necessitate that a warning be given. This firm stand should limit the endless appeals concerning corroboration warnings which were a feature of the old law.

It might have been thought preferable for Parliament to forbid the use of the corroboration warning altogether[438] rather than leaving the matter to the discretion of the judges. Although the Court of Appeal has dealt with the issue in a perfectly satisfactory way, research is required into whether its pronouncements are being followed by trial judges. Australian research suggests that the practice of giving corroboration warnings is hard to dislodge.[439]

432 Law Com No. 202, *Corroboration of Evidence in Criminal Trials* (Cm 1620, 1991).

433 Announcing the reform in Parliament, the Home Secretary Michael Howard denounced the requirement of a warning as 'outdated and demeaning to women': *The Times*, 16 Nov. 1993. However, the legislation was opposed by the Criminal Bar Association and leading criminal solicitors: the *Lawyer*, 23 Nov. 1993. It was also opposed by the Labour peer Baroness Mallalieu who led a group of peers against it: *The Times*, 19 May 1994.

434 [1995] 3 All ER 730.

435 i.e. so unreasonable that no reasonable judge could have exercised discretion in this way. See *Associated Provincial Picture Houses Ltd v Wednesbury Corporation* [1948] 1 KB 223.

436 [1995] 3 All ER 730, 733.

437 [1996] Crim LR 815; see also now *L* [1999] Crim LR 489.

438 This would not prevent a judge from an ad hoc warning where the particular circumstances of the case require it. In *L*, above, a warning was understandably given where a child's complaint of sexual abuse was made after her mother quarrelled with the defendant and where her evidence in court did not support all the allegations she made in a video-recorded interview.

439 Discussed below.

There has been one unfortunate development in the wake of this reform. It has always been accepted that evidence may be adduced of the complainant's demeanour at or around the time she complains of rape. Clearly, evidence that she was distressed will be of some assistance to the jury in assessing her credibility. Such evidence was, in some circumstances, also regarded as corroborative, as where it was noticed by an independent observer.[440] However, recently, in *Keast*,[441] the Court of Appeal has suggested that the use of such evidence should be restricted. Given the dearth of evidence that is available to complainants in sexual cases and given the importance which is generally attributed both in the adversarial system and in ordinary life to a person's demeanour, it is hard to understand the justification for this. It seems that in taking two steps forward, the law in this area may have moved one step back.

(d) Reform in Other Jurisdictions

In the United States in the early 1970s, seven states had the rule that the testimony of a female complainant had to be corroborated in order to sustain a conviction for rape.[442] A further eight required limited corroboration[443] or corroboration only under certain circumstances.[444] But many other states required the judge to give a special cautionary instruction to the jury.[445] In California, for example, the judge had to give the following instruction, which was based on Hale's notorious dictum:

> A charge such as that made against the defendant in this case, is one which is easily made, and once made, difficult to defend against, even if the person accused is innocent. Therefore the law requires that you examine the testimony of the female person named in the information with caution.[446]

In *People v Rincon-Pineda*, Judge Armand Arabian took a stand against the warning by refusing to administer it and calling for a review of the law. He stated:

> I find that the giving of such an instruction in this case is unwarranted either by law or reason, that it arbitrarily discriminates against women, denies them equal protec-

[440] *Redpath* (1962) 46 Cr App R 319.

[441] [1998] Crim LR 748 and see commentary by D. Birch at 749.

[442] Georgia, Idaho, Iowa, New York, Virgin Islands, District of Columbia, Nebraska. See 'The Rape Corroboration Requirement: Repeal Not Reform' (1972) 81 Yale LJ 1365; S. Estrich, *Real Rape* (Cambridge, Mass.: Harvard University Press, 1987), 42–7.

[443] Hawaii and New Mexico.

[444] e.g. where the complainant was a minor or complaint was made late. Texas, Massachusetts, Minnesota, Mississippi, Tennessee, and Missouri.

[445] e.g. California, Wyoming, Maine, and New Mexico. In some states, the instruction was given only where there was no corroboration. In others, it had always to be given. For a full account, see Arabian (1978).

[446] California Jury Instructions, Criminal 10.22 at 327 (3rd rev. edn., 1970). See Arabian (1978), 588.

tion of the law, and assists in the brutalization of rape victims by providing an unequal balance between their rights and the rights of the accused in court.[447]

The case went to the California Supreme Court, which in 1975 unanimously agreed to strike the cautionary instruction from the law of California in all sex cases. The position now is that in *all* criminal cases, not merely sexual ones, where there is no requirement of corroboration, the judge must instead direct the jury as follows: 'Testimony which you believe given by one witness is sufficient for the proof of any fact. However, before finding any fact to be proved solely by the testimony of such a single witness, you should carefully review all the testimony upon which the proof of such fact depends.'[448] While it might be thought that such an instruction is unnecessary, in so far as it does not rely on misogynistic assumptions about women and applies in all criminal cases, it is clearly a vast improvement on the previous law. By the end of the 1970s, most American states had repealed rules requiring either corroboration or a special cautionary instruction in sexual cases.[449]

In Israel, where there are no jury trials, it used to be the case that there could be no conviction for rape without corroborating evidence.[450] In 1982, the fight to abolish this requirement was partly but not entirely won. Whilst there is no longer a formal corroboration requirement, a court which convicts a defendant on the basis of the victim's testimony alone is obliged to specify what induced it to rely on this testimony.

In New South Wales, the requirement of a corroboration warning was abolished by the Crimes (Sexual Assault) Amendment Act 1981.[451] Judges are therefore permitted to give the corroboration warning but are no longer compelled to do so, as is the position in England and Wales. In his commentary on the NSW Act, Woods states: 'Under section 405C the judge will not be compelled to utilise the traditional formula of denigration which identifies women as especially untrustworthy'.[452] If the corroboration warning is indeed a 'formula of denigration', the question remains whether its use can be justified at all.

[447] 14 Cal 3d 864 (1975).

[448] California Jury Instructions, Criminal 2.27; see Arabian (1978), 590.

[449] See Schulhofer (1998), 30; Spohn and Horney (1992), 25.

[450] See L. Sebba, 'The Repeal of the Requirement of Corroboration in Sex Offences—A Symbolic Victory or a Symbolic Defeat for the Feminist Movement?' (1983) 18 Israel LR 125.

[451] Section 405C of the Crimes Act 1900 which specifically outlawed the requirement of a corroboration warning in sexual cases, has now been repealed and replaced by s164 of the Evidence Act 1995 which no longer applies specifically to sexual cases but has a general application. The absence of a specific provision stating that there is no requirement of a warning for sexual cases is perhaps regrettable.

[452] Woods (1981), 28. A similar provision to s 405C has been enacted in New Zealand: see Evidence Amendment Act (No. 2) 1985, s 3. In Western Australia, the judge is no longer required to give the warning and may only give it where it is considered to be justified in the circumstances: see Acts Amendment (Sexual Assaults) Act 1985, s15.

The subsequent history of the reform in New South Wales has not been a happy one. In *Longman*,[453] the High Court entered into the spirit of the legislation and commented that judges ought not to use their discretion in such a way as to convey to the jury 'a caution about the general reliability of the evidence of alleged victims of sexual offences'.[454] However, the NSW Court of Appeal in *Murray*[455] stressed that in all serious criminal cases where there was only one witness asserting the commission of a crime, it was customary for judges to stress that the evidence of that witness must be scrutinized with great care.[456] A further setback came in the shape of section 165 of the NSW Evidence Act 1995 which deals with warnings in relation to unreliable evidence. There is nothing in the section itself which refers to sexual cases in this context but the legislation provides an avenue for judges with stereotypical views about rape complainants to give jury warnings.[457] Indeed, the leading commentary on the Act specifically mentions the evidence of the complainant in a sexual offence trial where there are particular circumstances suggesting fabrication as an example of the type of case where such a warning should be given.[458] Some judges will readily construe rape cases in this way.

Research suggests that old judicial habits die hard. A NSW study found that corroboration warnings were given in 80 per cent of trials in a sample of 92.[459] Furthermore, in 40 per cent of the sample, it was old-style warnings which were given. The study noted: '. . . the harsh way in which corroboration warnings were delivered by some judges show some ongoing judicial scepticism towards complainants'.[460]

All states and territories of Australia apart from Queensland[461] have enacted legislation similar to that of New South Wales. In Victoria, the legislation takes a slightly stronger form. Rather than simply asserting that a corroboration warning is no longer a requirement in sexual cases, it states: 'The judge must not warn or suggest in any way to the jury that the law regards complainants in sexual cases as an unreliable class of witness . . . nothing in this subsection prevents a judge from making any comment on evidence given in the proceeding that it is appropriate to make in the interests of justice'. In the light of the New South Wales experience, this formula has much to commend it.

In Canada, reform of a similar type was introduced in 1982. Section 274 of the Canadian Criminal Code now provides that where the accused is charged with sexual assault or other listed sexual offences, 'no corroboration

[453] (1989) 168 CLR 79. [454] At 89. [455] [1987] 39 A Crim R 315.
[456] At 322. [457] See New South Wales Dept. for Women (1996), 195–6.
[458] S. Odgers, *Uniform Evidence Law* (Sydney: Federation Press, 1995), 268.
[459] New South Wales Dept. for Women (1996), 188. The study was conducted between 1994 and 1995.
[460] ibid. 192
[461] See ACT: Evidence Act, s 76; South Australian Evidence Act, s 341; Tasmania Criminal Code, s 136; Western Australia Criminal Code, s 50; Victoria Crimes Act, s 61.

is required for a conviction and the judge shall not instruct the jury that it is unsafe to find the accused guilty in the absence of corroboration'. In Canada, therefore, the judge is not permitted routinely to give a corroboration warning in sexual assault cases. However, the trial judge is in no sense inhibited from commenting upon the evidence and assisting the jury as to the weight that they should give to it.[462] Moreover, where there are serious reasons to be concerned about the credibility or reliability of the complainant in a particular case, a warning may be regarded as necessary.[463]

Conclusion

The last decade has witnessed a sea change in judicial perceptions of sexual offences. As a result of some legislative intervention and the combined efforts of the women's and victims' movements, judicial attitudes appear to have moved forward so that victims of sexual offending are no longer routinely perceived as liars or vindictive trouble-makers. The evidential rules surrounding sexual offences have, in some respects, developed to reflect this. However, the progress which has been made on, say, similar fact evidence must be weighed against the regressive movement of the case law in relation to, for example, the collateral finality rule. It remains to be seen to what extent the YJCEA has resolved the problem of sexual history evidence, but the early signs are not entirely promising. Moreover, the rule in *Turner* concerning evidence of the defendant's character continues to be interpreted in a way that discriminates blatantly in favour of the accused in rape cases.

[462] See Watt (1984), 176.

[463] See *R v Brooks* (1998) 20 CR (5th) 116 (Ont CA).

5

Assisting the Victim of Rape

In Chapter 1, some of the problems experienced by victims of rape were discussed. This chapter will consider their needs and ways of assisting them which go beyond reform of the substantive law of rape and the rules of evidence referred to in Chapters 2, 3 and 4. Attention will be focused on the implementation and operation of the Danish scheme which provides legal representation for sexual assault victims. Some consideration will also be given to other ways of protecting and compensating them, including changes in policing and in courtroom procedures, the control of publicity, and the bringing of civil proceedings.

The Victim's Need for Help

Today there is growing recognition of the enduring effects of crime and that time alone may be insufficient to heal the victim's wounds. In the 1980s, research studies began to reveal the deep need of many victims for active support and help. In Canada, Brown and Yantzi studied victims of a broad range of offences.[1] They found that victims desired to be treated caringly by the criminal justice system and to receive information about the progress of their cases and about compensation. Their need for informational support was expressed to be even greater than their need for emotional support. Victims of crimes against the person, including physical and sexual assaults, showed the highest degree of unfulfilled need.

In an English study of victims of a range of offences, Shapland, Willmore, and Duff found that the major determinant of victim satisfaction with the police was the attitude of police officers and the concern they expressed. Apparently uncaring or casual attitudes were the most frequent source of criticism. The major source of dissatisfaction was lack of information about what was happening in the case and a consequent feeling that the police did not care.[2] Eighty-eight per cent of victims felt that they should have received

[1] S. Brown and M. Yantzi, *Needs Assessment for Victims and Witnesses of Crime,* Report prepared for the Mennonite Central Committee and Ministry of Correctional Services, Ontario, Canada (1980).

[2] Shapland *et al.* (1985), ch. 5. They found that in Coventry and Northampton the sexual assault victims in their survey were more satisfied with the police than were physical assault or robbery victims. This was because the police had made a particular effort to keep them

some notification of the result of the case and, of these, most held the police responsible for this.[3]

A decade later, in 1996, a study by Victim Support which looked at the experiences of over 1,000 women who reported rape still identified lack of information as a central area of concern.[4] The second Victim's Charter published in 1996 focused on the victim's right to information, placing responsibility on the police to give victims information at every stage in the process. Subsequently, in 1998, the Glidewell Report recommended that the CPS should take overall responsibility for information.[5] Yet, writing recently, Dame Helen Reeves and Kate Mulley of Victim Support declared: 'Lack of timely information is the most common complaint we hear voiced by crime victims'.[6]

In 1982, Howley pointed to the discrepancy between police and victim attitudes. Thus, police officers thought that it was important to appear 'professional' and efficient, whereas victims were looking to the police for support and personal contact.[7] His findings were borne out by Kelly's 1982 study of 100 female rape victims in the Washington Metropolitan area.[8] Sixteen of those interviewed felt police officers made offensive comments regarding the veracity of their complaint. Others complained that the police pressed for information at a time when they were too distraught to provide it. Victims frequently felt used by the police. One stated: 'I was treated like an object, a set of keys, they didn't care about me at all—only about catching the guy'.[9] Similar findings were made in the Sussex and London studies over a decade later.[10]

In studies in the 1980s, the victim's need for support and assistance was found to carry over into the trial process. Once again it was largely a need that was unmet. In the early stages, the victims in Kelly's study were bothered by a lack of explanation. They understood neither their legal status nor court procedures.[11] Shapland *et al.* made similar findings in England.[12] Court delays were a further source of anxiety and frustration to Kelly's victims, particularly since most delays were occasioned by defence requests.

informed of what was happening in the case. However, these victims had all had their complaints accepted and recorded as crimes by the police. See particularly pp. 88–9.

[3] Shapland (1986), 214; 278 victims were interviewed in the study. Victims of sexual assault in the Scottish study received little information about case progress and were particularly dissatisfied about this: see Chambers and Millar (1986), 51, 55, 73, 75, 76, 80.

[4] Victim Support (1996), 11–12.

[5] I. Glidewell, *The Review of the Crown Prosecution Service: A Report* (1998), Cmnd 3960 (London: HMSO).

[6] Reeves and Mulley (2000), 130.

[7] J. Howley, 'Victim-Police Interaction and its Effects on the Public Attitudes to the Police', M.Sc. thesis, Cranfield Institute of Technology (1982).

[8] Kelly (1982).

[9] ibid.

[10] Temkin (1997, 1999). See below under the heading 'Changing Police Attitudes'.

[11] Kelly (1982).

[12] Shapland *et al.* (1985), ch. 4. For similar findings in Scotland, see Chambers and Millar (1986), 52–3.

Victims frequently cited delay as proof that the judicial system had little regard for their well-being. One stated: 'Everybody tells you from the date it happens to forget about it, but you can't while the case is still pending'.[13]

Fifty-nine per cent of the victims in Kelly's survey felt that they were denied participation in the case and 49 per cent felt that they were denied information about it. Victims were particularly dissatisfied with prosecutors.[14] Eisenstein and Jacob noted that in the United States there was frequently a conflict between the interests of the victim and the state and that prosecutors were more closely aligned with police, judges, and defence attorneys than with victims.[15] The National District Attorney's Association stated: 'Prosecutors are typically too pressed by time, heavy case loads and crises to reflect long on the situation of the crime victim'.[16] Kelly found that victim satisfaction with prosecutors depended upon how prosecutors treated them rather than upon whether a conviction resulted. The more they heard from the prosecutor, were consulted and informed about the case, the more satisfied they were. Victims who felt that the prosecutor represented their interests adequately were most likely to say that they were well treated. Twenty-eight per cent felt that prosecutors did not represent their interests.[17] Similar criticisms of the prosecution were made in the English context. Shapland *et al.* observed: 'The prosecutor [was] the most unsatisfactory courtroom participant as far as the victims were concerned'.[18] One of the victims put the matter thus: 'I was nervous, frightened because I hadn't been to a trial before. They didn't try to help me in any way . . . the prosecution solicitor should have explained to me what was going to happen—it would have been easier.'[19] It is not clear that a great deal has changed since then. In a recent study of barristers prosecuting in rape cases it was found that most had minimal contact with complainants and few routinely introduced themselves before trial.[20] One of the three main areas of concern expressed by the women in the 1996 Victim Support study was the way women were treated when they were called to give evidence at court.[21] Lengthy waiting periods and changes to trial dates were a continuing problem.[22]

Thus, victim studies in the 1980s confirmed the many individual accounts of the experiences of victims in the criminal justice system.[23] Victims expected that they would be treated with kindness and consideration, that

[13] Kelly (1982).

[14] ibid. This was also the case in the Scottish study; see Chambers and Millar (1986), 89.

[15] J. Eisenstein and H. Jacob, *Felony Justice: An Organisational Analysis of Criminal Courts* (Boston, Mass.: Little, Brown, 1977).

[16] Quoted in F. Cannavale and W. Falcon, *Improving Witness Cooperation: Summary Report of the District of Columbia Witness Survey* (US Dept. of Justice, Law Enforcement Administration, National Institute of Law Enforcement and Criminal Justice, Washington DC, 1976).

[17] Kelly (1982).

[18] Shapland *et al.* (1985), 67.

[19] ibid. 68.

[20] Temkin (2000), at 222–3.

[21] Victim Support (1996), 15.

[22] ibid. at 16.

[23] See e.g. L. Spry-Leverton, 'This is No Way to Treat a Victim', *The Guardian*, 2 May 1985; 'The Victim of Rape who Faces Trial by Ordeal', *The Times*, 31 July 1985.

they would be kept informed and consulted. They looked to police, prosecutors, and the courts for this and found themselves bitterly disappointed. Kelly concluded that the rape victims in her survey objected to the criminal justice system—'a system that, much to their surprise, was not geared to victims' perspectives'.[24] But almost two decades later Reeves and Mulley comment: 'All too frequently an individual's initial negative reaction on becoming a victim of crime is reinforced and intensified by their experience of the criminal justice process'.[25]

It is none the less true that today far greater attention is paid to the needs of victims and their concerns have become central in the public debate about criminal justice.[26] The Victim's Charter of 1990 and 1996 set out rights and standards of service for victims. Similarly, the Courts' Charter sets out standards of service for witnesses. The Crown Court Witness Service aims to help all witnesses, victims, and their families before, during, and after the hearing.[27] Along with all other victims, sexual assault victims have been the beneficiaries of this change in climate. However, it may be concluded that what has been done remains insufficient for their needs.

Radical Law Reform and the Rape Victim

It seems clear that modest alterations to the substantive law of rape as discussed in Chapter 2 can do little to improve the experience of most victims within the criminal justice system. Is the same to be said of more radical law reform? Research into the operation of the Michigan Criminal Sexual Conduct Act suggests that the ordeal of rape victims has been reduced as a result of the legislation. This was mostly due to the provision limiting the use of sexual history evidence.[28] The Act does not appear to have had much impact in changing the attitudes of criminal justice officials. Indeed, it was found that police officers exhibited a continuing concern with fabrication, and polygraphs remained a crucial investigative tool both for police and prosecutors.[29] In Detroit, the Women's Justice Centre initiated a class action suit against the Detroit Police Department for its routine use of polygraphs with rape victims. Legislation had finally to be introduced to prohibit law enforcement officials or prosecutors from requesting or requiring rape victims to take lie-detector tests.[30] Thus, as Marsh, Geist, and Caplan noted, 'Attitudes of criminal justice officials may change in time, but attitude change is clearly not a short-term effect of the law'.[31] So long as the attitudes of criminal justice personnel to rape remain the same, victims will not

[24] Kelly (1982). [25] (2000), 127.

[26] See e.g. P. Rock, 'Acknowledging Victims' Needs and Rights' (1999) 35 Criminal Justice Matters 4; Reeves and Mulley (2000).

[27] They will, for example, provide information on court procedures, accompany the witness into the courtroom when giving evidence, and talk over the case when it has ended.

[28] Marsh *et al.* (1982), 68. [29] ibid. 90–5. [30] ibid. 117. [31] ibid. 119.

receive the care and concern which they need and crave. On the contrary, they are likely to be treated, as they always have been, with suspicion and hostility and this can only intensify their original trauma. It seems, therefore, that reform of the substantive law of rape and the evidential rules is in itself not enough. Further steps are required. In this chapter, it is proposed to consider several strategies for improving the victim's lot.

Changing Police Attitudes

In the United States, the approach to policing rape changed radically in many places in the 1970s. This was undoubtedly a result both of the rapid increase in the number of reported rapes and of pressure from the Women's Movement. In 1972, the first Sex Crimes Analysis Unit was set up in New York after which similar units were set up in many other parts of the United States. Their principal characteristics were, first, the restriction of sexual offence investigation to dedicated teams; secondly, the selection and special training of officers; thirdly, high prestige; and finally, extensive collaboration with external centres for the treatment and after-care of victims.[32]

Harry J. O'Reilly, who supervised the New York Unit, devised a training programme for sexual assault investigators working in units of this kind.[33] He believed that the focus should be on the rape trauma syndrome and attitudinal training which involved breaking down the myths of rape. Police officers should be taught that rape does not only happen in dark alley-ways and deserted places, that the victim's dress is immaterial, that women do not enjoy rape, and most important of all, that few reported rapes are likely to be fabricated. He perceived the task of the sex crimes investigator as being empathetically to assist the victim at a time of acute crisis:

> I ask the officers to identify with the deep sense of violation experienced by someone who has been sexually violated and explain that if they can empathise and feel the kinds of feelings that victims experience, then they have probably got what it takes to deal sensitively with the victims of rape.[34]

O'Reilly was confident that it was possible to effect attitudinal change in police officers through training. His approach involved a non-judgemental attitude towards victims allowing them to express their feelings, limiting questions to what was strictly necessary, and maintaining contact with them afterwards. Indeed, he claimed:

> The New York City police have changed their whole rationale. We are now victim-orientated and have taken an active role in getting the entire helping network—lawyers, doctors, nurses, social workers, rape crisis centre workers—to talk and to interact together . . . We are then in a position to concentrate fully on the primary

[32] See Blair (1985), ch. 4. [33] See O'Reilly (1984). [34] ibid. 98.

goal that unites us all—helping victims of sexual assault to get their lives back together.[35]

This new approach to policing rape was studied by Detective Inspector Ian Blair of the Metropolitan Police in London, who had become 'acutely and personally aware of the impact of rape on its victims and their families'.[36] He returned from the United States a dedicated convert, advocating a complete reappraisal of existing police methods in rape cases and the adoption of a victim-orientated approach which would involve special training of the type devised by Harry O'Reilly, both for police officers and police surgeons. In his book, *Investigating Rape—A New Approach for Police*, he suggested that officers of the rank of detective sergeant, detective inspector, and detective chief inspector should be appointed and trained as sexual offence investigators. In order to ensure that the victim's trauma was not augmented by her experience at the police station, he further proposed that questioning should not take place until she had had time to rest and recuperate at home. Upon her arrival at the police station, only the most essential information should be elicited. He recommended that the police should abandon their devotion to clear-up rates and should keep cases on file and encourage women to pursue their complaints regardless of whether the offence was likely to be cleared up.[37] He was firmly of the view that the vast majority of rape complaints were genuine and that the police should not seek further to undermine a complainant by suggesting otherwise.[38]

Blair's research and recommendations added further impetus to the steps which the Metropolitan Police Service (MPS) had already taken to change practice in this area. In response to growing public criticism of police handling of rape cases, it set up a Sexual Offences Steering Committee in 1983 which has been responsible for the orchestration of a range of improvements to the system. These include the introduction of a chaperon system for adult women who report rape, to look after them 'at the beginning, during and end of the investigation'.[39] Chaperons are in the main female uniformed officers who spend most of their time on general policing duties.[40] They receive a special training and are in fact referred to as SOIT trained officers, that is, officers who have taken the Sexual Offences Investigative Techniques Course.[41] Male officers are now also trained as chaperons.

[35] See O'Reilly (1984), 103.

[36] Blair (1985), 5. Ian Blair is now Deputy Commissioner of the Metropolitan Police.

[37] ibid. 80.

[38] ibid. 53–62. For the approach to recording rape offences which the Metropolitan Police adopted, see p. 20 above.

[39] MPS (1995), 15.

[40] Occasionally, CID officers, previously trained as chaperons, may be called upon to act as such and in some cases to conduct the investigation at the same time.

[41] Chaperons are required to take refresher courses and in each police district they are supposed to meet to discuss problems and new developments MPS (1995), 17.

When a rape is reported in London, it is the duty of the CID officer in charge of the investigation both to appoint and to supervise a chaperon who will look after the victim. The MPS Policy Guidelines[42] clearly set out the roles and duties of chaperons and investigators in rape investigations. The chaperon is said to have two crucial functions: to ensure that victims are treated with kindness, sensitivity, and courtesy and to obtain the best possible evidence to aid an investigation and support any subsequent prosecution.[43] The Guidelines strongly emphasize that once appointed to a case the chaperon should not be changed.[44] They also state that chaperons should ideally undertake no more than two or three cases a year.[45]At some stations, call-out and rota systems operate, the purpose of which is to ensure that a trained chaperon is always available and that the same chaperon is not called out too often.[46] The task of investigating the case and dealing with the accused is that of CID officers.

Special examination facilities have been set up at different locations in the MPS area.[47] The MPS has made arrangements with a number of London hospitals for rape victims to be screened for sexually transmitted diseases (STDs). Women doctors have been recruited and trained to carry out examinations on female victims of sexual assault without having to take on the full range of police surgeons' duties. There are also some female photographers. MPS practice is to allow the victim who reports more or less immediately after the rape and is tired and distressed, to rest and recuperate after the medical once basic information has been obtained. The statement is then taken the following day or even several days later. In common with other police forces, the MPS has devised a useful booklet for complainants to provide them with information and useful addresses and contact numbers.

42 MPS (1995).

43 MPS (1995), 27–8. The Guidelines instruct chaperons to do the following MPS (1995), 27–31: 'Give the victim a plain cover copy of the MPS booklet *Advice for the Victims of Sexual Assault;* Make notes at all meetings with the victim regarding the history of the incident before taking the statement; Take a full evidential statement at a time most appropriate for the victim; Be present at the medical examination and secure exhibits where chaperon of same sex as victim; Make appointments with photographers and be present if necessary; Arrange priority appointments at genito-urinary clinics if the victim wishes and offer to accompany her; Assist with transport if necessary; If the victim wishes, contact family, friends etc; Offer to arrange contact with Victim Support and organise this if victim agrees. If victim declines, repeat the offer when appropriate; Inform victim about Criminal Injuries Compensation Board; Maintain contact with the victim during the investigation, up to and during any court case; Obtain a pre-trial or pre-sentence statement from the victim indicating the effects of the offence on the victim's life; Accompany victim to court in the absence of any other suitable supporting agency; Obtain support for the victim after the investigation or court case from whatever sources are available where victim obviously needs support.'

44 MPS (1995), 33. 45 MPS (1995), 17. 46 Temkin (1999), 19. 47 ibid.

Evaluating Changes in Police Practice

There can be no doubt that changes in the handling of rape complaints have taken place within the Metropolitan Police in the past two decades. However, what is less clear is exactly how far these changes have gone or how effective they are. What is the precise nature of the training which sexual offence investigators receive? Does it emphasize the genuineness of most rape complaints? If so, how likely is it that the police officers concerned will change their attitudes? The Report of the Policy Studies Institute on the Metropolitan Police, published in 1983, identified widespread sexism within the Metropolitan Police.[48] Subsequent reports confirm that sexual harassment by police officers of fellow police officers and civilian staff is a serious problem in police forces throughout the country.[49]

A further question is whether steps have been taken by police forces apart from the MPS to improve their handling of rape cases.[50] In October 1986, the Home Office, at the instigation of the Women's National Commission,[51] issued a new circular[52] addressed to chief constables throughout the country concerning the treatment of rape victims. It recommended that consideration be given to the setting up of special examination suites or, where this was impractical, that alternative arrangements be made for victims to be medically examined in hospital or in local doctors' surgeries. The need for victims to be provided by the police with information on the availability of pregnancy advice, Victim Support schemes, and criminal injuries compensation was also emphasized. It was suggested that the police should consider offering to make appointments at venereal disease clinics for complainants who might be too shy to do so. Chief officers were also invited to review their training policies to ensure that the special needs of victims of rape and serious sexual assault were given due weight. It is not clear to what extent this advice has been followed.

In 1990, Adler conducted a postal survey to discover how women who had reported rape or a serious sexual assault to the Metropolitan Police and whose cases had been recorded as crimes viewed their treatment by the

[48] D. J. Smith, *Police and People in London—III. A Survey of Police Officers* (Policy Studies Institute, No. 620, 1983), 193. In 1986, Commander Thelma Wagstaff of the Metropolitan Police stated that many rape victims continue to be viewed sceptically by the police. She mentioned in particular victims who offered no resistance and did not try to escape, cases where no violence was used and only one unarmed man was involved, or where a victim failed to report immediately, or did not show feelings of disgust, shame, or fear, or accepted a lift in a car, or where she was aged 14 to 17 with a history of promiscuity. See *The Times,* 1 Oct. 1986.

[49] See e.g. R. Anderson, J. Brown, and E. Campbell, *Aspects of Sex Discrimination within the Police Service in England and Wales,* Home Office Police Department (London: Home Office, 1993); B. Hilliard and C. Casey, '800 Women Officers Sexually Assaulted by Colleagues', Police Review, 12 Feb. 1993, 5 and Editorial, p. 4; J. Brown, 'Abusive Relationships at Work—Policewomen as Victims' (1999) 35 Criminal Justice Matters 22.

[50] On Sussex, see Temkin (1997).

[51] Women's National Commission (1985), ch. 2.

[52] Home Office Circular 69/1986: *Violence Against Women.*

police.[53] One hundred and three women who reported between May 1990 and February 1991 responded to a simple questionnaire. It was found that 89 per cent of respondents were satisfied or very satisfied with their treatment by women police officers and 76 per cent were satisfied or very satisfied with the male detectives investigating the case. Adler concluded, 'attitudes to victims of rape in the Met are now overwhelmingly caring and sympathetic. The vast majority of women speak very favourably indeed of their experience of reporting'.[54] It is noteworthy, however, that 24 per cent of women did not describe themselves as satisfied with the way in which they were treated by officers in charge of the case. Moreover, 'as time went by in the investigations, the proportion of satisfied customers declined to some 70 per cent, mainly because of lack of information from the police'.[55] Lees and Gregory,[56] in a study concerned mainly with attrition rates in sexual assault cases, interviewed 24 women who had reported sexual assault in North London between 1988 and 1990. (Only four had been involved in recorded cases of rape or attempted rape.) Their results were not dissimilar to Adler's. They found that 75 per cent of the women were generally satisfied with their treatment by the police. They concluded that 'the service provided by the police has greatly improved. The police are to be congratulated for these improvements.'[57] Several complainants, however, were very dissatisfied with their treatment by the police and few were told the outcome of cases.[58] In the Sussex study,[59] 23 women who reported rape to the Sussex Police between 1991 and 1993 were interviewed in depth. Twenty-two (96%) were positive about the officers (mainly women) who took their statements and 16 (70%) were satisfied with the way in which their cases were investigated (mainly by male officers). However, some complainants were highly dissatisfied with the investigation and the officers responsible for it and many were dissatisfied with the follow-up provided by the police. Overall, the majority of women, 57 per cent, were wholly or mainly positive about the service provided by the police, but 43 per cent were wholly, mainly, or partly negative. One conclusion drawn in the Sussex study, which also included in-depth interviews with police officers, was that 'old police practices and attitudes, widely assumed to have vanished, are still in evidence and continue to cause victims pain and trauma'.[60] Thus, although the results of the three different studies were in some respects similar, the Sussex study cast a shadow of doubt on optimistic assumptions about the new regime.

The London Study[61]

The doubts raised by the Sussex study have been reinforced by a small qualitative study conducted in the Metropolitan Police Area. The London study,

[53] Adler, 'Picking up the Pieces' Police Review, 31 May 1991, 1114–15.
[54] At 1115. [55] ibid. [56] Lees and Gregory (1993). [57] At 23.
[58] At 20, 23. [59] Temkin (1997). [60] At 527. [61] Temkin (1999).

which involved in-depth interviews with police officers and female rape victims, considered *inter alia* whether the overall experience of contact with the police had been positive or negative for each victim and those aspects of the experience which were particularly positive or negative.

There was a high degree of dissatisfaction on the part of some victims in the study with the way in which the police had dealt with their cases and most victims were negative about some aspect of their treatment.[62] As in the Sussex study, negative responses clustered around the disbelieving attitude of the police and the insensitive way in which the case was handled. But in London as against Sussex, it was what was perceived to be the uncaring, unhelpful, and unsupportive attitude of some police officers which was a particular source of criticism. A number of women expressed the view that the only concern of the police was to obtain a conviction. They had no care or concern for the victims themselves. One woman said: 'It's not like a service. They don't seem to be particularly interested and even less interested when it doesn't go to court.'[63] Women in the study were asked to sum up their feelings about the service provided for them by the police. Some of the criticisms and conclusions were scathing and several mentioned that, in the event of a similar occurrence, they would not report again.

Although victims were mostly well pleased with the police officers who took their statements, it was found that, despite the existence of a range of victim examination suites in the Metropolitan area, statements were still being taken in police stations even though this process takes many hours or days.[64] Most of the women in the study were negative about the investigation, mainly because of the attitudes of the officers concerned. The study found that, as is the case in Sussex,[65] CID officers who conduct the investigations receive no training which is geared towards an understanding of the victims of rape and the rape trauma syndrome or which challenges entrenched attitudes about rape and its victims. Training focuses instead on investigative and evidence-gathering issues.[66]

A majority of the women interviewed were also negative about the follow-up provided by the police. The study reveals that follow-up contact with victims is actively discouraged by some supervisors and regarded as a waste of time. It suggests that the pressures on chaperons and their heavy workload may also explain why follow-up is given low priority.[67]

IMPLICATIONS OF THE LONDON STUDY

Since the Metropolitan Police introduced changes to procedures for dealing with rape victims in the early 1980s, the number of rapes reported to the police each year has increased meteorically. In 1985, there were 1,842

[62] Temkin (1999), 34. [63] ibid. [64] ibid. 24. [65] Temkin (1997), 525.
[66] Temkin (1999), 36. [67] ibid. 37.

offences of rape recorded by the police in England and Wales. In 1995, this had risen to 4,986[68]—an almost threefold increase in a decade. Although recorded crime in general rose at an average rate of 3.5 per cent per annum during this period, the average annual rate of increase for rape was 10.8 per cent.[69] But, whilst the number of rapes recorded in the Metropolitan area rose from 1,369 in 1994 to 1,410 in 1995, to 1,512 in the year ending June 1996, in every other police area in England and Wales the annual return during this period did not even reach 300.[70] In the year ending March 2001, the number of rapes recorded in the Metropolitan area rose to 2,044. The highest number recorded outside London was in Greater Manchester where 508 rapes were recorded.[71] Thus, the problem of recorded rape is one that is overwhelmingly borne by the Metropolitan Police.

Faced with financial cutbacks and the demands of a performance culture, the rise in the number of women reporting rape presents the MPS with a considerable dilemma. Only a small percentage of reports will be translated into convictions. Yet each report of rape is very expensive to process given the cost of the medical examination, the length of time it takes to obtain a statement, as well as to provide follow-up. There must be a strong temptation in these circumstances to sift out the few cases which might seem likely to lead to convictions whilst moving the rest as swiftly as possible out of the system. Yet succumbing to this temptation could itself be a factor in declining conviction rates.

The findings of the London study must be set against this background and context. They indicate that, although the MPS Guidelines provide the framework for a model system of care for victims, in practice they are not always followed, neither are the promises contained in the MPS booklet always fulfilled. Little seems to be done effectively to challenge disbelieving and stereotypical attitudes about women who report rape.

Systems set in place in the 1980s may no longer be adequate either to sustain appropriate rises in conviction rates or to provide effective support for victims. The Metropolitan Police Authority has, at the time of writing, just published a review of MPS procedures.[72] It recommends, *inter alia*, that the

[68] Home Office, *Criminal Statistics England and Wales 1995* (Cm 3421, 1996), 51.

[69] At 37.

[70] The Home Office Research and Statistics Directorate kindly provided these statistics.

[71] Home Office, *Criminal Statistics England and Wales Supplementary Tables 2000*, vol. iii, table 3.1A.

[72] Metropolitan Police Authority, *Scrutiny Report: Rape Investigation and Victim Care* (April 2002). The Report supports dedicated and trained sexual offence investigation teams. Sussex Police has also initiated a review. The Northumbria and Durham Area Committee has developed an imaginative protocol for dealing with rape cases. Designated officers provide information to victims and are a link with the CPS, the courts, and other agencies. They also provide information to the court about the victim's situation before sentencing: see *Criminal Justice Consultative Council Newsletter* (London: Home Office, Feb. 1999), 3. Plans to improve the investigation of rape cases by the police were announced on 22 July 2002: see Home Office, *Action Plan* (2002).

much vaunted rape examination suites should be abandoned in favour of hospital-based facilities which encourage self-referral. It was impressed by the Haven-Camberwell scheme in south-east London[73] which is modelled on the highly praised scheme set up at St Mary's Hospital in Manchester. These schemes permit adult and child victims to seek assistance without reporting to the police. Medical attention is provided along with forensic examination and DNA sampling, counselling, care, and advice. The service is entirely confidential but police information may be enhanced even if victims finally decide not to lodge a formal complaint. There is much to be said for developments of this kind. But what seems to be needed above all is a change in management priorities. Without this, the plight of rape victims within the criminal justice system is unlikely to improve.

Victim Support

The victim's problems do not end once the police investigation has been completed. Victim Support is now firmly in place as a source of assistance for victims and the number of sexual assault victims contacting Victim Support is growing. In 1995, for example, it offered a service to over 15,400 victims of rape and other sexual offences.[74] In 1999/2000 there were 4,145 referrals for rape and 14,400 referrals for other sexual offences making a total of 18,545 referrals for sexual offences. In 2000–1 this rose to 4,813 referrals for rape and 15,462 for other sexual offences, making a total of 20,275 referrals for sexual crimes.[75] Victim Support volunteers who deal with sexual assault victims are all specially trained. They will visit victims in their own homes or elsewhere, accompany them to the police station, provide them with information about criminal injuries compensation, and assist with applications. They will also help victims to consider how they wish to proceed after an attack, allow them to discuss their feelings, provide information about urgent practical, medical, and personal issues, and refer them on to other agencies when appropriate.[76] The police may refer complainants to Victim Support but in 1995 almost one-third of the women offered help by Victim Support made direct contact with their local scheme.[77] In 2000–1, one in ten of those who contacted Victim Support directly were victims of sexual crime.[78] Victim Support's Witness Service provides information and support to victims, witnesses, and their families before, during, and after the trial. Since 1996 the Witness Service has been established in every Crown Court centre in England and Wales.[79] But there has been no recent evaluation of the efficacy of Victim Support's intervention in rape cases.[80]

[73] See Tina Orr-Munro, 'Care in a Crisis?' (2001) Police Review, 6 Apr. 2001.

[74] See Victim Support (1996), 3.

[75] Victim Support (2001), 14.

[76] Victim Support (1996), 3–4. Victim Support does not provide therapy.

[77] ibid. 3.

[78] Victim Support (2001), 14.

[79] ibid. 4.

[80] For an early study, see Maguire and Corbett (1987).

Legal Representation for Rape Victims

In Scandinavia, another solution to the problem of assisting rape victims has evolved. Complainants in Denmark, Norway, and Sweden are entitled as of right to legal representation from the moment that they report a sexual assault to the police.[81] The idea of legal representation, at least during the trial, is one which has been frequently mooted in common law jurisdictions,[82] but precisely how such a scheme would work has never been properly examined. It is proposed, therefore, to analyse in detail how the Danish scheme, which was subsequently adopted in Norway and Sweden, came to be introduced and how exactly it operates.[83]

(a) Representation for Victims—Background to the Scheme

In Denmark, the law of rape[84] has been less the focus of attention than the treatment of rape victims. In the 1970s, there was widespread criticism of the police, prosecutors, and courts for their unsympathetic and callous approach to victims and their failure to deal with offenders.[85] Legal representation for victims was introduced in this context.

[81] The Danish scheme is discussed below. In Norway, a similar scheme was introduced by Act No. 66 of 12 June 1981 which amended the Criminal Procedure Act 1887. The Swedish scheme was introduced in 1988 by the Legal Counsel for Injured Parties Act. See also Republic of Ireland, Sex Offenders Act 2001, s 34.

[82] For the United States, see e.g. Bohmer and Blumberg, 'Twice Traumatized: The Rape Victim and the Court' (1975) 58 Judicature 391, 399; Berger (1977), 84–7. For New Zealand, see Young (1983), i, 68–71. For England, see CLRC (1984), para. 2.100; Women's National Commission, (1985), para. 84. However, surprisingly, the matter was not discussed in *Speaking Up for Justice* (Home Office, 1998).

[83] The following analysis of the Danish scheme is based on research originally carried out by the author in 1984 in Denmark involving, *inter alia,* extensive interviews with judges, state prosecutors, other practising and academic lawyers and criminologists, as well as with members of the Joan Sisters who run the equivalent of the English Rape Crisis Centres. The material was updated in 2001.

[84] The substantive law of rape contained in s 216 of the Danish Criminal Code was amended in 1981 and there have been no major changes since then. Rape carries a maximum penalty of six years' imprisonment, rising to 10 where there are aggravating circumstances. Sentences of four years or more require a trial by jury which prosecutors are keen to avoid. Jury trials are far less common in Denmark than in England and Wales. Offences of indecent assault and buggery are dealt with identically to rape and carry the same penalties. There is also an offence of unlawful coercion which applies where sexual intercourse is obtained by threats other than of violence (s 217). It is also an offence to procure sexual intercourse by gravely abusing the victim's subordinate or economically dependent position (s 220). The Danish code depicts rape and related offences purely in relation to the conduct of the defendant without reference to the victim's consent. Evidence of sexual history may not be adduced except where it is of essential importance to the case (Danish Procedural Code, ch. 18, s 185(2)). For more detailed discussion of the evolution of the Danish law, see Temkin (1987), 163–5 and Rasmussen, 'Voldtaegt i retshistorisk belysning', in A. Kongstadt, ed., *Voldtaegt (sforskning) i fr Nordiske Land* (Copenhagen: Institute of Criminal Science, 1982).

[85] See e.g. Snare (1983).

One of the moving forces behind the scheme was Jytte Thorbek, a feminist lawyer.[86] She was much impressed by the forensic skills of the distinguished French advocate Gisele Halimi whom she had observed in action in France. She was equally struck by the plight of complainants in Danish rape trials. In the mid-1970s, the only source of positive assistance for rape victims was that provided by a group of women known as the Joan Sisters. Their activities closely resemble those of the English Rape Crisis Centres. Members of the Joan Sisters were prepared to accompany rape victims to the police station as well as to court. They were also a source of counselling and general assistance. In consultation with them, Thorbek resolved to take further action. One day in 1977, she turned up at a rape trial and asked for leave to represent the complainant, but the judge summarily dismissed her request. Subsequently, she tried again, this time before a higher court which was about to embark upon a jury trial for rape. It was declared that she could be appointed only if there were legislative provision to this effect. Such provision the judges obligingly discovered for her. In Denmark, as in some other European countries, victims of crime may make a civil compensation claim in a criminal trial. In 1969, an amendment was introduced to the Danish Procedural Code which permitted the appointment by the court of a lawyer to assist victims with such a claim. The cost of this appointment is met by the legal aid scheme. Thorbek thus found herself appointed under section 995A of the Danish Procedural Code to assist the complainant in bringing a claim for damages. This decision marked a turning-point. Hitherto, section 955A had scarcely been used at all in any criminal trials. Subsequently, Thorbek regularly applied to be appointed and was often, although not invariably, successful.

An appointment under section 995A enabled an advocate to advise her client about compensation, to gather information relevant to the claim, and to address the court on the matter. In a rape case, the advocate may, in her application for compensation, draw attention to the plight of the victim, to any emotional, psychological, or physical effects of the rape and to any economic loss she has sustained in consequence of it.

Appointment under section 995A did not permit the advocate to deal with any issue apart from compensation. There were thus limits to Ms Thorbek's achievement. However, her activities became a matter of public interest. She effectively drew attention to the unenviable position of the victims of sexual assault. Thorbek, herself a socialist, was soon to find that her initiative had caught the imagination of the Danish Conservative Party, then in opposition, which proposed in Parliament that certain victims of crime should be entitled to a more general form of legal assistance. It was the widespread support for this proposal from every point in the parliamentary political spectrum which persuaded the Ministry of Justice to consider

[86] For her own account of the scheme and its origins, see Thorbek (1981).

the matter. In 1979, it began a process of consultation with relevant interest groups, including the Danish Bar Association and the police, to ascertain their reaction to a scheme which would permit legally aided representation for victims in certain cases of sexual assault. The views of these interest groups were reflected in the Ministry's final proposal.

(i) The Ministry of Justice's Proposal[87]

REPRESENTATION FOR COMPLAINANTS IN SEXUAL ASSAULT CASES

The Ministry of Justice finally proposed that complainants in sexual assault cases should be provided with legal representation. However, a suggestion by the Danish Conservative Party that a range of victims of violence should be similarly represented was rejected. The Ministry stressed the singular nature of sexual assault proceedings in which the victim is often the only prosecution witness and whether or not she consented is a central issue.[88] It pointed out that complainants were for these reasons subjected to a particularly tough interrogation and cross-examination which was likely to be a considerable ordeal. Moreover, the Ministry was understandably concerned about the cost of a scheme which embraced all manner of victims and the administrative burden which this would impose. In 1977, there were 3,700 reports of assault contravening sections 244–6 of the Danish Criminal Code. By contrast, there were only 300 sexual assaults. The Ministry did not, however, reject the possibility of extending the scheme at a later stage.

REPRESENTATION BY A LAWYER

The Ministry gave consideration to whether the right sort of person to assist the victim was a lawyer: a number of Members of Parliament had expressed the view that it was not. The Ministry concluded that it was important to have someone who was well acquainted with the criminal justice system. Moreover, it decided to give certain powers to the victim's representative which could only be exercised by a lawyer. The proposal stressed that the role of the victim's advocate would be to explain to the victim the nature of the proceedings, to prepare her for the case, and to assist her in the police station and in court. But it would also be to provide her with guidance as to how she might obtain help of a different nature from other agencies. The Ministry appears to have had in mind counselling or medical assistance. The proposal also stressed the importance of securing continuity of assistance by ensuring that the person who looked after the complainant's interests in the police station represented her through to the end of the case.

[87] Dated 27 Nov. 1979 (*Forslag til lov om aendring af retsplejeloven—Advokatistand til den forurettede. Lovforslag*, no. L45).

[88] It is noteworthy that the absence of reference to consent in the definition of sexual offences has not avoided this outcome.

REPRESENTATION TO BE PERMITTED AT THE POLICE STATION

The Ministry considered that, since the victim of sexual assault might very well be in a distressed state upon arrival at the police station, the guidance and support of a lawyer at this stage and whilst she was being questioned would be of great assistance to her. It was therefore proposed that the police should be under a duty to inform the victim of her right to representation before any questions were asked of her and that the police report should state that the victim was so informed. It was also suggested that a list of advocates willing to act in these cases should be kept at the police station for victims who did not have a particular lawyer in mind or whose own lawyer was unavailable. The advocate would be appointed by the court, upon application by the police at the earliest convenient moment, but in order to ensure that victims were questioned without undue delay, advocates would be authorized to act at the police station before leave of the court was sought or obtained. However, it was felt that a victim who consented should be able to be questioned in the absence of an advocate. This is similar to the rules which apply to representation for the defendant in criminal cases. It was also proposed that the complainant's advocate should be able to be present throughout the interrogation and should be able to put further questions to her where she considered that the ground had not been fully covered by the police.

PREPARATION FOR TRIAL

Once the police had gathered all the statements and evidence in the case in preparation for trial, counsel for the complainant should, it was suggested, be entitled to have access to this evidence, including defence evidence. Counsel for the defence has access to evidence in police hands at an earlier stage but there was concern that the victim's statement should not be influenced either by that of the defendant or by other evidence. It was emphasized that counsel for the complainant should not be entitled to reveal any evidence to her client without police permission. It was proposed that counsel should be informed of the date of the trial.

THE ADVOCATE IN COURT

The Ministry's proposal contained little about the role of the advocate in court. It was intentionally left to the courts to determine the scope of her powers, and in particular to decide whether and to what extent she could question witnesses apart from the victim. It was clearly intended that she should be able to ask questions of the victim herself. However, the Ministry was at pains to stress that the advocate should not act as a supplementary prosecutor in the case. She should not address the question of the accused's guilt, she should not suggest what sentence would be appropriate for the defendant, and she should not advise her client how to respond to questions.

She should be concerned rather with issues such as whether the case should be dealt with in camera, whether the defendant should be excluded from court while the victim is giving evidence, and matters relating to compensation.

APPOINTMENT BY THE COURT AT THE EXPENSE OF THE STATE

The Ministry proposed that the appointment of counsel should be at the court's discretion. It should be up to the court to decide in each case whether the victim was in need of such assistance. Clearly, in most cases, the police would not be able to delay interrogation of the victim until the court had been presented with an application. Therefore, in practice, the victim would be entitled to representation at the police station since the proposed rules would make it mandatory for the police to provide or help provide such assistance. However, once the application came to court, the judge would be able to terminate such assistance. The proposal envisaged that the appointment could be limited to part of the case only and could be brought to an end where the need for it was considered no longer to exist. It was proposed that the state should meet the cost of the advocate's appointment and that the practice governing payment should be that which applied under the existing scheme for legal aid for defendants. On the basis of the 1977 statistics, it was estimated that if legal representation were provided for every eligible sexual assault victim, the public expenditure involved would be 500,000 Danish krone.[89]

(ii) The Parliamentary Debate

On 11 December 1979, a Bill containing the Ministry of Justice's proposal was given a first reading in Parliament. With one exception, all parties were enthusiastic in their support for it. The speakers in the debate demonstrated a high level of sympathy and insight into the plight of sexual assault victims. However, the Member speaking on behalf of the Christian People's Party, a former policeman, felt that the main advantage of the scheme would be in dealing with the problem of false allegations of rape. He argued that a sensible word with a lawyer might dissuade a complainant from pursuing her allegation.

Four main issues were to emerge from the debate.[90]

THE ROLE OF THE ADVOCATE

Some speakers felt that the proposed scheme did not go far enough. Many stressed the need which a victim might have for counselling or psychiatric

[89] In January 1987 there were approximately 11 Danish Krone to the pound sterling, 12 in 2001.

[90] Parliamentary pressure in this debate also led in 1981 to the provision of anonymity for sexual assault victims.

help. However, it was generally considered that, providing the advocate bore in mind that her role was both to provide legal advice and also to refer the victim to other sources of assistance, the scheme should prove to be an effective step in the right direction.

There was some discussion of the advocate's legal role which, in line with the Ministry's proposal, was not clearly spelt out in the Bill. It was pointed out that it was essential for the victim to be able to confer with her lawyer prior to interrogation by the police. Clearly, the advocate's usefulness would be much reduced if she were unable to reassure her client beforehand, prepare her in broad terms for the interrogation, and elicit any points material to her case which required mentioning to the police. As far as her role in court was concerned, it was considered appropriate for the courts to be left to work this out for themselves. One speaker also pointed to the problem of ensuring that complainants were represented by the appropriate sort of lawyers, since many would not be suited to work of this nature.

JUDICIAL DISCRETION

The Joan Sisters had made known their opposition to the discretionary nature of the proposed scheme for victim representation. They contended that the victim of sexual assault should be entitled to such representation as of right. Many Members of Parliament expressed firm support for this view in the debate.

THE SYMBOLIC SIGNIFICANCE OF THE SCHEME

A number of Members of Parliament spoke of the curiously negative social attitude towards victims of sexual assault and the double standard in sexual behaviour which was applied to men and women. They deplored the view that such victims had only themselves to blame and that there was a high level of fabrication in reports of rape. The proposed scheme for representation of the victim was thus perceived as a public statement of support for sexual assault victims, as a way of improving their image and reducing the stigma which attached unfairly to them.

EXTENDING THE SCHEME TO OTHER VICTIMS

A number of Members of Parliament expressed the view that other victims of violence should be included in the scheme. The victims of domestic violence were singled out for attention. It was argued that, while it was clearly not possible for all victims of violence to be represented, victims of marital violence should be regarded as an exception, since some of the problems associated with sexual assault applied equally to them. They often found it very hard both to report the matter to the police and to pursue it in court, and were thus in particular need of support. Reference was made to Erin Pizzey's book, *Scream Quietly, or the Neighbours will Hear*.[91] The Minister

[91] 1974. See above, p. 73.

of Justice did not reject this proposal outright but showed no particular enthusiasm for it.

(iii) The Committee Stage[92]

At the committee stage, several alterations were made to the original proposal. These were approved by representatives from all parties save the Progress Party which represents the extreme right in Danish politics.

The most significant amendment was to render the appointment of an advocate mandatory at the request of the victim. The power of the court to terminate the advocate's appointment otherwise than at the victim's behest was also removed. The Bill had further provided for application for legal representation to be made by the police where the complainant herself did not wish to be represented. The second amendment introduced in committee was to limit such applications so that they could not be made once the police had questioned her. Moreover, an appointment made at the request of the police would lapse automatically at this juncture. However, the complainant would be able to apply for counsel herself at this point and, upon such a request, an appointment would be mandatory. It was considered that there might be cases in which the interests of police and victim with respect to representation did not coincide and that once the police interrogation was over, the police interest in the matter would lapse.

The report on the committee stage notes that the likely cost of the scheme was in the region of one million krone per annum rather than the half million originally estimated. The extra half million would be the result of rendering the scheme mandatory but was also due to the rise in the number of reported sexual assaults from 300 in 1977 to 500 per annum by 1980.

The bill as amended was finally passed by 134 votes to seven.

(b) The Law

The law relating to the appointment of a lawyer for sexual assault victims was finally enacted on 16 June 1980 and located in chapter 66a of the Danish Procedural Code. Section 741 of this chapter provided that a lawyer was to be appointed at the victim's request in cases under sections 216, 217, 218(2), 224, and 225 of the Criminal Code. These cover rape, unlawful sexual coercion, sexual intercourse with a person 'who is not in a position to resist', buggery, and grave indecent assault whether the victim is male or female.[93]

[92] The Report of the Committee stage is dated 23 May 1980 (*Betaenkning over Forslag til lov om aendring af resplejeloven—Advokatbistand til den forurettede*).

[93] By virtue of s 224, the crimes of unlawful sexual coercion and sexual intercourse with a person who is not in a position to resist apply equally to sexual acts apart from intercourse.

In 1987, the Report of a Committee set up by the Danish Ministry of Justice[94] recommended *inter alia* that the scheme should be extended to cover the victims of incest and certain other sexual offences involving children. It also proposed that the courts should be given discretion to appoint counsel for victims of other sexual crimes and crimes of violence. These proposals have gradually been enacted[95] so that today the victims of a range of sexual crimes and crimes of violence including robbery may be represented. Legislation enacted in 1997 provided that in cases where there is discretion to appoint counsel the court may refuse to do so only where the offence is not serious and it considers that counsel is clearly unnecessary.[96] In all cases, where the victim does not request counsel, counsel may nevertheless be appointed at the request of the police for the duration of the police investigation.[97]

The police must inform the victim of her right to representation before questioning her and the police report of the case must state whether or not she was so informed. The police must then take her request to court so that a judge can make the necessary appointment. A victim who requests the appointment of a lawyer may nevertheless, if she so desires, make a statement to the police in the absence of a lawyer. If she is unwilling to do so, the police may call upon a lawyer to represent her pending an appointment by the court. The lawyer may be chosen from an official list of lawyers who are available for these purposes.[98] The lawyer must be informed when police questioning of the victim will take place, is entitled to be present, and to ask her further questions. The lawyer must be provided with a copy of her statement and, once an indictment is preferred, is entitled, as far as is practicable, to receive copies of the rest of the evidence in the case which is in the possession of the police. However, this material may not be passed on to the victim nor may its contents be revealed except with police permission. The lawyer must be given notice of court hearings.

[94] *The Victim in Cases of Rape and Violence*, Report No. 1102, Danish Ministry of Justice (1987). Judge Marie Louise Andreasen chaired the Committee.

[95] See Law No. 730 of 1988 enacted 7 Dec. 1988; Law No. 366 of 1994 enacted 18 May 1994 and Law No. 349 of 1997 enacted 23 May 1997. All the legislation on victim representation has now been consolidated in s 741a by the Administration of Justice Act (Consolidated Act No. 857, 12 Sept. 2000). Law No. 730 of 1988 also provided for the exclusion of the public at the request of rape and certain other victims during their testimony.

[96] Law No. 349 of 1997. In Sweden, victims of crimes of violence are entitled to free legal counsel during the police investigation and trial.

[97] s 741a(2).

[98] This list is also available to those arrested or indicted for the commission of any criminal offence. As a result of legislation introduced in October 1978, the latter have a right to have a lawyer present during police interrogation. The scheme for representation of suspects at the police station bears some resemblance to the scheme described here for complainant representation at the police station. For further details of the former scheme, see Leigh and Hall Williams (1981), 12.

(c) The Scheme in Operation[99]

(i) *Representation at the Police Station*

It seems that victims are not always represented at the police station, despite the legislation. There are a number of possible explanations for this. One is that some police officers do not inform them of their right to representation at this juncture. On the other hand, the view has been expressed that police officers are far kinder to sexual assault victims than they used to be so that many are content to proceed without a lawyer.[100] Members of the Joan Sisters considered that the police behaved perfectly properly if a Joan Sister were present but were far less amiable to victims who were on their own. In such cases, pressure was often brought to bear upon victims to permit the police to begin their examination without the presence of a lawyer, particularly as lawyers may be unable to turn up at the station immediately.

Some lawyers whose names appear on the official list of those available to represent victims are not particularly knowledgeable about sexual assault. The police sometimes refer cases to members of the Joan Sisters who are permitted to be present during the police examination of the victim even where the victim is also represented by a lawyer. However, since the Joan Sisters are few in number, their impact in this area is only marginal.

It is not clear that lawyers who do attend at the police station are necessarily provided with the opportunity to discuss the case with their client before police questioning begins. The lawyer is not expected to interrupt except where improper questions, for example, general questions about the victim's past sexual history, are put. It is considered to be improper for the lawyer either to advise her client how to respond to questions or to act as a co-investigator with the police. The lawyer's primary role is to ensure that the complainant is treated in a proper fashion, that she does not feel alone and vulnerable, and that any points she wishes to make are recorded.

(ii) *Legal Advice before the Trial*

Complainants are generally represented in court even if they are not represented at the police station. The complainant will be able to visit her lawyer to obtain legal advice before the trial. The lawyer's task on these occasions is essentially fourfold. She will first ask her client for a detailed account of what happened, including her experience after the assault. She must then prepare her for the trial by discussing the case with her and telling

[99] For an account of the scheme and criticism of its limitations, see Thorbek (1981). No Danish research has been conducted to evaluate the operation of the scheme but Swedish research into the equivalent Swedish scheme concluded that it had succeeded both in improving the quality of legal procedures and strengthening the position of victims: see Swedish Government (1998), 27.

[100] Both explanations were suggested to the author by members of the Joan Sisters and by academic researchers.

her what to expect in the courtroom. The police are, it seems, providing lawyers with the papers in the case efficiently and promptly. Many lawyers stress the importance of explaining to the complainant the significance of an acquittal, namely, that it means no more than that the case was not proved beyond reasonable doubt. The lawyer will also endeavour to give her client moral support and reassurance and will, if necessary, refer her for counselling. Finally, the lawyer will inform her client of her right to apply for compensation and will prepare the claim.

(iii) Representation in Court

Sections 741a–e of the Procedural Code set out the bare bones of the scheme. It has been left to the courts to work out some of the details. There are no fixed parameters on what counsel for the victim may or may not do in court. This is left to the court's discretion. However, it is recognized that counsel does have certain clear duties and functions. First, she may, and generally does, apply to the judge for leave for her client's evidence to be given in the absence of the defendant.[101] Such leave is often granted, although defending counsel may contest it. Counsel may further apply for her client's evidence to be given in camera or even that the case should be heard entirely in camera.[102] After examination and cross-examination by prosecution and defence, the judge will generally permit counsel to put additional questions to her client. These will generally concern her condition and circumstances after the rape, which will be material to her compensation claim. The answers to these questions may also throw light on her previous testimony. Thus, for example, evidence that since the alleged rape she has been so traumatized that she has been unable to continue in employment or that she has, through fear, been forced to move house, is clearly likely to support her allegations. Counsel's duty will also be to object to inappropriate questions put by the defence, particularly concerning sexual history.[103] She will, moreover, and most importantly, be there to explain to the complainant the course of events and to provide support and reassurance.

The question remains whether the courts should permit the advocate to play a greater role than that which has been described. Should counsel, for example, be able to question witnesses other than the complainant or object to questions put to them by the defence or even by the prosecution? Certainly there is general agreement as to certain things which counsel may not do. She may not advise her client how to answer questions but may advise her

[101] Such leave is applied for under s 848.1–848.2 of the Danish Procedural Code. See p. 318 below.

[102] Danish Procedural Code, s 29. Under s 29a the complainant is now entitled, if she so wishes, to have the public excluded whilst she gives her evidence.

[103] In a case in 1998 in which defence counsel asked the complainant whether she had a criminal record, it was held that neither she nor her counsel was entitled to challenge the question.

whether to do so if, for example, they relate to her sexual past. She must never address the court or comment on the question of the defendant's guilt.

Most lawyers who act for sexual assault victims appear to accept that their role is fairly circumscribed. Some are deliberately unassertive and low-key in court. Thus, in one case observed by the author, the lawyer did not appear in court until the moment before her client was due to give evidence, when she requested permission that the complainant be permitted to testify in camera. After the application was granted, she led the complainant, an 84-year-old woman, into court on her arm and stayed beside her throughout her testimony, occasionally explaining to her a number of points made by the judge. Her application for compensation was very brief. She mentioned, *inter alia*, that since the incident the complainant had been too scared to go out at night and requested a sum of money to cover taxi fares. She finally escorted the complainant from the courtroom and did not make a further appearance.

Afterwards, the lawyer explained to the author that it is her policy when representing sexual assault victims to keep quiet unless she feels that the judge has misunderstood her client. Since there is a tariff by which compensation is assessed, she did not feel that the lawyer could do much to influence the amount awarded and she therefore considered that it was best to keep her remarks brief. She felt that her role was to provide moral support for her client and for that reason she had preferred to remain with her outside the courtroom whilst she was waiting to give evidence. She felt that lawyers who attempted to act as second prosecutors might prejudice the interests of their clients, since the judges disliked this approach. The judge in the case explained to the author that, while he thoroughly approved of the discreet approach of this lawyer, she could have gone further without incurring the disapproval of the court.[104]

At the opposite end of the spectrum, one or two lawyers who act for victims are particularly assertive on their behalf. The judicial reaction has been to keep them on a tight rein. They may, for example, be prevented from putting any questions to the complainant until after the court has reached its verdict. In this way, the issue of compensation is treated quite separately from the issue of guilt. The disadvantage of this from the complainant's point of view is that the court will not hear additional information which may throw light on her previous testimony. It seems, therefore, that what counsel for the complainant is permitted to do in court may depend to some extent on her approach. The judge will stop her if she gives the impression that she is an adjunct of the prosecution or sails too close to the question of the defendant's guilt. If her approach is discreet and circumspect, she will be afforded more latitude.

[104] Another judge expressed the view that, on the whole, Danish judges prefer active advocates, provided that they do not overstep the mark.

It is because most lawyers acting for victims have understood the limitations of their role and have not sought to push beyond them that they have been integrated with ease into the trial process. The judges on the whole have responded positively, although some, mindful of the cost of employing counsel, have encouraged them to leave after the complainant has finished giving evidence. Prosecutors continue to be in charge of the prosecution and do not consider that the complainant's counsel has any role to play in this. They do not seek their advice nor will they liaise with them about the conduct of the case nor about whether or not to bring an appeal. Complainant's counsel may be seated next to the prosecutor and may sometimes suggest that a particular question be asked or a particular witness called. But the prosecutor is under no obligation to accede to counsel's suggestions. Certainly, prosecutors will brook no interference with the overall conduct of the case.

(d) The Advantages of the Scheme

It is generally agreed that the role of the complainant's lawyer is to provide her with support, to steer her through the legal process and to ensure that she is treated fairly and with respect. Her role is not to prosecute the case, to obtain a conviction, or to influence the sentence. Danish lawyers in general appear to have welcomed the scheme and to be satisfied with its present operation. There is a widespread feeling that victims of sexual assault do require the support which it provides. It is also recognized that judges, prosecutors, and defending counsel have in the past been insufficiently sensitive to the complainant's plight. Improvements in their conduct were noticeable before this innovation, but the scheme seems to have encouraged the trend. Very often, the mere presence in court of a lawyer for the complainant is sufficient to ensure that she is properly treated. Previously, complainants were frequently subjected to a very lengthy cross-examination. This no longer happens. It is felt that victims are becoming more willing to testify in court as a result of these developments and that this will encourage prosecutions. The case mentioned above, involving the sexual assault of an 84-year-old woman, provides an illustration of this. The complainant was initially resolutely opposed to testifying in court. The lawyer appointed to represent her wrote to her requesting a meeting, which took place at the complainant's home. After the lawyer had promised to provide her with every assistance, to fetch her by taxi, and remain with her during the trial, the complainant agreed to testify. The defendant, who had a previous conviction for similar conduct and was clearly dangerous, was convicted as a result.

(e) Criticisms of the Scheme

While moderate legal opinion in Denmark would appear to be broadly in favour of the scheme, there are a few lawyers who have vehemently opposed it. In the press, Søren Søltoft Madsen, a well-known defence lawyer, questioned whether a lawyer was any more suited to helping the complainant than a doctor, priest, social worker, or psychologist.[105] He warned that a victim who visited her lawyer to discuss the case might be over-prepared rather than spontaneous, both in giving testimony in court and in her statements regarding compensation. He argued that the judge could just as well assist the victim in making a compensation claim.

Senior Danish lawyers questioned by this author could find no substance to these criticisms. It was felt that if her lawyer had coached the complainant, this would be all too apparent in court. Compensation was in any case determined according to a tariff, so that however eloquently the complainant expressed her suffering, the award was unlikely to be greatly affected. The matter is essentially one of professional conduct and ethics. It would be wrong for any lawyer, whether appearing for the prosecution, the defence, or for a witness, to instruct a client what to say. The dangers are no greater where the client is a victim.

At the opposite extreme, it is felt by some that the scheme as it presently exists does not go far enough in the assistance it provides for sexual assault victims. It is considered that the complainant's lawyer ought to be able to take a more active role. She should be able to ask questions of the defendant and of witnesses apart from the victim and call witnesses herself. She should also be able to speak to the question of the defendant's guilt. It is felt that Danish prosecutors are all too often unsympathetic to sexual assault victims and do not pursue these prosecutions with sufficient vigour.[106] The Swedish Code on Judicial Procedure permits a victim making a damages claim to question the accused, witnesses, and experts. It has now been proposed that this right should extend to victims and their counsel whether a claim for damages is made or not.[107]

(f) Could the Danish Scheme Provide a Model for England?

Much has been spoken and written of the dangers of comparative research. In particular, academics have warned that institutions cannot simply be transported from country to country regardless of differences in culture, population, and legal system.[108] On the other hand, insularity and xenophobia are equally to be avoided, as is an inclination to dismiss ideas simply because they have been realized in a setting which is not quite identical to our own. Moreover, as Shapland, Wilmore, and Duff have remarked: 'At the moment, similarities in attitude between . . . victims in different countries are extraordinary. They tend to suggest similar roles for victims and a similar

[105] See 'Voldtaegt og retssikkerhed', *Politiken*, 4 Mar. 1984.
[106] See e.g. Thorbek (1981). [107] Swedish Government (1998), 28.
[108] See e.g. Leigh and Hall Williams (1981), 73.

perception of victims in different countries and in different systems.'[109] The Danish scheme was after all introduced to alleviate the plight of sexual assault victims in the Danish criminal justice system. Since that of English victims is very similar, a successful scheme of this sort ought to be of interest to us.

There are, however, certain differences between England and Denmark and between the English and Danish legal systems which might at first sight seem worthy of mention. The population of Denmark, five million, is clearly a small fraction of our own and the number of sexual assaults is likely therefore to be considerably fewer. This would not, however, appear to be a difference of any significance. The cost of the Danish scheme is, after all, met by considerably fewer taxpayers.

The Danish system, like our own, is adversarial in nature. It is, however, generally rather less combative. The emphasis is on consensus and co-operation rather than conflict between defence and prosecution.[110] The tone and style in court is more informal, less aggressive. Furthermore, the conviction rate tends to be higher in Denmark since cases do not tend to go forward to trial unless the evidence is fairly strong.[111] It must also be reiterated[112] that most Danish trials are before a judge and two lay assessors and relatively few are before juries.

It is not clear that any of these differences are material. If the Danish system is, generally speaking, somewhat less adversarial in style, it is also true that sexual assault trials are often fought hard by the defence and that convictions are by no means guaranteed. Furthermore, one of the principal concerns in setting up and operating the scheme in Denmark has been to ensure that the distinctive roles of prosecution and defence are maintained and that victim's counsel does not destroy the delicate balance between the two by identifying too closely with the prosecution. It is not clear that the prevalence of jury trials in England and Wales presents any particular problem. Indeed, if a complainant's representative were to become too closely involved with the prosecution, the likelihood is that this would operate in the defence's favour so far as the jury was concerned. However, the scheme should be so constructed as to ensure that this does not occur.

It might very well be argued, on the other hand, that if our system is more adversarial than the Danish and if rape trials are mostly by jury in England, then the case for victim representation is that much greater. Where the combat is more intense, it is the victim who will be caught in the crossfire. Where there is a jury to be persuaded, attacks on the victim and attempts to discredit her are that much more likely to occur and the need to protect her consequently greater.

[109] Shapland *et al.* (1985), 186.
[110] See Leigh and Hall Williams (1981), 73.
[111] See Leigh and Hall Williams (1981), 73.
[112] See n. 84 above.

It must also be recalled that the Danish scheme is not a Scandinavian invention. The idea of victim representation in sexual assault cases has been discussed for some years in the United States and in commonwealth countries.[113] In the Republic of Ireland, legal representation for sexual assault victims has recently been introduced on a limited basis.[114] The Scottish Executive Justice Department is currently considering a proposal by the Law Society of Scotland that a lawyer, to be known as an *amicus curiae,* should be appointed to represent the interests of complainers in sexual offence cases while they are cross-examined.[115] Jytte Thorbek herself obtained the idea from France. Victims in the civil law inquisitorial systems do play a far more active role than in common law adversarial systems. (In Germany, victims may opt to become victim-plaintiffs and thereby enjoy independent procedural status in criminal trials and, if they choose, be legally represented.)[116] But the Danish scheme is not the French scheme. The Danish have simply taken an idea and remoulded it to their own requirements. There would appear to be no sufficient reason why we should not do precisely the same with the Danish model. The Ombudsman, a Swedish invention, has after all been tailored to our own needs.

It might be argued, on the other hand, that although the legitimate needs of sexual assault victims are not currently met by the English criminal justice system and although a scheme for legal representation would do much to fulfil these needs, there is a crucial objection in principle to affording privileges to one class of victims as against all others.[117] The CLRC, for example, stated: 'If representation of witnesses in rape cases were allowed, it would be difficult to refuse it in other cases'.[118] The Danish scheme now provides for legal representation for victims of non-sexual violence subject to certain restrictions.[119] Certainly, Shapland *et al.* have demonstrated that victims of crimes of violence have in common an unmet need for guidance, information, and help. On the other hand, their study also revealed that sexual assault victims suffered greater and more persistent psychological and

[113] See n. 82 above.

[114] Sex Offenders Act 2001, s 34. See n. 151 and accompanying text.

[115] See Scottish Executive (2002), 26 and n. 117 below.

[116] The Victim Protection Law of 1986 (Bundesgesetzblatt 1, at 2496) enabled victims of sexual abuse, rape, sexual coercion, and grievous bodily harm to acquire victim plaintiff status for the first time. This also enables victims to bring private suits should the state decline to bring proceedings: see Goy (1996) at 335–6. The state may pay for the lawyer or, if he is convicted, the defendant may be made to pay the costs. Victims' organizations will also sometimes lend financial assistance.

[117] The Scottish Executive Justice Department has put forward for consideration a proposal that an *amicus* could be appointed by the court for any witness who might be particularly vulnerable. 'The *amicus* could ascertain the witness's needs and make application for whatever special measures for giving evidence he felt were appropriate, taking account of the witness's own views. The *amicus* could then ensure that the measures were properly used and protect the interests of the witness by intervening in questioning, or asking for breaks on behalf of the witness.' See Scottish Executive (2002), 26.

[118] CLRC (1984), para. 2.100.

[119] See above under the heading 'The Law'.

social effects than any other group in their survey.[120] It is suggested, moreover, that, within the criminal justice system, their needs are greater than those of other victims of violence. The Battelle Institute concluded after their two-year study on rape: 'In no other crime is the victim's complaint so suspect. In no other crime is it necessary to demonstrate that the victim did not consent [to a criminal act]. In no other crime is the victim less protected from abusive treatment by medical personnel, police, prosecutors and defence attorneys.'[121]

Thus, rape, 'while similar to other crimes . . . is in many ways unique'. For 'rape laws—more than any other criminal statutes—require victims to establish their status as victims'.[122] Sufficiently similar issues are raised by other forms of sexual assault to warrant similar treatment in such cases. But there may also be a case for providing representation to certain other victims as well, particularly those of domestic violence.

(g) Adaptation of the Danish Scheme

Danish sexual assault victims are now entitled to legal representation at the police station, legal advice thereafter, and legal representation in court. These three elements of the scheme are not inseparable. It is proposed to consider each in turn with a view to assessing to what extent it would be desirable to make similar provision in England and Wales and, if so, how this might be done.

(i) Representation at the Police Station

There can be no doubt that further action needs to be taken in this country both to ensure that all genuine complaints of rape are processed and that rape victims are properly treated by the police. Had the American approach to rape investigation pioneered by Harry O'Reilly been adopted over here by all police forces, the case for legal representation at the police station would be hard to sustain. The advantage of it is that it goes to the root of the problem by seeking to change both the behaviour and the attitudes of

[120] Shapland *et al.* (1985), 98, 101, 107.

[121] US Dept. of Justice, Law Enforcement Assistance Administration, National Institute of Law Enforcement and Criminal Justice, *Forcible Rape: Final Project,* Police vol. 1 (Washington, DC: Government Printing Office, 1977). The particular ruthlessness of defence tactics in rape cases is amply illustrated by the Scottish study which notes, 'Such tactics were all the more upsetting for the complainer since there was no scope for intervening or challenging the pattern of questioning': see Chambers and Millar (1986), 121; see also pp. 200–1 above. The study found that judges and prosecutors rarely intervened even where defence questioning was contrary to the rules of evidence and where the complainer was clearly very distressed. Complainers were generally in the witness box for as long as two hours. Victims in the study frequently expressed the view that they would have liked to have their own lawyer: see ibid. 53, 55, 83, 123, and 131.

[122] V. Rose and S. Randall, 'The Impact of Investigator Perceptions of Victim Legitimacy on the Processing of Rape/Sexual Assault Cases' (1982) 5 *Symbolic Interaction* 23, 24.

police. The Danish scheme, by contrast, does not demand the same degree of internal change from police officers. It seeks rather to curb their worst excesses. Indeed, the assumption which appears to underpin it is the inevitability of tough behaviour from the police. It will be recalled that in its proposal the Ministry of Justice asserted that, because of the centrality of the issue of consent, a robust interrogation by the police was bound to take place and the complainant would necessarily suffer an ordeal.[123] It is noteworthy, therefore, that Blair found that in Newark in the United States police officers were trained to approach the issue of consent very differently and to focus their attention upon 'the actions, criminal responsibility and possible culpability of the suspect' rather than upon the consent of the victim. He observed:

> Officers are encouraged to move the focus of their investigation from the rape itself to its surrounding circumstances and to divide those circumstances into five areas: initial contact; coercive efforts; intimidation; rape; and report. Attention is also given to the movements of the victim and offender and the manner in which those movements may indicate coercion and intimidation. In addition, officers are given careful instruction as to the nature of consent. The sexual assault investigators interviewed as part of this study endeavoured to ensure that their working definition of consent was neither based on assumptions of sexual dominance or compliance nor more extreme than that which would be accepted in a court of law. Detectives concentrated not only on proving that the victim had not consented but on obtaining evidence about the suspect's behaviour to determine whether or not he had sought consent.[124]

But some will no doubt query not merely whether police attitudes can be changed, but whether they should be to the extent which Harry O'Reilly and Ian Blair envisaged. It might be said that it is inappropriate for police to seek to empathize with the victim, since they, like the prosecution, are the servants of the state and must remain neutral as between victim and defendant. For police officers to assume a role which requires a clear involvement with the victim might be thought to entail a shift in the balance of the system, which is contrary to the interests of justice. Arguably, it is one thing to demand that the police forswear bullying and desist from questioning calculated to belittle and degrade complainants but quite another to insist that they act as social workers, advisers, and counsellors to them. Those who adopt this view might conceivably prefer the Danish system, which provides a check on the police without demanding any radical shift in their approach.

It is clear, however, that there is nothing in the American approach which is inimical to the interests of justice or which is in any sense improper. It does not follow that empathy with the victim will ensure bias against the defendant. A willingness to accept a complaint as genuine does not mean that police will be willing to bring prosecutions where sufficient evidence is

[123] See p. 283 above. [124] Blair (1985), 63.

lacking. Indeed, sympathy for the victim might conceivably discourage prosecutions, even though there is abundant evidence against the defendant, where this might exacerbate her trauma. The American approach is clearly to be preferred to the Danish—provided that it works.

Whilst legal representation of the complainant at the police station would be unnecessary if the American approach were fully and successfully implemented, a woman might still wish to be accompanied whilst she is there by a friend, counsellor, or rape crisis representative. In San Francisco, if a victim wishes, staff from the Sexual Trauma Service will remain with her during police interviews.[125] But American rape crisis counsellors questioned by Blair no longer felt the need to insist on being present at police interviews and were happy to allow the officer concerned to decide whether this would be in the victim's interest.[126] In England, Home Office Circular 25/1983[127] states that 'the complainant should normally be asked whether or not she would like a friend or other third party present during the interview: but the interviewing officer remains responsible for deciding whether there is a risk of this prejudicing the conduct of his enquiries'.[128] West Midlands Police Force Orders direct officers to inform rape victims of the existence of the Rape Crisis Centres and to allow them at their discretion to be accompanied by a representative of the centre.

Recent research suggests that whilst police practice in the investigation of rape offences has improved, Harry O'Reilly's approach has not been adopted in England and Wales and problems still abound.[129] There is therefore a strong case for providing the victim with greater assistance at the police station. But should the complainant be *entitled* to be accompanied and should the person concerned be a lawyer?

The presence of a friend or relative might well be sufficient to help the complainant cope with certain aspects of her ordeal at the police station. Shapland *et al.* found that sexual assault victims spent longer at the police station on first reporting an offence than other victims of crime. Of these, the rape complainants were there longest of all, for periods ranging from 3 hours 45 minutes to over 12 hours.[130] To remain unaccompanied at the police station for long stretches of time, having just experienced a sexual assault, could very well be a frightening experience in itself and the presence of a companion could do much to alleviate the situation.[131] On the other hand, a friend or parent is not necessarily the best person to help the victim even as regards her emotional state. Either may be too shocked or upset to

[125] Blair (1985), 44. [126] ibid. 33. [127] 'Investigation of Offences of Rape'.
[128] ibid., para. 5.
[129] See Temkin (1997, 1999) and discussion under the heading 'Changing Police Attitudes' above.
[130] Shapland *et al.* (1985), 26; see also Temkin (1997), 514, (1999), 22.
[131] As yet there is no research which indicates what effect, if any, Home Office Circular 25/83 has had. See also n. 132 below.

provide the right sort of assistance. Rape Crisis Centre and Victim Support representatives will accompany women to the police station but the former organization is beset with funding difficulties and, countrywide, there are few of its representatives available for this purpose. Victims who report to the police immediately are unlikely to be able to arrange for assistance from either organization.[132]

But the rape victim is not merely in need of a companion. The object of legal representation at the police station is, *inter alia*, to ensure that the victim's complaint is treated seriously and with due respect,[133] that her story is properly heard and taken down, that she is subjected neither to bullying nor to intimidation, and that only relevant and proper questions are asked of her. A lawyer is more likely to have the status, power, knowledge, and ability to see that this is done. It is for this reason that a lawyer is the best person to represent the complainant and that the complainant should be entitled to such representation.

Assuming, therefore, that England was to adopt the Danish system of legal representation as of right at the police station, how precisely would it operate? It is suggested that upon arrival at the police station, a rape complainant should be informed of her right to legal representation and should be permitted to contact her solicitor. Many women will not know of a solicitor and the question therefore arises how best to provide her with one. It would be possible for her to be advised by the duty solicitor, but there would be disadvantages in such an arrangement. The duty solicitor is there to provide assistance to those suspected of or charged with a criminal offence. Rape victims are not in this category and should not be seen in any sense to be linked with it. The symbolic disadvantage of the Danish scheme is that it parallels so closely the provision made for defendants who are equally entitled to legal representation at the police station.[134] It would be preferable, therefore, for a list of lawyers to be drawn up who were able and willing to act in such cases and who had attended a special training course. Complainants who did not have their own lawyer would be able to contact a lawyer on this list.

The complainant's lawyer might well take time to arrive. Questions relating to the whereabouts of any suspects would need to be asked immediately and the police should be entitled to ask them irrespective of the lawyer's absence. Similarly, the medical examination would have to be conducted

[132] Commander Thelma Wagstaff is reported to have stated that members of Victim Support 'can be with the victim right from the start of the police interview onwards if requested': *The Guardian*, 19 Aug. 1986. But unless victims are informed of this possibility, they are most unlikely to make such a request. There is no mention of it in the explanatory leaflet for victims produced by the Metropolitan Police. For a contrasting approach, seen n. 142 below.

[133] Despite recent changes in police practice, many rape victims are still treated sceptically by the police. See the statement by Commander Thelma Wagstaff, n. 48 above and Temkin (1997, 1999).

[134] See n. 98 above.

without delay. However, the victim should be entitled to await the arrival of her lawyer before further questioning begins. She should also be entitled to have a friend, relative, or representative from the Rape Crisis Centre or Victim Support scheme with her while she is waiting.

Upon arrival, the complainant's lawyer should be entitled first to discuss the case with her client and then to remain with her throughout the interrogation. The lawyer should not interfere with her client's answers but should see that she is fairly treated, that inappropriate questions about her sexual past are not asked, and that she is informed about her rights. Home Office Circular 25/1983 will provide the lawyer with clear guidance as to what can properly be expected of police officers in this situation. It states that the complainant should be informed that the law places strict limitations on the opportunity for the defence to cross-examine her about her previous sexual history. It also advises officers that

> it should not in general be necessary to ask a complainant questions about her previous sexual experiences . . . Before asking such questions, the limitations on the admissibility of such evidence in court should be carefully considered (if appropriate after taking legal advice). If questions about a complainant's previous sexual history do have to be asked, it should be explained to the complainant why they are necessary and that she does not have to answer them . . . The complainant should also be made aware that her statement will have to be disclosed to the defendant and to his legal advisers.[135]

Officers are further directed that a woman should be made aware at the earliest possible stage of her right to anonymity.[136] Her lawyer should clearly ensure that she understands the anonymity provisions and that the court does on occasion lift reporting restrictions.

Once the interrogation is over and the complainant allowed to leave the station, it would be the lawyer's task to keep her informed of the progress of her complaint.[137] This would require that the police keep the lawyer informed, but would not prevent them maintaining contact with the complainant directly. Home Office Circular 25/1983 states: 'The police should bear in mind the desirability of maintaining contact with the complainant pending the apprehension or trial of the alleged offender. This could be achieved through the designated officer who should also be responsible for informing the complainant of the outcome.'[138] Under the scheme proposed here, the victim would be less dependent on the goodwill and free moments of police officers and would stand a far greater chance of being kept abreast of the progress of her complaint.

135 'Investigating Offences of Rape', para. 6.

136 ibid. para. 8.

137 See text accompanying nn. 4, 5, and 6 above.

138 'Investigating Offences of Rape', para. 9.

(ii) Legal Advice

Once the complainant leaves the police station, she may receive some assistance from Victim Support. She may also need professional advice and information about the legal process in which she may be involved for a long period of time. Having experienced the trauma of rape, she is confronted with the prospect of court proceedings which may take many months to begin. She is likely to have heard that her forthcoming role in the courtroom drama is an unenviable one.

In the event that legal representation has not been provided at the police station, it is suggested that, on leaving it, the victim should be told, not merely, as Home Office Circular 25/1983 directs, about local services which might be of help to her,[139] but also of her right to legal advice. A list of specially trained solicitors should be given to her for this purpose. The victim could then in her own time contact a solicitor. Where she does receive advice at the police station, her legal adviser should be able to continue to assist her. The advice obtainable from the solicitor should encompass such matters as the stage her complaint has reached, the likely course of events, her claim for compensation, and the availability of other helping agencies. The solicitor would also prepare her for the trial. In Denmark, the victim's lawyer will obtain the papers in the case from the police and it would seem desirable that similar provision should be made here once the defence has received them.

Where a prosecution is not brought, the need for contact with the solicitor will clearly be reduced. However, the issue of compensation may still arise. Home Office Circular 25 instructs the police to discuss compensation claims with the victim before she leaves the station.[140] A complainant may not, however, be in a suitable state to grasp the information at this stage.[141]

(iii) Representation in Court

In England, the YJCEA 1999 and possible changes to the substantive law of rape should make some difference to the experience of rape victims at the trial. Moreover, the Witness Service will provide information on court procedures, arrange a visit to the court beforehand, and will accompany a witness into the courtroom. However, despite these positive developments, the sexual assault victim will remain in a particularly vulnerable position. In Los Angeles, where police methods of handling rape cases have dramatically improved, victims are informed of their right to have their own attorney present during legal proceedings.[142] There is clearly a strong case for permitting

[139] ibid., para. 7. [140] ibid. [141] But see n. 472 below.

[142] The booklet, *Survivor*, which informs sexual assault victims of their rights and is published by the Los Angeles Commission on Assaults Against Women is given to all victims of sexual assault by the Los Angeles Police Department. It states: 'You have the right to have your own attorney present during the proceedings . . . You have the right to have someone with you (a friend, relative, advocate etc) at police and court proceedings.' See Blair (1985), 44, 90, 91.

a complainant to be accompanied by a lawyer. The lawyer's presence is bound to be reassuring and should make the prospect of confronting the defendant, his family and friends less intimidating. The lawyer would also be able to explain precisely what is happening. But should she be able to play a broader role than this?

The CLRC received suggestions that complainants in rape cases should be entitled to legal representation in order to challenge defence applications to admit sexual history evidence. It responded entirely negatively to this proposal:

> The implementing of this suggestion would make a substantial change in criminal procedure which would be unnecessary and would probably have far-reaching consequences. In practice representation would be unlikely to make any difference to the judge's ruling. Our correspondents may not have appreciated that judges have a duty to protect all witnesses from unfair cross-examination by counsel, whether they be prosecuting or defending. In our experience they try to perform their duty. They do not need counsel appearing for witnesses to remind them of it. If representation of witnesses in rape cases were allowed it would be difficult to refuse it in other cases. Cross-examination about previous sexual behaviour may become relevant in cases of all kinds. One of our members was once counsel in what seemed a straightforward receiving case. Cross-examination about past sexual behaviour revealed that the allegation of receiving had been fabricated because of sexual jealousy. Further, cross-examination about such behaviour is not the only kind of cross-examination about past conduct which may cause distress to prosecution witnesses.[143]

The CLRC's objections are unconvincing. It is not unprecedented for persons who are not parties to proceedings to be legally represented. Several statutes make provision for this.[144] To state that the scheme is unnecessary clearly involves a matter of opinion. It is highly necessary to ensure that sexual history evidence is only admitted where it is truly essential to the defence's case. It is not clear that this result can be obtained under present arrangements. Judges do indeed have a duty to protect all witnesses from unfair cross-examination. The CLRC must have forgotten that it was precisely because the judges failed so lamentably to discharge this duty that section 2 of the SOAA 1976 was introduced. In the parliamentary debate preceding its enactment, the Lord Chancellor, Lord Hailsham, commented: 'My own view is that judges, on the whole, have not ridden defending counsel on a sufficiently tight rein. If they had ridden defending counsel on a tighter rein, I do not believe that [clause 2] would have been necessary.'[145] In the same vein, Lord Morris said: 'If judges face up to their duties they would deal with these matters without the necessity of having . . .

[143] CLRC (1984), para. 2.100.

[144] See e.g. The Criminal Justice Act 1972, s 36; Obscene Publications Act 1959, s 3(4); Coroners' Rules 1953 (SI 1953 No. 205), r. 16. See also Matrimonial Causes Rules (SI 1977 No. 344), r. 115.

[145] HL Deb., vol. 375, col. 1773 (22 Oct. 1976).

legislation'.[146] Moreover, studies illustrate the slackness of judges in controlling the cross-examination of witnesses.[147] Adler found that defence counsel often ignored section 2 altogether, not infrequently with the connivance of the judge. Indeed, some judges themselves asked questions of the victim about her past sexual experience in the absence of any application by the defence to do so.[148] It would appear, therefore, as if some judges do need counsel to remind them of their duties. To state, however, that 'representation would be unlikely to make any difference to the judge's ruling' seems to be unnecessarily damning of them. Presumably, judges would be prepared to listen to reasoned argument and would be open to persuasion if a good enough case were put. The CLRC did not explain its comment that 'legal representation would probably have far-reaching consequences' and it is not clear what it had in mind. It is true that sexual history evidence may be relevant very occasionally in crimes other than sexual assault. The legislature, however, has chosen to limit the use of such evidence in sexual offence cases only. The purpose of legal representation would be to assist the courts in the implementation of this legislation.

If section 41 of the YJCEA 1999 is to operate effectively to protect complainants, it requires counsel, where appropriate, to argue that sexual history evidence should not be admitted because either it does not come within one of the exceptional categories or, if it does, that the main purpose for which it would be adduced is to impugn the credibility of the complainant as a witness.[149] Prosecuting barristers cannot be relied upon to do this.[150] It is noteworthy that in the Republic of Ireland a scheme has recently been introduced which entitles the complainer in a sexual offence case to her own legal representative to represent her interest during a defence application to introduce evidence about her sexual history.[151]

The CLRC was not alone in opposing the idea of legal representation. One American writer has dismissed the suggestion on the ground that 'too many cooks spoil the broth'.[152] In the New Zealand study, judges and lawyers who were asked if they favoured legal representation for victims in court were nearly all opposed to it. They appeared to think that 'it would be likely to interrupt the smooth flow of the prosecution case and reduce the chances of conviction'.[153] In a small study of English barristers who prosecuted and defended in rape cases, all those interviewed were similarly negative about the idea.[154]

It seems clear that the Danish legislation which provides in broad terms for legal representation in court and leaves the courts to work out the details would not be acceptable here. It would be necessary to spell out in some

146 HL Deb., vol. 375, col. 1785 (22 Oct. 1976).

147 See e.g. Adler (1987); Lees (1996).

148 Adler (1982), 673–4.

149 s 41(4).

150 See e.g. Temkin (2000), 234.

151 Sex Offenders Act 2001, s 34. Representation only applies at the application stage.

152 Berger (1977), 87.

153 Young (1983), i, 70.

154 See Temkin (2000), 238.

detail precisely what the legal representative was entitled to do apart from providing comfort and reassurance to the victim and answering her questions. It is suggested that the victim's legal representative should be entitled to object to pre-trial applications for third party disclosure,[155] to contest the application for admission of sexual history evidence, and to object to improper defence questions put to the victim at the trial. She should also be able to make the compensation claim after the verdict if such a claim is appropriate.[156] If the legal representative's role were limited in this way, some of the objections voiced to the idea of legal representation would disappear. The smooth flow of the prosecution's case would in no sense be affected by a scheme of this nature. Since applications for the admission of sexual history evidence take place in the absence of the jury and since the compensation application is made after the verdict, it is only where the complainant's lawyer objects to defence questions that the jury would be in a position to be influenced by her remarks. Representation for victims is in itself likely to affect defence presentation of the case and the need for intervention may not as a result be too great. It seems unlikely that the jury would respond to objections from the complainant's lawyer by acquitting the defendant. It is more likely to acquit the defendant if defence counsel is permitted gratuitously to undermine her character and discredit her.

A scheme of this nature leaves the prosecution to prosecute. The complainant's lawyer becomes involved only to protect her client's interests. Such a scheme should suit prosecutors, whose role is not after all to represent the complainant but who have none the less been criticized for their failure sufficiently to take her interests into account.[157] It has been stated, for example, that 'most prosecution cases are not put well and the prosecution often does nothing to counteract the anti-female tenor of the defence's case. Many rape cases are defended by innuendo and prosecuted faithlessly.'[158]

If a scheme for legal representation were introduced, it would be desirable to ensure continuity of assistance. Thus, ideally the same lawyer who advises the complainant at the police station would continue to assist her at each stage of her involvement with the criminal justice system. Since solicitors with the requisite advocacy training now have rights of audience in the

[155] See Temkin (2002).

[156] In most cases, a conviction for rape will give rise to an immediate sentence of imprisonment. See further p. 36 above. Compensation orders are not generally made in these circumstances.

[157] The trial of a man charged with the rape of Tabitha Bryce had to be discontinued after the CPS had permitted a key prosecution witness to accompany her into court, remain while she gave her evidence and retire with her into a private room after she broke down during defence cross-examination. Attempts to sue the CPS for negligence failed: see *The Times*, 7 Dec. 1998. Had she been legally represented this would not have occurred.

[158] Rape Crisis Centre, *First Report* (1977), 21. The Scottish Report notes, 'The prosecutor's impartiality left complainers open to attack and created an imbalance in the conduct of trials and in the way evidence was presented': see Chambers and Millar (1986), 131.

Crown Court, in many cases this should pose no problem. The appointment of counsel should remain an option, however.

(iv) Assistance with Applications for Compensation

Rape victims frequently incur substantial financial loss. Some, for example, are too traumatized to continue in employment and many move house. Compensation for victims may be awarded by the court on conviction of the offender[159] and by the Criminal Injuries Compensation Scheme whether or not a conviction has taken place. It has already been suggested that rape victims should be entitled to legal advice about compensation and that their legal representative should make the compensation application in court if such an application is appropriate. It is also suggested that the legal representative should be able to assist with applications to the Criminal Injuries Compensation Scheme and this is discussed later on in this chapter.[160]

A scheme for legal representation for rape victims as they move from police station to court to Criminal Injuries Compensation Scheme could immeasurably improve their experience of the criminal justice system. There would be no valid reason for excluding from it other victims of sexual violence such as indecent assault. Moreover, since child victims might particularly benefit from this type of assistance, there is a case for extending it to, and adapting it for, victims of incest and other forms of child sexual abuse.

In addition to legal representation, there are other measures which could be taken to ameliorate the victim's position and these will now be discussed.

Anonymity

(a) Press Reporting

A further way of reducing the victim's ordeal is to protect her from the glare of publicity.[161] In *Socialist Worker and Others, ex p Attorney General*,[162] Lord Widgery CJ suggested that it was for Parliament to afford anonymity to rape complainants, since they did not fall within the category of witnesses who had traditionally been granted it by the courts. It was in these circumstances that the Heilbron Committee decided to review the matter.

(i) The Heilbron Committee

The Heilbron Committee concluded that there was a special case for granting anonymity to rape complainants. It considered that 'one of the greatest

[159] But not generally where the offender is sentenced to imprisonment as is almost invariably the case for rape: see *Jorge* [1999] 2 Cr App R (S) 1.

[160] See below under the heading 'The Criminal Injuries Compensation Scheme'.

[161] See further, under the heading 'Protecting the Complainant in the Courtroom' below.

[162] [1975] 1 All ER 142.

causes of distress to complainants in rape cases is the publicity they sometimes suffer when their name and personal details of their lives are revealed in the press'.[163] It pointed out that 'the complainant's prior sexual history (by any standard essentially her private concern) may be brought out . . . in a way which is rarely so in other criminal cases'.[164] It also emphasized that in rape cases publicity was a severe deterrent to bringing proceedings and that anonymity was necessary, as it was in prosecutions for blackmail in order to encourage victims to come forward.[165] The Committee might also have mentioned two further reasons for anonymity. There is, first of all, the unaccountable stigma which attaches to sexual assault victims and does not apply to other victims of crime. Secondly, there is the extraordinary salaciousness of the press which has time and again revealed itself to be ruthless in its desire to exploit sexual assault cases to the full regardless of the victim's feelings.

The Committee further considered but totally rejected a proposal that defendants in rape cases be afforded anonymity as well. It argued cogently that defendants are generally named in criminal cases, that in blackmail prosecutions anonymity has never been afforded to defendants, although it is customarily enjoyed by complainants, and that the main reason for affording anonymity to rape complainants is to encourage them to report. It concluded that it was erroneous to talk of equality between complainant and defendant in this respect. The true measure of equality was that between rape defendants and defendants in other cases.[166]

The Committee accordingly recommended that rape victims should be granted permanent anonymity in the sense of protection from identification in the press and on radio and television, as from the moment of reporting the offence to the police, and that any breach of it should amount to a criminal offence.[167] There should, however, be judicial discretion to lift reporting restrictions in circumstances where 'the complainant's identity is necessary for the discovery of potential witnesses, the Judge being satisfied that there are real grounds for supposing that the proper conduct of the defence is likely to be substantially prejudiced by a refusal'.[168] The Committee considered that this discretion should be exercised rarely, since 'the name and identity of the victim will not usually be of importance in seeking witnesses'.[169] Moreover, application by the defence should be before a judge in chambers and should take place before, at, or after the committal stage but no later than the commencement of the trial.[170] Since its brief was to consider rape alone, the Committee did not feel able to make suggestions concerning indecent assault, but it did recommend that the complainant should retain her anonymity if, during the trial, a charge of rape

[163] Heilbron Committee (1975), para. 143.
[164] ibid., para. 157.
[165] ibid., paras. 152–4.
[166] ibid., para. 177.
[167] ibid. 37.
[168] ibid., para. 165.
[169] ibid., para. 164.
[170] ibid., para. 165.

was reduced to one of indecent assault. On the other hand, where a defendant was originally charged with rape, but proceedings were started for some other offence, then anonymity should not apply.[171] Where the indictment contained offences in addition to rape, it was proposed that the complainant's anonymity should be preserved.[172]

(ii) The Sexual Offences (Amendment) Act 1976

The Heilbron Committee's proposals, though balanced and eminently sensible, were only partly implemented by the SOAA 1976. Under the Act, anonymity applied only after a person was accused of a rape offence[173] and the circumstances in which a judge might lift reporting restrictions were not confined in the manner which the Committee proposed. A further critical distinction between the Heilbron Report and the 1976 Act was that the latter afforded anonymity to defendants as well.[174] This came about as a result of an amendment introduced in Parliament. The defendant's anonymity automatically ceased on his conviction by the Crown Court[175] and the judge also had discretion to remove his anonymity in certain circumstances.[176]

The history of rape trials after 1976 strongly suggested that the legislation ought to have followed the Heilbron proposals far more closely. In the 1980s, there were strong calls to change the law by abolishing anonymity for defendants, limiting the discretion of judges to lift reporting restrictions, and further extending anonymity for complainants.

(iii) Abolishing Anonymity for Defendants

The CLRC expressed itself in favour of abolishing anonymity for defendants and endorsed the view of the Heilbron Committee on this matter. It appeared to consider, however, that 'as a matter of practical politics anonymity for defendants, introduced as recently as 1976, is unlikely to be abolished'.[177] It therefore proposed a far more limited statutory amendment to deal with a particular problem which arose, in its view, from the legislation. This concerned the situation in which the defendant was acquitted of rape but convicted of some other sexual offence. The Committee considered that the newspapers which reported the conviction in such a case could run foul of the law, since the public might be able to deduce that this defendant was the same man who had been charged with rape earlier on, but whose name had, at that stage, been omitted from press reports. It therefore proposed that the press should, as a general rule, be free to publish the defendant's acquittal of the rape offence if he was convicted of another sexual offence but that the judge should have discretion to allow his anonymity to continue in these circumstances.[178] This proposal, though well intentioned,

[171] ibid., paras. 170–1. [172] ibid., para. 172. [173] s 4 (1).
[174] SOAA 1976, s 6. [175] s 6(1)(*b*). [176] s 6(2) and (3).
[177] CLRC (1984), para. 2.92. [178] ibid., para. 2.93.

would have served both to complicate existing law and to create further anomalies. Many defendants charged with rape are convicted of non-sexual offences. Press reporting of such convictions could also have led to public recognition of the defendant as a man initially charged with rape. The proposed amendment would not have afforded protection to the press in such cases.

Disquiet about the anonymity of the defendant in rape cases was further expressed by David Mellor MP, who was then Parliamentary Under Secretary of State at the Home Office, during a Commons debate in November 1985. He referred to the CLRC's discussion and also pointed out that, if a dangerous criminal charged with rape escaped before conviction, publicity could not be used to trace him.[179] Further impetus for a change in the law came early in 1986 when it was revealed that the Wiltshire Police had felt inhibited by the anonymity rules from publishing the name of a man wanted for rape. He had subsequently raped another woman before being caught and sentenced to life imprisonment. In point of fact, the name and full details of the man concerned could have been issued, since anonymity did not apply until a person was accused of a rape offence. But as *The Times* pointed out at the time: 'The fact remains that they [the police] are often confused by the anonymity rule and fear to take any step which may be said later to have prejudiced a fair trial'.[180] In February 1986, the Home Office finally announced its intention of abolishing anonymity for defendants[181] and this was accomplished by section 158 (5) of the Criminal Justice Act 1988.[182]

There are some who oppose this change in the law. A number of defendants who have caught the attention of the press after their acquittal on rape charges have complained publicly about their lack of anonymity thus drawing even greater attention to themselves.[183] Implicit in these complaints is an assumption that allegations of rape are prone to be false, so that men require special protection from them. The absence of any evidence for this assumption and the increasing recognition that the guilty are all too often acquitted in rape cases may partially explain why successive governments have stood commendably firm against this backlash.[184] A private member's bill

[179] See *The Times,* 23 Nov. 1985; *The Times,* 17 Feb. 1986.

[180] *The Times,* 18 Feb. 1986.

[181] See *The Times,* 17 Feb. 1986.

[182] For discussion of anonymity in marital rape cases, see Ch. 2 under the heading 'Unlawful Sexual Intercourse—Anonymity'.

[183] e.g. the actor Craig Charles, see *The Guardian,* 6 March 1995; Austin Donellan, a student at King's College, London, see Lees (1996), 79–85. The acquittal of PC Michael Seear prompted further calls for the restoration of anonymity, see *The Times*, 22 Feb. 1995. See also Temkin, 'Putting the Clock Back on Rape' 143 NLJ, 5 Nov. 1993, 1575. The matter resurfaced after musicians Paul Weller and Mick Hucknall were arrested in connection with alleged rapes although no charges were brought in either case, see *The Times,* 23 Jan. 2001.

[184] See e.g. *The Times,* 22 Feb. 1995. The present DPP David Calvert-Smith QC has, however, stated that he would not be opposed to the reinstatement of anonymity for defendants. This statement is regrettable given the lack of confidence in rape complainants which it implicitly denotes: see *The Times,* 9 Jan. 2001.

designed to give anonymity to teachers and others charged with sexual offences against children under 16 was opposed by the National Union of Teachers and did not receive a second reading.[185] It has been suggested that the present law could be challenged under Articles 8 (protection of privacy) and 14 (unjustified discrimination) of the European Convention on Human Rights.[186] But, since defendants in sexual cases are treated identically to defendants in all other cases which, as the Heilbron Committee pointed out, is the only significant point of comparison,[187] this argument should not succeed.

Where a person under 18 is alleged to have committed an offence which is the subject of a criminal investigation, he is protected from publicity and once criminal proceedings have begun the court has the power to apply reporting restrictions to safeguard his anonymity.[188]

(iv) Limiting Judicial Discretion

The provisions contained in the SOAA 1976 permitting the judge to lift anonymity in certain circumstances remain largely unaltered and are now to be found in the SOAA 1992. Under section 3(1), reporting restrictions may be lifted upon application before the trial, where this is necessary to induce witnesses to come forward. Section 3(2) also permits the lifting of restrictions where the judge 'is satisfied that anonymity would impose a substantial and unreasonable restriction upon the reporting of proceedings at the trial and that it is in the public interest to remove or relax the restriction'. This discretion may be exercised at the trial itself. Section 3(3) specifies that the power to lift restrictions under section 3(2) is not to be exercised 'by reason only of the outcome of the trial', so that the mere fact that the prosecution case collapsed or the defendant was acquitted is not in itself sufficient reason for doing so.[189] Section 3(4) further permits the judge to lift reporting restrictions where the defendant is appealing after conviction and this is 'required for the purpose of obtaining evidence in support of the appeal'. While there might be something to be said for section 3(4),[190] section 3(2) would seem to give the judges a discretion which is altogether too broad.

For some years, there has been disquiet about the way in which judges exercise their discretion to lift the embargo on press reporting. The implications of so doing were horrendously illustrated in September 1984 in the Hutchinson case. Hutchinson received a triple life sentence for the murder

[185] See C. Cobley *Sex Offenders—Law Policy and Practice* (Bristol: Jordans, 2000), 168.

[186] D. Bentley, *The Times*, 23 Jan. 2001.

[187] Heilbron Committee (1975), para. 177.

[188] See YJCEA 1999, ss 44 and 45.

[189] This subsection derives from the Criminal Justice Act 1988, s 158(4): see commentary by I. Leigh, *Current Law Statutes Annotated* (London: Sweet & Maxwell Ltd. and Stevens & Sons Ltd., vol. ii, 1988), 33–171.

[190] Although the word 'necessary' might have been preferable to the word 'required'.

of three members of a family and the rape of another after breaking into their Sheffield home. At the outset of his trial, two Sheffield newspapers applied to have reporting restrictions lifted.[191] They argued that the accused was charged with murder as well as rape, that the whole of Sheffield knew about the crime and who was involved, and that it would be impossible to report the case at all unless the embargo was lifted. These arguments proved to be persuasive and the application was granted. As a result, the case was extensively reported, for the most part salaciously, in newspapers throughout the land. Photographs of the victim and her family appeared in papers ranging from *The Times* downwards.[192] Defence counsel, apparently at Hutchinson's insistence, cast every conceivable slur on the victim's sexual character. These allegations, as the prosecution pointed out, were 'wild and wicked fabrications',[193] but the 19-year-old victim, who had lost both her parents and her brother at the hands of the accused, was forced to defend herself before the nation. The Press Council accused many newspapers of 'an appalling lack of compassion or sensitivity'.[194] Had the Heilbron proposals been fully implemented, however, this disgraceful episode could never have occurred, since the Committee recommended that anonymity should apply even where the indictment contained offences apart from rape and should not be lifted save where this was necessary in order to seek out other witnesses.[195] This was not the ground for lifting restrictions in this case.

It is not known how often or for what reasons judges are prepared to override the anonymity provisions, but disquiet about their operation was expressed well before the Sheffield case.[196] Widespread criticism about the reporting of the latter led to calls for Parliament to remove discretion from the judges so that anonymity would be the inalienable right of rape victims.[197] It is noteworthy that in Canada the present law guarantees anonymity to sexual assault victims upon application to the court by the complainant or the prosecutor. Moreover, the judge must inform the complainant of her right to make such an application.[198] The ban is mandatory and there is no discretion to lift it. The Supreme Court of Canada has held that this limit on freedom of the press is justifiable and does not violate the Canadian Charter of Rights and Freedoms.[199]

The Heilbron Committee's proposals represented a fair compromise between those who would preclude the publication of the complainant's

[191] It was considered to be unprecedented for newspapers to make such an application.

[192] See *The Times*, 5 Sept. 1984, and *The Times*, 15 Sept. 1984. The Press Council criticized the publication of her photograph as 'unnecessary and unjustifiable': *The Guardian*, 15 Nov. 1984.

[193] *The Times*, 15 Sept. 1984.

[194] *The Guardian*, 15 Nov. 1984.

[195] Heilbron Committee (1975), paras. 172, 165.

[196] See *The Times*, 29 and 30 Oct. 1982.

[197] These calls were renewed in 1986 after the vicarage rape case, discussed below. See *The Guardian*, 13 Mar. 1986.

[198] Canadian Criminal Code, s 44(3) and (3.1).

[199] *Canadian Newspapers Co Ltd v Canada (Attorney General)* [1988] 2 SCR 122.

name in all circumstances and those who would give the judge a general discretion to override the ban. It is hard to envisage any circumstances, other than those in which it is necessary to encourage witnesses to come forward, where the desire of newspapers to publish the victim's name should override the interests of the criminal justice system in protecting her anonymity. Jack Ashley MP has pointed out that 'defence counsel in almost every rape case can argue that disclosure of the woman's name might help his client by encouraging witnesses to come forward'.[200] Whilst there is such a danger with a provision of this kind, the possibility of a genuine application is probably sufficient justification for it. On the other hand, it is disturbing that once a judge has lifted the publication ban, newspapers appear to exercise little restraint in reporting. Whilst freedom of the press, the right of the defendant to a public hearing, and the right of the public to know are all of the greatest significance, it is not clear that public fascination with the scandalous and the prurient should be indulged at the expense of victims who have already suffered trauma and humiliation. It is suggested, therefore, that there might be a case for vesting in the judge an additional discretion in cases in which they have withdrawn anonymity from the complainant, to preclude publication of certain parts of the evidence in the trial, where it would be reasonable to do so in order to avoid further distress to the victim.

Section 158(3) of the Criminal Justice Act 1988 provided a new defence of written consent to the offence of unlawful publication where the complainant has agreed in writing to publication provided that there has been no unreasonable interference with her peace or comfort to obtain this consent.[201] Since then a number of complainants have chosen to waive their anonymity in order to be able to speak out about their experiences and help other victims.[202]

(v) Extending the Anonymity Rules

Under the SOAA 1976, anonymity did not apply until after a person was accused of a rape offence. In March 1986, there was widespread press coverage of a violent assault by three men on a vicar at his vicarage. His 21-year-old daughter was also raped on the same occasion in front of him and a friend of hers seriously injured. The police eventually tracked down

[200] In a letter to the Lord Chancellor: see *The Times,* 30 Oct. 1982.

[201] Now contained in SOAA 1992, s 5(2) and (3).

[202] e.g. Muriel Harvey, a widow and magistrate: see *The Times,* 1 Mar. 1993, where Mrs Harvey was praised for 'an act of great courage and social responsibility'. Other victims who have abandoned anonymity include Merlyn Nuttall and Judy (surname undisclosed) who addressed the Conservative Party Conference in 1994. All three were victims of stranger rapists. Some American feminists, as well as Germaine Greer, appear to believe that anonymity perpetuates the stigma that attaches to rape victims and should be dropped, see *The Times,* 15 June 1990, *The Guardian,* 6 Mar. 1995. This ignores the experience of victims, the further violence they may encounter if their names are known, and the implications for the criminal justice system: see *The Times,* 10 Aug. 1994.

and arrested a number of persons in connection with these crimes. Before this occurred, however, and despite appeals by the police to have regard to the victim's 'horrendous ordeal',[203] the press and television reported the case in such a way that her identity became obvious. The *Sun* published a picture of her on its front page with her eyes blacked out. Of course, under existing law, there was nothing to prevent this from happening, as the Attorney General pointed out in Parliament after he had been requested to take action against the newspaper.[204] His statement led to the tabling of a Commons motion asking the Government to introduce appropriate legislation as a matter of urgency.[205] Section 158(2) of the Criminal Justice Act 1988 extended anonymity so that it applied from the time of the making of an allegation which remains the present position.[206] However, the anonymity which was afforded to the complainant before a charge was brought was strictly limited, merely prohibiting the publication of her name, address, or a still or moving picture and only if this was likely to lead to her identification.[207] This contrasted with the position after charge, where any matter likely to identify her was banned. This distinction was hard to justify. The law has now been tightened by the YJCEA 1999 so that pre-charge 'no matter relating to that person shall during that person's lifetime be included in any publication'.[208] This prohibition seems to apply whether or not the matter would be likely to lead to identification whereas, after charge, publication remains restricted to matters which would lead to identification. It now seems therefore that the protection pre-charge has become greater than the protection post-charge. The reasons for the distinction are not entirely clear. However, in both cases, the Act specifies that restrictions apply in particular to publication of name, address, identity of school or educational establishment, place of work, or any still or moving picture.[209]

Further issues were raised by the scope of the anonymity rules under the SOAA 1976 which granted anonymity to complainants only in cases of rape, attempted rape, being an accomplice to either offence, and incitement to rape.[210] The CLRC recommended that anonymity should extend to complainants in other offences involving rape, such as conspiracy to rape and burglary with intent to rape, but did not wish to see the law extending beyond this to other sexual assaults. It stated:

> We have looked at this subject in broad outline. We endorse the reasoning of the Heilbron Committee that led to complainants in rape cases being granted anonymity to encourage them to come forward. We do not consider that this is as significant a factor in other sexual offences and would therefore confine the anonymity of

[203] See *The Guardian*, 10 Mar. 1986.
[204] See *The Times*, 11 and 13 Mar. 1986.
[205] *The Guardian*, 13 Mar. 1986.
[206] See now SOAA 1992, s 1.
[207] For criticism, see the Press Council, *Report on the West London Rape Inquiry* (London: 1987).
[208] Schedule 2, para. 7(2) amending SOAA 1992, s 1(1).
[209] Schedule 2, para. 7(3A) amending SOAA 1992, s 1(3).
[210] s 7(2).

complainants to rape cases. It must not be overlooked, however, that the fact of anonymity increases the risk of false accusations.[211]

The CLRC's proposal was implemented in the Criminal Justice Act 1988[212] but it had failed to produce a logical or coherent argument for confining anonymity to rape offences and excluding other similar sexual offences.[213] As Professor Markesinis pointed out: 'To make privacy for the victim depend on who penetrates whom with what and where appears quite absurd'.[214] The SOAA 1992 extended anonymity to cover a full range of sexual offences,[215] leaving the SOAA 1976 to cover rape offences. The YJCEA 1999 has added several further offences to the 1992 list[216] and has also added rape offences so that the anonymity provisions of the 1976 Act will cease to apply. The 1999 Act also extends the ban on publication to Scotland and Northern Ireland.[217]

Section 4 of the 1992 Act provides special rules for cases of incest or buggery where both the parties concerned are charged as defendants. Thus, for example, where a man is charged with incest with his daughter over 16 under section 10 of the SOA 1956 and she is charged under section 11 with permitting him to have sexual intercourse with her, there is no anonymity for either party. It is not unlikely that a father who has been sexually abusing a girl over 16 will allege that she consented to sexual relations with him. She then runs the risk not merely that charges will be brought against her but that the matter will be fully reported in the press. This will be a powerful deterrent to reporting or pursuing the case which is the very outcome which anonymity is designed to avoid. Anonymity for both parties is a preferable solution.

There are other situations, too, in which a case for anonymity might be said to exist. Allegations of rape or sexual assault can give rise to prosecutions of the complainant for wasting police time or for perverting or attempting to pervert the course of justice. Whether or not there is substance in these allegations is, of course, the principal consideration in the case. But there is no right to anonymity during the trial of such cases or beforehand.[218] Thus, a woman who alleged rape by a number of police officers and was prosecuted for wasting police time had her name and details of the case fully reported in the press throughout the trial.[219] Certainly, where

211 CLRC (1984), para. 2.92.

212 s 158(6).

213 For further discussion of its proposal and the arguments against it, see Temkin (1987), 196–7.

214 *The Times,* 26 Mar. 1986.

215 See s 2.

216 s 17 of the SOA 1956 (abduction of a woman by force) has been added as have offences of acting as an accomplice to some of the listed crimes: see Schedule 2, para. 8(4) and (5).

217 Schedule 2, para. 14 amending s 8(6) and (7) of the Sexual Offences Act 1992. This amendment implements the recommendation contained in *Speaking Up for Justice,* Home Office (1998), 52.

218 This seems to be confirmed by SOAA 1992, s 1(4).

219 See *The Times,* 28 Feb. 1985, 5 Mar. 1985.

there is a conviction for such an offence the defendant can expect to be named in the press.[220] It might be thought that the possibility of a prosecution of this nature in which anonymity is forfeited might dissuade some genuine complainants from reporting. At the very least, anonymity should apply unless and until there is conviction for such an offence.

The case of *Meah v McCreamer*[221] revealed a further gap in the anonymity provisions set out in the 1976 Act which did not apply to rape victims who brought or who were named in civil proceedings. In March 1986, in response to a letter from Jack Ashley MP to the Lord Chancellor, the latter announced that he proposed to ask the Home Secretary to change the law. He could see no public interest in revealing the identity of victims and believed that the anomaly could be deterring rape victims from seeking redress in the civil courts.[222] Anonymity for rape victims in civil proceedings was introduced in the Criminal Justice Act 1988[223] and now applies across the board to all the sexual offences set out in the 1992 Act.

Quite apart from the complainant, other witnesses may be deterred from co-operating with the criminal justice process in sexual cases. Section 4 of the YJCEA 1999 now usefully permits the judge to impose reporting restrictions to protect such witnesses in certain circumstances.[224]

The 1988 Act confined reporting restrictions to the complainant's lifetime. There was no such limitation in the 1976 Act. This means that reporting restrictions will not ordinarily apply where a person is raped and murdered and will cease to apply once the complainant is dead. This demonstrates scant respect for deceased victims or their families, for whom the disinterment of unpalatable details, perhaps years after the events in question, could be particularly traumatic. Since courts have the discretion to lift the ban on publication during the complainant's lifetime, it is not clear why the ban on publication should not continue after death, leaving the courts with a discretion to lift it.

(b) Anonymity in the Courtroom

The general practice in criminal cases has always been for a witness to state in court his or her full name and address, which may be published by the press. It is for the trial judge to control the proceedings, and the inherent jurisdiction to do so includes the power to grant anonymity to witnesses in

220 See e.g. *The Times*, 20 Jan. 1999; *The Times*, 23 Mar. 2000.

221 [1985] 1 All ER 367.

222 *The Guardian*, 27 Mar. 1986.

223 Section 170(2) and Schedule 16 repealed s 4(7) of the SOAA 1976 which allowed matter likely to lead to the identification of a rape victim to be published in a report of certain legal proceedings, including civil proceedings.

224 The section permits judges to grant anonymity to witnesses in all criminal cases having taken into account a list of factors including the nature of the offence, the age and social background of the witness: see s 46(4).

certain cases. Certainly, courts have some discretion at common law to suppress the name and address of a witness where to reveal them would hinder the course of justice.[225] Indeed, in exceptional circumstances the judge may even permit a witness to conceal his identity entirely from the accused.[226] Moreover, judges have traditionally granted anonymity to complainants in blackmail cases, permitting them to write down these details.[227] The reason for doing so is to ensure that complainants come forward. In *Jones, Dee and Gilbert*,[228] six prostitutes appeared as witnesses at a trial involving charges of controlling prostitutes and attempting to pervert the course of justice. They were not required to provide their names and were referred to in court by a letter of the alphabet. Several of them had given up prostitution or had become engaged or married. The court was concerned to encourage witnesses of this kind to come forward in future cases. The same approach was applied in *Shaw v DPP*,[229] where prostitutes again appeared as witnesses, and also, occasionally in rape cases before 1976.[230]

The present anonymity provisions do not extend to giving a rape victim the right to give evidence in court without stating her name and address. A rape victim may be particularly concerned that the defendant, together with his friends and family, should not be given these details. The knowledge that they have such information may considerably increase her fear and trauma. The Heilbron Committee confined its anonymity proposals to press reporting only. Victims in a study by Victim Support felt that the protection of the anonymity rules was undermined by having their address read out in court or having details of their address revealed through insensitive questioning.[231] Subsequently, in July 1996, Lord Bingham LCJ approved the Criminal Justice Consultative Council's Trial Issue Group's Statement of National Standards of Witness Care in the Criminal Justice System which provides that, unless it is necessary for evidential purposes, witnesses should not be required to disclose their address in open court. This approval has never been published as a Practice Direction in any of the law reports;[232] however, it has now become the practice for the address of a witness to be removed from the witness statement and witnesses are no longer normally required to disclose their addresses in open court.[233] In New Zealand, the Crimes Amendment Act (No. 3) 1985, section 2, ensures that complainants are not required to state their address or occupation in court and that this information is not revealed in court by others involved in the proceedings, except where special leave is obtained from the judge. A legally enforceable statutory provision of this type clearly has much to commend it.

[225] *Gordon* (1913) 8 Cr App R 237.
[226] See *R v Taylor (Gary)* [1995] Crim LR 253.
[227] See Archbold (2001), para. 8–69.
[228] Central Criminal Court, Dec. 1973 (unreported). See Archbold (2001), para. 8–69.
[229] [1962] AC 220 and see Archbold above.
[230] See Archbold (1985), para. 4–291.
[231] Victim Support (1996), 54.
[232] Archbold (2001), para. 8–71A.
[233] See Home Office, *Speaking Up for Justice* (1998), para. 8.27.

Protecting the Complainant in the Court Room

(a) Trials in Camera

The presence of the public in court may considerably increase the trauma of the rape victim, particularly if neighbours or friends and relatives of the accused are there. From the complainant's point of view, a trial in camera would in most cases be preferable. In some states in the United States, rape trials may be held in camera.[234] In others, the public is excluded during the complainant's testimony at the trial.[235] In New South Wales, the court is specifically entitled to order that proceedings for sexual assault offences be held in camera.[236] In Canada, section 486(1) of the Criminal Code confers upon a trial judge in all criminal cases a statutory discretion if of the opinion that it is in the interest of public morals, the maintenance of order, or the proper administration of justice to exclude all or any members of the public from the courtroom for all or part of the proceedings. Section 486(2) of the Code now additionally provides that, where an accused is charged with a range of sexual offences[237] and the prosecution or the accused applies for an order under section 486(1), then the judge must give reasons for refusing the application.

In England, trials must generally be held in a courtroom that is open to the public. Article 6 of the ECHR provides that everyone is entitled to a public hearing:

> Judgement shall be pronounced publicly but the press and public may be excluded from all or part of the trial in the interests of morals, public order or national security in a democratic society, where the interests of juveniles or the protection of the private life of the parties so require, or to the extent strictly necessary in the opinion of the court in special circumstances where publicity would prejudice the interests of justice.

Arguably, English practice has been rather stricter than Article 6 demands. It is well established that the judge may, in certain exceptional cases, order the court to be closed or cleared where, for example, this is necessary for the administration of justice.[238] However, in *Scott v Scott*, it was pointed out by Viscount Haldane LC that the exceptions to the general rule of open trials are 'narrowly defined'[239] and that which is based on the administration of justice is to be 'applied with great care' and not to be 'stretched to cases where there is not a strict necessity for invoking it'.[240] He cited cases in

[234] e.g. New York: see New York Jud Law 4 (McKinney, 1968).

[235] e.g. North Carolina: see NC Gen Stat (1975), 25–166.

[236] Crimes Act 1900, s 77A.

[237] Including incest, offences against children, or any of the three sexual assault offences.

[238] See on this, *Att-Gen v Leveller Magazine* (1979) 68 Cr App R 342; *R v Governor of Lewes Prison, ex p Doyle* [1971] 2 KB 254.

[239] [1913] AC 417 at 434.

[240] ibid. 436.

which 'the evidence can be effectively brought before the court in no other fashion' or where 'the paramount object of securing that justice is done would really be rendered doubtful of attainment if the order were not made'[241] as examples of situations in which in camera proceedings would be justified. However, the Earl of Halsbury considered that the language used by the Lord Chancellor to describe the exceptions to the general rule was, if anything, too broad.[242] Therefore, it would seem that, without statutory intervention, it would be in rare cases only that the public would be excluded from a rape trial.

However, statute provides for trials in camera in certain limited classes of case. Section 47 of the Children and Young Persons Act 1933, for example, excludes members of the public from youth courts, although bona fide representatives of newspapers and certain other persons may be present. Similarly, under section 8(4) of the Official Secrets Act 1920, the public may be excluded during any part of the hearing. In the case of children and young persons under the age of 17, section 37 of the Children and Young Persons Act 1933 provides as follows:

> Where in any proceedings in relation to an offence against or any conduct contrary to decency or morality, a person who, in the opinion of the court, is a child or young person is called as a witness, the court may direct that all or any persons, not being members or officers of the court or parties to the case, their counsel or solicitors or persons otherwise directly concerned with the case, be excluded from the court during the taking of the evidence of that witness, provided that nothing in this section shall authorise the exclusion of *bona fide* representatives of a newspaper or news agency.

If it is assumed that sexual assault, incest, and intercourse with under-age girls are contrary to decency and morality, then the judge has discretion to exclude the public in such cases, provided that the child or young person is actually called as a witness.

The Heilbron Committee would not support what it described as 'the drastic step of holding rape trials *in camera*'.[243] But while it would clearly be undesirable for the public to be excluded automatically from all rape trials, there is clearly a case for a statutory provision conferring a discretion on the judge to permit the court to be cleared for part, if not for all, of the proceedings, where the presence of the public is likely to cause the complainant exceptional anguish, fear, or embarrassment. This would seem to come well within Article 6.[244] The reasons which the Heilbron Committee set out for granting anonymity to complainants might also be invoked in support of such a discretionary power. The need to encourage victims to come forward and the deterrent effect of an open trial, given the type of cross-examination to which complainants are often subjected, might be thought to justify such

[241] ibid. 438–9. [242] ibid. 443. [243] Heilbron Committee (1975), para. 148.

[244] See *X v Austria* (1965) App. No. 1913/63, 2 Digest 438.

a provision. In Chapter 4, it was noted that it was not unknown for judges to exclude the public during a defence application to introduce sexual history evidence. In Canada, such applications must be held in camera.[245] In *Speaking Up for Justice,* the difficulty for a complainant of giving evidence of an intimate nature in public was noted and it was proposed that the courts be given the statutory power to clear the public gallery in cases of rape and serious sexual offences during her evidence. The YJCEA 1999 implements this proposal and takes it slightly further. Section 25 permits the judge to exclude anyone from the court whilst *any* witness is giving evidence in *any* sexual offence trial. The exceptions are the accused, legal representatives, and an interpreter for the witness. Where such an exclusion order is made, the press can nominate one representative to be present.[246]

(b) Screens and Television Link

It is not only the presence of the public which may intimidate the complainant. She may be equally if not more disturbed by the sight of the defendant himself. The Women's National Commission pointed out that, while it may be necessary for defendant and complainant to *hear* each other, it is not clear why they should have to *see* each other as well. It suggested that consideration should be given to providing a covered witness box for the complainant, or one so placed as to be invisible to the defendant.[247] In Denmark, the defendant may be excluded from the courtroom while the complainant is giving evidence, where there is reason to believe that her testimony will be substantially affected if he is present. He has the right in these circumstances to be informed of her testimony or of its principal contents.[248] In *Speaking Up for Justice*, it was proposed that CCTV (closed-circuit television) links should be available so that sexual assault victims and others should be able to give evidence from another room within the court building or from a suitable location outside the court.[249] In this way the victim would not need to face the defendant or his supporters in the public gallery but he would be able to see her on the screen. It also proposed that screens should be made available in the courtroom as an alternative measure.[250] These provide less shelter for the witness but enable her to be present

[245] Canadian Criminal Code, s 246.6(3).

[246] Discretion to exclude the public at this stage is frequently exercised in Denmark: see p. 290 above. In Scotland, it is normal practice for the court to be cleared of the general public when the complainer gives evidence in a rape trial: see Chambers and Millar (1985), 86.

[247] Women's National Commission (1985), para. 84.

[248] Danish Procedural Code, s 848.1–848.2. See also J. P. Anderson, 'The Anonymity of Witnesses—A Danish Development' [1985] Crim LR 363.

[249] para. 8.7.

[250] para. 8.17. Courts had previously been reluctant to permit screens for adults: see *R v Cooper and Schaub* [1994] Crim LR 531, although in *R v Foster* [1995] Crim LR 333, the Court of Appeal showed more willingness to do so. Their use was approved by the European Commission of Human Rights in *X v United Kingdom* 1993 15 EHRR CD 113.

in the courtroom. Sections 23 and 24 of the YJCEA 1999 now implement these proposals. Section 23(2) provides that where a screen is used, it must not prevent the witness from being able to see or be seen by the judge, jury, legal representatives, or an interpreter for the witness. In line with Convention jurisprudence,[251] there is no provision that the defendant should be able to see the witness.

Where measures are ordered by the court under sections 23, 24, or 25, the judge must give the jury such warning as the judge considers necessary to ensure that the defendant is not prejudiced by them.[252] This will involve explaining to the jury that it should draw no adverse inferences from the fact that the witness is, for example, screened or that the public has been excluded from the courtroom.

(c) Other Special Measures

In response to the recommendations contained in *Speaking Up for Justice*,[253] the YJCEA 1999 introduces a new regime which has the potential to be of substantial assistance to complainants in sexual assault trials.[254]Alleged victims of sexual offences will be eligible for assistance in giving evidence unless they themselves do not wish to be so eligible and inform the court to this effect.[255] In addition to the special measures available under sections 23 to 25,[256] the judge may order the removal of wigs and gowns,[257]and the use of video-recorded evidence as a substitute for examination-in-chief and for cross-examination and re-examination.[258] Where the complainant or any other witness suffers from a physical disability or disorder or has a significant impairment of intelligence and social functioning,[259] additional measures are available. The complainant may be examined through an intermediary[260] who will be able to explain the questions and answers so that they can be understood. Use of communication aids may also be ordered.[261]

The judge will decide whether any or a combination of these measures are likely to improve the quality of the evidence which the complainant is able to give[262] and if so, which of them are likely to maximize the quality of the evidence.[263] The quality of the evidence relates to its completeness, coherence, and accuracy.[264] The statute defines coherence in terms of the ability of the witness in giving evidence to give answers which address the questions and can be understood individually and collectively.[265] Consideration will

251 See *X v United Kingdom* above. 252 YJCEA 1999, s 32.

253 Home Office (1998), 16.

254 For detailed commentary on these provisions, see Birch (2000) and McEwan (2000).

255 s 17(4).

256 Discussed above under the headings 'Trials in Camera' and 'Screens and Television Link'.

257 s 26. 258 ss 27 and 28. 259 See s 16(2)(a) and (b). 260 s 29.

261 s 30. 262 s 19(2). 263 s 19(2)(b). 264 s 16(5). 265 ibid.

be given to the complainant's views as well as to whether the measure in question would inhibit the effective testing of the evidence involved.[266] All these special measures are subject to availability in the area in which the court proceeding will take place.[267] They will be accompanied by a warning to the jury at the trial to ensure that they do not prejudice the defendant.[268]

(d) Personal Cross-Examination by the Defendant

Section 34A of the Criminal Justice Act 1988 prohibited unrepresented defendants from personally cross-examining child witnesses. The YJCEA extends these provisions and also prevents defendants in sexual assault trials from personally cross-examining adult complainants.[269] This latter provision was enacted in response to several notorious trials at which complainants were personally cross-examined by the men who had raped them.

(i) The Problem

In 1996, Ralston Edwards who was charged with the rape of Julia Mason, cross-examined her over the course of six days. He wore the same clothing which he had worn at the rape. His questioning appears to have been designed to relive the rape and to derive pleasure from doing so.[270] The trauma experienced by Ms Mason as a result of her ordeal in court led her to apply to the European Court of Human Rights to contend that her rights had been violated under the ECHR. At a subsequent trial, Milton Brown sacked his defence counsel and proceeded to conduct his own defence.[271] Sentencing him to 16 years' imprisonment,[272] Judge Pontius commented:

> It is a highly regrettable and extremely sad aspect of this case that despite my repeated efforts during the first two days of your trial you insisted on dispensing with the services of highly competent leading and junior counsel and solicitors, the third set you had been allocated at public expense, thereafter subjecting your victims to merciless cross-examination clearly designed only to intimidate and humiliate them. In the course of your questioning you made outrageous and repulsive suggestions to both witnesses.[273]

He also commented that 'the whole experience must, for those women, have been horrifying'.[274]

Similar behaviour took place in the later trials of Camille Hourani [275]and Patrick Simms[276] who, like Edwards and Brown, were also convicted. These

266 s 19(3).
267 s 18.
268 s 32. See discussion above under the heading 'Screens and Television Link'.
269 s 34.
270 See *The Times,* 20 May 1998; Home Office, *Speaking Up for Justice* (1998), para. 9.33.
271 See *Brown (Milton)* [1998] 2 Cr App R 364.
272 This sentence was not influenced by Brown's behaviour in court: see ibid. at 368.
273 ibid.
274 ibid. 369.
275 *The Times,* 5 Apr. 2000.
276 *The Times,* 7 Oct. 2000. Simms was sentenced to life imprisonment.

trials, reported extensively in the press, were, it seems, not the only cases in which the problem had arisen.[277]

(ii) Attempts to Tackle the Problem

In February 1998, in the House of Lords, Baroness Anelay of St Johns moved an amendment to the Crime and Disorder Bill which was designed to prohibit defendants charged with rape and indecent assault from personally cross-examining complainants.[278] Lord Ackner, Baroness Mallalieu QC, and Lord Thomas of Gresford spoke against it. Lord Ackner, apparently unaware of the decision by the European Court of Human Rights in *Croissant v Germany* in 1991,[279] considered that the amendment would be likely to conflict with Article 6 of the ECHR.[280] He also pointed out that Ralston Edward's cross-examination of Julia Mason, although 'grossly excessive', did not in fact take place for six days *continuously*. There were, after all, breaks and adjournments.[281] Baroness Anelay withdrew her amendment commenting, 'I imagine that, in this victim's case, for every minute of the six days, even if she was not physically answering questions, she was under the most appalling pressure'.[282]

In *R v Brown*, Lord Bingham LCJ attempted to respond to what Judge Pontius clearly perceived to be the helpless position of the trial judge in these situations.

He had commented in his sentencing remarks at Brown's trial:

> Although I took what steps I could to minimise that ordeal by repeated efforts to prevent repetitious and irrelevant questioning . . . the law as it stands permits a situation where an unrepresented defendant in a sexual assault case has a virtually unfettered right personally to question his victim in such needlessly extended and agonising detail for the obvious purpose of intimidation and humiliation.[283]

Lord Bingham emphasized both the judicial duty to do everything to minimize trauma for participants in the trial and the powers that judges have to protect witnesses and control irrelevant and repeated questioning.[284] He suggested several ways of tackling the problem. First, the judge could ascertain from the defendant before cross-examination of the complainant takes place, in the absence of the jury, the general nature of the defence and the specific points in the complainant's evidence with which he takes issue. The judge should then make it clear to the defendant that, after he has made a point in cross-examination, he must then move on to the next. Once cross-examination begins, if the defendant seeks to dominate or intimidate the

[277] According to Baroness Anelay of St Johns, research, conducted by Victim Support and other groups in the country and which had been sent to her, revealed more such cases: HL Debs., 12 Feb. 1998, col. 1359 .

[278] See ibid. cols. 1353–8.

[279] (1993) 16 EHRR 135.

[280] HL Debs., 12 Feb. 1998, col. 1355 .

[281] col. 1359.

[282] ibid.

[283] [1998] 2 Cr App R at 369.

[284] ibid. 371.

complainant, or even if there is a reasonable fear that he will do so, the judge could order the use of a screen as well as controlling the questioning. If the defendant is unwilling to comply with instructions, the judge could stop the questioning and, if necessary, take over the cross-examination.[285] Lord Bingham emphasized that the Court of Appeal would be slow to disturb a conviction where the judge has been forced to intervene to protect the complainant from inappropriate pressure.[286]

But this advice and guidance was criticized as inadequate by one of the complainants cross-examined by Milton Brown. In her view, the Lord Chief Justice had simply failed to recognize that *any* cross-examination by the defendant was likely to be highly disturbing to a complainant.[287] Indeed, it became clear that the Lord Chief Justice had seriously underestimated the lengths to which some defendants were prepared to go in rape trials and the difficulties which judges experienced in controlling them. In a subsequent case, the defendant Camille Hourani, forced the complainant to come to court six times to be cross-examined by him. On five occasions, he changed his mind. His rantings, accusations, and delaying tactics left her physically sick and tearful each morning before she was forced back into court. The Common Sergeant of London, Judge Neil Dennison, adjourned the case for three days to accommodate Hourani. Finally, five days later, the cross-examination took place, lasting for an entire day.[288] 'The woman was subjected to an extraordinary array of bullying, detailed questioning about her sexual activity and accusations about affairs with other men.'[289] The judge responded by urging Hourani to 'get on with it'.[290] After Hourani had demanded that the jury all stand up and give their names, it appears he finally went berserk and fled from the court, never to reappear. The judge, in desperation, turned to the jury and commented, 'I don't know what to do . . . There has to be an end to this . . . I can't put this girl through any more than I have.'[291]

In the same year, Patrick Simms, a convicted rapist charged with rape of a former girlfriend, also decided to cross-examine her personally. Despite repeated rebukes from the judge, this did not stop him from asking her intimate questions about sex, her sexual health, and her underwear.[292]

(iii) Changing the Law

At a press conference, after taking office in 1996, Lord Bingham LCJ made clear his opposition to any change in the law that would prevent defendants from cross-examining their victims personally and requiring them to employ a lawyer. Seemingly oblivious to growing public concern, he appeared to think that the public would object to what it would see as an attempt to

[285] [1998] 2 Cr App R at 371. [286] ibid. [287] *The Independent*, 7 May 1998.
[288] *The Times*, 5 Apr. 2000. [289] ibid. [290] ibid. [291] ibid.
[292] *The Times*, 7 Oct. 2000.

extend legal monopolies.[293] In *Speaking Up for Justice* there was clear support for legal change[294] in the form of a ban on personal cross-examination by the defendant in sexual assault trials. The Report noted that the European Court in *Croissant v Germany* did not consider that there had been any breach of Article 6 when a German court appointed a lawyer for the defendant against his will. This had been done in the interests of justice and to ensure that he was adequately represented. The Report provided a useful blueprint for legal change which was largely followed in the YJCEA. It was particularly significant that Justice, the campaigning organization traditionally concerned with the rights of defendants in criminal trials came out in favour of this proposed change in the law.[295]

SECTIONS 34–9 YJCEA 1999

The YJCEA now prohibits defendants from cross-examining adult complainants under any circumstances in trials for rape, burglary with intent to rape, indecent assault, USI, and various other sexual offences.[296] The prohibition applies equally to any other offences if these are dealt with in the same proceedings.[297] Whilst there is an absolute prohibition on personal cross-examination of adult complainants in sexual cases, the legislation also gives the judge a discretion to forbid it in other cases as well.[298] There is a list of criteria for the judge to take into consideration. Broadly speaking, these are concerned with whether the quality of the evidence given by the complainant is likely to be diminished by personal cross-examination and whether the interests of justice would be infringed by such a prohibition.[299] This provision responds to concerns expressed about the victims of such offences as stalking.[300]

The protection afforded to child witnesses has also been extended to cover kidnapping, false imprisonment, or abduction as well as other offences dealt with in the same proceedings.[301] Thus the protection afforded to children in this respect is greater than for adults in that it applies to a wider range of offences and also extends to witnesses in such trials who are not complainants and to child defendants.[302] The protection applies to children under 17 in trials for sexual offences and to children under 14 in other cases.[303]

Unrepresented defendants who are barred from personal cross-examination of adults or children will be invited to appoint their own legal representative for this purpose and to inform the court in writing of the name and address of their appointee.[304] Under section 34A of the Criminal

[293] *The Times*, 5 Oct. 2000.
[294] See paras. 9.39–9.55.
[295] Response of *Justice* to *Speaking Up for Justice* submitted to the Home Office, July 1998 (unpublished).
[296] See s 62.
[297] s 34(b).
[298] s 36.
[299] s 36(2).
[300] See Home Office, *Speaking Up for Justice* (1998), para. 9.41.
[301] s 35(3)(b).
[302] s 35(5).
[303] s 35(4).
[304] s 38(2); Crown Court (Amendment) Rules 2000, SI 2000 No. 2093 (L 17).

Justice Act 1988, where a defendant refused to appoint a legal representative, this left a vacuum in which there was no one to cross-examine the child witness. The judge had to put questions to the child and ask the defendant if there were any matters which he wished to have raised.[305] In *Speaking Up for Justice* this situation was considered to be unsatisfactory. Since the judge could not be expected to conduct a full cross-examination, it could be argued that the accused had not had a fair trial as required by Article 6.[306] It was proposed therefore that the court be empowered to appoint a legal representative. The Act accordingly provides that if a defendant fails to appoint counsel, the court is required to consider whether, in the interests of justice, it is necessary for cross-examination to take place. This seems inevitable in serious sexual assault cases. The court will then appoint a legal representative, who will be responsible not to the defendant but to the court itself, to conduct a cross-examination.[307] However, the defendant is permitted to adopt this person as his own representative to act for him.[308] Alternatively, he may still appoint his own representative even after a court appointment has been made,[309] although presumably this would not be permitted once the cross-examination of a witness has begun. There can be no justification for forcing a witness in these circumstances to be cross-examined more than once.

Where a court-appointed representative has conducted the cross-examination, he may not have been able to test the evidence of the witness as fully as a representative appointed by the defendant himself. The judge is accordingly required to consider whether it is necessary for the jury to be given a warning to ensure that the defendant is not prejudiced.[310] The judge is also obliged to consider warning the jury that it should not draw prejudicial inferences from the fact that the defendant has not been permitted to cross-examine personally.[311]

These carefully conceived provisions, embellished by procedural rules which have been drafted to provide maximum scope to accommodate the defendant,[312] are of vital importance. They ensure that complainants will not be deterred from acting as witnesses out of fear of a personal cross-examination by the accused.

(e) Child Witnesses

In the 1980s, an increasing number of prosecutions for child sexual abuse led to a growing recognition of the problems faced by children giving

[305] See *De Oliveira* [1997] Crim LR 600. [306] paras. 9.48–9.50.
[307] s 38(3), (4), and (5). [308] SI 2000, Crown Court Rules 1982, 24C.
[309] ibid. 24D(4). [310] See s 39 and *Explanatory Notes*, para. 142, 23. [311] s 39.
[312] See text at nn. 304, 308, and 309 above. Legal aid is also ensured for the defendant who appoints his own counsel, see s 40.

evidence in court.[313] It came to be appreciated that it was necessary both to protect them from the adverse effects of involvement in the criminal justice process and also to ensure that they were not too intimidated by court proceedings to act as effective witnesses. Earlier, in Scotland, the Thompson Committee considered whether children who have been the victims of sexual offences should be required to give evidence in court at all. Some of those who testified to the Committee were firmly of the view that children were so seriously affected by having to narrate the circumstances of the offence in evidence in court that the practice should be discontinued. However, this was not the majority opinion and the Committee did not adopt it.[314] The Women's National Commission Working Group recommended that trials involving child victims should be held in less intimidating premises than courtrooms and that diagrams of the body be made available to help children give evidence.[315] But it was clear that these very modest proposals did not go nearly far enough.

The first major legislative attempt to confront the problem came with section 32 of the Criminal Justice Act 1988 which gave the judge discretion to allow children under 14 to give evidence by CCTV. This meant that they would not need to be in the courtroom in the presence of the defendant, the jury, and members of the public[316] but would still have to give evidence and submit to cross-examination by counsel at the trial, a gruelling experience for children and a deterrent to prosecutions. The Government resisted attempts in the debates on this legislation to take the further step of permitting video interviews with child witnesses to be used in court in place of live testimony. Although they were routinely admitted in jurisdictions such as Texas,[317] their use in civil proceedings in England and Wales had been criticized.[318] The Government did, however, agree to the establishment of an advisory group to consider the matter.[319]

The Advisory Group on Video-Recorded Evidence chaired by Judge Thomas Pigot QC reported in 1989 producing a raft of radical proposals.[320]

313 See J. Spencer and R. Flin, *The Evidence of Children: The Law and the Psychology* (London: Blackstone Press, 1993).

314 *Criminal Appeals in Scotland:* Report of the Committee appointed by the Secretary of State for Scotland and the Lord Advocate (Thomson Committee), Cmnd 5038 (1972), para. 43.32.

315 Women's National Commission (1985), para. 85.

316 For the limitations of this provision, see J. Temkin, 'Child Sexual Abuse and Criminal Justice' (1990)140 NLJ 410.

317 See Tex Crim Proc Code Ann, art. 38.071 2, 4 (Vernon Supp. 1986). See G. Williams, 'Videotaping Children's Evidence' 137 NLJ, 30 Jan. 1987, 198, for the view that procedures, such as video interviews, should be evolved which would obviate the necessity for the child to have any involvement with the trial at all. See also *The Use of Video Technology at Trials of Alleged Child Abusers,* Home Office Consultative Paper (1987).

318 See *The Times,* 16 and 17 June 1986 and 10 Oct. 1986.

319 The announcement was made in the House of Commons on 20 June 1988.

320 See Home Office (1989), henceforth the Pigot Report.

These were designed to benefit child witnesses but also, eventually, vulnerable adult witnesses particularly in sexual cases.[321] It was proposed that video-recorded interviews with child witnesses under the age of 17 should be admissible in court where these had been conducted by police officers, social workers, or other comparable individuals.[322] No child witness should be required to appear in open court unless he or she wished to do so.[323] Instead, it was proposed that a preliminary hearing would be held in informal surroundings during which only the judge, lawyers, and a parent or supporter would be in the same room as the child. The accused would be able to see and hear the proceedings through closed circuit television and would be able to communicate with his lawyer. At this hearing, the video-recorded evidence would be used as a substitute for examination-in-chief although the child could be asked to expand upon any matters which the prosecution sought to explore. The defence lawyer would then be able to cross-examine the child. The preliminary hearing would be video-recorded.[324] At the subsequent trial, the jury would see both the examination-in-chief and the cross-examination of the child on video and the child would not appear in person.[325]

The Pigot proposals were partially adopted by the CJA 1991 which authorized the admission of video-recorded evidence as a substitute for examination-in-chief[326] provided that the child appeared in court and was available for cross-examination.[327] This half-way-house solution and the manner of its implementation proved to be less than satisfactory.[328] The uncertain and discretionary nature of the combined provisions for the use of CCTV and video-recordings made it hard to predict whether they would be permitted by the court, so that it was difficult to prepare children and allay some of their fears in advance of the trial.[329] Moreover, the video and CCTV provisions did not cover child witnesses in proceedings in the magistrates' courts. The Utting Report recommended that the Pigot proposals should be implemented in full,[330] as did a number of other public enquiries.[331]

321 Pigot Report, para. 9, 71.
322 ibid., para. 1. 69.
323 ibid., para. 3, 69.
324 ibid., para. 4, 70.
325 ibid., para. 7, 70.
326 See Home Office with Dept. of Health, *Memorandum of Good Practice on Video Recorded Interviews with Child Witnesses for Criminal Proceedings* (London: HMSO, 1992) which provides extended guidance for the conduct of video-recorded interviews.
327 s 54 amending the Criminal Justice Act 1988 by inserting s 32A. The child could not be examined-in-chief about any matter dealt with in the video. Subsequently, this legislation was modified to permit supplementary questions where the trial judge was satisfied that the matter was not 'dealt with adequately' in the recorded interview: Criminal Justice and Public Order Act 1994, s 50. This remained a stricter test than had been envisaged by Pigot.
328 See G. Davis, L. Hoyano, C. Keenan, L. Maitland, and R. Morgan, *An Assessment of the Admissibility and Sufficiency of Evidence in Child Abuse Prosecutions* (London: Home Office, Aug. 1999); Hoyano (2000).
329 See ibid. 253–4.
330 W. Utting, *People Like Us: The Report of the Review of the Safeguards for Children Living Away from Home* (London: The Stationery Office, 1997), ch. 20.
331 See Hoyano (2000), n. 12, 251.

Further support came in *Speaking Up for Justice*.[332] Finally, the YJCE Bill moved towards the full implementation of Pigot and its provisions were substantially strengthened at committee stage in the House of Commons.[333]

The YJCEA 1999 now provides that a child under 17, who is a complainant or other witness in a sex case is in need of special protection.[334] This means that the court must make a special measures direction which provides for the whole or part of a video-recording of an interview with the witness to be admitted as evidence-in-chief.[335] Alternatively, where the court considers that in all the circumstances of the case, in the interests of justice, the recording or that part of it should not be so admitted,[336] the special measures direction will provide that witnesses will give evidence at the trial by means of CCTV.[337] It is unfortunate that no criteria are provided as to when it will be in the interests of justice to exclude the video. Where the special measures direction orders the use of a video-recording as evidence-in-chief then it must equally provide for cross-examination and re-examination to be video-recorded.[338] The witness will then attend a pre-trial hearing at which the pre-recorded interview will be used in place of examination-in-chief[339] and where a cross-examination will take place which will be videoed. These special measures are subject to availability in the given area[340] and the witness may decline to use them by opting for cross-examination at the trial itself.[341] Whether the child gives evidence by means of video or through CCTV at the trial, the court must go on to consider further special measures[342] such as removal of wigs and gowns by counsel and the judge,[343] the use of communication aids[344] which will benefit especially those with disabilities, and the appointment of an intermediary who will put questions to the child in the place of counsel.[345] If the court considers that any such measures would be likely to improve the quality

[332] Home Office (1998), ch. 10.

[333] Hansard, Standing Committee E, 22 June 1999.

[334] YJCEA 1999, s 21(1)(b).

[335] s 21(3)(a).

[336] See s 21(4)(b) and 27(2). Where the issue is whether any part of a video should not be admitted, the court will need to consider whether any prejudicial effect on the accused in showing it is outweighed by the desirability of showing the whole or substantially the whole of the recorded interview, see s 27(3).

[337] s 21(3)(b). The witness could seek the permission of the court to dispense with this provision should she wish to give evidence in the courtroom: see s 24(2).

[338] s 21(6).

[339] Restrictions on the child giving additional evidence remain and have to some extent been strengthened: see s 27(5)(b).

[340] s 21(4)(a). As at August 2002 video-recorded pre-trial cross-examination was not yet available.

[341] s 21(7)(b). Whilst the statute specifically provides for the witness to opt out of a video cross-examination, there is no such specific provision for opting out of examination-in-chief by use of video-recorded evidence. The court could take account of any wishes of the witness in this regard under s 27(2) but would not be bound to do so.

[342] s 21(2)(b).

[343] See s 26.

[344] See s 30.

[345] See s 29.

of the evidence given by the witness,[346] it must give a direction that such measures be applied.[347]

The Act provides that the pre-trial hearing must take place in the absence of the accused, but he must be able to see and hear the examination of the witness and be able to communicate with his legal representative.[348] The judge and legal representatives must also be able to see and hear the examination of the witness.[349] These requirements would be fulfilled if the child gives her evidence by CCTV or, as envisaged by Pigot, where the child is in the same room as the judge and lawyers and it is the accused who is in another room connected to the proceedings through CCTV. There are disadvantages with the first alternative since the child would then be two stages removed from the trial. The jury would see a video of the child giving evidence from a room in which she is set apart from the rest of the dramatis personae and unable fully to interact with them.[350] An advantage of the scheme envisaged by the Act is that the trial judge will also preside over the pre-trial hearing.[351] This will ensure vital continuity.

One criticism of the Pigot package which was constantly raised as a reason for not implementing it was that the defence might require a further cross-examination of the child once the trial began if new issues were raised and that this would undermine the whole purpose of pre-trial proceedings. The Act provides that subsequent cross-examination or re-examination will not be allowed save where the party has become aware of a matter which it could not with reasonable diligence have ascertained at the time of the original cross-examination or where it is in the interests of justice to allow it.[352] Subsequent cross-examinations and re-examinations will be held outside the trial itself in the same conditions as the original cross-examination.[353] In other jurisdictions where Pigot has been implemented, they take place rarely[354] but the broad 'interests of justice' test may encourage defence applications. This will mean that until the trial is over, the child will be left uncertain as to whether her role as a witness has been completed. Difficult decisions as to whether and when to commence therapy will thus remain.[355]

There are clear advantages to the new regime which represents a bold step forward in the treatment of child complainants in sexual abuse cases.[356] Children under 17 should be able frequently to avoid a court appearance

[346] It will then be assumed for the purposes of s 19(2)(b) that they would be likely to maximize the quality of such evidence: see s 21(2)(b).

[347] s 19(2)(b).

[348] s 28(2)(a) and (b).

[349] s 28(2)(a).

[350] The Government will be creating detailed guidelines for all involved in the organization and conduct of these pre-trial hearings: see Hoyano (2000), 268.

[351] s 28(2).

[352] s 28(5) and (6).

[353] s 28(5).

[354] Hoyano (2000), 79, 270.

[355] See now Home Office, CPS, Dept. of Health, *Provision of Therapy for Child Witnesses Prior to a Criminal Trial* (London: CPS, 2001).

[356] But it has been criticized: see Birch (2000), at 244–6; McEwan (2000).

altogether. The pre-trial hearing will take place at any early stage,[357] when, in many cases, the evidence is fresh in their minds. They will thus be less likely to give contradictory evidence brought on by the lapse of time between interview and trial. It seems a pity that under the Act all the advantages of pre-trial hearings will be denied to those whose interviews with the police and social workers were not video-recorded in the first place. There is an all-or-nothing quality to the new provisions which may render them too inflexible to meet the needs of some children, particularly in complex cases where a video-recorded interview proved to be impossible.

It remains to be seen how juries and counsel will react to the lack of immediacy which video-recorded testimony inevitably involves. The option remains for children to be cross-examined at the trial with a host of measures to assist them.[358] But for those who are unable to face a trial, these new provisions ensure that cases which would otherwise never reach the courts can at least be prosecuted.

CIVIL PROCEEDINGS

(a) Legal Background

Historically, the law of tort has been little concerned with those wrongs and harms suffered most typically by women.[359] The devastating physical, social, and economic consequences of rape for women and children have not been its province[360] and yet it was happy to compensate men for a variety of consequential harms which they might sustain. Blackstone noted:

> It appears to be a remarkable omission in the law of England which with such scrupulous solicitude guards the rights of individuals and secures the morals and good order of the community that it should have afforded so little protection to female chastity. It is true that it has defended it by the punishment of death from force and violence but has left it exposed to perhaps greater danger from the artifices and solicitations of seduction. In no case whatever unless she has had a promise of marriage can a woman herself obtain any reparation for the injury she has sustained from the seducer of her virtue.[361]

'Seduction' was, as often as not, a euphemism for rape. According to Blackstone, even where there had been a promise of marriage, it had to have

357 Despite attempts to address the problem, delay remains a problem in prosecutions of this sort: see J. Plotnikoff and R. Woolfson, *Prosecuting Child Abuse: An Evaluation of the Government's Speedy Progress Policy* (London: Blackstone Press, 1995).

358 i.e. use of CCTV or screens, examination through an intermediary, video-recorded evidence-in-chief, removal of wigs and gowns, communication aids.

359 See generally J. Conaghan, 'Gendered Harms and the Law of Tort: Remedying (Sexual) Harassment' (1996) 16 OJLS 407.

360 See VanderVelde (1996).

361 Blackstone (1829), 142. In a footnote to this text Blackstone commented: 'The condition of the wife and that of the sex in general appear in the eye of the law to be that of a slave'.

been overheard or made in writing since the victim herself was not allowed to give evidence in her own cause.[362] Thus although single women were not subject to the same procedural barriers to bringing actions as married women, in practice there was scarcely any legal pathway for them. Married women could not sue in tort because, until 1882, they lacked capacity under the doctrine of couverture.

A husband who was deprived of his wife's services as the result of rape could, however, sue the party responsible in an action *per quod consortium amisit*. Similarly, where a daughter was seduced, her father could bring an action *per quod servitium amisit*.[363] In the latter case, he was required to prove loss of service by showing that she had assisted in housewifery and was rendered less serviceable to him by her pregnancy or illness. She had to be living in her father's household or be part of her father's family.[364] It is significant that, according to Blackstone, she was a competent witness in such an action because she did not necessarily receive part of the damages.[365]

An action for seduction could also be brought through the medium of an action for trespass. Where the seducer illegally entered the father's house and debauched his daughter this was regarded as an aggravation of the trespass and, as such, did not require proof of pregnancy or loss of service.[366] Hence husbands and fathers had certain remedies for the rape of a wife or child but the victims themselves in effect had none.

Lea VanderVelde has carefully documented the use of the writ of seduction in the northern and midwestern states of America from 1795 until the early twentieth century to provide retribution to fathers for the rape and sexual coercion of their daughters.[367] She points out that, whilst nineteenth-century working women frequently experienced rape, coerced sex, and unwanted pregnancy, they were largely without legal remedy. She explains:

> This lack of redress resulted primarily from the shadow cast by the doctrine of consent in criminal rape law which also carried over to the civil law of assault and battery and virtually barred recovery under any theory of intentional tort. Moreover, in several states, a variety of criminal law doctrines[368] designed to discourage private recovery for what many considered to be a public wrong and the general cultural reluctance to transform so serious a public wrong into a claim for monetary damages, inhibited the development of a civil action for the victim.[369]

The cultural barrier against compensating forced sex with money seemed to have had its roots in the perception that raped women were somehow to

[362] Blackstone (1829), 142.
[363] ibid. See further Conaghan (1998).
[364] Blackstone (1829), 142.
[365] ibid.
[366] ibid.
[367] VanderVelde (1996).
[368] VanderVelde argues that as well as misprision of felony there was also the doctrine of merger which prevented a tort action being brought before a criminal prosecution had taken place: see 847–9.
[369] ibid. 824.

blame for what happened to them. But the tort of seduction was not contingent upon lack of consent and, since it was concerned with loss to the father, it circumvented this cultural barrier. Until the mid-nineteenth century single women in America as in England had no effective means of direct action in tort for sexual injuries and were, because of the narrow ambit of the law of rape, unprotected by criminal law as well. They were consequently fair game. Their only recourse was to remain at home or marry.[370]

From the middle to the end of the nineteenth century, 11 American states enacted codes containing provisions which permitted women to bring their own seduction actions. This change seems to have been motivated less by concern for women than as a means of dissuading them from abortion and infanticide.[371] By the beginning of the twentieth century, women had begun successfully to bring civil actions for rape in certain American states.[372] Today, such actions are common in America and Canada. Indeed, one Canadian commentator has referred to 'an epidemic' of lawsuits for rape, incest, and child sexual abuse.[373]

In England and Wales, by the end of the nineteenth century, the crime of rape had expanded so that it ceased to be entirely dependent on proof of violence and resistance, and the doctrine of couverture had been abolished. However, the crime of misprision of felony[374] was still held to be alive in 1962[375] and was not finally abolished until 1967.[376] This is likely to have deterred civil suits based on criminal conduct such as murder and rape. Even today civil actions for rape are rare.[377] There are clearly reasons why victims might be reluctant to turn to the civil courts. If they have been through criminal proceedings, they may feel that they have had sufficient dealings with the legal system. In addition, there is the uncertainty and cost of civil litigation. In America, contingency fee arrangements are helpful to litigants. But in this country, the low level of legal aid, together with the distinct possibility that the defendant is the proverbial man of straw who is not worth suing, have acted as potent deterrents. The introduction of conditional fee arrangements may encourage more women to bring actions[378] but these are not without the risk of costs. Moreover, the Criminal Injuries Compensation Authority can award the victim compensation from state funds which are not, therefore, dependent upon the defendant's resources.[379]

370 ibid. 822.

371 ibid. 891–4.

372 See e.g. *Harris v Neal* 116 NW 535 (Mich 1908); Bublick (1999), 1420.

373 A. Linden, *Canadian Tort Law* (6th edn., Toronto: Butterworths, 1997), 44. See also B. Feldthusen, 'The Civil Action for Sexual Battery: Therapeutic Jurisprudence?' (1993) 25 Ottawa L Rev 203 which discusses 33 sexual battery cases litigated since 1985.

374 A person who failed to press criminal charges and brought a civil action instead could be held liable for this offence.

375 *Sykes v DPP* [1962] AC 528.

376 Criminal Law Act 1967.

377 Textbooks on the law of tort barely refer to them.

378 See Courts and Legal Services Act 1990, Access to Justice Act 1999.

379 See below p. 347 .

(b) Modern Developments

In 1985, two women brought a successful civil action against Christopher Meah who had been convicted of raping them and this was heralded as a major breakthrough which was likely to encourage more women to sue.[380] The case brought by Miss D. and Mrs W. was prompted by an earlier tort action which Meah had himself brought against the driver of a car in which he was a passenger. The car was involved in an accident as a result of which Meah sustained serious head injuries, brain damage, and, so it was held, personality change which turned him into a rapist and led to his imprisonment for life. He was awarded damages of £45,000.[381] In the subsequent proceedings, the same judge, Woolf J, awarded Miss D. £10,480 and Mrs W. £7,080, respectively. Miss D. had been raped, forced to engage in oral sex, and subjected to behaviour which the judge described as 'extremely obscene and terrifying'.[382] Her hands and feet had been tied with cord and she had been stabbed in the chest with a knife. At the time of the civil proceedings, over three years later, she continued to be worried by the dark and had nightmares once or twice a week. She also suffered from claustrophobia and found it difficult to travel on tubes and trains. She was very frightened of social contact and of sexual activity and had lost trust in men. Her own psychiatrist was pessimistic that she would regain the potential to make a satisfying sexual relationship, although a report by a second psychiatrist was slightly more optimistic. The judge commented that Miss D. was an attractive person who would, if she so desired, be able to resume relationships with the other sex.[383] This was reflected in the award he made.

The second victim, Mrs W., had been subjected to an ordeal lasting between four and a half and five and a half hours. Once again, Meah was armed with a knife. He forced her to have oral sex whilst her 4-year-old son was on her lap and afterwards engaged in 'appalling behaviour', including covering her with butter 'to obtain the gratification which he was seeking'.[384] At the time of the civil action, she continued to feel dirty and humiliated as a result of the assault and to suffer from depression. However, the judge said that her depression was also due to other causes and that this must be reflected in the level of damages. He also felt that at 26 she was still relatively young and should get over the experience by the time she reached her early thirties.[385]

There was considerable feeling in many quarters that the level of damages awarded to the two victims was too low in view of the horrific nature of the

[380] *W v Meah* [1986] 1 All ER 935. After the successful civil action brought against Michael Brookes for the murder of Lynn Siddons it was claimed that this would open the floodgates to actions of this sort but this has not transpired: see *The Guardian,* 1 Oct. 1991.

[381] *Meah v McCreamer* (No. 1) [1985] 1 All ER 367.

[382] *W v Meah* [1986] 1 All ER 935, 939.

[383] ibid. 940.

[384] ibid. 937.

[385] ibid. 938.

crimes against them, and particularly in comparison to the amount Meah himself had received. It was also felt that the judge's ruling manifested an inability to grasp the depths of distress and dislocation which rape causes.[386] The fact remains, however, that Miss D. and Mrs W. had received only £3,600 and £1,000 respectively from the Criminal Injuries Compensation Board, and although these sums had to be returned, they were considerably better off as a result of their lawsuit. Their action also served the useful purpose of focusing attention on the low level of awards made by the Board in sexual assault cases.[387]

Following *W v Meah*, there have been few reports of successful civil actions for rape in England and Wales. In *Griffiths v Williams*,[388] a jury awarded the claimant £50,000 damages for rape by her landlord. It heard that the defendant had frequently raped his own wife and that he took the view that there was no such thing as rape.[389] It was also told of the very serious consequences of the rape. The claimant had been suicidal and had been on anti-depressant drugs for six months. The Court of Appeal upheld the award. The significance of the case was not merely that the award of damages was much higher than in *W v Meah* but also that it had been made in a case where the CPS had declined to prosecute. In *Parrington v Marriott*,[390] the claimant was awarded £73,778.06 in damages after she had been raped on two occasions and sexually harassed for 18 months by a friend and work colleague. The Court of Appeal declined to reduce the damages on the ground that they were not out of proportion to the circumstances or so excessive as to justify its interference. In 1997, a woman was awarded £14,000 for rape by her husband.[391] At the time of the civil action she was divorced from him.[392]

These three cases demonstrate that it is possible successfully to bring civil proceedings for rape even where there has been no criminal prosecution. But the road is a rocky one which is likely to deter all but the most determined. There have been some notable failures. In *Miles v Cain*[393] the claimant was a student teacher who was allegedly raped by a self-styled physiotherapist. Unknown to her, Cain was in fact an electrician, unqualified as a physiotherapist, although he had taken some courses.[394] The Criminal Injuries

386 See e.g. 'Justice for Victims', *The Times,* 12 Dec. 1985.

387 See *The Guardian,* 17 Dec. 1985. For a defence of the Board by its Chairman, see letter, *The Times,* 28 Dec. 1985.

388 *The Times,* 24 Nov. 1995.

389 The Court of Appeal considered that the use of this evidence was in accordance with the decision in *R v P* [1991] 2 AC 447.

390 Unreported, Court of Appeal, 19 Feb. 1999, Lord Woolf MR, Mummery LJ, Mantell LJ (Lexis).

391 *The Times,* 10 Sept. 1997.

392 For discussion of the damages awarded in these three cases, see below under the heading 'Damages'.

393 *The Times,* 15 Dec. 1989; Court of Appeal, 14 Dec. 1989 (Lexis).

394 See *The Independent,* 26 Nov. 1988.

Compensation Board had decided that she had been raped and had awarded her compensation. She subsequently brought a civil action. There was evidence to support her claim both from her parents and from a friend and in the view of the judge, Mr Justice Caulfield, she emerged as a convincing witness even after a tough cross-examination. He awarded her £25,000 in damages. But the Court of Appeal took the highly unusual step of overturning the decision even though it had not had the benefit of seeing the witnesses and hearing the evidence. It was clearly puzzled by a number of features of the case[395] to which the judge in its view had not devoted sufficient attention. Having allegedly been indecently assaulted on one occasion, Ms Miles had nevertheless kept her next appointment. There was some evidence that other patients may have been present during the time of the alleged rape but they had heard nothing, even though only curtains divided the cubicles. Caulfield J had concluded that the surgery could have been empty for long enough for the rape to take place. There was evidence that Ms Miles came from a sheltered and inhibited background where sexual matters were never discussed. She was unable to tell her father about the indecent assault and thus felt compelled to attend the next session to avoid explanations. She was lacking in self-esteem and self-confidence and ill versed in the ways of the world. She claimed that she had been too shocked to move or scream during the rape. This is a not uncommon response in rape victims but it evidently excited the disbelief of the Court of Appeal. There are aspects of the Court's judgments which are disturbing. They are clouded by rape myths and stereo-typical expectations of how reasonable women behave in sexual assault situations. Sir John Donaldson even cited Hale's notorious and discredited dictum that such allegations are very easily made but most difficult to refute. He emphasized the need for great caution where corroborative evidence was lacking. There was scant understanding of Rape Trauma Syndrome. Psychiatric evidence brought to show that Lorraine Miles had suffered acutely from it was used against her and interpreted as an indication that she was hysterical and had manufactured the whole episode. She was thus characterized as mad rather than bad and Caulfield J, a judge whom the Court itself described as highly experienced, was implicitly depicted as foolish and susceptible. The Court took the unusual step of ordering a retrial before another judge, a daunting prospect for any claimant. It was not surprising that this option was not pursued.

In *Moores v Green*[396] M was awarded £12,500 in damages for her rape and subsequent pregnancy by G with whom she had previously had a relationship. M claimed that G had turned up at her home and persistently rung the doorbell and knocked at the door. She did not wish to let him in but was forced eventually to open the door in order to collect her child from school.

[395] Such as possible discrepancies concerning an appointment card.

[396] Unreported, Court of Appeal, 6 June 1991(Lexis); see also *The Guardian*, 13 Sept. 1990.

G, a bouncer and ex-boxer, had pushed his way into the house and raped her. There was no criticism of the way that the judge had dealt with the case or had directed himself. However, the Court of Appeal considered that fresh evidence of two phone calls made by a former boyfriend to her during the course of these events were of such significance that a retrial should be ordered. The trial judge had refused to order a rehearing. It is easy to understand why. It seems that in her affidavit M had said that she left the house to collect the child at 11.30 a.m whilst the phone call had ended at 11.38 a.m. It is plainly rather difficult to remember times precisely and remarkable that the Court of Appeal chose to set such store by this. The Court was also puzzled that the maker of the call was someone whom M had described as a former boyfriend. But there had been no suggestion by her that she had ceased to have contact with him. Remarkably, this evidence was regarded by the Court as meeting the requirement set out in *Ladd v Marshall*[397] that to justify the reception of fresh evidence it must *inter alia* be such that it would probably have an important influence on the trial. Hence, despite the principle of finality and the general reluctance to order retrials, a retrial was ordered. With admirable fortitude M decided to proceed with a retrial only to meet further obstruction. Both parties had been legally aided and G was granted legal aid to defend the action at the retrial. The Legal Aid Board then refused legal aid to M, essentially on the ground that costs in the action had already reached over £18,000. Since any damages she was likely to be awarded were less than this and costs were unlikely to be awarded against a legally aided defendant, there was no point in her continuing with the action. M was thus forced to apply for leave to move for judicial review of the action of the Legal Aid Board. This application went eventually to the Court of Appeal which granted it.[398]

In *J v Oyston,*[399] Owen Oyston, who had been convicted of rape, was sued by one of his victims. She set out his conviction in her statement of claim. He sought to adduce evidence to discredit her and to deny the assault and rape even though he had failed to have his conviction overturned on appeal. He thus sought to reopen the whole matter in civil proceedings even though the burden of proof in criminal proceedings is higher and even though it was not apparent that there was any fresh evidence. The Court of Appeal held that he was entitled to do so. Section 11 of the Civil Evidence Act 1968 provides that a person who has been convicted of an offence shall be taken to have committed it unless the contrary is proved. It appears, therefore, to allow the convicted party the opportunity to seek to prove that he was not guilty. However, in *Brinks Ltd v Abu-Saleh*,[400] it had been held that a convicted defendant must produce fresh evidence which 'entirely

[397] [1954] 3 All ER 745.

[398] *R v Legal Aid Board ex p Moores* unreported, Court of Appeal, 16 Dec. 1992 (Lexis). It is not known how the case was finally resolved.

[399] [1999] 1 WLR 694.

[400] [1995] 1 WLR 1478.

changes the aspect of the case'[401] to contest a civil action based on the same facts. But the Court of Appeal disagreed with this decision, preferring instead an earlier decision to the opposite effect.[402] In so doing it was condemning a young woman who had been proved beyond reasonable doubt to be a rape victim to go through the ordeal of examination and cross-examination once again about the self-same issues—an obvious deterrent to continuing with the civil action.

These three cases illustrate the very real obstacles which the courts have placed in the way of recovery of tort damages. But there is an abundance of further difficulties.

(i) Sexual History Evidence and Cross-Examination

Evidence of the claimant's sexual history may be used in civil proceedings since the provisions of section 41 of the YJCEA do not apply. Certainly, a claimant can expect to be put through a rigorous cross-examination. Indeed, in *Miles v Cain,* Caulfield J commented 'I have never heard a woman subject to so thorough and ferocious cross-examination as this plaintiff'. In *Griffiths v Williams,* it was noted by the Court of Appeal that the defence made very unpleasant allegations against the claimant which were tantamount to accusing her of prostitution. Unlike in criminal proceedings, the claimant may also be personally cross-examined by the defendant himself.[403]

(ii) The Burden of Proof

The burden of proof in civil proceedings involving allegations of a criminal offence has gradually been raised. Thus, although the burden in civil proceedings generally is on the balance of probabilities, it was held in *Halford v Brookes*,[404] where the claimant brought a tort action for damages against a man whom she claimed had murdered her daughter, that the burden was proof beyond reasonable doubt. Although this has not been followed in any of the decided rape cases, it seems clear that a standard rather higher than the balance of probabilities will be required. In *Miles v Cain,* Caulfield J applied the dicta of Lord Denning in *Bater v Bater*[405] that when a court is considering a charge of a criminal nature, the degree of probability must be commensurate with the occasion, an approach upheld by the Court of Appeal. This approach was cited with approval in *Moores v Green* where it was reiterated that 'in proportion as the crime is enormous so ought the proof to be clear'. Thus, what was once thought to be an advantage of civil over criminal proceedings, has been, to some extent, eroded.

[401] At 1482.

[402] *Nawrot v Chief Constable of Hampshire Police, The Independent,* 7 Jan. 1992.

[403] See e.g. *The Times,* 4 Jan. 2002.

[404] *The Times,* 3 Oct. 1991.

[405] [1950] 2 All ER 458.

(iii) Delay

Particular problems have arisen with respect to the rape of children where an inflexible approach has been taken to the time limits imposed by the Limitation Act 1980 to the bringing of tort actions. Adults who were raped in childhood may suppress the experience or fail to appreciate its damaging significance until much later in their lives, by which time they may well have passed the time limits specified by the Act. In *Stubbings v Webb*,[406] the House of Lords held that in an action for rape the normal limitation period of six years for tort actions applied so that any legal action was barred six years after the event or, in the case of children, six years after reaching 18. Leslie Stubbings alleged that she had been raped and sexually abused by her stepfather and stepbrother between the ages of 2 and 14. Whilst she had always been aware of what had happened to her, she had not appreciated that the mental illness she had suffered might be attributable to it until she consulted a psychiatrist at the age of 27, by which time the limitation period had been exceeded. The House of Lords concluded that there was nothing that could be done about this and the European Court of Human Rights upheld the decision.[407] Since it is frequently the case that adults damaged by sexual abuse which occurred in childhood do not gain an appreciation of this until they are older, the impact of this decision is to place a total embargo on civil proceedings in many cases of child rape. Other jurisdictions have displayed sensitivity to this problem by adjusting time limits or waiving them altogether. Indeed, even the Court of Appeal[408] was prepared to do so by holding that the action brought by Mrs Stubbings fell within section 11(1) of the 1980 Act which provides for a different limitation period in tort actions for breach of duty in respect of personal injuries. This limitation period runs for three years from the date of knowledge of the person injured. Since Mrs Stubbings did issue her writ within three years of discovering from her psychiatrist that it was the rape and sexual abuse which was the likely cause of the mental illness she had suffered, she was within the limitation period. In an almost identical case, the Supreme Court of Canada, overruling the decision of the Ontario Court of Appeal, approved the Court of Appeal's decision in *Stubbings*, noting that there was 'no public benefit in protecting individuals who perpetrate incest from the consequences of their wrongful actions'.[409] It held that the limitation period for a sexual battery based on incest does not begin to run until the victim discovers the connection between the harm

[406] [1993] 1 All ER 322.
[407] *Stubbings and others v The United Kingdom* ECtHR [1997] 1 FLR 105.
[408] *Stubbings v Webb* [1991] 3 All ER 949.
[409] *M (K) v M (H)* [1992] 96 DLR 4th 289 (SCC), 302.

she has suffered and her childhood history.[410] By contrast, the House of Lords in *Stubbings v Webb* refused to accept that the action was one for breach of duty within the meaning of the term used in section 11(1). However, in S *v W and another*[411] an incest victim whose father had been imprisoned for the offence attempted to bring an action against him and also against her mother who, knowing of the abuse, ignored it. It was held that, although the action against the father was time barred, the action against the mother amounted to a breach of duty within the meaning of section 11(1) and was therefore brought within the time limits and could proceed. The anomaly of the situation in which it was possible to sue the child's mother but not the perpetrator himself was remarked upon by the Court of Appeal which recommended that the matter be brought to the attention of the Law Commission.

The Law Commission has conceded the unfairness of the present law[412] and has recommended that the limitation regime for civil claims should be fundamentally reformed.[413] It has proposed a primary limitation period of three years starting from the date when the claimant knows or ought reasonably to know the facts which give rise to the cause of action or, if the claimant has suffered injury, that the injury was significant.[414] The primary limitation period would not run during the claimant's minority. There should also be what is referred to as a 'long-stop limitation period' of 10 years starting from the date of the accrual of the cause of action. However, in the case of personal injury claims, there would be no long-stop and the courts would instead have discretion to disapply the primary limitation period. The Commission had provisionally proposed that there should be no discretion to override the primary limitation period but that there should be a long-stop of 30 years where the claim was for personal injuries.[415] The Commission's final proposals, if implemented, would undoubtedly assist many victims who were raped as children to bring civil actions and are to be welcomed as an improvement on the present law. However, it could be argued that the proposed period of three years does not give victims long to bring a claim and that they are thereafter dependent on the exercise of judicial discretion. The Law Commission did not see fit to dispense with lim-

[410] Several provinces have amended their limitation legislation to incorporate this approach: see e.g. Prince Edward Island, SPEI 1992, c 63, s 1(b) and Nova Scotia. Some provinces have abolished limitation periods in actions based on sexual misconduct: see e.g. Saskatchewan Bill No. 15 1993. See further L. N. Klar *Tort Law* (2nd edn., Canada: Thomson, 1996), 45–6.

[411] [1995] 1 FLR 862.

[412] Law Commission Consultation Paper 151, *Making the Law on Civil Limitation Periods Simpler and Fairer* (London: The Stationery Office, 1998); Law Commission, *Limitation of Actions,* Report 270 HC 23 (London: The Stationery Office, 2001).

[413] Consultation Paper 151, para. 15.2.

[414] Report, para. 1.12. In Germany, there is a similar three-year limitation period but this is based on the actual knowledge of the claimant: see German Civil Code, s 852 BGB.

[415] Consultation Paper, para. 15.18.

itation periods altogether in the case of sexual abuse,[416] although there is a case for doing so given the particular difficulties for victims in bringing claims.

(c) Abuse of Trust

Whilst the climate in England and Wales has not been particularly conducive to the bringing of civil actions, there has been a far greater openness to civil suits in the United States and Canada. The Supreme Court of Canada gave a boost to the bringing of civil actions in *Norberg v Wynrib*.[417] In this case, an elderly doctor took advantage of a young drug-addicted woman by suggesting a sex-for-drugs agreement whilst declining to assist her to obtain medical assistance to deal with her drug habit. The Supreme Court's decision is notable for several reasons. First, in determining whether the tort of battery had been committed, the court was willing to take a broad view of what constituted lack of consent. It held that consent was not merely vitiated by force, threat, of force or fraud. 'The concept of consent in tort law is based on a presumption of individual autonomy and free will.'[418] Consent must be voluntary. This involved taking into consideration the power relationship between the parties. Where there was a power-dependency relationship, whether or not there has been legally effective consent depends on whether there is inequality between the parties and whether there has been exploitation. Here, there was an unequal distribution of power which the defendant had exploited. Consequently, there was no real consent.[419]

Two judges also considered that there had been breach of a fiduciary duty so that, quite apart from any liability which might have arisen in contract or tort, an equitable remedy was available.[420] The advantage of this analysis was said to be that equity holds trustees strictly accountable and foreseeability of loss is not a factor in equitable damages.[421] Moreover, defences based on alleged fault of the claimant may carry little weight when raised against the beneficiary of a fiduciary relationship.[422] It was said that a fiduciary relationship applies where the fiduciary has scope for the exercise of power and can unilaterally exercise it to affect the beneficiary's interests and where the beneficiary is peculiarly vulnerable or at the mercy of the fiduciary holding the discretion or power.[423] Thus the concept of a fiduciary

416 See Report, paras. 4.23–4.28.
417 [1992] 2 SCR 224.
418 At 228.
419 ibid.
420 At 231.
421 At 232.
422 At 231. In *B (M) v British Columbia* [2000] BC D Civ 275, an action was brought against the government of British Columbia for breach of fiduciary duty after a foster child was abused in a foster home where she had been placed by crown officials. It was held that although the Crown did owe a fiduciary duty towards her as it had become her legal guardian, since the child had not communicated the abuse to social workers and the abuse was not observable, there could be no liability. But it was possible that a finding of negligence could have been justified.
423 At 230.

relationship was by no means confined to the doctor–patient relationship. This novel analysis adopted by the two female members of the Supreme Court is indicative of a very different approach to civil actions for sexual abuse. It is one that recognizes the damage done by sexual exploitation and the justice of affording a proper remedy.

(d) Actions against Third Parties

Civil proceedings may be brought against persons or bodies other than the rapist who may be in a better financial position than he is.[424] Most such actions are brought in negligence which involves establishing a duty of care and a negligent breach of it. For example, in the Canadian case of *Q v Minto Management Ltd*,[425] Q, a rape victim, sued both Carl Halliday, the man who raped her, and the company employing him, which managed the apartment block in which she lived. The rape took place after Halliday had broken into her apartment. It was held that the management company had been negligent. It had failed to provide adequate locks, had maintained insufficient supervision over master keys, and had failed to take proper precautions after a previous rape had taken place in the same block, even though it had been informed by the police that the culprit could have been an insider. In these circumstances, Q, who had suffered a long-term emotional crisis as a result of the rape, was awarded $40,000 against Halliday and Minto Management. It is of further interest that her son who was 13 at the time of the rape was also awarded $1,000 in damages. The court accepted his claim that, as a result of his mother's emotional state after the rape, he had been deprived of guidance, care, and companionship that he might reasonably have expected to receive from her if the assault had not occurred.

Negligence involves establishing breach of a duty of care and may be hard to prove. Although, in England and Wales, actions involving allegations of negligently caused personal injury are no longer routinely funded as part of the Community Legal Service, this does not apply to personal injury arising from an alleged assault or deliberate abuse.[426]

(i) Actions against public bodies

Recently there has been a growing willingness to countenance actions against public bodies and to hold them responsible in a variety of different ways. Actions have been brought for events following upon rape as well as for the rape itself and by parents of victims as well as victims themselves. In *Jane Doe v Board of Commissioners of Police for Municipality of*

[424] Actions against third parties could have the effect of bringing pressure from their insurers to provide more protection for women: see Bawdon (1993), 371.

[425] (1985) 15 DLR (4th) 581 (Ontario High Court).

[426] See Access to Justice Act 1999, Schedule 2. The Funding Code Guidance, Legal Services Commission Manual, April 2002, para. 3.2(5).

Metropolitan Toronto,[427] the Ontario Court awarded general damages against the police of $175,000 to a woman who had been raped by a serial rapist. This was on the basis *inter alia* of their negligence in failing to warn her and other women living in first- and second-floor apartments that four other women had been raped in that area within eight months. It was held that there was a special relationship of proximity between the police and the women and a duty of care either to warn the women or to take steps to protect them.

In *Waters v Commissioner of Police of the Metropolis*[428] a police officer alleged that she was raped and buggered by a fellow officer when they were both off duty. She sued the Metropolitan Police for negligence in failing to deal properly with her complaint and for permitting officers to victimize her, thereby causing her to suffer psychiatric injury. 'At the heart of her claim lies the belief that the other officers reviled her and failed to take care of her because she had broken the team rules by complaining of sexual acts by a fellow police officer'.[429] The House of Lords held that her statement of claim should not have been struck out since it was arguable that the defendant did owe duties to a police officer and that by doing nothing to protect her, might be in breach of its duty. In this case, Waters was not suing as a member of the public but as an employee. But in *Osman v UK*,[430] the European Court of Human Rights held that the blanket immunity from suit for negligence by members of the public enjoyed by the police amounted to a breach of Article 6.

In *W and others v Essex County Council and another*,[431] a couple who had fostered a child who then went on to sexually abuse their own children, sued the local authority for negligence in placing the child with them. The authority knew that he had sexually abused his own sister and was being investigated for an alleged rape. The couple had specifically stipulated their unwillingness to accept any child who was known or suspected to be a child abuser. The House of Lords held that it was not clear that the parents' claim for damages as secondary victims who had suffered psychiatric injury as a result of what had happened to their children could be struck out as being too remote. They were accordingly given leave to pursue the matter to trial. The claims brought by the children themselves against the authority had been permitted to proceed by the Court of Appeal. In *X v Bedfordshire County Council*,[432] the House of Lords held that local authorities should not be held liable in respect of the exercise of their statutory duties safeguarding the welfare of children. But the children concerned appealed to the European Court of Human Rights which in *Z v UK*,[433] 'took a great stride

[427] (1998) 160 DLR (4th) 697.
[428] [2000]1 WLR 1607.
[429] At 1610.
[430] [1999] 1 FLR 198. But see now *K v Secretary of State for the Home Department* [2002] EWCA Civ 775; 152 NLJ (2002) 917.
[431] [2000] 2 All ER 237.
[432] [1995]3 WLR 152.
[433] [2001] (29392/95) 2 Family Court Reporter 246.

forward for children's rights'[434] and awarded substantial damages. It held that Bedfordshire County Council had failed to protect them from severe neglect and emotional abuse in breach of its statutory duty. The abuse amounted to inhuman or degrading treatment in breach of Article 3. Moreover, the applicants had been denied an effective remedy since there had been no procedure enabling them to obtain an enforceable award of compensation and therefore there had been a breach of Article 13 as well.

(ii) Vicarious Liability

The advantage of vicarious liability from the point of view of the claimant is that no fault needs to be established. So, for example, an employer can be held liable for the torts of his employee regardless of any fault on his part. But the concept of vicarious liability generally demands that the tortious conduct of the employee take place during the course of his employment and this has caused difficulties in this context.

In *J (A) v D (W)*,[435] the state of Manitoba was held to be vicariously liable for the negligence of one of its social worker employees who failed to investigate a complaint brought by a 14-year-old victim against her stepfather who, to the social worker's knowledge, had already sexually abused her. However, in the English case of *Trotman v North Yorkshire County Council*,[436] it was held that an act of indecent assault by a teacher on a pupil was an independent act outside the course of employment and that therefore the employer, the North Yorkshire County Council, could not be liable for it. For the same reason, in *Lister and Others v Hesley Hall Ltd*,[437] the Court of Appeal held that the company which owned a home for maladjusted children was not vicariously liable where Grain, a warden whom it employed to run the home, was convicted of sexually abusing some of the children. Similarly, in Canada, the Board of School Trustees which employed a school janitor was held not to be vicariously liable when the janitor raped a schoolgirl.[438] However, there has now been a radical shift in the direction of liability in these circumstances. The Supreme Court of Canada examined the social and economic implications of vicarious liability for child abuse in some detail in *Bazley v Curry*[439] and *Jacobi v Griffiths*,[440] concluding that there were sound reasons for imposing such liability. The House of Lords in *Lister*[441] was clearly and expressly influenced by these decisions and has now overruled *Trotman* and allowed the appeal. It held that Grain's torts took place whilst he was caring for the children in the performance of his duties and were so closely connected with his employment that it would be

[434] *The Times*, 11 May 2001, quoting Allan Levy QC.
[435] [1999] 87 ACWS (3d) 1052.
[436] *The Times*, 10 Sept. 1998.
[437] *The Times*, 13 Oct. 1999.
[438] *G (E. D.) v Hammer* [1998] BC D Civ 920.
[439] [1999] 174 DLR (4th) 45.
[440] [1999] 174 DLR (4th) 71.
[441] [2001] UKHL 22; [2001] 2 All ER 769.

fair and just to hold the company vicariously liable. It noted that 'experience shows that in the case of boarding schools, old people's homes, geriatric wards and other residential homes for the young or vulnerable, there is an inherent risk that indecent assaults on the residents will be committed by those placed in authority over them'.[442] This decision will facilitate civil actions for rape and indecent assault based on vicarious liability in this type of situation.

(iii) Problems with Actions against Third Parties

Whilst actions against third parties are becoming increasingly common, they are not without difficulty. In *F (B) v Saskatchewan Rivers School Division*,[443] an action brought against the province of Saskatchewan and against the school division which employed a teacher convicted of raping a pupil, was held to be statute barred because it was an action for negligence. Had it been an action for trespass, assault, or battery the limitation period would not have been exceeded.

In the United States, where actions against third parties are common and are permitted in most states as a means of distributing the costs of crime, defendants are able to take advantage of broad defences of rape victim fault. Hence, bus companies, hotels, landlords, and other third-party defendants will allege fault in order to reduce their liability. Where it is considered that the claimant's conduct subjected her to an unreasonable risk of rape this will affect the extent of the third party's liability. A reasonable woman does not go outside alone at night to hail a cab or walk to her car in a hotel parking lot. She does not take four or five steps inside her front door before closing it, does not open the door when someone knocks, or invite a salesman into her home.[444] She never drinks alcohol with a man, particularly if he is older or she has only recently met him. As Ellen Bublick has commented, 'One thing we know quite clearly about the reasonable woman from the case law: she is afraid of going out, of letting someone in, of rape. She is always on guard and her fear of rape shapes every aspect of her life and conduct.'[445] Contributory negligence is no defence to rape in criminal trials although defence counsel may try to allege fault on the complainant's part to sway the jury against her, but in American civil trials victim-blaming where third parties are involved is a recognized part of the script. In a minority of states, it is also permitted where no third parties are involved and rapists may argue that any liability on their part is reduced by the claimant's negligence.[446]

[442] *Per* Lord Millett at 800. [443] [2000] Sask D 920.
[444] See Bublick (1999), 1432–3. [445] ibid. [446] ibid. 1427.

(e) Damages

The successful claimant in a civil action will be compensated by general damages.[447] Special damages may also be awarded to cover specific items which can be pinned down, such as loss of earnings until the time of the trial and particular expenses which the claimant has incurred. Items which are less easy to calculate such as pain and suffering and loss of amenity will come under the head of general damages. Aggravated damages may also be awarded in tort claims where the court considers that the claimant has suffered more than the normal degree of anguish and that an enhanced level of compensation should be given. Punitive damages are awarded where the court considers that the defendant deserves to be punished. Although frequently awarded in the United States and Canada, the conditions for awarding punitive damages set out in *Rookes v Barnard*[448] would seem to preclude their award in rape cases in England and Wales. The Law Commission has proposed that punitive damages should be available if the defendant has deliberately and outrageously disregarded the claimant's rights. This should enable their award in rape cases. However, it also proposes that they should not be available where the defendant has been convicted of a criminal offence for the same conduct.[449]

The low level of damages awarded in English rape cases involving both adult and child victims has been the subject of strong criticism. It has been said that judges simply fail to grasp the enormity of the injuries inflicted.[450] For example, in 1996, in *Pereira v Kelman*,[451] three sisters who had been variously raped, buggered, and beaten by their father when they were children were awarded £16,965.58, £11,921.51, and £10,500 respectively. Recently, however, the level of awards has considerably increased.[452] In *Coxon v Flintshire County Council*,[453] the Court of Appeal approved a higher level of damages to compensate for psychiatric damage in the case of sexual abuse than is normal in run-of-the-mill personal injury cases. Amanda Coxon was awarded general damages of £70,000 for pain and suffering and loss of amenity that she had suffered as a result of physical and sexual abuse whilst in care.

In *Griffiths v Williams*,[454] the jury awarded £15,000 in general damages with a further £35,000 in aggravated damages. Although the Court of

447 In relation to family cases, see Conaghan (1998), 145–7.

448 [1964] AC 1129.

449 Law Commission, Report 247, *Aggravated, Exemplary and Restitutionary Damages*, HC 346 (London: HMSO, 1997). This is a stricter approach than applies in Canada, see below.

450 See above for comment on the damages awarded against Christopher Meah.

451 [1996] 1 FLR 428.

452 See Law Commission (1999) which recommended that damages for non-pecuniary loss, i.e. for pain and suffering and loss of amenity, should be increased. The Court of Appeal has now implemented this Report: see *Heil v Rankin and another* [2001] QB 272.

453 *The Times*, 13 Mar. 2001.

454 n. 388 above.

Appeal expressed some misgivings about the amount, it upheld the award.[455] In upholding the high award for aggravated damages, it took into account that during the proceedings the defendant had mounted a fierce attack on the claimant's character and behaviour. Rose LJ noted that 'attitudes towards rape have changed in the decade since *Meah* was decided'. He added 'As to the adequacy of Mr Justice Woolf's award in 1986 I make no comment'. Similarly Millet LJ stated: 'It is plainly arguable that Mr Justice Woolf awarded too little in 1985. There is today a far greater awareness of the gravity and seriousness of the outrage to a woman's feelings which is caused by the peculiarly intimate nature of this form of assault.' In *Parrington v Marriott*,[456] general damages of £25,000 were awarded and the court decided to award a further £30,000 in aggravated damages. The judge stated that he would be doing less than his duty if he did not award a large element of aggravated damages in the circumstances of this case. The claimant had suffered a complete breakdown, clinical depression, and PTSD and would continue to require treatment for the foreseeable future. The judge acknowledged that the award in *Griffiths v Williams* was at the top of the band but considered that this case was worse 'in terms of the conduct and indignity to which this lady was subjected'. Special damages of £11,154.96 were also awarded and interest on top of this, which in the case of special damages is payable on the whole period from the time of the accident to the date of the trial.

In Canada, courts have been willing to award punitive damages as well as awarding general and aggravated damages. In *Miers v Haroldson*,[457] punitive damages of $40,000 dollars were awarded in addition to $10,000 general damages where the defendant was said to have engaged in a relentless and vicious pursuit of the plaintiff at a social event and ensured her intoxication in order callously to rape her. Osborn J noted that punitive damages are often awarded 'where the tortfeasor has offended the ordinary standards of morality or decent conduct in the community or is guilty of moral turpitude . . . They are also awarded where the defendant's conduct amounts to arrogance and callousness.'[458] He noted that the defendant's conduct was 'conduct needing deterrence as the predominance of sexual assaults primarily by adult males upon females in our society is real and unabating'.[459] Punitive damages will not generally be awarded where the defendant has already been punished by conviction in criminal proceedings since this is regarded as amounting to double punishment. However, in *Glendale v Drozdik*[460] it was held that where the accused had, for example, been convicted but conditionally discharged, there was no reason why punitive

455 For the use of juries in the assessment of damages, see now Law Commission (1999).
456 n. 394 above.
457 [1989] 3 Western Weekly Reports 604.
458 At 614.
459 At 614.
460 [1993] BC D Civ 355.

damages should not be awarded as well.[461] In *Norberg v Wynrib*, the Supreme Court of Canada awarded punitive damages of $10,000 dollars against Dr Wynrib. Noting the Final Report of the Task Force on Sexual Abuse of Patients[462] it stated: 'An award of punitive damages is of importance to make it clear that this trend of underestimation [of sexual abuse by doctors of their patients] cannot continue. Dr Wynrib's use of power to gain sexual favours in the context of a doctor-patient relationship is conduct that is offensive and reprehensible.'[463]

As the criminal justice system is seen to be failing the victims of rape, growing attention is being focused on civil actions as an alternative means of seeking redress. It seems that the civil courts have now become the site of struggle as some courts attempt to keep a rein on such actions and to discourage them. Until the judiciary properly understands the harm of rape, claimants can expect to encounter every form of obstruction and difficulty. It is to be hoped that victims will not be deterred, for quite apart from the possible financial advantage of a civil action, it may have other merits. The victim, as claimant, has some control over the proceedings and may tell the story of what happened from her own point of view. Although, regrettably, she is not protected from cross-examination about her previous sexual history or from personal cross-examination by the defendant, she is, as in criminal proceedings, protected by anonymity. By contrast with a criminal trial, in which the prosecution represents the state, her lawyer is plainly there to represent her. It has even been suggested that:

> Whether or not they are willing to discuss the rape themselves, those who know the victim will be forced to recognise her suffering if she puts her case to a civil court. Like a funeral, the victim's civil action may provide a ceremonial context that brings her private grief into the open and helps her dispense with it.[464]

It may be concluded that civil suits are likely to be worthwhile in a minority of cases only, but such a course of action is nevertheless worthy of consideration by sexual assault victims. If a scheme for legal representation for victims who report rape to the police were to be introduced, lawyers should also be able to give advice as to whether a tort claim would be worth pursuing.

461 See also *B (A) v J (I)* [1991] 5 Western Weekly Reports 748, where the defendant was imprisoned for two years for sexual assaults but also had punitive damages awarded against him on the ground that evidence of further abuse was revealed at the civil trial which had not been considered in the criminal proceedings. In Germany, where punitive damages do not exist, the principle is that the level of general damages will be affected by the length of any prison sentence—the higher the sentence, the lower the damages: see Goy (1996), 347.

462 College of Physicians and Surgeons of Ontario, 1991.

463 (1992) 2 SCR 268.

464 Batt (1983).

The Criminal Injuries Compensation Scheme

The Criminal Injuries Compensation Scheme was established in 1964[465] to provide compensation on the basis of common law damages for blameless victims of violent crime,[466] including sexual assault. It was recognized that it was often impractical or pointless for such victims to seek compensation through the courts. In 1995, the link with common law damages was broken and a tariff scheme introduced instead.[467] This sets out a series of fixed levels of compensation for specified injuries and sexual assaults which was determined on the basis of awards previously made by the Criminal Injuries Compensation Board. This Board has now been replaced by the Criminal Injuries Compensation Authority (CICA), a non-departmental public body under the jurisdiction of the Home Office which makes the initial decisions on compensation. Appeals from its decisions can be made to the Criminal Injuries Compensation Appeals Panel (CICAP), an entirely independent statutory tribunal subject to judicial review.

The scheme is of considerable importance to and has significant advantages for rape victims. Not merely can it provide them with some financial compensation for the suffering they have endured, but it can also afford public recognition that a rape has taken place and acknowledgement of the harm that this has caused.[468] Moreover, compensation is not dependent on a guilty verdict [469] and may be awarded even where the defendant has been acquitted or where no prosecution has been brought. The ordeal of civil proceedings can be avoided and compensation is not contingent upon the means of the offender.

(a) Problems for Victims of Sexual Offences in Applying for Compensation

There are many pitfalls and difficulties for victims of sexual offences in navigating their way through the compensation system. It has been suggested above[470] that a scheme for legal representation for rape victims should include assistance with compensation claims.

465 The scheme has been amended and developed over the years. The Criminal Injuries Compensation Scheme 2001 is currently in place.

466 See Home Office Consultation Paper (1999), para. 3.

467 Criminal Injuries Compensation Act 1995 which came into effect in Apr. 1996.

468 On the other hand, a failed claim may increase the victim's trauma.

469 The Criminal Injuries Compensation Scheme 2001, para. 10. For further discussion, see Miers (2001), 385.

470 See above under the heading 'Assistance with Applications for Compensation', p. 305.

(i) The Application

Application to the Criminal Injuries Compensation Scheme has to be made in writing to the Criminal Injuries Compensation Authority within two years of the incident on a form obtainable from the Authority.[471] A rape victim suffering from the rape trauma syndrome may well be unable to cope with making such an application at the required time and for this reason it is important that the legal advice which she receives under a scheme for legal representation for victims should extend to assistance in the drafting of such an application.[472] It is not apparent why the limit should be any less than the three-year limit which generally applies to civil actions for damages. However, a claims officer may waive the time limit 'where he considers that, by reason of the particular circumstances of the case, it is reasonable and in the interests of justice to do so'.[473] Provided there is supporting evidence, the limit is frequently waived in the case of offences against children where applications sometimes relate to abuse suffered 20 or 30 years previously.[474] Adults who have suffered from rape trauma syndrome and, as a result, have been unable to bring claims are also dependent on a waiver being made.[475]

(ii) Proof of the Offence

The applicant has to prove her case on the balance of probabilities.[476] The Criminal Injuries Compensation Authority is not set up to undertake investigations or to hold a quasi-criminal trial. It cannot compel witnesses.[477] It is therefore largely dependent on evidence from police investigations, including witness statements, statements from the alleged assailant, and the

[471] The Criminal Injuries Compensation Scheme 2001, para. 18. The time limit was originally three years.

[472] In the leaflet produced by the Metropolitan Police, rape victims are informed that the chaperon dealing with the case or a member of Victim Support will be available to offer assistance with filling in the necessary forms for a compensation application. Victim Support provides this assistance free of charge throughout the country. Under the scheme proposed in this chapter for legal representation for victims, it would be preferable for the victim's lawyer who is dealing with all other aspects of her case to deal with the application, particularly as, under this scheme, she or he might have to represent her subsequently before the Panel. It was formerly the case that legal advice and assistance up to the value of £50 (or more if needed and agreed to by the Area Committee) could be obtained by applicants who were eligible, under the provisions of the Legal Aid Act 1974 (the 'green form' procedure). This would cover help in making an application or in deciding whether to apply for a review but not representation at a hearing: see Interdepartmental Working Party Report (1986), para. 23.11. The Community Legal Service now provides legal help which covers work previously carried out under the 'green form' scheme.

[473] Criminal Injuries Compensation Scheme 2001, para. 18.

[474] Criminal Injuries Compensation Appeals Panel Annual Report 1998–9, para. 4.1; Miers (1997), 144–5.

[475] See *R v Criminal Injuries Compensation Board, ex p A*, 1992 Lexis, 20 Feb. 1992 (DC), where it was held that consideration should have been given to the severity of the impact of a sexual offence.

[476] Criminal Injuries Compensation Act 1995, s3(2).

[477] See Foster (1997), 109.

evidence of the investigating officer as well as medical and forensic reports. In practice, where the police are satisfied that a rape has taken place, this will weigh substantially in the applicant's favour.[478] Victims who do not report to the police are most unlikely to be able to claim successfully. The majority of rape victims will thus be excluded.

(iii) Behaviour of the Victim

The purpose of the scheme is to provide compensation from the public purse for those who are considered to be deserving. Not all victims of violent crime are so regarded and previous convictions and the conduct of the applicant before, during, or after the incident will be taken into account and may reduce the award or even cancel it altogether.[479] The 2001 amendment specifically allows the Authority to take into account excessive consumption of alcohol or use of illicit drugs if these contributed to the circumstances which gave rise to the injury.[480] Victims are also expected to inform the police promptly[481] and to co-operate with the police in bringing the assailant to justice.[482] Failure to do either may result in the withholding or reduction of an award.

A further setback for victims is the decision of the Court of Appeal in *R v Criminal Injuries Compensation Appeals Panel, ex p August and Brown*[483] upholding the decision of the panel which rejected the applicant's claim. At the age of 13, August participated in acts of buggery with a 53-year-old man who was imprisoned for seven years as a result. August had been in the habit of soliciting men in public lavatories. It was held that the Scheme was not intended to compensate participants who consented or were willing and that they were not to be treated as victims of a crime of violence. This decision, interpreting the provisions of the Scheme, has serious implications, since it appears to challenge the law's approach to sexual activity with children whom it regards as non-consenting parties. A child's sexuality is easy to exploit. Children who become prostitutes are highly likely to have been previously sexually abused.[484] If child A, who has been so debased that

[478] ibid. 111.

[479] Criminal Injuries Compensation Scheme 2001, para. 13(d) and (e). For criticism of the way in which conduct has been taken into account in awards for rape, see Bawdon (1993), 371, 372.

[480] Criminal Injuries Compensation Scheme 2001, para. 14.

[481] ibid., para. 13a. In *R v Criminal Injuries Compensation Board, ex p S, The Times*, 18 Apr. 1995, Sedley J granted an order of *certiorari* to quash a decision of the Board which had denied a rape victim compensation because she did not report the attack until six weeks after its occurrence. He held that the extent to which the victim was traumatized by the attack should have been taken into consideration.

[482] Criminal Injuries Compensation Scheme 2001, para. 13b.

[483] [2001] 2 All ER 874. For more detailed discussion, see Miers (2001), 381–4.

[484] See e.g. D. Barrett, ed., *Child Prostitution in Britain: Dilemmas and Practical Responses* (London: Children's Society, 1997). August himself was described by a child psychologist as 'grossly psychologically disturbed and damaged': see [2001] 2 All ER 874, 885.

he resorts to prostitution, is to be regarded as consenting, what of child B who willingly succumbs to the seduction of a relative? If child B is covered by the Scheme, it would seem that the more corrupted and abused the child has been, the less likely he is to qualify for compensation. In purporting to distinguish between non-consent in law and non-consent in fact where children are concerned, the protection of children is undermined. A concept of consent which ignores factors such as age, maturity, exploitation, vulnerability, and power lacks moral credibility and is so wide as to be meaningless. These arguments should apply in the context of the Scheme just as they apply in the context of criminal liability. To suggest otherwise is to distort the way in which we think about and treat the sexuality of children. Rather than regarding his claim as excluded from the scheme from the outset, a better approach to the particular dilemma posed by August's behaviour would have been to consider his conduct as a factor to be taken into account in determining whether any award should be reduced.[485]

(iv) Families and Shared Households

Where the parties are members of the same family, the offender must in general have been prosecuted before an award will be made 'unless there are practical, technical or other good reasons why a prosecution has not been brought'.[486] In practice, where a child has been raped or otherwise sexually abused by a member of the family and no prosecution has been brought, the Authority will look for evidence from the police that an offence has taken place.[487] In addition, if the parties are adults and were living under the same roof at the time of the crime, the victim must have ceased to do so before the application was made and the claims officer must be satisfied that they are unlikely to share the same household again.[488] This places some limitation on applications for marital rape.

(v) Reviews and Appeals

A claims officer in the Criminal Injuries Compensation Authority will determine claims in accordance with the Scheme. Applicants are entitled to seek a review of a decision not to waive the time limit, not to reopen a case, to withhold an award, to make a reduced award or to seek repayment of an award.[489] Application for a review, made in writing and supported with reasons, must be received within 90 days of notification of the decision.[490] Once again, in the scheme proposed in this chapter, the complainant's lawyer would be able to assist with this. A claims officer who is more senior than the officer who originally determined the claim conducts the review. An applicant who is dissatisfied with a decision taken on a review may appeal

485 Under s13(d) of the Scheme. 486 ibid., para. 17. 487 Miers (1997), 131.
488 ibid. 489 See the Criminal Injuries Compensation Scheme 2001, para. 58.
490 ibid., para. 59.

against the decision by giving written notice of appeal to the Criminal Injuries Compensation Appeal Panel (CICAP) on a form provided by the Authority. It must again be supported by reasons and be received by the panel within 90 days of the date of the review decision. Again, assistance with preparing the appeal application will be essential for many applicants.

All applicants for criminal injuries compensation are entitled to be legally represented at an oral hearing set up by CICAP. However, the Authority does not pay for the cost of this; neither is legal aid available. The Panel may meet reasonable expenses. Although the scheme states that 'the procedure at hearings will be as informal as is consistent with the proper determination of appeals',[491] there is evidence that applicants find the hearings stressful.[492] Both the claims officer presenting the appeal and the Panel may call witnesses to give evidence and may cross-examine them as well as the applicant. The alleged rapist is always invited to attend and occasionally will do so. The task of calling and cross-examining witnesses is not one for the inexperienced lay person, particularly where sexual assault is alleged. As has been demonstrated, many of the issues are complex. The applicant will need to prove her case on the balance of probabilities. It is not surprising that, in general, applicants who do have representation are more successful than those who represent themselves.[493] Appeals are more likely to fail than succeed.[494] Moreover, appeals are not risk free since awards may be reduced as well as increased.[495] A majority (63% in 1999)[496] of all applicants are now represented. Some pay for representation, others are represented by trade unions, free representation units, or on a *pro bono* basis, but it is not known what proportion of alleged victims of sexual assault are represented or what proportion of such appeals brought by such victims fail. The particular trauma experienced by rape victims may render it difficult if not impossible for many to conduct their own case at the hearing. For those who do, the suspicion which surrounds rape victims is likely to make their task particularly difficult. The vast majority of CICAP members are male.[497] Moreover, it is plainly unacceptable for the alleged victim of a sexual assault to be faced with the possibility of having to cross-examine her assailant personally. The case for legal representation for rape victims before the Panel is thus particularly strong. Since the scheme for victim representation which has been outlined in this chapter entails legal aid for victims, it would be desirable for this

491 Criminal Injuries Compensation Scheme 2001, para. 75.

492 CICAP (2001), para. 3.4.

493 CICAP (2001), para. 3.26.

494 In the year 1999–2000, 40 per cent of appeals succeeded: CICAP (2001), para. 3.19. This was an increase on the proportion in 1998–9 where one-third were successful: CICAP (2000), para. 3.10.

495 Thirty-four appellants had their awards reduced in 1999: see CICAP 2001, para. 3.23.

496 CICAP (2001), para. 3.24.

497 Of the 146 listed in the 1999–2000 Report, 38 or 26 per cent are female: CICAP (2001), annex A.

to be extended to the representation of the complainant before the Panel.[498] Ideally, the lawyer who has assisted a complainant from the moment she has entered the criminal justice system should be the one to represent her.

(b) Compensation for Rape: The Tariff

The level of compensation which the Scheme awards for rape has been a matter of some controversy from its inception. In the beginning, since there were no civil cases upon which to draw in order to set the level of damages, the Board was forced to set its own guidelines which were criticized as too low. It subsequently dispensed with a guideline figure.[499] The tariff which came into effect in 1996 was designed to cut the costs of the scheme by reducing compensation to victims. It was the object of strenuous criticism, particularly with respect to rape victims.[500] It provided £7,500 for a rape. Rape by two or more attackers, or repeated rape over a period of up to three years, raised the tariff figure to £10,000. Where the rape resulted in serious bodily injury (a relatively rare occurrence), or repeated rape over a period of more than three years, it rose again to £17,500 and to £20,000 where there was permanently disabling mental disorder arising solely from the attack. The tariff for an indecent assault involving non-penile penetration or oral genital contact was £3,000. This included object penetration. There were no increases equivalent to those for rape. For sexual abuse of a child involving non-penetrative acts, the tariff was set at £1,000, an amount so low that it was criticized as 'grotesque' by Women Against Rape who condemned the whole package as 'outrageous'.[501] The Director of Victim Support also stated that the organization was 'deeply shocked' at the tariff figures which displayed 'no recognition of the catastrophic effects of sexual abuse'.[502] Tariff awards could be considerably smaller than under the previous scheme. It was noted in parliamentary discussion that under the old scheme, one applicant who had been assaulted for over an hour and raped in a public lavatory received £44,000, a much larger sum than she would obtain under the tariff.[503] But the Home Office Consultation Paper, which reviewed the tariff scheme in 1999, noted that payments for rape and sexual abuse were running at 20 per cent of all payments made under the Scheme

[498] An Interdepartmental Working Party concluded that the cost of legal representation at any criminal injuries compensation hearing should not be met by the Criminal Injuries Compensation Board, nor should it be covered by legal aid until such time as legal aid was available for representation before tribunals generally. This was because it took the view that the procedure at hearings was 'simple and informal': see Interdepartmental Working Party Report (1986), para. 23.11.

[499] See further, Foster (1997), 109.

[500] See HC Debs. Standing Committee A, cols. 156–8, 15 June 1995; Miers (1997), 196.

[501] *The Times*, 24 Feb. 1994.

[502] *The Times*, 12 Dec. 1993.

[503] HC Debs. Standing Committee A, cols. 156–8, 15 June 1995. Similarly, according to Women against Rape, another applicant, a victim of marital rape, received £25,000 with their assistance in 1992: *The Times*, 15 Dec. 1993.

and that any increases would have to be matched by savings elsewhere.[504] Yet the fact remains that applications under the Scheme are dominated by claims for non-sexual violence falling within sections 18, 20, and 47 of the Offences against the Person Act 1861.[505] Claims brought for sexual offences remain a small proportion of the total.[506]

On 1 April 2001, the scheme was again revised. One of its principal alterations was an increase in awards for rape and child abuse. The level of compensation for rape by one attacker has risen to £11,000, by two or more attackers to £13,500, to £22,000 where there are serious internal bodily injuries, and to £27,000 for permanently disabling mental illness confirmed by psychiatric prognosis. For repeated incidents lasting up to three years, the tariff payment is now £16,500 or £22,000 where the period exceeded three years. The extra payment of £5,000 where rape results in the birth of a child born alive which the victim intends to keep[507] has been abolished and replaced with a tariff amount of £5,500 where pregnancy results directly from the sexual assault. All pregnancies are thus compensated, irrespective of whether a child is born or kept. Where there has been a sexual assault or abuse, the tariff now specifically provides for an additional award of £5,500 for a sexually transmitted disease where there has been substantial recovery, £11,000 where there is permanent disability, and £22,000 where the victim has been infected with HIV/Aids.

Whilst these changes are a considerable improvement, non-penile penetrative and/or oral genital acts qualify for only £3,300, although the figure rises to £22,000 where serious internal bodily injuries have been caused. Improvements to the tariff made by the 2001 amendments still leave the level of award far below what can be achieved through a civil action. However, the same may be said of all tariff payments to the victims of crimes of violence.

Tariff payments are intended as token payments by society in recognition of the pain and suffering which the victim has sustained as a result of the sexual assault. The Scheme will also compensate for loss of earnings after the first 28 weeks following the injury[508] and for certain medical costs. But it does not cover many expenses commonly incurred by rape victims, such as the cost of self-defence classes, running a car, taking taxis, securing the dwelling with extra locks, and moving home to live in a safer area.[509] Successful applicants are obliged to repay any compensation awarded if they receive more in damages at a subsequent trial.

504 (1999), para. 29.

505 Miers (1997), 32.

506 Thirteen per cent—see Home Office Consultation Paper (1999), para. 39.

507 See Criminal Injuries Compensation Scheme 1996, para 27 for this requirement under the old scheme.

508 But not for such loss incurred during the first 28 weeks: see Criminal Injuries Compensation Scheme 2001, para. 30. Injury includes mental injury arising from a sexual offence where the victim did not consent: see ibid., para. 9.

509 Hall (1985), 145.

Conclusion

Dissatisfaction with the criminal process may encourage some rape victims to seek redress in the civil courts. Whilst this may be a worthwhile course to pursue for a few, it should not be seen as a substitute for improving the lot of complainants within the criminal justice system itself. The YJCEA 1999 introduces a new regime which has the potential to be of substantial assistance to complainants in sexual assault trials. But it does not go far enough. The Scandinavian scheme for legal representation for victims remains, it is submitted, the surest method of providing victims with the support which they need. This scheme may be justified on humanitarian grounds alone. One disincentive to its implementation would undoubtedly be its cost. It is suggested, however, that this would be more than offset by the greater efficiency which co-operative witnesses would produce. Victims who are assisted, protected, and treated with compassion will be more able and willing to play their vital role within the criminal justice system.

6

Conclusion

The problem of rape will not be solved by measures taken within the criminal justice system alone. Rape, and what would seem to be its growing incidence, has to do with the type of society in which we live, and the attitudes it fosters towards violence, women, and relationships between the sexes. Tackling the problem of rape, therefore, requires a broadly based strategy. It must entail an examination of those factors which promote sexual violence against both women and men, including the role of pornography; it must include projects of all kinds to render people less vulnerable; and it must involve education and re-education of children and adults to combat sexism which underlies and ultimately promotes rape.

For the foreseeable future, however, it will primarily be the criminal justice system which will bear the burden of regulating rape. This book has attempted to look at the difficulties entailed by this enterprise and how best they might be overcome. It has suggested solutions which involve law reform and has also emphasized the need for attitudinal change. As far as the former is concerned, a great deal has been accomplished since the first edition of this book was published in 1987. Husbands and boys under 14 are no longer exempt from liability for rape and, contrary to expectation, their prosecution is by no means a rare event. Male rape has been officially recognized. Corroboration warnings are no longer routinely required, the anonymity provisions have been considerably extended, and further restrictions have been placed on the use of sexual history evidence. The YJCEA 1999 introduces a bold new scheme which will provide procedural assistance to adult and child victims of sexual offences.

More, however, remains to be done. The substantive criminal law as it relates to sexual offences not merely lacks coherence and consistency, but fails fully to articulate the issues of autonomy which are the heart of the matter in this area of law. The decision by the Home Office to set up the Sex Offences Review in 1999 was a considerable step forward. The Review had the advantage of being able to evaluate law reform enacted elsewhere in the common law world over the past two decades. Its proposals have been fashioned so as to avoid some of the pitfalls to which legislation of this type is prone. Two broad principles underpin its conclusions. The first is that, where adults are concerned, the law should protect sexual autonomy by seeking to ensure that individuals are protected from sexual relations to which they do not freely agree[1] and, by the same token, do not suffer interference if they engage in sexual relations to which they do freely agree. The second is that the law must seek to give special protection to children and adults who are particularly vulnerable to sexual abuse. The Review's proposals,[2] which are both practical and measured, require implementation.

As far as the law of evidence is concerned, much has been achieved not only through legislation but also in the development of the common law. The decision of the House of Lords in *DPP v P* illustrates a new judicial understanding of the problem of child sexual abuse which has been carried forward in *H* and also in *Christou*. However, the Law Commission's report on bad character evidence fails adequately to address the imbalance in sexual cases in which the character of complainants is routinely trashed whilst the past behaviour of defendants remains obscured from view. Indeed, its proposals may even exacerbate the problem. This issue remains of central importance if fairness to the victim as well as to the defendant is to be achieved in rape trials.

There is a case too for further procedural reform. Implementation of the Danish scheme for legal representation of sexual assault victims[3] could conceivably do more to improve the present system of dealing with sexual assault than any alteration in the substantive criminal law or rules of evidence.

But reform of the kind advocated here is, in its practical aspect, only as good as the people charged with its implementation. In the 1980s, the police began to come to terms with past errors. New systems were set up, new protocols devised. Impetus in this area seems, however, to have been lost and research suggests that these systems are now under strain. Suspicion of complainants, and the stereotypical view of what true rape is, persist among police officers. Much more needs to be done to overcome this.[4] Judges today are less inclined to make foolish remarks about complainants or defendants in rape trials, but the training they receive about gender issues and aspects of sexual violence, other than the purely legal, is limited[5] and, for barristers, non-existent. Although teachers of law are now more inclined to consider with their students the problem of sexual assault, it is not clear how often the law is discussed in the context of its operation within the criminal justice system or to what extent the experience of victims and the myths of rape are examined. But unless there is an alteration in the attitudes of lawyers,

[1] On the meaning of 'free agreement', see Ch. 2, pp. 97–107.

[2] They are considered in detail in Ch. 2.

[3] See Ch. 5.

[4] For example, the Women's National Commission recommended that special training about rape needs to be extended to male officers of all ranks: see Women's National Commission (1985), paras. 33–8. This author's research in the 1990s found that CID officers were not receiving adequate training in either London or Sussex: see Temkin (1997, 1999). See now Home Office, *Action Plan* (2002).

[5] See Ch. 1 under the heading 'Sentencing'.

including those in the CPS, very little in the way of real change can be achieved. There is as much a need for the teaching of criminal law and procedure in this area to be reconsidered as there is for police to be retrained.

Attitudinal change takes time to accomplish, although law reform can assist its progress. In the meantime, much can be done to provide assistance for sexual assault victims. More research is necessary—there has been very little in this country—to discover the extent of sexual victimization and to test the legal procedures which have evolved for dealing with it. There is a need for proper counselling services to be made available which go beyond the limited help which can be offered by police or Victim Support schemes. The 'one-stop shop' in which medical, forensic, and counselling services are contained under one roof, as at St Mary's Hospital, Manchester and the Haven-Camberwell project in London, may be the way forward.

Anxiety about rape continues to grow—and with justification. It is fuelled by the statistics of rape which reveal a system patently failing to deal with the problem, as increasing numbers of women, men, and children come forward to report it. The culture of human rights has not been seen sufficiently to embrace the basic human right to be free of unwanted sexual interference, coercion, and violence. At a time when women are better represented in Parliament than ever before, it must be hoped that the measures available to improve the situation will be taken, for it is clear that dissatisfaction with the present state of affairs is increasing and that the call for change will not abate.

Select Bibliography

Adler, Z., 'Rape—The Intention of Parliament and the Practice of the Courts' (1982) 45 MLR 664.

——*Rape on Trial* (London and New York: Routledge and Kegan Paul, 1987).

Amir, M., *Patterns in Forcible Rape* (Chicago: University of Chicago Press, 1971).

Arabian, A., 'The Cautionary Instruction in Sex Cases: A Lingering Insult' (1978) 10 Southwestern ULR 585.

Archbold: Criminal Pleading, Evidence and Practice (42nd edn., London: Sweet and Maxwell, 1985); (London: Sweet and Maxwell, 2001).

Attorney General's Legislation and Policy Branch (Victoria), *The Crimes (Rape) Act 1991: An Evaluation Report*, Reports 1 and 2 (Melbourne, 1997).

Auld LJ, *Review of the Criminal Courts of England and Wales: Report* (London: Stationery Office, 2001).

Batt, S., 'Our Civil Courts—Unused Classrooms for Education about Rape'. Paper presented at annual conference of the Canadian Research Institute for the Advancement of Women, Vancouver, November 1983.

Bawdon, F., 'Putting a Price on Rape' (1993) 143 NLJ 371.

Berger, V., 'Man's Trial, Woman's Tribulation: Rape Cases in the Courtroom' (1977) 77 Columbia Law Review 1.

Bienen, L. B., 'A Question of Credibility: John Henry Wigmore's Use of Scientific Authority in Section 924a of the Treatise on Evidence' (1983) 19 Calif Western LR 235.

Birch, D., 'A Better Deal for Vulnerable Witnesses' [2000] Crim LR 223.

Blair, I., *Investigating Rape—A New Approach for Police* (Kent: Croom Helm, 1985).

Blackstone, W., *Commentaries on the Laws of England*, vol. cxi (18th edn., London: S. Sweet, 1829).

British Medical Association, 'Revised Interim Guidelines on Confidentiality for Police Surgeons in England, Wales and Northern Ireland' (1998).

Bonney, R., *Crimes (Sexual Assault) Amendment Act 1981: Monitoring and Evaluation: Interim Report No. 3: Court Procedures* (Sydney: NSW Bureau of Crime Statistics and Research, 1987).

Boyle, C., *Sexual Assault* (Toronto: Carswell, 1984).

——'The Judicial Construction of Sexual Assault Offences', in J. V. Roberts and R. Mohr, *Confronting Sexual Assault: A Decade of Legal and Social Change* (Toronto: University of Toronto Press, 1994).

Bracton, H., *Bracton on the Laws and Customs of England,* vol. II, fo. 147 (Thorne's edn., Cambridge, Mass.: Belknap Press of Harvard University Press, 1968).

Brown B., Burman, M., and Jamieson, L., *Sexual History and Sexual Character Evidence in Scottish Sexual Offence Trials* (Edinburgh: Scottish Office Central Research Unit Papers, 1992).

Brownmiller, S., *Against Our Will* (Middlesex: Penguin Books, 1976).

Bublick, E. M., 'Citizen No-duty Rules: Rape Victims and Comparative Fault' (1999) Columbia Law Review 1413.

Butler, S., *Conspiracy of Silence—The Trauma of Incest* (Calif.: Volcano Press, 1978).

Cambridge Department of Criminal Science Report, *Sexual Offences* (London: Macmillan, 1957).

Canadian Department of Justice, *Sexual Assault Legislation in Canada: An Evaluation: Overview Report No. 5* (1990).

Cavallaro, R., 'A Big Mistake: Eroding the Defence of Mistake of Fact about Consent in Rape' (1996) 86 Journal of Criminal Law and Criminology 815.

Chambers, G., and Millar, A., *Investigating Sexual Assault* (Edinburgh: Scottish Office Central Research Unit, 1983).

——— *Prosecuting Sexual Assault* (Edinburgh: Scottish Office Central Research Unit, 1986).

Chappell, D., 'Rape: Changing the Law (and Attitudes . . . ?)' (1977) Legal Services Bulletin 302.

Childs, M., and Ellison, L., eds., *Feminist Perspectives on Evidence* (London: Cavendish, 2000).

Clark, L. M. G., and Lewis, D. J., *Rape: The Price of Coercive Sexuality* (Toronto: The Women's Press, 1977).

Clark, L., *Evidence of Recent Complaint and Reform of Canadian Sexual Assault Law: Still Searching for Epistemic Equality* (Ottawa: Canadian Advisory Council on the Status of Women, 1993).

Clark, S., and Hepworth, D., 'The Effects of Reform Legislation', in J. V. Roberts and R. Mohr, eds., *Confronting Sexual Assault: A Decade of Legal and Social Change* (Toronto: University of Toronto Press, 1994).

Conaghan, J., 'Tort Litigation in the Context of Intra-familial Abuse' (1998) 61 MLR 132.

Criminal Injuries Compensation Appeals Panel, *Annual Report 1998–1999*, Cm 4670, 2000.

—— *Annual Report 1999–2000*, Cm 5081, 2001.

Criminal Law Revision Committee, Eleventh Report, *Evidence (General)*, Cmnd 4991 (1972).

—— *Working Paper on Sexual Offences* (1980).

—— Fifteenth Report, *Sexual Offences*, Cmnd 9213 (1984).

Cross, R., and Tapper, C., *Cross on Evidence* (6th edn., London: Butterworths, 1985).

Cunliffe, I., 'Consent and Sexual Offences Law Reform in New South Wales' (1984) 8 Crim LJ 271.

Damaska, M., 'Propensity Evidence in Continental Legal Systems' [1994] 70 Chicago-Kent Law Review 55.

Danna, M. K., 'The New Federal Rules of Evidence 413–415: The Prejudice of Politics or Just Plain Common Sense' [1996] 41 Saint Louis University Law Journal 277.

Darbyshire, P., 'Previous Misconduct and Magistrates Courts—Some Tales from the Real World' [1997] Crim LR 105.

Davies, A., Wittebrood, K., and Jackson, J., 'Predicting the Criminal Antecedents of a Stranger Rapist from his Offence Behaviour' (1997) 37(3) Science and Justice 161.

Dennis, I. H., *The Law of Evidence* (London: Sweet and Maxwell, 1999).

Easteal, P., ed., *Balancing the Scales: Rape, Law Reform and Australian Culture* (Sydney: The Federation Press, 1998).

Explanatory Notes: Youth Justice and Criminal Evidence Act 1999 (London: The Stationery Office).

Firth, A., 'Interrogation', Police Review, 28 Nov. 1975.

Forrester, J., 'Rape, Seduction and Psychoanalysis', in S. Tomaselli and R. Porter, (eds)., *Rape* (Oxford: Basil Blackwell, 1986).

Foster, D., *Claiming Compensation for Criminal Injuries* (2nd edn., Croydon: Tolley, 1997).

Freeman, M. D. A., 'But If You Can't Rape your Wife, Whom Can you Rape?: The Marital Exemption Re-examined' (1981) XV Fam Law Q 1.

Gardiner, S., 'Appreciating *Olugboja*' (1996) 16(3) LS 275.

Giles, M., 'Judicial Law-Making in the Criminal Courts: the Case of Marital Rape' [1992] Crim LR 407.

Goy, A., 'The Victim-Plaintiff in Criminal Trials and Civil Law Responses to Sexual Violence' (1996) 3 Cardozo Women's LJ 335.

Grace, S., Lloyd, C., and Smith, L. J. F., *Rape: From Recording to Conviction*, Home Office Research and Planning Unit, Paper 71 (1992).

Hall, R. E., *Ask Any Woman: A London Inquiry into Rape and Sexual Assault* (Bristol: Falling Wall Press, 1985).

Harper, R., and McWhinnie, A., *The Glasgow Rape Case* (London: Hutchinson, 1983).

Harris, J., and Grace, S., *A Question of Evidence? Investigating and Prosecuting Rape in the 1990s*, Home Office Research Study 196 (1999).

The Heilbron Committee, *Report of the Advisory Group on the Law of Rape* (1975) Cmnd 6352.

Henning, T., and Bronitt, S., 'Rape Victims on Trial—Regulating the Use and Abuse of Sexual History Evidence', in P. Easteal, ed., *Balancing the Scales: Rape, Law Reform andAustralian Culture* (Sydney: The Federation Press, 1998), 76.

Her Majesty's Crown Prosecution Service Inspectorate (HMCPSI) *A Report on the Joint Inspection into the Investigation and Prosecution of Cases Involving Allegations of Rape* (London: HMCPSI, 2002).

Holmstrom, L. L., and Burgess, A. W., 'Sexual Behaviour of Assailants during Reported Rapes' (1980) 9 *Archives of Sexual Behaviour* 427.

Home Office, *Report of the Advisory Group on Video Evidence* (1989). (The Pigot Report).

——*Criminal Statistics England and Wales 1997*, Cm 4162, (London: The Stationery Office, 1998).

——*Speaking Up for Justice: Report of the Interdepartmental Working Group on the Treatment of Vulnerable or Intimidated Witnesses in the Criminal Justice System* (London: Home Office, 1998).

——*Criminal Statistics for England and Wales 1999*, Cm 5001 (London: The Stationery Office, 2000).

——*Criminal Statistics for England and Wales 2000*, Cm 5312 (London: The Stationery Office, 2001).

——Consultation Paper, *Compensation for Victims of Violent Crime: Possible Changes to the Criminal Injuries Compensation Scheme* (1999).

Home Office, *Setting the Boundaries: Reforming the Law on Sex Offences* vols. 1 and 2 (London: Home Office Communication Directorate, 2000).

——*Statistical Bulletin, Recorded Crime*, Issue 12/01 (London: Home Office, July 2001).

——Research Study 237, A. Myhill and J. Allen, *Rape and Sexual Assault of Women: The Extent and Nature of the Problem—Findings from the British Crime Survey* (London: Home Office Research, Development and Statistics Directorate, 2002).

——*Action Plan to Implement the Recommendations of the HMCPSI/HMIC Joint Investigation into the Investigation and Prosecution of Cases involving Allegations of Rape* (London, July 2002).

——Lord Chancellor's Department, CPS, *'Justice for All'—Responses to the Auld and Halliday Reports*, Cm 5563 (London: The Stationery Office, 2002).

Howard League Working Party Report, *Unlawful Sex: Offences, Victims and Offenders in the Criminal Justice System of England and Wales* (London: Waterlow, 1985).

Hoyano, L. C. H., 'Variations on a Theme by Pigot' [2000] Crim LR 250.

Interdepartmental Working Party Report, *Criminal Injuries Compensation: A Statutory Scheme* (London: HMSO, 1986).

Johnson, H., and Sacco, V. F., 'Researching Violence against Women: Statistics Canada's National Survey'(1995) Canadian Journal of Criminology, July 281.

Kalven, H., and Zeisel, H., *The American Jury* (Boston: Little Brown, 1966).

Karp, D. J., 'Evidence, Propensity and Probability in Sex Offence Cases and Other Cases' (1994) 70 Chicago-Kent Law Review 15.

Kelly, D. P., 'Victims' Reactions to the Criminal Justice Response', Paper delivered at the 1982 Annual Meeting of the Law and Society Association, 6 June 1982, Toronto, Canada

Kelly, L., *A Research Review on The Reporting, Investigation and Prosecution of Rape Cases* (London: HM Crown Prosecution Service Inspectorate, 2002).

Koss, M.P., *et al., No Safe Haven: Male Violence against Women at Home, at Work and in the Community* (Washington: American Psychological Association, 1994).

Krahe, B., *The Social Psychology of Aggression* (East Sussex: Psychology Press, 2001).

Lanham, D., 'Hale, Misogyny and Rape' (1983) 7 Crim LJ 148.

Law Commission, Working Paper No. 116, *Rape within Marriage* (London: HMSO, 1990).

——Report No. 205, *Rape within Marriage* (London: HMSO, 1992).

——Consultation Paper No. 139, *Consent in the Criminal Law* (London: HMSO, 1995).

——Consultation Paper No. 141, *Evidence in Criminal Proceedings: Previous Misconduct of a Defendant* (London: HMSO, 1996).

——Report No. 245 *Evidence in Criminal Proceedings: Hearsay and Related Topics*, (London: HMSO, 1997) Cm 3670.

——Report No. 257, *Damages for Personal Injury: Non-Pecuniary Loss*, HC 344 (London: Stationery Office, 1999).

——Report No. 273, *Evidence of Bad Character in Criminal Proceedings*, Cm 5257 (London: Stationery Office, 2001).

Law Commission Policy Paper, *Consent in Sex Offences* (Law Commission: 2000).

Lees, S., *Carnal Knowledge: Rape on Trial* (London: Hamish Hamilton, 1996).

——*Ruling Passions: Sexual Violence, Reputation and the Law* (Buckingham: Open University Press, 1997).

——and Gregory, J., *Rape and Sexual Assault: A Study of Attrition* (London: Islington Council, 1993).

Leigh, L. H. and Hall Williams, J. E., *The Management of the Prosecution Process in Denmark, Sweden and the Netherlands* (London: London School of Economics and Political Science, 1981).

Lloyd-Bostock, S., 'The Effects on Juries of Hearing About the Defendant's Previous Criminal Record: A Simulation Study' [2000] Crim LR 734.

Los, M., 'The Struggle to Redefine Rape in the Early 1980s' in J. V. Roberts and R. Mohr, eds., *Confronting Sexual Assault: A Decade of Legal and Social Change* (Toronto: University of Toronto Press, 1994).

McEwan, J., 'Law Commission Dodges the Nettles in Consultation Paper No. 141' [1997] Crim LR 93.

——'In Defence of Vulnerable Witnesses: The YJCEA 1999' (2000) International Journal of Evidence and Proof 1.

McIntyre, S., 'Redefining Reformism: The Consultations that Shaped Bill C–49' in J. V. Roberts and R. Mohr, eds., *Confronting Sexual Assault: A Decade of Legal and Social Change* (Toronto: University of Toronto Press, 1994).

Maclean, N. M., 'Rape and False Accusations of Rape' (1979) Police Surgeon 29.

Maguire, M., and Corbett, C., *The Effects of Crime and the Work of Victim Support Schemes* (Aldershot: Gower, 1987).

Marsh, J. C., Geist, A., and Caplan, N., *Rape and the Limits of Law Reform* (Boston: Auburn House, 1982).

Meredith, C., Mohr, R., and Cairns Way, R., *Implementation Review of Bill C-49* (Ottawa: Dept. of Justice, 1997).

Metropolitan Police Service, *Investigation of Serious Sexual Assaults—Policy Guidelines for Investigators and Chaperones* (London: Directorate of Public Affairs and Internal Communication, New Scotland Yard, 1995).

Mezey, G. C., and King, M. B., eds., *Male Victims of Sexual Assault* (Oxford: Oxford University Press, 1992).

Miers, D., *State Compensation for Criminal Injuries* (London: Blackstone Press, 1997).

——'Criminal Injuries Compensation: The New Regime' [2001] Journal of Personal Injury Law, Issue 4/01 371.

Mitra, C. L., 'For She Has No Right or Power to Refuse Her Consent' [1979] Crim LR 558.

Model Criminal Code Officers Committee of the Standing Committee of Attorneys-General, *Discussion Paper, Model Criminal Code*, ch. 5, 'Sexual Offences Against the Person' (Barton, ACT: Attorney-General's Department, 1996).

Mohr, R. M., 'Sexual Assault Sentencing: Leaving Justice to Individual Conscience' in J. V. Roberts and R. Mohr, eds., *Confronting Sexual Assault: A Decade of Legal and Social Change* (Toronto: University of Toronto Press, 1994).

Morgan-Taylor, M., and Rumney, P., 'A Male Perspective on Rape' (1994) NLJ 1490.

National Children's Home, *The Report of the Committee of Enquiry into Children and Young People who Sexually Abuse Other Children* (London: NCH, 1992).

New South Wales Bureau of Crime Statistics and Research, *Crimes (Sexual Assault) Amendment Act 1981—Monitoring and Evaluation—An Interim Report No. 1—Characteristics of the Complainant, the Defendant and the Offence* (New South Wales: Attorney-General's Department, 1985).

New South Wales Department for Women, *Heroines of Fortitude: The Experiences of Women in Court as Victims of Sexual Assault* (Canberra, 1996).

New South Wales Law Reform Commission, Issues Paper 14, *Review of Section 409B of the Crimes Act 1900 (NSW)* (Sydney, 1997).

Newby, L., 'Rape Victims in Court—The Western Australian Example', in J. Scutt, ed., *Rape Law Reform* (Canberra: Australian Institute of Criminology, 1980).

O'Reilly, H. J., 'Crisis Intervention with Victims of Forcible Rape: A Police Perspective', in J. Hopkins, ed., *Perspectives on Rape and Sexual Assault* (London: Harper and Rowe, 1984).

Paciocco, D., and Stuesser, L., *The Law of Evidence* (2nd edn., Toronto: Irwin Law, 1999).

Painter, K., *Wife Rape, Marriage and the Law: Survey Report—Key Findings and Recommendations* (Department of Social Policy and Social Work, University of Manchester, 1991).

Pattullo, P., *Judging Women* (London: National Council for Civil Liberties, 1983).

Percy, A. and Mayhew, P., 'Estimating Sexual Victimisation in a National Crime Survey' (1997) 6 Studies on Crime and Crime Prevention 125.

Pigot Report (see Home Office 1989).

Pizzey, E., *Scream Quietly or the Neighbours will Hear* (Harmondsworth: Penguin, 1974).

Post, J. B., 'Ravishment of Women and the Statutes of Westminster', in J. H. Baker, ed., *Legal Records and the Historian* (London: Royal Historical Society, 1978).

Quraishi, A., 'Her Honour: An Islamic Critique of the Rape Laws of Pakistan from a Woman-Sensitive Perspective' (1999) 38(3) Islamic Studies 403.

Raitt, B. F., and Zeedyk, M., 'Rape Trauma Syndrome: Its Corroborative and Educational Roles' (1997) 24 Journal of Law and Society 552.

Reeves, H., and Mulley, K., 'The New Status of Victims in the UK: Opportunities and Threats', in A. Crawford and J.Goodey, *Integrating a Victim Perspective with Criminal Justice* (Aldershot: Ashgate, 2000).

Resnick, H. S., Kilpatrick, G., Walsh, C., and Veronen, L. J. 'Marital Rape', in R. T. Ammerman and M. Hersen, eds., *Case Studies in Family Violence* (New York: Plenum Press, 1991).

Roberts, J. V., *Sexual Assault Legislation in Canada: An Analysis of National Statistics* (Ottawa: Department of Justice, 1990).

——and Grossman, M. G., 'Changing Definitions of Sexual Assault: An Analysis of Police Statistics', in J. V. Roberts and R. Mohr, eds., *Confronting Sexual Assault: A Decade of Legal and Social Change* (Toronto: University of Toronto Press, 1994).

——and Mohr, R. eds., *Confronting Sexual Assault: A Decade of Legal and Social Change* (Toronto: University of Toronto Press, 1994).

Rumney, P. N., 'When Rape Isn't Rape: Court of Appeal Sentencing Practice in Cases of Marital and Relationship Rape' (1999) 19 OJLS 243.

Russell, D. E. H., *Sexual Exploitation—Rape, Child Sexual Abuse and Workplace Harassment* (Calif.: Sage, 1984).
——*Rape in Marriage* (Bloomington, Ind.: Indiana University Press, 1982; 2nd edn., 1990).
Sallman, P. A., 'Rape in Marriage and the South Australian Law', in J. Scutt, ed., *Rape Law Reform* (Canberra: Australian Institute of Criminology, 1980).
Schiff, S., *Evidence in the Litigation Process* (4th edn., Toronto: Carswell, 1993).
Schulhofer, S., *Unwanted Sex: The Culture of Intimidation and the Failure of Law* (Cambridge, Mass.: Harvard University Press, 1998).
Scottish Executive, *Vital Voices: Helping Vulnerable Witnesses Give Evidence* (Edinburgh, 2002).
Scutt, J., 'Consent versus Submission: Threats and the Element of Fear in Rape' (1977) 13 W Aust LR 52.
——'Consent in Rape: The Problem of the Marriage Contract' (1977) 3 Monash Univ LE 255.
——ed., *Rape Law Reform* (Canberra: Australian Institute of Criminology, 1980).
Sentencing Advisory Panel, *Sentencing Guidelines on Rape—Consultation Paper* (London: Home Office, 2001).
Shapland, J., 'Victims and the Criminal Justice System', in E. A. Fattah, ed., *From Crime Policy to Victim Policy: Reorienting the Criminal Justice System* (Basingstoke: Macmillan, 1986).
——Willmore, J., and Duff, P., *The Victim in the Criminal Justice System* (Aldershot: Gower, 1985).
Shute, S., 'The Second Law Commission Consultation Paper on Consent' [1996] Crim LR 681.
——'Who Passes Unduly Lenient Sentences? A Survey of Attorney-General's Reference Cases, 1989–1997' [1999] Crim LR 603.
Silber, S., 'The Law Commission's Work on Hearsay and Previous Misconduct' (1997) 37 (2) Med Sci Law 125.
Smart, C., *Feminism and the Power of Law* (London: Routledge, 1989).
Smith, J. C., and Hogan, B., *Criminal Law* (9th edn., London: Butterworths, 1999).
Smith, L. J. F., *Concerns about Rape*, Home Office Research Study No. 106 (1989).
Snare, A., 'Sexual Violence against Women', in *Sexual Behaviour and Attitudes and Their Implications for Criminal Law,* Report of 15th Criminological Research Conference (Council of Europe, 1983).
Spencer, J., 'Reforming the Law on Children's Evidence in England: The Pigot Committee and After', in H. Dent and R. Flin, *Children as Witnesses* (Chichester: Wiley, 1992).
Spohn, C., and Horney, J., *Rape Law Reform: A Grassroots Revolution and its Impact* (New York and London: Plenum Press, 1992).
Statistics Canada, *Violence against Women—Survey Highlights and Questionnaire Package* (Canada: Statistics Canada, 1993).
Sturman, P., *Drug Assisted Sexual Assault: A Study for the Home Office,* (London: Metropolitan Police, 2000).
Swedish Government's Commission on Crime, *Victims of Crime: What Has Been Done? What Should be Done?* (SOU, 1998: 40).
Tapper, C., *Cross and Tapper on Evidence* (9th edn., London: Butterworths, 1999).

Tasmanian Law Reform Commission, Report No. 31, *Report and Recommendations on Rape and Sexual Offences* (1982).
Temkin, J., 'Towards a Modern Law of Rape' (1982) 45 MLR 399.
——'Regulating Sexual History Evidence—The Limits of Discretionary Legislation' (1984) 33 ICLQ 942.
——'Women, Rape and Law Reform', in S. Thomaselli and R. Porter, eds., *Rape* (Oxford: Basil Blackwell, 1986).
——*Rape and the Legal Process* (London: Sweet and Maxwell, 1987).
——'Sexual History Evidence—The Ravishment of Section 2' [1993] Crim LR 3.
——'Plus Ça Change: Reporting Rape in the 1990s' (1997) 37 Brit J Criminol 507.
——'Medical Evidence in Rape Cases: A Continuing Problem for Criminal Justice' [1998] MLR 821.
——'Reporting Rape in London: A Qualitative Study' (1999) 38 Howard Journal of Criminal Justice 17.
——'Rape and Criminal Justice at the Millennium', in D. Nicolson and L. Bibbings, eds., *Feminist Perspectives on Criminal Law* (London: Cavendish, 2000).
——'Prosecuting and Defending Rape: Perspectives from the Bar' (2000) 27 (2) Journal of Law and Society 219.
——'Digging the Dirt: Disclosure of Records in Sexual Assault Cases' (2002) 61 CLJ 126.
Thomas, D. A., *Principles of Sentencing: The Sentencing Policy of the Court of Appeal Criminal Division* (2nd edn., London: Heinemann Educational, 1979).
——*Current Sentencing Practice* (London: Sweet and Maxwell, 1982).
Thorbeck, J., 'Valdtaksoffrets rattsliga stallning = systemvald?' (1981) 3 Kvinnovetenskaplig tidskrift 47.
Toner, B., *The Facts of Rape* (London: Arrow Books, 1982).
Torrey, M., 'When Will We Be Believed? Rape Myths and the Idea of a Fair Trial in Rape Prosecutions' (1991) 24 UC Davis L Rev 1013.
VanderVelde, L., 'The Legal Ways of Seduction' (1996) 48 Stan L Rev 817.
Victim Support, *Women, Rape and the Criminal Justice System* (London: Victim Support, 1996).
——National Association of Victims Support Schemes, *Annual Report and Accounts* (London, 2001).
Walby, S., and Myhill, A., 'New Survey Methodologies in Researching Violence Against Women' (2001) 41 Brit J Criminol 502.
Walmsley, R., and White, K., *Sexual Offences, Consent and Sentencing* (Home Office Research Study No. 54, 1979).
Watt, D., *The New Offences against the Person* (Toronto: Butterworths, 1984).
Weinrott, M. R., and Saylor, M., 'Self-report of Crimes Committed by Sex Offenders' (1991) 6 Journal of Interpersonal Violence 286.
Williams, J. E., and Holmes, K. A., *The Second Assault: Rape and Public Attitudes* (Westport, Conn.: Greenwood Press, 1981).
Williams, G., 'The Evidential Burden: Some Common Misapprehensions' (1977) 127 NLJ 156.
——*Textbook of Criminal Law* (2nd edn., London: Stevens, 1983).
Wilson, P. R., *The Other Side of Rape* (Queensland: University of Queensland Press, 1978).
Wolfram, S., 'Eugenics and the Punishment of Incest Act 1908' [1983] Crim LR 308.

Women's National Commission, *Violence Against Women—Report of an Ad Hoc Working Group* (London: Women's National Commission, 1985).

Woods, G. D., *Sexual Assault Law Reforms in New South Wales* (Sydney: Department of the Attorney General and of Justice, 1981).

Wright, R., The English Rapist', *New Society*, 17 July 1980, 124.

——'Rape and Physical Violence', in D. J. West, ed., *Sex Offenders in the Criminal Justice System,* Cropwood Conference Series No. 12 (Cambridge Institute of Criminology, 1980), 100.

——and West, D. J., 'Rape—A Comparison of Group Offences and Lone Assaults' (1981) 21 Med Sci Law 25.

——'A Note on the Attrition of Rape Cases' (1984) 24 Brit J Criminol 399.

Young, W., *Rape Study—A Discussion of Law and Practice* (Wellington, New Zealand: Dept. of Justice and Institute of Criminology, 1983).

Zander, M., and Henderson, P., *Royal Commission on Criminal Justice, Research Study No. 19 Crown Court Study* (London: HMSO, 1993).

Index